THE MISSING THREAD

ALSO BY DAISY DUNN

In the Shadow of Vesuvius: A Life of Pliny

The Poems of Catullus: A New Translation

Catullus' Bedspread: The Life of Rome's Most Erotic Poet

THE MISSING THREAD

A Women's History of the Ancient World

DAISY DUNN

VIKING

VIKING
An imprint of Penguin Random House LLC
penguinrandomhouse.com

First published in hardcover in Great Britain by Weidenfeld & Nicolson, an imprint of The Orion Publishing Group Ltd, London, in 2024

First United States edition published by Viking, 2024

Image credits may be found on page 437.

Text credits may be found in the Acknowledgments on pages 439–40.

Maps by John Gilkes.

ISBN 9780593299661 (hardcover)
ISBN 9780593299678 (ebook)

Printed in the United States of America
1st Printing

Aliciae sorori,
optimae feminarum

Contents

Maps xiii
Family Trees xviii

Introduction 1
Chapter I: Of Breasts and Bulls 9
Chapter II: The Work of Giants 29
Chapter III: Decline and Change 45
Chapter IV: The Tenth Muse 61
Chapter V: The Oracle is Corrupted 82
Chapter VI: Horsewomen and Queens 98
Chapter VII: Atossa's War 111
Chapter VIII: A Shared Blanket 132
Chapter IX: The Rough End of the Cheese-Grater 153
Chapter X: Olympias' Games 178
Chapter XI: Dido's Curse 199
Chapter XII: The Price of Punic Figs 214
Chapter XIII: Educating Gracchus 231
Chapter XIV: Conspiring at Crossroads 252
Chapter XV: From the Bed-Sack to the Bed 275
Chapter XVI: This One's for Fulvia 298
Chapter XVII: The Exiles 317

Chapter XVIII: Empresses in the Shadows 336
Chapter XIX: Broken Body, Valiant Mind 362
Conclusion 377

Notes 381
Bibliography 421
Picture Credits 437
Acknowledgements 439
Index 441

Italy
N
ALPS
CISALPINE GAUL
Verona
Placentia
Cremona
Mutina
Ravenna
Lucca
Rubicon
Ligurian Sea
ETRURIA
Perusia
APENNINES
Tiber
ILLYRICUM
Adriatic Sea
Planasia
CORSICA
Veii
Rome
Ostia
Antium
Arpinum
Isole Tremiti
Dyrrachium
Cannae
Beneventum
Canusium
Cumae
Vesuvius
Pandateria
Baiae
Neapolis
Pompeii
Capri
Paestum
Brundisium
Tarentum
SARDINIA
Heraclea
Thurii
Tyrrhenian Sea
Croton
MAGNA GRAECIA
Messana
Rhegium
Locri
Ionian Sea
Trapani
Mediterranean Sea
SICILY
Agrigentum
Syracuse
Carthage
0 50 100 Miles
0 50 100 150 Kms

The Greek World
N
MACEDONIA
Philippi
THRACE
Amphipolis
Pella
Aegae
Pydna
CHALCIDICE
Stageira
Samothrace
Hellespont
EPIRUS
Mt Olympus
Lemnos
Sigeum
Troy
TROAD
Dodona
Larissa
Aegean Sea
THESSALY
Pharsalus
LYDIA
Corfu
Lesbos
Pergamon
Mytilene
Actium
Thermopylae
EUBOEA
Phocaea
Ithaca
PHOCIS
Delphi
Lefkandi
Smyrna
BOEOTIA
Eretria
Chios
Thebes
Colophon
Mt Helicon
Plataea
Marathon
Ionian Sea
Athens
Ephesus
Corinth
Samos
Mycenae
Olympia
Argos
Tiryns
Salamis
Miletus
Aegina
Delos
Sparta
Naxos
Pylos
Melos
Cythera
CRETE
Mediterranean Sea
0 50 100 Miles
0 50 100 150 Kms

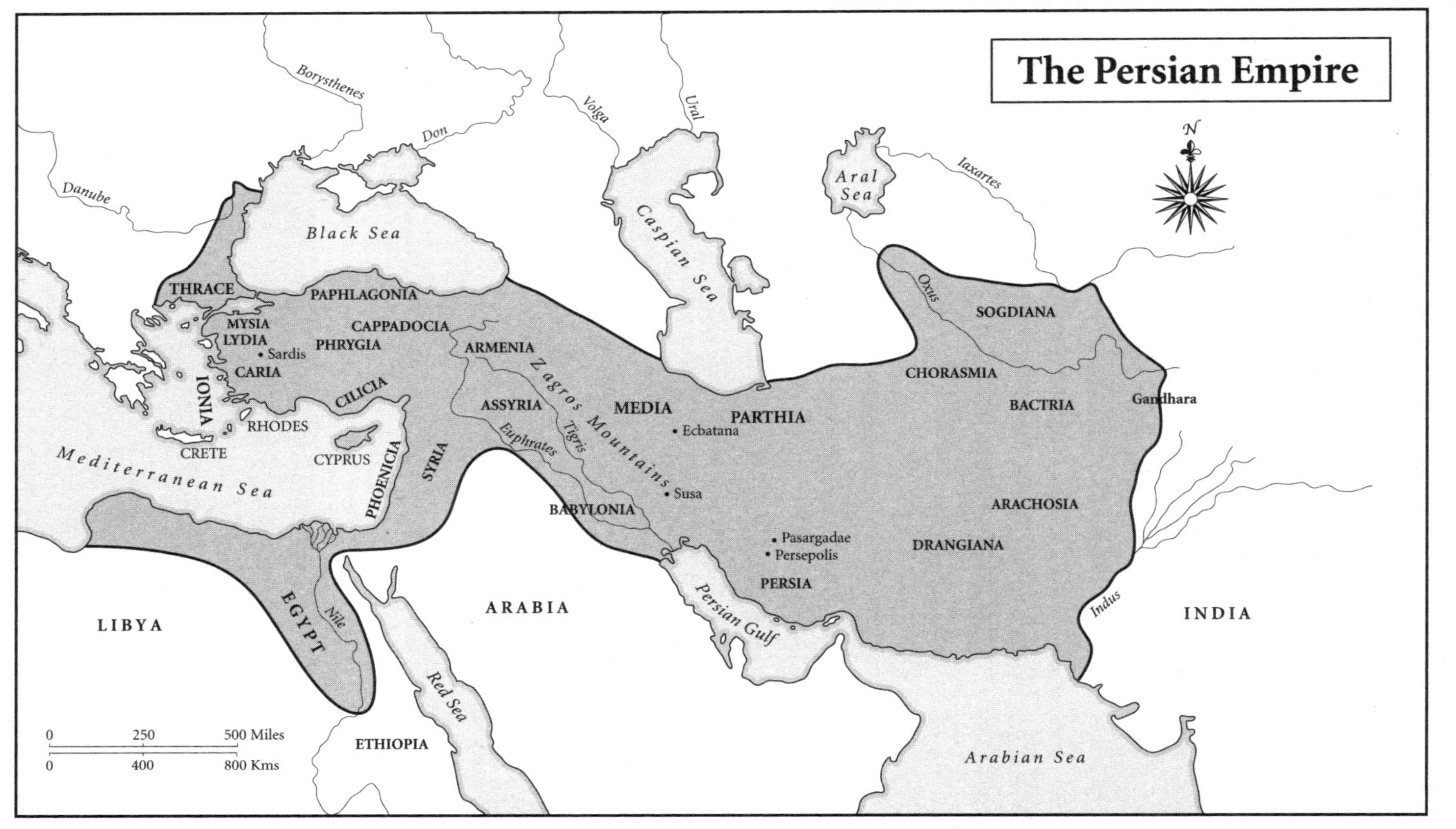
The Persian Empire
N
Borysthenes
Volga
Ural
Danube
Don
Aral Sea
Iaxartes
Black Sea
Caspian Sea
THRACE
PAPHLAGONIA
MYSIA
LYDIA
Sardis
CAPPADOCIA
PHRYGIA
CARIA
IONIA
ARMENIA
Zagros Mountains
CILICIA
ASSYRIA
MEDIA
Ecbatana
PARTHIA
Oxus
SOGDIANA
CHORASMIA
BACTRIA
Gandhara
RHODES
CRETE
CYPRUS
Mediterranean Sea
PHOENICIA
SYRIA
Euphrates
Tigris
Susa
BABYLONIA
ARACHOSIA
Pasargadae
Persepolis
DRANGIANA
PERSIA
LIBYA
EGYPT
Nile
ARABIA
Persian Gulf
Indus
INDIA
Red Sea
ETHIOPIA
Arabian Sea
0 250 500 Miles
0 400 800 Kms

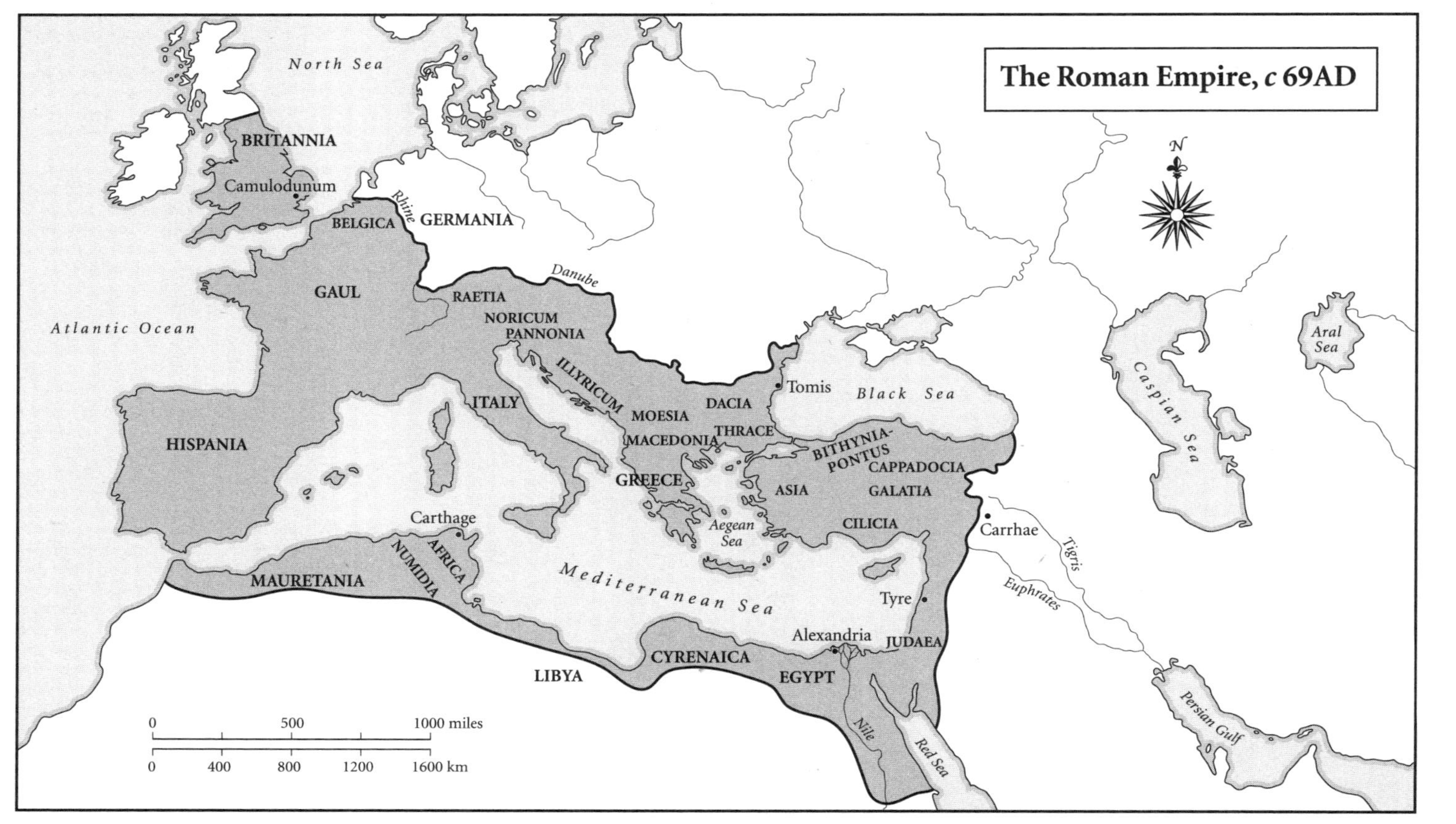
The Roman Empire, c 69AD
N
North Sea
BRITANNIA
Camulodunum
Rhine
BELGICA
GERMANIA
GAUL
Atlantic Ocean
Danube
RAETIA
NORICUM
PANNONIA
ILLYRICUM
HISPANIA
ITALY
MOESIA
DACIA
Tomis
Black Sea
THRACE
MACEDONIA
BITHYNIA-PONTUS
CAPPADOCIA
GALATIA
ASIA
GREECE
Aegean Sea
CILICIA
Carrhae
Tigris
Euphrates
Caspian Sea
Aral Sea
Carthage
AFRICA
NUMIDIA
MAURETANIA
Mediterranean Sea
Tyre
Alexandria
JUDAEA
CYRENAICA
EGYPT
LIBYA
Nile
Red Sea
Persian Gulf
0
500
1000 miles
0
400
800
1200
1600 km

The House of Macedon

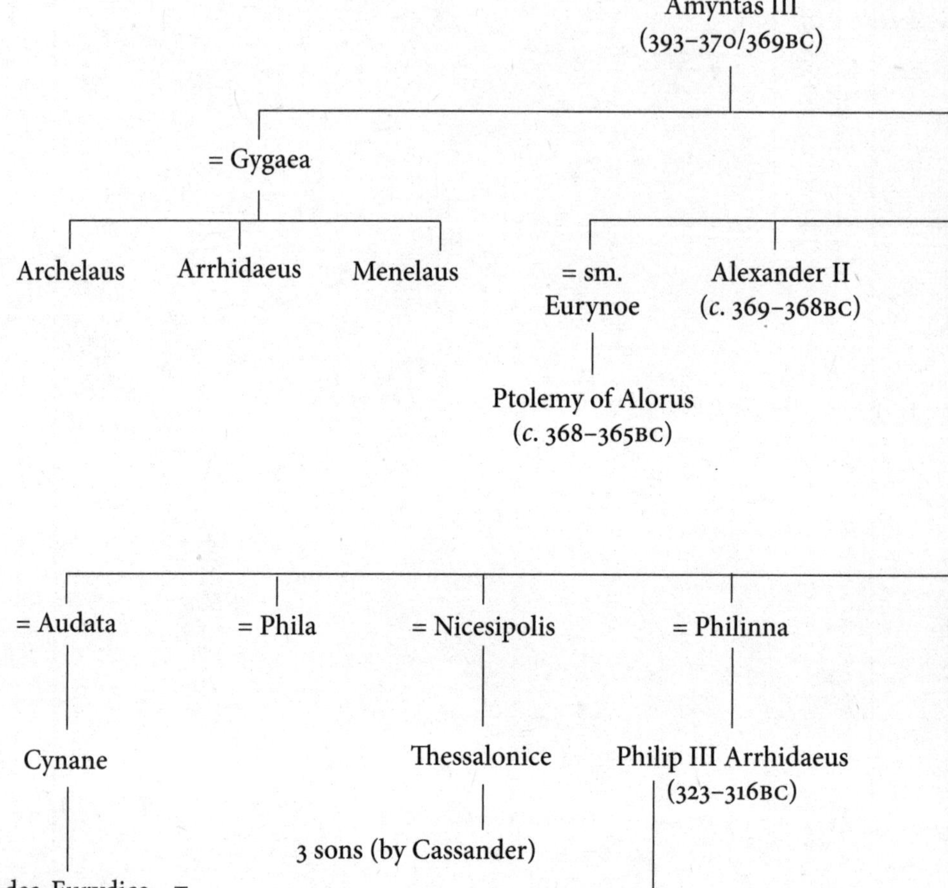

= married
= sm. speculated marriage
+ mistress
(bracketed dates) reigns of throned kings

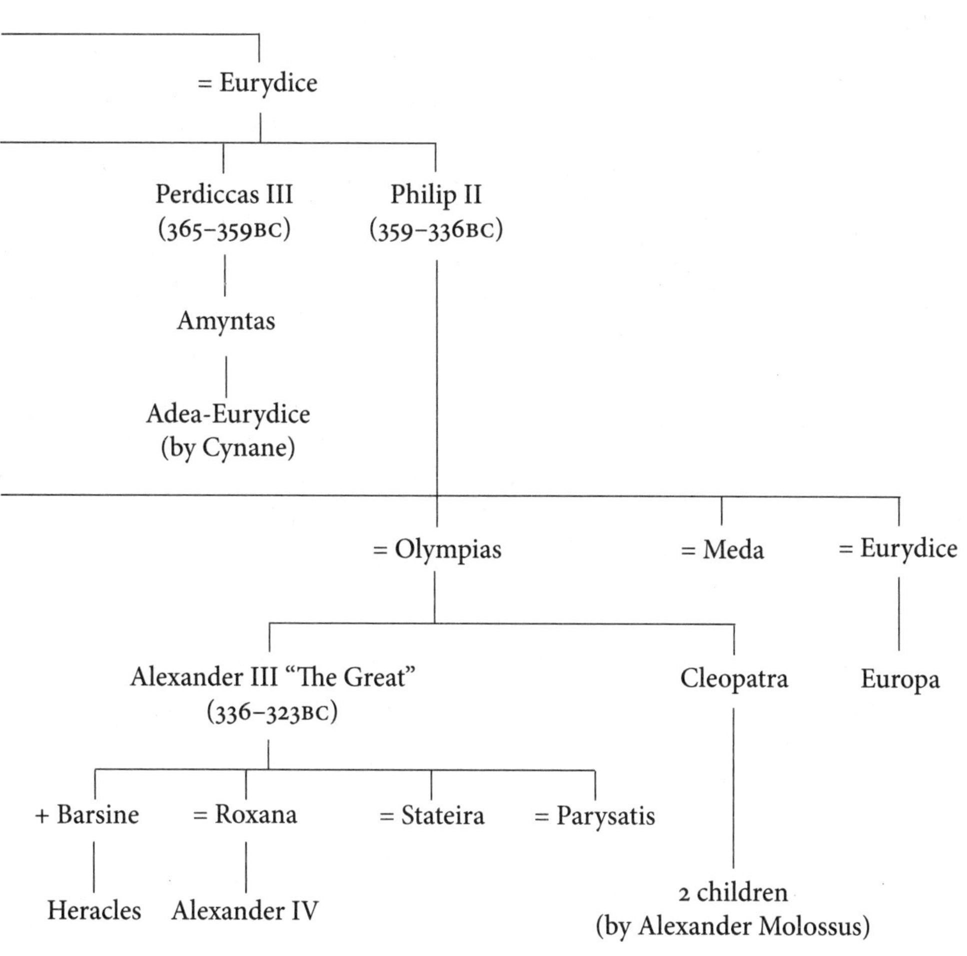

The Julio-Claudians

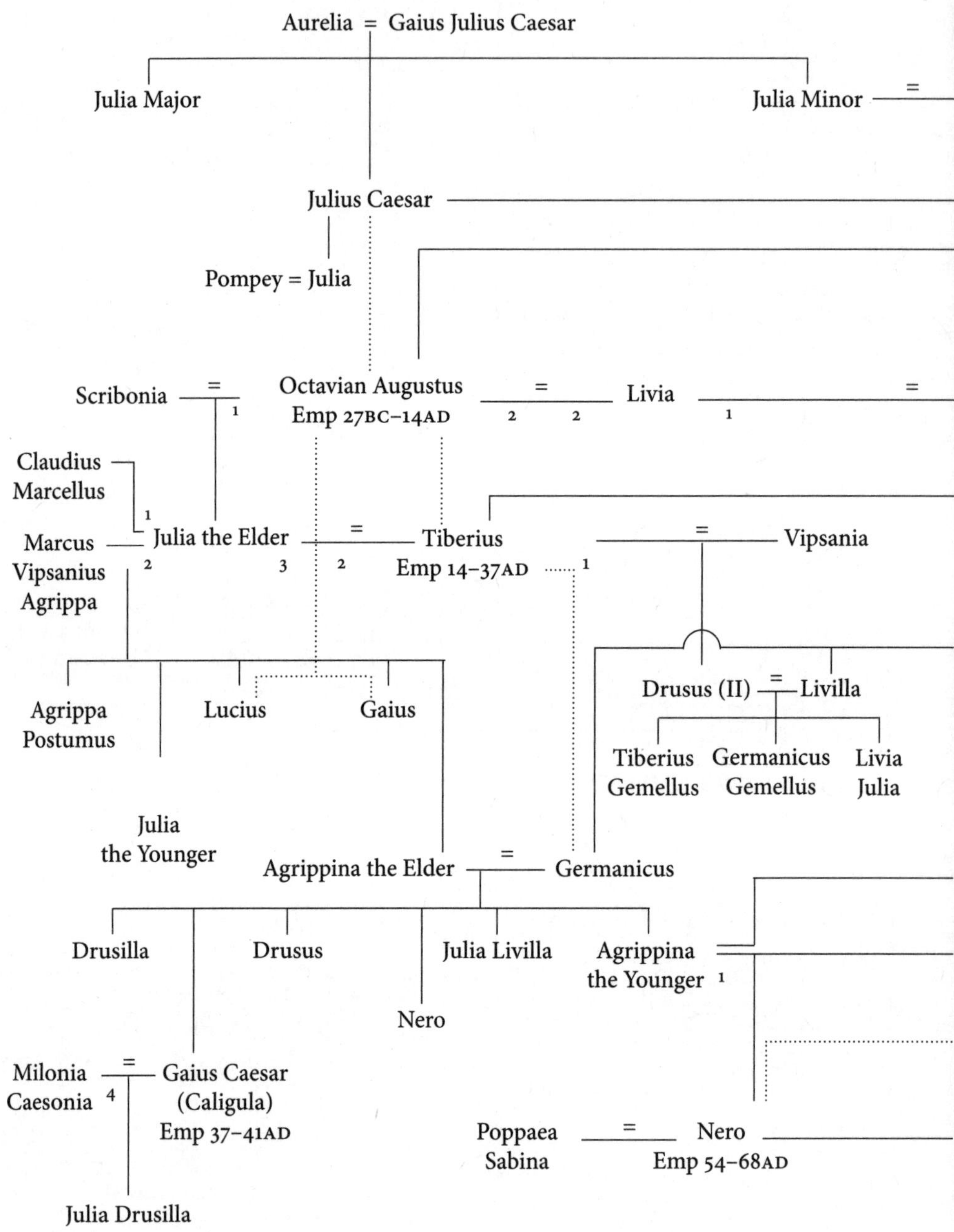

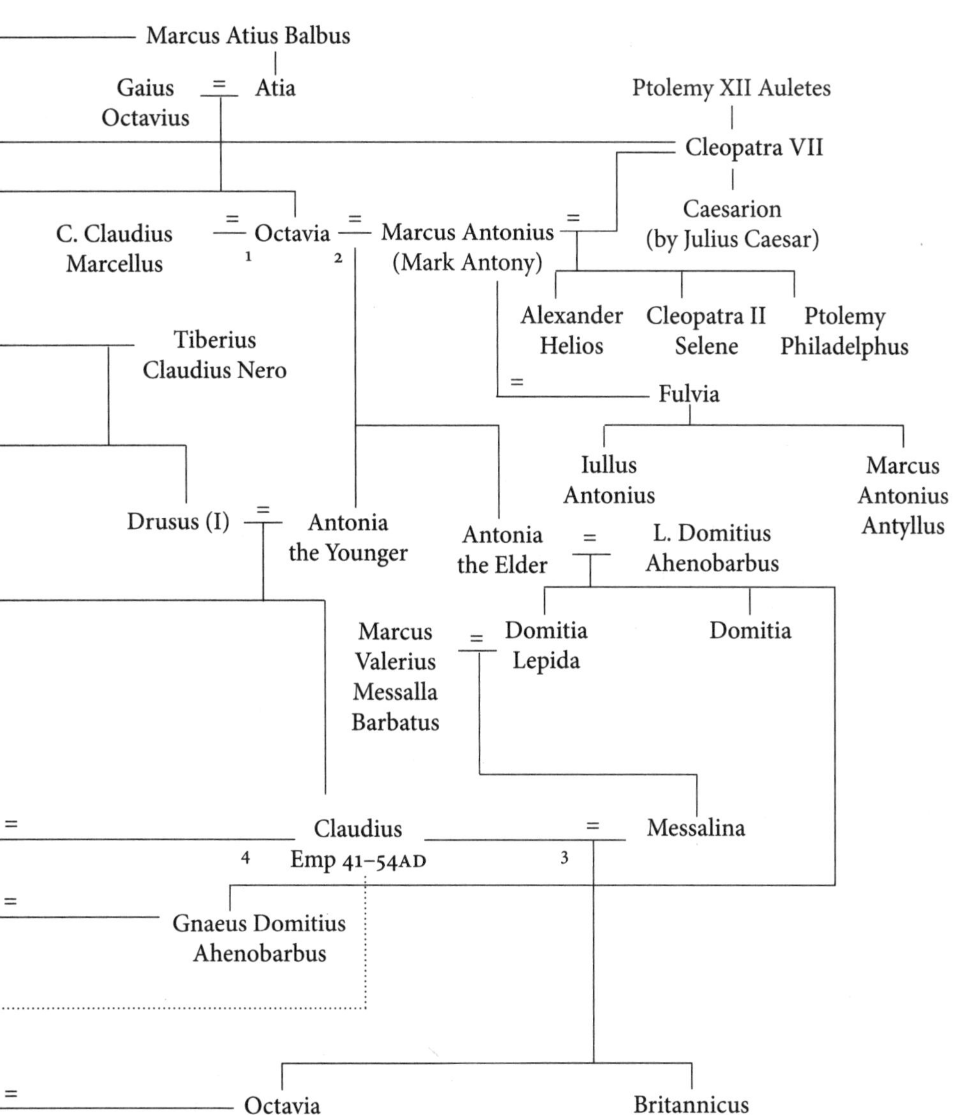
son/daughter
adopted son
= marriage
1, 2, . . . number of marriage
Marcus Atius Balbus
Gaius Octavius
Atia
Ptolemy XII Auletes
Cleopatra VII
Caesarion (by Julius Caesar)
C. Claudius Marcellus
Octavia
Marcus Antonius (Mark Antony)
Alexander Helios
Cleopatra II Selene
Ptolemy Philadelphus
Tiberius Claudius Nero
Fulvia
Iullus Antonius
Marcus Antonius Antyllus
Drusus (I)
Antonia the Younger
Antonia the Elder
L. Domitius Ahenobarbus
Marcus Valerius Messalla Barbatus
Domitia Lepida
Domitia
Claudius Emp 41–54AD
Messalina
Gnaeus Domitius Ahenobarbus
Octavia
Britannicus

Introduction

Women were invented to make men's lives more difficult. Many men had always known this, but even so, it was comforting to hear it said by someone who had met the Muses, who knew the gods, who knew everything. Hesiod worked as a farmer in Boeotia, central Greece, and the Muses haunted Mount Helicon nearby. They met, in whatever way mortals usually meet divinities, and Hesiod came away a poet with words as golden as the grain he sowed and as sharp as the scythe that cut it.

'Let no woman deceive your mind with her shapely bottom / And wheedling conversation,' he urged, 'it's your barn she is seeking.'[1] Women were good for ploughing with the oxen, bearing children, and scoffing the food they were supposed to store away. For everything else they were worse than hopeless. This was not entirely their fault, poor dears, but they paid the price for their descent from what Hesiod described in Greek as *kalon kakon* – a beautiful evil.

The beautiful evil, Pandora, was the first woman. Zeus, king of the gods, summoned the divine craftsman Hephaestus to sculpt her out of earth and water and give her the face of a goddess. Athena taught her to weave and dressed her in silver-white clothes and a finely wrought veil.[2] The Seasons crowned her with flowers and the Graces placed gold around her neck. Aphrodite imbued her with sexual desire and Hermes gave her the mind of a treacherous dog. Each of the immortals had something to bestow – *Pandora* was 'all-gifted' and 'all-giving' – but she was above all Zeus' creation.

Pandora was intended as a punishment for men, the unfortunate pawns in an argument between the king of the gods and a Titan. Zeus was offended because Prometheus had tricked him by serving him a dinner of bones wrapped in fat instead of the finest cut of meat. In the heat of their dispute, gigantic Prometheus stole fire from the gods and gave it to humans so that they could fend for themselves. Prometheus' act triggered the end of the Golden Age, an Edenic era in which men (there were only men) lived off the land without work or disease or the need or even desire to travel overseas. With fire they acquired the means to build ships and cook and live faithlessly. And then Zeus sent Pandora down to earth. All man's troubles originated in her and the jar she carried with her.

There were variations on the myth (sometimes Prometheus rather than the gods was the sculptor and animator of the clay that created man), but the fundamental idea established by Hesiod in the seventh century BC persisted. Woman was a figment of the male imagination, formed between his fingers as a scapegoat for his woes. She could come in many forms: a poet named Semonides of Amorgos working in the same period as Hesiod described pig-like women who cleaned neither their houses nor their bodies but spent all day fattening themselves; fox-like women, who noticed everything; donkey-like women, who had sex with everyone; disobedient dog-women; tempestuous sea-women; gluttonous earth-women; thieving weasel-women; idle horse-women; ugly ape-women; and bee-women, industrious and brilliant, the only good kind in existence. Pandora, like her Christian counterpart Eve, lingered in men's minds as the raw essence of femininity. Women wove as she wove, deceived as she deceived and, if they seemed lascivious, which any who enjoyed themselves in the bedroom might, loved as she had loved.

It was only in the Byzantine period that more enlightened writers began to realise that Pandora was more than a hideous *objet d'art*. She represented what was possible after Prometheus cleverly hid fire in the stem of a fennel plant and gave it to mortals to play with. She was creative potential, art object and allegory of art rolled into one.

The transformation of Pandora began long before men were even aware of it. All through antiquity women were engaged in acts of making, writing, politicking and engineering that passed many men by. Male writers were quite happy to imagine mythological women turning their daily chores into creative exercises in self-expression. In Homer's *Odyssey*, which dates to just before Hesiod, Penelope cleverly unpicks by night the threads of a shroud she has been weaving by day to avoid marrying a grasping suitor. In Ovid's *Metamorphoses*, Philomela weaves the story of her rape into a tapestry after her tongue is cut out and she is deprived of the power of speech. It did not always occur to men that real women might be up to something just as interesting. These women are the focus of this book.

'An army of horsemen, some say, or infantry, / Or a fleet of ships is the most beautiful / Thing on black earth, / But I say it's what one loves.'[3] There is such confidence in Sappho's poetic voice. Reading her words can make you feel like you are entering the space between two people caught in the middle of something. They have been having a row, perhaps, or they are trying to say goodbye before one of them leaves on a voyage from which the other fears they will never return. The air between them is yet to clear, but somehow Sappho has swept it up, carried it away to somewhere even more private to scrutinise with what transpires to be the very opposite of an objective eye. Even – especially – when she herself is one of the two people involved and has fair claim to be the injured party.

Sappho was the great poet of longing and jealous desire. Born on the island of Lesbos perhaps eighty years after Hesiod, she did for love poetry what Homer did for epic. People called her the Tenth Muse because her verses appeared to have flittered down from the godly heights of Helicon.[4] She composed hymns for weddings and competitions in addition to the more private, romantic verses for other women that won her lasting fame. '. . . As far as the memory will stretch,' wrote a male geographer some six centuries after she lived, 'I do not know of any other woman who has been noted to be any match for her in the art of poetry.'[5]

Sappho may well have been superior to most, but already by the first century, the writings of many of her competitors had been lost, making a fair judgement impossible. The ensuing centuries have been even crueller to the survival of women's work. We know the names of many female artists and writers, but possess the works of few.[6] On an Etruscan perfume jar made in Italy in Sappho's lifetime there is inscribed something like a love poem by the otherwise enigmatic Asi Akarai. In the Peloponnese in the third century BC, a woman named Anyte composed touching epitaphs and epigrams about animals and art, more than twenty of which are extant. I have translated some of these together with fragments of other women's writings at the head of each chapter in this book. Erinna, a talented female poet of the fourth century BC, wrote an astonishingly beautiful poem for her childhood friend Baucis, who had died. It was probably the only work that Erinna circulated prior to her own early death at the age of nineteen. In solemn hexameters she recalled how she and Baucis had once played together at being tortoises and fussed over their dolls like little mothers. Erinna related that Baucis' obsessions of new love following her marriage had obtruded on her own childhood memories. Erinna's tribute was known as *The Distaff* because it interwove passages on weaving with imagery of the mythological Fates spinning the thread that determined the shape and length of mortal lives. Weaving, Pandora's craft, was not only the principal occupation of most women in antiquity, it was a daily reminder of the approach of death.

Weaving made artists of all women, but not all women were content just with weaving. The great first-century encyclopaedist Pliny the Elder credited one Kora of Corinth with the discovery of the art of portraiture after she traced the shadow of her lover's face on a wall and had her father work up the outline in clay. Pliny knew of six other professional artists who were women – Timarete, Irene, Calypso, Aristarete, Iaia and Olympias – but not one of their pieces has survived. Other kinds of works by women were just occasionally recorded in inscriptions. Phile of Priene in Greek Ionia was an interesting rarity. In the mid-first century BC she became not only a magistrate in her city, but the first known woman to have a reservoir and aqueduct constructed at her own expense.

The importance of ancient women's work exceeds the contributions of extraordinary individuals. Together women helped to make antiquity as we know it. They were *creators of history*. It feels only right to think of them in this collective sense given how many died without being able to leave their own mark upon the world. Millions who perished in childbirth disappeared without so much as their names being carved in stone. As Pericles said in the fifth century BC, 'Great is the glory of the woman who is least spoken about, whether for good or for ill.' Most women followed this trajectory and were therefore lost to history. Even those who were documented in the literary and historical sources were prone to being overshadowed and wilfully miscast. They are too often presented as meddlers in men's lives, bad Pandoras, *les femmes à chercher*. Good women were defined in Latin by words that need no translation: *modestia*, *pudicitia*, *castitas*, *pietas*. Such qualities may not stir much excitement in the modern woman, but were we to seek out the rebels alone, we would risk overlooking some of the most fascinating characters in history. It was sometimes by conforming to these very expectations that women achieved immortality. It could be both the greatest compliment and the gravest insult to say, 'She did not act like a woman.'

Classical historians privileged the deeds of men over the loom-work of their wives and daughters, and modern historians have typically followed suit. There are many histories of the ancient world on my bookshelves, and for all that they are 'epic', 'sweeping', 'definitive' and 'extraordinary', they are, it has to be said, ineluctably male. 'The Story' of antiquity is one of warlords, conquerors and kings with imposing beards and do-not-cross-me sceptres. We could attempt to counter this trend by stitching together a collection of chapters on Cleopatra, Boudica and half a dozen lesser-known women, but the result would never add up to a complete history.

My challenge has been to write a book that holds its own as a new history of the classical world while emphasising women's roles within it. This is not a book *about* women, but a history of antiquity written *through* women as far as this is possible. It aims to bring women to the fore without distorting the reality of events by pretending that men were not usually in charge. Remove the Ptolemys and Caesars, Pericles and Alexander, Xerxes and Juba entirely, and one ploughs a spartan field. Push them to the borders slightly, and light may fall upon the clearing to reveal the women in their shadow.

Many of these women *are* shadow. They now exist in no more than a few sentences or engravings on a fragment of marble. Some may say there is no value in writing of those we know so little, but I have always thought it wrong to leave people in the dust for the simple fact that they seemed unremarkable to others at the time. Some figures from history owe their survival to serendipity but many more owe it to design. The disappearance of so many women was not simple chance. The men who penned the vast majority of the surviving sources simply wrote them out of the narrative as unimportant.

There are women we can lift out of antiquity and give some muscle to, especially in the Roman period, when the merest hint of brazenness stirred the fashionable writers' pens. But there are also women who remain spectral and mizzled. If they cannot be made all flesh and blood again, their existence can still be acknowledged, taken up and used to tell the story of the world they helped to create. With every chapter, with every century, the sources grow richer, and we may inch a little closer to this goal.

Researching this book has required me to go back and re-read the Greek and Latin texts I have studied throughout my life. The process has reinforced my belief that, in order to find something, you should search for it rather than wait for it to filter through to you. Regardless of how well you *think* you know a poem or a work of art, there is always another way of looking at it.

Actively looking for women in the literary and archaeological sources has led me to uncover material I never knew existed. Most of us are familiar with Mark Antony as the doomed lover of Cleopatra, for example, but relatively few remember his wife Fulvia. Classical historians tell of this astonishingly accomplished woman fighting a war in Antony's name while he continued his affair in the east. I had read these passages with suspicion until I learned of the excavation of lead bullets referencing Fulvia at the site of a siege. These bullets bore messages of abuse. 'I'm aiming for Fulvia's clitoris', reads one.

The complicated relationships between women and men are an inescapable part of this story. Antony was, in my view, an unworthy husband for Fulvia, and an unworthy husband, too, for his next wife, Octavia. I have repeatedly been struck by the ill-treatment that wives received at the hands of their husbands, fathers, guardians and politicians, and by the courage with which these women sought to forge their own paths. It may be true that behind every great man is a great woman, but it is often also the case that in front of every great woman is a man who believes he is great. It is a bold and subjective claim to make, but the sources speak clearly for themselves.

As the culmination of research I have conducted over the past fifteen years, this book naturally reflects my specialism as a classicist, which is to say a pursuer of the worlds of Greece and Rome. It is at the same time a global story, proceeding from Minoan Crete to Mycenaean Greece, from Lesbos to Asia Minor (modern Turkey), from the Persian Empire of ancient Iran to the royal court of Macedonia, from Dido's Carthage in

Africa to Cleopatra's Egypt via Rome and its growing empire. It covers a stretch of almost 3,000 years up to the collapse of the Julio-Claudian dynasty, a watershed in classical history, which provided the starting point of my previous book on the two Plinys. I write with new awareness of how fragile yet fortifying a woman's words may be.

Chapter I

Of Breasts and Bulls

Purple reins have the kids put on you, goat,
And on your shaggy face a muzzle
As they teach you to race like a horse round the temple of the god
That he might watch over them delighting in childish games.

Anyte, Greek Anthology 6.312, third century BC

In ninth-century Constantinople a scholar, bibliophile and soon-to-be saint named Photius is rifling through his papers. Hopes of retrieving anything from his tottering compendium of reviews, titbits and other people's thoughts are growing more remote by the day, but a couple of lines of text catch his eye. The note, jotted down from a piece of papyrus from ancient Egypt, makes the astonishing claim that Homer copied his epics from a woman.[1]

Her name was Phantasia, and she had deposited her books about the Trojan War and the adventures of Odysseus in a temple at Memphis, south of Cairo, where Homer found them. Impressed by what he read, the would-be poet asked the temple scribe for copies, which he then used to compose his *Iliad* and *Odyssey*. The man celebrated for producing the earliest recorded poems in the western world might have been a genius, but he was apparently also a plagiarist, a thief, a claimant to a woman's intellectual property.

A few centuries after saintly Photius discovered this curious piece of intelligence, Eustathius, archbishop of Thessalonica in Greece, stumbles upon another reference to Phantasia.[2] His source, a mysterious Naucrates, identifies her as a poet from Memphis and Homer as a student or an

Egyptian poet. Phantasia is said to have placed her finished works in a Temple of Hephaestus.

Three-quarters of a millennium later the novelist Samuel Butler is on a boat from Dover to Calais when he strikes up conversation with a passenger who has read of the archbishop's heart-stopping discovery. As the gentleman reveals 'the truth' about the origins of Homer's epics, he sows a seed in Butler's mind that will never be dislodged. It seems unthinkable that a woman could have composed the *Iliad* with all its descriptions of martial warfare, but the *Odyssey* has long seemed to Butler a more domestic poem, a poem of women and goddesses, a poem brimming with mistakes that a man would never make. No man would be so thoughtless as to give a ship a rudder at both ends! No man would be so simple-minded as to propose that dry timber could be cut from a living tree! In 1897 Butler publishes a book with a wryly informative title: *The Authoress of the Odyssey: Where and when she wrote, who she was, the use she made of the Iliad, and how the poem grew under her hands.*

Some decades after that, Robert Graves, author of *I, Claudius*, reads Butler's book and finds in it a reflection of his own thoughts on the *Odyssey.* Butler had proposed that Phantasia was a pseudonym for Nausicaa, helper of Odysseus and princess of Scheria, a magical island where the trees are forever in fruit. She was, in Butler's words, 'a high-spirited, headstrong girl who had been accustomed to have her own way', living, very precisely, at Trapani on the west coast of Sicily.[3] Graves now imagines Nausicaa, a young woman, 'neither tall nor particularly beautiful', as the original bard.[4]

'Oh, Muses,' she prays in *Homer's Daughter*, Graves's novel of 1955, 'enter into the heart of your servant Nausicaa, and teach her to compose skilful hexameter verses!' Nausicaa's prayer is answered. Over many years she produces an epic poem, writes it out on Egyptian papyrus and entrusts it to a male poet to sing across the courts of Greece. 'The *Iliad*, which I admire, is devised by a man for men,' she promised. 'This epic, *The Odyssey*, will be devised by a woman for women.' And so, in Graves's mind, the *Odyssey* was born.

There was just one problem with these men's theories. Phantasia was a fantasy. The earliest reference to her may be traced to the writings of a grammarian of second-century Alexandria named Ptolemy Chennus ('the Quail'). Despite being surrounded by serious-minded scholars, the

Quail was something of a jester, with a keen appetite for the absurd. He frequently supported his alleged facts with spurious citations and also claimed that Homer was inspired by one 'Helen'. The truth was staring scholars in the face: 'Phantasia' is the Greek for 'a parade', 'a display', almost 'a front'.

Phantasia may be one of the most protracted hoaxes in literary history. In hailing her as the originator of Homer's tales, the Quail and his adherents pulled wool over the eyes of some of the most learned readers in history.

Not many men of the nineteenth and early twentieth centuries would have thought a woman capable of composing one of the greatest poems in the world. The likes of Samuel Butler and Robert Graves deserve some credit for their free-thinking. Their efforts besides say something interesting about the nature of Homer's poems and the world from which they came. The two epics were set some 400 years before they were completed. Looking back to the Trojan War from the vantage point of the late eighth or early seventh century BC was the equivalent of looking back to the Spanish Armada from the present day. When we remember that the poems consciously evoke the Late Bronze Age, a time when women not only worked, but held considerable authority within their societies, the longevity of the Phantasia legend suddenly seems less bewildering.

The story of Phantasia serves to remind us that, in order to understand the position of real women in antiquity, we need to look further back in time to the period before Homer and the advent of literature. We must go back to the Mycenaeans of early Greece, who thrived in legendary Odysseus' time, and before that, to the people the Mycenaeans learned from, the women-revering Minoans of Bronze Age Crete. It is with the Minoans that our history must begin.

Crete has always been an island of bulls. Even in shape it is peculiarly bovine – a taut, long body stretched out to the south of the Aegean, culminating at its north-west end in a pair of elegantly distinguished horns. In antiquity, disputes arose over the precise measurements of the land mass – home to the fabled King Minos, Queen Pasiphaë and the half-man, half-bull Minotaur – and the question of whether its isthmuses and promontories ought to be included in the calculation, or just the torso, chest to rump.[5] One estimator claimed that the strip exceeded 2,300 stadia in length and 5,000 in circumference. Too fat, cried another, who believed that precision was everything: it was 4,100 stadia all around at the very most. No, no, no: 2,000 stadia long, insisted somebody else. No consensus was reached.

The size of Crete (later confirmed to be 260 kilometres – roughly 1,400 stadia – by 60 kilometres at its very brawniest) mattered because it brought the island into close proximity to not one continent, like many of the smaller islands, but three. Two days and two nights at sea could carry a Cretan from the south coast to Cyrene in Libya, and twice as many would take them from the north-east down to Egypt.[6] The journey to Asia Minor was comparatively direct, and mainland Greece lay within such easy reach that the archaeologist Sir Arthur Evans would hail ancient Crete as 'the first stepping-stone of European civilisation'.[7]

The island was home from about 3000 BC to the Minoans, a spectacularly enterprising and industrious people, whose civilisation developed at the beginning of the Bronze Age and reached its zenith a millennium and a half later following the construction of palatial buildings so intricate as to resemble labyrinths. Named by a nineteenth-century German scholar in honour of their legendary king, the Minoans were non-Greeks, whose way of life was startlingly unlike that of any other people in the world.[8] Much about them remains mysterious. They developed a language to write in, but left behind no literature, no chronicles and no citizens' names. They built sunken rooms in their halls but did not document what they used them for. They sculpted figures of buxom women with snakes enwrapping their arms like lace, of men leap-frogging over bulls, of cats nesting snugly on people's heads, but they provided little clue as to whether these were episodes drawn from life, or symbols for something else. Their surviving art and architecture nevertheless give the impression that, in their richly creative society, women were often more prominent than men.

The origins of the Minoans have long been argued over. Scholars have proposed that they came to Crete from North Africa, Asia Minor or the Near East, but a ten-year study on mitochondrial DNA extracted from bones discovered in one of the island's caves has lent some credence to the hypothesis that they were in fact more local.[9] The results of DNA investigations are never uncontentious as their accuracy can be difficult to establish, but the ancestry of the deceased examined in this investigation was traced predominantly to the Aegean and western Turkey; there was little to differentiate their bones from those of modern Cretans.[10] The Minoans were relatively tall, the average man standing at 167 centimetres, and the average woman at 154 centimetres.[11] His life expectancy was about thirty-five at the height of Minoan civilisation and hers, reflecting the dangers of childbirth, just twenty-seven or twenty-eight.[12] Both osteomyelitis, an infection of the bone, and brucellosis, a disease transmitted through animal products, especially milk, have been detected in the skeletal remains.[13]

We would describe many Minoan clothes today as characteristically feminine. Minoan men liked to dress in skirt-like sarongs with codpieces and carried swords and axes made of bronze. Women wore long patterned skirts with belts and corset-like tops, or no tops at all; in surviving art they very often have their breasts fully exposed to view. Both men and women tended to wear their hair long in flowing curls and were fond of gold jewellery. It is thought that the Minoans invented the sandal; the Greek word *sandalon* is believed to have derived from their language.[14]

Cretan hieroglyphs were developed in the north of the island about 2000 BC but were superseded early on by a different form of syllabic script known as Linear A. The art of writing was by then already well-established in other parts of the world including Egypt. The Sumerians, who controlled Mesopotamia and established powerful cities in the east, had been the first to stamp the wedge-like shapes of cuneiform on clay tablets in the fourth millennium BC. The earliest named author in the world was a Sumerian woman named Enheduanna, a poet and priestess, to whom we shall return. Minoan Linear A looked quite different from the existing cuneiform, consisting of a series of line-heavy signs and ideograms designed to represent common objects and items of produce, including olive oil, wine and cattle.[15] Linear A was used for list-making and accountancy rather than extended writing. It is yet to be fully deciphered.

Crete was known among later Greek historians for being the first place to raise a navy and master the Aegean.[16] Minoan ship-sheds have been discovered at a number of sites, including at Kommos on the southern coast and at Katsamba near Heraklion in the north.[17] Boats varied according to use, some practically equipped for trade, others so charming in appearance as to evoke the promise of a pleasure cruise, with strings of bell-like decorations stretching from mast to stern and bow to mast, and long, luxurious awnings shielding the rowers labouring beneath. The first Minoan shipwreck ever to be found was excavated earlier this century by Elpida Hadjidaki-Marder, a marine archaeologist who grew up in Chania in north-west Crete.[18] Guided by intuition, Hadjidaki-Marder directed her search off Pseira, an islet in Mirabello Bay, at the north-east of the island, and alighted upon something extraordinary. Although all trace of the wooden vessel had gone, its cargo, consisting predominantly of ceramic jars for transporting oil or wine, still lay on the seabed. The Minoan ship had sunk about 1750 BC.

Expertise in shipbuilding enabled the people of Crete to establish themselves widely overseas. Minoan settlements arose on neighbouring islands, including at Triánda on Rhodes, Kastri on Cythera, Akrotiri on Thera (Santorini) and further afield; Gaza was at the very least a Minoan trading station. Like Pompeii and Herculaneum in AD 79, the Minoan port town of Akrotiri was preserved after being smothered in ash during a catastrophic volcanic eruption sometime between about 1600 and 1530 BC, allowing later excavators to reveal the extent of its own networks with Crete, Egypt, Syria and beyond. The city possessed a central square or, technically, a triangle, surrounded by elegant streets lined with many-storeyed houses. One of the Minoan-style wall frescoes discovered beneath the debris features a species of monkey believed to be native to the Indian subcontinent.[19] Identified only recently by their unusual downward-pointing tails, the grey langurs were painted an exotic blue, just as African baboons were in wall paintings on Crete in an artistic convention that emphasised their exoticism.[20] These wall paintings provide tentative but thrilling evidence of the existence of the Silk Roads over a millennium earlier than previously thought.

The Minoans exchanged goods with the peoples of the Cycladic islands and Egypt from almost the very beginning of their civilisation. The first delegations were depicted in Egyptian art in the early fifteenth century BC when the female pharaoh Hatshepsut was on the throne. It would have been characteristic of Hatshepsut to initiate the trade link. She was, even more than her husband/half-brother Thutmose II, exceedingly partial to new enterprise.

Defying convention, Hatshepsut ruled as a female 'king', possibly following the example of her first-dynasty predecessor Meritneith, while serving as co-regent with her young stepson following her husband's untimely death. How her stepson felt about this arrangement is unknown. In works of art, Hatshepsut was often depicted wearing male clothes, and even a false beard.[21] Her building works included the pair of extraordinary obelisks, almost 30 metres tall, still visible in the Temple of Amun at Karnak. Episodes of her life story were narrated in sculptures at the mortuary temple in which she was laid when she died, probably of natural causes, some twenty years into her rule.[22] They began with her conception as the daughter of Thutmose I, shown as the sun god Amun-Re, and his wife Ahmose, and progressed to show her being modelled, Pandora-like, from clay. Some of the most vivid artworks documented her expedition to the Land of Punt, in east Africa. The treasures Hatshepsut brought back from here included frankincense and myrrh. In Sinai, she established mining interests to extract copper and turquoise. The Phoenicians (Canaanites) of the Levant she persuaded to supply her with wood for shipbuilding. Hatshepsut probably arrived at an agreement with the early Cretans as well. The Egyptians came to speak of the Minoans as dwellers of 'Keftiu' (Crete) or of the 'islands in the middle of the Big Green [sea]'.[23] The tomb paintings of Rekhmire, a vizier of the same dynasty as Hatshepsut, reveal just some of the items the Minoans carried over. Minoan men, since altered to resemble the later Mycenaeans, are shown in profile wearing kilts and bearing large pots, metal vessels and sculpted animal heads.[24] In exchange for items such as scarabs, the Minoans also supplied the Egyptians with textiles and wood so that they could build further monuments and ships of their own.

Revering the water and the life that swam beneath it, the Minoans covered their ceramics in paintings of fish, dolphins and enormous octopuses with flailing arms and staring eyes. Their pottery was produced on clay potters' wheels which were typically freely revolving so as to enable rapid production.[25] The finest Minoan clothes glowed purple with the product of another sea creature. Piles of Minoan-era murex shells discovered across Crete, especially at Palaikastro, Kommos and Malia, provide evidence that the Minoans were using the molluscs to make purple dye thousands of years before the Romans made 'Tyrian' purple fashionable.[26] Fish and shellfish also formed part of the Minoan diet, but in smaller quantities than meat, such as mutton, fowl, hare, goat and pork, which was cooked on braziers, and wheat, millet and barley, legumes, figs, grapes, pomegranates, almonds, pistachios and saffron. Wall paintings show Minoans gathering saffron with such devotion as to suggest that the spice played a role in ritual as well as cooking and textile-dyeing.

Life on Minoan Crete could be comfortable but unpredictable. The 'Town Mosaic', a series of small plaques made about 1700–1600 BC, reveals their houses (some square, others taller than wide) to have been built from mudbrick with multiple storeys and windows arranged on the upper levels alone.[27] Many homes had terracotta bathtubs, cisterns and inner courtyards. The grander properties were built of ashlar masonry with large central halls, storage wings, the mysterious sunken rooms and light wells to flood even the darkest corners in sunlight.[28] Most spacious of all were the 'palaces'. Their construction on Crete coincided with the development of Linear A following a period of dramatic upheaval. From about 2200 BC, a number of early settlements on the island were destroyed and deserted, perhaps in connection with a drought. Further devastation followed the erection of the first palatial complexes.[29] This time, earthquakes or warfare were probably to blame, and led to many of the newer buildings being razed. The palaces were subsequently rebuilt on such a grand scale as to exceed in splendour all existing architecture in the western world.

The palaces were so-named by the aforementioned Arthur Evans, the Oxford-educated son of a wealthy paper manufacturer, who arrived on Crete at the turn of the nineteenth century with an ambition far greater than his experience. His half-sister Joan described him as 'small and rather insignificant' as a boy, with a 'peering' stance owing to severe myopia.[30] While he 'had not eyesight enough for cricket', the diminutive scholar did have an eye for art, which he put to good use when he became Keeper of Oxford's Ashmolean Museum in his mid-thirties. A man of boundless energy, Evans transformed the haphazard jumble of things he found there into a world-class collection by relocating the museum to a more spacious building nearby, reorganising the displays and enriching the holdings through inspired acquisitions. His chance purchase of some Cretan seal stones at an Athenian market awoke him most palpably to the mysteries of the Minoans.

Knossos, near Heraklion in northern Crete, was already by then a known archaeological site. Inhabited since the Early Neolithic era, circa 6000 BC, it became home to one of the great centres of Minoan civilisation when it was chosen as the setting for a palatial complex extending to hundreds of rooms. A wealthy Cretan businessman named Minos Kalokairinos had discovered it in 1878 and combed the soil in which the so-called Second Palace stood, but much remained alluringly earthed-over, like crabs buried deep in the sand. Kalokairinos had been prevented from carrying out a full excavation for fear that any finds could be removed to Constantinople.[31] Crete was still subject to Ottoman control. To Kalokairinos's frustration, a Cretan official allowed Evans to purchase part of Knossos after Crete gained its autonomy in 1898, and a new law was passed permitting the Englishman to commence his own excavation. It was Kalokairinos who had first introduced Evans to the site. He later launched an unsuccessful legal case against him.

Evans had no formal archaeological education – he acquired most of his knowledge from digs conducted by private means since his youth – but he did have his trained, near-sighted eyes, and considerable funds. The sudden death of his wife Margaret while they were both still in their forties provided the impetus he needed to lay aside his dislike of water ('that uncertain element'), select his team, and make the rough crossing to Crete.[32] Over the coming years, Evans would make headlines around the world for leading what remains one of the most exciting excavations ever to have taken place. But while his large company of labourers, male and female, were sifting through the earth, another archaeologist was looking on.

Harriet Boyd was born in Boston in 1871 and studied at Smith College, Massachusetts, before volunteering as a nurse with the Greek army in the Graeco-Turkish War. Less celebrated than Evans in the ensuing decades, but better qualified for fieldwork, she defiantly brushed aside the many people who told her that archaeology was no pursuit for a woman and undertook her own dig on Crete. Using the funding she had received through an academic fellowship, she completed three seasons at Gournia, in the north-east of the island, from 1901. She consequently became the first woman in history to direct her own excavation on the island and publish the results.[33] It so happened that Boyd had visited Knossos a year earlier in time to observe and sketch some of Evans's most intriguing discoveries. In April 1900 there came to light a large compartment with a carved gypsum chair built into one wall, surrounded by vibrant red frescoes of griffins. 'In sport,' Boyd recorded, Evans named this chair 'the throne of Ariadne', daughter of Minos, as if the historicity of Ariadne was firmly established.[34] The joke, however, was on Evans, as Boyd apparently recognised. Believing the throne's seat too narrow for a female derrière, the Oxonian abandoned this improbable attribution in favour of the equally romantic idea that he had discovered at Knossos 'The Throne Room' of a priest-king or King Minos himself.

Stories of the mythical Cretan ruler had circulated for thousands of years after Homer's epics. In death, Minos was said to have sat with a golden sceptre at the threshold of Hades as a judge of the spirits of the Underworld.[35] In life, he was a much-feared ruler, blighted by misfortune. Legend held that his wife, Pasiphaë, a daughter of the Sun, was consumed by unnatural lust. Minos had failed to sacrifice the fine bull he had promised to Poseidon, and to punish him, the sea god put Pasiphaë under a spell. Overcome by feelings she could not satisfy in human form, the queen commissioned Daedalus, the most skilled of the craftsmen on Crete, to build her a wooden cow. Daedalus fashioned a shell-on-legs just large enough to hold her in the most amenable fashion for having sex. By some miracle she conceived within the carapace a hybrid child.

Daedalus was kept in lucrative employment after the monstrous Minotaur was born. He designed and built the enormous labyrinth that concealed the bull-man, who feasted on a regular tribute of seven girls and seven boys sent from Athens in recompense for the murder of Minos' son in the city. In the myth, Theseus, a so-called hero, arrived from Athens and won the heart of the princess Ariadne to bring the gruesome practice to an end. Hopelessly enamoured, Ariadne gave Theseus the ball of thread he needed to weave himself free of the twisting lair, and with it the confidence to slay the beast.[36] Daedalus made his escape from Crete and the changeable king's rule by soaring to the sky on wax-sealed wings. It was during their flight that his beloved son Icarus flew too close to the sun, whereupon the wax of his wings melted and he tumbled to his death. The Cretan tragedy was doubled when Ariadne awoke to find that Theseus had abandoned her on the island of Naxos without a parting word. Her lovesickness and despair at the heartlessness of men would be immortalised by poets through history, never more poignantly than by the love poet Catullus in a first-century BC poem inspired by the decoration on a bedspread.

Evans had studied antiquities in Bosnia, Italy and Sicily before turning to Knossos, but for all his worldliness, his view of Minoan culture was influenced predominantly by his experience of the British Empire. His assumption was that buildings as grand as those at Knossos could only have supported a king-led monarchy. While it was reasonable to suppose that the ancient complex was home to the most authoritative members of the elite, there was no evidence of a real King Minos – no evidence, indeed, that Minoan Crete was ruled by men. The buildings at Knossos did not constitute a 'palace' in the conventional sense. They consisted rather of a cultural centre with workshops, spaces for enormous *pithoi* storage jars, rooms for administration and the archiving of writing tablets, places to perform religious sacrifice, a central court, stately suites and well-functioning sewers. In ambition and range, the establishment paralleled the walled city of Erlitou in China, which had been constructed slightly earlier, about 1800 BC, in the Yellow River valley, and was thick with workshops and tombs.[37] Other palatial complexes existed elsewhere on Crete, including at Malia, Phaistos and Galatas, but the Second Palace complex at Knossos, which replaced the earlier destroyed structure, was by far the largest and most intricate, extending to almost two hectares.

Visitors who entered the complex from the south proceeded through the porch to a long corridor, which led them slowly into a central court larger than four modern tennis courts combined (the courts at the palace of Phaistos in central-southern Crete could similarly host hundreds of people). Those coming from the north-west passed a grander room with central columns. In Minoan culture, columns tended, most unusually, to taper downwards, so as to be slimmer at the base. While 'The Throne Room' lay just west of the central court, the suites Evans associated with the royal family of Knossos were in the east wing. Of these, the 'queen's quarters' were the more lavish, as they contained a bathtub and toilet which were connected to the sophisticated underground drainage system. These quarters offer further evidence of the prominence of women within the Minoan court.

An exquisite fresco of dolphins adorned one of these regal rooms. Like so many of the artworks discovered at Knossos, it was heavily restored by an artist-architect under Evans's watch. The restorations or 'reconstitutions' made to various parts of the palace by Evans and his artistic associates were rightly a source of contention from early on. Repairs to columns and roofs were justified by the need to protect the site from the elements. Knossos was rocked by earthquakes in 1926 and

1930 as it had been in the past. The erection of a new floor allowed for the exhibition of many of the works of art that would otherwise have remained unseen. But Evans went further than was strictly necessary. The Greek archaeologist Spyridon Marinatos criticised him for 'tak[ing] liberties beyond what is desirable' in his repairs to doors, window openings, and the arrangement of some of the frescoes.[38] The repainting of frescoes themselves, many of them by Swiss artists Émile Gilliéron *et fils*, invited even fiercer complaints. The faces of three Minoan women standing against a blue wall were more or less recreated *ex nihilo*. 'Mais, ce sont des Parisiennes!' exclaimed a French scholar on seeing some of the paintings of *femmes élégantes* with their red lips and flawless coiffure.[39] The novelist Evelyn Waugh, visiting the site in the late 1920s, likened the appearance of the re-painted women to that of models gracing the covers of *Vogue*.[40]

While some of Evans's interventions were wrongheaded, his interpretations were understandable, even where they were unsound. Some of the least realistic elements of the Cretan myth were readily discernible in the remains. There may have been no Minotaur, but the palace itself was a labyrinth, deep and mysterious, stirring stories of what lurked within. Images of labyrinths appeared on an early fresco at Knossos, on writing tablets from about 1200 BC, and on coins from the fifth century BC.[41] Sir Arthur Evans came to see the palace as a labyrinth quite literally. Many of the walls, columns and artworks bore a symbol of a double-axe which he described using the Greek word *labrys*.[42] The connection Evans drew between *labrys* and the palace as a *labyr*inth is dubious, but the Greek *labyrinthos* is etymologically linked to 'da-pu-ri-to', which appears on tablets at Knossos. It is possible that the palace or another destination on Crete was indeed known in the Bronze Age as a labyrinth.[43] The fact that the double-axe is very often shown in the hands of women, as if a symbol of female power, adds weight to the argument that women stood at the centre of this labyrinthine world.

Like the 3,000-chambered 'labyrinth' built at Hawara near Crocodilopolis in Egypt about 1800 BC and identified as a mortuary temple for Amenemhat III, the Second Palace at Knossos drew visitors into a network of corridors so tight and expansive that, like the Minotaur, they might never have found their way out again.[44] There may have been no Daedalus, but craftmanship was so central to Minoan culture that considerable parts of the cities and palatial complexes were given over to the workshops. Knossos was home to potters, stone-cutters and other artisans, and at Gournia, Harriet Boyd (Hawes after her marriage to the British anthropologist Charles Hawes) uncovered crafting centres where ivory and gold were used as raw materials. One of the most striking Minoan objects took the form of a solid gold pendant shaped to resemble bees and a honeycomb.[45] Crete was an island full of Daedaluses and Daedalusai. It is highly likely that many of the craftspeople were female. If women arranged the trade of their textiles, which is most probable, they contributed significantly to the Minoan economy.

There may never have been a queen named Pasiphaë who mated with a bull, but Minoan Crete was saturated in bull imagery, which only reinforced the power of the myth. It featured in everything from wall crenelations and paintings to drinking vessels (among the most impressive, discovered near the palace at Knossos, a black steatite *rhyton* used for pouring liquids, shaped as a bull's head with golden horns and eyes glowing blood-red).[46] No challenge was considered greater on the island than that of leaping over a charging bull. There was no fixed method of performing the feat, known as *taurokathapsia* (bull-leaping), and no certainty that it was ever actually achieved. Nevertheless, intrepid leapers were immortalised in wall frescoes and seals, on sarcophagi and vases, in terracotta and bronze, flinging themselves over the bulging torsos of the beasts or using them as pommel horses upon which to perform acrobatics. An ivory sculpture, made circa 1500 BC, captures the look of determined concentration on a leaper's face as he moves over a (now missing) bull.[47] A bronze from a similar period shows a leaper performing a somersault between a bull's horns.[48]

Most leapers mount their bulls from the front rather than from behind. Modern bull-handlers deny that this is possible owing to the bull's habit of tossing its head.[49] This was where women came in useful. One of the wall paintings at Knossos shows a male leaper performing a handstand on a bull's back while two figures, seemingly women presented in male clothes, assist.[50] One of these mysterious figures is standing before the long-bodied animal and grasping its horns to steady it. The other waits at its rear with her arms in the air as a 'spotter' to support the leaper as he prepares to dismount. The artist went to some effort to emphasise the assistants' roles in the bull-leaping. It was artistic convention to depict men with brown-red flesh suggestive of outdoor labour, but to paint women with white skin to emphasise the time they spent indoors. In Egypt, by contrast, Ahmose-Nefertari, Chief Royal Wife in the eighteenth dynasty, was most often shown with blue or black skin, suggestive of her priestly role as God's Wife of Amun, a divinity also typically depicted in blue paint. In the Cretan wall-painting, a starker than usual distinction has been made between the women's whiteness and the men's brownness. The choice of colour might have been determined by the subjects' status rather than their gender, but it is more tempting to view the white figures as female and portrayed in such a way as to illustrate the novelty of their involvement in a male exercise.

While the bull-leapers of ancient Crete immediately evoke the image of Minos and the Minotaur, the myth of Minos' mother, Europa, and another bull was just as important. Europa, a legendary princess, came from the region of modern Lebanon inhabited by the Phoenicians, whose civilisation emerged about the same time as that of the Minoans.[51] Spying her from afar, Zeus pulsated with lust. Assuming the shape of a handsome white bull, he made his approach and stole her away to Crete, where in her innocence she delivered his child. Minos was therefore the son of one bull, and the stepfather to the monstrous product of another.

Where later artists would explore the raw violence of the Minotaur, the Minoans appreciated the bull's potential to tame and be tamed. Bull-leaping represented an act of extraordinary intimacy between human and animal.[52] Minoan young men were perhaps taught to master bulls as a means of mastering themselves. Their success as bull-leapers might well have marked a rite of passage to adulthood. There is evidence that the Minoans also sacrificed bulls. They clearly believed that the animal possessed some potency on earth and beyond it.

Zeus' connection with Crete ran deeper still because his mother, Rhea, was supposed to have given birth to him at Lyctus in its heartlands.[53] Rhea's husband, Kronos, had swallowed each of their previous children alive when they were born because he feared that one of them might usurp him. Thickly forested Mount Dikte offered Rhea's new child the best possible chance of survival. The baby, Zeus, was safely delivered here, and grew up to fulfil his father's nightmare by taking his place as king of the gods. The most cavernous parts of Crete subsequently assumed significance among worshippers – especially pregnant women and new or hopeful mothers. While the earliest offerings deposited in the caves of Mount Dikte probably pre-dated the myth of Zeus' birth, the connection between the setting and Rhea's labour was firmly established in the period after the Minoans. The votives, some of which were discovered in the cave's stalagmites and stalactites, included weapons, figurines, both male and female, a terracotta female head with enormous eyes and long lashes, and part of what would have been a colossal sculpture of a woman or a goddess, perhaps Rhea herself.[54] Clay models of women in labour have also been discovered at Amnisos, northern Crete, in a cave Homer said was dedicated to the worship of Eileithyia, a goddess of childbirth.[55] They are less detailed than examples from other cultures, such as the teeth-baring Dumbarton Oaks Birthing Figure, discovered in South America and associated with Aztec tradition, but equally charged with emotion.[56]

Some of the most interesting sculptures of women came from Knossos itself. One of the oldest, made in the fourteenth century BC, is a figure of a woman or goddess raising her huge plate-like hands to the skies while a bird rests on her head.[57] Three 'Snake Goddesses' were also discovered at the complex in a very poor state of repair. Reconstructed after Evans excavated them using bits and pieces found near them in the ground, they resemble divinities, but might just as well have been inspired by priestesses or other prominent Minoan women. They stand bare-breasted in floor-length skirts with snakes in their hands or slithering up their arms. A cat, which originally belonged to another sculpture, sits on the headdress of the most striking of the three. The sculptures are faience – quartz crystal crushed to form ceramic which is then glazed – and date to about 1600 BC when the palace complex at Knossos was at its most splendid.

Controversy surrounds the authenticity of a number of similar figures held in museum collections around the world. The Goddess in the Museum of Fine Arts Boston, a 16-centimetre-tall statuette of a topless woman grasping snakes, is now widely believed to be a fake.[58] Her face is reminiscent of that of a woman in a statue group from the later Mycenaean civilisation. The restorations and series of copies have made the interpretation of the Snake Goddesses only more complicated.

Sculptures of women with snakes have been found at so many sites on Crete, including Gournia, that they must have been central to Minoan belief. But what did they represent? Were they fertility figures? Protectors of the household? Symbols of death and, via the sloughing of snake skin, rebirth? Did they represent a predecessor of the Greek goddess Athena? Or were they based on Minos' daughter Ariadne? They are less obviously associated with fertility than some of the earlier sculptures discovered on the island. The so-called Goddess of Myrtos is an Early Bronze Age ceramic (c. 2500 BC) with prominent round breasts affixed in clay, a painted triangle for her *mons pubis*, and a vessel held like a baby with such affection that it would take a brave soul to wrest its contents from her.[59] A number of other Minoan terracotta wares (not to say jugs) were shaped as breasts with the nipples sometimes serving as spouts. The female breast, so often exposed to view, was important in Minoan culture, not only as a symbol of fertility and the fount of life-nurturing milk, but for its beauty. Given how ubiquitous they were in society, the breasts of the Snake Goddesses would not have been the first things a Minoan noticed. These women must have been celebrated less for their fertility than for their prowess at snake-handling. Lower Egypt was presided over by a cobra goddess named Wadjet (Upper Egypt, by contrast, had Nekhbet, a vulture goddess), who was believed to protect the pharaoh. She wore snakes and an elaborate headdress. Perhaps the Minoan 'Snake Goddesses' had a similar function and offered protection to whomever ruled Knossos. Snake-handling appears to have been an activity associated exclusively with women on Minoan Crete. It is possible that Minoan women, or the goddesses they revered, learned to master snakes in the same way as men learned to master bulls.

Arthur Evans argued that Minoan religion centred on the worship of one central goddess in various forms, but appearing most often with animals, plants or the double-axe. In Egypt in the fourteenth century BC, Queen Nefertiti and her husband and equal, Akhenaten, had presided over the establishment of a form of monotheism focused on the sun god Aten. The line between one goddess in various forms and several different goddesses is, however, a difficult one to draw in Minoan culture, and it is perhaps more helpful to recognise the separate qualities for which they were idolised. A female figure in a landscape with aggressive animals such as lions, for example, evokes the idea of divine power over the wildness of nature.

The prominence of female divinity in Minoan culture might well have reflected the prominence of Minoan women in daily life. In Shang dynasty China, the authority of goddesses such as the Eastern and Western Mothers was echoed to some degree by the authority of women in elite society and even the army. Fu Jing and Fu Hao, wives of King Wu Ding, led men into battle before being honoured in death with monumental tombs containing the victims of human sacrifice, battle axes, knives and arrowheads.[60] In Egypt, many of the images of Hatshepsut were destroyed or defaced after her death when her name was removed from the official list of rulers by her male successors, who sought to claim direct descent from her husband. It is possible that images of powerful Minoan women were subject to similar mistreatment. While there is no evidence that Minoan women ruled in the same manner as Hatshepsut, or joined battle like the women of Shang China, the sheer number of artworks depicting them centrally placed and on a larger scale than men has prompted some historians to speculate that Minoan society was matriarchal or matrilineal. 'Neopalatial Crete,' writes one scholar, 'presents the best candidate for a matriarchy – if one ever existed.'[61] There is nothing to say that the position of Minoan women was in any way secondary to that of men.

Minoan women were certainly not confined to the weaving room. Sculptures show them playing lyres, flutes and zithers, sashaying in flounced chevron-patterned skirts and raising their arms in the air in ecstasy.[62] In the 'Grandstand Fresco' from Knossos the women are more carefully delineated in paint than the men. Each woman has her own identity, her own style. The women appear to occupy the main rooms of the palace while the men congregate as an anonymous mass beyond. Women depicted seated – a sign of divinity or authority – are often being approached by men or animals. A highly enigmatic fresco at Thera (Santorini), for example, features a woman wearing large hoop earrings, a snake in her hair, and a neck-chain of ducks, sitting on a dais with a griffin beside her while a blue monkey pays her court.[63] On a gold ring, a female deity, we may presume, is seated beneath a tree, where she receives flowers from two women. A smaller figure of a man with a double-headed axe over his head hovers between them.[64] By depicting the man beneath the axe, and on a smaller scale than the women, the engraver of the ring perhaps hoped to convey that he was a divine vision, almost a thought-bubble, originating in one of the female worshipper's heads. Trees, as Arthur Evans recognised, were sacred in Minoan culture, and were perhaps believed to be capable of inspiring divine visions in those who honoured them. Such artworks contribute to the picture of Minoan women exerting considerable religious authority in the palace complexes and society more widely.

Minoan women also played a crucial role in ritual. The early Minoans sometimes interred their dead twice by exhuming the bones of their family members and resettling them later in jars. The more usual custom, however, was to bury the dead in chamber tombs or stone beehive-shaped 'tholos' tombs, clay sarcophagi or, in the case of infants, under the floorboards of the home. The colourful paintings on a rare limestone sarcophagus from Hagia Triada, circa 1400 BC, show three men carrying young animals and a model boat to the deceased, who stands in front of his tomb, ready to receive his provisions for the afterlife.[65] There are also three women present, the first of whom pours a libation into a cauldron placed between two upright axes mounted by birds; the second carries further vessels; the third – darker skinned like the men and thus possibly of lower social status – has a lyre. On the other side of the sarcophagus the women assist in the sacrifice of a bull on an altar. Other wall paintings show women involved in rituals of their own involving blood. A fresco from Akrotiri features a group of women, one of whom sits beside a sunken room or 'lustral basin' with a bleeding foot.[66] A tree also bleeds. It is possible that lustral basins were used for purification by women during or after menstruation.

The Minoans lived with a keen awareness of the precariousness of life and the threat of early death, but nothing could have prepared them for the devastation wrought at Akrotiri in the sixteenth century BC. It was at some indeterminate date in the first three-quarters of the sixteenth century BC, likely in spring or summer, that the disaster occurred. The volcanic eruption, one of the most violent in history, threw a Plinian column cloud dozens of kilometres into the sky before enveloping what lay beneath in swathes of ash. Modern Santorini and the archipelago to which it belongs form part of the caldera created during the eruption.

The effects of the eruption must have been felt across the Aegean, Mediterranean and perhaps further still. Volcanic pumice has been found at Tell el-Dab'a in Egypt, but in a workshop where it was used as a material for crafting objects; it could have been collected from a site nearer the volcano. It has been argued that unusual weather patterns documented in the Bamboo Annals in China were also triggered by the events at Thera. Crete lay just 150 kilometres south of the epicentre but miraculously experienced little pumice fall. There is evidence, however, that the north coast of the island and its harbours were struck by an ensuing tsunami. Even at Palaikastro, inland from the north-east coast, deposits have been discovered containing ash from Thera, shells and marine microfauna.[67]

The vision of Crete being submerged came to be associated with the story of Atlantis.[68] Plato described a utopian kingdom of that name being swallowed up by the sea following a natural disaster.[69] The island he evoked in two separate dialogues in the fourth century BC bore some similarities to Minoan Crete. His Atlantis was sacred to the sea god Poseidon, who settled upon it the children he had by a mortal woman named Cleito. A mighty power, Atlantis was subsequently ruled by a confederation of kings, who held sway over neighbouring islands and territories as far away as Italy. It was rich in metals, wood and fruit. There was a monumental palace marked for its fine workmanship and its furnishings of ivory and gold. There were harbours, ship-sheds, a channel built to the sea. And bulls, kept in precincts of Poseidon, which the princes of Atlantis used to hunt and sacrifice and pour libation to in a pledge to obey the laws inscribed upon a sacred pillar. But there were also important differences between Plato's Atlantis and historic Crete. The former – surely fictional – was described as larger than Libya and Asia Minor combined, and as located off the Strait of Gibraltar, a long way from Crete. More obviously, whereas Atlantis was said to have vanished following an earthquake, throwing up so much shoal mud in the process that the water around it became unnavigable, Crete manifestly did not sink.

If the myth of Atlantis can be linked to Crete at all, it is as an allegory for the demise of Minoan civilisation that commenced in the aftermath of the disaster. The Minoans might have been fortunate enough to escape submersion, but their culture, utopian in its way, began to wallow a century or so after the tragedy at Akrotiri occurred. What happened may never be recovered, but trade on Crete was disrupted as a result of the destruction caused to Akrotiri and the broader region, and the most prominent palatial sites were abandoned with the exception of Knossos, which survived for a further two centuries.

It was probably no coincidence that a new people, the Mycenaeans, had since arrived on the island. Was there a struggle between two rival civilisations? There is some evidence of Minoan artworks being destroyed. The Minoans had already spread their influence to the Mycenaeans' homeland in mainland Greece when the two came together. Recent studies reveal their genetic make-up to have been similar, though the Mycenaeans, defined now as early Greeks, had additional ancestry derived from the Eurasian steppe.[70] They managed to coexist on Crete for a time and the Mycenaeans remained indebted to the Minoans long after they established their own traditions on the island. In the longer term, however, the merging of the two peoples proved problematic, especially for women, whose powers diminished in the Mycenaean age. By the twelfth century BC, the newcomers had superseded the Minoans on their home soil, and had set their sights far beyond the bull-shaped isle.

Chapter II

The Work of Giants

But when you went to a man's bed, you forgot
All the words you heard from your mother as a child,
Dear Baucis: Aphrodite sowed forgetfulness in your heart.
I mourn you but now I look past your [scruples] . . .

From Erinna, *The Distaff*, fourth century BC

According to the myth, Danaë, princess of Argos in the Peloponnese, was impregnated by Zeus in the form of a shower of gold. The king of the gods poured into her while she was lying quite innocently in bed. Her father had locked her in a tower in a vain bid to avert a prophecy that said that, if she ever took a lover and conceived a son, the boy would grow up to kill his grandfather. Perseus, born of the union, inadvertently did precisely that by striking the old man with a discus. Although he would be more famous for killing the snake-haired Gorgon Medusa, whose look could turn a man to stone, Perseus was also recognised as the founder of one of the central cities of the Mycenaeans. Mycenae was said to have acquired its name after the hero plucked a mushroom (*mykes* in Greek) from the soil there and drank from it like a cup.[1]

The historical Mycenaeans established themselves all across the Peloponnese with magnificent centres at Tiryns, Pylos, Iolcus, Greek Thebes and Gla as well as Mycenae – cities that most of us would struggle to locate on a map today. They were both financially prosperous and globally curious. The extent of the trade networks into which they fed have been laid bare by the discovery of a fourteenth-century BC shipwreck off Uluburun in southern Turkey. The vessel was carrying a vast quantity of exotic items when it sank: copper ingots from Cyprus, ebony from Egypt,

Canaanite jars of terebinth resin, herbs and spices from the Middle East, the shells of ostrich eggs and twenty-four stone anchors (there is an especially sad irony in those).[2] A likely hypothesis is that it was travelling from the west coast of Israel towards the Aegean at the arrangement of an Egyptian pharaoh. The Mycenaeans might well have been the intended recipients of its cargo. The broad perspective these early Greeks gained through trade and travel on their own long-oared galleys was reflected in their cosmopolitan palatial complexes which rose as kingdoms within kingdoms, cities within cities, stout and bewilderingly monstrous.

The Mycenaeans are important to the history of the classical world and its women because they were central to the histories ancient peoples told themselves. There was their architecture, and there was their wealth, but there was also the delicious possibility that they inspired Homer's tales of the Trojan War and the struggle over beautiful Helen.

Writers and historians of ancient Greece and Rome believed almost unanimously that the war immortalised in Homer's *Iliad* was an historical event. Waged between the Trojans and the avenging Greeks, it marked a watershed between the old world and the new. Children grew up believing that an Age of Heroes had preceded their own Age of Iron. The inhabitants of this fortunate age were imagined as bigger, stronger, more courageous and closer to the gods than the people of their own time. Accordingly, in Homer's Age of Heroes, men claim descent from the gods without a hint of hubris, women launch a thousand ships, and kings inhabit palaces with gold walls, ever-fruitful orchards and mechanical guard dogs in the porch. Completed most probably in the late eighth century BC, the *Iliad* and its sequel, the *Odyssey*, tell of events which were imagined to have occurred when Mycenaean culture was at its peak.[3] Homer's impressionistic portrait of the world was coloured by remnants of the glorious civilisation the Mycenaeans left behind.

The scale at which the real Mycenaeans built was mesmerising. The Late Bronze Age citadel of Mycenae was enclosed by a strong, limestone-block wall which has been described, not inaccurately, as 'pork-chop-shaped'.[4] The stone chop was so large that it was said to have been the work of the gigantic one-eyed Cyclopes who threatened Odysseus' men during their homecoming in the *Odyssey*. It was besides so thick that storage spaces were created within it.[5] On the north-west wall, forming the main entrance to the citadel, is the 'Lion Gate'. Still standing at over three metres high and just under three metres wide, it is topped by a lintel so enormous (4.5 metres long by 1.9 metres deep) that it, too, was anciently believed to have been raised by Cyclopes.[6] The gate has been misgendered, for the early relief sculpture at its summit features not lions, but a pair of stately lionesses.

The palace within the citadel possessed a large hall with a round hearth at its centre surrounded by wooden columns, a grand staircase, and a substantial network of rooms and working spaces, at least one of which was used for weaving. Among the objects discovered in this room were a number of spindle whorls. Used as weights to spin wool, spindle whorls resemble terracotta or stone beads and are far from the most exciting things to look at. Their discovery is nevertheless important because it offers firm evidence of women working within the space. At Mycenae, the whorls were found with other accoutrements for making clothes and accessories, including gold foil, a carnelian bead, and a glass bead shaped like a grain of wheat. The presence of an arrowhead among these items offers a small clue that the women of the palace were not strictly segregated from the men.[7]

One of the reasons the theory of Phantasia as authoress of the *Odyssey* gained traction in the past was that the epic features highly creative women. Samuel Butler scandalously cast doubt upon the virtue of Penelope in the poem – 'Sending pretty little messages to her admirers was not exactly the way to get rid of them. Did she ever try snubbing?'[8] Robert Graves, by contrast, recognised Penelope's creativity as part of her virtue, and saved her from the accusation of 'living riotously with fifty lovers' by emphasising her ingenuity at the loom.[9] Graves's Penelope, like Homer's, is so loyal to her ribaldly adulterous husband during his absence (ten years at Troy and ten years returning home) that she not only weaves his father Laertes a funeral shroud, but unweaves it by night, informing the 108 suitors who crowd upon her that she will not marry any of them until the piece is complete. Penelope is not simply a weaver, but an artist, like her real-life Mycenaean counterparts.

Mycenaean women put their own spindles to splendid use, producing luscious cloaks and long, richly patterned or striped skirts. Far from resigning themselves to the weaving rooms, they travelled in chariots, performed songs or poetry to the accompaniment of lyres, and carried wheatsheaves for public ceremonies and rituals, as vibrantly coloured frescoes from the palace at Mycenae reveal. In one of the most enigmatic paintings, one woman holds a sword, another a spear, while two tiny men, one painted red and the other black, float mysteriously between them, like toy models or thought bubbles.[10] Through their contact with the divine, perhaps, the women pictured gain agency over the men's fate. Hera, Zeus, Poseidon and a female birth and death goddess known as Potnia were among the deities the Mycenaeans are known to have worshipped.

While Mycenaean women clearly played an important role in religion, their political position within the palaces was weaker than that of their Minoan counterparts, and secondary to the men's. Each Mycenaean palace complex was presided over by a male 'wa-na-ka' or *wanax*. Echoing this practice, Homer described Agamemnon, king of Mycenae and leader of the Greek army at Troy, as *anax* or 'lord' in the *Iliad*. The historical *wanax* was served by a deputy, known as a 'ra-wa-ke-ta', as well as 'hek-w-etai', probably a personal military guard. The immediate authority of the *wanax* was over his palace, but his influence was felt across a wider territory. Homer's Agamemnon lords over Corinth and much of the north-eastern Peloponnese in addition to Mycenae.[11] The poet reflected the historical prominence and wealth of the city in the second book of the *Iliad*. In Homer's 'Catalogue of Ships', Mycenae is described as supplying 100 vessels – more than any other city – for the Trojan War. Pylos, another thriving Mycenaean centre, sends ninety. Other ships come from Boeotia and Thebes, Phocaea and Euboea, Athens and Salamis. From Sparta, Elis, Argos, Tiryns and Rhodes. These ships, says Homer, are too many for even ten mouths and ten tongues to enumerate.[12] While they, too, are populated by men, the vessels intrigue the women of the epics, Penelope envisaging them romantically in the *Odyssey* as 'horses of the sea'.[13]

Drawn from all quarters of the Greek world, the ships of the *Iliad* assemble at the bidding of both Agamemnon and his brother Menelaus, king of Sparta, for the sake of Menelaus' wife Helen, a woman presented as the antithesis of loyal Penelope. Homer did not describe the long-term cause of their campaign because the story was already well known. According to a very ancient myth, Leda, princess of Aetolia, was raped by Zeus in the shape of a swan, and produced two eggs, from which there emerged two girls and two boys. Clytemnestra and Castor bore the blood of Leda's husband. They were mortal. Helen and Polydeuces pulsated with a more vivid lifeforce, Ichor, the substance of immortal veins, and were therefore semi-divine. Helen married Menelaus but found herself pushed into the bed of another man after the wedding of a sea nymph, Thetis, to a mortal, Peleus. During the nuptials, a vengeful uninvited guest named Eris (Strife) threw a golden apple into the congregation inscribed 'to the fairest', but who was that? The judgement of this contest lay with Paris. The Trojan prince wavered over the persuasions of fair Hera and Athena when fairer Aphrodite promised him sex with the fairest mortal. Helen, deemed to be the most exquisite woman on earth, was forced to leave Menelaus for Paris. She is probably the figure being led by the hand towards a boat full of rowers on one of the earliest narrative vase paintings in existence.[14] Her brothers are among the men who join Menelaus and Agamemnon to reclaim her and her dowry and punish the Trojans for their bloodless crime in the ensuing Trojan War.

The allied Argives, Achaeans, Danaans – Greeks – of the *Iliad* make land near the Hellespont. The historic city of Troy was located at nearby Hisarlik on the north-west corner of Asia Minor. Excavations of the site in modern times have revealed some similarities with the city of legend.

Inhabited as early as 3000 BC, it covered seventy acres and consisted of a small but heavily fortified citadel overlooking a larger lower town, and a plain that was well-watered to the point of being boggy. Living between two seas, the Black and the Aegean, might have been more advantageous for crop-growing than for riding, but the Trojans excelled in horsemanship. They were, said Homer, *hippodamoi*, 'horse-breakers', with fine foals and experience in taming them. The first horses were bred at Troy in the Late Bronze Age, the period in which the city reached its greatest architectural heights and, if the story is to be believed, the Trojan War was fought.

Herodotus, hailed in Roman times as the 'Father of History', supposed that the Trojan War had erupted almost 800 years before his own time, perhaps 1250 BC. The astronomer Eratosthenes produced a more precise date of 1184/3 BC for the war's conclusion. There was no way of proving either man right in antiquity, but the excavation of Hisarlik in modern times has cast light on the possibility that both excelled in their calculations. Within the ten main settlements excavated at Hisarlik, the grandest Late Bronze Age cities are traditionally identified by archaeologists in the sixth and seven layers as Troy VIh and Troy VIIa. The destruction of the former coincided approximately with Herodotus' estimation.

The destruction of the latter coincided with that of Eratosthenes.

Around the time of the war, historic Troy became a vassal state of the mighty Hittite Empire, which stretched all the way from the Aegean to modern Iraq. Women were central here too. When Tutankhamun died in Egypt at the end of the eighteenth dynasty, it was to the Hittite king that his young widow, Ankhesenamun, appealed for a new husband. Ankhesenamun, daughter of Nefertiti and Akhenaten, wrote King Suppiluliuma a very direct letter requesting that he send her one of his sons, seeing as he had so many, for she wanted to produce an heir.[15] Ankhesenamun had already delivered two daughters but both were stillborn, one at twenty-four weeks, and the other at thirty-six weeks.[16] Their tiny mummified corpses were interred in their father Tutankhamun's tomb. Rather than risk causing an insurrection by selecting a man from among her own subjects, or marrying one of her late husband's grasping relatives, Ankhesenamun looked overseas. 'I am afraid,' she told the Hittite king as she contemplated her options. Zannanza, one of the younger Hittite princes, travelled to Egypt to satisfy her request, but died soon after arriving. Violence erupted between the two kingdoms when the Hittites accused the Egyptians of murdering him. It is not known whether Ankhesenamun ever achieved her wish of remarrying and having more children, but Ay, the relative she most feared, rose to become pharaoh in her lifetime.

The Hittites had regular dealings with the Egyptians, but fewer with the Greeks, whom they viewed increasingly circumspectly from across the water as potential rivals. A trove of roughly thirty Hittite texts found at Boğazkale in Turkey refer to a place called Ahhiyawa. Although the location of Ahhiyawa continues to be disputed, a strong argument has been made since the 1920s for identifying it with Mycenaean Greece.[17] Homer often referred to Greece as 'Achaea', a word that seems to be linked to 'Ahhiyawa', which was evidently a place of some importance. The texts reveal that the Hittites and Ahhiyawans were in contact since at least the fifteenth century BC. When a Hittite king became unwell around 1300 BC, divine idols were brought to him from Ahhiyawa as well as from Lazpa, identified with the island of Lesbos.[18] In a similar period, the Hittites wrote of a queen being exiled to Ahhiyawa, some distance away.[19] The Hittites and Ahhiyawans had also exchanged gifts or at least traded.[20]

The historic Hittites almost certainly knew Troy or the broader region in which it lay as 'Wilusa'. A thirteenth-century text written in Luwian, an Indo-European script used in the vicinity of Troy, contains the line, probably from a lost poem, 'When they came from steep Wilusa'. Homer frequently used the epithet 'steep' to describe Troy or, as he more often referred to the city, 'Ilios', a word etymologically derived from 'Wilusa'. About 1280 BC the Hittites approached the king of Wilusa, whose name was Alaksandu, to forge an alliance. By the terms of the treaty, Alaksandu agreed to supply the Hittites with manpower in the instance of war in exchange for greater protection.[21] The identification of Paris, prince of Troy, also known to Homer as 'Alexandros', a Greek form of 'Alaksandu', with Alaksandu, king of Wilusa, remains tentative. But it is clear that in the Late Bronze Age the Hittites and Trojans were making preparations for their collective safety.

In the *Iliad*, the sea god Poseidon describes building Troy's 'wide and very beautiful wall' in the hope 'that their city might be indestructible'.[22] The walls constructed in the sixth archaeological layer uncovered at historic Troy were similarly monumental to those at Mycenae. Formed of limestone blocks arranged up to 4.5 metres thick, they looked so imposing that a visitor could well believe they were built by divine hands. Homer described the palace at the heart of the Trojan citadel as 'surpassingly beautiful, furnished with polished porticoes', and as containing 'fifty rooms of polished stone'.[23] No trace of this has been found. The sixth-layer city was mysteriously destroyed about 1300 BC and much of its brickwork was dislodged. While repairs were being made, however, new fortification towers went up along the boundary wall, the most magnificent of which, the south tower, overlooked the main entrance to the citadel like Homer's Scaean Gate, the main entrance to Troy. (It was only fitting that the modern city built on top of these ruins should be named Hisarlik – 'Place of Fortresses' in Turkish.) Within decades of its foundation, however, this newer city also met with disaster. The fall of Troy was evidently not a one-off.

The battlefield was a male domain, but the ways in which men comported themselves in combat had an important impact upon the women they left behind. In the *Iliad*, Andromache foreshadows her own fate and that of many of the other Trojan women in a conversation with her husband Hector, the greatest of Troy's warriors. It would be better to die, she tells him, than to face the alternative. Hector envisages this vividly: led off in tears to Greek Argos as a slave, Andromache would sit at the loom and weave at another woman's instruction, fetch water from the spring, look to the floor as onlookers whispered cruelly.[24] Knowing what other abuses await them if their husbands are defeated, the wives of the warriors strive to influence events by offering the kind of tactical advice that could only come from observing the fighting closely. Andromache is confined to the palace but there are windows. Her name means 'Man Fighter' in Greek and she certainly lives up to it. She discovers where the Trojan walls are most vulnerable to assault. Having counted three attempts on the section 'by the fig tree', she urges Hector to station men there to prevent the wall from being scaled. Hector unappreciatively instructs her to return to her weaving.

As intensely as Andromache fears losing her husband to his bravery, Hector fears losing face, which is more than can be said for his younger brother. When Helen scolds Paris in their bedchamber it is not because she is afraid of his courage. It is because, like Hector, she fears shame. Ten years on from the outbreak of war, Helen is still chiding herself for the turmoil unleashed in her name and cursing Paris, a man she now despises. Pandora may have been 'dog-minded', but Helen is, by her own account, 'dog-faced'.[25] Most of the Trojans hate her, but Priam, king of Troy and Paris' father, does not. He is old and wise and he knows that this war was brought about by the gods. He speaks to Helen affectionately, as any true father-in-law would. He tells her of the time he travelled east to Phrygia, central Asia Minor, and witnessed Amazons, 'equals of men', allying with the armies.[26] Contemporary legend related that there were Amazons among the Trojans' supporting forces. Priam remains hopeful that a band of warrior women might still rise to bolster his army's defence.[27] In an episode later captured by Greek vase painters, Achilles, the foremost fighter among the Greeks, fell tenderly in love with the Amazon queen Penthesilea the moment he drove his spear into her neck.

The prospect soon arises of a duel between Paris and Helen's husband Menelaus.[28] The duel was very much the showpiece of real Late Bronze Age conflict. An unbelievably accomplished seal stone from the grave of the so-called Griffin Warrior (probably *wanax*) of Pylos, one of the most astonishing finds of the past decade, demonstrates the skill involved in such an encounter.[29] Paris is no natural dueller and fails to emerge the hero.

The drama of Homer's *Iliad* is driven less by physical duels than by duels of words – and then silence – between Agamemnon and Achilles over an enslaved woman. Described as being of immortal beauty, Briseis had been married to Mynes, king of Lyrnessus, when Achilles sacked their city on his way to Troy. Having witnessed Achilles kill both her husband and her brothers, Briseis was forced to become Achilles' sex slave. She is, in a word, his *geras* or war prize. Agamemnon's decision to seize her for his own pleasure bruises Achilles' sense of honour so deeply that he departs from the battle at Troy. Through history, classical writers would blame 'Helen the Ship-destroyer, Helen the Man-destroyer, Helen the City-destroyer' for the bloodshed of the Trojan War.[30] But after nine years in the field, the Greeks are no longer fighting over Helen; they are fighting for Troy itself, for glory, and in the weeks that occupy the plot of the poem, it is rather Briseis who divides the army. Through no fault of her own, the former queen consort leaves the Greeks ailing, as Achilles, their strongest fighter, wallows in self-pity in his tent.

The spoken word, so important to the plot, was also central to the poem's composition. The ancients were generally in agreement that both the *Iliad* and the *Odyssey* were the work of Homer. Quite who this Homer was, however, none of them could say for certain. His name was connected to the poems since at least as early as the sixth century BC but was not a standard one in Greek. How to translate it? 'Hostage' summoned a fanciful image of a pale, ascetic bard labouring over his lines in captivity. 'Blind', another possible rendering, raised the possibility that Homeros had concealed himself in the *Odyssey* as Demodocus, a sightless poet who sings stories to the accompaniment of a lyre in the royal court of Scheria, the home of the Phaeacians and the eponymous hero's last landfall before his return to Ithaca and Penelope. Singers calling themselves the *Homeridae* ('Children of Homer') began performing Homer's epics within perhaps a century and a half of their completion, but they were hardly his biological children, and they left no indication of who they thought their great father figure was.[31] Seven different places claimed Homer for their own: Athens, Chios, Argos, Rhodes, Colophon, Salamis and Smyrna. The island of Ios, said to have been the poet's final resting place, minted a silver coin bearing the earliest known portrait of him. This bard was bearded, with long wavy hair held back in a headband, large eyes and a fine-pointed nose. It cannot be a true likeness. It has been dated to the fourth century BC and is therefore many centuries too late. But clues in the principal dialect used in the *Iliad* and *Odyssey* make it almost certain that they originated on one of the Aegean islands off the west coast of Turkey, possibly the coastline itself, in the region known historically as Ionia. It is probable that one of the seven cities was the true home of these poems.

The idea of a single poet named Homer – or Phantasia – was partly dislodged in the early twentieth century through the work of the American scholars Milman Parry and Albert Lord. Discerning a parallel in the poems' structure and the performance of poetry in former Yugoslavia, Parry put forward a thesis on the 'oral culture' of antiquity. The repetition of formulaic phrases and epithets offered evidence that the epics were composed in song prior to the establishment of writing in Greece. The poems' hexameter lent itself perfectly to rhythmic performance. There could not be one poet, it was argued, when so many were involved in composing and editing the verses by performing them. Products of an illiterate age, the *Iliad* and the *Odyssey* developed over several generations and only began to be fixed when the art of writing was reborn in Greece in the eighth century BC. Innumerable bards shaped the stories they passed down, with established formulae providing the building blocks, and the hexameter providing the beats.

This does not mean that Homer was a fiction. Someone must have come up with the storylines of the *Iliad* and the *Odyssey* in the first place, and someone must have marshalled the many forms of the oral poems into two distinct works of literature when they were finally written down. They would have been familiar with earlier epics from other cultures, especially the twelfth-century BC Mesopotamian *Epic of Gilgamesh*, which told of a legendary king of Uruk's quest for eternal life, and influenced the Homeric tale of Odysseus' ten-year *nostos* or homecoming after the Trojan War. There is still space for a single Homer, the original rhapsode, the inventor of tales, spinning the stories into song. Or for Homer, the master editor at the other end of the process, distilling the inherited material into the complete poems. 'Homeros' can also mean 'the fitter' in the sense of one who pieces things together. His name may as such be little more than a shorthand for the two epic poems, evoking the spirit of a bard rather than anyone knowable, but 'Homer', originator or compiler, rightly still hovers over the maze of the poems' composition.

Like an historical novelist, the poets of this era strove to resurrect the earlier period through conscious archaisms and descriptions of cities based on their visible archaeological remains, some of these Mycenaean. At the same time, by virtue of being preserved orally, the poems retained genuine traces of older language and memories which had become attached to the stories over the long period of their composition. Many of the myths merely alluded to, as we have seen, were already well known before the epics came into being. Through both accident and design, the Homeric poems sounded older than they really were, which only deepened the mystery that surrounded them.

In contrast to the Greeks of the ninth century BC and earlier, the Mycenaeans, Hittites and Trojans – female and male – were keen correspondents. Like the Babylonians, Assyrians and Egyptians, they inscribed their words on tablets and other objects. A remarkable bronze seal made slightly after the period of the Trojan War, for example, bears the name, in Luwian, of a man on one side, and of a woman on the other. The seal probably belonged to a husband and wife, who would have used it to sign documents together, or separately, as the need dictated. A solitary seal may only reveal so much, but the extensive use of similar equipment by women in neighbouring regions makes it likely that elite women in Troy oversaw business matters of their own.

One of the most influential women among the Hittites was also a writer of letters. Puduhepa, a former priestess, ruled as coeval with her husband, King Hattusili III, in the mid-thirteenth century BC, when Herodotus believed the Trojan War took place. As well as being heavily involved in the politics of the court at the royal capital of Hattusa (Boğazkale, central Turkey), Puduhepa corresponded regularly with both Nefertari and her husband, Rameses the Great, in Egypt. When the Hittites found themselves suffering in a famine, it was Puduhepa who wrote to Rameses for assistance, signing her letter with her own seal.[32] Barley and wheat were duly shipped over.[33] Nefertari, a prolific letter-writer in her own right, was clearly fond of the Hittite queen, whom she addressed as a sister and furnished with magnificent jewellery and clothes.[34]

It was no coincidence that the sole reference to writing in Homer's poetry was made in relation to the conduct of a woman from the east. In the *Iliad*, a soldier named Glaucus tells of how Queen Anteia of Lycia, a kingdom in Asia Minor, took a fancy to his ancestor, Bellerophon, when he was visiting her and her husband in Argos in Greece. Bellerophon rebuffed Anteia's advances, knowing that it would be dishonourable to have sex with a married queen, and Anteia took offence. Seeking revenge, the queen told her husband that Bellerophon had sexually assaulted her and should be put to death for his crime. Reluctant to do the deed himself, the king drove Bellerophon to his wife's native country with *sehmata lugra* ('grievous symbols') written on a folded clay tablet.[35] The symbols, presumably a form of cuneiform, were given to Anteia's father. The shocked king punished Bellerophon by sending him on a series of Herculean challenges which included fighting the Amazons and killing the lion-snake-goat hybrid Chimera. Against all expectations, Bellerophon emerged victorious, earning a position in the royal household as husband to the king's other daughter.

Surviving clay writing tablets provide just as fascinating an insight into the lives of women in the real palaces of the Mycenaean era. The fullest collection of tablets comes from a pair of rooms in the palace complex of Pylos, but Knossos, the former Minoan capital, was also a key repository. A total of 4,476 tablets have been preserved across the two sites.[36] Among these there are references to more than 2,000 different women. Unlike Linear A, the Minoans' writing system, the Mycenaeans' similarly syllabic Linear B has been successfully deciphered. Working (as opposed to non-working elite) women were denoted by signs resembling an abstract impression of the female form. 'Woman' was conveyed by two dots for breasts, legs joined to suggest a long skirt of the kind Mycenaean women wore, and a curved line where her head would be, suggestive of long or dressed hair (in the sign for a man, by contrast, there is a straight line for the head).

The women referred to in the tablets were employed in a wide range of jobs, many of them familiar from the Homeric epics. In the *Odyssey*, women grind wheat and barley, 'the marrow of men', at mills.[37] There were 'flour-grinders' at the palace in Pylos. In both epics, women weave, whether royal or servile. Andromache works in the Trojan palace with a loom and distaff while ordering her servant women about their work. Helen embroiders a purple cloth with scenes from the Trojan War as if she were telling the story of the poem herself. And as we have seen, Penelope weaves and unweaves a funeral shroud for her father-in-law, Laertes. The women who wove at Pylos and Knossos were no less versatile in their handiwork. They managed something like a textile industry, producing goods for export as well as the palace community, and worked in groups according to specialism. There were wool-spinners and carders, linen- and leather-workers, finishers and headband-makers for horses. These women usually worked separately from men, but at Pylos there is evidence that at least two women, Wordieia and Amphehia, formed part of a mixed leather-making group.[38]

Working groups were the *modus operandi* at the Mycenaean palaces. Women were usually accompanied by boys and girls, presumably their own children, as they went about their tasks.[39] Many were divided also according to their geographical region. Pylos was split into sixteen districts over two provinces, Nearer and Further, separated by Mount Aigaleo.[40] The palace-workers came from more than 200 named places, some of which may have been local streets, while others, including Lemnos, Miletus and Knidos, lay further afield.[41] It is possible that, like the Sidonian (Phoenician) women carried to Troy by Paris in the *Iliad* to weave fine robes for the court, some of the women working in the Mycenaean palaces had been enslaved.[42]

Although the women were engaged in hard, practical labour, their work was recognised as highly skilled, and the Mycenaeans took some pride in it. Men were sometimes described on tablets as being the offspring of women of particular crafts, for example, 'sons of flax-workers'.[43] Female workers were allocated the same amount of food in the regular distributions as their male counterparts, and twice as much as their children, whereas in Babylonia, men typically received three times the female ration.[44] A mysterious senior class of priestess at Pylos known as 'keybearers' (did they open and close shrines within the palace complex?) even owned land.[45] A landowning keybearer named ka-pa-ti-ja ('Karpathia') was wealthy enough to donate almost 200 litres of grain to the palace, probably for a religious festival.[46] Given the historical prominence of women at the court of Pylos, it is fitting that a mythical Pylian king should intervene in the dispute over Briseis in the *Iliad*. Old Nestor urges Agamemnon to return the woman to Achilles and to end their feud.

Architecturally, Pylos was as extravagant as Mycenae and is excellently preserved. The Late Bronze Age palace that has come to bear Nestor's name stood on a hill at Ano Englianos, south-west of Chora in the Peloponnese, and had a footprint approaching 6,000 metres squared. Built about 1300 BC, it was divided into three main sections, the stateliest of which possessed courtyards, a columned hall with central hearth like the one at Mycenae, and running water, carried via an early aqueduct from a spring a kilometre away. There was also, as at many Mycenaean palaces, a throne, or at least a ceremonial seat, from which the *wanax* might have greeted his guests. Visitors were well catered for at Pylos. One storeroom alone contained 2,853 cups; another held large vats of olive oil, and an outbuilding was used as a wine cellar.[47]

When Odysseus' son Telemachus travels to Nestor's palace in the *Odyssey* in search of information about his father, he is treated to a bath by the king's youngest daughter, Polycaste, who washes and anoints him with olive oil before dressing him in fine clothes for dinner. This is quite some bath, for Telemachus emerges from it looking 'like the immortal gods'.[48] The poet must have been familiar with the extraordinary Mycenaean bathtub at Pylos. Short and lozenge-shaped, it was set into a stucco-coated base along one wall of a narrow room in the palace. Made of terracotta, the bathtub had a pattern of concentric circles in its interior, which would once have been brightly painted.[49] There was even a step up for ease of access. Found nearby were two jars for filling the tub, each measuring over 1.2 metres tall, and inside them, a number of smaller vessels and cups for rinsing the bather.[50] At least thirty-seven 'bath-attendants' ('re-wo-to-ro-ko-wo') were recorded as working at the Mycenaean palace of Pylos.[51] Every one of them was female.[52]

From Pylos, Telemachus travels to Sparta, where Menelaus has been reunited with Helen after the fall of Troy. Agamemnon, who ultimately led the Greek army to victory over the Trojans, has been less fortunate. To secure a fair wind for his voyage out to Troy ten years earlier, he had sacrificed his daughter Iphigenia to the goddess Artemis, an act for which his wife Clytemnestra could never forgive him. The sight of Priam's daughter Cassandra accompanying Agamemnon home as his prize concubine only makes matters worse. In a fit of rage, Clytemnestra butchers Agamemnon with an axe, remembering how her husband had butchered Iphigenia. In the fifth century BC, the playwright Aeschylus would dramatise the bloodbath in the first part of a trilogy of plays about the former war leader. The episode, alluded to only briefly by Homer in the *Odyssey*, was purely legendary, but evidence of child sacrifice has been found in the Late Bronze Age Aegean, even at Minoan Knossos, where it appears to have been carried out in an attempt to avert earthquakes.[53]

Historians and later writers were eager to locate the final resting places of Agamemnon and his compatriots. Visiting Mycenae in the second century AD, the Greek geographer Pausanias saw what he believed to be the heroes' tombs. The grandest were *tholos* or beehive-shaped, built into hillsides and sealed by stone walls. The round 'Treasury of Atreus', optimistically linked to the family of Agamemnon, was constructed about 1300 BC and possessed what was, at 13 metres tall, the highest known domed roof in the world.[54] The Tomb of Clytemnestra, rumoured to have belonged to Agamemnon's vengeful wife, was built to similar splendour, and housed the remains of a wealthy woman and some of her possessions, including mirrors and fine pottery. A wealthy German businessman and self-taught archaeologist, Heinrich Schliemann, followed in Pausanias' footsteps in the 1870s and paused by a grave circle.

Schliemann, who made his fortune in the indigo and gold trades, had excavated Troy a short time earlier, digging zealously through the archaeological layers to reach what he thought must be the treasures of Homer's world, only to realise that he had gone too deep. Close examination revealed that much of the pottery and gold jewellery he had found at Troy belonged to an earlier age. At Mycenae, in a grave circle discovered close to the Lioness Gate, he repeated his mistake. 'I have gazed upon the face of Agamemnon,' he allegedly proclaimed, peering at the gold masks that covered the faces of the dead. The 'Mask of Agamemnon' that came to be connected with this story showed the face of a bearded man with large eyes, a long slim nose and prominent ears, and dated to about 300 years before the Mycenaean warlord was supposed to have lived. The same grave circle contained deceased women and children, too, all members of Mycenae's elite, surrounded by goods, including gold and silver goblets, pots, daggers and other weapons.[55] There was no strict segregation of the sexes in death; several of the graves contained both male and female remains. But while gold masks rested on the faces of men, gold diadems and headbands were placed on deceased women, and a baby was wrapped in gold foil.

The graves of Mycenae were remarkable for the light they shed upon the world of Homer's poems. What might have struck readers in the past as mere fantasy was often revealed to have been based in fact. In the *Iliad*, the warriors of former times are described as bigger and stronger than their notably big and strong descendants. Nestor of Pylos takes delight in telling his allies that no one at Troy could come close to conquering the men he knew three generations earlier. Agamemnon taunts his fellow Greek warrior Diomedes (who stole the famous white Thracian horses during a bold night raid) with the idea that he is inferior to his father. This is the Diomedes who wounds Aphrodite with his spear and lifts a stone so heavy that not even two men of Homer's time could manage it. The kind of Golden Age thinking that infects some of the older members of the Greek army remained endemic to post-Homeric Greece. Much as Homer's warriors fight in the shadow of their ancestors, men – it was mainly men – living in Greece later on consistently compared themselves unfavourably to Homer's warriors. One look beneath the ground of the grave circles at Mycenae would have confirmed their worst fears. The men interred there were on average about 5 feet 7 inches tall and the women 5 feet 2 inches. This was approximately four inches taller than most people living around Athens some centuries later. The dead of Mycenae, moreover, were interred with just the sort of terror-inducing armour that Homer described. The Greeks of the poems fight with large rectangular or figure-of-eight shaped shields.[56] They hold scabbards and spears and, in the case of certain heroes, including Odysseus, wear helmets adorned with rows of boar tusks.[57] Wall paintings show men holding precisely the kind of shield Homer described, but brightly painted. Much has decomposed within the Mycenaean graves, but lavishly adorned swords, daggers and fragments of boar tusk have not. One grave alone contained three men, two women, and more than 27 swords, 16 knives, 38 arrowheads and 92 boar's-tusk plates in addition to 1,290 Baltic amber beads.[58] Many of the men had died while still in their thirties. They looked like warriors and their wives resembled queens.

Chapter III

Decline and Change

And when Colonus had passed judgement, the brothers of Ochne fled, and she meanwhile threw herself from a precipice, as Myrtis the lyrical poet of Anthedon has told.

Plutarch's paraphrase of part of a poem by Myrtis of Boeotia, teacher of Pindar and Corinna, fifth century BC, *Greek Questions* 40

The Trojan War marked symbolically the death of one age and the birth of another that would prove far less progressive for women. Even if the narrative was broadly fictional, so much of what Homer described – the mindset of the soldiers; the feuds; the unpredictability of conflict, swinging one way and then the other, as if two camps of gods were playing a game; the armour; the horror; the enslavement of women – was only too true to life. The *Iliad* was a story of the last heroes of the Late Bronze Age told in the knowledge that their world was coming to an end.

There is historical evidence that the Mycenaean inhabitants of the palace at Pylos were preparing themselves against attack in the late thirteenth century BC. Their defensive plans included the dispatch of hundreds of rowers from five locations to a mysterious place called 'Pleuron' located somewhere near a sea-border.[1] The rowers would have been striving to offer a first wall of defence and drive the enemy away from their territory.[2] According to a surviving writing tablet, 'watchers' were also 'guarding the coast'.[3] While the rowers and watchers were probably male, women, namely the 'keybearers', contributed to the defence effort by donating bronze for emergency use.[4]

Across the Aegean, about 1250 BC, the Hittites, too, were growing increasingly nervous. They had lately lost a vast swathe of territory to the

Assyrians and anticipated disruption from further in the west. Trouble was also brewing at home. A nobleman named Tawagalawas had lent his support to revolutionary forces who threatened the authority of the Hittite king.[5] Tawagalawas, probably known to the Greeks as Eteocles, was then living in Millawanda, which is believed to be Miletus in Greece. His brother was king of Ahhiyawa, which we have tentatively identified with Mycenaean Greece, and aided the campaign by providing sanctuary for the ringleader of the revolutionaries. The king of the Hittites demanded that the ringleader be returned. An exchange of hostages later took place, and the city of Miletus, formerly controlled by the Mycenaeans, became occupied by the Hittites.[6]

After keeping a fair distance from one another, the Hittites and Ahhiyawans had begun to spar, and Troy became a source of contention on at least two occasions. One dispute over the city was resolved, but another arose in the mid-thirteenth century BC when a Trojan king, Walmu, was removed from his throne and the Hittites attempted to reinstate him.[7] Troy was presumably still under Hittite control at this time. Mycenaean tablets, written in Linear B, reveal that women in this period were being carried off from the west coast of Asia Minor – the area of Troy – to staff the palaces on the Greek mainland. The combination of elements bears obvious parallels to the story of the Trojan War. It was around this date that Troy VIh, the illustrious city with the enormous walls, was destroyed. Evidence of collapsed masonry (plus a crushed human skull) led one team of twentieth-century archaeologists to suggest that the cause of the destruction was an earthquake.[8] Hisarlik lies just north of a major fault line and has been struck numerous times in the past. There would have been a bitter irony to Homer's description of 'earthshaker' Poseidon building the walls of Troy so as to make them indestructible, only to knock them down himself.[9] But there were weapons among the debris: bronze arrowheads, stemmed arrowheads; knives; axes; slingshots with terracotta bullets.[10] Might these have been the tools of the people of Ahhiyawa? Were these the paltry remnants of a Trojan War?

No historian today would countenance the possibility that an army of men descended upon Hisarlik in 1,186 ships, as enumerated by Homer, for the sake of a woman, made war on its people for ten years, and stormed the citadel in a wooden horse. Even Pausanias, the geographer, described it as common knowledge that the wooden horse was in fact 'a machine to breach the walls' – what we would call a siege engine.[11] But the surviving Hittite tablets show that wars were waged over Troy in the Late Bronze Age, and the citadel was destroyed. If there really was a war at Troy, it is likely to have formed part of a broader phenomenon – a network of invasions and attacks – which disturbed large territories of Asia Minor and Greece in the Late Bronze Age. The *Iliad* is scattered with reminiscences of battles fought and habitations overrun by the Greeks on their way to Troy. The impact upon women, in particular, is borne out in the descriptions of Achilles sacking twenty-three cities, including Briseis' Lyrnessus, and Thebe, where he butchers Andromache's father and seven brothers in a single day.[12] Priam's father Laomedon had also seen Troy sacked by Heracles in an earlier Trojan war.[13] Homer's war was perhaps an amalgamation, perhaps an allegory, of the accomplishments of an earlier generation raised in Mycenaean splendour, and of their impending decline.

The destruction of Troy VIh, whether by earthquake, man, or both, was followed by a period of hasty rebuilding. New, makeshift houses consisting of just one or two rooms were constructed in unhealthily close proximity to one another along the previously spacious streets. Almost every one of them had vast ceramic jars sunk beneath its floors for grain and other provisions. The appearance of simple accommodation with storage for food built into its floors is strongly suggestive of efforts to batten down the hatches in a period of uncertainty. Just decades later, around 1180 BC, this newer city, too, was devastated and severely burned. Homer stops short of describing the fall of Troy in the *Iliad* in favour of ending the poem with the funeral of Hector and lament of the women closest to him. The death of the Trojans' most robust defence at the hands of Achilles in a duel stands within the poem for the death of Troy itself. But the poet does subtly anticipate the day when the citadel will be sacked by the Greeks and set ablaze. Later poets would describe the heroic escape of a band of refugees, led by Aeneas, who was destined to found a new settlement in Italy. If the fire that consumed Troy the second time was not a product of warfare, it was almost certainly a product of a period of unrest.

The fall of Troy as immortalised in poetry coincided with the fall of the main centres of Mycenaean culture. Despite the best efforts of the rowers and keybearers to put up a rigorous defence, the palace of Pylos burned to the ground about 1180 BC. People had been enjoying a large animal sacrifice there a short time earlier. Burnt offerings of cattle and deer, and the presence of cups set out nearby, provide evidence of ritual and feasting.[14] The gods rewarded this display of piety by seeing that the feasters escaped the desecration of the palace; the remains at the site were purely animal. Elsewhere in the Peloponnese, the sites of Thebes, Iolcus and Tiryns ceased to be inhabited. Mycenae was also put to flame and eventually abandoned. Baked in the heat were the clay writing tablets which preserved mere glimmers of the civilisation which had flourished there for hundreds of years.

The destruction of the Mycenaean palaces was followed by a period of dramatic decline. In south-west Peloponnese, the number of known inhabited sites fell between the thirteenth and the twelfth century, and similarly dramatic population shrinkage occurred elsewhere, including in Attica and Boeotia.[15] It has been estimated that the number of inhabitants of Mycenaean Greece had dropped from about 500,000–700,000 to 250,000–300,000 by 1000 BC.[16] Trade dried up, partly as a result of the collapse of the palaces with their workshops, and art generally became less ambitious. Maritime-inspired 'Octopus Style' vase paintings, popular in Mycenaean times, ceased to be made after about 1200 BC.[17] Floral patterning was replaced by concentric circles drawn rapidly with compasses on pots in Athens. The age of the grand beehive tomb was over.

It used to be said that the fall of the Mycenaeans was caused by an invasion of Greek-speaking peoples from the north. Historians described 'Dorians' descending on the Peloponnese from somewhere – perhaps the Balkans, perhaps Epirus – and achieving dominance over the region. The Dorians were not a mythical people. Homer described them as living on Crete 'with waving plumes'.[18] Human skulls with broader crania than those of the indigenous population on Crete have enthusiastically been identified as 'Dorian' by some modern archaeologists.[19] In later centuries, the peoples of Corinth, Argos, Crete, Rhodes, Syracuse, Sparta, Halicarnassus and other cities would be known collectively as 'Dorian' as opposed to 'Ionian' (the eastern Greeks of the Aegean islands and western Asia Minor as well as Athens) or 'Aeolian' (those who inhabited Boeotia and Lesbos) by virtue of their geography and dialect. But there was no firm evidence of an invasion of a northern people in the Peloponnese, no sudden emergence that could account for the fate of the Mycenaeans.

The 'Dorian Invasion' was rather an attempt to explain the upheaval and displacement that ensued after the palaces were destroyed.

Reports were also made of the arrival of 'Sea Peoples' – mysterious, piratical fighters travelling across the water and targeting various territories. Seaborne raids had been commonplace for some time. Scenes of this nature feature in some of the frescoes at Akrotiri and on an early Mycenaean silver rhyton discovered in one of the graves at Mycenae. References to 'Sea Peoples' specifically occur in a number of written sources. Pharaoh Merneptah of Egypt claimed a victory over an alliance of Libyans and so-called 'Sea Peoples' in 1208 BC.[20] The Great Harris Papyrus, now housed in the British Museum, records further victories over 'peoples of the sea' by Rameses III in about 1180 BC. These peoples, it is recorded, included 'Sherden' and 'Weshesh'. None is identifiable, but 'Danuna', also listed, could conceivably denote Greeks, like Homer's 'Danaans'. Egypt was certainly weakened through the loss of territory in the twelfth century BC. It was also about 1180 BC that the Hittites abandoned their capital, Hattusa, and other cities, including Tabikka (Maşat Höyük). The Hittites, too, were apparently subject to invasion from overseas. The Sea Peoples, whoever they might have been, appear to have been migratory and of no fixed abode. Among them, perhaps, were some of the Mycenaeans displaced by the fires in the Peloponnese, and even, very possibly, veterans of war. The second destruction of Troy, also circa 1180 BC, could well have been brought about by migrants targeting an already weakened city.

The Mycenaeans were certainly on the move. In the twelfth century BC they began to travel away from the palatial centres to coastal settlements to their east, including Perati in Attica – the territory of which Athens formed a part – Ialysos on Rhodes, and Lefkandi on the fertile Xeropolis promontory of Euboea. The appearance of large houses, likely multi-storeyed, and a new kind of pottery in the Argolid and at Lefkandi from the mid-twelfth century BC may be evidence of their handiwork. There are signs that Mycenaeans were well settled on Crete by 1200 BC, and in Cephalonia, Eastern Attica, Cyprus, and across the Cyclades and broader Dodecanese in the century that followed.[21]

Their travels were prompted in part by the need for fresh trade ventures and well-watered land. A period of drought is believed to have affected mainland Greece, Egypt and Asia Minor in the Late Bronze

Age. A rise in temperatures and northward shift of latitude of the polar front in relation to other air currents might have plunged the Aegean into desert-like conditions in the summer months.[22] It has been estimated that southern Greece endured up to eight months of drought a year as a result of the climatic change, with interior and east-coast regions wholly deprived of rain.[23] Unusual weather events may partly explain the decline of human populations. But the Mycenaeans must also have needed to find new homes after their palatial kingdoms were ravaged. The temptation to connect their migrations to warfare, or at least raids on cities following the collapse of their palatial economies, is overwhelming. In antiquity, a specific link was drawn between the fallout of the Trojan War and the upheavals which followed. The fifth-century BC Greek historian Thucydides, for example, wrote of how 'the return of the Greeks from Troy after so long gave rise to many changes, and factions sprung up in many cities, and those banished as a result founded more cities'.[24] The Homeric tales of a Trojan War and of Odysseus, the wanderer, striving to find his way home to Penelope, encapsulated perfectly the decline and displacement endured across the real Mycenaean world.

The period following the collapse of Mycenaean civilisation used to be known as the Dark Age. An era of uncertainty and listlessness, it witnessed the steady abandonment of settlements, of collaboration and trade between peoples, and of writing, in favour of an increasingly itinerant way of being for both women and men. Thucydides appears to have been describing it when he wrote of a time in the distant past when migrations in Greece were commonplace, but commerce and reliable communication by land and sea barely existent.[25] The soil remained unplanted, 'it being uncertain when someone might attack – and when they did arrive, there were no walls to protect it'. New cities were few and far between and the rootless life was as flat as it was precarious. It is no longer fashionable to call this period 'dark', just as it is no longer fashionable to label the Middle Ages the Dark Ages, but by comparison with the preceding age, it was markedly introspective.

For women, this was an especially fraught time, for their husbands, sons and brothers often sailed away from the Greek mainland without them as they made for Asia Minor and the islands just off it. The women had little way of knowing if and when they would see their menfolk again. They might have been promised new beginnings – told that they would follow as soon as a suitable home had been found – but hope could be sustained for only so long. If the protracted silences were unbearable, the reports that began to filter in from across the Aegean were worse. Many of the men did find places to settle, but not all of them did so peaceably, or with any intention of reuniting their families. One group of Athenians travelled to Miletus in south-west Asia Minor, slaughtered the men and raped the women before making them their wives.[26] It was said that the Milesian women swore an oath never to dine with their new spouses, nor to address them by name, and enjoined their daughters to maintain this custom down the ages. The misery of the women abandoned on the mainland was now that of the women of Asia Minor and beyond.

From Greece to the east, a change had occurred, as the lights that guided the previous centuries of high culture began to flicker and dim. The sun no longer dazzled off bronze greaves and swords as it had on the battlefields of Troy. By the mid-eleventh century BC, a duller metal had begun to be produced on a mass scale on Cyprus, hitherto known for its copper. Hesiod, the farmer poet, spoke of the misery caused when Prometheus stole fire for man, precipitating the end of the Golden Age and the beginning of an inferior Age of Silver. The Bronze Age and ensuing era of heroes had now given way to a lamentable Iron Age. This age, like the iron smelted on Cyprus and across Greece, seemed at first flat and uninspiring, at least by comparison with its shiny predecessors. No longer did people trouble themselves to inscribe clay tablets with Linear B. The art of writing was forgotten everywhere in the Greek world except for Cyprus, where a syllabic system not unlike the Mycenaeans' began to be used. Inhumation of the dead was generally replaced by cremation. The grand ambition that had driven developments down the earlier centuries had apparently evaporated with them. This pattern was reflected further east when thwarted King Di Xin of China set fire to his own palace and committed suicide in 1046 BC, bringing the Shang dynasty to an end. The ensuing Zhou dynasty would place new restrictions on women's lives, particularly towards the end of its 789-year rule, when the genders were strictly segregated.

It wasn't until about 1000 BC that the first signs of recovery began to appear following the long period of lassitude. If one had to pinpoint where, precisely, the transition took place, the map would fall open upon Euboea, in the north. Lefkandi, situated in the South Euboean Gulf, had been well known to the Mycenaeans, whose grand warrior tombs have been uncovered there. Well-fortified and fertile, the settlement became home around the turn of the millennium to the earliest proto-temple in Greece. Measuring almost 50 metres long, the building had a rounded, 'apsidal' end, mudbrick walls set into a stone base, and wooden columns erected along two of its sides. Within were two tombs, one of which held the skeletons of four horses, the other, a cremated man and a buried woman. They were clearly very wealthy. He had been interred with weapons made of iron, and she with embossed gold discs over each of her breasts, gilt hair coils, bronze, bone and gilt iron pins, and a pendant from the east dating back to 1600 BC. Their tomb building is of great importance because it presaged the use of temples throughout Greece and heralded an explosion in monumental building that would reach its peak in the eighth century BC. By about 800 BC, a roofed temple some 100 metres long had been erected beside a pre-existing altar on the island of Samos, and dedicated to the goddess Hera.

The new age of construction was aided by a surge in the populations inhabiting the Greek world following the dramatic declines of the previous centuries. Ironically, the reawakening which occurred in the nascent Iron Age is most perceptible in the sleeping, the number of graves and the quality of their contents offering the clearest evidence of growth. By far the most tantalising of these is associated with the 'Rich Athenian Lady'. She had been heavily pregnant or in premature labour at the time of her death aged between thirty and forty about 850 BC.[27] Her cremated ashes were placed underground in a funerary amphora painted with an ornate geometric pattern. A not dissimilar amphora from the period, also from Athens, features an illustration of the death rites she would have received.[28] The central scene on the vase shows a woman laid out on a bier beneath a woven shroud, which is depicted using cross-hatching from a bird's-eye perspective to allow a full view of her body before it is carried to the pyre. All around her figures stand tearing their hair in a traditional Greek gesture of mourning.

The authority of the Rich Athenian Lady, who received the grandest early burial yet found in this part of the world, is clear from the goods interred with her: bronze brooches, gold earrings and rings, a glass bead necklace from Egypt or Syria, ivory stamp seals, jars for cosmetics and, most interestingly of all, a beautifully painted terracotta chest topped with five sculpted beehive-style model granaries, which in shape echo the beads of her earrings. The granary box is so unusual that it is tempting to conclude that the woman was involved in an agricultural business. It was at precisely this time that Athens and surrounding Attica were starting to flourish again through trade. Female farm managers, owners or similar were not unheard of in the ninth century BC, although there is little evidence that they were commonplace. To have interred the deceased with a form of her work in miniature, ivory seals and all, her relatives must have felt immense pride in the lady's accomplishments.

In the period the Rich Athenian Lady died, arts and crafts were beginning to enjoy a renaissance in Athens and Corinth in particular. The creation of the intricate granary chest coincided with the development of increasingly decorative pottery. An ensuing 'Orientalising Revolution' inspired the appearance of intricate new patterns and shapes on Greek vessels, including lotus and palmettes as well as swastikas.[29] In the east, the Assyrians had established a new capital at Nimrud in 884 BC using spoils from the territory they gained in Syria and Babylon. The Euboeans now set up a trading post in Syria, at Al Mina, which brought them into regular contact with a wide range of eastern wares. The arrival of craftspeople from the east in Crete and central Greece drove the artistic revolution further. Through the eighth and seventh centuries BC, the Hellenes combined the incoming ideas with their own tradition for geometric styles to great effect. Attractive new pots began to be exported in some numbers to the Levant, Sicily and the Italian mainland.[30] It has been suggested that the use of cross-hatching, used to depict the funeral shroud described above, as well as clothing and patches of pattern on other pots, was inspired by weaving, of which women had the most intimate knowledge.[31] It is most probable that women were among the pot-painters of this period.

Not content with setting the precedent for temple-building and facilitating trade with the east, the people of Euboea also took an early lead in learning to write. According to an ancient myth, a group of Phoenicians followed Europa's brother Cadmus, king of Greek Thebes, out of the Levant to settle in Boeotia, central Greece, bringing their learning with them.[32] The alphabet the Phoenicians taught the Greeks was known thereafter as 'Cadmean Letters' and consisted of twenty-two syllabic signs, each of which represented a consonant and a vowel. Occasionally, myths contain kernels of truth, and this one proved quite accurate. The

Greek alphabet did derive from the Phoenician, though Boeotia, Hesiod's home, was a less likely point of contact than Crete, Al Mina or Euboea.

One of the earliest known examples of writing in the new alphabet appears on a cup from c. 715 BC and describes the power of a goddess. Deposited in a boy's grave at Pithekoussai, Ischia, a Greek colony in the Bay of Naples, the cup was probably made in Teos or Rhodes.[33] Adapted slightly from the Phoenician prototype, the letters upon it celebrate the divine magic of love. 'I am Nestor's cup, good to drink from,' the three-line inscription begins, before continuing in epic verse, 'and he who drinks from this cup, the desire of most beautifully crowned Aphrodite will seize at once.'[34] The text evokes the memory of Nestor drinking from a cup in the *Iliad*, only there Nestor's cup is described as heavy and gold-adorned, with four handles featuring decorative doves.[35] Heinrich Schliemann subsequently named a two-handled cup he discovered at Mycenae the 'Cup of Nestor'. Made of clay and painted with black geometric patterns and shapes, the Pithekoussai cup pales in comparison to both. Its maker may have been laughing as he likened his fine but comparatively modest creation to the gold masterpieces of the heroic age.

Many of the stories that went into the *Iliad* and the *Odyssey* were still being told when the cup was made. After being circulated orally for generations, the two poems were now set down in hard copy. They were among the very first works to be transcribed in the new, Phoenician-inspired Greek alphabet. Far fewer people would have been able to read the poems than recite them from memory at this stage, but the reintroduction of writing to Greece ensured that versions of them were preserved for posterity. The translation of the poems from spoken words to written texts also helped to fix the ideas they contained.

As the Pithekoussai cup of Nestor shows, Aphrodite was also by now well known in Greece in her Homeric guise as a goddess of lust. Although she was first named in the eighth century BC, when the epics were written down, worship of a love and sex goddess had existed for centuries, not least of all on Cyprus, her sacred island, where a sanctuary was built to her at Paphos as early as 1200 BC.[36] Enticing fertility figures with female genitalia and phallus-like necks had been crafted from limestone and other materials on the island up to three millennia earlier, but the poems of Homer and Hesiod added colour to the story of a sex goddess's origins. In the *Theogony*, Hesiod explained that Aphrodite was born when

Kronos, father of Zeus, castrated his father Ouranos (Sky or Heaven), and the dismembered body parts foamed up on the sea near the Greek island of Cythera. 'Aphrodite' was the Greek for 'foam-born'. Kronos carried out the bloody act at the bidding of his mother Gaia (Earth), who was desperate to be relieved of the agony she felt as, repeatedly, Ouranos had sex with her while she was in labour.

As an offspring of this dysfunctional family, Aphrodite had the ability to inspire both fear and love, a duality for which she had her Mesopotamian counterparts to thank. The goddess Inanna, who featured in the *Epic of Gilgamesh*, was known for her aggression as well as her powers of seduction. She was often depicted with bull-like horns. Such was the anxiety Inanna spread that Sumerian kings envisaged themselves having sex with her in order to gain her protection in war, thereby uniting her two chief attributes. The first temple to her was erected in Uruk (southern Mesopotamia), of which she was considered the patron goddess. Worshipped from about 3000 BC by the Sumerians and Akkadians, and later by the Babylonians and Assyrians as Ishtar, she was a truly paradoxical goddess.

Inanna owed her reputation in no small part to the imagination of the earliest named author in the world. Enheduanna was a Sumerian poet of the third millennium BC. Her father, Sargon, was king of Akkad, a capital some believe to have been located close to modern Baghdad. Her mother was Tashlultum. The family presided over an extraordinary empire that spanned the distance from the eastern Mediterranean to the Persian Gulf. Enheduanna held the position of high priestess of a Moon deity called Nanna in Ur for several decades. She composed lively temple hymns and poems which she had the forethought to sign with her name. She often sang the praises of Inanna and her many attributes.[37] Enheduanna admired the goddess's fearsome battle cry and stood in awe of the mourning she carried to people's homes by laying men low in the field. In the 'Exaltation of Inanna', the most celebrated of Enheduanna's hymns, the goddess is the gatherer and protector of the greatest powers of the heavens. She is capable of breathing poison onto the world below, of overwhelming the land and of flattening the crops simply by raising her voice.[38]

Inanna's voice was important to Enheduanna because she very nearly lost her own. The poet spoke openly to the Moon-god Nanna in the same hymn of her maltreatment by a man named Lugal-anne. An enemy of her father, the brutish Lugal-anne moved to seize power himself, slobbered over his hand then placed it over her mouth. He held up a dagger – a symbol for something else – and told her that it suited her well. He raped her, dragged her from her post, forced her to wander among the thorn bushes. 'My talent for lifting spirits,' wrote Enheduanna, tragically, 'has turned to dust.'[39] We can appreciate how her sentiments would have resonated with the later women of Miletus.

Enheduanna's mouth was a poet's mouth, 'honey-sweet' and innocent. It was a mouth that could no longer speak yet refused to be silenced. Enheduanna used her hymn to incriminate and curse the man who had assaulted her and to implore Inanna to punish him. The goddess inspired Enheduanna in turn to regain something of her strength. The poet had reason to believe that Inanna was at her side when her nephew Naram-Sin quelled Lugal-anne's rebellion. Enheduanna, bruised but defiant, was able to return to the centre of the largest empire in the world at that time. A contemporary artist depicted her on a carved limestone and calcite disc shaped like the moon. She wears a hat and her hair in neat plaits and is attended by three more plainly dressed people who assist her in offering thanksgiving presents to the goddess.[40] Enheduanna's name appears in an inscription on the back of the object. The art of writing, associated with women from the Trojans to the Hittites and the verses of Homer, preserved Enheduanna from the common fate of anonymity.

A few hundred years before Enheduanna was born, another woman had either single-handedly ruled or held a significant position of power in the city of Ur. Her name was Puabi and she was known as 'queen'. Her colourful funeral clothes and golden headdress, discovered in her tomb, are among the most astonishing finds from the period. The Mesopotamians' tolerance of female displays of power helps to explain why Enheduanna's portrait of the goddess Inanna endured. There was no apparent reaction against the hymns that described her for being the products of a female poet. Enheduanna's authority was respected. The Greek conception of Aphrodite as a goddess to be feared certainly echoed the Mesopotamian ideas voiced by Enheduanna. Readers of Homer understood the duplicity of Aphrodite's act when she united Helen with Paris. This was not a love-match – it was a declaration of war.

*

At the same time as artistic and literary inspiration was entering Greece from the east, inhabitants of various eastern cities were beginning to move west. The eighth and seventh centuries BC were marked by considerable migration and resettlement. Hesiod told of his father's decision to relocate from Cyme in Asia Minor to Ascra in Boeotia, a place he deemed wretched in winter and summer alike. Conversely another poet, Mimnermus, wrote of leaving Pylos, where Nestor had kept his palace, and travelling east to longed-for Asia, where he settled at Colophon.[41] Ischia, where the ceramic Cup of Nestor was buried, was popular with travellers seeking a new home away from the Greek mainland. And Sicily received an influx of newcomers after the Phoenicians first settled there about 800 BC.

The first Greeks on Sicily were said to have been Euboeans from the city of Chalcis.[42] The sight of them pouring in was enough to persuade the Phoenicians to abandon their coastal spots, where they had lined the promontories, and make their way inland. Many Phoenicians set up home at Motya, Soluntum and Palermo, hoping they might face less competition for supplies, and continued to cultivate their own gods, including the fertility god Baal Hammon.[43] In the longer term, their migration proved fruitless, for the Greeks only spread themselves out over Sicily during the later eighth century, founding Messana, Catania, Leontini and Naxos. Incoming Corinthians, led by one Archias, were credited with establishing the still more influential city of Syracuse. Located at first on Ortygia, a land mass separated from the Sicilian mainland via a channel, Syracuse was later re-established on the south-east coast. It would become one of the most powerful city-states of Magna Graecia ('Greater Greece'), as this region was later known. Westward migrations to Sicily were followed by eastward migrations of Greek peoples to Thrace, the Hellespont and the shores of the Black Sea.

From 776 BC, and very probably long before, the increased circulation of ideas brought about by these movements helped to inspire the establishment of the first panhellenic games. Held in honour of Zeus at Olympia, the Olympic Games took place every four years and necessitated further travel, as thousands of people came to participate and spectate from all corners of the Greek world. As the competition approached, heralds were dispatched to announce the start date and initiate a truce for peace, the *ekecheiria*, which would last for the duration of the games and up to three months surrounding them.[44]

The invention of the games heralded a new freedom for women, who had until now travelled predominantly out of necessity rather than pleasure. At the beginning, this freedom was hard to find, for rules were imposed to limit their participation. No woman could have been surprised to find herself banned from entering the various chariot races and vicious wrestling contests, for the sports were practised only by men. Many women would surely have been disappointed, however, to find that they were also prohibited from watching their sons and husbands take part. A peculiarly punitive law dictated that any woman spotted in the vicinity of the games while the men were competing could be cast off the cliffs nearby.[45] The ruling was intended to protect her virtue: men generally competed in the nude. Pausanias knew of only one woman who had dared to put the law to the test. A widow was so eager to see her son compete that she attempted to disguise herself as his male coach in order to enter the arena. As the boy stormed to victory, she boldly exposed herself, prompting new measures to be introduced to strip-search all future 'coaches' at the games. The widow was forgiven out of respect for her family and her son's success.

Women were given an opportunity to experience triumph for themselves following the introduction of a women's footrace. Held at Olympia every four years in honour of Hera, queen of the gods, the competition required women to run on a slightly shorter track than the men, and in heats according to their age. The competitors dressed in short tunics which left their right shoulders exposed.[46] As it was also a religious occasion, sixteen married women were commissioned to weave the goddess a luscious new robe for each new set of races. As in the men's competitions, the prizes were modest, the winners receiving olive crowns and sacrificial meat. Winners were also occasionally permitted to dedicate statues bearing their names. The fact that it was usual in the Greek world for the keepers rather than the riders of winning horses to be crowned victors enabled more women to succeed in otherwise male competitions. Most famously, in the fourth century BC, a Spartan princess named Cynisca would become the first woman to win a victory – in fact two consecutive victories – in the equestrian events at the Olympic Games as owner of the winning steeds.[47] She was then aged about fifty. Sculptures of Cynisca with her horses and chariot were erected at Olympia.[48]

While the Olympic Games offered some women the chance to win fame outside their own cities, the establishment of new cult practices saw others enter deeper confinement. A particular tradition developed in Locris near Euboea requiring women to shave their heads and take up a life of religious solitude. The process appears to have arisen in response to a story told in the aftermath of the Homeric epics. Such was the appetite for the *Iliad* and *Odyssey* that a series of poems known as the Epic Cycle came into being to extend their storylines or offer prequels. One poem told of Cassandra, daughter of King Priam, and her rape by the Greek warrior Ajax, son of Oileus, during the fall of Troy.[49] The heinous act was said to have occurred while Cassandra was clinging to a statue of the goddess Athena. Ajax compounded his crime by proceeding to take refuge himself at the goddess's altar. To punish him, Athena sent a plague upon his countrymen at Locris, just as Apollo had sent a plague upon the Greeks at Troy at the beginning of the *Iliad*. In a bid to appease Athena, the Locrians sent two women to Troy to tend her temple.[50] Each chosen pair had to make their way to the goddess's precinct while the Trojans enacted a ritual attempt to hinder their path. Once they had reached the temple, the women dispensed with their shoes and agreed to be shaved.[51] In exchange, their parents were paid money, and the Locrians were granted certain privileges, including inviolability for some of their leaders in wartime.[52] It is uncertain whether the women served Athena for the rest of their lives or until they were released to marry. The tribute is likely to have begun in the early seventh century BC, when the Epic Cycle of poems began to circulate. The *Iliupersis*, largely now lost, contained the story of Cassandra's rape by Ajax. The boundary between literature and life had once again been crossed.

By the seventh century BC, the heroic world immortalised by Homer and his adherents felt nearer than it had for generations. The vestiges of enormous boulder 'cyclopean' walls and grand tombs filled with gold might have towered mockingly over the efforts of intervening centuries, but something of the spirit that had propelled the Mycenaeans had now been rekindled through the travels of their heirs. The experience of women over this period had been highly mixed, ranging from abandonment and sexual assault to the freedom to compete for the first time, but new commerce of ideas and knowledge, especially of writing, made this also a time of anticipation. The Iron Age might have struck a dull note after the glories that had come before, but its subjects were now dancing to a sweeter tune as they faced the uncertainties of a new era. Archaic Age Greece would bring women the opportunity to sing their own songs as they strove not simply to sustain, but to build upon Homer's legacy.

Chapter IV

The Tenth Muse

I hear that you're raising the children indulgently. It is the task of a good mother not to pay attention to her children's pleasure but rather to steer them in the direction of wisdom.

Theano to Euboule, correspondence between
Pythagorean women, sixth century BC

Lying in the eastern Aegean, about half a day's journey from the west coast of Asia Minor, was the rugged Greek island of Lesbos. Known to the Mycenaeans, at least through trade (fragments of their exported pottery turned up habitually in the ground), it received its first great influx of settlers in the eleventh or tenth century BC, when the Hellenes were displaced from their homes in northern and central Greece.[1] While Agamemnon, Menelaus and Odysseus were all said to have travelled there in the Homeric epics, the island became better known for its women, and best of all for its female poets.[2]

Readers of the *Iliad* were assured that Lesbos was an island of beautiful women. When Achilles withdrew from battle, smarting at his maltreatment over Briseis, Agamemnon strove to tempt him back to the field with gifts which included seven Lesbian women chosen for their beauty.[3] By the second half of the seventh century BC, the real women of Lesbos had grown used to being judged on their appearance as part of an annual contest.[4] Participants dressed in their most elegant trailing robes and paraded before a panel deemed to be expert in such things. But not every woman was considered worthy of a prize. Sappho, so people said, was not beautiful at all.[5] She was short, dark and very unattractive. Not one of the writers who described her as such could possibly have seen her, but that did not stop their words from gaining currency down the ages.[6] There was something very appealing in the idea that the woman who grew famous for writing about love was herself unlovely to look at. The unflattering rumours did Sappho no harm in the long term. In fact, they helped her to become the first woman of Lesbos to be remembered for something other than good looks.

Lesbos had a long-established reputation for poetry when Sappho plucked her first notes. The head and lyre of Orpheus were said to have floated over the seas in very ancient times and served as a kind of divine spark. The musician had formerly lost his wife Eurydice to a snakebite and tragically turned back to look at her as he was trying to lead her free of the Underworld. Some Thracian women then tore his body to pieces in the madness-inducing ecstasy of worshipping Dionysus. A number of male poets had arisen on Lesbos in Orpheus' wake, including Terpander, who outperformed the singer-poets of all other lands, and Lesches, poet of the *Little Iliad*, part of the post-Homeric Epic Cycle.[7] But it was Sappho and her male contemporary Alcaeus who retained the 'Aeolian' dialect of Lesbos in their verse and cemented the island's renown as the cradle of lyric poetry.

Sappho composed in a variety of styles, leaping effortlessly between epigrams, funeral dirges, wedding hymns, epic-like pieces and romantic verses, many of them inspired by the enigma of women she admired. She invented her own poetic form, the Sapphic Stanza, a light but penetrating triplet of eleven-syllable lines rounded off by a final five-syllable flourish.[8] And like the Homeric bards, she performed her verses to a melody, holding in her hands a lyre constructed from a tortoise shell with seven strings derived from the intestines of a sheep.

She lived on the south-east coast of Lesbos at Mytilene, the most powerful city-state in all the Greek East, after being born into a wealthy family either there or in the west, at Eresos, a city largely since swallowed by the sea. Described by Homer as *euktimenos* ('well laid-out'), Mytilene had two harbours around which most of the houses were clustered, and a set of surrounding walls constructed in Lesbian style from vast polygon-shaped stones. Beyond these walls and the divine protection offered by Mount Olympus, situated 840 kilometres to the west across the Aegean, there was little in the way of a defensive system. Other cities on the island possessed more robust barricades and towers. The lack of large-scale buildings reflected the Mytilenaeans' broad outlook.[9] They were less anxious to defend themselves from attack than to expand their interests abroad. As Alcaeus wrote, cities consist not of stones, beams and buildings, but of people who gather together in unison.[10]

This was a bold assertion given how unsettled life on Mytilene had become. At the time of Sappho's birth in the mid-seventh century BC, the city was ruled by the Penthilidae, an aristocratic dynasty with origins in Thessaly, north-east Greece. Members claimed descent from Agamemnon via his son Orestes. Historically, theirs had been a harsh rule, which authorised the flogging and clubbing of citizens in the street.[11] During Sappho's early childhood, the Penthilidae were overthrown and a man named Melanchrus was installed as the wealthy new ruler of Mytilene. Some years later, when Sappho was about twenty, Melanchrus was in turn unseated in a coup in which Alcaeus' brothers played a part.

In many cities of the Greek world, something like a revolution was taking place as populists emerged to usurp their elite rulers.

In Athens, shortly before Sappho's birth, a former Olympic champion named Cylon attempted to seize the Acropolis. The city was still in the early stages of its development. All freeborn men (but no women) were entitled to attend the Athenian Assembly, where nine *archons* were habitually elected as civil rulers, and these archons typically came from the oldest and wealthiest families. In a bid to challenge the domination of the elite, Cylon assembled the forces of his father-in-law, the king of Megara.[12] A priestess advised him to await the arrival of a particular festival to launch his attack, but Cylon believed he knew better, and he led his men to the Acropolis during the Olympics. He was soon thwarted. The Athenians put the majority of the invaders to flight and the archons voted to slaughter the stragglers. While Cylon and his brothers fled, some of their soldiers sought refuge at a shrine and wrapped a thread around a cult image to claim divine sanctuary. On seeing the thread snap, the archons concluded that the divinities did not support the invaders, and proceeded to break the religious code which dictated that suppliants ought to be spared.[13] A curse was believed to linger over the descendants of the offending archons for centuries afterwards.[14]

While the political situation in Mytilene, Athens and beyond remained febrile, Sappho was able to live a relatively peaceful life in her younger years. Since her earliest childhood she learned to weave, first at the loom, then more freely; the women of Lesbos were keen weavers of floral garlands.[15] As a poet, she was interested in the idea that the first woman, too, was a weaver. Hesiod had described Athena endowing Pandora with the requisite skills to produce fabrics and dressing her in fine clothes, as if to teach her by example what she could weave for herself.[16] It is likely that Sappho followed Hesiod in characterising Pandora as the archetypal weaver in one of her lost poems.[17] Outdoing Pandora, Sappho steadily earned a reputation as 'a weaver of tales', as she once described Eros.[18] She grew up to weave stories, and garlands, and songs about those garlands, so making local women's handiwork the subject of celebration. Her words preserved their blooms for centuries after they withered away.

Floral garlands were made for weddings as well as religious festivals in ancient Lesbos. Sappho's dual talents made her welcome at these occasions, where the bride's bedchamber had to be draped with flowers, the hair of the cult image of Aphrodite dressed with hyacinths and a long hymn composed and performed.[19] Sappho learned from her mother, Kleis, that while a purple headband was a fine adornment for most women, blonde hair was best shown off with fresh flowers.[20] Women on Lesbos sometimes brightened their locks using *thapsos*, fustic, a wood-based dye.[21] Just as the Graces made Pandora irresistible by adorning her with gold necklaces, and the Horai, goddesses of the seasons, made Pandora beguiling by placing a floral crown upon her head, so Sappho believed that women made themselves most pleasing to the Graces by weaving beautiful flowers into their tresses and dousing their skin with richly spiced fragrances.[22] It was part of the ritual of mourning on Lesbos for women to shave their heads with sharpened iron. By contrast, dressing the hair was a way of celebrating life.

In garlanding their hair, women made themselves pleasing to Sappho, too, as some of the most erotic of her verses reveal. She wrote to a female lover about the time they had adorned each other with flowers, and on a soft bed, Sappho reminded her, 'you would quench your desire'.[23]

Of all the many kinds of poem Sappho composed, it was the ones in which she expressed a romantic interest in women that proved the most memorable, especially in later years. Like 'sapphism', the word 'lesbianism' would come to be applied exclusively to relations between women only from the late nineteenth century and in the light of Sappho's verses. Already in antiquity, a connection developed between Lesbos and subversive sexual practices. While the Greek verb *lesbiazein*, 'to act like a woman of Lesbos', could be used of oral sex performed on people of both genders, the island came to be associated particularly with women who refused to submit sexually to men. Homer's portrait of Lesbos as an island of beautiful women was supplanted by descriptions of 'masculine-looking' women liking other women 'as if they were men'.[24] This was a subtle way of saying that women on Lesbos had sex with each other using dildos.

The mechanics of their relations were deemed too shameful even for satirists to explain. Still in the second century AD, literary allusions to women learning to 'love like a man' remained brisk, coy, red-cheeked. Artists were characteristically less bashful. One male vase-painter, working a century or so after Sappho's time, portrayed a naked woman raising one dildo to her lips while inserting another into her vagina in a scene more redolent of male fantasy than reality.[25] Another vase-painter depicted a woman inspecting a veritable production line of moulded phalluses in varied shapes and sizes.[26] Dildos could be made from just about anything – leather, bread – but in this painting, they are of clay. The woman sprinkles water on the instruments to prevent the terracotta from drying out (a problem familiar to potters in general) or to help them grow. A reference to a woman receiving something, possibly *olisboi* ('dildos'), appears in one of the very many barely decipherable fragments of Sappho's work uncovered from the deserts of Oxyrhynchus, 'City of the Sharp-Nosed Fish', in Egypt.[27] If Sappho ever did make use of a dildo, she was not the only woman to do so on Lesbos, the island of transgressive love.

Despite achieving fame for her love poems for women, Sappho apparently married a wealthy male trader. No one living within the influence of the Greek world could have taken seriously the suggestion made in a prominent Byzantine encyclopaedia that her husband was named Kerkulas, meaning 'Cock', or that he came from Andros, the 'Isle of Man'.[28] But while his identity is unknown, his existence is plausible, for several of Sappho's poems feature a daughter named Kleis after her maternal grandmother. It may even be that some of Sappho's surviving verses are addressed to him: the object of Sappho's affections was often left ambiguous. In one desperate plea, the poet summons Aphrodite, 'weaver of stratagems', *doloploke*, to help her as she suffers the pangs of unrequited love.[29] The goddess agrees to assist, promising that the one she loves will not only love her back, but even pursue her against her will. A single word, 'against her will', reveals the beloved's gender in the Greek, and even that is uncertain from the condition of the papyrus.[30]

While some of the poems commonly assumed to be addressed to women might actually have been addressed to men, Sappho's professional life revolved predominantly around women and girls. When she was not falling in love with them, she was teaching them, and listening to them sing. Sappho stood at the head of what she called 'a house serving the muses'.[31] Later described as 'one of the first literary salons', it was, in practice, a school for girls specialising in poetry and music.[32] The pupils were *tas aristas*, 'the best girls', a phrase that referred predominantly to their noble birth – to *aristocrats* – but might also have reflected their poetical prowess.[33] They came to Sappho's school in Mytilene from as far away as Ionia and included one Andromeda, an Atthis and a Telesippa.[34] Kleis, Sappho's daughter, was apparently also of their number; a fragment of poetry describes her wailing in a building sacred to the Muses and being told off by her mother.[35]

Sappho's profession as a teacher of girls was also undertaken by men in this period. A male poet named Alcman wrote *partheneia*, 'maiden songs', which he taught to choruses of girls in Sparta.[36] As his own poems reveal, poet-teachers were by no means immune to becoming enamoured of their pupils. Alcman found much to admire in talented 'fair-haired Megalostrata', and Sappho developed a near-romantic attachment to several of her tutees.[37]

Some people detected a romance between Sappho and her fellow poet Alcaeus too. 'I wish to say something to you, but shame holds me back,' wrote Alcaeus in one of his verses. '. . . If you had something good or noble in mind, and your tongue were not conceiving something wicked to say, shame would not envelop your eyes, you would speak,' Sappho replied.[38] The pair would often be portrayed together on Greek vases in the centuries after they lived.[39] Their poems were very probably performed at the same festivals and competitions even though female performers were formally segregated from male ones.[40]

Sappho was nothing if not competitive. Even love was portrayed as a war. When Aphrodite came to her in answer to her prayers, it was as her 'fellow warrior' in a battle chariot drawn by sparrows.[41] The Aphrodite she worshipped shared much in common with the Mesopotamian Inanna. It was perhaps only natural that the people of Lesbos, living on the fringes of Asia Minor, should have cultivated an Aphrodite imbued with the bellicosity of her eastern forebears.[42]

The island's main religious centre was at Mesa, near modern Kryoneri, where worshippers congregated at a temple dedicated to Zeus, Hera and Dionysus.[43] Further temples have been discovered at Klopedi, near the centre of the island, one with columns topped by capitals particular to the region (the two volutes associated with Ionic capitals were turned 90 degrees so as to stand upright), and another nearby, possibly dedicated to the sun and arts god Apollo.[44] Most striking was the early temple near Mytilene's north harbour. Constructed with an apsidal end, it was dedicated to Cybele, a formidable eastern mother goddess.[45] Originating in Asia Minor, Cybele had her chief sanctuary in the heartlands of Phrygia, at Pessinus, and was often shown in the company of lions. A sculpture in the temple at Mytilene showed her taming a lion in her lap.[46] Hundreds of years later, Cybele would become an unlikely heroine for the Romans as they faced their darkest hour in conflict with the Carthaginians of North Africa.

Fascination with Cybele would have spread to Mytilene from another of her cult centres, a place of some significance to Sappho and the broader population of Lesbos. Situated on a busy trade route, the kingdom of Lydia, Asia Minor, was as famous as Lesbos for the beauty and creativity of its women. Legend held that its ruling dynasty, the Mermads, had come to power in the first decades of the seventh century BC through the vengeful act of a former queen consort named Nyssia. Her husband, Candaules, had boasted to his friends that she was the most beautiful woman in the world. *Don't just take my word for it*, Candaules said to his guardsman, Gyges, *see for yourself.* Gyges was reluctant. He did not particularly want to see Nyssia in the nude when doing so would involve creeping into her bedchamber, hiding in a corner of the room, and ogling her before making a swift escape. Candaules, however, was insistent, so Gyges did as he was told. He watched Nyssia undress for bed and slowly turned away. As he was leaving, Nyssia caught sight of him. For whatever reason, it occurred to her that her husband might have been responsible for leading his most trusted guardsman to her bedchamber. Without saying a word, she summoned Gyges to a private meeting the following day, held out a dagger and told him that he must either die for having shamed her by seeing her naked, or kill the man who put him up to the deed and take her as his wife. Faced with an impossible choice, Gyges accepted the weapon and hid himself in the same place as he had on the previous night. He assassinated Candaules in his sleep.

Despite public outcry at the slaughter of the king, the coronation of Gyges was sanctioned by the Pythia of Delphi, who emerged as the world's leading oracular priestess in the seventh century BC. A Greek hymn composed in this period related that Apollo had founded her sanctuary on the plain of Crisa, beneath the snow-capped peaks of Mount Parnassus, so that he could issue divine guidance through her.[47] From that moment on the Pythia was recognised as the most valued mouthpiece of the god on earth. She was awarded her place at Delphi after Apollo vanquished a monstrous serpent that guarded the site.[48] In a splendid Greek vase painting, the creature was depicted with female anthropomorphic features, her long tail curling over the end of the tripod upon which the priestess of the oracle perched.[49] The memory of Apollo's victory over the beast lived on in the Pythia, whose name derived from the Greek for 'rot' (referencing the serpent's mouldering corpse) and gave us the word 'python'. The priestess offered her wisdom on just nine days a year after entering an almost trance-like state from inhaling, it is believed, natural gases issuing from the Delphian rocks. The early priestesses were young virgins, but after one was raped, a rule was imposed requiring them to be aged fifty or over and celibate.

With the Pythia's blessing, Gyges of Lydia became the first man to be described formally as *tyrannos*, 'tyrant' or 'king', a word probably derived from the Lydian for 'lord', *turan*. In its original context, the term was employed neutrally and denoted a sole ruler who could pass his power down. Only later, from the fifth century BC, would 'tyrant' carry with any consistency the negative associations of 'tyranny'.[50] While Gyges was entitled to rule with impunity, the oracle warned that the fifth generation of his family would be sure to suffer the repercussions of his murderous act.[51] And so it would prove.

The day for vengeance was fast approaching, for by Sappho's time, Lydia was ruled by Alyattes, who belonged to the fourth generation of Gyges' family. Alyattes was a successful diplomat, who succeeded in conquering the coastal city of Smyrna (Izmir), and agreeing peace terms with the people of the Greek city of Miletus after a war.[52] The betrothal of one of his daughters, Aryenis, to a prince named Astyages sealed his treaty with the Medians, who inhabited the sprawling kingdom abutting his own. The marriage of another daughter to the tyrant king of Ephesus, on the west coast, further secured Lydia's pre-eminence within Asia Minor.

The people of Lesbos and the Greek world associated Lydia predominantly with its wealth and fine exports. Some of the most splendid objects at Delphi were dedicated by Alyattes, among them an enormous silver bowl on a welded iron base, delivered in thanksgiving for his recovery from an illness.[53] Tapestries and embroidered headbands made by Lydian women were highly coveted. (In the *Iliad*, Homer had likened the appearance of Menelaus' skin after it was punctured by an arrow to an ivory bridle of a king's horse dyed deep crimson by a woman of Lydia or neighbouring Caria.)[54]

The Lydians' reputation for high living was compounded by their invention of coins for use as currency.[55] Sappho was a young woman when the first 'slaters' were circulated. Irregular in shape, though roughly oval, the novel coins were stamped with lion's heads and made from electrum, an alloy of gold and silver found in great abundance in the Pactolus River which ran through Lydia's royal capital of Sardis at the foot of the Tmolus Mountains. King Midas was said to have bathed in these waters in his desperation to cleanse himself of the curse of turning everything he touched to gold. The residue of his repeated ablutions lined the riverbed. While the first Lydian coins were minted under Alyattes, the wife of another King Midas – a ruler, perhaps, of nearby Phrygia in Asia Minor – was credited with being the first person to strike coins in the coastal city of Cyme.[56] Hermodike was Greek by birth and, if she existed at all, queen consort at Cyme in the late seventh or early sixth century BC. The gold that wasn't used for minting was most often used for jewellery. Lydian women were particularly partial to pomegranate-headed gold pins, gold appliqués for clothes, and gold necklaces strung with electrum beads.[57]

Sappho knew more than a few women who left Lesbos for the riches of Lydia after marrying Lydian men. Watching girls graduate from her poetry school and enter into marriage, typically in their early to mid-teenage years, did not always bring her happiness. In one poem, Sappho staged a conversation between a woman and her virginity, which sings back to her, mournfully, that she will never return once taken.[58] Marriage was an irreversible process for girls. While young men were encouraged to gain sexual experience early on, young women were expected to keep their virginity intact until their wedding night. Wedding hymns usually celebrated this moment for the possibilities it brought for new life. Sappho lingered rather on what marriage took away.

Her sorrow at seeing her girls leave to marry was matched only by the disgruntlement she felt when they abandoned her teaching for the sake of their poetic careers. At least one of Sappho's former pupils went on to establish a rival school. Young Andromeda might have expected her teacher to be pleased at her following in her footsteps. She instead found Sappho overcome by bitterness and jealousy. The elder poet branded the younger or her inamorata a 'country bumpkin' and proceeded to mock her for failing to cover her ankles with her rough, ragged drapery.[59]

This was only the beginning. When some of her existing pupils deigned to leave her school and join Andromeda's, Sappho took to her tablets once more, positioning herself as a pitiable lover who had been forsaken cruelly for another. She described the girls fleeing her House of the Muses in the same language she would use to describe them fleeing her embrace. They were not merely abandoning her school. They were abandoning her. Sappho was unrelenting in her interpretation of the facts. That Atthis 'flies to Andromeda' is offered as proof that she, Sappho, has become 'hateful' to her.[60] Another girl, Gorgo, is savaged for an unknown crime. According to Sappho, other people, too, had 'had enough of Gorgo'.[61] At least one of these girls belonged to the Polynax ('Much-Ruling') family with which Sappho had some familial connection. A blood tie could only have made the perfidy harder to bear. Sappho's competitive spirit might have aided her when it came to composing poetry for festivals, but in daily life it could be a destructive force. Sappho underestimated how far she influenced her own pupils. Her demands for absolute loyalty were bound to be broken by women she raised in her own mould.

Within a century or two of arriving on Lesbos, the Aeolian Greeks had assumed control of several cities surrounding the Hellespont as well as much of the Troad – the region in which Troy lay – including Assus, Lamponia and Sigeum.[62] The Lesbians consequently had a strong trade base, with connections stretching from North Africa to the Black Sea. They exported their goods, especially wine, in *bucchero*, a particular style of pottery made on the island.[63] Plain, grey, practical, the amphorae were similar in shape to those made in Phrygia in central Asia Minor, and have been found in abundance in the Nile Delta at Naucratis ('Power in Ships'), home to the earliest Egyptian port the Greeks had access to, and the first Greek settlement in Egypt.[64]

Naucratis was founded shortly before Sappho's birth during the reign of the pharaoh Psamtik I, possibly by Milesian Greeks. On coming to power in 570 BC in the wake of a Babylonian invasion, Amasis II of Egypt would encourage Greek visitors to establish their own religious precincts in the area in order to revive trade and replenish the coffers.[65] With Amasis' blessing, citizens of Mytilene, Rhodes, Halicarnassus, Phocaea and elsewhere founded the holy precinct of Hellenion at the site. The Halicarnassan historian Herodotus would be astonished by the sight of Egyptian women attending the markets and handling trade while some men stayed at home weaving. Naucratis was by no means a male-only zone.

Already in Sappho's time, it was a richly cosmopolitan centre, with trade coming in from every direction. One of the poet's three brothers, Charaxus, was a trader with direct experience of the port town.[66] The journey between Mytilene and Naucratis carried Charaxus over long stretches of difficult water. Sappho prayed to Aphrodite and the Nereids (water nymphs who protected seafarers) that he would make it home safely. In a papyrus rediscovered in 2014 and still being examined for authenticity, she expresses her frustration with people who utter casually that Charaxus will be fine, as if they *know* this, when only the gods could truly tell what fate awaited him.

Given his sister's anxiety, Charaxus might have assumed that he would receive a warm welcome upon returning to Lesbos intact, but Sappho was Sappho. News reached her that he had met a woman at Naucratis. Her name was Doricha, though some called her 'Rhodopis' ('Rosy-Cheeks'), and she was a courtesan.

Herodotus believed that Doricha was born in Thrace, on the Greek border of the Black Sea, and that she was a slave belonging to a man of Samos, who also owned the fable-maker Aesop.[67] Whether this was true or not, Doricha had clearly come to Egypt to sell her body, and it was presumably in this context that Charaxus made her acquaintance. Swayed by love, pity, or both, Charaxus put down a large sum of money to buy her freedom, and allowed her to remain in Egypt as a free woman.

Surviving fragments of Sappho's poetry hint that her family became the subject of slander on account of Charaxus' extravagance.[68] Using prostitutes may have been generally acceptable in the Greek world, but on Lesbos there was an attitude among certain men that they might as well throw their money in the sea.[69] Alcaeus, Sappho's fellow poet, surprises in his revelation that men who paid for sex suffered 'shame'. The circles in which Sappho moved seemingly sympathised with Alcaeus' sentiments. Islanders turned, sharp-tongued, against Sappho's family, and Sappho against Charaxus for being such a fool.[70] 'My helpless brother was set aflame in his love for a whore / And suffered unspeakable losses muddled with shame,' wrote Ovid centuries later, assuming Sappho's voice.[71] The later poet delighted in presenting the female perspective in his early work the *Heroides*. It was obvious to him as a keen-eyed reader that Charaxus' affair had caused a division between brother and sister.

In her suspicion of her motives and snobbery towards her social class, Sappho overlooked the fact that Doricha was very much a woman after her own heart, eager for longevity and fame.[72] Their mutual ambition to be known and remembered made them unusual, for very few women of their time managed to achieve immortality through their work and on their own merits. Most of the epitaphs Sappho wrote for deceased women are limited to describing their marital status. 'Here lies the dust of Timas,' begins one, 'Who died before her marriage and was received by the dark blue chamber of Persephone.'[73] Marriage dominated descriptions of the female dead. Sculptures of young women known as *korai* had recently begun to be erected as grave-markers or votive offerings around Greece. One of the first was dedicated circa 650 BC by a woman of Naxos named Nikandre to the goddess Artemis at Delos. The inscription that accompanied it identified Nikandre as the daughter of one man, sister of another, and wife of one more. Subsumed by their drapery (the slightly earlier male *kouroi* were nude), the Egyptian-inspired figures were stiff and lifeless and no substitute for the words the women might have spoken themselves.

Reluctant to be reduced to a lump of stone or a handful of lines by somebody else, Sappho aspired to *kleos*, a glorious and undying reputation. It was what the heroes of Homer's epics fought for. It was what they obtained by being commemorated in the poems themselves. In a sign of just how closely she associated poetry with longevity, Sappho took to taunting an 'uneducated woman' who showed no interest in verse with the threat of being forgotten *post mortem*.[74] Of course, by writing of Doricha, Sappho unwittingly carried her name to the stars as well.

Doricha used her freedom to make her own bid for *kleos*. With a tenth of the money she acquired from Charaxus, she purchased a collection of iron spits made for roasting sacrificial oxen, and sent them to Delphi. Thousands of travellers would be able to see them and learn her name.[75] Herodotus was one of them.[76] Doricha's fame only grew as time went on. Mesmerised by the idea of her, the third-century BC Macedonian poet Posidippus wrote dreamily of her enveloping naked Charaxus in her perfume-soaked shawl.[77] Outlandish tales even arose of her financing the construction of one of the pyramids in Egypt. Doricha proved Sappho right. Given the correct set of circumstances, ambition and perseverance, a woman, even a servile woman, could outlive her mortal years and be remembered far beyond the walls of her home town.

The Greek city of Sigeum lay in the Troad, at the mouth of the Scamander River surrounding Troy. People said that Archeanax of Lesbos had built Sigeum's walls using Trojan stone.[78] The city was certainly of heroic dimensions. For the first three decades of Sappho's life, no one had thought to question the Lesbians' authority over the conveniently located harbour town. 'Sigeum' meant 'silent place', and while the name was ironic, as anyone who experienced the around-sound howl of the sea could testify, the port was much less talked-about than Naucratis. By the end of the seventh century BC, however, the Athenians had begun to look towards Sigeum while internal politics continued to threaten revolution at home.

A new system of legislation had been introduced to Athens in 621 BC. It bore the name of Draco ('Serpent'), of whom little is known, and aimed to take lawmaking out of private citizens' hands and thereby diminish common blood feuds. Citizens accused of murder were now entitled to a trial by the state so that their fates were not decided by interested parties. More draconianly, the code made even petty crimes, such as stealing vegetables, punishable by death.[79] Inscribed on public tablets so that they could be read and cited, Draco's laws benefited the wealthy and educated over the poor and illiterate. While granting the vote to hoplites (spear-wielding citizen soldiers) and other men in possession of specialist military equipment, the laws did nothing to address the broader inequalities of the time, such as those experienced between landowner and labourer. Many farmers were sold into slavery as a result of being driven into debt by their employers.

It was against this background that the Athenians made their bid for Sigeum. Travelling to the Hellespont about 600 BC, they established a base at nearby Achilleum, home to a monument to the Greek warrior, and watched as their general stepped forward and offered the Lesbians a suitably Homeric challenge. Phrynon was a former Olympic athlete.[80] He had triumphed in the vicious, boxing-like sport of *pankration*, participants in which were, to judge by surviving vase paintings, exceptionally large and terrifying. Who, Phrynon asked, would be bold enough to fight him man-to-man?

Alcaeus was among the Lesbians who had come over to defend the territory. Poets were not generally known for their martial prowess, but here Alcaeus was, dusting his feet in the same sand as Homer's heroes. Might he earn his place in the next generation of heroic verse? The reality was too frightening. The Athenians stripped him of his armour while he hesitated and hung it up in a temple of their patron goddess Athena.[81] Afraid of endangering his life any further, Alcaeus fled the field and sought a herald to carry a message home to Lesbos.[82] He was safe, he panted, but only just. His armour – and that of many others – was gone.

Another man emerged from Alcaeus' shadow. His name was Pittacus and he had once banded with Alcaeus' elder brothers to depose one of the tyrants of Mytilene.[83] A Roman copy of an earlier Greek portrait shows him as bearded, with wavy hair reaching down to his earlobes, close-set eyes and a mouth turning naturally downwards in a frown. He was not, as far as one can tell from a bust, of *pankration* proportions. Pittacus, a nobleman with Thracian blood, did not fancy his chances at wrestling Phrynon, but he was ambitious to rule Mytilene himself. Inching forward, he threw an enormous fishing net around his foe, and brought him down with a thrust of his spear. The scene ought to have inspired a hundred vase paintings. On one side would be slender Pittacus spreading his arms wide and preparing to strike the fatal blow. On the other, bulky Phrynon, struggling like a mullet in his net, speared like a kebab.[84]

Inspired by Pittacus' victory, the Lesbians gained the upper hand over the Athenians, but their success was evanescent. The two sides soon reached a stalemate. With no clear path for either to achieve victory, a neutral party was called in from Corinth to arbitrate, and the vote was cast in the Athenians' favour.[85]

The loss of Sigeum to a rival city-state was a disaster for morale in Mytilene. Only Pittacus felt sufficiently emboldened by his act of heroism to address what had cost the Mytilenaeans this victory. Not one of their tyrants had been able to control the factions that had been forged across the island. Numerous attempts had been made to install someone capable of leading, but when it came to uniting the citizenship, each candidate had been found wanting. Myrsilus, the current ruler, lacked vim. It occurred to Pittacus that he might round up Alcaeus' brothers and others to displace him. But what good had displacing a tyrant done them before? To the shock of his former co-conspirators, Pittacus changed tack, and went over to Myrsilus' side.[86]

To many on Lesbos, this was a gross act of betrayal, nothing more. Pittacus had pitched himself against the tyranny, then simply decided that he had been thwarted too many times, and defected. Ambition had trumped loyalty to the cause. Disgusted by his slipperiness, his former co-conspirators, among them Alcaeus, turned against Pittacus. The poet might have won admiration for abiding by his principles, but without Pittacus he had little hope of succeeding in his aims of changing the mode of rulership in Mytilene. Alcaeus helped to launch another plot against the tyrant but he was again defeated. He and his co-conspirators were soon making their way to the other side of the island in a voluntary exile in a bid to stay alive. They could only imagine the misery others were suffering as Myrsilus, devilish trampler of oaths, 'devoured' their dear city of Mytilene.[87]

For all the ructions it caused, Pittacus' decision to go over to the other side was vindicated when Myrsilus died a short time later and the Mytilenaeans lent Pittacus their support to take his place. It would be only so long, smirked Alcaeus, before Pittacus resembled every other tyrant who had come before him.[88] With a powerful metaphor the poet begged his compatriots to extinguish the smoke from the log before it became fire.[89] For the moment, Sappho held her tongue, if not for her own sake, then for the safety of her daughter Kleis. Sappho was to witness Alcaeus lead his fellow exiles in revolt against Pittacus, only to be driven out of Lesbos in a second exile.[90]

While Alcaeus seems to have gone to Egypt, Antimenidas, one of his brothers and co-conspirators, joined the army of Babylon.[91] The capital of the Neo-Babylonian Empire had become increasingly dominant in recent years. In 612 BC the Babylonians had joined forces with the Medes, of modern Iran, to overthrow the august Assyrian royal capital at Nineveh (in modern Mosul). The Babylonian king, Nebuchadnezzar II, now sought to extend his influence over Syria, Palestine and Egypt. In 587/6 BC he captured Jerusalem, leaving the Jews to be transported to Babylon, then laid siege to the Phoenician-founded city of Tyre on the coast of modern Lebanon. Nebuchadnezzar's marriage to Amytis, daughter (or possibly granddaughter) of Cyaxares, king of Media just east of Lydia, carried his name to Asia Minor.[92] Word must have spread there of the wondrous Hanging Gardens he commissioned at Babylon in honour of his wife. The gardens, later declared one of the Seven Wonders of the Ancient World, have never been found, but are known to have been planted over elevated terraces of stone so as to resemble mountains and remind Amytis of the lush landscapes of her homeland.[93]

At some uncertain point during the upheavals that saw Alcaeus and his brothers banished, Sappho, too, landed in exile. Despite marrying into the Penthilidae, the old ruling family of Lesbos, Pittacus was anxious to loosen the grip that monied factions had long had on the island. Ridding Mytilene of the aristocracy from which Alcaeus and other conspirators had risen would enable him to proceed unhindered with his plans for reform. Sappho was probably little more than an innocent victim of Pittacus' efforts to consolidate his power. She might also have been a victim of Andromeda's revenge. Her former pupil, who had set up a rival poetry school, was part-Penthilidae by blood.[94] At the very least, Andromeda could not have been sorry to see the woman who branded her a 'country bumpkin' ousted from Lesbos.

Ancient historians were less concerned with why Sappho left than where she went. In the mid-third century BC a great marble *stele* was erected on the Greek island of Paros and inscribed with events dating back over a millennium. Amid the list of kings coming to power and battles being waged was a reference to Sappho leaving for Sicily during the archonship of Critias of Athens, somewhere between 605 and 590 BC.[95] A fragment of Sappho's poetry contains the words 'sailors', 'large gales', 'brightness' and 'dry land'.[96] If these were not allusions to her brother

Charaxus' perilous travels to Naucratis and back (cargo is also mentioned in the papyrus), then they were perhaps remnants of her reflections on the journey out. Alcaeus' words supplement Sappho's portrayal of a treacherous sea voyage, his own exile on a storm-tossed ship with leaking sides lending itself as a seminal metaphor for the political turmoil that had thrown him overboard.[97] On finally beaching, Alcaeus sang a prayer to the gods: Bacchus, the Muses, Aphrodite and Eros.[98] His prayer of thanksgiving – his invocation to the gods that he might be rescued from the hardships and grief of exile – was not perhaps so very different from what Sappho uttered when she made land in Sicily.

The historical inscription does not record where on the island Sappho settled, but Syracuse, where she was later honoured with a statue, is a likely spot. The city, initially founded just east of the mainland on the islet of Ortygia, was incidentally steeped in myths of women in flight. The north arm of one of Ortygia's harbours was home to the freshwater fountain of Arethusa. The story goes that the nymph stumbled upon a ravenous river god while she was bathing in his waters. Chased through valleys, over mountains, down cliffs, she ran as fast as she could to escape him. As the river came closer, panicking Arethusa offered prayers to the chaste goddess Artemis, who concealed her by enveloping her in a cloud. Steadily, Arethusa metamorphosed into water and passed into the earth through a gap Artemis opened up before the river god was able to flow into her. Arethusa emerged as a fountain at Ortygia.

A second harbour spring was named after Cyane, a Sicilian nymph famed for her attempt to halt Hades' abduction of Persephone. Despite stretching her arms as wide as possible, Cyane had proved unable to restrain the vehement god, and literally dissolved in tears as she watched him take the young virgin by force. A Greek hymn composed in the sixth century BC described the tragic desperation of Persephone's mother, the grain goddess Demeter, as she tried to locate her missing daughter. Arethusa came to Demeter and told her that she had swum beneath the earth and seen Persephone. Persephone was afraid, Arethusa said, but she now possessed considerable power as queen of the Underworld. Driving her chariot furiously to Mount Olympus, Demeter begged Zeus to release her daughter, but found him immune to her distress. Zeus was Hades' brother and defended his crime as an act of love.[99] An arbitrary loophole meant that Persephone could leave provided she had not eaten a morsel since arriving in the darkness. News of the rule came too late. Persephone's innocent consumption of a small handful of pomegranate seeds sealed her fate as mournful mistress of the Underworld for six months of the year, and joyous bringer of summer for the remainder.

By the time Sappho embarked on her own voyage into the unknown, the Syracusans had extended their city beyond Ortygia and its nymph-haunted springs to the mainland, establishing an *agora* (marketplace) at Achradina, a small temple to Athena, and a larger one to Apollo.[100] The beauty of the architecture could not, however, distract from the troubles that had taken root. Ambitious young men on the island were as eager as Pittacus and Cylon to overthrow their existing leaders – a landowning elite known as the *Gamoroi* – and seize power themselves. The *Gamoroi* were descended from the founders of Syracuse, who had arrived from Corinth in the eighth century BC and proceeded to enslave some of the native 'Sicel' population. The revolutionaries would have to wait until the beginning of the fifth century BC to see the *Gamoroi* toppled and the city become subject to rule by a tyrant. Their frustration was keenly felt. Sappho had escaped the political turmoil of one city for the political turmoil of another. Alcaeus was wistful for the Mytilenaean assembly, the council, the temples, the voices of women at festival time.[101] Sappho missed the days when she could make her daughter smile with the present of a headband from Lydia.[102]

Fearing for the future of their trade relations with Lesbos, the Lydians took pity on the exiles and attempted to intervene in Lesbian politics on their behalf. Croesus, Alyattes' son by a woman of Caria, could only have been a young prince at the time, but he had 2,000 staters (ancient coins) with which to attempt to talk Pittacus of Lesbos round. Croesus tried, but to his astonishment, Pittacus rejected the bribe. He had inherited quite enough money from his late brother, he reasoned, and that had served him no political advantage. 'Cunning fox,' uttered Alcaeus about Pittacus' response.[103]

While Alcaeus kept up his vitriol towards the new tyrant, branding him variously 'Drag-Foot', 'Cracked-Foot', 'Boaster' and 'Pot-Belly', Sappho wisely refrained from passing judgement in public.[104] It steadily became apparent that, far from being the criminal Alcaeus feared, Pittacus intended to keep his word and revitalise life on Lesbos. The remaining residents of Mytilene were sufficiently impressed to appoint him *aisumnetes* – a form of dictator – to deal with the troublesome exiles and rule over them for the next ten years.[105] Wiser than his predecessors, and more determined, Pittacus appeared to offer them the best hope for stability. His vendetta against the elite delighted the common workers. Working women particularly praised his willingness to disregard the conventions of his class and assist them in their flour-making. 'Grind, mill, grind,' one woman sang, 'for even Pittacus, king of mighty Mytilene, grinds!'[106]

In time, Pittacus was credited with restoring peace after years of political unrest and hailed as an accomplished lawmaker.[107] His legislation targeted causes of social unrest, especially alcoholism, so that anyone who committed a crime while drunk faced paying a larger fine than those who committed a crime while sober.[108] Such measures were unlikely to win over Alcaeus, who composed an exhortation to drink that would be rendered more famous in Latin as *nunc est bibendum* by Horace some centuries later.[109] Pittacus was wise to act with Mytilene's long-term well-being in mind. As he himself said, 'painted wood' – public writing tablets inscribed with laws – offered the best civil protection.[110]

The innovation of these laws on Lesbos coincided with the emergence of a new set of painted tablets in Athens. There, the strains of social and political inequality, deepened by Draco's legislation, had very nearly led to civil war. Solon, one of the most extraordinary figures in Athens's political history, was entrusted with the task of overhauling the existing legal code and reforming the justice system. An archon, he came from a noble family but hoped, like Pittacus, to diminish the prominence of the louche elite and improve the lot of the labourers. Solon would later be credited with lifting Athens's men out from their luxuriant and 'effeminate' ways and encouraging them to more 'manly' deeds.[111]

A part-time poet, Solon had held a command in a war between Athens and Megara for possession of the island of Salamis, and demonstrated all-round creative flair. According to his biographer, Solon had a message sent to the Megarians luring them to a city in Attica with the suggestion that they might carry off the women, who were preoccupied performing sacrifices to Demeter.[112] As the Megarians approached, Solon had the female worshippers ushered to safety, and told the youngest men to put on their clothes. The Megarians approached only to be slaughtered by the cross-dressing Athenians, who went on to win Salamis.

Solon recognised that women had as important a role to play in a well-functioning society as men. When it came to establishing new laws for Athens, he repealed all of the legislation that Draco had laid down except the rules pertaining to homicide, which were largely concerned with protecting women's chastity. Under Solon's system, a man was still permitted to kill another man if he caught him *in flagrante* with his wife or another female relation. The adulteress would then be divorced and banned from public sacrifices. While a man with adulterous intentions took his life in his own hands, the onus was upon the woman to remain faithful. Given that the rape of a freeborn woman could result in no more than the payment of a fine, however, the family stability the Athenians hoped to achieve was strictly limited.

In some ways the lives of women in Athens became more restricted as a result of Solon's pernickety laws. Women were henceforth permitted to wear no more than three items of clothing in public for fear of promoting ostentation; the baskets they carried were to be no taller than the length of their forearms; they were not to mourn excessively nor to tear their flesh at funerals, nor to travel by night except by lamp-lit wagon.[113] It could be said that Solon prefigured Confucius, who rose to prominence in China following the violent collapse of the Zhou dynasty and helped nurture a way of life in which women were increasingly cloistered. A famous story was told of Boji, a woman of Song, who burned to death in a palace fire because it was deemed improper for women to proceed through the hall without male guardians to protect them. Athenian women were in danger of falling subject to equally stringent methods of control.

The one advantage for the women of Solon's Athens was that their futures were no longer determined by how much money their families kept in their coffers. Dowries were abolished except among the very richest citizens, meaning that most women could enter into a marriage on their own virtue, bringing with them no more than three changes of clothes and modest household goods. The free male population of Athens was divided into four classes according to wealth. Although only members of the richest bands could hold political office, the poorest could serve as jurors and participate in an Assembly and, later, a new Council of 400, to deliberate on public affairs. The fact that men had the potential to progress up the ladder as they earned more afforded their families greater opportunities than they had possessed to date. Together with Solon's great 'shaking-off of burdens', which involved the cancellation of existing debts, the new societal structure liberated many women from the oppression of poverty.[114] Athenians were now protected from being enslaved by one another, and much land was restored to its rightful owners.

Solon's laws, like those of Pittacus, were written out on wooden tablets. The two lawmakers were subsequently counted among the Seven Sages of Greece. This list – which also included the philosopher Thales, intellectuals Bias and Myson, poet Cleobulus and Spartan adviser Chilon – was written out by Plato in his *Protagoras* in the early fourth century BC, but probably already existed in the seventh century BC.[115] Pamphila, a seminal first-century AD female historian from Epidaurus in Greece (her thirty-three-book work of *Historical Commentaries* is sadly lost but was quoted from by male writers in antiquity), claimed that Pittacus had distinguished himself by forgiving the man who hacked his son to death in a barbershop.[116] 'Forgiveness,' the tyrant had said, 'is better than revenge.'[117] Pittacus earned his place in the record of sages by living up to one of his many other truisms, 'Power reveals the man'. He resigned, as promised, after ten years of harmonious dictatorship.

Sappho and Alcaeus and the other exiles returned to a significantly more settled island. What became of them, no one recorded, though a number of fanciful tales were written of Sappho hurling herself from a cliff in unrequited love for a man. Handsome Phaon, the object of her affections, was said to have been a favourite of Aphrodite, who concealed him in a bed of lettuces, known for their aphrodisiac qualities. A similar story was told of Aesop. The enigmatic fabulist had allegedly dined with the Seven Sages before setting out for Delphi with armfuls of gold from Croesus. He was apparently thrown from the cliffs on being accused of stealing treasure.

The greatest story was the true one. Sappho died on Lesbos when she was at least middle-aged and fulfilled her ambition to be remembered. Her verse had reached the Greek mainland, where Solon overheard his nephew singing one of her songs and was so enamoured that he asked to be taught it.[118] Later poets would assume Sappho's voice to tell of her escape from the clutches of Hades by means of being spoken about each and every day in the world above.[119] Poetry had bought Sappho everlasting fame.

Chapter V

The Oracle is Corrupted

Most beautiful is the light of the sun I leave behind,
Second most beautiful are the shining stars and the moon's face;
Also cucumbers and apples and pears in season:
For simple-minded is the man who puts cucumbers and the rest
On a par with the sun and moon.

Praxilla, From the *Hymn to Adonis*, fifth century BC

The ladies of Lydia achieved new prominence following the death of Alyattes circa 561 BC. The king had ruled for almost half a century and succeeded in conquering Greek Smyrna, on the west coast of Asia Minor, and expanding his territory across Mysia and Caria as far east as the c-shaped River Halys (Kızılırmak). His remains were interred in a burial ground of suitably magnificent dimensions.[1] Located near the Lydian capital of Sardis, at Bin Tepe, the site encompassed more than a hundred *tumuli* or earth mounds, the largest of which has been identified as the home of Alyattes' white-marble and limestone chamber.[2] Measuring some 350 metres at base diameter, the royal mound was marked by five cornerstones inscribed with the names or professions of the Lydians who had financed its construction.[3] Several groups contributed the money, including *agoraioi* – market-going men or merchants – but the majority share, according to Herodotus, was raised by female prostitutes.

Only one of the limestone markers has so far been excavated.[4] The other stones are likely to have been broken up or repurposed; the mound has been raided by tunnellers regularly since Roman times. There was no reference to female funders on the surviving stone and, at first glance, one could not be surprised if Herodotus' testimony on this point proved to be entirely fictitious. The historian also claimed that the Lydians prostituted their daughters to raise their dowries.[5] Other writers added that these daughters were permitted to select their own husband and that Lydian girls were the first in the world to be transformed into eunuchs.[6] However, Herodotus grew up in Halicarnassus (Bodrum), not too far south of Sardis, and could hardly have got away with inventing what was still legible on the cornerstones in the fifth century BC. Even though he was writing for Greeks, and could not read Lydian himself, Herodotus knew that other visitors could easily discredit his account. That the courtesans of Lydia pooled their funds and contributed to the king's burial is suggestive of not only the respect they held for him, but of the acceptance they themselves enjoyed among their own people.

These women, like much of the population, expected that Alyattes' power would pass to one of his natural sons, Croesus being the eldest and heir apparent. As far as anyone could tell, the prince was perfectly capable. The order of succession often proved, however, more complicated in practice than it appeared in conversation around the deathbed. It was a godly monarch who slipped away believing their will be done. Alyattes' widow, a second wife, certainly had little regard for the rights of blood. She – her name has not been preserved – had children of her own and could see no reason why one of them should not come to the throne instead. She hatched a plan to remove Croesus from the line of power by having his baker poison his bread.[7]

Bakers in Greece and Asia Minor in this period tended to be women. They proved and rolled and baked for their families, and they proved and rolled and baked for their townspeople. They were inexhaustible in their flour-clothes. So Pittacus was praised by the flour-grinding women of Mytilene for his willingness to assist them in their labours. Men permitted their wives and daughters to bake because they deemed it to be a 'safe' profession, as it was conducted in the home or in bakeries in the company of other women. Men also happened to believe that there was something innately female about bread itself. In their literature, the uterus is frequently likened to an oven, and the foetus to a loaf.[8] In the heat of their bodies, women 'baked' their babies into being, delivered them fully cooked. Baking was, in this sense, the most natural activity for a woman to pursue.

The metaphor was powerful enough to inspire superstition. A medical treatise of the fifth century BC suggested that if a pregnant woman baked bread at a low temperature and the loaf turned out well, then she would have a boy, whereas a loaf with a cracked top signified that she was expecting a girl.[9] Bread continued to play a symbolic role in her life after she had given birth. Women in the Greek world had to endure a post-partum confinement of at least forty days. Before re-entering society, they would undergo a process of purification, which often included a visit to a religious sanctuary to make offerings of clothes, fruit and bread – or terracotta models of bread and bakers – in thanksgiving for their safe delivery.[10] These were small gifts of gratitude when on average one in three women died in labour or post-partum.

Terracotta figures of women working dough in bowls balanced on high spindling tripods survive from many different cities, including Tanagra in central Greece. The most striking example, made not far from Tanagra in Thebes in the sixth century BC, features four women together at a bread-making station.[11] They roll their dough enthusiastically, putting their whole bodies into it, as though they fear being swallowed up by a pocket of air. Beside them a flautist plays music. The scene calls to mind descriptions of sailors by Greek poets: rowers lean in to their oars from their benches and time their strokes to the rhythm set by a musician. The female bakers lean in to their rolling pins from their benches and seemingly roll in time to the music. The production process is well-organised and sanitary – each woman wears a hat to prevent stray hairs from falling into her mixture – and might form part of a commercial enterprise. Female bakers depicted in groups were very likely baking bread to sell or to distribute.

It would not have been difficult for the baker responsible for making Croesus' bread to knead something deadly into her dough. Whether she was prepared to risk her own life in doing so was another matter. Croesus' baker proved to be as disobedient as she was cunning. She ignored her orders, fed the poison to the children of Alyattes' widow, and told Croesus what had happened. The thirty-five-year-old prince was consequently able to claim his birthright and succeed to the Lydian throne. The narrative may seem incredible, but it does not end there. The intriguing finale to the tale of the baker woman occurs slightly later, when Croesus is making one of a number of generous offerings to the Pythia at Delphi.[12] He sends gold, and he sends silver, but most strikingly of all, he sends a gilt sculpture of a woman, three cubits tall, modelled to resemble his court baker. If he did not believe that she had saved his life and aided his rise to power, then he must have been truly evangelical about her bread.

The early years of Croesus' rule demonstrated the scale of his ambition. His troops laid siege to Ephesus and subjugated the majority of the Greek cities along the western seaboard of Asia Minor. Non-Greek Phrygians, Thracians, Bithynians and Pamphylians soon bowed to his authority. Such rapid expansion might have unnerved the rulers of neighbouring territories, but Croesus managed to remain on friendly terms with many of the Greek peoples, and was anxious to impress one Greek man in particular. This presented a challenge, for Solon, the ageing sage he admired, had received invitations to travel all over the world since establishing his laws in Athens two decades earlier. Moreover, Solon had already agreed to visit Egypt, which had recently undergone the greatest transformation of all.

Giant sphinxes and other colossi peered over cities from Memphis in the south to Sais in the Nile Delta.[13] The cobra goddess Wadjet, who was invoked as a protectress of the pharaoh, had been promised new temples at the cities of Buto and Athribis; Isis, divine mother of the ruler and protectress of the dead, was honoured with her own brickwork at Philae. The philhellenic pharaoh Amasis II, a man of extremely refined aesthetic tastes, had done well to rejuvenate Egypt's economy in the sixth century BC. While Greek settlers continued to pour into the port town of Naucratis in the western Delta, Amasis was able to strengthen his power-base further thanks to his marriage to Ladice, princess of Cyrene, west of Egypt on the north coast of modern Libya.

Founded some decades earlier, circa 630 BC, Cyrene had been ruled over by Ladice's mother Pheretime since the death of her father King Battus III and the banishment of her brother Arcesilaus. The young man had unwisely demanded an extension to his powers and seen himself exiled to the Aegean island of Samos. Desperate to recover her son, Pheretime prevailed upon the Greek king of Cyprus for forces, only to be patronised for being female with a present of a golden spindle, a distaff and a ball of wool.[14] While Arcesilaus was eventually able to raise an army himself, he was assassinated in the Libyan city of Barca a short time later, prompting Pheretime to prove that she was no docile woman. She could tolerate the taunts of foreign kings but this was too much. First, she called upon the people of Persia to assist her as she laid siege to Barca. Then, she had her son's killers rounded up and impaled publicly together with the breasts of their wives and lovers.

Ladice might have lacked her mother's fierceness of spirit, but she was clever and knew how to handle Amasis' temper. She would never be the most prominent woman at court when there was already Tentkheta, who had given Amasis sons, and Ankhnesneferibra, the senior priestess known as God's Wife of Amun, whose brother Amasis had overthrown to assume power. (Ankhnesneferibra's black sarcophagus, now in the British Museum, depicts her as a beautiful nude with her arms raised above her head.) But Ladice could play her part in strengthening the relationship between Egypt and her native region of Cyrenaica. That was if she could win her husband's trust. Their marriage got off to a difficult start when Ladice proved to be the one woman Amasis was unable to have sex with.[15] Perturbed by his sudden inability to perform his marital duties, he accused her of placing a curse on him, and threatened her with bad fortune. Ladice therefore made a vow. If ever her marriage was consummated, she would have a statue of Aphrodite put up at Cyrene. The dedication of a statue of the sex goddess in the city sometime later was taken as confirmation that the pharaoh had overcome his sexual difficulty. Ladice's authority was restored.

Despite the growing splendour of Amasis' Egypt, Croesus continued to hope that Lydia would stand out as the most wondrous place Solon ever beheld.[16] Whether the two men actually met is uncertain. The story Herodotus told of Solon's visit to the Lydian court in his *Histories* became not merely proverbial but firmly embedded within Greek tradition. At its centre lay a question. Was a man as rich as Croesus truly blessed? As a guest of the king, Solon was under intense pressure to answer *yes*. But how could he? There were a few people, all Greeks, Solon told Croesus, who were very blessed. The brothers Cleobis and Biton, for example, won the admiration of their native Argos for yoking themselves to their priestess mother's chariot to convey her to a temple when there was a shortage of oxen. The boys died after performing this feat, but the fact that they would be remembered for making their mother the envy of all women made them indisputably blessed. Solon's point was that one needs to look to the end of someone's life before counting them truly fortunate. Croesus was still alive and did not even yet have a grandson. It was too early to say whether he was blessed or not. Naturally, the Lydian was displeased with this response, and dismissed Solon as an impertinent fool. The Hellenes held this to be the king's first mistake.

In the real world, Croesus was facing a crisis, for a man almost equally matched in his ambition had approached the borders of Lydia. Cyrus was the son of the king of Anshan, a city located in the Zagros Mountains in the Fars Province of modern Iran. His father, Cambyses, was Persian, but his mother Mandane, or so it was claimed, was the daughter of Astyages, king of the Medes and father-in-law of Croesus' sister.[17] The kingdom of Media lay just south of the Caspian Sea, to the east of Lydia, in what now forms part of northern Iran. It was worryingly close.

According to common folklore, Astyages had given orders for Cyrus to be killed soon after he was born in order to avert the fulfilment of a prophecy. The Median king had dreamed that a vine grew from Mandane's vagina and overwhelmed his territory. Like Kronos, the former king of the Greek gods overthrown by his own son Zeus, Astyages feared usurpation by one of his bloodline. And like Oedipus, the infant Cyrus was duly handed over to a servant on Astyages' orders to be left to die. Only many years later did Astyages learn that his grandson had been saved and raised by a herdsman and his wife. In his wrath Astyages invited his servant to dinner and served him the flesh of his own son.

The colourful tale provided the backdrop to the historic moment in 550 BC when Cyrus overthrew ageing Astyages and conquered the kingdom of Media.[18] Astyages, dressed according to Median custom in purple garb, plentiful jewellery, a wig, eyeliner and rouge, had raised an army to march against Cyrus' forces.[19] But Astyages' troops rebelled and handed him over as a prisoner to the enemy.[20]

Cyrus' next, most pressing concern was to legitimise his rule, which was something he could only do through marriage to a suitable woman. He already had one wife, Cassandane, who had provided him with several children, including an heir, Cambyses. He also had a number of favourite concubines. In the biblical Book of Ezra, Zerubbabel describes the Persian as falling dangerously in lust with a concubine named Apame, who sits with him, playfully tries on his crown, and becomes the subject of his infatuation.[21] For the purposes of strengthening his authority over Media, Cyrus needed to lay aside any feelings he had for her and seek a more politically advantageous match. Amytis, who became Cyrus' second wife, was a daughter of Astyages, which would also make her Cyrus' aunt.[22] It seems so unlikely that Cyrus would marry his mother's sister that we must question whether he had a blood connection to Astyages at all. It is possible that Cyrus lied about his maternity in order to strengthen his claim to the kingdom of Media. No mere pawn in this arrangement, Amytis allegedly ordered Cyrus to arrange for one of her father's former eunuchs to be blinded, flayed and crucified for disloyalty.[23] The eunuch had left her father Astyages to die of thirst in a desert.

Amytis' marriage marked the beginning of the foundation of the first Persian or 'Achaemenid' Empire, so-named after Achaemenes, a legendary ancestor of Cyrus. At its height, the Persian Empire would be the largest empire in the world, spanning the distance from Libya to Pakistan by the beginning of the fifth century BC. The union of Cyrus and Amytis set the process in motion.

As Croesus scrambled to find a way to stop Cyrus in his tracks, it was however the priestess at Delphi rather than Amytis who came to the fore of international politics. In the years since the courtesan Doricha dedicated her oxen spits, the holy precinct had achieved an unparalleled reputation among religious sites. A stone, allegedly thrown by Zeus, marked Delphi out as the *omphalos* or navel of the world. Centuries of trade and religious tourism had brought considerable wealth to the city-state, with the people of Corinth, Attica, Sparta and Lydia among its most ardent supporters. A new set of 'Pythian' panhellenic games had even been instituted at the sanctuary in 582 BC to be held every fourth August in the year before the Olympics.[24] But the popularity of the oracle had also brought trouble to the region. When inhabitants of the nearby Crisaean plain attempted to capitalise on the growing industry by charging people who passed through, a group of city-states headed by Athens, Thessaly and Sicyon had resolved to defend the site. On the oracle's advice, or so they said, they made war on the inhabitants of the plain in 590 BC and poisoned their water supply with hellebore (this was Solon's idea) so as to make prisoners of the sick.[25] The attacking Greeks, known collectively as the Amphictyony, captured Delphi and rededicated the plain to Apollo, Artemis, Leto and Athena.

Croesus, eager for advice over the best course against Cyrus, tested the powers of the oracles of Delphi, Dodona, Lebadeia (Trophonius) and Siwa, home to Ammon, in the Libyan desert. 'What am I doing at the moment?'

he asked each. The Pythia might not have ascertained every detail – Croesus had engaged himself in the unlikely task of boiling a tortoise and a lamb in a bronze cauldron – but she satisfied him the most with her wisdom. In a bid to win her favour, he proceeded to lavish her with gifts of gold and silver bowls, necklaces and belts, his shining baker woman, and a colossal sculpture of a lion cast in gold and supported on a base of gold ingots.[26] Many of these offerings were destroyed in 548 BC when the sanctuary at Delphi caught fire, but at least two of the gifts he sent – a pair of gold and silver mixing bowls which had been positioned at the temple's entrance – were removed in time to be saved. A potential third present from Croesus, a chryselephantine sculpture of Artemis, Apollo and Leto, was found badly burned beneath the Sacred Way in Athens in 1939.[27] The Amphictyony oversaw the beginning of the reconstruction of the site.

Croesus might have taken the disaster as a bad omen and turned his back on Delphi, but he had asked the Pythia what to do about Cyrus, and the Pythia had given him advice he liked the sound of. The question he had asked was simple. Should he, alone or with allies, send an army against Cyrus and the Persians? The Pythia gave Croesus a characteristically slippery reply to the effect that, if he crossed the River Halys, his empire's eastern border, he would destroy a mighty empire.[28] The perennially optimistic king took this prophecy as assurance that he would destroy Cyrus' growing empire. Whether this episode is true or another piece of influential folklore, Croesus certainly proceeded in confidence to plan for a war by seeking alliances with the most powerful Greek city-states. As relieved as he was to secure the support of Athens, he realised that, to succeed, he would also need the help of Sparta.

The Spartans of the south-eastern Peloponnese, like the Lydians and Athenians, had long trusted in the prophecies of the Pythian priestess. This was only to be expected from a culture that valued women's opinions on war. While Spartan boys were given a strict military upbringing away from their families, Spartan girls were taught to race, wrestle, hurl javelins and ride horses before their marriage at the relatively late age of eighteen or so. The idea was to transform the girls into strong future mothers of even stronger sons within a process that inculcated staunch beliefs about masculinity and warfare.

Spartan women would long for their sons to return from battle in glory or else die in the field. A religious festival was once held in Sparta following the deaths of 700 male citizens, and while the widows and mothers of the deceased celebrated, the women whose sons and husbands had surrendered actually mourned. The first-century Greek biographer Plutarch, author of the celebrated *Parallel Lives*, collected an astonishing compendium of utterances and quips attributed to Spartan women, nearly all of which are marked by ruthless military aggression.[29] Argileonis, mother of a well-regarded military officer named Brasidas, declares that there were many better men in Sparta than her own son who had died in battle. Another woman, who had sent five sons to war, purported to accept their deaths when she heard that the Spartan forces had been victorious. Spartan women were even described as killing their own sons for cowardice or desertion. One mother allegedly killed her son by hurling a roof tile at him after he told her that Sparta was on the losing side.

Some of these statements must have been exaggerated by Greeks horrified by the prospect of female bellicosity. The Spartans would certainly not have recorded such statements themselves when not even their constitution was set in stone. The 'Great Rhetra', purportedly an oracle from Pythian Apollo, was attributed to the legendary figure Lycurgus, who commanded that his edicts were circulated orally only. Under his laws, not even tombstones could be inscribed with names unless the deceased happened to have died in childbirth or on the battlefield. This culture of orality was only too convenient for the Spartans as they endeavoured to justify their expansionist policy by citing prophecies and laws that may never truly have existed.

Until now, the policy had served the Spartans well, for their city-state was fast emerging as one of the wealthiest in all of Greece.[30] It was ruled by two kings in what was known as a dyarchy and the system had so far proven more stable than might have been anticipated. Between the late eighth and early seventh century BC, the Spartans had waged war against the Messenians of the south-west Peloponnese, annexed their territory and enslaved their citizens to become the wealthiest people in the Greek world. They had recently assumed control over the south-west Peloponnese more widely, but the victory came at a cost, namely for Sparta's girls.[31] In the course of the conflict, a number of Spartan youngsters were captured by the Messenians while they were performing a dance in honour of the goddess Artemis. The leader of the Messenians tried to prevent his men from raping the girls, but in many cases he was too late. The young victims were returned to Sparta only on payment of a heavy ransom.[32]

When Croesus approached them, the Spartans were invading Tegea, a territory of Arcadia in the central Peloponnese. Propelled, once again, by an oracle issued by the priestess at Delphi, they had taken chains with them with which to enslave the enemy, but ended up being enchained themselves.[33] The rare defeat did little to dampen Croesus' confidence in the Spartans' ability. An alliance was sealed between the two peoples in 546 BC through an exchange of presents.[34] As Croesus set his heart on conquering the mighty empire to his east, his men fought an inconclusive battle at Pteria across the Halys in Cappadocia in what would prove to be the first of many blows. Croesus returned to Sardis with the intention of invading the territory again the following spring with military attachments from Sparta, Egypt and Babylonia. Before he could execute this plan, however, Cyrus launched a surprise attack on the very same Lydian city. Knowing that the Persians could not compete with the famous 'Lydians' chariots and armed infantry', Cyrus led camels into the fray.[35] The Lydians' horses, fearing the strange beasts, fled the plain, allowing the Persians to lay siege to Sardis. Women were dragged from the court by the merciless enemy.[36] By the time the Spartans arrived to lend the Lydians their aid, the city had been captured, and Croesus taken prisoner.

It was only now that the true meaning of the Pythia's prophecy began to be understood. The mighty empire to be destroyed was Croesus' own. Despite all he had achieved in taking control of swathes of Asia Minor and dispatching riches across the Greek world, the king was now entirely helpless. He was described as sitting atop a funeral pyre together with fourteen Lydian boys, one for each year of his rule. An Athenian vase painting dated to the early fifth century BC shows him wearing a laurel crown and pouring a libation to the gods while the fire is stoked beneath him.[37] Archaeologists believe that Croesus' father, Alyattes, was cremated on an oak pyre on top of the chamber covered over by his enormous funeral mound. The punishment of Croesus, if true, was perhaps the most wilful subversion of the Lydian custom of honouring their deceased royals.[38] A poet, born not long after the event, described the king's bravery while his wife and daughters screamed.[39] Croesus' mother allegedly threw herself from the city walls in despair.[40] As he sat there on the pyre,

Croesus was said to have called out the name of Solon, whose words now proved depressingly wise: count no one fortunate until they have reached the end of their life.

Croesus' moment of understanding transcended history. It would be described for generations to come, the playwright Sophocles drawing most poignantly upon it a century later when he had his tragic Chorus reflect on Oedipus' fate and declare that no mortal should be deemed happy until their final day. But this was no victory for Solon. It was no victory for the Pythia at Delphi, either, who had warned that the fifth generation of Gyges' family would suffer the consequences of his usurpation of the Lydian throne. Croesus' confidence in his riches, his blind belief that the oracle portended the destruction of Cyrus' empire, when it meant his own, had led him to commit an act of hubris worthy of his great-great-grandfather. Some said that Cyrus was so perturbed by the sight of Croesus repenting of his mistakes, and so anxious that he might suffer a similar downfall, that he ordered the pyre to be quenched. Apocryphal tales were spread of a sudden rainfall extinguishing the flames, and of Apollo whisking Croesus away to the mythical land of the Hyperboreans 'beyond the North wind', where it was forever spring.[41] The truth of the matter was that Cyrus had conquered Media, and now Lydia, and was well on his way to a conflict further west. The coastal Greek Ionian cities swept up by Croesus were given no choice but to submit and pay tribute to the Persian conqueror.

In 546 BC, the year Cyrus took Lydia, Peisistratus was tyrant of Athens. His mother was a cousin of the mother of Solon, and over the past decade and a half he had demonstrated something of the family's verve for emerging at the centre of public life. Defying Solon's efforts to inhibit the self-appointment of the elite, Peisistratus had employed a band of men armed with clubs to seize control of the city-state before being driven out. Athens was still heavily factionalised, and Lycurgus, leader of the people 'Of the Plain', and Megacles, leader of the people 'Of the Coast', had successfully joined forces to oust this ambitious man 'Of the Hill'.[42] Peisistratus, a former hero in Athens's war with neighbouring Megara, was left to flounder outside the city gates. One row with Lycurgus, however, and Megacles was making overtures to the embittered exile. A new alliance was forged between the former enemies to neutralise Lycurgus.

At the centre of the bargain was Coesyra, daughter of Megacles, who was given to Peisistratus in marriage to secure the pact.

At least three women by the name of Coesyra have been identified in the sources of the period.[43] In Aristophanes' *Clouds*, a comedy first performed in 423 BC, a farmer named Strepsiades describes his haughty, expensively dressed wife as 'Coesyrafied'.[44] A niece of one Megacles and granddaughter of another, this Coesyra was probably a descendant of the woman Peisistratus married. The bride's family was notoriously grand. Her father Megacles was an Alcmaeonid. It was his ancestors who had held high office in Athens at the time of Cylon's thwarted revolution. Their decision to hack down the revolutionaries as they sought religious sanctuary on an altar had given rise to the rumour that the Alcmaeonids were cursed. Nevertheless, Megacles was chosen above a host of other suitors to marry Agariste, daughter of Cleisthenes, tyrant of Sicyon in the northern Peloponnese.[45] The arrangement was sealed after one of Megacles' chief rivals, another Athenian aristocrat, made the mistake of dancing drunkenly on a table at a feast.

Together Megacles and Agariste had three children: Cleisthenes, who would one day be hailed as one of the architects of Athenian democracy; Hippocrates, whose grandson, Pericles, would be the supreme ornament of that democracy; and Coesyra, who now married Peisistratus. Names were reused so frequently within this family that it is difficult to tell whether the inscription naming Coesyra, Hippocrates and Megacles discovered on a potsherd in Athens's potters' quarter referred to her generation, or to another.[46] Coesyra almost certainly shared her name with her paternal grandmother.[47] What is clear from the marginalia of an ancient scholar is that the younger Coesyra married Peisistratus just as he was angling to become tyrant of Athens.[48] She was therefore crucial to his success.

In spite of their arrangement, it was not Coesyra who accompanied Peisistratus back into the city from exile, but a female garland-seller named Phye.[49] Described as unusually tall and preternaturally beautiful, she probably came from Paeania in Attica, but was striking enough to pass for a goddess from Mount Olympus.[50] Peisistratus had her dressed in armour so as to resemble Athena and sat alongside her as their chariot pulled into Athens. He hoped to show his countrymen that his return was sanctioned by the patron warrior-goddess of the city herself. Few onlookers could have been taken in by such an elaborate piece of theatre, but the object was not to deceive so much as to amuse. *What a performance Peisistratus put on! Did you ever see a woman so strong and noble-looking? You'd think the goddess herself had driven in from the battlefield!* The people of Athens were persuaded to give the old charmer a second chance.

Phye was subsequently married to Peisistratus' younger son Hipparchus. The tyrant's elder son, Hippias, had a beautiful wife of his own, whose father, Charmus, was also rumoured to be his lover. As for Peisistratus, his marriage to Coesyra helped him out of a difficult political corner, but the thought that it could be anything more than an alliance of convenience was as far away from his mind as it was firmly embedded in hers. Peisistratus had no desire for more children and must have expected that the sons he had would succeed him. Coesyra hoped to become a mother. Their wedding night came and went and she remained *virgo intacta*. To her deeper shame, Peisistratus took his pleasure in her, only not in the manner she had expected.

Anal intercourse was seldom spoken of outside relationships between men. In Athens, it was traditional for youths to be eased into adult life by forging relationships with older men, who shared their wisdom with them as well as their bodies. In these pairings, the boy was the *eromenos*, or loved one, passively described in the Greek, while the older man was his *erastes*, the active sexual partner. By the time the *eromenos* was old enough to marry, it was considered shameful for him to carry on performing a submissive role. There was a strong societal expectation that he would transfer his affections to his bride and ensure that he satisfied both families' prayers for healthy children as soon as possible. This did not mean that grown men did not sometimes have sex with their wives in the way that their former lovers had had sex with them. To judge from surviving vase paintings, it was neither rare nor unacceptable for married women or prostitutes in Greece to be penetrated from behind at least. Nor is it likely that non-vaginal intercourse was preferred simply for reasons of contraception. But a newly married woman like Coesyra was entitled to feel slighted if her husband denied her the chance to conceive. Hers was very far from the sexual initiation that young virgins were prepared for.

At first, Coesyra felt unable to tell anyone what was happening, or not happening, in her marriage. When she did summon the courage to speak, she confided in her mother, who related what she had said to her own husband. Megacles was rightly outraged. He had given Peisistratus his daughter to help him return to Athens, and Peisistratus had insulted not only Coesyra but her entire family. Excuses came easily: Coesyra was a cursed Alcmaeonid and Peisistratus did not need any more bad luck. But Megacles was unmoved by Peisistratus' half-hearted defence. In his rage, the Alcmaeonid at once severed their allegiance, and reunited with his former faction in order to drive Peisistratus into exile once again. Little more is recorded of Coesyra.

For ten years, Peisistratus plotted his return, relying on the advice of his sons to call in the loans he was owed and use the money to hire mercenaries from the Peloponnese. Steadily, he fought his way back and, after a successful battle in 546 BC, established his tyranny firmly over Athens. Later Greek historians praised him as a moderate. He lent money to the poorest citizens so that they could forge careers for themselves as farmers.[51] He constructed roads. He patronised the arts. His rule witnessed the development of important silver mines at Laureion in south-east Attica, the minting of the first Athenian silver coins, and the completion of the city's first aqueduct. Homer's epics were refined and performed at the city's principal annual festival of Athena, the Panathenaea, for the first time.[52] While gaining control of the Cycladic island of Naxos and recapturing the formerly Lesbian territory of Sigeum after it was seized by the Mytilenaeans, Peisistratus also gained a reputation for peacekeeping. He worked so hard at this, asserted Aristotle some centuries later, that people were often heard comparing his tyranny to 'the [golden] age of Kronos'.[53]

This 'golden age', however, was a flawed one for women and moreover did not endure. When Peisistratus died in 527 BC, his power passed to his elder son Hippias, while his younger, Hipparchus, assumed a supporting role. The Peisistratid tyranny endured for thirty-six years altogether before unravelling in a dramatic fashion. In 514 BC, Hipparchus promised an aristocrat named Harmodius that his younger sister could play the role of basket-carrier during the Panathenaea, only to go back on his word.[54] A feud soon broke out between Harmodius and his older male lover Aristogeiton, and Hippias and Hipparchus, resulting in the former pair making an assassination attempt on the latter. Concealing daggers beneath their festive myrtle wreaths, the lovers located the brothers and brutally stabbed Hipparchus to death, but Hippias escaped. The killers struggled to make a similar exit through the crowded festival streets. Captured there and then, Harmodius was executed and Aristogeiton subjected to torture.[55] A number of late sources describe one of Aristogeiton's female lovers, a courtesan named Leaena ('Lioness'), enduring an intense interrogation as well and biting off her own tongue so as to avoid leaking the names of the other conspirators. A bronze sculpture of a tongueless lioness erected at the Propylaea (monumental entrance) on the Athenian Acropolis perpetuated the myth.[56] Half a dozen years after the event, the tyrannicides, Harmodius and Aristogeiton, were immortalised with bronze statues of their own.[57] In the aftermath of their deaths they were hailed as liberators for their attempt to free Athens of tyranny. The episode served to pave the way for the establishment of an early form of democracy.

It was largely the fault of Hippias that the two assassins ended up on the right side of history. In the wake of his brother's murder, the elder Peisistratid grew so paranoid, that he put to death anyone he suspected even slightly of plotting against him. It was for his own security that he married off his daughter, Archedice, to the son of the tyrant of Lampsacus, a Greek city just north of the Hellespont, which was allied with Persia. While Hippias descended into despotism, Archedice earned the admiration of the Greek people for her modesty and lack of pride. A popular praise-poet, Simonides, lauded her for displaying no arrogance at being married to one powerful man, and the daughter of another.[58] But Archedice's heritage was to prove most significant after her father-in-law was overthrown.

The enmity that had arisen between the Alcmaeonids and the Peisistratids as a result of Coesyra's unconsummated marriage reached a head in 514 BC. Capitalising on the old belief that the Alcmaeonids were polluted as a result of a decades-old curse, Hippias had the family's tombs exhumed and surviving members exiled.[59] His attempt to quell their influence ultimately proved unsuccessful. In spite of the violence directed towards them, the Alcmaeonids had managed to retain their wealth until now, and offered to use it to complete the reconstruction of Delphi following the fire that had incinerated so many of Croesus' priceless presents. Their money helped to buy a splendid new Doric temple, fifteen columns long by six wide, adorned with sculptural scenes of the Gigantomachy (a battle waged between the Olympian gods and giants) and Apollo, Artemis and Leto, with shining Parian marble.[60] Such generosity afforded the Alcmaeonids the power to bribe the Pythia. Their express instructions to her were to put it in the minds of her next Spartan visitors to free Athens from tyranny. It was on the priestess's word that Croesus had launched his invasion. Whether she was manipulating or being manipulated, the Pythia was fast revealing herself to be a key player in international politics, capable of reshaping alliances and dynasties.

The Spartans had entered into a ritualised guest-friendship with the Peisistratid family but, as a result of the Pythia's intervention, they recognised the need to act. Archedice had brought Persia into friendly relations with Athens. Sparta's position within the Greek world was potentially under threat.

The Spartans' first attempt on Athens, launched by sea in 511 BC, was a failure. The second, led by one of their kings, Cleomenes I, brought about what the Alcmaeonids desired. In 510 BC, Hippias retreated to the Athenian acropolis under pressure from the invading forces. The Spartans snatched his children as they were trying to make their escape and used them as a bargaining chip to force the despot out of Attica within five days. Hippias and his family withdrew to Sigeum, then to Lampsacus, and finally to the Persian court.[61] Some years later, Hippias reappears in the ancient histories urging Darius, king of Persia, to invade Greece, before joining battle himself at Marathon in 490 BC. Aged eighty or thereabouts, he would almost certainly have been too old by then to have served, but the legend prevailed. The downfall of the Peisistratids marked a significant turning point in the history of both Athens and Sparta and a woman, the Pythia, had played a central part in it. By accepting the bribe and persuading the Spartans to liberate Athens from tyranny, the priestess, endowed with powers above any other woman at this time, altered the power dynamic between two of the most significant Greek city-states.

Chapter VI

Horsewomen and Queens

As girls we cradled our dolls in our bedchambers
Like new wives without a care in the world; once it was dawn
Your mother, who assigned wool to her working wool-women,
Came and summoned you to help with the salt-sprinkled meat.

From Erinna, *The Distaff*, fourth century BC

The Massagetae tribespeople had been roaming the eastern borders of the Caspian Sea for hundreds of years when the Peisistratid dynasty collapsed in Athens. They were robust and bellicose and always most secure in the saddle. As they made their way west in their horse-led wagons, horsehair wigs and sprawling body tattoos, they displaced many of the other nomads to whom they were related by blood, including the mighty Scythians or 'Saka' of the Eurasian steppe. In a society in which men openly dangled quivers from women's wagon doors to initiate sexual affairs, it was considered nothing strange to bow before the authority of a female ruler, and in the later sixth century BC it was Queen Tomyris who held sway over the Massagetae. Tomyris had a grown son, Spargapises, but had carried on ruling in his place long after her husband died. She had no intention of ever marrying again.

Tomyris would never have been known to the peoples of Greece had she not received a marriage proposal from Cyrus of Persia in 530/29 BC. Since forcing the cities of Ionia to submit, the king had succeeded in absorbing Babylonia, permitting the Jews held captive there to leave for Jerusalem, where he supported the reconstruction of the Temple, and expanding his reach from the Aegean coast to modern Afghanistan and Pakistan. Tomyris was the first person to anticipate what Cyrus desired next. The Massagetae hovered threateningly over the easternmost marches of his empire. Marrying Tomyris would enable the Persians to expand into her territory, neutralise the threat from the unpredictable nomads, and strengthen their border. Tomyris was adamant that Cyrus should not get his way and neuter her, and so she firmly rejected his proposal.[1]

Cyrus, sensing he would never win her over, prepared to invade Tomyris' territory. As news of his preparations reached the tribe, Tomyris dispatched a herald with a message for the haughty king. Male historians felt at liberty to invent women's speeches in their narratives and Herodotus had Tomyris' run thus:

> . . . King of the Medes, stop striving after what you're striving after. You can't know if these things will be accomplished to your advantage. Give up, be king of your own people and watch and allow me to rule mine. If you're not minded to take this advice, by all means be at peace. Indeed, if you are so zealous to put the Massagetae to the test, quit bridging the river and cross over into our territory once we have made three days' retreat from it. But if you would rather receive us into your country, first go to where I have said.[2]

Tomyris' attempt to bargain with her suitor was only partially successful. Cyrus agreed that the queen should withdraw with her forces, but declared that he would invade her territory after she had done so. The Massagetae proceeded to slaughter a number of the men who piled in on Cyrus' orders. They then, however, made the mistake of drinking what the enemy laid before them. Nomads, as the Achaemenids knew, were hardened milk-drinkers with little experience of alcohol. In the seventh century BC, Cyaxares, king of the Medes, had defended his territory from Scythian tribes by plying the chiefs with wine and then killing a number of them. Intoxicated Massagetae were similarly taken unawares by the Persians and led away drunk into captivity.

On hearing that her own son was among the prisoners, Tomyris sent another herald to Cyrus with a message even more threatening than the last. He had tricked her, she complained, and prevailed through guile alone. Either he was to return Spargapises to her and leave their land, or she would be forced to take stronger action. 'If you do not do this,' Tomyris threatened the Persian, 'I swear by the sun, the master of the

Massagetae, that I shall give you your fill of blood, seeing as you are so insatiable for it.' Cyrus was unmoved. Spargapises chose suicide over prolonged internment.

Tomyris knew it was unlikely that Cyrus would change course over the invasion. And so, without pausing to allow him to consider his next move, she rounded up her forces and prepared them for battle. The two sides began by shooting arrows at each other and progressed to fighting at close quarters with spears and daggers. It was rare for a woman to initiate war, but Tomyris displayed no hesitancy. Herodotus described what ensued as 'the hardest of all the battles ever fought by non-Greeks'.[3] Tomyris' Massagetae proved the stronger of the two sides and massacred the Persian forces. It is highly likely that Cyrus died in the fray. Tomyris, far from being appeased by the victory, fulfilled her earlier threat to give the Persian his fill of blood by carrying out the foulest act of revenge for the death of her son. She first obtained an animal skin and filled it with human blood, and then retrieved Cyrus' head and deposited it in the bag. 'Though I conquered you in battle while you still lived,' she proclaimed over the floating mass, 'You have utterly destroyed me, taking my son by trickery. In keeping with my threat, may you have your glut of blood.' Writers of the Roman period would consider this one of the most memorable deeds ever performed by a woman in ancient history. The episode – entirely credible – was viewed less with disapproval than with awe.[4]

Tomyris' act assumed significance beyond the death of Cyrus. In the narrative of Persian history, it served to foreshadow the difficulties that awaited future leaders on the outskirts of their empire, where women were more in the habit of taking strangers by surprise. Within just two decades of Cyrus' death, another king would be forced to accept that he had underestimated the strength of a nomadic people. Darius, Persian 'King of Kings', would face his toughest challenge from the Massagetae's neighbouring Scythian tribes and their strident 'Amazon' queens.

Darius came to power in mysterious circumstances. Cyrus' son and successor Cambyses died without issue from a gangrenous wound after just seven and a half years in power.[5] Intent on taking his place, a pretender allegedly arrived at the Persian court in the guise of Cambyses' younger brother Smerdis and married Cambyses' grieving widow Phaedyme. Several sources suggest that Cambyses had had his real brother killed some time earlier. Amytis, the boys' mother, poisoned herself in despair.[6]

When word arose that Smerdis was not who he said he was, Phaedyme's father encouraged her to feel beneath her new husband's hair for his ears while he was sleeping. If he had ears, he said, he was the son of Cyrus. If he had none, then he was the man he feared, a Mede whom Cyrus had formerly punished by subjecting to the surgeon's knife. Phaedyme did as she was told and discovered that her husband was earless. She informed her father, who helped to orchestrate a plan by which a band of seven Persians would come together to overthrow the false Smerdis. Darius was the lead assassin.

Behind this story, told with much vim by Herodotus, lay a coup d'état by a handful of noblemen set on installing Darius on the throne. The details are peculiar, but the series of events echoes the story that Darius spun for himself following his power grab in 522 BC. There was a cliff at Bisitun, modern Behistun in western Iran, on the main road between Babylon and Ecbatana in Media. Semiramis, a ninth-century BC queen of Babylon, had come by it when she was constructing an irrigated park and commissioned artists to carve her portrait into its lower section. An inscription commemorated her successful scaling of the ridge.[7] Darius now added, but further up the cliff, a relief sculpture of his own. The artwork featured the earliest known image – a winged disc symbol – of the Achaemenid creator-god Ahuramazda. The accompanying inscription was written in three different languages – Old Persian cuneiform, Elamite and Babylonian – and so proclaimed Darius' message far and wide. It asserted that Darius had slain the pretender Bardiya (Smerdis) to reclaim and restore the kingdom that 'his' family (actually Cyrus') had formerly held. If the real Bardiya was not already dead, it may be that Darius and his fellow conspirators killed him and then launched a propaganda campaign to cover up the assassination. More boastful than Queen Semiramis, Darius gloried in quashing rebellions and creating stability. It was by the grace of Ahuramazda, he claimed, that he had become king of the Persian Empire.

The new king succeeded in putting down the numerous revolts that broke out against his rule in Egypt, Babylonia and beyond to establish himself firmly at the Persian court. The principal royal centres lay at Pasargadae (Cyrus' great marble-adorned former court), Elamite Susa (the administrative capital), Median Ecbatana (today's Hamadan) and Persepolis (Darius' ceremonial capital, in Fars Province), the last of which grew into an extraordinarily luxurious complex. Sitting at the foot of Kuh-e Rahmat in south-west Iran, the site was surrounded by a secure triple wall and dominated by a vast terrace accessed by two sweeping staircases. The terrace was occupied by a series of buildings, including the palace, a greeting hall known as an Apadana, and numerous other reception halls and brightly coloured sculptures.[8]

Darius' first wife, by whom he had three sons, was the daughter of one of his fellow conspirators.[9] The king now sought to legitimise his rule by marrying into Cyrus' family as well. Rather than take one bride, he took four, making wives of Phaedyme, who had felt no ears, Parmys, daughter of Cyrus' son Bardiya (Smerdis), the real one, and two of Cyrus' daughters, Artystone and Atossa. With each wedding he tightened his association with the older ruling family and drew a veil over his status as an outsider. Just as importantly, the unions ensured that the women closest to Cyrus were unavailable to marry anyone else who might desire Darius' throne. The king was so alert to the kind of threat that could arise within his own family that he had also added his own niece, Phratagune, to his roster of brides.[10]

The royal wives of Persia were accustomed to dine with their king but would depart when the evening's drinking began to make way for female musicians and concubines, many of whom would have been captives of war.[11] According to one Greek source, the queens tolerated this for two reasons.[12] First, because they had no choice, as the king was their master. Second, because the concubines showed them respect and understood that there was a feminine hierarchy.

Of the six royal women now embedded in the Persian court, Artystone, known in Elamite as Irtasduna, was Darius' favourite. Unlike his other wives, who had been married previously, Artystone was a virgin when he met her, so he might have felt that she alone was truly *his*. She had two sons by him, and he had a portrait of her made in hammered gold.[13] Artystone kept at least three estates in the region of Persepolis, one at a place named Mirandu, another at Kukkannakan, and a third at Matannan, the last of which had its own workforce and substantial storage facilities for grain and figs.[14] Some of the transactions from these estates are documented within a collection of more than 30,000 baked clay 'Fortification Tablets' from the first half of the fifth century BC discovered at Persepolis. Artystone received, for example, 100 sheep and a generous 2,000 quarts of wine, presumably to equip one of her residences for a series of banquets, at Darius' direction.[15]

But Artystone was by no means dependent upon Darius to spoil her with wine and sheep. She enjoyed a degree of financial independence as well as the use of her own seal. Astonishingly, her seal is believed to have been found, and is one of the most elaborately decorated on record. The cylinder-shaped object bears an intricate yet highly enigmatic narrative scene, at the centre of which stands a male bearded figure grasping the hooves of two bearded anthropomorphic winged creatures. Various symbols float around them, including seven dots, which represent the constellation of the Pleiades. A small figure in the foreground has been identified as the Egyptian god Horus as an infant sitting on a papyrus bed.[16] The images must have had religious significance for Artystone but they are difficult to interpret today. By contrast with the seal of Artystone's male chamberlain Shalamana, which has also been found, it is highly elusive. Shalamana's seal shows a standing female figure, who may be presumed to be Artystone, confidently holding up a large flower, while he sits rather conservatively on a chair waiting on her with wine.[17] It is not difficult to see who is in charge.

Artystone regularly authorised the release of provisions from her estates to selected people. The Fortification Tablets contain her direct instructions for 1,000 quarts of wine to be sent from her Kukkannakan estate, 3,000 quarts of grain from Matannan, and yet more wine from Mirandu.[18] Of particular note is her arrangement for supplies of grain to be dispatched to nursing mothers in her employment.[19] In Persian culture it was usual for women to care for their children entirely independently of their husbands for at least the first five years of the youngsters' lives. At court, they did so in their own private quarters, known as the *harem*. Artystone, seldom sequestered there, knew precisely how much she had to bestow from each of her estates and, just as importantly, when she needed to replenish her stocks by ordering in produce from elsewhere. She would have confounded the Greeks' belief that Persian women were the most closely guarded from public view in the world.[20]

Artystone may have had Darius' heart, but Atossa, daughter of Cyrus, had his head. Herodotus gave it as his personal view that Atossa held 'the totality of power', *to pan kratos*.[21] She was certainly involved in her husband's political affairs and would have welcomed delegations. In the absence of more than a handful of surviving Persian texts naming her, we must rely upon Greek sources to form a more precise impression of the sort of influence Atossa exerted. A near-contemporary described her as the first person to compose letters independently without a scribe.[22] This may have been an exaggeration, but Atossa was clearly dominant at court, not least because she was the mother of the man Darius chose – or was persuaded – to make his heir. Xerxes was the first of four sons born to Atossa after Darius came to power. The king's elder three sons, whom he had by his first wife, were products of the years before he came to the throne. If Xerxes therefore had the strongest claim to legitimacy, not least as the grandson of Cyrus the Great, then Atossa held the distinction of being the daughter of the first king of the Achaemenid Empire, a wife of another, and mother of another still.

Darius might well have been accustomed to taking advice from women. His mother is thought to have been Irdabama who, like Artystone, managed her own estates, their workshops and stock, and travelled widely.[23] Atossa's role in Darius' life certainly went beyond that of wife and mother. She roused him to action and gave him a sense of direction when his ambition was hot but aimless. Her brother Cambyses had added Egypt to Persia's empire during his brief rule in 525 BC. Amasis' wife Ladice was sent safely back to Cyrene in the process.[24] Darius hoped to go further. When, in about 513 BC, he conceived the idea of pushing the empire's eastern frontier out towards what is now Uzbekistan and Turkmenistan, Atossa suggested that he might invade land held by the Greeks instead.

Atossa's advice was said to have been influenced by anxieties over her health. The Persian queen had lately noticed a swelling on her breast. At first, she avoided telling anyone about it and did her best to cover herself up. When the lesion increased in size, however, and began to seep, causing the problem to spread, she had little choice but to seek help.

The first in-depth description of breast cancer would appear only half a century or so later in the medical writings ascribed to Hippocrates of Cos, but Atossa clearly recognised the risk of this disease, which would have affected women she knew. The cause of breast cancer was a mystery – Hippocrates would attribute the development of most cancers to the accumulation of black bile in the body – but the effects were only too familiar.

Her doctor, Democedes of Croton, a Greek colony in southern Italy, had initially arrived in Persia as a prisoner of war. Having proven his talents as a physician, he hoped to expand his remit by taking on a military command, and recognised that Atossa had the power to help him to achieve that. When she summoned him to examine her breast, he said that he would be able to cure her, but that he wanted something in return. What he wanted was nothing shameful, he assured her, but rather practical. Democedes longed to lead an expedition against the Greeks with a view to escaping home. Atossa agreed to talk to her husband (what choice did she have?) and took the topical lotion Democedes prescribed.

According to Herodotus, Atossa supported the prospect of a Greek expedition because she was eager to acquire the women of Sparta, Corinth, Argos and Athens as slaves, but this could hardly have been her true motivation.[25] In focusing on the demands of her doctor, indeed, Herodotus underplayed the depth of her own persuasions. The Persian queen had every reason to deter Darius from pursuing an expedition through the landscapes of the Scythians in favour of an expedition against the Greeks. Not only did these landscapes have less to offer him materially than a broad sweep of the Peloponnese, but they had been the death of her father. If mighty Cyrus could be reduced to a brain in a blood-filled bag by a nomadic queen, what fate could Darius look forward to by invading a land occupied by an equally aggressive tribe? Atossa's desire to save her husband from the Scythians was paramount.

Dissuading Darius from pursuing this course proved harder than she anticipated. Her arguments against the expedition could readily be contorted into arguments in favour. The very fact that Cyrus had failed in the face of the nomads meant that his descendants had a score to settle. If Darius prevailed, he would prove himself an even greater man than Cyrus, whose legacy was never in doubt. Darius was also reluctant to entrust a man as inexperienced as Atossa's doctor with too much responsibility. He was nonetheless unable to tell her no. Because it was his wife who was asking, he said, Democedes could lead a small detachment of fifteen Persians to reconnoitre the Greeks' territory. This might have been smaller than either the doctor or Atossa had hoped for, but it was a start.

After applying the solution to her breast, Atossa began to notice an improvement, which is the surest sign that she was not suffering from the cancer she feared. Her infection appears to have been fairly shallow:

she was perhaps suffering from a severe ulcer or inflammatory mastitis.[26] The expedition of her doctor proved less successful. Having run into trouble, Democedes had to abort the enterprise, which did not bode well for a larger-scale Greek invasion. There was, for the moment, little Atossa could do as Darius began to prepare his troops and draw up plans to bridge the Bosphorus. Against her best advice he was going for the Scythians.

Locating the enemy was the first challenge that confronted the invading Persians. The nomads had spread themselves over the Eurasian steppe from the northern littoral of the Black Sea to the borders of modern China. The landscape was not only difficult to traverse and navigate, but extremely unforgiving. The Scythians originated in Siberia and were well used to the freezing climate. Several pairs of long, insulating felt stockings have been discovered in the permafrost of the Altai Mountains at Pazyryk (near modern Kazakhstan). Well preserved in burial mounds, the men's and women's stockings were of a similar size and finely embroidered around their tops with colourful geometric patterns.[27] The Scythians favoured earthy colours derived from natural sources such as cochineal and indigo. On top of their stockings they wore thick leather and fur boots (fragments of women's exquisitely beaded shoes have also been found), and wool-lined coats constructed from various animal pelts including weasel, sable, squirrel, sheep and horse, often adorned with decorative appliqué work in leather or metal.[28] They also fabricated elaborate headdresses.[29] Wealthy Persian men usually wore the same vibrantly coloured robes as women and plentiful gold jewellery. Their beautiful textiles were no match for thick Scythian coverings in the biting cold.

As the Persians soon realised, the Scythians were also unabashedly itinerant. As a contemporary Greek writer noted, 'They do not live in houses, but rather in wagons. The smallest of these wagons are four-wheeled, and the others are six-wheeled. They are covered in felt and constructed, much like houses, in two or three parts. These provisions render them waterproof and protect against snow and wind as well as rain.'[30] One of these wagons has been preserved in a Pazyryk tomb.[31] Although it postdates the Persian expedition by at least a couple of centuries, it bears a close resemblance to the vehicle described, with a 3.2-metre-long central draught pole from which horses would have been harnessed and wheels extending to 1.6 metres in diameter.[32] It is likely that the Scythians also had yurts.

The Greeks had first encountered the Scythians in the Black Sea region in the seventh century BC while they were establishing their colonies on the northern shore nearby.[33] Even before their first sighting of them, they had contemplated Scythian culture with a mixture of wonder and disgust. Scythian youth were said to undergo a rite of passage that required them to drink the blood of their first human kill.[34] Members of the tribes scalped their enemies and attached the skins (some of which have been preserved) to their horses' bridles as trophies. Human teeth served very nicely as beads for earrings. Herodotus, who might well have encountered Scythians during his travels, also described their delight in drugs. The Scythians would roast hemp seeds on special braziers within small tents and lean forward in order to inhale the vapours.[35] Scythian men generally preferred taking drugs to bathing, but Scythian women habitually cleansed their faces and bodies by anointing them with a paste made from ground cedar and cypress wood.

The Scythian women were of particular interest to the Greeks. We can now say with some confidence that they were the real-life inspiration for the mythical Amazons. Paintings of the warrior women began to appear on pots in Greece from the seventh century BC, around the time Homer described them in his poetry and the first travellers returned from the Eurasian steppe, where they roamed. Contrary to the suggestion of many later Greek writers, the real-life 'Amazon' women did not remove their right breasts to facilitate the use of bow and arrows.[36] Scythian women were nevertheless often striking to behold, with shaved heads, wigs woven from their own tresses and strands of horsehair, and elaborate tattoos. Grafts of skin which have been preserved are inked with images of animals and animal fights. A grave uncovered in the Orenburg region of modern Russia contained the skeleton of a woman in her fifties who had been buried with a tattooing kit consisting of an iron knife, a bone needle and spoon, a bronze mirror and a palette.[37] The jazzy, highly patterned sleeves and trousers worn by Amazons in Greek vase paintings were probably intended to represent the Scythian women's body art.

We can tell from examining female skeletal remains that Scythian women were, like the mythical Amazons, highly experienced horse-riders. These riders were in many cases overcome by brutal injuries of a kind typically sustained in battle. One woman interred in the fourth century BC at the Chertomlyk burial ground in Ukraine had an arrowhead lodged in her spine. A collection of weapons – knives, arrowheads and an iron lance head – was arranged with jewellery around her body.[38] An exceptionally ancient grave dated to the end of the second millennium BC in modern Tbilisi contained the skeleton of a woman who had died in her thirties. In the course of her lifetime she had sustained a wound to her skull. She was buried with her sword and other weapons and part of a horse's head.[39] Scythian women were very commonly buried with spears.

The fact that Homer had presented the Amazons as 'equals to men' made them the perfect foe for male heroes to engage in close contests in literature and art. For one of his twelve labours Hercules was required to obtain the belt of the Amazon queen Hippolyte. The Athenian artist known as the Niobid Painter made Hercules and his fellow men roughly the same height and build as the spear- and shield-wielding Amazons on a fifth-century BC volute crater, used for mixing wine.[40] Many other artists painted the famous episode from myth in which Achilles fell in love with the Amazon Penthesilea at the very moment he killed her. Among the best was the master painter Exekias, who flourished in the mid-sixth century BC, a few decades before the Persians launched their expedition against the Scythians. On a celebrated vase painting he showed Achilles, all in black, inserting his spear into white-skinned Penthesilea's neck as their eyes meet.[41] *Amazonomachies*, mythological battles, always popular, often presented heroic men conquering the mighty women.

According to Herodotus, the real Amazon women first arrived among the Scythians around the seventh century BC, after they were carried off from the banks of the Thermodon (Terme) River near the Black Sea by some Greek sailors. The Amazons attacked and defeated their captors and drifted into Scythian territory, raiding and fighting as they went. The Scythians initially assumed that the assailants were men. It was only when they went over the bodies of those they had killed that they discovered they were female. Changing course, the Scythians dispatched their youths to camp out near the Amazons, imitate their actions, and see how the women reacted. As the trust between the two groups grew, one man took hold of one of the Amazons while she was out walking and had sex with her when it was clear she had no objection. At her signal, he returned the following day with another man, and it went from there until the Amazons had coupled up with the Scythians.

While the Scythian men struggled to learn the Amazons' language, the Amazons had little trouble in acquiring the early Iranian dialect of the Scythians. But language was far from the only barrier between them. When the Scythians suggested that they might come to live with them in their community, the Amazons demurred, saying something to the effect of, 'We could not live with your women, for they have their customs, and we have ours. We shoot arrows and hurl javelins and ride horses, but did not learn to do the work your women do. And your women do none of the things we have described, but stay in their wagons doing women's work and never go to hunt or anywhere else. And so we could never get along.'[42] Instead, the new couples crossed the River Tanais (The Don), and travelled three days north. Here, they established themselves as a new tribe, to be known historically as the Sauromatae. A number of graves containing the remains of female warriors have been discovered in the area in the vicinity of the river.[43]

As Darius and his forces came within sight on their expedition, the Scythians summoned the Sauromatae to their aid. They summoned other tribes, too, including the Agathyrsi, a sexually promiscuous people with a particular fondness for gold; the Tauri, who revered Iphigenia, the sacrificed daughter of Agamemnon; the Men-Eaters – savage cannibals, according to Herodotus; the Geloni, who were former Greek settlers; the Budini, who inhabited a city built of wood; and the Neuri and Black-Cloaks, who of course wore black cloaks. Not every tribe agreed to become involved in the impending conflict. The Scythians who took charge of the campaign therefore decided against meeting the Persians on an open plain in favour of drawing them into the woods. It was in their interest to remain elusive.

On this occasion, the Scythian women chose to go north with their children and some of their flocks rather than join combat with the strangers. They had extensive experience in the saddle and were well-prepared to defend themselves if the enemy were to catch up with them. Each woman in the Sauromatae tribe was tasked with killing one enemy soldier before she married. (Another writer claimed it was three.) It was, said the Roman geographer Pomponius Mela, a grown woman's 'military obligation' in these parts to bloody her hands in this way.[44] No excuse was made for gender among the Scythians and associated tribes. Women rode, women fought, women wore trousers. If they excused themselves from battle it was because they considered it tactical to do so. These Scythians' strategy was to draw as far away from the Persians as possible. It was only wise that as the Scythian men lured the puzzled Persians into the shadows and laid waste to their own land in order to deprive them of resources, the Scythian women should have retreated even further with provisions.

Darius was eager to engage the Scythians, but the Scythians contrived to evade contact, thereby denying him a war. Darius therefore forged a plan. He would proceed by night to the River Ister (Danube) with his best men and leave the majority of his forces behind him. The abandoned Persians woke the next morning and were so rattled by their leader's apparent treachery that they signalled to the Scythians to inform them of Darius' whereabouts. A division of Scythians promptly rode out to a bridge on the Ister. They had broken cover at last, just as Darius had hoped. The Persian's plan might have worked, had the tribesmen not overtaken his men, who took rather longer to navigate their way to the bridge over strange terrain. Instead of Persians, the Scythians encountered some Ionian Greeks by the bridge. In a demonstration of their aggressive foreign politics, the Scythians urged the Ionians to break the bridge and escape, for if they did so, they could declare themselves free from Persian control. The Scythians themselves would see to Darius and his men.

One of the Athenians who happened to be at the bridge was in favour of following this through. But as Histiaeus, tyrant of Miletus, told him, each ruler in Ionia held power over his city-state because of Darius. If the Persian were to be overthrown, then they would be too, and what good was there in that? Histiaeus' argument proved persuasive. The Ionians therefore put on a show of destroying the bridge in order to deceive the Scythians. The Persians, still no closer to engaging the tribesmen, were consequently able to make their way back over an only partially dismantled bridge. In his extensive inscriptions at Bisitun, Darius proclaimed total victory over the Scythians. The reality was a non-event. It might have been worse. The Scythian cavalry was equipped with the most striking array of handmade weapons, mainly of iron, including daggers, knives, short swords, pointed battleaxes, and especially bows and arrows.[45] Their knowledge of the terrain was second to none. Had the Scythians met the Persians in close combat then it is probable that Darius would have suffered the same fate as Cyrus at the hands of the Massagetae, much as Atossa had feared.

Chapter VII

Atossa's War

And Artemis, ye maidens,
Fleeing Alpheus.

Telesilla, PMG 717, fifth century BC

Atossa had to wait more than twenty years for her Greek invasion. By the time it came, she was approaching sixty years old and was obliged to accept that she might never see her husband return to her again. Darius, who was of a similar age, was no more enthusiastic about the venture at this point than he had been when he embarked upon his campaign against the Scythians in 513 BC, but world events had conspired in such a way as to give him little choice but to launch the campaign belatedly. His actions would anticipate the outbreak of the Graeco-Persian Wars, some of the most viciously fought battles of the fifth century BC, in which men dominated but a number of exceptional women and girls demonstrated both fortitude and ingenuity.

One of the unlikely witnesses to the beginnings of the struggles was a girl named Gorgo. She was the daughter of Cleomenes I, co-ruler of Sparta and leader of the force that had driven Hippias out of Athens during the collapse of the Peisistratid dynasty. Her name meant 'gorgon' and evoked the image of the monster of myth that featured widely on Spartan art as a symbol to strike fear in the enemy. Gorgo was still a young child – eight or nine years old in 499 BC by one account – but her keen eye and precocious observations had already won her admiration at court.[1]

Once, when her father asked her to pay a man in grain because he had given him some good advice about wine, Gorgo cautioned prudence, 'Oh father, but then more wine will be drunk and the drinkers will become more lackadaisical and worse behaved.'[2] It had not perhaps escaped Gorgo's notice that her own father was inclined to over-drinking. Cleomenes would descend into alcoholism in his older years.

The king's affection for his daughter was so deep that, when an unexpected visitor arrived at court to petition him for military support, he insisted she stay in the room and hear the negotiations. Their guest, Aristagoras, was the tyrant king of Miletus. The Ionian city-state, which lay on the Aegean coast of western Asia Minor, had grown through the intermarriage of Athenian settlers and its native female population before becoming a vassal of the Persian Empire. It remained best known as the birthplace of some of the leading Greek philosophers and stargazers of the previous century, including Anaximander and Thales, the latter of whom achieved fame for calculating the height of the pyramids in Egypt simply by using their shadows.

When a group of exiles from the island of Naxos landed in Miletus and asked for help in finding their way home, Aristagoras agreed to approach the Persians, who were in possession of the greater sea power.[3] He secretly believed that he had a fair chance of conquering Naxos and knew just how to convince Darius to help him achieve this end. Supply the islanders with ships, he bargained with the king, and the Persians could use Naxos and its dependent islands in the Cyclades as a base from which to launch an attack on wealthy Euboea on the mainland. Darius was tempted by this idea and agreed to send 200 triremes. The mission, however, was a failure, owing in large part to Aristagoras' dispute with Darius' admiral Megabates. Naxos held.

What Aristagoras truly desired was to revolt against the Persian Empire, and in this ambition, at least, he knew he could be confident of gaining the support of many other Ionian city-states. People in these parts were growing increasingly resentful of having to pay tribute to the Persians, who took advantage of their lucrative trade routes and luxuriated in the grand estates that had once been Greek. The tyrants Persia had imposed upon them had degraded them, Aristagoras complained to Cleomenes during their meeting, but it did not need to be this way. Change was possible. All they had to do was to set their hearts on liberating themselves.[4]

The Athenians had shown the fruits of liberation and established an important precedent for the disgruntled peoples of Ionia with the foundation of a new democracy. The path to change had not however been smooth. Freed from the Peisistratids, the people of Athens had enjoyed a brief period of calm, during which they continued to live by the precepts of Solon's constitution. But then came the storm, as a power struggle erupted between Cleisthenes, of the cursed Alcmaeonids, and Isagoras, a member of a rival family.[5] Both Sparta and Persia were drawn into this struggle. While Sparta intervened on Isagoras' behalf, Cleisthenes appealed to Persia and succeeded in securing an alliance with Sardis, their satrapal capital in former Lydia. Cleisthenes eventually prevailed and, as leader, divided the people of Athens and the surrounding region of Attica into ten tribes, each of which was entitled to select fifty members to join his new Council. The population was also divided into about 140 parishes or *demes* to manage their own internal politics. This meant that, although women were still excluded from holding positions of power, they were better represented through their male relations on a local level than they had been previously. Cleisthenes' democracy-inspired reforms were a beacon to the other Ionian city-states.

Cleomenes of Sparta had been on the losing side in Athens's battle and therefore had all the more reason to resent Persia. But while he could see the appeal of improving his lot by revolting and winning a share of Persia's riches, he worried for his men, who would need to travel quite some distance – about three months' march – in order to participate. As Cleomenes wavered and prevaricated, Aristagoras changed tack and implored him for his help as a suppliant, getting down on his knees in a gesture of respectful subjugation.

It was at this point, as he knelt there, his arms wrapped tightly around Cleomenes' legs, that Aristagoras asked that the young princess Gorgo be dismissed from the room. The Spartan king would not stand for this. Cleomenes, clearly mistrusting his guest, insisted that Gorgo stay, adding that there was no reason to hold back for her sake. Aristagoras therefore continued. He promised to pay Cleomenes if he agreed to lend his support to an uprising. Each time Cleomenes declined, Aristagoras increased his offer and intensified his plea, prompting Gorgo to interject, 'Father, our visitor will corrupt you with his bribes if you do not withdraw and leave.'[6]

Whether Gorgo actually said these words is doubtful. Male historians, as we have seen, conventionally invented speeches for their characters, especially women. In the narrative of Herodotus' *Histories*, Gorgo's voice serves as that of Cleomenes' conscience. It is so insistent, so persuasive, that it prevails. Aristagoras is left to make his own way out of the Spartan court. As the Milesian pauses to have his shoes put on by an attendant rather than tie them on himself, Gorgo utters a final passing quip: 'Father, our visitor doesn't have hands!'[7] Plutarch, who recorded the quote, was giving a foretaste of the person Gorgo would become. A mere child when the Milesian arrived, she would be a woman by the time the effects of Aristagoras' petitioning could be felt, and in a position to play a significant role of her own.

In the meantime, another woman emerged at the fore of the mounting conflict and won renown for her bravery. Her name was Telesilla and she came from Argos in the Peloponnese. The Pythia at Delphi predicted that Sparta would triumph against this city-state.[8] And so, in 494 BC, Cleomenes invaded. As his Spartans went on the rampage, slaughtering many of the inhabitants directly, servile 'helots' in their service killed many more by setting fire to one of the nearby groves. Telesilla assumed control of the interior defence while the land blazed, the women of Argos gathering closely around her inside the city walls, obedient to her commands.

Telesilla, too, had taken the advice of the Pythia in the past. When she became chronically ill, she called upon the oracle, who advised her to write poetry as a means of managing her condition. It can be easy to forget that Delphi was a place of pilgrimage for ordinary people suffering from common problems, not just kings and politicians seeking flattery for their ambitions. The Pythia's advice to Telesilla was eminently practical and showed some consideration of her mental state. The oracle had essentially told her to seek distraction. Telesilla took the advice she was offered and discovered that poetry was not only a valuable source of comfort when she was ailing, but also a salutary means of entering the consciousness of other people. Women, in particular, came to admire her work.[9] Only one short fragment of Telesilla's poetry survives, but we know that she was fond of writing lyric choruses for girls, and of gods and goddesses.[10] She wrote of Artemis fleeing the embrace of the same libidinous river god who had pursued Arethusa in Sicily, and of Artemis' sibling Apollo and his love of the sun. Her verses were so accomplished that 'most glorious Telesilla' was hailed alongside Sappho as one of the great female poets in Greek history.[11]

The later commemoration of Telesilla in public works of art was inspired by her courage during the Spartan invasion as much as her talents as a poet. When Argos was placed under siege, she directed the slaves, youths and elderly people to mount a human defence along the city's perimeters. Then, she flew around the houses and temples, gathering any weapons the men had left behind. With these, she armed the younger women, and saw that they took up position to confront the oncoming enemy. Her fellow Argives appeared so unfazed by their rousing battle cry that the Spartans withdrew in order to avoid a nebulous victory over women – or so it was reported. Of all the city-states, the Spartans were surely the least likely to demur at the opportunity to battle down the female sex. What actually happened at this moment in Argos will never be recovered, but Telesilla had played a crucial role in stockpiling reserve arms and aiding her city's defence, and for this she would always be remembered. A male artist, Niceratus, was commissioned to sculpt a monument of her to be erected beside the local Temple of Aphrodite.[12] On the stone *stele* she held her helmet in one hand and her books lay at her feet.[13] She was both poet and fighter combined. Not only that, but 'because of Telesilla', the war god Ares began to be worshipped at Argos as a women's god as well as a figure of reverence by men.[14] A festival was celebrated upon the anniversary of the Spartan invasion, during which women dressed in men's clothes, and men in women's.[15] And so a tragedy was transformed into a triumph for the women of Argos.

After failing to obtain the support of Sparta against the Persians, the combative Milesians succeeded elsewhere. Eager to present an Ionian revolt as a bid for freedom, Aristagoras laid down his tyranny and declared *isonomia* over his city-state.[16] In Greek, this meant something akin to 'political equality', and was precisely what Cleisthenes had declared in Athens as part of his reforms. A shift, symbolic at first, was beginning to occur with the dissemination of power from the top to the free male citizenship, especially among the Greek city-states with Persia-imposed tyrannies.[17] Many more rulers laid down their powers across Ionia at Aristagoras' suggestion. In some places, including Samos and Chios, tyrants were overthrown by their own people. The inhabitants of Mytilene, Sappho's former home, went so far as to kill theirs.[18]

Aristagoras next turned towards Athens. The fact that the Persians had taken in their ex-tyrant Hippias and refused to hand him over made the Athenians all the more eager to join the campaign. They contributed twenty ships. The Eretrians, the Milesians' old-time allies, lent a further five triremes.[19] And so began what would be known as the Ionian Revolt. At Aristagoras' instruction, the Athenians, Eretrians and peoples of Asia Minor marched on Sardis. They showed no mercy as they piled in with torches and laid waste to the finest buildings. Not even the great Temple of Cybele, the Mother Goddess, was spared. Incensed by the desecration, the Persians pursued the Ionians as far as Ephesus and put many of them to death. Their thirst for revenge following these dramatic days would fuel many more years of conflict ahead.

For the women of this part of the world the sudden escalation of war was extremely unsettling. While Aristagoras built up further support among the people of Byzantium, Caria, Phrygia and Cyprus, many women travelled west with their children to the Aegean island of Chios in the hope of reaching safety. When the Persians pursued them there, the Chians took them to the Milesians' allies on Lesbos, and thence to Doriscus in the northern Aegean, and finally back home. The emotional toll of these repeated upheavals can only be imagined.

The conflict intensified as the Persians sought to recapture Cyprus and besiege the revolting city-states. The Persians very soon led Cypriots, Egyptians, Phoenicians and Cilicians against Aristagoras' Miletus and remaining allies.[20] The Ionians chose to confront the enemy at sea near Lade, just off Miletus, in 494 BC. This was a mistake. The Persian triremes outnumbered those of the Greeks by 600 to 353. When a disagreement erupted among the rebels, the majority of the sailors needed little excuse to sail away, rendering the Persians the victors by default. There was no mercy for the Milesians. Their city was besieged, the male inhabitants slaughtered, and the women and children sold into slavery to the people of Ampe near the Red Sea.[21] Aristagoras had meanwhile escaped to Thrace where he was killed in a siege. Still worse came to pass the following year, when the Persians subdued Chios, Lesbos and Tenedos. It was said that they linked hands to form a line across each island and harried the inhabitants into the equivalent of a hunter's net.[22] Boys were snatched from the Ionian mainland and transformed into eunuchs. The prettiest girls were taken to the Persian court. The Ionians had little choice but to submit once again, their bid for liberation a failure.

Atossa had urged her husband to invade Greece more than two decades ago and he had chosen to pursue the Scythians instead. The Ionian Revolt had dragged them into a war of quite a different nature, for they were starting on the back foot. To Darius it was clear that Persia needed to punish Athens and Eretria for lending ships to Miletus and setting Sardis ablaze. But there were other Greek city-states that needed disciplining too. Darius dispatched heralds to each with the request that they send him a symbolic gift of water and earth. Any that refused to do so were branded uncompliant and in need of subjugation. One of Darius' nephews and chief generals, Mardonius, was accordingly sent after the Thracians, Macedonians and Eretrians. The people of Naxos were enslaved. Athens and Sparta proved to be stubbornly resistant, but Aegina offered up the requested gifts of earth and water.

A Persian naval taskforce led by a son of Darius and a Mede first torched Eretria in Euboea and then landed at Marathon, a broad plain near the Euboean coast, in 490 BC. According to Herodotus, it was Hippias, son of Peisistratus, who chose to lead the Persian fleet to this particular location. The Athenians wasted no time in applying for reinforcements. The fastest long-distance runner among them, Pheidippides, was dispatched some 240 kilometres to Sparta to request help. In a remarkable feat of human endurance, he managed to arrive there the very next day, only to find he was too early.[23] While the Spartans welcomed the 'marathon' runner, as Pheidippides would later be remembered, they remained reluctant to fight Persia, explaining that they could not send men until the next full moon because they were in the middle of celebrating the festival of the Carneia, which was a time for peace. In place of the Spartans, the Athenians welcomed a contingent from their allies in Plataea, a small city south of Thebes, in Boeotia.

Their combined forces proved highly effective at Marathon. Even though they were vastly outnumbered, they charged full tilt at the Persians, who could not believe their confidence. The Athenians' strength lay in their hoplites – infantrymen armed with wooden shields, long spears and all-over bronze Corinthian helmets – who proved particularly strong on the wings. Having routed part of the opposing army, the 9,000 or so Athenians joined their wing to that of the 1,000 Plataeans, and worked inwards to the centre of the fray. The Persians were obliterated across the plain. As stragglers fled to the coast, the Greeks hacked them down and seized seven of their ships. On the Persian side there were said to have been roughly 6,400 casualties. The 192 Athenians who lost their lives were covered over with a burial mound, roughly 12 metres tall, still visible today.

Marathon was neither the largest nor the most strategically significant battle ever fought, but politically it became symbolic of the division between east and west. The nineteenth-century political scientist John Stuart Mill went so far as to declare it more important in English history than the Battle of Hastings.[24] Certainly it marked a watershed in east-west relations. There was no going back to the earlier period of coexistence. As the surviving Persians sailed away from Marathon, dragging with them Eretrian slaves, Darius erupted in fury and vowed to raise an expedition against the Greeks.[25] He spent three years building up an army. In the fourth year, the Egyptians and Babylonians followed the Greeks in revolting against Persia, which decided Darius on a dual campaign. The king, however, was starting to get old. In 486 BC he fell ill, and a month later, at the age of sixty-four, he was dead.[26] He left behind an empire that stretched from Macedon to the Indus. He also left unfinished business. Two crucial wars now hung in the balance. His widow would need to take stock.

Atossa had always wanted a war with Greece, but the prospect of entrusting her eldest son with the responsibility of orchestrating it was fraught with anxiety. Xerxes was about thirty-two years old when he succeeded Darius as king of Persia and had a young family to support. Like his father, he was polygamous, but we know the name of only one of his wives. Amestris, daughter of one of the conspirators who had helped to bring Darius to power, was also Xerxes' cousin. They would have at least three sons – Darius, Hystaspes and Artaxerxes – and two daughters – Amytis and Rhodogune. A Babylonian tablet survives recording a grain-payment to the wet nurse of a further, possibly illegitimate daughter, Ratahsah.[27] (For many mothers of daughters, wet nurses were essential. A text from Persepolis reveals that, among a set of weavers, new mothers of daughters received precisely half the ration of food given to new mothers of sons.)[28]

Xerxes' daughters stayed behind in Persia while he set out to reconquer Egypt and place it under his younger brother Achaemene's control. Having succeeded there, the king's plan was to bridge the Hellespont, lead the Persian army over it, set Athens and Eretria aflame in recompense for the burning of Sardis and, only later, begin rebuilding the Persian dominion. His ambitions were so great that the people closest to Xerxes feared he would overreach. The playwright Aeschylus, a veteran of the Battle of Marathon, would later describe Atossa's sense of foreboding in his *Persians*. The tragedy, put on in Athens in 472 BC, had the queen suffer nightmares about the potential loss under her son of everything her husband had achieved. Aeschylus showed the Greeks what they wanted to see but also reflected the reality. Xerxes really was warned to tread carefully. He really did resent being told what to do. 'Abide here with the women,' he shrugged at one particularly tentative adviser.[29]

After some years of seeking advice and failing to heed it – of building up the army and stockpiling supplies – the king finally set out to fulfil his mother's dream of invading Greece in the spring of 480 BC. He brought with him several members of his family, including a number of illegitimate sons, but as before his daughters stayed behind in Persia. There was nevertheless a strong female contingent to his crew. The *pallakai* or concubines he kept at court numbered 300 or 360 according to credible Greek estimates.[30] In the Book of Esther, virgins are described as being brought to Xerxes (called 'Ahasuerus') at Susa from all around and subjected to a rigorous series of beauty treatments.[31] A six-month immersion in myrrh would be followed by a six-month immersion in incense, perfumes and make-up. Only then were the virgins led to the king's bedchamber. Legend held that Xerxes favoured Esther, a cousin of Mordecai, a Jew who lived at Susa, above all the other women and crowned her as his queen. It is probable that many new concubines were brought in for the purpose of joining his campaign. They were accompanied on the Persian ships by female 'bread-makers' and cooks.

While the women prepared for the long days ahead, the men had first dug a canal through the Mount Athos peninsula in north-east Greece. A number of Darius' ships had been wrecked here in the past, but Xerxes' motives in constructing the canal were less practical than psychological: the sight of the Persians taking up such a challenge would be sure to unnerve the enemy.[32] The completed canal appears to have crossed the highest ground of the isthmus via a deep man-made trench.[33] Once the canal was completed, the Hellespont needed to be bridged, ideally between the cities of Abydos and Sestos. It was said that Xerxes' Phoenician builders attempted to do this with ropes made of flax, and the Egyptian builders with ropes of papyrus, but neither held up. In his frustration, the king had the builders beheaded and proceeded to vent his anger on the sea itself, lashing the waves over and over, as if he might whip them into better shape than his forces. To the Greeks, who believed in the divinity of the sea, this was deeply sacrilegious. Eventually, a second set of builders was brought in and a plan was made to construct a pair of bridges out of boats. The craftsmen positioned hundreds of vessels alongside each other, lowered their anchors, and stretched cables of flax and papyrus woven together from shore to shore. It was a triumph.

The Persian advance had begun in a slow but stately manner. As Xerxes mustered his land army to Sardis, he fronted a magnificent procession, which showcased the skills of Persian women. Colourful garlands and pieces of tapestry were required to adorn the soldiers as they marched forth in undampened optimism. The women of Persia would have been exceptionally busy ahead of the spectacle. A thousand of the best spearmen and 1,000 horsemen were followed by 10,000 infantrymen, a tenth of whom carried silver spears topped with golden pomegranates, while those nearest Xerxes had spears with golden apples. Another 10,000 horsemen followed.[34] The king also had at his disposal an elite section of 10,000 splendidly dressed soldiers known to the Greeks as 'the Immortals': whenever one of them died, he would immediately be replaced.

The dazzling brigade proceeded to the site of former Troy before a devastating storm blew up south of the city at the foot of Mount Ida. When Xerxes surveyed the damage and realised how many of his men had been killed, he began to cry at the brevity of human life and the thought that the thousands who remained in his midst would also have died before the century was out.[35] Herodotus' account of the king's depression and premonition of death lent dramatic tension to his narrative but could well have been based on fact. It was with defiance that the king dried his existential tears and crossed the new bridges, the animals over one, men over the other.

The Persians marched through Chersonese, the modern Gallipoli Peninsula, and came to Doriscus, Thrace, where they were reunited with their fleet. In total, according to Herodotus' suspiciously high estimate, they numbered 1.7 million.[36] It can at least be said that, having already subjugated peoples as far as their allies in Macedonia, the Persians were able to expand their army as they made their way towards Greece. They counted upon the support of Medes, Assyrians, Indians, Parthians, Arabians, Bactrians, Scythians and Ethiopians. The last of these painted their bodies with gypsum and vermilion and wore lion and leopard-skin pelts. Their commander was Arsames, a son of Artystone and Darius. Otanes, Xerxes' father-in-law, stood in command of the Persians, and Hystaspes, one of Atossa's sons by Darius, led the Scythians and Bactrians. For all the hundreds of thousands it involved, the campaign remained, at heart, a family affair.

News of the impending Persian invasion of Greece – Xerxes' potential fulfilment of his parents' dream – reached the precocious 'gorgon-girl' Gorgo in Sparta through the intervention of a Persian defector. Demaratus had formerly served alongside her father within the kingly dyarchy but fled to Persia after being deposed. Despite his ill fortune, he outlived Cleomenes, who fell prey to his demons – and a scandal involving bribery of the Pythia – and died about 490 BC in a suspected suicide. The Spartans had a new king in the shape of Cleomenes' half-brother, Leonidas, to whom Gorgo, now aged about twenty-seven, was married. When Demaratus sent warning of the Persian attack to the Spartan court, Gorgo was the only person able to make sense of his message, which was so subtle as to be near invisible. She alone knew what to do with the blank wax tablets he sent. It is uncertain whether Spartan women were conventionally taught to read and write, but Gorgo understood the nature of writing tablets, and realised that the wax could be melted and scraped away. When the surface of the blank tablets was removed at her instruction, a secret message appeared, etched into the wood behind. Demaratus had inscribed all he knew of Xerxes' plans into the support, then disguised his intelligence by melting wax on top of it.[37] While news of Persia's approach had undoubtedly already reached the Greek mainland, the inhabitants of which had forged an alliance of resistance with Sparta, Gorgo's quick thinking as an early code-breaker provided the Spartans with fair warning and enabled them to alert other communities to the impending danger.

As they prepared to defend their territory, the Spartans rejected an offer from Gelon, tyrant of Syracuse, of 200 triremes, 20,000 men, 2,000 horses – and more – smarting at the thought of bowing to a Sicilian Greek.[38] With Athens choosing to stay away for the moment, the Spartans had an opportunity to predominate among the 10,000 soldiers who travelled to Thessaly by sea. Their primary objective was to ward the Persians off Greek territory by guarding the pass of Tempe, which ran from lower Macedonia along the River Peneus between Mount Olympus and Mount Ossa. When news came that the enemy was approaching by a different pass, however, they had little choice but to retreat to the Isthmus. The Spartans' new objective was to guard the somewhat narrower pass of Thermopylae ('Hot Gates'), so-named for the sulphurous thermal springs located nearby. By halting the Persians here, the Spartans could keep them outside central Greek territory.

Gorgo understood how dangerous a feat this would be. Her husband Leonidas was the leader of the crack force of 300 Spartans selected to descend upon the pass in August 480 BC. As he left, she asked him whether he had any instructions for her, and he said that if anything were to happen to him, she should marry well and bear noble children.[39] The Pythia at Delphi had told the Spartans, in her usual ambiguous way, that either their city must fall, or their king. Leonidas knew that he was very likely going to his death.

From the beginning, nonetheless, Xerxes underestimated the strength of the enemy. He had sent a spy ahead to ascertain how many Greeks were there, and the spy had reported seeing the Spartans exercising and combing their hair, which seemed to epitomise their vanity. Although Leonidas was rumoured to be a descendant of Heracles, he was neither vain nor self-important, but wholly committed to the success of Sparta. He certainly exhibited nothing short of a hero's courage as he stepped forward to meet the Persian onslaught. Over the course of two days, he succeeded in leading his men in the resistance. The enemy withdrew but Leonidas knew they would return. The near-certainty of death propelled him out into the open field while the Persians wheeled back on themselves to approach from higher in the pass.

Gorgo, waiting at home, could only imagine the horror her husband was encountering. The fact that he was still alive on the third day of the conflict offered little comfort. That morning, in fact, Leonidas bade his men eat their breakfast as if it were their last in unflinching belief that they would be dining in the Underworld.[40] He inspired them to fight to the very end by example. His earlier premonition was well-founded. The Spartan 300 were hacked down almost to a man. Leonidas was among the fallen. His head was cut off and impaled upon the orders of Xerxes, who lost two of his half-brothers, sons of Darius and Phratagune, in the fight. A praise-poet named Simonides later commemorated the Spartan heroes who had died and highlighted the particular *kleos* of Leonidas. The hero had given his life to slowing the enemy advance and earned immortality in the process.

While the dire news was carried to Gorgo and the other men's wives, the Persians set their hearts on victory at sea. With the wealth generated from their silver mines at Laureion the Athenians had amassed over 200 warships. Even so, the Persians claimed superiority, for their navy was dominated by Phoenicians who possessed the best war vessels known to man. Their two-banked galleys were less cumbersome than other contemporary models because they allowed for some rowers to sit on an upper deck while most laboured beneath. They also had in their possession a three-banked trireme with the capability to travel at almost 9 knots.[41] In an attempt to make quick work of the Athenians, the Persians dispatched their ten quickest vessels ahead of the main fleet, successfully capturing three ships. A larger contingent of Athenians and other naval allies had meanwhile made its way to Artemisium, on the northern coast of Euboea, in the territory of Histiaea.[42]

Despite their strength in ships, the Persians endured a challenging voyage with three of their vessels running foul of a reef on the passage to Cape Sepias, in Magnesia, Thessaly. It was perhaps here that the Thessalian courtesan Thargelia made Xerxes' acquaintance. Disappointingly little is known about her, though it was said that she was Milesian by birth, immensely beautiful and married some fourteen times.[43] Thargelia was said to have been instrumental in spreading pro-Persian sentiment in Thessaly and further afield.[44] A number of Greek cities 'medised' in the course of the wars, including, further south, Thebes itself. That a well-connected *hetaera* should have played a part in influencing allegiances in pro-Persian Thessaly is entirely credible.

While the Thessalians allowed the Persian ships to anchor when they arrived, neither the weather nor the inhabitants of the opposite coast proved to be quite so accommodating. After passing the night comparatively soundly, the crews awoke to a dramatic storm stirred up by the notorious Hellespontian east wind off Mount Pelion.[45] The Pythia at Delphi had allegedly predicted this tempest. At the approach of the Persians, the Delphians had consulted the oracle and followed its advice to pray to Boreas, god of winds, and his wife Oreithyia for deliverance. The Persians had had no such warning. When night fell once again over Mount Pelion, the storms moved in, whipping up the waters where the Persians had moored their ships so they could rest before engaging the Greeks the following day.

While the Persians slept, two figures approached the harbour walls, one male, the other female and considerably younger. Taking advantage of the howl of the wind, the two figures made a sudden dash, paused briefly and dived into the freezing water.

Growing up in Scione, a port town of Chalcidice on the north Aegean coast, the girl, Hydna, had had little choice but to become a strong swimmer and diver under the instruction of her father Scyllias.[46] A contemporary painting created for a tomb at Paestum, southern Italy, depicts a naked man diving joyfully off a wall into a void below.[47] He may well be plunging metaphorically into the depths of the Underworld – a keen swimmer in life eager to find his way to his next destination. Whoever he was, he arched his body so gracefully that anyone who saw him would have assumed he was a champion sportsman. Little else is known of Hydna and her father, but we might imagine them looking no less graceful as they launched themselves expertly into the abyss.

Over the course of several hours, they swam out towards the horizon, undetected under cover of night. When finally they reached the Persian ships, they set about their task of cutting and fraying the anchors and ropes beneath. As each mooring became loose, the hulls began to knock against each other in the wind. The damage the pair caused with their knives was minimal compared to the damage one ship inflicted upon another once untethered. The more the ships clashed, the more holes opened up, waterlogging the decks and orlops beneath.

In a desperate effort to calm the squalls, the Magian priests among the Persians employed spells and offered sacrifice to Thetis and her fellow Nereids, women of the sea, who were said to occupy this stretch of Sepian headland. It was in these very waters that Peleus had famously captured Thetis (the mother of Achilles) before making her his wife. Like Peleus, Hydna and her father risked their lives in pursuit of a near impossible quest, and succeeded in buying the Greek navy more time to prepare for battle. An estimated 300 Persian ships were destroyed in the course of the three-day storm. Many were supply ships laden with corn.

Despite their losses, the Persians looked strong as they proceeded with their Egyptian allies to Artemisium at the northern tip of Euboea, where they were met by a smaller number of Greek ships from Corinth, Sparta, Eretria and Athens. The filtering in of news of the disaster at Thermopylae did nothing to help Greek morale. The naval battle proved brief and anticlimactic. After just three days, the Greeks withdrew, too depleted to continue, granting the Persians a hollow victory, but a victory nonetheless.

Anticipating the dangers that lay ahead, the women and children of Attica fled their homes and made their way to safety in Troezen, Aegina and, especially, Salamis, an island near Athens. The women and children of Delphi similarly sought refuge in Achaea, western Greece, while the men did all they could to conceal the sanctuary treasures in a cave. These women were fortunate to escape in time. Many women fleeing Phocis, the region in which Delphi lay, were caught by the Persians on their return from Thermopylae and gang-raped to death.[48] They are the forgotten victims of the Graeco-Persian Wars, not the men who fought and fell in the field, destined to become the subject of glorious poetic verse. It was these women who paid the price of Xerxes' ambition.

The priestess of the oracle at Delphi at this time, Aristonice, was said to have predicted the Persians' next movements.[49] She envisioned their unstoppable forces pouring into Attica, setting fire to Thespiae, Plataea and Athens, laying waste all around. It was upon her advice that most of the inhabitants of these cities fled to safety. A small number stayed behind in a vain attempt to save their homes from destruction. One group of stalwarts stood at the crown of the Athenian Acropolis and tumbled boulders down onto the arrow-flinging invaders below. Still, the Persians fought their way up the hill, intent on taking revenge for the destruction of the Temple of the Mother Goddess at Sardis by burning the sanctuary of the patron goddess of the Athenians. What took place was in one sense a war over rival goddesses. Both Athena's temple and the building known as the Older Parthenon were plundered and destroyed. The Persians destroyed a statue of Nike, the goddess of Victory, and carried home a bronze sculpture of the 'Tyrannicides', the two men credited with helping to bring down the Peisistratids.[50] Some of the other female figures, the so-called

Korai in marble, were preserved at the site while their human defenders were killed.

Attica was now subject to Persian control. With nothing more to lose, the Athenians agreed to offer battle once more, this time off the waters of Greek-held Salamis. Only Xerxes was uncertain of the best course to take. While the majority of his men were in favour of vanquishing the Greeks at home, the queen of Halicarnassus (Bodrum) counselled against it, and her words of caution lingered in his ear.[51]

Artemisia held the distinction of being the sole female commander on either side of the Graeco-Persian Wars. Being Halicarnassan on her father's side, Cretan on her mother's, she had come to power after the untimely death of her husband (their son was still too young to rule) and held sway over Cos, Nisyrus and Calydna as well as Halicarnassus itself. The five ships she contributed to the Persian fleet were reputed to be second best only to the Phoenician warships. Spare the ships, she urged Xerxes' deputy Mardonius, and refrain from fighting the Greeks on water. 'It is right,' she said, 'for me to share my opinion, such advice as I think best for your situation.'[52] Her reasoning, as paraphrased by Herodotus, was that 'their men are stronger than yours by sea just as men in general are stronger than women'.

Mardonius was not unaccustomed to conversing with decisive women. His wife, Artazostre, a daughter of Darius, had seldom been one for resigning herself to the harem. Quite contrary to the claims of Plutarch, who related with some Greek bias that Persian men guarded their wives and concubines so jealously as to keep them tightly sequestered, Artazostre was an inveterate traveller.[53] A clay tablet reveals that she received a sizeable ration of 360 quarts of flour to take with her on a journey in the company of another woman and her father-in-law Gobryas.[54] Artemisia must nevertheless have taken Mardonius and Xerxes by surprise in her vehemence. Her words were not recorded verbatim, but Herodotus, who attributed them to her, was her fellow Halicarnassan and a contemporary:

> And why must you endanger yourself in sea battles at all? Have you not control of Athens, for which you set out on this campaign? And do you not have control of the rest of Greece? Nobody is standing in your way; those who opposed you gave over as befitted them. I will show you how I think the situation will turn out for your enemies. If

> you do not press to fight at sea, but stay your ships and remain here or even advance to the Peloponnese, then easily, master, will you achieve what you came for. For the Greeks are not the sort to be able to withstand you for very long, but you will disband them, and they will flee variously to their cities. For they have no food on this island, as far as I can ascertain, and, if you drive your land army into the Peloponnese, those who have come from there will not stay put, so they will be without shelter, too. Nor will they be minded to fight at sea for Athens's sake. But if you press to fight at sea at once, I am worried your fleet will suffer and damage your land army too. Moreover, my king, consider this in your heart: that while the slaves of good men tend to be bad, the slaves of bad men tend to be good. And you, who are the best of all men, have bad slaves. They claim to be your allies, these people of Egypt, Cyprus, Cilicia and Pamphylia, but are of no help.

When the Persian men heard Artemisia's advice, many of them feared for her safety, knowing how short-tempered Xerxes could be. Others smiled inwardly at the thought that this lofty woman might have endangered her position as the king's confidante. It was to the astonishment of both groups that Xerxes declared Artemisia's to be the best advice he had received so far. And yet, he did not take it. His generals' eagerness to beat down the Greeks even further than they had already propelled him to disregard everything the queen had said. And so Xerxes issued orders for his troops to sail for Salamis and to march to the Peloponnese, where Spartans, Corinthians, Athenians and others had encamped under Gorgo's brother-in-law Cleombrotus.[55]

It did not take long for word to travel of Xerxes' plans. The Athenians reacted by sending a deceiving message to the Persians at sea telling them that they were planning flight. The Persians, taking the Greeks at their word, approached Salamis by night, intending to hem in their ships. At that moment the Greeks sprang into action and began to engage.

The oracle at Delphi had proclaimed that a campaign at Salamis would culminate in the deaths of women's sons at the time the harvest was gathered in. The Athenians' highly regarded admiral, Themistocles, had interpreted the oracle as a signal that they should fight to victory at sea. When the sceptre of a woman appeared to one of the other Greeks to reproach him for not pushing forward, any lingering fear – on the part of the man experiencing the vision, at least – evaporated. The Hellenes proceeded in full conviction of their chances of success in spite of being dramatically outnumbered.

Such was the disorder on the enemy side that Artemisia resorted to sinking an allied ship so that she could steer herself free of peril. With some forethought, she had the colours taken down before ramming the vessel, intent on confusing the Greeks who surrounded her.[56] When the admiral of one of the Greek ships witnessed the ramming, he supposed that Artemisia's ship was either Greek or was commanded by a defector, and turned on the ships nearest hers in the belief that they were Persian or Persian-allied. This enabled Artemisia and her crew to make their escape. Said one of the Persians to Xerxes: 'Master, do you see Artemisia, how well she fights and has sunk an enemy ship?' The king asked whether it truly was Artemisia who had orchestrated this plan. It was still broadly assumed that the ship she had downed was the enemy's. 'Then my men have become women, and my women, men,' Xerxes proclaimed upon receiving confirmation of Artemisia's act. This was not so much a criticism of his men as an acknowledgement of Artemisia's naval prowess.[57] An anonymous work of famous women's deeds rightly evokes her 'personal bravery'.[58] It was later said that Xerxes rewarded Artemisia with a full set of Greek armour while sending the ship's male captain a distaff and spindle.[59]

A great many Persians died at Salamis or while attempting to swim away from it. Atossa alone lost six grandsons in the fight.[60] The Greeks had carried the day, but the vision of Artemisia gasconading in her minor victory riled them so deeply that they moved to put a price of 10,000 drachmas on taking her alive.[61] Few were more relieved at her escape than Xerxes, who was in a perilous position, given that the Greeks were now free to entrap his men by breaking the bridges he had erected between Asia and Europe.

Mardonius – indeed 'all men and women' – urged the Persian king to save face, either by launching an attack on the Peloponnese, or by returning home and sending 300,000 men to deliver the Greek territory to him.[62] As Xerxes contemplated his options, he once again sought Artemisia's guidance. This time, he took care to dismiss his male advisers, so that the two of them could talk alone. It was a difficult decision, Artemisia conceded, but instinct told her that he should march home and leave Mardonius behind to complete what he had proposed. The most important thing was that the Persians had a king to rule them. In burning Athens, Xerxes had done precisely what he had promised to do, and in almost every other matter he had good reason to anticipate a warm reception from his people. This was the best time for him to return home. Artemisia's advice was welcomed by Xerxes, who entrusted his bastard sons to her care, urging her to convey them safely to Ephesus.[63] No other woman played such an important role in his political strategy.

The decisive battle of the Graeco-Persian Wars was fought on land in 479 BC at Plataea, a city already obliterated by the Persians. It began on the lower slopes of Mount Cithaeron and culminated beside the former city itself. In spite of their confidence, the Persians found themselves swiftly overwhelmed by the might of the Spartans, and were forced to flee. For the Greeks, this was, in the words of Herodotus, 'the handsomest victory of all we know'.[64] For the Persians, it was nothing short of a disaster, overshadowing their former achievements and placing them on the losing side of the Wars. Mardonius was among the many who fell in the field. The Hellenes cemented their success with a final naval victory off the Asian coast at Mycale later that year.

Mindful of the need to strengthen their defence for the future, the victorious Athenians oversaw the establishment of an anti-Persia alliance that would become known in the modern world as the Delian League. While they made off with war spoils, it was up to individual Persians to try to save themselves. One woman who had served as concubine to a leading Persian approached the Spartans as a suppliant in her finest clothes and gold jewellery and begged to be spared from enslavement.[65] She had been taken violently from her home on Cos and held as a Persian prisoner. By a stroke of luck, the Spartan commander she approached had been a friend of her father. He showed her mercy by sending her to Aegina. Few other women were so fortunate as to escape enslavement.

Towards the end of Aeschylus' *Persians*, a distressed Atossa tells the ghost of Darius how blessed he had been in life. The real Atossa is thought to have survived just long enough to have witnessed Persia reduced to ruins and her son returned to her, defeated but alive and still king. It is difficult to imagine how she greeted him, but in Aeschylus' play her character makes no secret of her disappointment at his impetuousness and arrogance. The Athenian bias of the tragedy is clear, but it was true that frustration among the vanquished Persians ran extremely high. One of Darius' other sons went so far as to accuse a chief admiral of being worse than a woman. 'Now,' wrote Herodotus a few decades later, 'it is the greatest of all taunts in Persia to be called worse than a woman.'

Women may have played a comparatively minor role in the Graeco-Persian Wars, but they had made their mark both on the battlefield and off it and contributed to the liberation of the cities of Ionia. Statues of Hydna and her father, the brave swimmers who had sabotaged the Persian fleet by swimming out at night, were erected at Delphi. Centuries later, Emperor Nero carried the Hydna back to his palace in Rome, leaving the sculpture of her father behind.[66] Artemisia, who had done so much to aid the Persians at sea, was depicted alongside Mardonius on a white marble portico built at Sparta using war spoils.[67] Centuries later, she became the focus of a legend, according to which she fell in love with a man from Abydos, only to be rejected. Heartbroken Artemisia poked the man's eyes out while he slept and threw herself off the very rock that Sappho allegedly chose for her death-jump in her own throes of unrequited love.[68] The idea of a woman achieving fame for her brilliance – and then losing her mind to passion – was fast becoming a trope.

Back in Susa, about 478 BC, Xerxes became embroiled in a not dissimilar domestic tragedy at the hands of his wife. He had formed a romantic attachment to his sister-in-law, and planned to betroth his son to her daughter, Artaynte, but then he found that he preferred the daughter for himself. He asked young Artaynte what he could give her as a present to most please her. *Your cloak*, she replied. Xerxes' wife Amestris was a renowned weaver, so much so that the various tracts of land she owned were named after pieces of women's clothing, including 'the veil' and, more expansive, 'the girdle of the king's wife'.[69] Amestris had made Xerxes the most colourful and unusual cloak Artaynte had ever seen.[70] How was Xerxes to give it to her without his wife finding out? He tried to persuade the girl to choose something else. He offered her cities, gold, an army. Artaynte wanted only the dream-cloak. Worn down, Xerxes finally handed the item over, but naturally Amestris discovered what had happened and began to plot revenge. Her intended victim was neither Xerxes, nor his paramour, but Artaynte's mother, the original object of his desire.

Every year, on his birthday, Xerxes hosted a banquet at which he distributed gifts to family and friends. For her own present, Amestris requested Artaynte's mother, and Xerxes reluctantly agreed to hand the woman over. Rather than employ her as a slave, as Xerxes might have expected, Amestris had her breasts, nose, lips and tongue cut off and thrown to the dogs.[71] It was the most savage act to be overseen by a woman since Pheretime of Cyrene had her sons' killers impaled together with their wives' breasts. The deceased's widower and sons, namely Xerxes' brother and nephews, reacted to the outrage by travelling to Bactria to stir up a revolt. Xerxes had no option but to send his army after them and kill them. He would cling to power until 465 BC when he was murdered by Artabanus, commander of the royal bodyguard and the most powerful member of the Persian court, who desired the throne himself.

Chapter VIII

A Shared Blanket

Nothing is sweeter than love; all other riches
Come second. From my mouth, even, I drool honey.
It's Nossis who says this, Nossis whom Cyprian Aphrodite doesn't love,
Whose blooms she knows not, whose roses elude her.

Nossis, Poem 1, third century BC

Although the Greeks had triumphed, the history of the Graeco-Persian Wars was written by a native of the losing side. Herodotus of Halicarnassus, born about 484 BC, had been just a boy when most of the battles were fought, and his home city was part of the Persian Empire. He was too young to make sense of the news as it drifted in from Artemisium and Salamis and places that sounded too exotic and beguiling by far to have witnessed such bloodshed. Although he was able to compose his account with some even-handedness from the vantage point of middle age, he felt no particular embarrassment in laying bare his still-childlike fascination with Artemisia, the adamantine fellow Halicarnassan who had steered such a valiant course at sea and exerted a rare female influence upon the Persian campaign. What became of his queen after she led Xerxes' children to safety, Herodotus did not record, but within a few decades of her return to Asia Minor, a tyrant named Lygdamis – her son, grandson or possibly nephew – was in power.

Life in Halicarnassus was to be very different after the wars. No longer subject to control by Persia, Artemisia's former kingdom came within the orbit of Greece as the Hellenes built up their defensive alliance with the liberated cities of Ionia and Asia Minor. The establishment of the so-called Delian League on Delos in 478 BC coincided with a period of unprecedented turbulence in Halicarnassus. While Herodotus left for the Greek island of Samos, one of his cousins, a celebrated poet named Panyassis, stayed behind only to be killed by Lygdamis' regime.[1] According to a late biography, the historian returned home in the wake of the tragedy and succeeded in driving the tyrant from power.[2] If this is true, which it may well be, he would not have acted alone. In the most probable scenario, Herodotus worked within a faction as part of a larger Athens-backed campaign to remove the tyranny so as to bring Halicarnassus more securely under the influence of the new alliance.

Leaving his home for a second time, Herodotus made his way across the seas to Thurii, in the foot of Italy, where he remained a good while. A century later, Aristotle would describe him simply as 'Herodotus of Thurii'.[3] The colony was founded in the period Herodotus arrived, circa 444 BC, predominantly by Athenians.[4] Since the late eighth century BC, migrants from Greece and the Near East had arrived in numbers to settle in this region of Magna Graecia, establishing themselves at Sybaris, Cumae, Croton and other cities.[5] While Herodotus wrote little of Thurii itself, he was perfectly placed to witness the extraordinary period of change endured by its residents' oldest trading partners, the Etruscans.[6]

Long before the rise of Rome, the Etruscans dominated the Italian mainland and filled it with a culture in which women were not only visible, but celebrated. Having come to prominence by 900 BC, they had extended their reach from north of the River Arno in the area of modern Tuscany to the Bay of Naples in the south. In the eighth century BC, when Rome was just one of a number of developing Italian settlements, they had established a string of successful communities between the Po and the Tiber in the nearby region of Etruria, founding the cities of Caere, Veii, Tarquinii, Vulci and Poggio Civitate (in Murlo, Siena).[7] They had also forged an alliance with the people of Carthage (modern Tunis), who conquered Sardinia to the Etruscans' further advantage.

Greek speakers who encountered these domineering Etruscans could not help but wonder where they came from. A lesser-known ancient historian from Halicarnassus speculated that they had sprung from 'Pelasgian' Greeks, probably of Thrace, who had settled at Croton near Thurii before spreading northwards through Italy.[8] The Etruscan language was non-Indo-European. Looking around him, Herodotus could not believe that the Etruscans were so local, and traced their origins to Croesus' former kingdom of Lydia. Natives of Thurii had told him that a terrible famine had struck in the second millennium BC and forced half of their population to sail away from Asia Minor and re-establish themselves in Italy.[9] Selected by lot, the travellers were led by a Lydian prince named Tyrrhenus; the Greeks knew the Etruscans as 'Tyrrhenians'. Modern science has lent some credence to the story. In 2007 a genetic variant in the DNA of men whose families had lived in a town in Tuscany for at least three generations was found to be common only to native Turks, and closest to that of residents of Izmir, which lay in ancient Lydia.[10] And almost 60 per cent of the mitochondrial DNA in cattle in the region of ancient Etruria matched that of cattle in Asia Minor, making it credible that the plague-fleeing Lydians took their livestock with them.[11] The implications and reliability of these results have not gone unquestioned, however, and the possibility remains that the Etruscans were rather indigenous to central Italy, or had their origins in Northern Europe. If the Lydian connection is taken seriously, then the presence of maternal mitochondrial DNA in the scientific samples suggests that women were among the migrants.[12]

Origins aside, Etruscan women fascinated Greek men because they seemed so otherworldly – so sexual and brazen. One Greek author claimed that they raised their children communally because they could rarely be sure of their paternity; this was not surprising considering that they went to bed with men quite openly after parties.[13] He said that they preened themselves endlessly and exercised naked even though members of the opposite sex were watching. They offered toasts, he said, whenever the fancy took them, and sat beneath the same blankets as their husbands at dinner. Most shocking of all was that much of this was true.

Etruscan women did pay close attention to the way they looked. They dressed extravagantly in long tunics and cloaks and donned boat-shaped caps known to the Romans as *tutuli*. They wore their hair in single long plaits and put on slipper-like shoes with elegant upturned toes. The striking sarcophagus of Seianti Hanunia Tlesnasa, now in the British Museum, is topped by a sculpture of the fifty-year-old deceased woman in her younger years wearing fine jewellery and the kind of make-up that only a practised hand could apply.[14]

It is unlikely that women raised their children communally or exercised with men, but they liked nothing better than to drink and dine with them. In early Rome, women would sit decorously upright while their husbands reclined to eat, but in Etruria, women and men relaxed together, often, as noted, beneath a single blanket. A lovely fresco from a tomb in the Etruscan city of Tarquinii depicts a bearded man reclining on his left elbow and his beautifully dressed wife reclining on her right. They look at one another affectionately while he tenderly strokes her face.[15] They are not alone. A slave is at hand to ladle out their wine and a dog waits patiently for crumbs. Nearby, a similarly dressed woman gazes at a naked man, who is perched on her lap in a complete reversal of what a Greek viewer was primed to expect. Some sarcophagi featured intimate carvings of husbands and wives embracing in bed.[16]

The sexual openness of the Etruscans, whatever the Greeks said, was more loving than lewd. Even their most explicit art was charming. An incense burner discovered in an eighth-century BC tomb near Lake Bolsena, north of Rome, was adorned with a series of male and female figures touching their own and each other's genitals and breasts.[17] It would be perverse to speak of consent in relation to these tiny individuals, but they appear to be free and inquisitive and thoroughly enjoying themselves. The object was interred with the remains of a wealthy woman; jewels and metal brooches were also discovered around her.[18] Like the Egyptians, the Etruscans gave their dead the objects they believed would be most useful in the afterlife – funeral urns were sometimes even dressed in women's or men's clothing – so it is intriguing that this particular incense burner with its pulse-quickening decoration was chosen to accompany the woman on her way.[19] We may assume that women appreciated erotic art for the simple reason that it captured one of many interlocking aspects of their lives. The Etruscans were never so prudish as to pretend that lovers could not also be companions and friends. A beautiful bronze mirror from Praeneste in Lazio, central Italy, shows a young man and woman, both nude on the top half, playing a backgammon-like game at a table.[20] 'I'm going to win,' the woman says in the inscription. 'I don't doubt it,' he replies.

Etruscan women still maintained their own sphere as in other parts of the world. The lady with the incense burner also had a shuttle and spindle in her tomb. Spindles, distaffs, loom weights and whorls are among the most common finds in the graves of elite Etruscan women. Part of an extraordinary bronze *tintinnabulum* or wind chime placed in a tomb near modern Bologna in the late seventh or early sixth century BC documented the process by which the Etruscans produced their tapestries.[21] One scene on the *tintinnabulum* shows a woman in profile spinning wool using a spindle and distaff. Beneath her, in the lower register of the image, two women sit facing one another in comfortable, highly decorated curve-backed chairs, each pulling onto her spindle skeins of wool from a large communal jar positioned at the centre of the room. The other side of the object features two more pairs of women working together beside high-warp vertical looms. Their weaving is done in unison and is a clearly sociable activity.

The intricately designed *tintinnabulum* demonstrated Etruscan metalwork as well as weaving. The Etruscans were so adroit at the former that they were among the first pioneers of dentistry and orthodontics, fashioning a wide range of gold bands, bridges and braces to fill gaps in the gums or to secure loose teeth.[22] Wealthy women – and only women – wore gold bands in place of missing teeth.[23] One such device, found in a tomb in Etruria and thought to date from the early fifth century BC, held an anterior tooth in place in a woman's mouth by looping around two of her more stable teeth.[24] Other appliances incorporated false gold teeth. None of these pieces was subtle. It would have required some confidence to sport one. Toothsome additions were splendidly set off by chunky gold jewellery and hoop earrings.[25]

The visibility of women in Etruscan society was reflected in the use of matronymics. By contrast with the Romans, who would simply bestow upon their daughters the female form of their father's familial name – a Claudius might find it useful to distinguish his daughters as Claudia, Claudia Two (Secunda) and Claudia Three (Tertia) – the Etruscans had given names for girls. These names were often added to inscriptions on tombs and vases.[26] Statue bases have been discovered bearing the names of former slave women as well as freeborn women. One Kanuta, a freedwoman (ex-slave) who married a man with an Etruscan name, Aranth Pinie, dedicated a statue in the late sixth century BC at Volsinii (in Orvieto).[27]

It was unusual among ancient societies for the mother of a deceased man to be named together with the father on his tomb, but in Etruscan culture this was commonplace. Motherhood was considered important. Household objects were commonly adorned with scenes of childbearing and nursing.[28] Like the Minoans, the Etruscans revered Eileithyia, goddess of childbirth, and are thought to have honoured her alongside Leukothea, a goddess of the sea, and Uni, the Etruscan equivalent of Hera/Juno, at an important sanctuary in the port town of Pyrgi (Santa Severa), Caere, north-west of Rome.[29] Three gold tablets in the National Etruscan Museum in Rome reveal that a temple to Uni in her dual guise as the eastern goddess Astarte was constructed in the same area.[30] They were written in both Etruscan and Phoenician and so reveal close contact between the two peoples.

Mothers appear to have dedicated statuettes of their sons to the gods, presumably in prayer or thanksgiving for their health and well-being, or for that of their spirits. An 8-centimetre bronze dating to the late fourth century BC was moulded to resemble a young boy holding fruit in his hands. The inscription upon it bore the name of a woman, Larthia Ateinei, and a god, probably a figure from the Underworld.[31] It has been noted that, on the evidence so far found, Etruscan women appear not to have dedicated statues of themselves or of their daughters.[32]

The city of Locri in Magna Graecia nurtured some particularly artistic women. An aristocratic and highly educated Greek woman named Nossis found fame here around 300 BC for her epigrams. She wrote in praise of love – nothing was sweeter – and of the Olympian goddesses.[33] She described herself weaving and dedicating a robe to Zeus' wife Hera in a shrine.[34] She wrote of a woman named Kallo presenting Aphrodite with a portrait she considered to be very lifelike.[35] Another woman, Polyarkhis, won Nonnis' admiration for dedicating a golden statue to Aphrodite paid for out of the profits of prostitution.[36] Women were at the heart of Nonnis' poetry, which was read and enjoyed by men, too. Her literary interests in art and patronage were typical of her city and culture.

There is good evidence of literacy among servile as well as non-servile women in central Italy. A large roof tile survives from Pietrabbondante, near Abruzzo, bearing the shoeprints and inscriptions of two female tile-makers.[37] One of the slaves was named Amica and the other Detfri. The former wrote in Latin and the second in Oscan, and yet they could clearly communicate with one another, for they left similar messages in the wet tile. Each wrote her name followed by a line to confirm that they were signing the object. Detfri clarified that she was doing so with her foot.

The Etruscans had long exported their artistic wares overseas, though by the time Herodotus arrived in southern Italy their trade with Greece had slowed and the quality of the goods they produced and deposited in their tombs had deteriorated. In 474 BC, Hiero, tyrant king of Syracuse, had led the navies of Syracuse and Cumae to victory over the Etruscans at sea, weakening them and rendering them vulnerable to further attack. At the beginning of the fourth century, the Etruscans of Veii would be battled down by the ascendant Romans, marking a significant turning point in their fortunes. Etruria hovered on the precipice of decline. Herodotus' relocation from Halicarnassus following Artemisia's demise coincided with the beginning of the Etruscans' fall following an astonishing period of supremacy.

Romans traced the origins of their hostilities with the Etruscans to their legendary early history and the contest for a woman's hand in marriage. The conflict formed an integral part of their foundation story which otherwise had its roots in Homer. We have to look forward several centuries to Virgil's *Aeneid* to find a satisfyingly complete telling of this story. Arranged across twelve books, the first-century BC epic follows Aeneas, the son of Venus and the mortal Anchises, as he leads a band of refugees free from burning Troy at the end of the Trojan War in search of a new home. By the time he has crossed the border of the city, Aeneas is a widower, his wife Creusa lost and presumed dead. Their son Ascanius is protected by the survivors. After making false starts in Carthage and Sicily, the party lands at Latium in Italy, where a king named Latinus holds sway.[38] Although his daughter Lavinia is already betrothed to a man named Turnus, Latinus agrees that she can marry Aeneas so as to seal an alliance with the incoming heroes. Turnus, unsurprisingly, is furious. In the second half of the poem, he declares war, prevailing upon the Etruscans of Caere for support, knowing full well that the Trojans threaten their supremacy as well. As the Trojans battle down Turnus and his men, they suffer heavy losses, the heaviest of all being Aeneas himself.

Ascanius is still just a boy, so it follows that his stepmother, Lavinia, should be regent. 'Lavinia had such innate quality,' wrote the Roman historian Livy, a younger contemporary of Virgil, in his seminal history of Rome, 'that the Latin kingdom of his father and grandfather was preserved intact for the boy.'[39] Lavinia was accordingly hailed a heroine of early Rome. Without her, Aeneas' dream would have been thwarted, his legacy unfulfilled. Not a single attack was made on her people by the Etruscans from the other side of the Tiber for the duration of her rule. Lavinia went down in history as a highly capable pacifist.

There is a problem that confronts every reader of ancient history who seeks to discover how the Romans emerged from the Etruscans' shadow to dominate the Italian mainland. Rome's earliest historians found themselves not merely reluctant, but incapable of separating truth from legend. For the now obscure historians Quintus Fabius Pictor and Lucius Cincius Alimentus in the third century BC, as well as for Livy, Dionysius of Halicarnassus and many other respected Romans, the journey of Aeneas and regency of Lavinia constituted credible passages in history. The opening books of Livy's 142-volume history *ab urbe condita*, 'from the foundation of the city', are consequently saturated in myth. They describe Ascanius stepping into Lavinia's role as soon as he has come of age and going on to found a new city, Alba Longa, at the foot of the Alban Hills, 20 kilometres south-east of modern Rome. They describe Ascanius being succeeded by a son, Silvius, and Silvius being succeeded by his son, Aeneas Silvius, and Aeneas Silvius being succeeded by a son also, Latinus Silvius. Power passes down Aeneas' male line until one of the rulers, Numitor, is overthrown by his younger brother, who murders his nephews and makes his niece, Numitor's daughter Rhea Silvia, a Vestal Virgin. Rhea Silvia is the future mother of the founder of Rome. There is no evidence that any of these people existed. Most likely they did not.

Although the two most prominent women in this early part of Rome's 'history', Lavinia and Rhea Silvia, were fictional characters, aspects of their story were based in reality. Lavinia's home town of Latium prided itself historically upon the accomplishments of its local women. The earliest known piece of alphabetic Greek writing in all of Italy has been discovered here and relates to a woman who died about 775 BC.[40] The inscription, which appears on a terracotta urn in the necropolis of Osteria dell'Osa, 20 kilometres east of Rome, spells out the word EYLIN, which has been interpreted as an Etruscan form of the Greek word for 'good spinner' or 'weaving well'. While the word evidently referred to the woman cremated in the jar, the epithet was also associated with the spinning of fate and was sometimes used of the birth goddess Eileithyia, who set each person's fate in motion.[41] A woman was not just a weaver of thread, she was a weaver of a much larger story.

Rhea Silvia was identified as a Vestal Virgin by Livy. Six women at a time were selected to be Vestals throughout Rome's history, most usually from wealthy, influential families. They served as revered priestesses of the hearth-goddess Vesta, sister of Jupiter, for a minimum of thirty years and were entitled to make their own wills. While most other women in Rome were watched over by male 'guardians', usually their fathers or husbands, who limited their movements through the city, the Vestal Virgins were not; their lives were deemed restrictive enough already. The earliest Vestals resided in a building known as the Regia on the edge of what became the Roman Forum, but by about 575 BC a circular temple had been built for them at the foot of the Palatine Hill nearby.[42] The women were responsible for keeping the flame of the goddess alight for the well-being of Rome. Any extinction of the flame was interpreted as a bad omen for the city and as a reflection of the impurity of one or more of the priestesses. Lapsed Virgins – or Virgins merely suspected of losing their sexual purity – could be punished by being buried alive. The rationale behind this practice was that a woman who broke her vow of chastity was no longer inviolable as she had sinned against the very gods who entrusted her with powers.[43]

The mythical Vestal Rhea Silvia was presented as a lapsed Virgin, though she did not lose her virginity voluntarily. The war god Mars raped and impregnated her.[44] The Vestal was subsequently imprisoned and her twin sons, Romulus and Remus, carried away to be drowned in the River Tiber. As so often in classical myth, the second part of the plan was unfulfilled, and the Moses basket in which the boys lay drifted gently onto dry land. While few images were more famous in Rome than that of a she-wolf suckling the infants and thereby saving their lives, the lupine episode was but a brief one.[45] Before long, a shepherd chanced upon the scene and carried the babies home to be raised by his wife Larentia. The future founder of Rome would never have survived had it not been for the two females: the wolf and the mortal.

The Romans were hard-pressed to unite the legend of Aeneas with the tale of Romulus, Remus and the she-wolf. The timelines of the two foundation stories were hopelessly incompatible. Nonetheless, writers imagined the twins, powered by their wolf milk and bellicose bloodline, throwing their support behind Aeneas' descendant Numitor and reinstating him as king of Alba Longa. To commemorate their astonishing survival as infants, each twin then founded a city, Romulus on the Palatine Hill, and Remus on the Aventine Hill, whereupon a power struggle erupted between them. When Remus leapt mockingly over his brother's rising walls, Romulus took offence and, in a fit of rage, cut him down. And so it was that Romulus became king of Rome. The city that bore his name was later given an official foundation date of 753 BC.

Peeling back the layers of legend woven over this moment in history, it is clear that there was a significant settlement on the Palatine Hill – Romulus' hill – by the eighth century BC. While the site had been in use since the Late Bronze Age, the earliest domestic dwellings so far discovered on the mount date to the ninth century BC and took the form of timber-framed huts with thatched roofs. One of these constructions was still standing in the fourth century AD because it was popularly believed to have been Romulus' own dwelling. The early houses overlooked a large burial ground. By contrast with the Etruscans with their elaborately painted tombs and intricate tomb goods, the earliest Romans were usually cremated or interred in oak-tree logs with fairly rudimentary objects, such as pieces of pottery and brooch pins. As in Greece, however, the eighth century BC witnessed considerable change, and the burial ground was steadily redeveloped into a public square. The foundations of the Roman Forum – the commercial and legal centre of Rome – were probably laid at the close of the century. A furrow was drawn around the perimeter of the nascent city and a series of stones positioned at the foot of the Palatine Hill to mark the boundary.[46] As Cicero later noted, Rome was perfectly positioned for trade on the bank of the Tiber, rendering it from the very beginning a likely centre of power.[47]

The earliest stages in the political development of Rome were manifestly male. Romulus was said to have established a primary set of laws, appointed the first hundred senators known as *patres* (their descendants would be the 'patricians' or aristocrats of Rome), and selected twelve officers known as lictors, who probably came from the same class of people from which the Etruscans chose their own magistrates.[48] But how was Rome to develop and grow without women? The question occurred as an afterthought.

The story that came to be told of the origins of women in Rome may have been an addendum to the narrative of Romulus, but it proved equally enduring and violent. Still millennia later, it has the power to unsettle, not because it preserves an accurate chronicle of events, necessarily, but because it captures a universal truth about the status of women in times of war and conquest, and their unique vulnerability when they are made to trust the wrong people.

At the beginning, Romulus is confounded to discover that the peoples of neighbouring towns have relatively little appetite for drawing up marriage contracts between their finest women and his male citizens. As far as the neighbouring rulers are concerned, the Romans ought simply to open their doors to women who are in need of sanctuary. Women eager to escape poverty or other troubles would surely flock to the new city and be only too happy to find stability through marriage. Why force the issue? Their response strikes Romulus as the height of impertinence. He cannot countenance the idea of welcoming unfortunate and desperate women to his city to be wives to his excellent men. And so he proposes to host some games. Invitations are issued far and wide, and many people accept, but in this story the ones that matter are the Sabines. They lived historically just east of the Tiber, next to Etruria. They have few qualms about setting out all together – men, women, children – to join in the entertainment.

The Sabines place their trust in the Romans and the Romans almost immediately break it. No sooner have the guests relaxed than a signal is raised and Romulus' men make off with the Sabine women. They seize them by force, reserving the prettiest for the patricians, and bring them before Romulus so that he can address them in person and offer something by way of an explanation. They have been taken, Romulus tells them, because their parents were too proud. Had they only welcomed the Romans into their families, they would never have had to endure the sight of their daughters being dragged away. Now that they were there, Romulus told the women, they were to live honourably as wives and, even better, become mothers to Roman kin. They could even have a share in the men's property as a special privilege.

Writing centuries later, Livy claimed that 'the blandishments of their husbands sanitised the deed through conscientiousness and passion; blandishments are very effective at appealing to a woman's character.'[49] In other words, the women were taken violently, and provided with an excuse in the aftermath of the crime. No woman reading Livy's account could possibly have believed that the Sabines were appeased by such words; desire offered no grounds for rape. For Livy, however, the act was justified by the need to populate the new city, and emolliated by Romulus' words. It was committed 'not through hubristic daring', added Plutarch a century later, 'but out of necessity'.[50] The male writers of Rome were incapable of understanding the significance of what had occurred for these women's livelihoods.

Whether the story was an elaboration of real events, or simply an aetiology – an origin tale – composed to account for the arrival of real Sabines and women in Rome, it transcended history. Ovid, writing centuries after the alleged events, likened the women to doves attempting to elude an eagle, and to lambs struggling to escape the hungry mouth of a wolf. Being Ovid, he could not help but subvert the image, adding how well fear became the women as they turned pallid in their desperation.[51] Others took a more sympathetic approach. The late sixteenth-century sculptor Giambologna was just one in a long line of artists to capture the struggle and distress of a Sabine, depicted nude, as she was carried away in a Roman man's muscular grip. The Sabine women came to encapsulate the words *raptus* and *raptio*, which in Latin described both the act of being seized, and rape itself.

The families of the Sabine women were certainly not ready to accept Romulus' overtures and forgive him. The two sides were soon at war. Caught up unwillingly in this conflict, the Sabine women 'took themselves bravely into the midst of soaring missiles . . . their hair flying everywhere and their clothes ripped,' as Livy put it, doubtful that the battleground was any place for a hairnet.[52] In one of the most celebrated but surely mythical episodes of the war, a young noblewoman named Tarpeia opened the doors of Rome to the leader of the Sabines, eager to be rewarded with some of the beautiful gold jewellery worn by Sabine men. Historians could not agree on her precise role in the ensuing events, but Tarpeia was credited with ending the Sabines' siege of Rome and honoured as such for centuries after her death. She was hailed a heroine in spite of her betrayal of her home city. She had acted, after all, in the interest of peace.

It was left to another woman to bring the war to a conclusion. Hersilia was Romulus' wife. She was already married with a daughter when he first met her, but as his actions towards her fellow Sabines showed, Romulus was seldom deterred by such formalities.[53] Hersilia, taking pity on the women of her country, petitioned her new husband on their behalf to make peace with their parents. It was said that she also urged Romulus to grant them citizenship of Rome. It is difficult to believe that a woman who witnessed her own daughter being seized by the Romans would be so willing to sue for peace, but perhaps, after so much bloodshed, peace was the most anyone could truly hope for. Romulus issued the citizenship and the Sabines and Romans were finally united by a peace treaty as well as treaties of marriage.[54] Had it not been for Hersilia and the Sabine women there would have been no Rome in this story.

The identities of the majority of the Sabine women involved in the war, if it ever happened, were lost to history. When it came to dividing the three existing Roman tribes into new *curiae* (wards) for political purposes, however, Romulus could not help but think of their service. The thirty *curiae* bore Sabine women's names. Most of these, too, have been lost, but one, devastatingly, was simply 'Rapta' – 'The Seized Woman'.

The Sabines became firmly integrated into the history of Rome when Romulus died and was succeeded by a Sabine king named Numa Pompilius. It is with Numa that the narrative of early Rome begins to shift steadily, tentatively, from the mythological to the historical realm.

Numa was viewed as the second king to have ruled Rome between the mid-eighth and late sixth centuries BC. Although he remains a shadowy figure in himself, he was widely credited with establishing Rome's priestly offices and constructing the Temple of Janus, the double-faced god of gateways, beginnings and endings. The temple occupied a particularly important position in the city's political and cultural life. Its doors were kept open at all times but ceremoniously closed in a symbolic gesture when peace was declared across Rome and her dominions.[55] Between the rule of Numa and the first emperor, Augustus, they were shut only twice. The first Regia, where the king presided over religious rites, was constructed between the Roman Forum and the Sacred Way in the late seventh century BC. A terracotta sculptural frieze, believed to have adorned it, showed a Minotaur.[56] The historicity of Rome's early kings is supported by a piece of pottery discovered at the site inscribed with the Latin word *rex* or 'king'.

Within the traditional narrative of kingly successions, it can be easy to forget that women, too, were at the centre of life in early Rome. There was one woman in particular who achieved notoriety for setting an example to others and willingly making the transition from the world of the Etruscans to the developing world of Rome. Her name was Tanaquil, and she came from Tarquinii, the Etruscan town on the west coast of central Italy. Although her historicity has also been questioned, there is arguably enough detail in the sources – and enough tributes to her in the years after she lived – to restore her to the historical narrative of the sixth century BC.

Claudius, fourth emperor of Rome, certainly believed in Tanaquil's existence. He had an intense interest in both family history and Etruscan history. His first wife Plautia Urgulanilla was Etruscan and perhaps inspired him to write his now-lost twenty-volume history of the Etruscan people. Familiar with Etruscan sources (he also produced an Etruscan dictionary), Claudius identified Tanaquil as the wife of a man named Lucumo, the son of a well-born but penniless Etruscan mother and a Corinthian father named Demaratus.[57] Demaratus was also attested in other sources. He had come over to Italy with a group of sculptors and helped introduce plastic art to the country.[58] He was clearly a highly skilled man, but even so his status as an immigrant cast a shadow over his son's reputation at Tarquinii, and rendered him an outsider. This troubled Tanaquil even more than it did Lucumo, and it was allegedly at her suggestion that they relocated to Rome in search of a better life.[59]

Tanaquil was described historically as *bona femina*, a good woman or wife. She washed and anointed her husband.[60] Like most women from Tarquinii (over three-quarters of the female burials there have been found to contain textile tools) she also made and repaired his clothes.[61] But Tanaquil's particular flair for design led her to secure a legacy beyond that of her husband's seamstress. Astonishingly, Tanaquil was credited with inventing the *tunica recta* ('straight tunic'), a garment worn by both women on the eve of their wedding and boys as they marked the transition to manhood in Rome. It is unclear whether 'straight' referred to the cut of the cloth or the way it hung from the body, but the piece was easily recognisable at the time as part of the ceremonial dress. Tanaquil was also believed to have inspired the Roman custom by which women carried a distaff and spindle with thread during their wedding processions. Brides would traditionally wreathe their new husband's door with wool for good luck.[62] Such was the importance of these inventions that a bronze statue of Tanaquil holding her distaff, spindle and wool was erected in a temple of a Sabine god on Rome's Quirinal Hill, and remained standing until at least the first century AD.[63]

More significant still to Tanaquil's enduring reputation was the toga displayed in the Temple of Fortuna in Rome. Tanaquil wove it for her future son-in-law Servius Tullius (known to the Etruscans as Mastarna), a bright young man who was widely rumoured to be the son of a slave and a female prisoner of war named Ocrisia, who had entered Tanaquil's service.[64] Although his status was considerably lower than her own, Tanaquil believed that the boy enjoyed some kind of divine support, and had agreed to help raise him before seeing him marry her daughter Tarquinia.

However influential a figure he was among the Etruscans, Servius Tullius was able to establish himself in Rome only after his father-in-law became locked in a dispute over the kingship. On arriving in the new city, the half-Corinthian outcast Lucumo had adopted a Roman name, Lucius Tarquinius Priscus, and through his wealth and kindness, secured a job as guardian to the presiding king's children. When the king died, the increasingly ambitious Lucius Tarquinius sent the princes on a hunting expedition, and set about ingratiating himself with the Roman people. His popularity bought him the throne. Naturally, his coming to power did not sit well with the two boys, who plotted to bring him down. As if it was not painful enough to see a man with Greek blood in their father's palace, it now looked as though Servius Tullius, a son of slaves, was being lined up to succeed him.

The princes carried out their coup. As Tarquinius lay in a pool of his own blood, Tanaquil prepared dressings for his wounds, desperate to do something. At the same time, with remarkable clear-headedness, she called her son-in-law to the bedchamber. If he should see the king as he died, she realised, he would be only more inflamed to avenge the murder. With still greater cunning, Tanaquil moved to the window of the palace and addressed the people as they gathered anxiously below. Her husband's life hung in the balance, she announced, but she was confident that his wounds would heal. In the meantime, she said, it was his majesty's express instructions that they obey Servius Tullius in his place. Tanaquil thereby delayed announcing the news of her husband's death to smooth the transition of power to her son-in-law. Although Servius proceeded to have a law passed confirming his right to rule, Cicero would later identify him as the first man to govern with the support of the people rather than official legal backing.[65]

The rule of Servius Tullius, traditionally dated from 579 BC, was associated with a number of new additions to Rome. The king was held responsible for pushing out the boundaries of the city so as to incorporate the Viminal and Esquiline hills for housing, though in reality Rome probably had its full complement of seven hills by 600 BC, a little before Servius' putative dates.[66] The Etruscan king was also credited with establishing the first Roman census; a people's – albeit elite people's – assembly known as the *comitia centuriata*; and the first boundary line since Romulus. The so-called *pomerium* served as a sacred perimeter to the city. A number of new temples were also built in the period associated with Servius' rule, including those of Diana and Fortuna, where Tanaquil's weaving was displayed. And yet it was the tall tale of Servius' daughters that made the deepest impression upon Roman historians.

The two women, both named Tullia, were married to two brothers, their uncles Lucius Tarquinius and Arruns, sons of the late king Tarquinius Priscus, who had died in Tanaquil's arms.[67] The four individuals could not be more different from one another. While the younger and more ambitious Tullia was frustrated to find her husband Arruns lacking in drive, Lucius Tarquinius had real fire in his belly, which the elder Tullia did little to nurture. The more she saw of her brother-in-law, indeed, the more the younger Tullia felt that she ought to be with him instead. With her help, she believed, he would be capable of great things. Tarquinius agreed, and together they plotted the murder of their brother and sister respectively, their hearts set firmly on power.

The story was clearly inspired by that of Tanaquil.[68] Within the fiction of the narrative, indeed, Tullia the younger is even spurred on by her irritation at Tanaquil's success. It pains her that an Etruscan woman has succeeded in seeing her son-in-law rise to the throne, whereas she, a royal Roman, lacks the authority to confer or remove power.[69] Tullia therefore bullies Tarquinius into bringing charges against her own father, King Servius, with a view to removing him from the throne. At first, Tarquinius attempts the diplomatic route, calling into question the legitimacy of the law Servius Tullius had passed at the beginning of his reign, and highlighting his failure to consult the Senate before distributing land to the people in a reputation-enhancing move.[70] Then, Tarquinius resorts to violence, raging, without a hint of irony, that a king should owe his success to a mere woman. He picks up the older man and throws him down the stairs of the Senate House. The construction of the Senate headquarters belongs to roughly the period this story was set. Dating to about 600 BC, the building was rectangular in shape with a gabled roof, and large enough to accommodate 300 men.[71] It stood at one edge of the Roman Forum, which meant that as Servius fell he would have rolled directly into the most public space in the city. Tarquinius had gathered a group of armed men, who now stepped forward and finished Servius off.

Whose idea was this but Tullia the younger's? It was, Livy said, wholly in keeping with her wicked nature. Women had no place in the Senate House, which served also as a court of law, but Tullia had travelled there anyway and proclaimed her new husband Tarquinius king. Propelled 'by the avenging spirits of her sister and husband', she even had the driver of her carriage run over her father's corpse, before sweeping up some of his blood as an offering to her household gods. The street in which this incident occurred, close to the site where the Colosseum would be built in the first century AD, was named Vicus Sceleratus, 'The Street of the Crime'. The crime was remembered principally as a woman's.

As king from about 535 BC, Tullia's husband was known as Tarquinius Superbus, or Tarquin the Proud. He allegedly earned his sobriquet by denying his father-in-law due burial and proceeding to rule by fear. He made a peace treaty with the Etruscans and called upon craftsmen from Etruria to adorn a temple he established to Jupiter on the Capitoline Hill as a monument to his rule. The temple was distinguished by its fine Etruscan detailing. The work was paid for out of the public treasury and completed under duress by the common people, the plebeians, who were also instructed to dig the Cloaca Maxima, the first public sewer in Rome. Architecturally, the city was starting to take shape in this period, which may indicate that the leadership was more assured than the sources on these fraught family battles suggest.

The most famous and important story attached to the rule of Tarquinius Superbus concerned the sexual assault carried out on a woman by one of his sons. This episode, known to later writers and artists as the Rape of Lucretia, was significant because it presaged a profound moment in the history of Rome: the birth of the Republic. It could even be argued that, without Lucretia, there would have been no Roman Republic at all.

To begin with, the prince, Sextus, hosts a dinner. As he and his friends settle into their food and wine the conversation turns naturally enough to their wives at home. They grow more and more drunk until their descriptions turn to boasts, and their boasts to a contest to decide which of them truly is married to the most virtuous woman. A senator named Collatinus pledges to prove that his wife is worthiest of all. They should all go and spy on their spouses, he suggests, and test how honourable they are. And so they go. Sure enough, while most of the women are found feasting, Collatinus' wife Lucretia is weaving at her home in Collatia, north-east of the city.

Seeing as they are there, the men agree to spend the night at Collatinus' house. This means that when Sextus returns a few days later, his pulse quickened by the sight of Lucretia at her loom, he is already familiar to the household. He has some dinner before making his way to the bedchamber he had visited with Collatinus earlier. Lucretia is alone. Sextus draws his sword so as to silence her and attempts to coax her into having sex with him. Lucretia says no. Finding her resolute, Sextus threatens to kill a male slave and place his body beside her own, so that everyone will think that she has been killed *in flagrante* and consider her an adulteress. Lucretia feels that she has no choice but to agree to his demands. She is raped.

Somehow, Lucretia finds the strength to send a message to her father and husband, asking that they come to her with reinforcements because something terrible has happened. Four men arrive and find her in tears. For all the shame she feels, Lucretia swears openly that, while her body was defiled, her mind was not. Her argument – that rape does not take away one's purity or sully the victim so as to render them in any way less valuable or complete – would prove enormously influential down the decades, not least during the Fall of Rome, when nuns were assaulted by invading forces. Lucretia's words would indeed help to negate the prevalent belief that a woman who had been taken by force lost her virtue – was damaged goods – on the grounds that she had engaged in extramarital sex. It was not beyond men of the period to assume that women who had been raped had taken some pleasure in a forbidden act.

When Lucretia implores her husband and father to take vengeance on Sextus Tarquin, they agree to do so, declaring that 'no unchaste woman shall live by Lucretia's example'.[72] Their actions are welcome but their words show how thoroughly they miss the point. They are propelled more by the fear that Lucretia's experience could be hijacked by women less virtuous than by the desire to punish her attacker. Before they have so much as laid hands on the prince, Lucretia has taken a knife to her chest, and wounded herself fatally.

One of Sextus' cousins, Lucius Junius Brutus, an ancestor of the Brutus who would one day plot the assassination of Julius Caesar, arrives and removes the weapon from Lucretia's body. On her blood he swears that he will drive out the king, his wife – their entire family – and abolish Rome's monarchy once and for all. His words, and Lucretia's death, will not be in vain. Lucretia's body is carried to the forum so that everyone can see the consequences of Sextus' crime. This allows Brutus to work on the passion of the crowd and to speak at length. The brutality of the prince; the suffering of noble Lucretia; the agony her death caused. These were grounds, he stressed, for revolution!

Seldom had a man spoken so extensively of a woman in public. Brutus might have limited himself to expounding the evils of Sextus' crime, but Lucretia's death had provided him with an opportunity and an ambition beyond that of revenge. He was determined to whip up resentment towards the king himself. And so, he reminded the gathered Romans of how wretchedly they had toiled over the Cloaca Maxima. What reward had they for their efforts? What had they to gain from living under a king at all? The crowd was impressionable and quickly swayed. With the help of forces gathered from both inside and beyond Rome, Brutus succeeded in deposing the royal family and driving them into exile. Sextus Tarquinius was killed for old feuds. And so it was that 244 years of monarchy were brought to an end for the sake of one woman's virtue. The Roman historians would date this seismic event to 509 BC.

How much of this could Lucretia have foreseen? She might have anticipated that her instructions to her father and husband would spark civil unrest. But that she should set in train the process by which Rome became a republic could not possibly have crossed her mind. For later Romans, Lucretia's role in this transition was beyond doubt. As one historian put it, 'by so courageous a death, she granted the Roman people a reason to change rulership by king to rulership by consul'.[73] The nature of Lucretia's ordeal contributed to the negative emotions stirred by the prospect of monarchy in later Roman thought. After centuries of kings, the Romans developed a horror of returning to one-man rule in any form. Their distaste for it was so deep-seated that it appeared to flow through their blood. Such a visceral reaction was heavily shaped by the story of Lucretia.

There was certainly no place for the politics exercised by the Etruscan kings after the revolt. Rome was now *res publica* – literally 'the affairs of the people' – which was technically a misnomer. Although power would no longer be vested in one man, the 300 senators who stepped into the breach were hardly representative of 'the people' of Rome. Every year, they elected as their leaders two senior magistrates, initially known as praetors but later as consuls, and continued to bar women from the Senate House. This is why the story of Lucretia is so important. The first pair to take the helm of the Senate were Brutus and Collatinus. They owed their positions – and the Senate their enduring authority – to her.

Whether Lucretia was based in history, as Tanaquil most likely was, or rather in myth, she remained a central figure in historical accounts of Etruria and Rome. Her political role was often overshadowed by discussions of her virtue. She was admired not simply as 'mistress' or 'queen' of Roman chastity but as ***dux*** *Romanae pudicitiae*, a word borrowed from military contexts to denote a leader or general. She was viewed as masculine in her strength. Men were moved by her story, one describing Lucretia, 'whose manly spirit [literally 'spirit of a man'] by a cruel error of Fortune was allotted to a woman's body'.[74] The philosopher Seneca the Younger meanwhile upheld Lucretia as a worthy model for other women. Who was it who claimed that nature had restricted women's virtues, he asked a mother who was grieving for her son? Women were more than capable. They could endure grief, they could endure toil, they were well accustomed to both. 'To Brutus,' Seneca continued, 'we owe liberty, and to Lucretia we owe Brutus.'[75]

Parallels would continue to be drawn between Lucretia and other women who suffered sexual violence.[76] She was the daughter of one nobleman, and the wife of another, but Romans of lower social standing were still able to identify with her as a woman wronged. In the fifth century BC a senator named Appius Claudius outstayed his term as a senior magistrate and attempted to seduce a young woman named Verginia. When she failed to respond to his advances, he had her abducted, and forced her to become a slave. Verginia's father, a soldier, tried in vain to achieve justice. Appius Claudius was among the men entitled to pass judgement in court by virtue of his position in the Senate. This was said to have driven the desperate father to desperate measures. To free Verginia, he killed her, sparking a popular uprising of the kind that had attended Lucretia's suicide.

When Gaius Marcius Coriolanus, a Roman general, waged war on the city in the same century, the spirit of Lucretia could be felt in the women who put up a defence. Rome's male ambassadors had failed to persuade Coriolanus to give up the alliance he had forged with the neighbouring people of Volsci and make peace with his own people. Patrician by birth, he had been ousted from Rome by the junior consuls, who bristled at his arrogance. Coriolanus' wife and mother therefore led a sizeable detachment of women to the Volscian camp to shame him into changing course. Their success was so celebrated in Rome that the Senate agreed to the creation of a holy precinct and temple to Fortuna Muliebris ('Women's Fortune') at the fourth milestone of the Via Latina, which ran south-east from the city. The anniversary of the Volscians' retreat was celebrated every December. Coriolanus' wife, Valeria, served as priestess in the temple and, collectively, the women of Rome funded the creation of one of the two statues erected therein. One historian claimed that this statue could talk.[77]

Rome at the turn of the fifth century BC was still small – the most realistic estimates place its population at 20,000–30,000 – but it was now a city to be reckoned with.[78] The next century would witness the Romans vanquish their former Etruscan rivals once and for all, taking the city of Veii in 396 BC, Caere in 353 and Tarquinii in 351. The same period would see plebeians rise to challenge patricians for roles in the Senate. Rome's earliest system of laws, prescribed by ten magistrates in 451 BC and known as the Twelve Tables, initially banned intermarriage between the two classes – P and non-P, one might say – though this rule was repealed six years later. From the mid-fourth century BC it was obligatory that one of the two chief senators originated from the plebeian class. The laws, inspired by those of Solon in Greece, were to prove better for social mobility than for enhancing the position of women in Rome. Lucretia, Tanaquil, Lavinia and the women of Etruscan history had nevertheless established a precedent for later women to look up to.

Chapter IX

The Rough End of the Cheese-Grater

Damatrius, who transgressed our customs, was killed by his mother. He was a Spartan, so was she.

Damatria of Sparta, epigram, quoted by Plutarch, *Sayings of Spartan Women*

While Rome was rising in the west, a new religious centre was growing up on and around the Athenian Acropolis on the other side of the Mediterranean. The ruins of one of the temples the Persians had destroyed beneath a cloud of arrows during the Graeco-Persian Wars had now been cleared, allowing a far more magnificent structure to emerge on the south side of the outcrop. Begun in 447 BC and completed the following decade through the use of slave and free labour, the Parthenon was Doric in style, seventeen columns long by eight wide, and dedicated to the virginal, indomitable warrior-goddess Athena.

The Parthenon was 'the temple of the maiden' in more than just name. Its marble pediments, carved so subtly that they appeared to have emerged just-so from the quarry, showed Athena being born from the head of her father Zeus before battling her paternal uncle Poseidon for control of Attica, the territory of which Athens formed a part. On the relief metopes, Amazons fought Attic men while furious Lapiths (a legendary Greek people of Thessaly) confronted half-mortal, half-horse Centaurs. Most enigmatic of all was the Ionic-style frieze. Enveloping the temple like a cummerbund, it measured 160 metres when unwound and bore the shapes of some 400 humans and 200 animals, many of them in procession. Its prevailing theme continues to bewilder, but clearly revolved in part around the worship of Athena. The piece of fabric being held aloft by one sculptural group on the frieze is probably a dress; every year, as part of the festival of the Panathenaea, the women of Athens embroidered a new garment for the goddess. Another section of the frieze has been linked to the myth of Erechtheus, legendary king of Athens, and the sacrifice of his daughter. A now-lost play of Euripides featured a scene in which Athena ordered one new temple to be dedicated to the girl and her sisters, and another named in their father's honour.[1] This accounted for the creation of the Parthenon and, beside it, the holy Erechtheion with its elegant porch of 'caryatid' maidens.

Overseeing this divinely inspired redevelopment was Pericles, son of Xanthippus and Agariste, a woman from the 'cursed' family of the Alcmaeonids. Making use of the same process of ostracism that had seen his father removed from the city, Pericles (born c. 495 BC) came to prominence after helping to quell the rise of the politician Cimon, who had attempted to lend support to the Spartans during a helot uprising in 462 BC. While championing Athenian democracy, Pericles accepted his election to the post of *strategos* or general every year unchallenged between 443 BC and his death in 429, to the delight of his many followers, but fury of his enemies. Few would have denied that his position looked unassailable at the time the Parthenon was topped off, but then, they had not looked between the lines of its elegant carvings.

Pericles was a key member of the commission appointed to manage the employment of artists and architects to complete the building work. Two men, Ictinus and Callicrates, were in charge of laying the architectural plans for the Parthenon, while a third, Phidias, oversaw the design of the artworks. Ordinary people served as models for the sculptural gods and goddesses, their firm thighs, round breasts and touch-me torsos immortalised forever after in marble. Phidias had a predilection for handsome boys. A young champion wrestler, Pantarces of Elis, was said to have inspired him.[2] There might have been something of Pantarces in the rippling body of the river god Ilissos from the Parthenon's west pediment.

There was nothing exceptional in an artist's use of friends and lovers as muses, but Phidias' particular blending of the private and professional was ultimately to prove his undoing. Comic poets in the city stirred up the false rumour that he was pimping women from wealthy families to be Pericles' lovers.[3] The ladies were said to arrive at the Acropolis on the pretence of admiring his exquisite sculptures. One of the highlights of Phidias' artistic scheme was a colossus of Athena, almost 12 metres tall, consisting of a wooden core enveloped in ivory and gold. The goddess wore a helmet adorned with griffins and a sphinx and a breastplate bearing the face of the Gorgon Medusa. She held a spear and a model of Nike (Victory) and stood on a pedestal engraved with the image of Pandora's birth.[4] The first woman continued to occupy a significant place in the panoply of divinities. As if the vision of Pandora coming to life in the goddess's temple were not striking enough, Phidias allegedly incorporated portraits of himself and Pericles battling Amazons on Athena's shield, an act of impiety for which he could not be forgiven. Phidias' friendship with Pericles became a source of envy for his opponents. One went so far as to persuade the artist's assistant to accuse his master publicly of stealing gold from the sculpture.[5] The total quantity was weighed to reveal that none was missing, but even so Phidias was prosecuted and given little option but to flee Athens. The beleaguered artist settled in Olympia where he established a new workshop and created the Zeus of Olympia, later adjudged a Wonder of the World.

In spite of the blow to his reputation, Pericles stood proudly by his work for the Acropolis, which was an expression of Greek ambition as well as Greek accomplishment. Some decades earlier, in 472 BC, he had served as *choregos* or financial sponsor of the production of four plays that included Aeschylus' *Persians*. The Theatre of Dionysus on the south-east slope of the Acropolis now became the focus of the city's cultural rebirth. These were the years in which Sophocles and Euripides joined Aeschylus on the roster of popular playwrights. Their dramas were routinely performed at the City Dionysia, an annual festival held in honour of shape-shifting Dionysus, who supplemented his passion for wine with patronage of the theatre.

Lawcourts and businesses shut their doors as citizens hastened to watch the opening procession each spring. Offerings of bread and model penises were made to the hedonistic god ahead of sacrifices and celebrations in the streets. Early in the morning, 15,000 or so spectators made their way to the theatre and took their seats on the bleachers built into the sides of the Acropolis. Boys who had lost their fathers in battle and received their education at the state's expense were paraded before visiting dignitaries from other city-states and provided with a suit of hoplite armour. Each of the playwrights then put on three tragedies followed by a humorous satyr play. Their entries were judged as a set by the assembled crowd.

This audience was solely or predominantly male; it remains uncertain whether some groups of women were allowed to watch select performances. The stage itself was certainly the preserve of men, two or three of whom played all the parts in the tragedies, foreshadowing Shakespearean practice. The use of costumes and masks with lavish in-built wigs enabled the audience to distinguish between the various roles. The most prominent characters in the plays, however, tended to be female.

Here was Clytemnestra, stepping forth to hack down her husband Agamemnon with an axe upon his return from the Trojan War; and Phaedra, destroying the life of her too reverent stepson, Hippolytus; and Antigone, daughter and half-sister of Oedipus, defying the laws of her maternal uncle to grant one of her two brothers, Polyneices, due burial; and Medea; and Jocasta, mother-wife of Oedipus; and heroically self-sacrificing Alcestis. The twentieth-century classicist Gilbert Murray observed how these were 'all of them free women, free in thought and spirit, treated with as much respect as any of the male characters, and with far greater minuteness and sympathy'. The characterisation of women in the plays prompted Murray and many later scholars to question whether women in Athenian society were not also more liberated than has traditionally been supposed. On the available evidence this view is difficult to support.

As Pericles declared, 'Great is the glory of the woman who is least spoken about, whether for good or for ill.'[6] Her very clothes made her inconspicuous, a long tunic-like *chiton* covering her body as far as the ankles, and a *himation* resting on her shoulders and doubling as a veil when she was in public, which was rare. Only men could attend the Athenian Assembly; there were about 30,000 adult male citizens in the mid-fifth century BC, some 5,000–6,000 of whom would gather monthly on the Pnyx (official meeting place) underneath the Acropolis. Below the Pnyx was the Athenian *agora* or civic centre; it was in a lawcourt there that Phidias was prosecuted and sentenced. There, too, lay the Bouleuterion or Council Chamber. Candidates for the Boule of 500 men were chosen annually by lot, and officers involved in administering public finances and foreign policy were elected by male Athenian citizens, a group that by definition excluded slaves but also free foreign residents. Pericles, by sponsoring a law in 451 BC, narrowed this group still further by ruling that 'Athenian citizen' applied only to those born of both an Athenian father and an Athenian mother.

Athenian women, wholly deprived of a political voice and severely limited in their purchasing power, were also restricted in their movements. A male guardian – usually her father and then husband as in Rome – watched over her 'for her protection', especially on occasions when she needed to leave the house. The women of Dynastic Egypt, by contrast, were guardian-free and permitted to own their own property. Even where her housekeeping and child-rearing responsibilities were concerned, the Athenian woman was reliant upon her husband to make important decisions, which could be as stark as between life and death. If she had a baby, it was the right of the child's father to choose whether to raise or abandon it, according to his assessment of its health, strength and legitimacy. (In Sparta a collective group, male 'elders of the tribesmen', similarly decided whether or not the child should be reared, and the Twelve Tables legislation in Rome specified that it was the prerogative of the father alone to say whether his newborn child ought to be nurtured or rejected.)[7] If the infant satisfied his expectations, he would lift it up on its fifth or seventh day of life, then carry it around the hearth in a rite known as the *amphidromia*. The rate of infant mortality was so high – about one in three in the first year of life, according to one modern estimate – that it was considered imprudent, not to say unlucky, for the father to choose a name for his son or daughter before day ten.[8]

Unwanted babies were typically 'exposed' or abandoned in known public areas where they were sometimes retrieved and allowed to grow up either as the silently adopted children of otherwise childless parents or as slaves. Girls were more frequently exposed than boys, but in Sophocles' *Oedipus Rex*, first performed at the City Dionysia about 429 BC, Laius, king of Thebes, orders his son to be left on Mount Cithaeron after being warned by an oracle that, should he live, the boy would one day kill him. The infant Oedipus is handed over by Laius' slave herdsman to the slave herdsman of the childless king of Corinth, who adopts Oedipus and brings him up as his own. Ignorance of his true identity leads Oedipus to fulfil the terrible prophecy. He not only kills his natural father, but marries and has four children by his mother.

From the moment she married, typically at the age of fourteen to a man of about thirty, a young Athenian woman was under pressure to produce a healthy child. It was thought that sex and pregnancy could treat a number of ailments considered endemic to her gender, especially ones characterised by emotional instability. One of the treatises of the Hippocratic Corpus warned that virgins were liable to become unbalanced and even suicidal at the onset of puberty. The given reason for this was that their wombs had not yet been fully opened by intercourse, meaning that menstrual blood accumulated in the body, especially in the heart and diaphragm.[9] Marriage and pregnancy were prescribed as cures. Even once married, a woman was told that she needed to have sex regularly, or risk damage to her health. That she could experience pleasure from friction during intercourse was thoroughly attested in the Corpus.[10] This pleasure was said to be less intense but longer lasting than a man's. His ejaculation was said to serve as cold water to her flame. The Hippocratic medical texts, which date largely to this period, further stipulated that the womb required frequent watering with semen to prevent it from wandering around the body in search of moisture elsewhere. A 'wandering womb' was deemed a prime source of madness termed *hysteria* or 'wombiness'.

A bride might recognise the opportunistic nature of this advice, which was commonly given by male doctors and no doubt perpetuated by other men, but it was usually in her interest to take it, because she would struggle to gain acceptance otherwise. Women in this period were often treated as subservient outsiders by the families they had married into until they gave birth.[11] This did not make married life easy to begin with. Procne, a mythological character in one of Sophocles' tragedies, spoke for many real women when she described being taken away from a happy childhood home and installed in a joyless household with a stranger for a husband. 'And this, as soon as one night has yoked us,' she said, 'we must commend and deem to be quite lovely.'[12] The arrival of a baby offered the prospect of warmer relations between husband, wife and in-laws. The birth of a child, especially a boy, yoked the two bloodlines in deed, whereas a formal betrothal followed by marriage did so merely in name.

The Hippocratic Corpus contained a number of pieces of advice for women who sought to conceive. Although some doctors believed that only the man played an active role in reproduction (a woman was merely a receptacle), most realised that both contributed to the process, with conception depending upon a battle between male and female seed. A boy was believed to result from the triumph of the male seed, and a girl from the triumph of the female seed, which was weaker.[13] Girls were thought to grow from the left side of the womb and boys from the right 'correct' side. The Hippocratic Corpus recommended that men tie their left testicle if they wanted a boy, and their right if they wanted a girl. A woman could help by eating plenty of lettuce and cold foods for a girl and hot and spicy dishes for a boy. Women were in general characterised medically as cold and wet, while men were hard and hot.

A woman who was fortunate enough to conceive and carry a baby to full term had next to endure the uncertainties of labour. Surviving relief sculptures show that women generally wore loose clothing throughout pregnancy and delivery and untied their hair whereas usually they would wear it up in chignon-like buns.[14] They might give birth sitting up, or lying down, with female midwives (typically women beyond childbearing age) or close female relatives assisting. Men would stay away unless the worst happened. A sculptural stele from the fourth century BC shows a man holding the hand of a woman who has just given birth while another woman holds her from behind.[15] She has either died or is just slipping away. Artists usually stopped short of illustrating such tragedies in bloodied detail.

The child's future was heavily determined by their gender. Boys were educated at schools or by private tutors and formally introduced into hereditary pseudo-kinship groups known as *phratries* in Attica, or inducted into their military training in Sparta from the age of seven. Girls had to be content with learning what they could from their brothers and participating in a small number of highly selective religious practices.

Two girls were habitually invited to dwell near the Parthenon and perform regular rituals in honour of Athena at night. One of these involved passing into an underground passage beneath the city, placing a symbolic object there, and receiving in return something to carry up to the world above.[16] Another ritual, associated principally with the sanctuary of Artemis at Brauron, eastern Attica, was known as the *arkteia* after the Greek for 'bear'. Girls under the age of ten were encouraged to strip naked and play, untethered by societal convention, to demonstrate the wildness considered innate to the female sex. It was widely believed that this inner wildness could and should be tamed by men through marriage and defloration. The sanctuary at Brauron was presided over by a priestess rather than a priest.

The lifestyle imposed upon most women in Athens was usually sufficient to keep a free spirit in check. Although many poor women were compelled to work for a living outside the home, this was ethically frowned upon. *Poastria* worked in the fields removing weeds and *Kalametria* collected up the stalks and stubble. Others might serve as small shopkeepers or as wet nurses. Prior to her wedding, an aristocratic woman might be elected to serve as High Priestess of Athena Polias, protector of the city, a highly honourable and probably salaried role. Other known priestesses included the democratically selected priestess of Athena Nike (of Victory). These women were exceptions to the rule.

A dialogue written by a pupil of Socrates in the mid-fourth century BC provided an explanation as to why it was considered so important for women to remain indoors. Resembling an early guidebook to household management, the *Oeconomicus* ('Treatise on Household Management') of Xenophon featured a discussion between Socrates and a wealthy Athenian named Ischomachus on the respective roles of husband and wife. This topic was, perhaps, of personal interest to Socrates, whose wife Xanthippe was described by Xenophon as 'the most difficult of women who are, and were, and will ever be'.[17] As Socrates himself supposedly said, having learned to live with her, he could get along with just about anyone. The gods made women better suited to being indoors, ran Ischomachus' argument, and men hardy and robust so they could withstand the elements outdoors. Within the safety of the house, a wife could organise the slaves and teach them to be useful to her. She could also take the lead in apportioning the produce that came in so that the household had enough in reserve throughout the year. It was her duty to oversee the grain store and ensure that the grain – mainly barley but also wheat – remained in good condition. She also had to manage the manufacture of clothes. Ischomachus likened her role to that of the queen bee.[18] While remaining in the hive, she would raise the young, preside over the weaving (of combs), and take charge of the produce the worker bees brought in after she set them about their tasks. 'The sweetest thing of all,' Ischomachus addressed her, 'is if you emerge appearing better than me, and make me your servant . . .'[19]

It was only to be expected that a man marrying a pubescent girl

– Ischomachus wed a girl of fifteen – would issue her with instructions so that she would know the right way to do things. After that, in the words of Xenophon, she became the person her husband entrusted household matters with the most, but spoke to the least.[20] Ischomachus showed pride in his wife's ability to take care of domestic affairs by herself.[21] But quite a different portrait of her appeared in the contemporary account of another male author. The conservative politician Andocides alleged that she had an affair with her son-in-law, and that her daughter was so distraught by this that she attempted suicide.[22] The daughter eventually fled, leaving her mother to cohabit with her husband and raise their new baby.

Whether this story was true or not, there were certainly occasions when women were shamed for falling short of what was expected of them. In the late fifth or early fourth century BC an Athenian named Euphiletos went on trial in Athens for the murder of a man he had caught having sex with his wife. The defendant denied the charge on the grounds that he had committed a legitimate form of homicide. At the beginning of their marriage, he told the all-male jury (we have only a version of the speech composed for him by his barrister Lysias to deliver in person), he had kept a close watch over his spouse. After their son was born, however, he allowed her greater control over his property. He now recognised that this was a mistake. For while she had initially satisfied him in her management of the household, her head was turned when she attended his mother's funeral and met a certain Eratosthenes, who 'corrupted' her.

The seducer sent her messages through the family's female slave. By liaising with the slave, whom he met in the *agora*, Eratosthenes gained entry to the house, and proceeded to have his way with Euphiletos' wife in the women's quarters. Ordinarily, these would have been upstairs, but Euphiletos had suggested that she sleep downstairs to facilitate child-care. Euphiletos, meanwhile, was sleeping soundly upstairs. It was only when the female slave of another of Eratosthenes' lovers informed on him that Euphiletos understood what was happening. Under threat of death, the slave of Euphiletos' wife agreed to help him entrap her mistress, ensuring that Eratosthenes would be caught in the act. So it came to pass that Euphiletos burst in upon his wife and Eratosthenes in bed together and killed his love rival. Lysias, a resident alien of Syracusan origin and one of the foremost speechwriters in Athens, aided Euphiletos' defence. Frustratingly, the outcome of the trial is not known, but it seems likely that Euphiletos would have been absolved on the justification that it was lawful in fifth- and fourth-century Athens to kill a man caught *in flagrante* with a lawfully married woman. Justifiable homicide, not murder.

Given the nature of Athenian society and his own professed feelings on the status of women, it seems remarkable that Pericles chose the woman he did to be his life partner. He had divorced his aristocratic wife of many years, the mother of his two sons, when he took up with Aspasia of Miletus.

Aspasia was one of the most dazzling women of her age. Like her fellow countrymen, the philosophers Thales and Anaximander, she was exceptionally intelligent and well-read, and gave her opinions freely.[23] Her birth outside of Athens had afforded her the opportunity both to learn and to teach rhetoric, and on coming over from Asia Minor at the age of about twenty she became famous for her speaking lessons. Socrates held her in such high regard that he used to visit her with his pupils and encourage friends' wives to go to hear her converse.[24] According to one of Plato's dialogues, Aspasia indeed educated both Socrates and Pericles in the art of oratory.[25] She was, said Plato, a strong advocate of combining improvisation with preparation for her speeches.[26]

One modern scholar has argued that Aspasia also taught a lovesick Socrates about love.[27] The theory hinges upon her identification with a mysterious character in one of Plato's dialogues. In Plato's *Symposium*, written about 380 BC, Socrates receives lessons from a highly intelligent woman named Diotima. She speaks eloquently and at length and teaches him that love is neither wholly good nor wholly evil, neither mortal nor divine, but rather an intermediate spirit with the power to traverse the space between both. Socrates stands in awe before her wisdom. There can be no proof that Plato was thinking of Aspasia when he developed Diotima's character, but it should not be doubted that Aspasia moved in Socrates' circle and was capable of holding her own in intellectual argument.

In this respect she was everything Pericles said a woman should not be. And yet, in spite of himself, he was smitten. While he could not make her his wife, for this was forbidden under his own citizenship law of 451 BC, he formally acknowledged her as his permanent concubine or *pallake* and lived openly with her for the rest of his life. Every time he left the house to go to work, and every time he returned in the evening, he would kiss her, which was scorned as an excessive public display of affection.[28] They soon had a son together they named Pericles.

Aspasia's evident magnetism and unusual domestic situation did not fail to rouse suspicions in Athens. Cratinus, a contemporary comedian, described her as Hera to Pericles' Zeus but also, more insultingly, as 'a prostitute who can't be shamed'.[29] Prostitutes in Athens were of two main kinds. There were streetwalkers or brothel workers known as *pornae*. And there were 'companions' or courtesans known as *hetaerae*. *Pornae* were the most common and affordable prostitutes. They were often born into the profession or forced to pursue it through poverty or widowhood. *Hetaerae* were distinguished by their high culture and prices. They were seen to constitute a professional class and were taxed on their earnings. There was inevitably some crossover between the two types, and shades in between; *pallake*, for example, could occupy a role akin to courtesan. Athenian citizen women were debarred from becoming *hetaerae*, whereas women from overseas, like Aspasia, were tolerated or even welcomed into the profession. While other women were largely limited to the company of women, *hetaerae* learned to converse freely with men and attended their symposia. The wit, musicality and charm of *hetaerae* were considered as important at these occasions as their beauty and sexual prowess.

Some prostitutes who reached a certain age in Athens also became bordello madams, and it was as a madam, jested Pericles' critics, that Aspasia was supplying her husband with women of ill repute. Similar slurs were made of Aspasia in Persia. The prince known as Cyrus the Younger was said to have named his favourite concubine, a modest and highly educated woman of Phocaea named Milto, after Aspasia in the late fifth century BC.[30] The malicious accusations were notably all made in reference to Aspasia's power over Pericles rather than her rabid appetites. This was why Plutarch likened her to Thargelia of Miletus, the Thessalian with fourteen husbands whom he credited with spreading pro-Persian sentiment during the Graeco-Persian Wars.[31] Aspasia's threat was deemed to be political rather than sexual.

The association between Aspasia and prostitution developed only too naturally in the culture of fifth-century Athens, where the more visible a woman was, the less honourable she was believed to be. Men were sometimes besotted enough to grant their favourite *hetaerae* freedom from prostitution and aid their social or even political elevation. A notorious case arose in the mid-fourth century BC when one man attempted to help a free, resident, non-Athenian woman named Neaera to buy her way out of her existing lifestyle. The evidence we have – a lawcourt speech of prosecution – is far from unbiased, but it had to be plausible enough to convince an Athenian jury of hundreds of ordinary poor citizens. According to the main prosecutor, Neaera had grown up working in a brothel in Corinth (notorious as a port city for its prostitution). Two clients eventually purchased her for their own pleasure, but on proceeding to marriage agreed she could buy her freedom if she left Corinth. One of the Athenians who helped her to do so, however, had other ideas. He took her away with him to Athens where he proceeded to prostitute her among his friends. Neaera managed to escape, and once again began to look forward to a brighter future after meeting an Athenian citizen named Stephanus, who she might have hoped would marry her. In reality, this was unlikely to happen, for she would have needed to be freed and accorded Athenian citizenship in order to wed him. Stephanus, besides, was a minor politician and had political enemies. They saw Neaera put on trial under accusation of concealing her status as a foreigner and presenting herself and her daughter as legitimate citizens of Athens.

The outcome of the trial is unknown, but perhaps Neaera escaped prostitution. She strove hard to protect her daughter from having to enter the same profession. But the politician who prosecuted her ensured that she could never gain acceptance in Athenian society and thereby also ruined Stephanus' career. The prosecutor Apollodorus, himself the son of an ex-slave, outlined only too clearly the distinction men made at this time between different classes of women: 'We have *hetaerae* for pleasure, concubines (*pallakae*) for the day-to-day ministration of our bodies, but wives to make legitimate children and to be loyal guardians of indoors.'[32] The collapse of boundaries between the groups was believed to pose a threat to social and political stability.

Had Aspasia of Miletus been merely a *hetaera* she would hardly have attracted the attention she did. The label arguably became attached to her metaphorically rather than literally. There was simply no other vocabulary to describe a woman in Athens who had the power to influence men. In the case of Aspasia, it was this power that worried people, not her made-up role as a procuress, or as a prostitute in Pericles' bed. The most severe accusation brought against her, indeed, related not to her sexual *mores*, but to her supposed part in stirring up war in Athens's name.

In 440 BC, Aspasia's native city of Miletus came into conflict with Samos, home to Hera's temple, over control of the city of Priene in Ionia. In their hour of need, the Milesians prevailed upon the Athenians for aid, and Pericles agreed to persuade the Athenians to supply some, it was said at Aspasia's insistence.[33] The Athenians took the early advantage, rounding up Samian men and children as hostages, and establishing democracy in place of the existing oligarchy. When the oligarchic Samians revolted, the Athenians met them at sea and initially appeared to be victorious. The Samians were bolstered by a fleet of Phoenicians, however, and managed to take some Athenians captive. The hostages of Samos had been branded with boar heads, so the Samians branded their Athenian prisoners' heads with owls of Athena. Hearing the news, Pericles turned around and ordered his engineer to launch his latest invention. Ephorus, who was disabled, had designed a powerful new siege engine, and put it to effective use against the Samian defences. After nine months the Samians surrendered. The Athenians destroyed their city walls, took further hostages, restored Samos to the Athenian alliance, and imposed a heavy fine upon the remaining population. Pericles returned to Athens to a crowd of well-wishers. Even the women came out to crown him with victory wreaths. With one exception.

Elpinice, daughter of Miltiades, had met Pericles before. When Cimon, her half-brother, was put on trial for bribery, she had begged Pericles to be gentle on him. Pericles had complied and Cimon was acquitted. In the process, however, Pericles had curtly told Elpinice that she was too old to be meddling in these affairs.[34] Elpinice was now about fifty and certainly too old to be deterred by his unthinking prejudices. Stepping forward from the throng, she reminded Pericles that he had just lost Athens many of its bravest citizens in a war not against a foreign enemy, but against a fellow Greek city.[35] Pericles simply smiled and feigned amusement. At her time of life, he said, it was unbecoming to anoint oneself with perfumed oil. The line came from a poem of the seventh century BC and served as a metaphor for overstepping one's station.[36] While married to a wealthy Athenian named Callias, Elpinice was rumoured to have had an affair with an artist, Polygnotus, on the basis that the face of a Trojan woman he painted on a public stoa looked suspiciously like hers.[37] Pericles had more in common with her than he cared to admit.

Might Elpinice have taken up her cause with Aspasia instead? Pericles may have been unwilling to heed the advice of other women, but Aspasia had his ear – of this, the Athenians were certain. It was no secret that Aspasia had been born in Miletus. Blame for Athens's involvement in the Samian War was laid squarely at her door.[38] There was something horribly familiar in the way she seemed to linger there in Athens, carefree, while young men crossed the seas to their deaths. It took a comedian to say what others were thinking: Aspasia was the new Helen of Troy.[39] She had whipped up trouble behind closed doors and allowed Pericles to claim a hollow victory. But at what cost?

As so often in this city, the playwright exaggerated the woman's role, making it appear that men were only too pleased to take direction from members of the opposite sex. *Hetaerae* may have had more opportunities than other women to shape the decisions of men, but they were very far from plotting points to conquer on the world map. Comedians and tragedians skewed the reality because they were curious to explore what would happen in a topsy-turvy world in which men took second place. Their resulting plays illustrated just how anxiously they entertained this prospect. Powerful Medea kills her own children to spite their father, Jason, who was unfaithful to her. Vengeful and adulterous Clytemnestra butchers her war hero husband Agamemnon. Phaedra falsely accuses her stepson Hippolytus of rape. Give women free rein to their desires and civilisation, the playwrights suggest, would quickly crumble.

Aspasia had become a victim of the freedom of speech that flourished under the Periclean democracy. Pride in the cultural renaissance he had nurtured made it very difficult for Pericles to take too strong a view on such matters. Comedians were free to jibe at public figures in the name of entertainment. If politicians were primed to expect this and to deny whatever they pleased, the women in their lives had little option but to close their ears, shut their eyes, and do their best to forget. Being blamed for the Samian War was merely the beginning of Aspasia's woes.

The rebirth of the Athenian Acropolis and strengthening of the harbours did not go unnoticed by the inhabitants of other *poleis* (city-states). The Delian League had been established in the interest of protecting Greek city-states from future Persian aggression and taxation. The discovery that Athens had used money from the collective fund to help finance its urban redevelopment was guaranteed to cause upset.

Athens and Sparta had sworn an agreement for a Thirty Years' Peace in 446/5 BC to settle tensions that had already resulted in warfare. The peace had been tested a number of times, not least when Pericles introduced a decree banning citizens of Megara, the *polis* just west of east Attica, from trading with what was now, effectively, an Athenian empire of league states. It had been in Pericles' interest to force the situation to a head, seeing as the insulted and inconvenienced Megarians would now appeal for assistance from Sparta, head of a rival 'Peloponnesian' league. The effects of the decree on the oligarchic Spartans might have been limited, but they contributed to the souring of relations with Athens, whose rapid growth and influence over the other league city-states was a growing source of concern. When Corcyra (on Corfu) sought an alliance with Athens for protection against an invasion by Corinth, a Spartan ally, the Athenians agreed to send in ships. That by itself did not constitute a breach of the Peace, since Corcyra was not a party to the sworn treaty, and the alliance that Athens made was deliberately defensive-only. However, the inevitable clash between the Athenian and Corinthian navies could be *construed* as a breach, and as a cause of war between Sparta and Athens just fifteen years into the contract.

The year 431 BC marked the beginning of the most defining war in Classical Greece's history between Troy and the war of Middle-Eastern conquest conducted by Alexander the Great in the 330s and 320s BC. The Peloponnesian War was fought between Athens and the Delian League, which included most of the Aegean islands and western Asia Minor, and Sparta and its allies across the Peloponnese. Later likened to the First World War of twentieth-century Europe, it would draw in almost the entire Greek world, pitching Ionians against Dorians from Sicily to the approaches of the Black Sea, and endure for almost thirty years. The lives of women throughout the Greek world would be irreparably changed as a result.

In a highly political comedy put on at Athens in the sixth year of the conflict, Aristophanes urged his audience to refrain from blaming the Spartans entirely for their misery. Consider, too, suggested one of his male characters, the role Aspasia had played. She, not the Spartans, was the root cause of the trouble with Megara that led to the Peloponnesian War. In Aristophanes' version of events, some drunken Athenian youths had travelled to Megara and carried away a prostitute named Simaitha, prompting the Megarians to retaliate by taking 'two common prostitutes of Aspasia', cast here once again as a brothel madam.[40] The fictional Pericles exploded in Zeus-like fury. He cast the Megarians out of Athens and blockaded their exports. Had it not been for the women, there would have been no need for an embargo on trade, and no need for Sparta to intervene. So it was, by Aristophanes' interpretation of events, that all of Greece was suffering for the sake of 'three harlots'.

Aristophanes was writing comedy. There was no real embargo on trade with Megara. The prostitutes were very probably fictional. Aspasia was not responsible for sparking war between Athens and Sparta. But while the comedian's argument was ridiculous and wholly untenable in view of the facts, it grew out of the urgency many people in Greece felt to find a scapegoat for what they were now living through. Women provided that scapegoat. By the end of the first year of the war, the death toll was so great that Pericles had begun to speak of the need for women to have more children.[41] Aristophanes might have said that this was the least women could do to compensate for the trouble they had caused.

At the beginning of the Peloponnesian War, the Athenians were content to await the Spartan approach from within their city walls, protected further by their Long Walls – a newly completed series of fortifications running from the city to the two ports at Phalerum and Piraeus. Each summer, the hardy soldiers of Sparta would make their way over the mountains of the Peloponnese and march east into Attica. Contrary to the Athenians, their strength lay on land, and the abandoned countryside of Attica was theirs for the taking. The Spartans wasted little time in torching the crop fields at harvest time when the barley was almost ripe. Nestled within their city, the Athenians remained relatively untroubled for a time, as they were able to collect food and other supplies as it was shipped into their harbours. Pericles' decision to pack the people of Athens and surrounding Attica into the city walls for up to forty days at a time did, however, have significant drawbacks. Between the existing buildings and the makeshift camps, living conditions were cramped and highly unsanitary, and the shelters grew especially hot in the summer months. And so it was that when a plague broke out in the second year of the war, it spread with catastrophic speed, cutting short thousands of already harrowed lives.

Herodotus appears to have been in Greece, possibly even in Athens, when the Peloponnesian War erupted. His *Histories* of the Graeco-Persian Wars were already being read aloud in the city. Although he was potentially very well placed to document the latest conflict, he apparently chose not to, perhaps aware of the fact that he was nearing the end of his life. It was instead one of the young men who listened eagerly to his *Histories* being performed who took up the challenge.

Thucydides was related to Cimon and maintained his connections with Thrace (roughly modern Bulgaria), the home region of Cimon's maternal grandfather. When it came to Athenian politics, however, he was firmly on Pericles' side. He began writing his *History of the Peloponnesian War* soon after 431 BC when he was likely still in his twenties. The thoroughness of his research and minute attention to detail were extraordinary. Even in spite of the passages praising Pericles, the work reads like an early form of reportage, almost entirely devoid of the supernatural elements that had coloured Herodotus' *Histories*. The war would occupy the best part of Thucydides' life and require him to join the front line. His perceived failure as a general during a command in 424 BC would land him in exile for twenty years. It was astonishing he survived that long given he was among the thousands to contract the plague.

The first people fell ill a matter of days after the Spartans arrived in the summer of the second year. Fever, inflammation of the eyes, and bleeding from the tongue and throat were followed by coughing, sneezing, chest pain and the vomiting of bile. The skin of the afflicted became so ulcerated that their clothing became unbearable. Many suffered from insatiable thirst and insomnia. The disease (interpreted variously by modern historians as Ebola, smallpox, bubonic plague or typhus, most likely a strain of the latter) was so virulent that any birds or animals scavenging on the bodies also perished. Nothing as severe had ever been witnessed before.

Suspicions immediately fell upon the Spartans for poisoning the water supply. But as Thucydides recorded, the plague struck many other parts of the Greek world besides Athens, and had probably originated in North Africa. It could not have taken more than a few days to spread from the harbour of Piraeus to the crowds taking refuge in the city. The Long Walls built for the Athenians' protection served to seal them in with the disease.

As bodies began to fill the tents and the fountains, survivors and citizens yet to contract the illness turned to easy, empty pleasures, their minds newly focused on what it meant to be flesh. Some women achieved a rare and momentary sexual liberation at the cost of their own lives.

Devastated by their losses, angered by the outwardly passive approach Athens had so far adopted in the war with Sparta, the men of the city demoted Pericles from his generalship and fired him, only to re-elect him less than a year later.

In 429 BC the Spartans laid siege to Plataea. The Athenians followed with a victory of their own in the Corinthian Gulf, but it was too little, too late. They stood further from a final triumph than they had at the beginning of the conflict. The plague was unrelenting. Pericles lost his two legitimate sons by his first wife. He barely had time to mourn his losses when he himself was carried away by the plague. It is estimated that up to a third of the population of Athens perished. Aspasia, at once fortunate and unfortunate to survive, wasted little time in contracting a new partnership with another democratic politician. Her new partner, Lysicles, was mocked as a mere sheep-seller by the comedians. Just a year into their relationship he too died.

Pericles was succeeded as the leading democratic politician by his former enemy Cleon. In 425 BC, against all expectations, Cleon was elected *strategos* and led Athens to a much-needed victory at Pylos in south-western Messenia within Sparta's own territory. It was not long, however, before the Athenians were again feeling rudderless. The Spartans launched a campaign against Athens's north Aegean allies and while Thucycides lost his post (he failed to save the Greek city-state of Amphipolis, which was captured by the Spartans), Cleon lost his life. By 421 BC, with no clear end to the war in sight, the two sides agreed to a fifty-year peace under a treaty forged by Cleon's chief rival Nicias. As part of the peace treaty, Sparta agreed to surrender Amphipolis to Athens in exchange for their prisoners at Pylos and, for the moment, it looked as though the stalemate had been resolved. People could once again travel through Greece freely to visit temples, oracles and each other.[42] It proved to be a false dawn. The treaty drew a veil over several inconvenient facts. Not only were the people of Amphipolis reluctant to be returned to the Athenians, but the Corinthians were disgusted at being abandoned by the Spartans, and the Thebans were unwilling to sign the agreement at all. It took less than three years for all sides to accept that the treaty they had made was as good as void.

After five years of uneasy peace interrupted by one major battle – won by the Spartans at Mantinea in 418 BC – the Peloponnesian War entered a devastating new phase, for women as well as men. It began when the Athenians laid siege to the volcanic island of Melos in 416 BC. Being some 335 kilometres from the Greek mainland, north of Crete, the islanders had hoped to remain neutral (though their sentimental connections were with the Spartans) and declared in rousing rhetoric that they would defend their liberty to do so. When they refused to pay tribute or submit, the Athenians sent a force of 3,000 against them, and showed no mercy to the prisoners.[43] Men of military age were executed. Woman and children were enslaved and sold abroad. The Athenians proceeded to colonise the island with 500 of their own settlers.

Bolstered by their success, the Athenians then turned their attentions to Sicily, which they fooled themselves into thinking they could conquer in its entirety so as to come away with a limitless grain supply. Exaggerated reports of the wealth concealed in the temples of non-Greek Segesta, in the island's north-west, were sufficient to persuade the already war-inclined Athenian Assembly to launch a Sicilian expedition.

Only one of the three men entrusted with the command was prepared to outline the risks.[44] Nicias, whose eponymous peace was being broken, warned the Athenians that they would only incur more enemies in their quest for something they were unlikely to achieve. The threat of a Spartan-Sicilian alliance was real. Alcibiades, another of the appointed commanders, smarted at Nicias' speech. Having lost his father as a boy, Alcibiades had grown up as a ward of Pericles and was evidently eager to prove that he shared his ambition. Alcibiades perhaps owed something of his fighting spirit to his mother, a cousin of Pericles and an Alcmaeonid, whose name, Deinomache, meant 'Terrible in Battle'. The commander had received an injury on the battlefield just before the Peloponnesian War and was allegedly nursed back to health by his mentor and possibly lover Socrates. He later repaid the favour by helping to save Socrates' life in the war. The charming hero had since won the hearts of many more men besides and had little difficulty in persuading the Assembly that they should proceed with the expedition.

An unusual occurrence on the eve of the launch nevertheless gave even the most strident members of the party reason to pause. It was a common practice in Athens to place herms – pillars with portrait heads of the travellers' god Hermes and erect male genitalia – outside houses and temples. The monuments were considered sacred and apotropaic. They provided protection for the families residing indoors as well as their guests. In the middle of the night, just as the final preparations for the journey were being laid, a group travelled through the city mutilating the herms and breaking them to pieces. The desecration of the holy stones shook the confidence not only of Nicias and his colleague Lamachus, but of Alcibiades and the city more widely.

No one discovered who was responsible, but an official message was swiftly dispatched to assure potential informers that they would not be punished for any intelligence they supplied. A number of slaves subsequently came forward and reported that similar acts of destruction had taken place at the hands of some youths and various other characters. By far the most surprising name on their list was that of Alcibiades, who was accused simultaneously of profaning the solemn Mysteries of Eleusis.[45]

The handsome young general had a reputation for dishonourable behaviour. His wife Hipparete ('Virtuous with Horses') had long ago tired of his excessive womanising. A daughter of one of the wealthiest men in Athens and Pericles' first wife, Hipparete had brought a sizeable dowry to the marriage, and blessed Alcibiades with two children. He repaid her by continuously cavorting with prostitutes, even installing them at the home of her brother.[46] It was by no means common for women in Athens to seek a formal separation, but Hipparete was never one to be held back by convention. Athenian law permitted a woman to appeal to the Eponymous Archon for a divorce. This official, selected annually by lot, stood at the head of the Athenian state and would ordinarily negotiate the terms with the woman's male guardian. Hipparete preferred a direct approach. In an extraordinary scene, she went to meet the archon alone, only to be intercepted by Alcibiades. He would not stand for being divorced. He seized hold of her, dragged her through the *agora*, and forced her back into the marital home. Hipparete was unable to secure her divorce. She would remain living under Alcibiades' roof and rules until her early death.

Seizing the opportunity to remove Alcibiades from power, a group of Athenians perpetuated the unlikely charge that he had smashed the herms, adding that he had taken to profaning religious rites in order to subvert democracy itself. The trial of Alcibiades was delayed until after he had set sail for Sicily to allow time for a stronger case to be established against him. When, finally, he was recalled from southern Italy, Alcibiades chose rather to flee. He treacherously sought refuge with the Spartans.

The Sicilian expedition continued in Alcibiades' absence with predictably dire results. The funds promised at Segesta were minimal. South Italian and Sicilian allies were few and far between. As Nicias had anticipated, the Athenians had overstretched themselves, and even with formidable triremes from Chios and Lesbos, and the very best crews of their own, they proved incapable of defeating the might of the Syracusans, well-defended as they were behind a strong complex of city walls. The Athenians' naval defeat in the Great Harbour of Syracuse in 413 BC was near total. Survivors were unable even to gather up their dead which included Nicias himself. About 7,000 Greek and Italian-Greek survivors were imprisoned in stone quarries in terrible conditions.[47] Those who did not die and decay in their midst were sold into slavery. It was later alleged that the poetry-loving Sicilians agreed to let go any prisoner who could recite verses of Euripides by heart.[48] On their return to Athens the survivors were said to have thanked the playwright for their lives.

The Sicilians' passion for Euripides would have taken the Athenians by surprise. Of the three leading tragedians of the city, he was not only the youngest, but also the least successful in terms of prizes won at the City Dionysia. Euripides was nevertheless emerging as a most sensitive critic of the Peloponnesian War. Performed in Athens during the Sicilian expedition, his *Trojan Women* brought home the terror of the preceding Melian siege that had resulted in the slaughter and enslavement of so many Greek citizens. The story was set in the aftermath of the sack of Troy and explored what became of the women left behind in its wake. Enslaved, sacrificed, or taken into the beds of the victorious Greeks, the sisters and wives of the Trojan leaders endured a fate that was only too familiar to the women of fifth-century BC Melos. As Hecuba, wife of King Priam and the queen consort of Troy, lamented:

Born of a king, I married a king,
And then delivered the best of children,
Not a mere lot, but the very crown of the Phrygians:

Children such as no other woman of Troy, Greece,
Or foreign lands could ever produce and boast of.
These I have seen fall to Greek spears.
I have cut off my hair at the tombs of their corpses,
And hearing of Priam, who gave them life, I wailed,
The news coming not from others, but to my own eyes,
After he was slaughtered at his own hearth,
And his city was captured. The girls I raised
To enter worthy marriages, I raised to be snatched
Away in the hands of strangers.
I can hope neither to be seen by them
Ever again, nor to see them myself.
Lastly, the cornice on my cake of misery,
I shall go to Greece as a slave woman in my dotage.[49]

Euripides was only too familiar with the impact of the war upon the women of Greece. It was very probably because there were too few men to go around that he took two wives. Bigamy, rare in Greece to date, became a means of overcoming the dramatic shortfall. A law passed by Pericles in 413 BC permitted Athenian men to have legitimate children by two citizen women to repopulate the city.

It is difficult to gauge how the women of Athens felt about this, but two years after the law was passed, their fertility became the subject of a new comedy by Aristophanes. The *Thesmophoriazusae* ('Women Celebrating the Thesmophoria') was set during a religious festival attended each autumn by married women in Greece in honour of Demeter, the goddess of grain, and her daughter, Persephone. Men were strictly forbidden from witnessing the fertility rites, which included periods of fasting, sexual abstinence, and the sacrifice and hurling of piglets into snake-filled ditches and recovery of their remains to dedicate on altars. In Aristophanes' satire, Euripides persuades a male relative to infiltrate the festival in female clothes, perturbed to discover that the women of the city are preparing to punish him for his cruel portrayal of their gender in his tragedies. Given his tender characterisation of the women of Troy, the claims of misogyny were peculiar, but Aristophanes could point to Medea and Phaedra and their crimes. Far from championing women himself, Aristophanes chose to portray them as slovenly, conniving and, with a stroke of dramatic irony, outrageously duplicitous. Euripides emerges from their ruse intact.

Aristophanes followed in Euripides' footsteps by exploring the Peloponnesian War from a female perspective. The panhellenic crew of women from both sides of the War who feature in his *Lysistrata*, also staged in 411 BC, orchestrate a sex strike in a bid to force their husbands to bring the fighting to an end. Athenian Lysistrata, the title character, is a vibrant creation. In the face of quite considerable opposition and doubt, she prevails upon the women of the various city-states to follow her lead and practise abstinence. She is not afraid to use humour. Women must deprive men of their bodies, she declares, and give up their usual sexual positions, even the 'Lioness on the Cheese-Grater'! The crowd rallies. Vegetable-sellers and market workers and mothers march to the top of the Acropolis. They know that this is where the treasury containing the war funds stands. They seize control of the surrounding area.

It is widely believed that the character and name of Lysistrata were inspired by a real woman, Lysimache, who was serving as chief hereditary priestess of Athena Polias and her Erechtheum shrine in the year the play was performed. The idea that women should physically take charge of the Acropolis may be outlandish, Aristophanes seems to be saying, but it is merely an extension of the reality, in which a woman presides symbolically over the city's most sacred space. He here acknowledges indirectly that a sex strike would not by itself bring about peace. Stunned by the audacity of their wives, the men of his play threaten to burn down the gates to the Acropolis. The women respond by pouring water, literally, upon their plans.

Amid the comedy, there is a highly poignant scene in which Lysistrata speaks to a male official of the frustrations endured by women, especially in wartime. For years, she says, they have had to remain silent, even when eager to cut in. Husbands would talk of the war, and their wives would ask them what had been said in the Assembly. The conversation seldom developed, for the men simply told the women to keep quiet and carry on with their weaving. This was not easy when they were mourning for the sons they had lost in battle. If the war is dire for married women, says Lysistrata, many of whom were widowed, it is even worse for unmarried women, who are being deprived of the opportunity of marrying altogether. Men, too, grow old, the official retorts. Yes, says Lysistrata, but there is a difference. Men may return home grey-haired and marry whenever they please. Women may not. Their window of opportunity is all too brief.

Lysistrata offers a number of pseudo-practical solutions in the play as to how women might adapt their daily lives to contribute to the war effort. They are used to cleaning wool, she says, so they could scrub the city clean of political parasites. They are used to weaving, so they would have little trouble in weaving a new cloak of state. Like their real-life counterparts, the women of the *Lysistrata* are denied the opportunity to step outside their usual spheres, but their sex strike plus occupation is ultimately successful. The men grow so desperate for sex that they initiate peace talks. And it is a metaphorical female figure, Reconciliation, who brings the men of Athens and Sparta together to make a swift agreement. Thanks are offered to Athena, a goddess of chastity, for the happy conclusion.

It is extraordinary that a comedian living in fifth-century Athens was able to communicate the female experience of war to an auditorium of men. Was Aristophanes encouraged to do so because women had begun to fill some of the theatre seats ordinarily taken by their husbands? It is plausible that this happened in wartime. In either case, Aristophanes had shown that gender was no barrier to his understanding of what life was truly like for women in society, especially at a time when they keenly felt they could be of service. Aristophanes' Lysistrata had become the mouthpiece for the half of the population that lacked the right to speak. Yes, the power of Lysistrata and her female companions rested in their bodies, but they had demonstrated their intellectual clout in masterminding the strike, taking the Acropolis, talking the official round to their way of seeing things. Historians of the Peloponnesian War should never underestimate the role that Euripides and Aristophanes played in presenting the female viewpoint, while Thucydides and Xenophon were busy focusing their energies upon chronicling the actions of men.

By the time *Lysistrata* premiered, the people of Greece had been at war, on and off, for two decades. In 411 BC, Sparta made an alliance with Persia, striking such fear into the Athenians that they recalled Alcibiades, in spite of his connections with both. After fleeing to Sparta during the Sicilian expedition, the slippery commander had taken refuge with the Persians, always valuing personal safety over loyalty. His return to Athens was brief. In 410 BC he masterminded a naval victory over Sparta before retiring to the Black Sea coast. It was here that he received news of an astonishing victory by the Athenians in a naval battle at Arginusae near Lesbos. As so often in the Peloponnesian War, the resulting joy was tempered by tears as reports came in that the younger Pericles, son of Aspasia and Pericles senior, had been executed for failing to rescue survivors. He had been specially legitimised and given Athenian citizenship on the death of his natural father and elected *strategos* for 406 BC only to be put to death, along with five other generals, for culpable dereliction of duty. Aspasia was now entirely bereft, having lost her husband and son.

Against Alcibiades' advice, the Athenians proceeded to Aegospotami, in the Hellespont, to confront the Spartans under their charismatic new commander, Lysander. This was to prove a disastrous final offensive for an already beleaguered Athens. By spring 404 BC the men who had taken up arms despite Alcibiades' recommendation had little choice but to admit defeat, and prepared to accept peace terms with Sparta.

The following years were ones of misery and instability for much of the Athenian population. Democracy was overturned as Lysander installed an oligarchy of Thirty Tyrants to rule the city with a heavy hand. In 403 BC a band of exiled Athenians succeeded in deposing the tyrants and reinstating their democracy, but peace, so easy to aspire to, failed to take hold. The first decades of the fourth century BC witnessed a continuation of hostilities between Greek city-states. It was only in 386 BC, with the establishment of a King's Peace by Persia, that the people of Athens and Sparta could begin to see a way forward. By the conditions of the agreement, most Greek city-states could continue to be self-governing, but Persia would control Cyprus and regain those territories of Asia Minor she had lost to the Hellenes in the Graeco-Persian Wars. Athens had come full circle. The optimism that had followed the earlier conflict and fuelled the regeneration of the city was permanently lost. A shadow had fallen over Athens and her women at the very moment another power was rising in the north.

Chapter X

Olympias' Games

Eurydice of Hierapolis offered this
To the Muses, seizing the desire in her soul for knowledge.
As the mother of sons in the prime of youth she finished learning
Letters, which become the records of spoken words.

Eurydice, mother of Philip II, on her pride at learning to write in the fourth century BC, quoted by Plutarch

For as long as the people of Macedon could remember, their homeland had been dismissed by members of the Greek city-states as a cultural backwater by comparison with lofty Athens. It was the very last place anyone would think to go in search of something beautiful. The Athenian democratic orator Demosthenes claimed it was impossible to buy so much as a decent slave there, though his vendetta against the Macedonian king was well known.[1] Philip II, the victim of Demosthenes' barbed 'philippics', was well aware of the rumours. The poor reputation of his kingdom ought to have been dispelled by Euripides' bold decision to end his life serving at what was, by all accounts, a highly artistic court in the Macedonian capital of Pella. But like the inhabitants of the contemporary Qin state in China, the Macedonians were destined to remain barbarians in the eyes of their neighbours until they could prove themselves otherwise.

Their opportunity came in 336 BC when Philip's daughter Cleopatra became betrothed to her maternal uncle. The wedding would provide the ideal setting to show the world how sophisticated life was in the north. Invitations would be sent out far and wide bidding distant friends to bring other friends to join in games, dances and meat-rich banquets in Cleopatra's honour.[2] Little could Philip have anticipated that his wife, the mother of the bride, would use the occasion to concentrate power in her own hands. The king's wish to host a party to remember would soon become a regret.

The problems within the Macedonian court had arisen many years earlier. Since coming to power almost a quarter of a century ago following the death of his elder brother in battle, Philip had attempted to Hellenise his kingdom, but his own way of life was so extraordinary that his efforts had only left his Greek peers bewildered. The people of Macedon lived by a most un-Greek set of traditions. They paid respect to Philip and his cavalry of *hetairoi* ('Companions'), drank their wine neat rather than mixed with water, and viewed it as perfectly acceptable for women to manage their own finances and move about freely, unimpeded by male guardians. There was no *polis*-style self-government but rather an unrestricted hereditary autocracy. And more significantly still, Philip was wildly polygamous, and owed much of his influence abroad to his selection of superbly connected brides.

First there was Audata, a woman from Illyria (on the western shore of the Balkan Peninsula); the marriage helped Philip to secure power following his defeat of the Illyrian king. She and Philip had a daughter named Cynane.[3] The girl would grow up to accompany Philip into battle and show him undying loyalty – even when he returned to war in her motherland.

Then there was Phila of Elimeia, which lay within the borders of Macedon on the south-west. And then Nicesipolis, who gave Philip another daughter, Thessalonice. And Philinna, who gave him a son, Arrhidaeus. Both Nicesipolis and Philinna were women of Greek Thessaly, over which Philip had been eager to consolidate his control. Then there was Meda, daughter of a king of Thrace, whom he married after subduing the territory.

But the most prominent and politically involved of Philip's wives would prove to be Olympias. She belonged to the old Greek family of the Aeacidae, which claimed kinship with both Achilles and Helen of Troy and had long been prominent in Epirus, just east of Corfu, some way south of Macedon. Olympias' mother is unknown, but her father had ruled Epirus as Neoptolemus I, and her brother Alexander was the current monarch. This was the man Cleopatra was to marry, further solidifying the alliance with an uncle-niece union.

Olympias and Philip had met in the green of youth while attending some religious *mysteries* on the north Aegean island of Samothrace.[4] Olympias was particularly partial to impassioned religious observance. She was an ardent devotee of Dionysus and practised snake-handling as part of a well-established Macedonian cult in his honour. She very much took the lead in showing off the snakes, removing them from baskets and allowing them to twirl themselves exotically around her garlands and her wand-like pole while men looked on in horror. The fact that Olympias and Philip had devoted themselves to the worship of deathly *chthonic* deities on Samothrace proved to be no impediment to a budding romance. It was undoubtedly politically expedient for the teenage Philip to secure an alliance with Epirus in order to strengthen the Macedonian defence against Illyria, not least because it was the Illyrians who were responsible for his brother's death. But that apart, Philip was bewitched by the snake-charming Olympias in all her otherworldly devotion and proposed marriage almost immediately. Within a couple of years, they had produced a son, Alexander, and their daughter, Cleopatra.

Olympias was known by a number of names – Polyxena, like the daughter of King Priam of Troy; Myrtale, perhaps in relation to her religious rites; and Olympias only from the time of Alexander's birth in 356 BC. News had arrived of the victory of one of Philip's horses at the Olympic Games at the same time as she was delivered of her son.[5] This was believed to be deeply auspicious. Arrhidaeus, Philip's son by Philinna, may have had the stronger claim to power as the elder of the two boys, but he was said to have suffered from a disability that hindered his mental and physical development. Rumours that his condition had resulted from drug-poisoning at the hands of Olympias were baseless.[6] Whatever was wrong with Arrhidaeus, it was deemed grave enough to thwart his prospects as a successor.

Many signs over the past twenty years had given Olympias reason to hope that Philip was raising her son to follow in his path as ruler. Alexander alone of the children at court was entrusted to Aristotle for tuition, for example. Reputed to be the greatest philosopher among the Greeks, Aristotle had accepted a handsome wage to come to Macedon, despite knowing that Philip had been responsible for the destruction of his home city of Stageira and the exile and enslavement of many of his fellow countrymen.[7] He had arrived in Macedon when Alexander was thirteen years old and proceeded to teach him everything from ethics and politics to medicine in the comfortable surroundings of a shrine sacred to the nymphs.[8] Despite their less than ideal beginnings, the two men grew close over the years. In his adulthood, Alexander would carry Aristotle's version of the *Iliad* with him on campaign and sleep with it under his pillow.

The young man's own first taste of military life came sooner than he or the increasingly ambitious Olympias might have expected. Alexander was just sixteen when Philip set off on an expedition against Byzantium, leaving him regent of Macedon, and eighteen when he was allowed to launch his first major cavalry charge.[9] For Olympias, it was an especially promising indication of Philip's intentions that Alexander should accompany him to Chaeronea, north-west Boeotia, in 338 BC. The engagement would be of signal importance to both Macedon and the Greek world at its greatest extent.

The Battle of Chaeronea took place against a fraught political backdrop. Since the Peloponnesian War, Athens and Sparta had continued to spar, but other city-states, particularly Greek Thebes, were on the rise.[10] Macedonia had a growing military might of its own and Philip was proving to be an impulsive leader with a sly political acumen. The engagement at Chaeronea was to be the grand finale of a series of strategic moves.

Philip had originally lent Thebes his support in order to maintain a passage for his kingdom to the mainland via the pass at Thermopylae. But at Chaeronea, democratic Thebes had chosen to side with Athens, leaving the 30,000-strong Macedonian infantry to confront an Athens-Thebes coalition. Alexander, eighteen years old but with several victories already behind him, commanded the cavalry on the left wing of the Chaeronean plain and led the way in wearing down the Thebans' crack infantry force, known latterly as the Sacred Band. Formed of pairs of male lovers, this special contingent, ordinarily so stalwart, proved no match for the aggression of Alexander's warriors and was utterly annihilated. Some of the 254 skeletons discovered in a mass grave at the site from 1880 still had blades embedded between their ribs and others were missing body parts.[11] A further 1,000 Athenians died in the field and twice as many survivors were taken prisoner. Philip imposed a garrison and oligarchy upon Thebes but was relatively gentle towards Athens. He had no war fleet of triremes and anticipated that Athens's might prove useful. His victory was so decisive that it secured him a Macedonian hegemony over the city-states of the Aegean and the Greek mainland, exclusive of Sparta, as well as over the Balkans. The Greek *poleis* were gathered together under a new confederation known to later historians as the League of Corinth.

Alexander had been poised to assist his father in the next arm of his campaign, which was to carry him east with the Greeks to reclaim the cities taken from Hellas during the Graeco-Persian Wars. Just lately, however, the relationship between Alexander, Olympias and Philip had begun to sour. The king, now in his mid-forties, had fallen violently in love with Eurydice, the teenage niece of Attalus, one of his chief courtiers.[12] A well-born Macedonian, Eurydice was even younger than Alexander.

At the wedding – Philip's seventh – Attalus made an ill-judged remark about what distinguished his niece from the king's other wives. At last, he said, in marrying a Macedonian, Philip would be able to produce legitimate children to contrast with the bastard sons he had already brought into the world.[13] It was probably no accident that Alexander should have overheard this. Incensed, the prince picked up his wine cup and hit Attalus with it. Although he would become notorious for his drinking, Alexander was usually capable of making a cup last the duration of a conversation, so Attalus was probably drenched as well as cut.[14] Attalus fought back in kind, but the dispute did not end there. In defence of his new relative, Philip raised his sword against Alexander, but wisely decided to take it no further. The evening had been a disaster. Shortly after the wedding, Alexander left for Illyria, now one of Macedonia's western territories, and Olympias for her homeland of Epirus.

Plutarch, Alexander's later biographer, interpreted Olympias' departure as evidence of her jealous temperament. Philip had taken a new, younger, Macedonian bride, who would now take pride of place at court. But Olympias knew that Philip had many wives. Plutarch underestimated Olympias' need to protect her dignity and preserve the family until the tension eased. Philip had commissioned a gold and ivory monument of himself with her and Alexander and his parents at Olympia following his victory at Chaeronea.[15] Olympias was determined that her position and Alexander's within the royal household remained adamantine. While all eyes focused on Philip's new bride and the slightest sign of pregnancy, Olympias was wise to make her exit.

Eurydice had given birth to a daughter, Europa, by the time Olympias returned to Macedonia the following year for Cleopatra's wedding. Attention turned once again to the Epirote bloodline. Overnight, the old ceremonial capital of Aegae ('Place of Goats'), at modern Vergina, became the centre of the world as well-wishers poured in all around to pay King Philip and Olympias court and mark their daughter's nuptials.[16] There could have been little expectation among the guests of what was about to occur.

Early one morning during the course of the celebrations, the wedding party was invited to congregate at the theatre, just north of the palace, for a special performance. The seats of the auditorium, wooden but for a single stone row closest to the stage, filled rapidly, and a procession began to feed across the floor. Macedonian artisans had crafted the most spectacular models of the twelve Olympian gods and added to their number an august thirteenth figure, unmistakeable as Philip.[17] The king followed his effigy in a striking white cloak. To make even more of an entrance, he had his guard proceed before him, meaning that he would stroll into the theatre without them. Philip was now doubly recognisable and wholly exposed.

He was in high spirits as he prepared to receive his audience's applause. One might have been forgiven for thinking it was yet another of *his* weddings they were there to celebrate. All eyes were upon the king when, apparently out of nowhere, a man ran at him with a dagger and stabbed him hard between the ribs. Was this an actor, or a murderer, a stage tragedy or an actual assassination? Hopes that Philip had been playing a part began to fade soon after he collapsed. While onlookers hastened to revive the king, the assassin fled the theatre for the city gates, where he had tethered his horses, the royal guard chasing rabidly after him with javelins. It was said that the culprit tripped on a vine just as he was about to mount his horse, allowing the guard to close the gap and pierce him through as he stumbled to his feet. The assassin did not know for certain as he died that he had fulfilled his mission. Philip, too, was dead.

It did not take long to identify the perpetrator as a former member of Philip's personal bodyguard. Pausanias had once enjoyed the king's favour on account of his good looks. Even with seven wives to satisfy him, Philip took a number of male lovers, which was in itself sufficient to stoke Pausanias' ire. The guardsman was not the sort to be satisfied with being one of a number. The sight of Philip admiring another man had inspired in him a jealousy worthy of Sappho. When the love rival threw himself in front of Philip to save his life in battle, Pausanias' envy reached fresh heights.[18] How could Pausanias compete with such a show of heroism? Since he could not have Philip for himself, he was determined that no one else would either.

Pausanias did not kill out of sexual jealousy alone. His obsession with the king had begun to waver following a deeply unpleasant incident at court. Attalus, the uncle of Philip's wife Eurydice and friend of Philip's lover, had deliberately got Pausanias drunk and had him sexually assaulted. Pausanias recovered and lodged a complaint with Philip, but Philip had refused to take action against Attalus.[19] Pausanias concluded that Philip had never truly loved him, planned revenge, and found it at Cleopatra's wedding.

It seemed as unlikely at the time as it does today that Pausanias was solely responsible for the assassination of Philip II. There were other people in Macedon with less personal reasons for wanting the king dead. Certainly, Alexander behaved as though he believed that others had been involved in his father's murder, too, presumably as part of a coup. In the aftermath of the tragedy, he had a number of individuals put to death to avenge his father and to protect himself, including three of Pausanias' sons; two sons of a former commander of Philip who had fallen foul of him; Attalus; and a cousin, who might otherwise have threatened Alexander's position as Philip's successor.

But suspicion also fell, with good reason, upon Alexander himself and upon Olympias for inciting Pausanias to the deed. Memories of their grievance at Philip's wedding to young Eurydice were still fresh.

Thousands of years later, in the 1970s, a series of grand tombs was discovered beneath a mound at the site of ancient Aegae.[20] Tomb I had vibrantly painted walls bearing scenes of Hades' rape of Persephone and contained the remains of three people. One was an unusually tall man of about 1.8 metres with a severe left-knee trauma that would have given him a limping gait.[21] Philip, a strong fighter, is known to have developed a limp through a severe lance injury to his left knee (he also lost his right eye during a siege). The other skeleton belonged to a woman about eighteen years old and 1.65 metres in height. Interred with her was a newborn baby whose gender could not be determined. It would appear on the basis of this evidence that Eurydice and her daughter died – or were killed – in the aftermath of Philip's assassination along with Alexander's other victims.[22] While it certainly cannot be ruled out that they died of natural causes such as a post-partum infection, the timing of the double tragedy makes it at least plausible that Olympias and Alexander helped pull the strings behind not only their demise, but Philip's, too.

King Alexander III of Macedon enjoyed a smoother accession than his mother had anticipated, but for many of the Greek city-states conquered by his father the moment of transition felt ripe for revolution. No sooner had the twenty-year-old been crowned than revolts broke out in pockets of the League of Corinth. Alexander, determined to quash the most ardent dissenters as swiftly as possible, sent an army as far as the Danube before making war on the rebel Thebans.[23] About 6,000 Thebans were killed and many more enslaved, including the city's women, before Alexander's men set fire to the city-state in 335 BC. The former house of the praise-poet Pindar and some religious shrines were all that survived the flames. A *hetaera* and artists' model named Phryne later offered to pay for the reconstruction of the city walls. The wealthy woman had escaped prosecution for impiety after allegedly inventing a new god and assembling a motley band of devotees. It was no doubt a fiction that she was acquitted after baring her breasts to the jury. The condition of her offer, which was apparently rejected, was that a plaque should be erected at Thebes explaining that she, a *hetaera*, had rebuilt what Alexander had destroyed.

Having made an example of Thebes, Alexander endeavoured to do as little as was needed to secure his position; he simply shrugged off the Spartans when they failed to bow. An unusual story is told in the sources of his willingness to reward people's loyalty. It features Timocleia, a young mother from Thrace, who is raped at home by a group of men from her own city. The criminals ransack the house, demanding to know where she keeps her gold and silver, so Timocleia leads them to the well in her garden in which she claims she deposits her treasures.[24] As one of the Thracians bends over to peer into the dark well, she pushes him in, casting stones after him to ensure he is dead. The other Thracians lead the woman to Alexander to be punished. The king is impressed by the calm dignity of her entrance. More than that, he is moved when he discovers that she is the sister of a man who died fighting on the opposite side to him and his father at Chaeronea. She is therefore allowed to carry on living with her children as a free citizen.

There may be little truth to this tale, but it was characteristic of Alexander in this period to deal with matters arising swiftly as he strove to move forward with the campaign begun by his father. Within just two years of becoming king, Alexander would have launched an expedition against the Persian Empire and set out east with more than 30,000 infantrymen, 5,000 cavalry, and recruits from across the Greek city-states. Olympias, remaining in Macedon with Antipater, his late father's loyal adviser and general, would prove herself once more.

Alexander had already led the Macedonians to victory against the Persians once by the time he reached Issus, a town close to the Levantine coast, in November 333 BC. The opportunity to enjoy first a tour of Troy and perform honours for Athena, Priam and Achilles, his particular hero, proved too much to pass over. Alexander was in the land of the men he most aspired to emulate. Homeric *thumos* ('fighting spirit') drove him on to the Granicus (Biga), one of the great rivers of the Troad, where he experienced little trouble in pushing the Persians back across the far bank. As he worked his way down through Asia Minor, he granted the formerly Greek cities he passed through freedom from taxation and independence from Persian rule, and in this way began chipping away at the Persian Empire's edges. He liberated Troy, granted it a democracy, and laid siege to Artemisia's former kingdom of Halicarnassus in Caria and other cities in the process.

The Carians were unusual in permitting women to succeed their fathers as monarchs even if they had surviving brothers, and Alexander used this local custom to his advantage. The late ruler of Caria, known as the satrap, had passed his power to his daughter Ada upon his deathbed in 344 BC.[25] Ada, who was married to one of her brothers, had since been usurped and driven into exile by another of her brothers. She retained rule over one part of Caria alone. By the time Alexander arrived, however, the usurping brother had died and another male satrap had been installed in his place. Rather than rely upon him for support, Alexander went directly to Ada, believing he had a better chance of striking a deal with her. In exchange for a portion of her territory known as Alinda he was prepared to grant her command of the final siege of the acropolis at

Halicarnassus.[26] Ada was only too happy to agree because the deal fell in her favour. After fulfilling the command at Halicarnassus she was able to reclaim her position as ruler of both Alinda and Caria more widely.[27] Macedonian troops and a general were put at her disposal rather than imposed strictly upon her. Few could doubt the sincerity of her loyalty to Alexander when she proceeded to adopt him as her son. Alexander honoured her with the title 'Mother' and she offered him parcels of meat and use of the finest cooks she knew.[28] We can only imagine that Olympias was prepared to lay aside any maternal jealousy towards a middle-aged woman with no children of her own.

As Alexander prepared for his second major engagement against the Persians, at Issus, word of his extraordinary capabilities began to spread. It was said that the young Macedonian had already achieved the impossible and with his sword released the knot in the cornel-bark yoke of the king's carriage at Gordian in Phrygia. An oracle had proclaimed that whoever achieved this feat would be destined to rule all of Asia.[29] The moment had arrived for Alexander to meet Darius III and fulfil what was written in the stars.

The Persian king had come to power around the time of Philip's death and held the undisputed advantage in manpower. There were perhaps 30,000 more men in his charge than Alexander's. In the event, the numbers meant little, for Alexander was able to lead a confident cavalry charge against the Persian left wing, throwing the enemy into confusion. Thousands of Persians met their deaths. Rumour spread that Darius was one of them.

The women of the Persian court, unlike the women of Macedon, customarily accompanied their men to war. They were among the first to receive the confused reports of Darius' fate. As word went around that Alexander had been seen driving back to camp with Darius' armour, they began to scream, Darius' mother, Sisygambis, standing beside one of his wives (and possibly sister) Stateira, two of his daughters, Stateira II and Drypetis, and his six-year-old son.[30] Their cries were so loud that they reached Alexander in his tent. The Macedonian, at first confused by the commotion, took pity on them. He sent one of his men to reassure Darius' family that Darius was alive and well and that they would be shown clemency in spite of his defeat.[31]

On the following day, Alexander went to visit Darius' family in person with his adviser (and very probably male lover) Hephaestion. Darius' mother, Sisygambis, stood up. She knew all about Alexander, had been in close proximity to him, but she had not seen him until now. The sight of two Macedonians approaching side by side proved quite confounding. Looking from one to the other, she made an unconscious assumption and addressed the taller and more handsome of the pair as Alexander. While blessed with long leonine hair and compelling eyes, Alexander was not an especially tall man, and his habit of tilting his head to one side did little to help his inches.[32] Sisygambis realised her mistake. Alexander could see how embarrassed she was and told her not to worry. He addressed her warmly, like Ada, as 'Mother'. She would be allowed to retain her servants, he told her, and he would give her more in addition to jewellery taken from the spoils.[33] Her daughters would have dowries and he would treat Darius' son as his own. They would remain at Susa, the Persian capital, and each of them would be tutored in Greek.[34] The women had no need to fear male intrusion for they would be granted secure bedchambers. They were, all the same, Alexander's prisoners.

The other Persian women of the camp received no such treatment. Darius usually travelled with 300 concubines, a female army so peculiarly large, that any Persian who thought to question the statistic could not have been surprised to learn that it originated in a Greek source.[35] If not quite 300-strong, the female contingent was still large, and now exceptionally vulnerable. Following the battle, Alexander's soldiers began to tear through the enemy camp, assaulting whomever they encountered, their ears closed to all appeals as Persians begged for mercy at their feet. These women were dragged away as captives and sex slaves.

There is no suggestion that the women closest to Darius were subject to similar attacks. Historians indeed praised Alexander repeatedly for the sexual restraint he exhibited towards Darius' beautiful wife Stateira in particular. Whether he was worthy of this praise remains questionable. Within a couple of years of being granted a secure bedchamber at Susa, Stateira became pregnant, and the father of her child was never named.[36] When she died in labour, Alexander gave Darius every assurance that he had remained true to his word and never touched her, but it is possible that he lied.

Alexander was unmarried when he set out on campaign and only too familiar with the precedent his father had set with his seven wives and other lovers. It is interesting that, while he had his pick of women following his victory at Issus, he now chose to forge a lasting relationship with someone he had known as a child at his father's court at Pella. Barsine was the half-Greek daughter of a Persian satrap who had risen up against the Persian king many years earlier and fled to Macedon with his family.[37] Alexander must have come to know her over the course of about a decade while she benefited from Philip's hospitality. She had since returned to Persia, where her father pledged his allegiance to Darius, and had married an uncle and had a daughter. Following her husband's early death, Barsine had married another uncle and had a son, only to be widowed a second time. She and her children ended up at the court of Darius in Damascus for their own protection.[38] The Macedonian army took her captive nonetheless as they sought to triumph over the Persian enemy.

Although Barsine was a prisoner, there is no indication that she was coerced into becoming Alexander's mistress, and one might imagine she felt some relief when she was reunited with her childhood friend in the midst of the frightening ordeal.[39] Barsine and Alexander would remain lovers for several years in spite of enforced separations. Syria and Phoenicia, an important Persian naval base, still awaited Alexander as he moved south.

By the time Alexander came up against Darius again, he had achieved notoriety for his feats in the Levant, which included a seven-month siege of Tyre that resulted in the execution of 6,000 Tyrians and crucifixion of 2,000 more along the shoreline; further triumphs in Egypt, where he was hailed as pharaoh; and the establishment of the first of several cities he would name Alexandria in the Nile Delta.[40] With an iron helmet on his head and a breastplate lined with linen from Issus wrapped around his body, he mounted his loyal steed Bucephalus and steeled himself for the fight.

The site of his meeting with Darius lay just inside northern Iraq at Gaugamela ('Camel's House'). The Persian infantry and cavalry which gathered there were vaster by far – one report claimed there were a million soldiers – but this was not the first time Alexander had been outnumbered.[41] He led a bold charge, and while he endured heavy losses, he ultimately routed his royal rival. Alexander pursued Darius across the Zagros and Alborz mountains. The Persian was later killed by his own men in an attempted coup to save him from death at Alexander's hands.

In a final act of compassion, Alexander had Darius' body laid out in state and returned to his mother, Sisygambis.[42]

It was a small gesture given the carnage the Macedonians were to unleash on Persepolis following their victory. They had covered a vast distance – more than 2,000 kilometres separate northern Egypt and Iran – but energy never failed them. No sooner had they reached the Persian capital at the end of 331 BC than they had pillaged all that was left, murdered the civilian population, and enslaved the women. Soon, all that was left of the once bustling centre was the palace complex, but it was not long before the finest part of that, too, was obliterated.

An Athenian courtesan named Thaïs threw the first firebrands at Xerxes' glorious building.[43] She had once served Alexander's bed and would later become the mistress or wife of Alexander's friend and military general, Ptolemy, later Ptolemy I Soter, ruler of Egypt.[44] She had been dining with Alexander and his men in the palace when the idea of torching it came to her. Unusually for a woman in this society, she was allowed to stand up and make a dinner speech, which she used to reflect on what a difference it made to be luxuriating here after journeying across Asia. There would be greater pleasure still, she declared, in setting fire to the building Xerxes had formerly called home.

Thaïs' motivation was allegedly to prove to future generations that the women in Alexander's entourage had inflicted an even greater punishment upon the Persians than the men. She had perhaps heard of the viciousness of Persian women such as Parysatis, consort of Darius II and mother of Cyrus the Younger, and her infamous poisoning of her daughter-in-law and others at the beginning of the century. The harsh decisiveness of Thaïs' words penetrated the drunken crowd and inflamed further passions. In the exhilaration of the moment, Alexander agreed to Thaïs' plan and led his company through the palace to drop torches on the grandest hall. The flames spread more quickly than anyone had anticipated and soon engulfed the building. It was said that regret flashed upon the face of Alexander as he realised he had been seized by pyromania. It is telling that Ptolemy did not mention Thaïs' role in the conflagration in his history of Alexander's campaigns. The pharaoh would be far prouder of his wife for giving him three brilliant and successful children.[45]

*

Back in Macedon, the relationship between Olympias and Antipater, Alexander's regent, had grown increasingly difficult. Letters had begun to wend their way east detailing their ongoing animus. Olympias complained to her son of Antipater's repeated insolence towards the court. Antipater wrote Alexander an exceedingly long and trying letter bemoaning Olympias' meddling. Olympias was exacting a heavy rent for her place in the kingdom, Alexander sighed, knowing only too well how involved she liked to be in his affairs.[46] He had often grown impatient of this himself, but when it came to weighing up her grievances against those of Antipater, there was no doubting the weight of his mother's tears.[47] So ground down was he by the correspondence that he considered removing Antipater from power for a more peaceful life. Before Alexander could act, however, Olympias left Macedon for her native Epirus just as she had at the time of Philip's seventh wedding.[48]

The couple's daughter Cleopatra had recently lost her husband in battle and now resided in Molossia as regent of Epirus. Her responsibilities over her maternal homeland were considerable. In addition to caring for her young son, she had to take charge of the grain supply when famine struck, receiving in quantities from Cyrene in her own name, just as the women of Persia had done centuries earlier. She also dutifully oversaw the dispatch of grain to Corinth in its hour of need.[49] Beyond this, Cleopatra had an important role to play in international diplomacy; in a surviving inscription, she is named as a *thearodoch*, which was the title given to the official who welcomed ambassadors.[50] Cleopatra's authority was not unique. In China the Qin had revealed themselves as anything but backward in their unification of the country and willingness to recognise women as heads of household and contributors to local industry.[51] Cleopatra was, however, unusual among the women of her time as a potential threat to the male regent of Macedon.

Olympias certainly believed that Antipater could be thwarted by a female-led coalition. On returning from Epirus in 331 BC, she prevailed upon Cleopatra to help her forge a faction against the regent and assume his position. The mother would take Epirus while Cleopatra sought authority over Macedonia.[52] All they needed Alexander to do was to recall Antipater so he was no longer in their way. Alexander, seldom one to say no to the women of his family, duly summoned his beleaguered regent to his current base in Babylon, effectively ending his control at home.

Olympias' decision to retreat to Epirus was, once again, less defeatist than it looked. She had chosen the perfect moment to reassert herself.

A few years later, in 327 BC, Alexander's childhood friend Barsine gave birth to his son, who was named Heracles in honour of his father's alleged ancestor. About the same time, Alexander decided to get married. He might have chosen to propose to Barsine to legitimise their child, but he was now twenty-nine and believed that his future lay elsewhere. He met Roxana ('Little Star') at a banquet in modern Afghanistan and was dazzled by her beauty.[53] She was, like him, an experienced traveller, and in coming years she would visit Athens to dedicate a gold drinking cup and jewellery to Athena on the Acropolis. More pressingly, her father, Oxyartes, was a local chieftain among the Sogdian people, north of Bactria, whom Alexander hoped to win over to his side. Alexander understood the power of a geopolitical match. The pair were married in accordance with local customs. While Roxana is thought to have accompanied Alexander on his ensuing travels in India, her political role, like that of Barsine, was to be limited by comparison with that of her mother-in-law and sister-in-law.

When the widowed Cleopatra embarked upon a new relationship of her own, Alexander gave her his blessing, stating that it was only right that she, too, should enjoy the privileges of royal power.[54] It was incredibly rare that a woman received such encouragement from her own male kin. Alexander appears to have recognised that women were just as capable as men of forging politically useful connections.

Within three years of his wedding to Roxana, he had followed in the footsteps of his polygamous father and married again. Almost a decade earlier, he had promised to provide the two captive daughters of Darius with dowries. Improving upon that offer, he married the younger Stateira, and Stateira's sister Drypetis was yoked to his handsome adviser Hephaestion. Both weddings took place at Susa in 324 BC as part of a mass ceremony involving multiple marriages between Alexander's Companions and Persian women. At the same time as marrying Stateira, Alexander married Parysatis, the daughter of a former Persian king.[55] A total of ninety-two bridal chambers were prepared for the ninety-two weddings expected to take place.[56] Sumptuous fabrics of gold, red and purple were rolled out, and Alexander's wedding bed was elevated upon gold feet. The main banqueting tent was supported by columns and curtains embroidered with animals. Five days of music and performance followed. Before the brides were led in for the first time, the grooms were seated all together in a row. Each kissed his new wife on her right hand before leading her away.

Alexander bestowed dowries upon every one of the brides. Over 10,000 other marriages were said to have taken place between Macedonians and Asian women in this period. The weddings represented the marriage of two empires and provided a happy gloss on a difficult period in Alexander's campaign. The Macedonian's ambition to push beyond the borders of modern Pakistan was thwarted by mutinies among his exhausted men. Next to what was to follow, indeed, these long wedding days seemed halcyon.

Alexander had incorporated his new Persian territories into his kingdom and extended Macedon's reach as far as the north-west frontier of the Indian subcontinent when he returned to Babylon in 323 BC and fell ill. He had been enjoying a bout of feasting and drinking when he developed a fever.[57] Some reported that he also had a pain in his back. He was thirsty, but drinking more wine only caused him delirium, and his temperature continued to rise. He was still bedridden two weeks later at the palace of Nebuchadnezzar II when, on 10 June, a cloudy day, he died, aged just thirty-two.[58]

The cause of Alexander's death continues to be debated. Malaria, typhoid, pancreatitis and liver disease have all been proposed as diagnoses. Certainly, in the immediate aftermath of the event, there was little speculation that the cause of death was anything other than natural. It was only five years later that suspicions arose.

Alexander was said to have grown fearful of Antipater and his sons, quarrelsome Cassander, and his younger brother Iolas, who served as his cupbearer.[59] A fictional biography fancifully attributed to Alexander's court historian Callisthenes would implicate Antipater in an unlikely plot involving the concealment of poison in the hoof of a mule.[60] That Antipater and his sons had anything to do with Alexander's death is highly improbable. The chances of establishing the truth of what happened are small. The king's corpse was laid in a gold sarcophagus filled with honey and carried first to Memphis by his friend Ptolemy, who was to establish the next great dynasty in Egypt, and then to Alexandria, where it remained for hundreds of years. The current whereabouts of Alexander's sarcophagus are unknown.

The death of Alexander meant freedom for the people of Athens and other Greek city-states, many of whom rejoiced at the prospect of extricating themselves from Macedon's grip. Among the Persians, however, there was some cause for tears. Sisygambis, mother of Darius and Alexander's grandmother-in-law, was said to have been devastated by the loss of the young man. She was now an old woman and was allegedly so shaken by the news that she ceased eating and consequently died five days later.[61] Her granddaughter Stateira, Alexander's widow who may have been pregnant, was killed on the orders of Roxana, Alexander's little star of a wife, who was carrying his child too. With her mind firmly focused on the succession, Roxana had forged a letter summoning Stateira and her sister to a meeting, which ended with the two Persian women at the bottom of a well. A short time later, Roxana gave birth to Alexander's posthumous son, another Alexander.

The death of Alexander, soon hailed 'the Great', triggered nothing short of civil war between his potential heirs and those who sought to inherit his kingdom by force. The following years would witness particular strife between his mother and a newly emergent female member of the family, eager to stake her own claim to the succession.

Adea was the granddaughter of Philip II, and daughter of Cynane of Illyria. Her mother had once accompanied Philip into battle and covered herself in glory by killing an Illyrian queen through a single blow to the throat. Widowed young, she chose to remain single and to raise Adea in her own mould, as a fighter. She had every hope that Adea might stake her claim to the succession. Since Alexander had no firm designated heir, an agreement was initially reached whereby his power passed to his half-brother Arrhidaeus conjointly with Roxana's new son, Alexander, with Antipater acting as regent. Cynane now moved to betroth her daughter to Arrhidaeus.

In her determination, Cynane crossed over into Asia with an army and pledged to die if the wedding did not come about. The general who told her to stand down or do precisely that must have believed she was bluffing. Cynane's subsequent death at the hands of one of Alexander's former generals sparked immediate outrage. Unnerved by the sudden sequence of events, the army resolved to do everything possible to see Adea married to Arrhidaeus, and a wedding was duly arranged. In homage to her paternal great-grandmother, who had taught herself to read and write, Adea acquired the additional name Eurydice after her marriage. Adea-Eurydice, as she was now styled, was not yet twenty, but the onus was very much upon her to capitalise on the void left by Alexander's will. Her new husband, as has been seen, was deemed mentally incapable.

There is no record of Adea-Eurydice excelling in battle like her mother, but it has been suggested that a pair of greaves interred in one of the royal tombs and formerly associated with Philip II were in fact hers.[62] Cynane had certainly educated her in the Illyrian art of war.[63] While Adea-Eurydice might have drawn on her military expertise to further her interests, when it came to dealing with Antipater and his enduring authority, she found words more powerful than weapons. In the immediate aftermath of Alexander's death, the regent had turned his hand to quelling the rebellions which broke out in Athens and other city-states, imposing an oligarchy on the former. Adea-Eurydice now stirred up accusations against him and delivered a speech reinforcing the same points in a bid to persuade his soldiers to revolt and cast him out for her.[64] Her plan worked and Antipater only narrowly escaped with his life.

Antipater was not the last of Adea-Eurydice's troubles. Reinstated by his cavalry shortly after his displacement, he died in 319 BC, leaving another of Alexander's former generals as regent. Polyperchon was well aware of the messiness of the situation and, so Adea-Eurydice believed, determined to turn the balance of power against her. It was at Polyperchon's invitation that Olympias made her way back from Epirus to care for her grandson, Roxana's boy, in Macedon.[65] If there was any doubt in Adea-Eurydice's mind that Polyperchon was plotting to install the young Alexander on the throne, it soon dissipated. The new regent began raising an army in Epirus.

As Olympias made her way to Macedon with the child, Adea-Eurydice frantically sought help for her own cause and alighted upon Cassander, Antipater's son, as a potential ally. Cassander had hoped to marry Cleopatra in the aftermath of Alexander's death. He was clearly hungry for power. To Adea-Eurydice's relief he agreed to draw up an army of his own among the Macedonians.[66]

A classical historian described what followed as the first war to be waged by two women.[67] One army of men lined up behind Olympias, another behind Adea-Eurydice, both under orders to do a woman's bidding. To differentiate the two sides in his narrative, the historian described Olympias as raging like a bacchanalian maenad, drums beating, hair flying, while Adea-Eurydice advanced calmly like a Macedonian general. It is difficult to believe that the middle-aged mother of Alexander the Great revelled so passionately in the field. Had she done so, the soldiers posted under Adea-Eurydice would hardly have been moved to go over to her side, as they did through loyalty to her. Their revolt left Adea-Eurydice and her husband deserted.

The pair was soon put under armed guard at triumphant Olympias' command. Arrhidaeus was stabbed to death, but for her haughtiness, Olympias declared, Adea-Eurydice deserved a harsher punishment. A parcel arrived bearing the young woman's name. It contained a noose, a sword and some hemlock. Adea-Eurydice was to choose her own way out.

While Adea-Eurydice took the noose, Olympias took a new name, adding Stratonice ('Victory') to her long list of sobriquets. If only she had stopped there, she might have recovered her breath and seen her grandson raised to power. As it was, the anxiety of unfinished business compelled Olympias to go after the allies of Cassander, who had aided Adea-Eurydice. More heinous even than the assassinations she oversaw of Cassander's relatives was the ensuing desecration of Cassander's brother's tomb.[68] The Macedonian people believed that Olympias had gone too far this time. Isolated, Olympias fled the city with her daughter-in-law Roxana and the young Alexander, and sought refuge in the fortified seaside town of Pydna.

Thirsty for vengeance, Cassander pursued the fugitives there in 317 BC and raised a lengthy siege. Many of the people trapped within the walls with Olympias died of famine together with their horses and elephants. The situation at Pydna was so desperate that it was said that some people even turned to cannibalism. It was the following spring, 316 BC, before Olympias felt in a position to launch a quinquereme (a galley with three banks of oars) to make her escape. Cassander came after her and seized her ship. Olympias admitted defeat, and Cassander's men overran Pydna, Pella and Amphipolis.

The assembly at Macedon voted to condemn Olympias to death. The only concern for Cassander was that, if she was to return to the city first, the Macedonians might pity her and attempt to save her at the eleventh hour. He therefore sent Olympias a ship with a message instructing her to travel to Athens. There was always a chance the vessel would sink. Olympias refused to go. A short time later she was met by a band of Cassander's soldiers. The very sight of her so overwhelmed the would-be assassins that they proved unable to fulfil their orders out of respect for her position. It was left to the relatives of Cassander's allies to carry out the deed. Olympias made no plea as she died. So it was, wrote one historian, that the widow of Philip and mother of Alexander attained the highest dignity possible.[69]

With Olympias dead, there was little hope for Roxana and the young boy who might have been Alexander IV. Both were captured by Cassander and put to death. Olympias' daughter, Cleopatra, died a couple of years later in 308 BC. She had travelled to Sardis in Lydia in the wake of Alexander's assassination. Despite having had a number of suitors eager to ally themselves with her as the sister of the late king, she was yet to remarry, perhaps preferring to retain her own power like Cynane. Antigonus the One-Eyed, a former general, ordered the governor of Sardis to keep Cleopatra in his city so that she had little opportunity of becoming involved in the fraught affairs of Macedon.[70] Little light can be shed on Cleopatra's final years in captivity, but it was said that Antigonus had her killed by a group of women to conceal his part in the crime.

The contest between Alexander's male 'Successors' continued apace. Antigonus took control of Asia Minor, Greece and Phoenicia and in 306 BC declared himself king of Macedon. While he competed with Ptolemy and Seleucus, former governor of Babylon, to acquire Cyprus, the Cypriot king committed suicide, prompting his wife Axiothea to kill their daughters to prevent them from being enslaved.[71] Axiothea then fell on her sword together with other female members of the family. The impact of Alexander's death could hardly have been more devastating or widespread.

In the midst of the continuing succession wars, the Athenians succeeded in shrugging off their oligarchic constraints and resurrecting a weakened version of their former democracy. In 302 BC, Seleucus defeated the eighty-year-old Antigonus in battle and, just over twenty years later, in 281 BC, saw off Lysimachus, another of the warring successors, too. What had briefly been the largest empire in the ancient world fragmented into a series of smaller kingdoms. The Seleucids, who traded India for war elephants, acquired power over Asia from Syria to Iran; the Ptolemies over Egypt; and the Antigonids over Macedon. Olympias, Eurydice and Cleopatra had all played their part in ensuring that no one outside the family could singly capitalise upon Alexander's short-lived conquests.

Chapter XI

Dido's Curse

Delighting no more in the sea I bob upon
I shall rouse myself from the depths and hold up my neck,
Not blow around the beautiful prows of ships
Gasconading over a bust of my own image;
The purple sea threw me onto dry land,
And I lie here on this coast.

Anyte, *Greek Anthology* 7.215, third century BC, on a dolphin

The people of Rome had stood largely aloof from the Wars of the Successors. While Alexander's former empire was being carved up, the Romans were greedily eyeing the grain supplies of Sicily beyond its borders. After decades of war with the peoples of Italy and Gaul, they had extended their reach across the Italian mainland as far south as the Bay of Naples and hoped that they might go further still. Their moves on Thurii and surrounding cities in Magna Graecia ('Greater Greece') prompted the people of the Greek city-state of Tarentum (Taranto) in Apulia to retaliate. It was in the course of their ensuing conflict with the Tarentines that the Romans came into contact with a new enemy, destined to stymie their expansion efforts.

Pyrrhus, king of Epirus, was Olympias' first cousin once removed. A man of few teeth and startling countenance, he had, in spite of his unconventional appearance, made a string of expedient marriages, which enabled him to establish himself with some force internationally.[1] His first wife, Antigone, was a great-great-granddaughter of Antipater, Alexander's former regent, and a daughter of Berenice I, wife of Ptolemy I Soter of Egypt, who gained the Egyptian slice of Alexander's empire.

When Olympias' old foe Cassander deposed Pyrrhus in his teenage years, Ptolemy had come to his rescue and seen him reinstated. And when a plot was made against Pyrrhus as an adult, Antigone had handled the intelligence and helped to save his life.[2] She died young, leaving behind a daughter, another Olympias, and a baby son, Ptolemy.

Lanassa, daughter of the king of Syracuse, became Pyrrhus' second wife and stepmother to his children. Through his marriage to her Pyrrhus gained control of the islands of Corfu and Lefkada in the Ionian Sea. He showed Lanassa his gratitude for these by embarking upon a series of romantic affairs. Steadily ground down by Pyrrhus' emotional attachment to several of the women, especially those he chose to make his wives (an Illyrian princess named Bircenna among them), Lanassa left him for his former brother-in-law, Demetrius I, who was then king of Macedon. Lanassa ought to have had the final word, but Pyrrhus was so affronted by her behaviour, and so covetous of everything his rival now possessed, that he resolved to take revenge. Pyrrhus drove Demetrius from power and for a short time shared the throne of Macedon with Alexander's successor Lysimachus. Demetrius' eventual demise at the hands of Seleucus, another of the Successors, only partly alleviated the burden on Pyrrhus, whose ambition would ultimately prove greater than his capability.

Pyrrhus was said to have been eager to conquer Sicily, Carthage and even parts of Italy in a bid to establish dominion there. He therefore agreed to support the Tarentines in their struggle against Rome. Demonstrating the scale of his plans, he set out with a sizeable army, including 20,000 infantry and twenty elephants. This was the first time that elephants had been seen on Italian soil and there was some doubt among the startled soldiers as to whether they were animal or machine. The Romans' fascination with the beasts would grow over the centuries as they discovered their aptitude for performing tricks and even learning the Greek alphabet. It was no reflection of their novelty at this stage that the elephants were overshadowed by the phantom of Pyrrhus himself.

The hubris of the man was quite unprecedented in the field. He led his men to 'victory' over the Romans near the cities of Heraclea and Ausculum so boastfully that anyone would have thought he had annihilated the enemy and returned with his full contingent intact. In reality, the losses he endured were so heavy that his victories were as good as void; they were, proverbially, 'Pyrrhic'. Confidence is nevertheless a valuable asset, and it continued to serve Pyrrhus well as he proceeded in his career. The leading men of Syracuse, Lanassa's city, nodded approvingly at the inroads he had already made in southern Italy and summoned him to their aid in 279 BC. They promised him he could be lord over their city – as well as Agrigentum and Leontini – if only he could help them to drive one particular group of people from their island, the Carthaginians.[3]

The Sicilians had long viewed Carthage with suspicion. Some of the earliest myths characterised the city as hostile or even inimical to Italian progress. The Phoenician princess Elissa, known to Virgil and others as Dido, had tried to detain Aeneas in a Calypso-like embrace in Carthage when it was his destiny to carry on and establish a new home for himself and his band of Trojan refugees on the Italian mainland. It would have been especially inauspicious for Aeneas to have settled in her city given its grievous backstory.

Legend held that Dido had built Carthage in the wake of a foul tragedy. Her brother Pygmalion, king of Tyre, had murdered her husband Sychaeus (Acerbas) out of lust for his treasure.[4] The ghost of Sychaeus had appeared to her in a dream and told her to take the gold he had concealed and escape. A number of Phoenician men, despising Pygmalion's tyranny, had followed Dido out of Tyre as she directed a voyage to Cyprus. There was supposedly an ancient tradition on that island of prostituting young women to raise funds for their dowries. A perverse logic dictated that Venus, mother of Aeneas, would protect these women's chastity in future years. Dido gathered together about eighty Cypriot women and put them on board her ship with a local priest and his family with the idea of populating a new kingdom swiftly and efficiently.[5] Living up to her name, which meant 'Wanderer', Dido steered a long course to the northern tip of Africa. Making land in Tunisia, just across the water from Sicily, she prevailed upon a local king for a patch of land of such a size as to be covered by a single ox-hide.[6] The king met her modest request and was astounded when she proceeded to slice the ox-hide up into the slenderest strips imaginable. Ingeniously, Dido laid the strips out on the ground, end to end, to form the perimeter of a city far larger than anyone could have pictured.

Carthage, located on the northern coast of modern Tunisia, was accordingly named from the Phoenician for 'new city', *Qart Hadasht*, and occupied the southern slopes of a hill known thereafter as *Byrsa* from the Greek for 'ox-hide'. Consistent with the myth, which places the foundation of Carthage in 814 BC, there is evidence that the city was inhabited from the ninth century BC and possessed Phoenician connections from the start.[7] A record of the kings of Tyre, drawn up by one Menander of Ephesus, contained the detail that King Pygmalion's sister fled from him in the seventh year of his forty-seven-year rule and, after leaving Tyre, built the city of Carthage.[8] Carthage was, in each tradition, a female-founded city. The earliest inscription so far discovered in Carthage, engraved on a ninth-century BC gold pendant placed in a tomb, refers twice to 'Pygmalion', possibly this king, as well as to Astarte, the eastern goddess or a woman who shared her name.[9] A further inscription on what is known as the Nora Stone attests to Tyrian colonisation in the same period in Sardinia.

Carthage lived on in the Roman imagination as a city of dominant women. Virgil described it as 'rich in resources and most aggressive in the pursuit of war' and wrote of Aeneas' surprise upon discovering that the women who had relocated there from Phoenician Tyre, with their quivers and huntress-style purple boots, were as bellicose as the men.[10] When Aeneas arrives, the Carthaginians are still building their city, but a temple to Juno, wife of Jupiter, has already taken shape. As the Trojan surveys the temple sculptures he finds scenes from the Trojan War bearing his own portrait as well as the figures of bare-breasted Queen Penthesilea and her fellow Amazons. All pale beside beautiful Dido. The Phoenician queen stands by the temple like Diana thronged by nymphs, only, it is not nymphs who surround her, but loyal followers of both sexes. Dido and Aeneas share a common plight in Virgil's poem in their struggle to resettle their people. The queen soon longs for her handsome visitor to stay and take a share in her new kingdom.

No trace of an historic Dido exists, but for the people of Carthage, she was real insofar as she was inseparable from their origin story. Byrsa, the hill which evoked the memory of Dido's ingenuity with the ox-hide, remained at the centre of their heavily fortified citadel, and as late as the fourth century BC, Carthaginians in Sicily were still minting silver coins bearing the portrait of a woman in an elegant pleated headdress who is presumed to be her.[11] Dido was remembered as the founding queen of Carthage because she was extraordinary. In the centuries following its establishment, the city was ruled by one man after another, mostly from an extremely limited number of bloodlines. The two *sufetes* (magistrates) elected annually by a people's assembly from the fifth century BC to serve as governors were always male. Like their Phoenician forebears, the women of Carthage resided predominantly in the home and were known for their high-quality weaving and baking. A far smaller proportion found work beyond their four walls. The epitaph of a Carthaginian woman named Shiboulet describes her as a 'city-merchant', an occupation usually associated with men.[12] Like the female Chorus members of Euripides' *Phoenician Women*, who leave their homes voluntarily to serve as priestesses of Apollo in Thebes, the women of Carthage would also have had opportunities to enter religious service. But there is no evidence of real women achieving anything like the authority of mythical Dido.

The legacy of Dido was felt most palpably in the Carthaginians' appetite for enterprise. In the sixth century BC, long before the birth of Pyrrhus, the Carthaginians had come to the defence of the Phoenicians when the Sicilians were attempting to drive the latter from their settlements at Palermo and Motya. The Carthaginians had been ambitious to extend their reach beyond their existing foundation. In the same period a Carthaginian ruler named Hanno wrote an account of his circumnavigation of the north-west coast of Africa. Known from a Greek translation of the lost original, the *Periplus* of the fifth century BC documents Hanno's thrilling adventures and encounters with hairy-bodied 'people' on an island within an island in the continent. Hanno's interpreters made history in pronouncing these creatures to be 'gorillas'. The males of the species are described as escaping the travellers by climbing out of reach. The females, who are dominant, are less fortunate. Hanno's companions – he claimed improbably to have led 30,000 men and women with him on his voyage in sixty ships – captured three of the females and killed them for their disobedience. They then flayed the victims and carried their skins back to Carthage. Such tales of derring-do might have been worthy of a place in Homer's *Odyssey*, but the Romans were willing to believe that Hanno had indeed intruded upon a rare tribe. The first-century historian Pliny the Elder recorded the survival of two of the supposed female gorilla skins in the Temple of Juno at Carthage.[13]

The object of Hanno's travels had been to establish Carthaginian cities along the perimeter of Africa. Among those he was credited with founding was Cerne, off the west coast, which became home to an important Carthaginian trading base.[14] Historically, the Carthaginians achieved a reputation for their excellence at growing crops, especially olives, which they exported all across North Africa. Their merchant ships were anchored at the ready in a large harbour beyond the public square in which they sold their produce to locals. It would be fair to say that Carthage had achieved commercial pre-eminence when Pyrrhus of Epirus finally landed in Sicily at the Tarentines' bidding in the third century BC. And it was from this moment that the legend of Dido came into its own.

In the *Aeneid*, Venus urges Aeneas to approach the queen, anxious to see her son settled and relieved of his burdens, and the Trojan survivors recompensed. With her blessing her other son, Cupid, sets Dido's heart aflame for Aeneas by striking her with his arrow. The hero is recounting his experience of the Trojan War and, as he speaks, Dido falls more and more deeply in love. As Dido confides to her sister, Anna, this is the first time since her husband's murder that she has been tempted by a man. She needs little encouragement from Venus and Cupid to abandon herself to her feelings, which are stirred not only by Aeneas but by the tender sight of his young son Ascanius. Reluctant to leave anything to chance, all the same, Venus and Juno plot to bring Dido and Aeneas together completely. In a cave, in the middle of a storm, the young travellers consummate their relationship. Their union, in Dido's eyes, represents the first part of a marriage contract.

It does not take long for rumours of the widowed queen's broken celibacy to spread through Carthage. The rumours may be painful to hear, but they are nothing compared with the words that reach Dido a short time later, just as she is beginning to reconcile the conflict she is feeling between passion and guilt. Aeneas is preparing to leave. He cannot stay with her, far less be her husband, when he has a destiny to fulfil. Aeneas' mission to found a city of his own dominates the remainder of Virgil's narrative, and yet some of the most moving passages of the poem describe not his heroism, but Dido's heartbreak and humiliation. The queen rails at him repeatedly:

You are neither the son of a divine parent nor a descendant of
Dardanus,
You traitor. Rather, the dread Caucasus gave birth to you
On its harsh rocks, and Hyrcanian tigers fed you on their udders.
For why should I dissemble it or hold back to deeper agony?[15]

Dido steadily gives way to what Virgil defines – in the tradition of the Greek Hippocratic medical writers – as female instability. Harried by her emotions, she falls desperately upon her sword on her own funeral pyre while Aeneas sails away, quite oblivious. In an alternative version of the legend, Dido dies on the pyre after defiantly trying to resist the advances of a local king, who is forcing her to marry him on threat of war.[16] This version was recorded by a second-century male writer named Justinus but also, quite probably, by Pamphila of Epidaurus, the early female historian whose writings have been lost but for a few fragments.[17] Instinct told Dido to remain unattached. Her experience echoes that of Ariadne, the tragic heroine of Crete, who sacrificed everything to help Theseus in the Minotaur's lair and then awoke on Naxos to see his ship disappearing over the horizon. Denied her audience, like the Cretan princess, Dido is reduced to venting her frustration on the breeze and cursing her absent lover and the Trojans who worshipped him.

'May there be no love nor pacts between our peoples,' she cries, praying that the gods take vengeance on Aeneas in future generations for his callousness.[18] These words weigh heavily upon the poetic metre for they were written with a poet's hindsight. Virgil's *Aeneid*, composed in the last third of the first century BC, acquired a status equal to that of the *Iliad* and the *Odyssey* in Rome because it was seen not only to celebrate the city's past, but to portend its future, most usually with optimism. Dido's curse, as uttered here, was more than rhetoric. It served as an explanation for the historic Punic Wars that erupted between her descendants, the Carthaginians, and Aeneas' descendants, the Romans, in the third and second centuries BC. There would be no love – and no enduring pact – between the Carthaginians and Romans for generations to come. The development of this tension and its significance for the future of both peoples was attributed most profoundly to Dido's vengeful words.

Rome and Carthage had not always been enemies. The two sides had signed treaties of friendship since as early as the expulsion of the Etruscan kings.[19] Strict lines had been laid down prohibiting one from plundering or founding cities on territory belonging to the other. The Carthaginians could not touch Roman cities in Latium, for example, and the Romans were barred from exerting their influence upon Libya and Sardinia. About the time of Pyrrhus' invasion, they had agreed to help each other if either was attacked, and treaties to this effect were inscribed on bronze tablets in Rome. But Pyrrhus' efforts to dispel the Carthaginians from Sicily disrupted the already strained agreements between the two superpowers.

After some initial success on Sicily, Pyrrhus turned his attention to Libya, only to fall foul of the Sicilians themselves. They resented being coerced into manning his ships and, besides, took exception to his haughty and aloof attitude towards them.[20] The king then had little choice but to retreat to the Italian mainland, where he was defeated by the Romans at Beneventum, before returning home, trailing his threadbare forces behind him. His war had catastrophically crashed the currencies of the major cities of Magna Graecia and reduced him to raiding, among others, the Temple of Persephone at Locri, home town of Nonnis, the poetess with a passion for art.

Pyrrhus eventually met his end in 272 BC at the hands of a woman armed with a roof tile. He had just completed a series of land-grabs in Macedon, determined to recover what remained of his pride, when he became entangled in a further battle in Argos. The mother of an Argive soldier was standing on the rooftops with other women of the city watching the fighting proceed below when Pyrrhus came within a spear's throw of the action. Fearing for her son, the impecunious but impassioned local woman lifted a tile from her house and threw it down hard on Pyrrhus' head. Incapacitated, he fell from his horse, and was thereupon decapitated by another soldier. Antigonus II, king of Macedon, received his severed head. The story – true or not – was often repeated and contributed to the rumour that the women of Argos were a peculiarly aggressive breed.[21]

When the Romans had proposed making peace with Pyrrhus, an elderly ex-senator named Appius Claudius Caecus ('The Blind') urged caution. Claudius came from an old patrician family but had always worked hard to further opportunities for lower-class citizens. During his time in office he had overseen the introduction of sons of freed slaves to the Roman Senate for the first time in history. He was also responsible for commissioning the Appian Way, which ran between Rome and the south, as well as the first aqueduct, both of which bore his name. People therefore listened when he argued that there should be no agreement with Pyrrhus. It was eventually decided that the invader must leave Italian soil before a peace settlement was formally concluded. The fragility of the agreement had been as obvious to Pyrrhus as it was to sage old Claudius. 'Dear friends, what a wrestling-ground we are leaving behind for the

Carthaginians and Romans,' Pyrrhus had uttered as he departed Italy, and for once, he had been right.[22]

Not long after Pyrrhus' retreat, a wedding was held at Syracuse between Philistis, daughter of Leptines, the most powerful man in the city, and Hiero, a military commander.[23] Little is known of Philistis, though her portrait appears on several coins with Nike, goddess of Victory, riding her chariot-of-four on the reverse. Like the goddess, Philistis is shown with a star, her authority underlined by the words, 'Basilissas Philistidos' ('Queen Philistis'). The same inscription has been discovered in the theatre at Syracuse built by Hiero I, tyrant and victor in the chariot race of the Pythian Games in 470 BC.[24] Depicted on her coins with wide eyes, a long elegant nose and curly hair emerging from beneath a veil, Philistis earned her royal title after her own Hiero was appointed king in 270 BC. The Greek city of Messana, on the north-east tip of Sicily, had been overrun by mercenaries from Campania, and Hiero had helped to disperse them. The least the Syracusans could do was to hail their hero king.

The difficulty arose when the same mercenaries appealed successfully to Rome for assistance against their enemies, who included the Syracusans. They called themselves 'Mamertines' in honour of the war god, Mars, and were suitably threatening. The Romans were afraid that if they refused to help them, the Mamertines would simply turn to the Carthaginians, who might then have the means of gaining supremacy over all of Sicily. The men of Rome therefore voted to send one of their most senior senators, Appius Claudius, a younger brother of Appius the Blind, to Messana in 264 BC.[25] Hiero allied himself with the Carthaginians and proceeded to the same city. A game of cat-and-mouse ensued while Appius drove back the Syracusans, prompting Hiero also to retreat, before the Roman attack began in earnest in what marked the beginning of the First Punic War. A pact would ultimately be agreed by the Romans permitting Hiero to continue ruling the kingdom of Syracuse comparatively unfettered. This only further inflamed Carthage's ambitions for power in Sicily.

Cultural differences which had always existed between the two sides became increasingly marked. Roman historians reflecting on the Punic Wars would characterise the Carthaginians as unremittingly hostile and bloodthirsty by drawing attention to their performance of child sacrifice. One Greek historian wrote emotively of young victims rolling from the outstretched hands of a statue of Kronos into a pit of fire beneath.[26] Romans noted that even freeborn boys were offered up to the god.[27] The archaeological record provides a fuller picture. While the written accounts were strongly coloured by hatred of the enemy and the heat of the conflict, it is clear that the Carthaginians did sacrifice both boys and girls, usually infants, and that Baal Hammon, their equivalent to Kronos, was a common recipient, together with his goddess wife Tanit. One area of Carthage, known to archaeologists as a *Tophet*, contained an estimated 20,000 urns, many containing infants' bones, dating from between 400 and 200 BC. Writers of Greece and Rome did not feel hypocritical in pouring scorn on this practice while remembering that Agamemnon of Mycenae had sacrificed his own daughter Iphigenia. That was a myth, this was reality. The extremes to which the Carthaginians were prepared to go to secure divine support were alarming. Little could the Romans have anticipated at this point that their conflict with Carthage would prompt them to perform human sacrifices of their own.

Tensions, for now, centred on the Carthaginians' base at Agrigentum, in southern Sicily. The Romans laid siege to the city until it was broken by the onset of famine. The Carthaginian commander, Hannibal Gisco, had little choice but to send to Carthage for reinforcements. Hannibal Gisco's fellow general, another man named Hanno, gathered men and elephants from nearby Heraclea and proceeded, in turn, to besiege the Romans in that city. When the two sides came to face each other in battle, the Romans utilised supplies sent over by Hiero of Syracuse, and secured the advantage. They seized Agrigentum and savagely enslaved its population. The Carthaginians there were dispersed and deprived of their war elephants. The Romans back home were so encouraged by the news that they voted to make a bid for the whole of Sicily.

The chief problem that confronted the Romans as they proceeded was the Carthaginians' known superiority as a sea power. They maintained hundreds of ships, including quinqueremes, which were rowed by 300 men each. In the 260s BC the Romans had sourced a Carthaginian ship that had run aground and used it as a blueprint for constructing vessels of their own. With some difficulty, they managed to build 100 quinqueremes and twenty triremes, but the challenge lay in using them effectively.[28] Particular distress arose at the defeat of Gnaeus Cornelius Scipio, the man selected to command the navy, after he steered a course to

Lipari, off the north coast of Sicily. After being trapped in the harbour by the Carthaginians he chose to surrender. Defeat in a crucial naval battle against the Carthaginians at Drepana (Tripani) in western Sicily in the course of the war in fact led the Romans to withdraw from the oceans altogether.

The Roman people's wrath at this state of affairs was such that, three whole years after the humiliation, the sister of the consul (senior senatorial magistrate) who led the doomed flotilla, Appius the Blind's son Publius Claudius Pulcher, was fined simply for mentioning it in public. Claudia had been trying to push her way home through an enormous crowd following some games in 246 BC when she voiced an idle wish. If only her brother could lose another fleet, she sighed, then the streets would be free of plebs again![29] Claudia had said the unsayable. For her loose talk, she became the first woman in Rome to be trialled by the people for treason, which was all the more extraordinary given her noble birth. The fact that the trial took place at all was a sign of how tense life had become in Rome in view of Carthage's progress.

Claudia was punished by being fined a considerable 25,000 asses by the aediles (junior magistrates) of Rome.[30] In the long term this was less a punishment than an opportunity for the young woman to achieve a legacy equal to that of the male politicians of the city. Claudia's money went towards the construction of a temple to Libertas (Freedom) on the Aventine Hill.[31] For a woman's name to be associated forever after with one of the city's prime religious monuments was no small achievement. Generations later, Claudia's descendant, Clodia Pulchra, would court a similar line between public censure and enduring fame after being accused of helping to fund the assassination of a foreign dignitary.

The Romans needed to play to their own strengths. Their most ingenious invention was the *corvus* ('raven'), a moveable addition to their boats, which could be let down like a bridge to enable the crew to cross over onto their enemies' decks by foot. The equipment effectively transformed a naval battle into a land battle characterised by close physical combat. The ravens proved most efficient on calm water. The Carthaginians lost fifty ships in the first engagement in which they were used. Unfortunately for the Romans, Hamilcar, commander of the Carthaginian land forces, retaliated by attacking their camp near the hot springs at Himera, and killed 4,000 soldiers. Hannibal Gisco, meanwhile, went to Sardinia with renewed naval forces, only to be crucified by his own men after the Romans established a blockade.

Emerging at the forefront of the Carthaginian forces in this war was another Carthaginian named Hamilcar Barca. In the eighteenth year of the conflict, he led the navy to the Sicilian harbour town of Panormus (Palermo), valued for its lookout points, and established a base from which to launch an assault on the coast of Italy as far as Cumae.[32] The Carthaginians led a trail of devastation across the mainland for three years before the conflict reached a climax on the slopes of Mount Eryx in Sicily. They seized a town here in which the Romans kept a garrison and succeeded in cutting them off further up the mountain. Polybius, an Achaean Greek sent to Rome as a hostage in 167 BC, became the chief historian of the Punic Wars and likened the standoff to a pair of well-bred birds engaged in a struggle to the death. Their wings had lost all function, but their determination was ripe as they clung on to one another, mid-flight, and waited to be the last to drop.

The Romans and Carthaginians were no less exhausted than those birds of prey. The drain on both sides' resources had been considerable. Although they had now been worsted at sea many times, the Romans found the strength and courage to return to the water once more, their objective being to cut off the supplies being shipped to the Carthaginians at Eryx. This proved to be the turning point in the conflict. The Romans intercepted the Carthaginian supply boats as they made their way across the water. The ships were weighed down, and the men steering them lacked experience in combat – it had been assumed that they would simply be delivering reinforcements. The Romans sank fifty of their vessels and captured seventy more together with their crews. Hamilcar Barca, left to find a way forward following the defeat, took the only sensible course left open, and sued for peace with the Romans. The war had rolled into its twenty-third year and both sides were spent. In accordance with the terms agreed, the Carthaginians left Sicily and the surrounding islands, gave up their prisoners, handed over 2,200 talents, and pledged never to make war on Hiero or the Syracusans and their allies again. Significantly, Sicily became the first Roman province.

From the beginning, the terms imposed on Carthage gave rise to internal tensions, which culminated in a civil war in North Africa. Particular demands were now made of women. After almost a quarter of a century of suffering while their husbands and sons waged war on Rome, the women of Carthage were asked to give up their last possessions to fund another conflict entirely.[33] Their jewellery was melted down to mint coins. Although Hamilcar Barca eventually succeeded in bringing about the wholesale submission of North African cities to Carthage, his work was far from complete. Over the course of a further nine years, he would lead a campaign in Spain with the aim of reducing that country, similarly, to Carthaginian control. He would be accompanied there by his nine-year-old son by a woman whose identity is now unknown. The boy's name was Hannibal.

The Romans added to their gains in the third century BC. Following their victory over Carthage, they transformed Sardinia and Corsica into a new province and made their way, for the first time so far north-east, to Illyricum in the Balkans, where they encountered a woman of rare obstinacy. The former king of Illyricum, Agron, had died of pleurisy following a drunken celebration.[34] His son was supposed to succeed him, but as he was still too young to rule, power fell to the boy's stepmother, Teuta, as regent.

From the start, Teuta was eager to make her presence felt beyond the borders of her kingdom, far across the Peloponnese. She sent a fleet to raid and pillage Elis and Messenia and helped to orchestrate a plan through which Illyrians in Epirus fell in with a garrison of 800 Gallic soldiers in a bid to capture the local city of Phoenice.[35] The ensuing attack on the Epirote city was so severe that the local population had to appeal to the Aetolians and the Greeks of the Peloponnese for support. It was at that point that Teuta was forced to abandon the operation and recall her men to stem an uprising at home. The Illyrians gave up Phoenice, not before emptying it of resources and potential slaves and forcing its people to pay a ransom, and made a truce with the Epirotes. The effect of these events was such as to inspire widespread fear in the surrounding coastal Hellenes.

Teuta now set her sights on a larger and more comprehensive campaign in Greece. Plutarch believed that her appetite had simply been whetted by the spoils of Phoenice, but Teuta's ambition certainly went far beyond the desire for material goods. Through her alliance with Epirus, she dispatched troops to capture Epidamnus and Corfu, the desperate inhabitants of which sent envoys to the Achaeans and Aetolians, who were her chief targets. Only a dispute with Rome hindered her from fully realising her plan to sweep these territories into the net of Illyricum. While it is unlikely that Teuta would have been able to conquer all the cities of the Achaean and Aetolian League, she was arguably powerful enough to weaken them.

The queen regent was in the process of besieging the city of Issa on Lesbos when two Roman ambassadors arrived to confront her. She met them with a contemptuous air. While the Illyrians would commit no wrong against the people of Rome, she asserted, their rulers were not in the habit of preventing their people from seeking spoils overseas.[36] Startled by her curt manner, the younger of the two ambassadors replied that the Romans had a most excellent custom of their own, which was to pursue private grievances publicly. Teuta was so affronted by his retort that, the moment the ambassadors left, she sent her own men after them with instructions to kill the Roman who had addressed her so menacingly. The deed was done. Teuta continued besieging Corfu and set about imposing a garrison upon the island.

News of the ambassador's murder so incensed the Romans at home that they voted to launch an expedition against Illyricum in 229 BC. There is no doubt that the territory was already in Rome's sights for trade, but Teuta's transgression of common decency – and a formal custom that granted sacrosanctity to ambassadors – provided the requisite justification, and the timing. The queen had inadvertently invited the Romans to make territorial gains at her own expense.

The Illyrians had little time to mount a defence. In the desperation of the moment, Teuta was betrayed by one of her governors and left with little option but to take cover for her own protection. As she fled to safety in the fortified city of Rhizon, in modern Montenegro, she awaited news of Corfu, which the Romans had gone after most rapaciously. To her regret (but not surprise) the island fell into Roman hands. Teuta sued for peace. From a Roman perspective, Teuta had had her comeuppance for daring to believe that she, a woman of a country of no particular distinction, could insult Rome, and still she benefited from the magnanimity of the Romans, who established no permanent province on her land.

In accordance with the peace terms, the Illyrians paid tribute to Rome and agreed never to sail further into Greek territory than the Lissus on

Crete with more than two vessels. Illyrian garrisons were removed from Greek cities. But Rome's greater conflicts with Carthage were far from over, and tensions with the Illyrians would flare up in the course of the ensuing wars. While the Romans' continuing success in the Balkans would enable them to establish a growing mountain of booty, Illyricum remained a live threat. The memory of Teuta, the proud woman who challenged Rome, would live on.

Chapter XII

The Price of Punic Figs

Terpsichore calls me to sing
Beautiful songs for the women
Of Tanagra in their white robes,
And much does the city delight
In my clear-voiced songs.

Corinna, Fr. 1, third century BC

The year Teuta was defeated, Hamilcar Barca fell victim to one of the tribes he had attempted to reduce in Spain, leaving his son-in-law, Hasdrubal the Fair, to take over his command. Hamilcar had made significant progress in conquering the Iberian Peninsula, to which Hasdrubal added by founding a new city, another *Qart Hadasht*, New City, to be known as Cartagena.[1] Such activity provided the Romans with worrying evidence of the Carthaginians' recovery from the terms of the Punic War. With one eye open, the Romans agreed, for the moment, to form a treaty with the Carthaginians in Spain and focused on engaging the Gauls of northern Italy who neighboured the Etruscans.[2] The assassination of Hasdrubal the Fair by a Gaul following a private dispute and ensuing change in leadership altered the dynamic between the Romans and Carthaginians once again.

Hasdrubal was succeeded in the field by Hamilcar Barca's eldest son Hannibal. As a nine-year-old boy, Hannibal had accompanied his father on campaign and experienced the taste of success as well as the humiliation of defeat. Growing up in the aftermath of Rome's victory over his country, he had developed an appetite for vengeance, so much so that the Romans would come to believe that he had inherited a hatred of their empire in his blood. 'Skilled at nurturing fury,' wrote the Roman poet Silius Italicus of Hannibal's father in the first century, 'Hamilcar sowed Roman warfare in the heart of the boy.'[3]

Hannibal was in his late twenties before he was ready to launch his assault on Rome. In 219 BC he laid siege to Saguntum, a port town under Roman protection near modern Sagunto in Valencia. In addition to making it very difficult for the Romans to campaign in Iberia, the siege struck fear in the local tribes, who were left in no doubt of the monumentality of Hannibal's ambition. The peace between Rome and Carthage had lasted fewer years than the First Punic War, and there was no telling how the latest conflict would develop. Hannibal certainly appeared to be thinking in the long term. According to Silius Italicus, Hannibal's son was born during the siege and swiftly sent away with his mother, Imilce, to safety.[4] It could not have eluded Imilce that her husband intended to march his troops over the Alps and invade Italy.

Hannibal had married Imilce when they were both still in their youth. Her name is known only from Silius Italicus, who describes her as coming from Castulo in Andulasia, a detail also provided by Livy in his history of Rome.[5] In his poem, the *Punica*, Silius Italicus likens Hannibal's departure from Imilce to that of Hector from Andromache in the *Iliad*. Just as Hector spoke to his wife of the future of their son Astyanax, mindful that the boy might never come to know his father, so Hannibal urges Imilce to remember him to their son and allow him to join battle once he is old enough so that he can continue the fight against Rome. Hannibal assumes that Imilce's glory will grow solely from her relationship with him and the exploits of their boy, but on this point she corrects him. Women are strong, Imilce reminds Hannibal, and it is perfectly within her capacity to climb the mountains alongside him to pass into Italy.

Imilce longs to go to war, but like Andromache, she is obliged to stay behind and pray for her husband's safe return. The farewell scene between Hannibal and Imilce in the *Punica* has often been compared in turn to the scene in which Aeneas takes leave of Dido and Carthage in the *Aeneid*, but the comparison undermines Imilce's fortitude and defiance. Imilce does not despair as Dido does. She is very far from throwing herself onto a funeral pyre. Had Hannibal not prevented her we can well believe she would have led soldiers across the Pyrenees by his side. What became of the real Imilce during Hannibal's absence is unclear, for she vanishes from the historical record at this moment. If her character in the *Punica* is anything to go by, we might imagine her actively seeking news of Hannibal's progress as he ventured forth against the men of Italy.

The writers of antiquity were less interested in Imilce and the home front than in the resilience required of Hannibal as he climbed the mountains she had hoped to attempt herself. His first task was to cross the River Ebro in Spain with an army of about 90,000 infantrymen, 12,000 cavalry and countless Gallic recruits. Contrary to some reports, these men were well-equipped for the journey, being hardly reckless enough to attempt it without adequate planning.[6] Hannibal had posted soldiers in Africa and Spain for their defence and made advance enquiries of Gauls who had followed the same path. One of the Carthaginian commanders, Hanno, to whom Hannibal assigned a large army of his own, took some of his men plus the baggage, allowing Hannibal's forces to proceed more easily as they then approached the Rhone. Horses were tethered to boats and made to swim ahead of them, three or four abreast, and elephants were towed along on a bridge of rafts, two females leading each pack.

Hannibal and his forces marched for ten days along the bank of the Isère before beginning their ascent of the Alps. At this point the Gallic tribe of the Allobroges began to mass against them. Hannibal took several prisoners among the Gauls and made a point of mistreating them in order to remind his men of the punishments that would await them if they fell into the hands of the Romans. While there were heavy losses on both sides, the Carthaginians prevailed, helping themselves to the Gauls' corn and cows as they went. They overcame further obstacles from local tribes to reach the summit of the mountains in just nine days. Their elephants offered them some protection owing to the fear they inspired in unwitting tribesmen.

The descent proved more treacherous, with snow and landslips carrying many men and animals to their deaths. After fifteen days in the Alps, Hannibal reached the plain of the River Po with roughly half the number of men he had set out with and just one of his elephants. He now led 12,000 African and 8,000 Iberian infantry plus 6,000 horses into battle against Publius Cornelius Scipio. Hannibal was astonished to find the Roman consul encamped and awaiting his arrival. The boldness and speed with which the Carthaginians made the journey had in fact taken the Romans by surprise. Scipio had been dispatched to Spain but told to turn around in time to meet the oncoming forces. The Romans' war preparations had indeed been limited, even counterproductive. While sending their other consul, Tiberius Sempronius Longus, to Africa, they had fortified their position in Cisalpine Gaul through the establishment of further colonies at Placentia and Cremona, which served predominantly to trigger revolts by the Boii tribe in particular.

Hannibal was able to forge an alliance with the Boii and other tribes after his men confronted the Romans and injured Scipio. Hannibal's Numidian cavalry had proven almost unbeatable on the wings. While Scipio rested, a new commander, Tiberius, took over and pressed to launch another attack sooner, in winter, rather than later, in spring, while the Romans still had the advantage of numbers. A winter offensive of this kind was rare and ultimately proved costly. The Roman javelin throwers were no match for the Numidians, who overwhelmed them with their band of elephants in the pouring rain. Many men died of hypothermia. Even robust Hannibal was not impervious to the perils of close combat under the elements. In the course of the Punic War, he lost one of his eyes to a disease, which rendered him dangerously conspicuous. He took to sporting a series of wigs in an attempt to foil a feared assassination attempt.[7]

For all his anxieties, Hannibal appeared to be triumphing over the Romans, who were swiftly falling into disarray. While in Spain the Romans had enjoyed some success and taken the Carthaginian general Hanno prisoner, on Italian soil they were faring so badly that they took the unprecedented step of appointing a first and then a second dictator.[8] The appointment of dictators was rare in Rome's history because it was antithetical to the premise of a republic. It signified desperation.

Such a dramatic course was justified in Rome by the sudden display of a number of ill-omened portents. Weapons took to combusting spontaneously; something resembling blood began to drip through water and grain; the sky appeared to be ripped in half; cocks started metamorphosing into hens.[9] Alarmed by the troubling reports, the Senate urged offerings to be made to appease the gods, and all eyes fell upon the women of Rome to play their part. While Jupiter received a golden thunderbolt, Juno on the Aventine Hill and Feronia, goddess of abundance, were treated to as much money as each woman in Rome – even former slaves – could put forward. This was not the first and nor would it be the last time that women were required to give up their wealth in the Punic Wars.

In this case, the women's offerings were of little consequence, for Hannibal succeeded in ambushing the Romans in Etruria and laying waste to the surrounding countryside. About 12,000 men fell to his forces during a momentous battle at Lake Trasimene in Umbria in June 217 BC and a further 15,000 were taken prisoner. The Romans suffered even more dramatically the following spring when Hannibal seized the well-supplied town of Cannae in Apulia at the end of a further landmark battle. Although the Romans had proceeded with eight strong legions (predominantly infantry forces) against a Carthaginian force just half the size, they were enveloped on the wings by the Carthaginians and their allies, and suffered annihilation. It is estimated that up to 70,000 Romans lost their lives. The Carthaginians prevailed to gain much of the south Italian coastline, including the city of Tarentum, where the memory of Pyrrhus lived on. Hannibal ought to have advanced upon Rome from there. The fact that he did not is a clear sign that he believed he was on a winning streak. Little could he have anticipated that he had peaked.

It was in the aftermath of the Battle of Cannae that the unlikeliest heroine of the Second Punic War came to prominence. Busa was reputed to be the richest woman in all Apulia.[10] Nothing is known of the origins of her wealth, but Livy wrote admiringly of the way she used it to help Rome at a time when help was in short supply. She lived in the town of Canusium (Canosa di Puglia), 16 kilometres from Cannae. Some 10,000 Romans sought refuge there after fleeing the field.[11] While the people of Canusium were generally quick to open their doors to the exhausted soldiers, Busa very much led the way, gathering food and clothes as well as coins to aid them.

Busa's generosity was important because it established a precedent. When the people of nearby Venusia heard of it, they were so determined not to be behindhand that they followed her in bestowing clothes, arms and money on the Romans who made their way there so that they 'would not be beaten by a woman from Canusium in their kindnesses'.[12] Most significantly, without these supplies it is doubtful that the Romans would have been able to rebuild their forces.[13] One of the survivors, in particular, became extraordinary for his resilience as a result of Busa's work. Publius Cornelius Scipio welcomed her generosity and then rose up to receive a supreme command and rally the Romans to defend the Republic from Hannibal once again. We have often seen that behind a successful man there was a hard-working woman. In Scipio's case that woman was Busa. She was formally recognised for her role in Rome's recovery at the end of the war, when the Roman Senate voted her honours, a privilege seldom bestowed upon any woman, especially a woman living outside of Rome.

Busa exemplified what was expected of women at a time when female behaviour was being closely scrutinised. The senators of Rome were increasingly at a loss to explain why their countrymen were faring so badly in their struggle against the Carthaginians. Rather than attribute blame to numbers or tactics, they alighted upon the conduct of the women left behind in the city. It suddenly occurred to the Senate that the women of Rome were being too excessive in their grief for the fallen. Their tears, they said, were devastating to morale. A new rule was introduced to limit the mourning period to a maximum of thirty days. But members of the house also turned their attention to the mothers and wives who were not wallowing in their widow's weeds. The wanton display of colourful fabric and jewels by these women, they concluded, was the real reason for the Romans' losses in the war. The women of Rome were so wedded to their luxuries that they were denying their menfolk the resources they needed to win! There was no longer any doubt in the senators' minds. Rome needed a new law to limit female ostentation. Women must give up their usual fashions for the salvation of the city.

Many women were only too pleased to do this and willingly donated their gold and silver to the public treasury. The new Oppian Law, named after one of the tribunes or junior officials, nevertheless made further demands. The law made it obligatory for women to part with a significant proportion of their goods and change their lifestyles.[14] Specifically, it stipulated that a woman could possess no more than a half-ounce of gold, must abstain from wearing multi-coloured clothes, and must give up taking a carriage in a city or town within a mile of where she was going except for religious reasons. The message behind the legislation was clear. Women were at least partly culpable for Rome's fate in the war despite playing no active part in it.

The implications of this reasoning were particularly devastating for the Vestal Virgins. The six priestesses, replaced whenever one retired or died, had continued to guard the flame of the Temple of Vesta in the interest of Rome's safety. It was now argued that the dire portents observed in Rome were a reflection of the lapsed chastity of two of them. There was no formal opportunity for either woman to refute the charges. The beautifully named Opimia and Floronia were abruptly condemned to death accused of breaking their solemn vows. One chose to end her own life there and then. The other was buried alive near Rome's Colline Gate in the traditional punishment.[15] The priest accused of being Floronia's lover died following a public flogging.

The people of Rome hoped that the gods would proceed to show them their favour. But in bringing about the deaths of three of their own citizens, two of them sacred persons, they inadvertently infected their city with what was known historically as religious 'pollution'. A new, more pernicious fear began to take root. What if they were all now subject to ill fortune and in an even worse predicament than they were before the Vestal Virgins died? The alarming continuation of portents appeared to confirm the worst. The strange occurrences continued and were interpreted as manifestations of the religious stain that now lay across the city.

To remove the stain and atone for their crime, the Romans needed a new strategy, and for this they turned to the Sibylline Books, a collection of oracular sayings which were supposed to offer guidance in times of extreme uncertainty. According to legend, Lucius Tarquinius Superbus, the last king of Rome, purchased the books from the all-seeing Sibyl of Cumae – the priestess of Apollo in southern Italy who was the near-equivalent of the Pythia at Delphi – and entrusted them to the Senate for safekeeping. Ten custodians still kept guard over the scrolls on the Palatine Hill and consulted them at the Senate's request. The interpretation of the text was more unwavering than anyone could have hoped for. Claiming to act in accordance with religious advice, the Romans buried alive a Gallic woman, a Gallic man, a Greek woman, and a Greek man, in the old cattle ground known as the Forum Boarium on the east bank of the Tiber. Rarely had such an extreme action been taken in the interest of preserving Rome's military. It would no longer be so straightforward for the Romans to claim the moral high ground over the child-sacrificing Carthaginians.

Believers in the power of the Sibylline Books felt vindicated when some of the enemy proceeded to defect to Rome. This was particularly noticeable in southern Italy, where it had become apparent that Hannibal's promises of freedom were never going to be fulfilled. Syracuse was unusual in going the other way, renewing its earlier allegiance with

Carthage following the death of the tyrant Hiero, who had done so much to aid the Romans. By 205 BC, however, the senators were once again seeking explanations for peculiar portents.

In a renewed effort to appease the gods, young girls were instructed to sing a hymn, but while they were practising the Temple of Juno on the Aventine was struck by lightning. Predictably, the soothsayers drew a further connection between the female population of Rome and the gods' displeasure. Women living in Rome or within ten miles of it were summoned to the Capitol. They were to select twenty-five from among their number to gather together all their dowries and purchase a gold basin for Juno. Further offerings to the goddess would follow.

Prompted by a sudden unexplained meteor shower, the senators again sifted through the pages of the Sibylline Books, and happened upon some unexpected advice.[16] Should a foreign enemy bring war upon Italy, they read, victory could be theirs if they brought the 'Mother' of Mount Ida to Rome. The statement seemed to be supported by the Oracle at Delphi that had proclaimed, or so the Romans interpreted it, that they would soon prevail in the war.

Who was this mother and what did it mean to bring her to Rome? Even though the advice of the Sibylline Books rivalled that of the Pythia for ambiguity, the interpreters perceived that it was Cybele, the Mother Goddess, who needed to be transported from the east. Cybele, the lion-taming goddess we encountered in Sappho's Mytilene, was a prime figure of worship in Phrygia, Asia Minor. A black stone 'sent from the sky' – a meteorite – was housed in the Phrygian city of Pessinus and worshipped as a representation of the goddess. It would be easy enough to ship the meteorite from Pessinus with the assistance of King Attalus of Pergamum. The greater challenge would lie in establishing the goddess's cult in the comparatively conservative city of Rome. Cybele had never been one to promote restraint in her devotees. Tambourines and cymbals were crashed in her honour and her followers were eunuchs known as Galli. In the first century BC the Verona-born love poet Catullus would describe one of Cybele's acolytes, Attis, cutting off his genitals with a stone to become 'she', only to regret the act later. This level of fanaticism was most un-Roman.

Buoyed by the promise of victory nonetheless, the Romans dispatched senators to Cybele's native Asia Minor in five quinqueremes, fetched the meteorite, and turned around to begin the journey home. The Pythia declared that the goddess should be welcomed to Rome by the best of men. Publius Cornelius Scipio Nasica, a cousin of the man who had enjoyed the assistance of the heroine Busa, was selected as a worthy candidate.

In April 204 BC the women of Rome – mothers, daughters, Vestal Virgins – formed a circle as the ship bearing the meteorite came within sight of the harbour. They were poised to receive the symbol to pass to Scipio when suddenly the vessel juddered and rooted itself firmly in the shallows.[17] The goddess seemed reluctant to go any further. While a group of men began to tug at the ropes in an effort to free the ship and drag her to land, a woman stepped forward from the crowd. Claudia Quinta was quite notorious in Rome, less for her noble birth than for her fashionable hairstyles, which the gossips interpreted as evidence of sexual immorality. Their cruel words had floated back to her. Sensing an opportunity to clear her name, Claudia raised her hands to the sky, gazed at a cult statue of the goddess, and prayed to be proven chaste and true in accordance with the oracle by being the one person capable of dragging Cybele to land.[18] One tug on the rope, and the goddess was free and, with her, Claudia's reputation.

The women passed the precious stone between them before it was taken to the Temple of Victory on the Palatine Hill. A new temple would be built for the goddess just here. While the streets were filled with well-wishers, eager to bestow presents of thanksgiving, further prayers were offered up to the gods for Cybele's propitious entry to Rome.[19] A new festival and set of games, the Megalensia, were established to commemorate this day in Rome's history. In homage to the eastern cult worship of the goddess, a train of eunuchs processed through the city to the accompaniment of cymbals and drums, marking a considerable breach with Roman tradition.[20] Whether it was the acceptance of Cybele and her rowdy entourage that was responsible, or Roman perseverance through belief, the Carthaginians ultimately proved incapable of sustaining their pre-eminence in the field. The goddess would be hailed for playing her part in sealing Rome's victory in the Second Punic War.

Publius Cornelius Scipio – later known as Scipio Africanus – also took much of the credit for changing the direction of the conflict, but fell short of obtaining everything he desired, namely to take the highest-ranking members of the enemy alive and parade them in Rome. There was one figure in particular who escaped his grasp through the most extraordinary act of courage, and that was not a general, but the daughter of the Carthaginian Hasdrubal Gisco, one Sophonisba.

Sophonisba was well known in Carthage for her intelligence as well as her beauty. Even one of Rome's historians had to concede that she was supremely well educated in literature and music, as well as very charming.[21] Her husband Syphax was king of the Masaesyli of western Numidia, formerly a Roman ally, and it had allegedly been at Sophonisba's pleading insistence that Syphax broke from Rome and allied with Carthage in the war. As Syphax himself told Scipio, he had lost all sense of reason the moment he fell in love with her. Try as he might, he simply could not say no when Sophonisba urged him to forge an alliance with her people, the Carthaginians, against Rome.[22]

Roman historians took Syphax's words to Scipio at face value and laid blame for the Numidians' ensuing misery squarely at Sophonisba's door.[23] Had seductive Sophonisba not stolen his heart, Syphax of Numidia would have done the sensible thing and avoided confrontation with Rome. But Syphax had a motive when he spoke to Scipio of Sophonisba's persuasion. The Romans had besieged the Phoenician-founded city of Utica, between Carthage and Hippo Diarrhytus (Bizerte), in 204 BC, before setting fire to the Carthaginian and Numidian camps with their flammable reed huts, killing up to 40,000 men in the process. Despite these depletions, Hasdrubal and Syphax had consequently redoubled their efforts against Rome, but proved powerless against the highly organised Roman forces. Scipio was aided by Syphax's enemy, Masinissa, king of the eastern Numidians. Scipio and Masinissa stormed to victory at the so-called Battle of Great Plains and took a number of further Carthaginian cities. Syphax was now their captive. Masinissa led his royal prisoner in chains through the streets and made his way to his enemy's palace to claim Sophonisba.

The following moments would leave a considerable imprint upon the imagination of writers and artists down the centuries. As Masinissa approached, Sophonisba stopped him, and bent down to grasp him by the knees. She was his suppliant and had just one favour to ask. Please, she implored, might her fate not be decided by the Romans? All she desired was to be saved from the Romans' cruelty and death at their command. In the speech Livy wrote for her, Sophonisba declared, most defiantly, 'If I had been nothing but the wife of Syphax, I still would have preferred to test the pledge of a Numidian, born in the same Africa as me, than that of someone born in another country.'[24] It was true that a Carthaginian woman could expect no mercy from Rome. There is no reason to doubt the contents of Sophonisba's prayer.

Masinissa was mesmerised by the woman clinging to his knees and, more than that, interested in the support her family might lend him in his ambition to broaden his control in Numidia. He therefore gave her his word and withdrew from Syphax's palace. The only way Masinissa could think to fulfil his promise and save Sophonisba from the Romans was by marrying her himself, and quickly, before Scipio could orchestrate a plan to ship her to Rome. The marriage rites were performed just in time. No sooner had the candles gone out than a Roman general was attempting to prise the bride away from the marital bed.

When Syphax told Scipio that he had lost his head and rebelled from Rome because of Sophonisba, he was mindful that he was a prisoner, and Masinissa was not. The surest way of harming his old foe was by incriminating the woman they both professed to love. And so it happened that Scipio informed Masinissa that Sophonisba was to be brought before the Roman Senate for judgement. They would decide the fate of the woman alleged to have estranged an allied king from Rome and driven him to war against them.[25]

To honour his vow to his wife, Masinissa withdrew and immediately ordered a slave to mix poison and take it to Sophonisba (another source asserts that Masinissa gave it to her himself).[26] With it, the Numidian sent a message to the effect that he was doing all he could to fulfil the promise he had made her as a husband, a promise he was unable to keep otherwise. She need not enter Rome alive, but the decision was very much hers to make. Masinissa advised her to think of her father, of Carthage, and of the two kings she had married, and to make up her own mind. Sophonisba did not need to think for long. Historians gloried in the drama of her accepting the poison 'as a wedding gift'. Yet there was no hint of irony in her utterance that this was the best present a husband could give his wife. Sophonisba had just one message for Masinissa in return. Tell him, she said to the messenger, that it would have been easier to die had she not married at her own funeral. She drained the cup fearlessly.

News of Sophonisba's death soon reached Scipio. The first thought that crossed the general's mind was that Masinissa would be so shaken by the tragedy that he might take his own life. Scipio therefore summoned Masinissa at once and tried to console him. More than that, he addressed him as king and gave him a curule chair, a sceptre, an embroidered toga and a gold dish – the accoutrements of royalty also enjoyed by Roman consuls – and assured him that, with Syphax gone, he would have control of all of Numidia. Sophonisba had escaped the fate of her first husband, and yet it was perhaps only now that the harsh truth became apparent. Sophonisba's death had brought Masinissa precisely what he had wanted.[27] The more cynical historian would say that he had foreseen everything when he handed Sophonisba the poison in a cup. Sophonisba of Carthage, like Dido before her, had died for a man's gain.

Her body was handed over to Scipio after her funeral. The Carthaginians sued for peace, but Scipio stipulated that they must first return the Romans they had taken as slaves, withdraw their troops from Italy and Gaul, pull out of Spain, abandon the islands between Italy and Africa, hand over warships, wheat and barley, and pay financial reparations. The Carthaginians professed to accept these conditions, but secretly they were biding their time until they could summon Hannibal to their aid.

Hannibal had withdrawn to Calabria in recent years following news that his younger brother, Hasdrubal Barca, had been decapitated in battle. Hannibal had very little hope of gaining ground in Italy when, in 202 BC, he was recalled to Zama, five days' march from Carthage, to confront the combined forces of Scipio and Masinissa in what marked the decisive battle of the Second Punic War. If only Hannibal had capitalised on his victory at Cannae, he might have found himself master of Rome rather than marshal of a melee of panicking forces in a Carthaginian backwater. Scipio's forces were victorious. Hannibal became *sufete* in Carthage before dying in Bithynia, in his mid-sixties, after the local people slipped him some poison because they feared he would reignite the war with Rome. His fellow countrymen were obliged to agree to the harsh conditions they had previously only pretended to accept, and more, for the Romans demanded that they be deprived of all the territory they held outside Africa. The Romans took all but ten of Carthage's warships.

Scipio earned a triumph – the highest military reward available to a Roman for victories overseas – and the sobriquet 'Africanus' in acknowledgement of his success. He became nothing short of a hero in Rome. For his wife, Aemilia Tertia, this was a mixed blessing, for a man who was hailed a hero received immunity from censure in almost all aspects of his life. It is difficult to argue with a man who can do no wrong in the public eye. Aemilia chose not to confront him over his alleged affair with one of her female slaves for fear of being seen to reproach the man who had given everything for his city.[28] Historians would praise her for displaying such dutifulness to her husband, but the desire to avoid gossip and maintain her sense of honour were perhaps Aemilia's prime motivations. When, later, Scipio died, she magnanimously awarded the other woman freedom from slavery.

Until the passage of the Oppian Law against luxury, Aemilia Tertia had been highly recognisable in Rome for the extravagance of her entourage. Even the cups she used to pour libations to the gods were made from silver and gold according to the historian Polybius, who knew her personally.[29] She was just one of many women in Rome whose lives continued to be affected by the legacy of the war and the restrictions it had placed upon them.

As the years went by, it became increasingly difficult for the Senate to justify a continuation of rules which served no practical purpose now that the war was over. The Roman coffers were so full that there would soon be no need to tax the population directly at all. By 195 BC the Oppian Law had been in place for two decades and the women of Rome had had enough. In an extraordinary display of disaffection, *matronae* (married women) left their family homes and blockaded the streets leading to the forum, demanding that they be allowed to return to their former way of life. They were joined by women from the countryside, who spread themselves out over the Palatine Hill and marched down towards the forum to confront the consuls and other magistrates face to face. This was the most visible act of protest mounted by the women of Rome since the earliest years of the city's foundation.

The female protesters encountered particularly stiff opposition from the consul Marcus Porcius Cato ('Cato the Elder'), and a tribune, Publius Iunius Brutus, and his brother Marcus. Tribunes of the plebs held their own assemblies and could propose legislation and veto the acts of senatorial magistrates. When these men looked outside their doors, they saw not female fortitude, but the signs of a deeper and more nefarious problem in the current culture.[30] As Cato explained:

> If each of us, citizens, had seen to it that he retained the rights and authority of a husband over his own wife, we all would have fewer issues with womankind. But as it is, our freedom has been eroded and trodden under foot by female fury at home – and indeed here in the forum – because we have shied away from restraining women, both individually and universally.[31]

Cato was a man easily shocked. He disapproved of Greek theatre, Greek philosophy, Greek medicine – most things Greek – while unwittingly absorbing the influences of each.[32] That a woman could be so brazen as to address another woman's husband in public, when she might more respectably have aired her grievances to her own husband behind closed doors, rankled with his innate puritanism. That hundreds of women should do so, in full view of the men of the city, was an abomination. Cato believed that men were at least partly to blame. Where were the husbands and guardians and why were they not speaking on the women's behalf?

Brutus stepped forward to fulminate further on the matter. The old cliché that women were animals that needed taming reverberated through his speech. This moment appeared to offer a turning point. If women were allowed to carry on in this vein, he asked, what would they do next? The tribune grappled with what he believed to be a very real threat to Rome's future. It struck him that women were on the verge of achieving equality with men. If they were to do this, he pondered, then they would, in practice, be men's superiors, for there would be no stopping them from proceeding even further. The tables of the sexes would be turned irrevocably.

Another of the tribunes of the people countered by arguing that what the women were doing was neither new nor revolutionary. Women had interceded in the battle at the heart of Rome with the Sabines, he reminded his colleagues, and then again following the expulsion of the kings. They had seen off the Volsci and handed over their gold to support Rome's war effort against the Gauls. Many years later, a woman named Hortensia would describe this voluntary sacrifice of personal goods as contributing to the salvation of the empire itself.[33] In giving up their fineries and receiving the Mother Goddess, women had also played a part in Rome's victory in the Second Punic War. Moreover, as the tribune reminded Cato, women had lived respectably before the law was introduced, so its repeal was hardly likely to make them slaves to luxury. The women of Rome, like the men, were surely entitled to enjoy the fruits of victory and prevailing peace. The tribune recognised that members of the Senate were pedalling an empty myth concerning women's addiction to money and fine things. Was it right, he asked, that men could wear purple-trimmed togas while women continued to abide by rules that banned them from wearing purple altogether? There was very little chance of women gaining the kind of foothold that Cato and Brutus feared. The tribune was of course correct.

The women returned to central Rome the following day, and in even greater numbers, to gather outside the house of Brutus' family. Under the pressure they applied – and against the best efforts of Cato and Brutus – they finally saw the Oppian Law repealed.

Cato was incensed. In spite of his plebeian roots – as a *novus homo* ('new man') he was the first of his family to enter the Senate – he was supremely conservative. His overriding ambition was to safeguard the old traditions of Rome and the usual social hierarchy. He had always despised luxuries – he once gave a polemical speech 'On clothes and vehicles' – and felt strongly that the Oppian Law still had a place in Roman society. By 184 BC he would have risen through the Senate and come out the other side as a *censor*, the magistrate in charge of maintaining the census and safeguarding public morals. He would oversee a number of new building projects in Rome, including the construction that year of the Basilica Porcia, a novel and monumental civic hall on the edge of the forum. He continued to play an active part in steering events, and it was with his support that a new law was introduced to limit women's financial freedom even further.

The Lex Voconia, passed in 169 BC, was ostensibly concerned with limiting inheritance allowance, but in practice it served to cut women out of family wealth altogether. Female members of families worth 100,000 sesterces or more were prohibited from being made heirs in a devastating repression of their rights.[34] Even female slaves could be listed as heirs in Rome and inherit property after manumission. The misguided assumption, as before, was that women with wealth – even modest wealth, for 100,000 sesterces was about half the price of a house in Rome – had the potential to achieve equality or superiority to men. Decades later no less a figure than Cicero would remark upon the injustice and inhumanity of this ruling for women.[35]

The Lex Voconia had a particularly notable impact upon Aemilia Tertia. Her husband Scipio died in Campania about 183 BC after being driven from Rome by his political enemies, among them Cato the Elder. Although the main beneficiaries of his will were Aemilia, their daughters and their sons, the new law prevented Aemilia from being able to pass her portion of the property to their daughters after she died. Her nephew (and also grandson via adoption) Scipio Aemilianus instead became her primary heir because Scipio's sons were heirless and received from her 'a sizeable fortune'.[36] The young man's divorced mother became the envy of Rome when he paid for her to ride in Aemilia's ornate carriage.

It was largely through his inheritance from Aemilia – and the Lex Voconia which made it viable – that Scipio Aemilianus was able to rise to the forefront of the next frontier against Carthage. While many Romans had hoped to draw a line under past events, a Third Punic War erupted in 149 BC, bringing further despair to both territories. The trigger was allegedly Cato the Elder's decision to bring a fresh fig from North Africa to the Senate House in Rome. With a theatrical flourish, Cato asked the senators when they thought the fig had been picked and shocked them by telling them – with an ounce of exaggeration – that it had still been on its branch two days earlier. In actual fact it would have taken about five days to ship the fruit from Carthage to Rome, but Cato's point held: the enemy was still close and could erupt upon them at any moment without warning.[37] At this, or so the Romans liked to claim, the Third Punic War was fought to see off the Carthaginian menace once and for all and achieve supremacy. Scipio Aemilianus would use his position as Aemilia's heir to take the reins.

The Third Punic War narrowly preceded a similar quest for domination by the Han Chinese. But while the 'Northern Desert Wars' saw unprecedented numbers of soldiers press upon the Yellow River to broaden Han frontiers, Rome's latest war with Carthage was relatively compact. Echoing the heroism of Scipio Africanus, his adoptive grandfather, Scipio Aemilianus was able to subjugate the Carthaginians, raze their city after a siege, and bring the war to an end within just three years. Of the Carthaginians who were not savagely killed, 50,000 were taken prisoner to be sold as slaves. Carthage was ransacked and reduced to form part of the new Roman province of Africa. Over the next century, Latin would replace Punic and Libyan as the chief language in former

Carthage, where it had seldom been used before.[38] The Senate had some of the Carthaginians' books shipped over and translated for a Roman readership. The twenty-eight volumes of an agrarian tract by a writer named Mago proved surprisingly popular.[39] Other spoils taken from the city helped to fund the renovation of Rome and its harbour.

By the mid-second century BC, thanks in no small part to the financial sacrifices of women, the Romans were beginning to look unassailable. Not only had they conquered Carthage, the largest and most powerful of her enemies, but they had overcome the lingering aggressors of Macedon, the Achaean League in Greece, including Corinth, and the Syrian kingdom of the Seleucids. The ceilings of the Capitoline Temple of Jupiter Optimus Maximus ('Greatest and Best'), Juno Regina and Minerva, the chief deities of Rome, were clad in gold.[40]

Chapter XIII

Educating Gracchus

My greetings to you, Rome, daughter of Ares,
Golden-mitred, war-obsessed ruler,
Dweller of holy Olympus on earth,
Forever unbroken.

Melinno, 'Ode to Rome', date unknown

A story was told of Aemilia and Scipio Africanus and a row they once had over the future of their younger daughter.[1] It began with Scipio going to lunch with members of the Senate and ended with him explaining to his bristling wife that the wedding they had arranged for little Cornelia would be going ahead whether she agreed to it or not. Roman mothers liked to have a say in who their daughters married and certainly did not want to be the last to know. *Even if* the suitor in question were Tiberius Sempronius Gracchus, a senator of some distinction, Aemilia said, she would have appreciated being consulted. It is not difficult to guess who the suitor was.

Scipio was dead before Cornelia was of an age to marry. Thanks to his exile by those men who feared he was becoming too powerful for Rome, he missed seeing his match bear glorious fruit. Cornelia and Tiberius Gracchus produced or at least conceived twelve children, of which three survived, namely a daughter, Sempronia, and two sons, Tiberius and Gaius Gracchus.[2]

One of the great women of Mid-Republican Rome, Cornelia won fame in her own time, not because she was intelligent, which she was, but because she raised two of the most forward-thinking politicians in history – and outlived them both. Her parents had given her an unusually rich education. Like her brothers, she and her sister had learned Greek literature as well as Latin, and were familiar with the leading intellectuals of the day. It was this grounding that enabled her to oversee her children's studies. She taught them Greek from the earliest age and, when they were a little older, had them instructed by some of the many masters she befriended.[3] Diophanes was a Greek orator from Mytilene on Lesbos and Gaius Blossius was a philosopher from Cumae, home of the Sibyl in southern Italy. Diophanes was renowned for his eloquence and Gaius Blossius had studied stoicism in Asia Minor. They probably taught Sempronia as well as the two boys.

A large age gap between Cornelia and her husband meant that she was widowed while still in her thirties. Young matrons were ordinarily encouraged to remarry following their customary ten months of mourning, but Cornelia had had her children and was determined to remain *univira*, a one-man woman. She was praised for this, especially when she had the tenacity to reject an offer of marriage from a king, Ptolemy VIII Euergetes II Physcon, of the Ptolemaic dynasty in Egypt.[4]

Ptolemy had initially ruled with his brother and sister before being driven out by the former. With the help of Rome, he took control of Cyrenaica, on Egypt's western border, and eventually succeeded in proclaiming himself pharaoh of Egypt itself. While he had a strained relationship with his co-rulers, his sister-wife Cleopatra II and niece-wife Cleopatra III, he believed he had most to fear from the intellectual class of Alexandria. The prospect of marrying the well-born widow of a man who had risen rapidly through the Senate, serving twice as consul, next as censor, naturally appealed to a paranoid Ptolemy seeking influence in Rome. To what little charm he had Cornelia remained utterly impervious. 'Physcon' is the Greek for 'Fat'. Cornelia had only to turn over one of his coins to confirm that he did not bear the name ironically.

Cornelia instead invested herself wholly in her children and became the subject of countless celebratory anecdotes on the theme. It was said that when a woman showed off her jewels, for example, Cornelia quipped that *her* most precious baubles were her offspring.[5] Cicero and Quintilian, two of the leading orators of future generations, believed that she raised her children in her own mould. Quintilian was a keen advocate of educating women (most were home-schooled) so that they could be good examples to their future sons, and Cicero believed that oratorical skill could be passed down through the blood. Both were convinced that Cornelia's *doctissimus sermo* ('most learned conversation') flowed into her boys and shaped their rhetoric well into their adult years.[6]

We may see Cornelia's influence, perhaps, in a speech her younger son Gaius delivered on the subject of a woman's bath in a town just north of Naples:

> Recently a consul came to Teanum Sidicinum. His wife said that she wanted to bathe in the men's baths. The task of ejecting the men who were bathing there was entrusted to the Roman quaestor Marcus Marius. The wife reports to her husband that the baths were not given up to her quickly enough and were not clean enough. And so a stake was set up in the forum and the most noble man of his city was led there – Marcus Marius. His clothes were stripped off him and he was beaten with branches . . .[7]

It is surprising that a woman could ask to use the men's baths and order them to be cleaned for her especially. Nowhere else in the records of Rome do we find a woman making such staunch demands, carrying out a personal inspection of a cleaning job, and prompting the punishment of a Roman official for failing to maintain the high standards she expected. Gaius Gracchus for one could not conceal his fascination with the woman's clout. The way he described it – with short, sharp sentences, an unexpected slip from past to present, passive verbs for the beleaguered consul – only emphasised the woman's authority. A Greek orator analysing the same passage observed Gaius' preference for direct narration over the imagery-rich storytelling favoured by Cicero. It is perhaps here that we detect Cornelia's influence. Finding her voice in the words of her son is extremely difficult, but she, too, would prove herself to be extraordinarily unflinching in her manner of speaking. Impassioned, unpretentious oratory would be the making of both her sons.

Tiberius, the elder of her boys by nine years, was the first to embark upon the political ladder. He ran successfully for the position of tribune of the plebs in 133 BC and committed himself from the very beginning to improving the lives of the urban poor. The existing system of land distribution in Rome favoured the wealthy, who crowded out their impecunious competitors by paying a higher rent than the treasury demanded for the use of common land. Previous attempts to rectify the problem by limiting the area that any single person could acquire had failed because the rich realised that they needed only to submit a false name in order to purchase more acreage. The poor had grown so disaffected that they were reluctant to complete their military service. Angry graffiti calling for the return of public plots covered the walls of porticoes and monuments around Rome. Tiberius was determined to reform the system.

Tiberius inherited at least some of his interest in the plight of the disadvantaged from his mother.[8] Although Cornelia had enjoyed a prosperous upbringing, the Cornelii and Gens Aemilia being two of the oldest patrician families in Rome, she knew that little now distinguished successful plebeians from unsuccessful patricians. Wealthy plebeian families now outnumbered patricians in the city. Tiberius' wife Claudia similarly shared his interest in improving the lot of the lower classes. She was a descendant of Appius 'the Blind' who had been such a trailblazer for broadening opportunities in Rome. Her father, another Appius Claudius, put himself firmly behind Tiberius in his efforts to introduce an effective programme for change.

Tribunes of the people were entitled to propose legislation to the popular assembly which could then be voted on and implemented. Tiberius Gracchus hoped that a new bill requiring citizens who had unlawfully taken land to return it in exchange for remuneration would satisfy the majority. On the day of one important vote, however, the urns in which men placed their voting tokens were stolen, most probably by someone wealthy and resentful. After some deliberation, Tiberius perceived that he would need to bring the matter before the Senate, even though the house was dominated by members of the elite whose powers of purchase he was attempting to curtail.

Tiberius Gracchus was able to remove one veto-ready tribune from office as he proceeded, but his greatest coup was to deliver a speech on the disadvantages endured by honest farmers and to persuade voters from outside Rome to travel to the city to exercise their suffrage rights. With their help, he was able to get his agrarian law through and to establish a panel consisting of himself, his brother Gaius and his father-in-law, to oversee a major redistribution of land. The Senate did its best to hinder this process by refusing to allocate the required funding.

Tiberius Gracchus antagonised many senators further by proposing to redirect some newly received funds to impoverished settlers. Attalus III, king of Pergamum in Asia Minor, had bequeathed his kingdom to Rome upon his death in 133 BC so as to protect it from destruction by rival successors. The Romans thereupon established a new province called Asia. To Tiberius it seemed only fair that the Roman people should have a say in how the endowment was used. The Senate disagreed. When Tiberius took the unusual step of running for the tribuneship a second time in place of seeking higher office, the senators practically exploded at his flouting of tradition and apparent attempt to court further popularity. A brutal fight erupted on the Capitol. The Senate, rattled by Tiberius' agenda, branded him a tyrant.

Few senators were more affronted by Tiberius' approach than his cousin Publius Scipio Nasica, the Pontifex Maximus (chief priest) of Rome. At his call, a stream of senators made their way to the popular assembly, many of them trembling with rage. They beat and stoned Tiberius and some 300 of his supporters to death. The bloodied corpses were hurled into the Tiber. And so one of Rome's brightest politicians was carried off on the river that bore his name. He was not yet thirty.

Ten years passed. Tiberius' younger brother Gaius followed in his footsteps and ran for the tribuneship more than once. Cornelia was naturally filled with dread. The letter she wrote to dissuade him is one of the most extraordinary survivals of the ancient world. It contains two substantial passages of text in which she expresses concerns over Gaius' plans. The extracts were preserved by a trusted biographer named Cornelius Nepos in the first century BC and were widely believed to be authentic. Cicero put it in writing that Cornelia was an ardent correspondent. The letter has nevertheless suffered the scrutiny of modern scholars, who know how rare it is for women's writing to be preserved from antiquity, especially in extensive passages. Few would suggest that the letter is a modern invention; the style of the writing is so characteristic of the period that suspicion falls rather upon Gaius' contemporaries in the Senate. Did his rivals forge a letter from Cornelia in order to discredit him? The correspondent is noticeably at odds with his outlook:

> You will say it is a beautiful thing to take revenge on one's enemies. To no one does this seem greater or more beautiful than it does to me – provided it can be done without causing harm to the Republic.

> But seeing as that is not possible, our enemies will not die for ages for the most part, and will carry on as they are now rather than see our Republic overthrown and obliterated.[9]

Senators hostile to Gaius would have been only too pleased to contemplate the possibility that he lacked even his own mother's support. But there is no evidence that they sought to blacken his character by penning fraudulent letters. It was, on the other hand, only natural for Cornelia to justify her private concerns in writing when her son was endangering his life in an attempt to achieve justice for his brother. This part of the letter feels authentic in the clarity of its prose as well as in the light of what happened next.

On being elected tribune in 122 BC, an accomplishment he would repeat the following year, Gaius did precisely what Cornelia feared he would, and attempted to pursue Tiberius' enemies. He first introduced a law to prevent any magistrate who had been removed from office by the people from ever holding post again.[10] This was clearly intended to incriminate one of the politicians who had been deposed and re-elected under Tiberius. He then introduced a law that would render a magistrate who exiled a citizen without trial liable for public prosecution. One of Tiberius' former rivals had exiled several of his allies without just grounds.

Cornelia took the astonishing step of urging Gaius to withdraw the first of these laws because she felt that the man it incriminated, Marcus Octavius, ought to be spared in spite of the opposition he had posed to agrarian reform. This was an intentionally populist move on her part. Surprised, perhaps, that the mother of the Gracchi brothers should intervene so decisively in political affairs, the Roman people supported her call for the repeal of the law, and Gaius had little choice but to heed their demands. Cornelia had scored a rare victory in a political world governed by men.

No one could have blamed Gaius if he felt embarrassed at having to change course at his mother's say-so, but had he truly resented her interference, he might have framed his volte-face in a different way and kept quiet about her in his speeches. As it was, he named her often, aware of the tactical advantage this would bestow. It was in keeping with the *mores* of the time that he drew attention to Cornelia's fertility, chastity and position as mother of the Gracchi rather than her political intelligence.

This last quality is easily discerned in the second part of Cornelia's letter. No enemy, she told Gaius, had caused her as much distress since the murder of Tiberius as he had. Why had he shown her no compassion in her dotage? Why had he not aimed to please her in the short time she had left? Where would it all end? Cornelia had had enough of her family's *insanity* and the suffering it caused. If Gaius had to seek the tribuneship, he could at least wait until she was dead. Her most contentious question came next. Did he feel no shame, she asked, in rocking the Republic? At first sight this looks suspicious – the sort of question a fraudster might have been eager to put in Cornelia's mouth. But the accusation is notably non-specific. We might have expected a senator-forger to highlight the shakier points of Gaius' policy rather than speak with such passion. Cornelia, on the other hand, would have spoken from the heart. It does not seem unlikely that she would have posed such a question to her son.

Gaius was seeking to address the lingering problems in land distribution. He put forward a new agrarian law, offered grain to the poor at a lower price, and proposed to free soldiers from the burden of paying for their own uniforms, grant Roman citizenship to 'Latin' peoples beyond Rome, and distribute a less comprehensive set of rights to the people of wider Italy. To the disgruntlement of existing members of the Senate, Gaius also planned to double their number from 300 to 600, with the newest recruits selected from the equestrian class – a wealthy minority, one rung down from a senator in the social hierarchy, whose members possessed an income deemed sufficient to maintain a horse for war. The senators were particularly riled by Gaius' plans to share among the equestrians their powers to judge criminal cases in the Senate.

Cornelia understood how controversial Gaius' manifesto was but, in spite of her concerns, did everything in her power to see it through. She even hired farmers from outside Rome to enter the city to build pressure for the passage of the agrarian law. These were not the actions of a woman who truly feared causing harm to the Republic. Her dramatic words to Gaius in the letter look like the anxious products of a mother's love.

Certain aspects of her son's programme invited a strong reaction from the Roman public. Gaius' establishment of a colony on top of the site of former Carthage in 122 BC was attended by a burst of what could only be interpreted at the time as bad omens over the city. The very idea of founding a new settlement upon Dido's cursed territory struck many as abhorrent. The colony was to collapse within decades, though Octavian-Augustus, future first emperor of Rome, would reoccupy Carthage by building a Roman forum on Byrsa, Dido's hill, the summit of which was shaved off and flattened. Gaius' decision to relocate from his house on the expensive Palatine Hill to a poorer neighbourhood beside the forum had the opposite effect and delighted his plebeian supporters.[11] To the Senate his move was only further evidence of his alienation from their ranks.

There was only so much Cornelia could do to protect her son when he proceeded to lose the election to a further tribuneship the following year. A public meeting held after one of the successful candidates proposed to repeal the law that had enabled Gaius to establish the African colony rapidly descended into a bloody brawl. The death of a consul's assistant in the struggle provided the senators with the grounds they sought to take action against Gaius. For the first time in history, they issued an early form of the *senatus consultum ultimum* ('the last decree of the Senate'), an emergency motion which effectively marked him out as a threat to national security. Opimius, the senator leading the opposition, placed a bounty on Gaius' head worth its weight in silver and gold.

Urged on by his supporters, Gaius fled to the Aventine Hill in little more than his toga, sweat dripping down his face. Where to go but to the Temple of Diana to seek sanctuary like a suppliant?[12] Gaius' wife Licinia fainted. By the time she came round it was too late. Gaius and his closest ally had been slain and beheaded. One of Gaius' former friends poured not gold but molten lead into the mouth of his decapitated head. In so doing he made a mockery of both the value of the bounty and the memory of a Roman general who had suffered the more expensive fate at the hands of an eastern king.[13] It was reported that 3,000 of Gaius' allies were killed in all. Among them was his young son. Licinia, left destitute, would only later have her dowry restored to her. It was little compensation for the double loss she had endured.

Cornelia was praised for her stoicism and strength of spirit in the wake of the assassination. She withdrew from Rome but never from the joys of life. A grand villa she owned at Misenum, the promontory of the Bay of Naples where Pliny the Younger would one day survive the eruption of Vesuvius, became her permanent base. Purchased by Cornelia for an extraordinary 75,000 drachmas, it would later become home to Lucius Licinius Lucullus, one of the most louche politicians of the Late

Republic.[14] For Cornelia, it offered the perfect setting for a *salon* for literary friends, who would come from Greece and further afield to stay with her. Even kings (their identities have not been disclosed) honoured her with presents.[15] If anything she became more widely respected after the death of her sons.

Cornelia's daughter Sempronia came to live with her at the villa after the breakdown of her marriage. If the sources are correct and Sempronia was physically disfigured, this would have been used as an explanation for why she had failed to have children. The sudden death of Sempronia's husband/cousin Scipio Aemilianus one night many years earlier as he lay in bed had been deemed suspicious. Scipio had been preparing to compose a speech for the Senate the following day and was not obviously unwell. Shortly after his death, some of the household slaves testified that strangers had entered through the backdoor and suffocated their master, triggering his untimely demise. This accounted for the lack of wounds but offered no clue as to whodunnit. As the mystery deepened, a rumour spread that the true culprits were none other than his childless wife and her mother.[16] Their motive? To stop Scipio from cancelling the Gracchan laws. Few could have believed this improbable tale.

Cornelia had told Gaius in her letter that she was nearing the end of her life. Actually, she carried on for many more years, probably into her eighties. When she spoke to people of her sons then, she did so with a strange detachment, as if they had lived hundreds of years ago in the era of Rome's kings. People listening to her often assumed that she had been numbed by the onset of dementia, but this was not necessarily the case. Over time she had learned to reflect with less sorrow than pride upon the accomplishments of her boys.

Cornelia was honoured with a number of statues after her death. One, in bronze, was inscribed 'Cornelia, Mother of the Gracchi'.[17] The surviving marble base of another monument also bears her name.[18] The date of her death has not been recovered, but it is likely to have been around 115 BC, before that of her daughter. Sempronia later returned to Rome at the request of a tribune to testify as to whether or not a man claiming to be her brother Tiberius' illegitimate son was truly him. Despite being threatened by a mob, Sempronia confirmed before the people of the city that the man was an imposter, and certainly not her kin.[19] Support for the Gracchi had not died with them.

There was indeed a strong feeling in certain quarters of Rome that the political system could not return to the way it was before the brothers rose to prominence. Gaius and Tiberius Gracchus had riven the Senate in two. A rising number of *populares* within the Senate House were continuing to champion Gracchan causes while the traditional class of *optimates* ('best men') struggled to accept that the threat to their authority was permanent. The following decades would be marred by civil war and diminishing opportunities for women as the tension between the inveterate *optimates* and the forward-thinking *populares* came to a head.

At the centre of the new struggle was a tribune named Gaius Marius. Born of common labourers in Arpinum, a pretty hill town some 120 kilometres south-east of Rome that would also be the birthplace of Cicero, Marius was raw, agrestic even – a boor by comparison with most senators. He had never studied Greek, but his aptitude as a soldier had marked him out in the eyes of Scipio Aemilianus as a compelling potential leader. Marius completed a military tribuneship before running successfully as a tribune of the plebs in 119 BC. His ambition and unaffected manner earned him the admiration of a great many voters as well as his future wife Julia.[20]

Julia suffered a fate common to many Roman women in being more famous in death than in life. She became only the second woman in the city to be eulogised in public after a consul, Quintus Lutatius Catulus, delivered an elegy for his mother Popilia in 102 BC.[21] Both women happened to belong to the same family: they were Caesars. When Julia died in 69 BC her nephew and eulogist, Julius Caesar, was at the very beginning of his political career. The speech he delivered from the speaker's platform in her honour served to illuminate his own merits as vividly as hers. The distinction of Julia's bloodline, upon which Caesar dwelled in the surviving, opening section of his eulogy, was also his. Julia was the daughter of Marcia, whose father was a senator, and of Julius, whose father was a consul. Further back in time, Julia's ancestry, Caesar claimed, could be traced to the fourth king of Rome on her mother's side, and to no less a figure than Venus, goddess of love, on her father's. It would have taken a genealogist of impeccable credentials to provide proof of these connections, and one of great courage to challenge them.

What mattered to Marius was that Julia could help him to broaden his appeal to members of the elite who might otherwise have discounted him on the basis of his lowly birth and ineloquence. Marriage to Julia would be crucial to his success.

Having achieved the consulship for the first time in 107 BC, Marius found himself re-elected to the post a second time in 104 BC, and again during the following years. Consecutive consulships were illegal – ordinarily a candidate needed to wait ten years before returning to office – but members of the popular assembly overrode the Senate's authority to keep Marius in place between 104 and 100 BC. From what they had seen of him so far, they believed that he was the best chance they had against the new threat emerging on their borders.

In the time of the Gracchi, the Romans had established a new province to their north, on the other side of the Alps, known as Gallia Narbonensis. No sooner had they dealt with the ensuing disturbance than streams of Germanic tribespeople had begun to cross the mountains in search of fresh land for their burgeoning population. Driven in part by the devastation wrought by a particularly severe period of flooding, 300,000 armed men and 'much larger throngs of children and women' were marching into the province and beyond.[22]

The first tribes the Romans needed to confront were the Cimbri and Teutones – Marius would receive a triumph for his victory over them – but it was the Ambrones who stood out for the fearlessness of their women. The tribe, consisting of men, women and children, came from the area of modern Jutland and had made it as far as Aquae Sextiae (Aix-en-Provence) when they encountered Marius and his forces.[23] The Romans burst upon them unexpectedly as they bathed in the hot springs. Even the most hardened soldiers would have struggled to leap from wallowing in the waters to fighting, but the Ambrones showed no difficulty in making the sudden transition; they simply retrieved their swords and axes and strove to push the Romans back. Many of them were hacked down by the water but their compatriots kept up their attack. Every so often they called out their tribe's name, 'Ambrones!', either to spook the enemy or rouse each other to further hand-to-hand combat. The Romans could not fail to be astounded when tribeswomen leaned forward and simply plucked their shields or swords from their grasp. The Ambrones did not seem to mind the blood dripping from their wounds: they carried on as though they felt no pain. Their spirit appeared unbroken even when it became clear that the Romans were gaining the upper hand. It was only much later, after the battle was concluded and the two sides had retreated to their camps, that the women fighters finally gave vent to their emotion. The cries they sent out into the valleys of the night were so piercing and animalistic that the Romans feared impending attack.

Germanic tribeswomen repeatedly confounded Roman expectations. Some of the most astonishing scenes played out after Marius' defeat of the Ambrones' neighbouring Cimbri tribe. So as to avoid torture at the hands of the Romans, the surviving women among the Cimbri hurried back to their wagons, killed their husbands, and strangled their children before committing suicide. The speed and ruthlessness with which they did so astounded the Romans who witnessed it. While the women's first plan had been to hang their survivors, a shortage of trees meant that they were reduced to casting them beneath the wheels of wagons or the feet of cattle.[24] Some even hanged from cattle horns. The body of a woman was said to have been found dangling from a wagon pole with her two children hanging from her ankles. Although the Romans managed to take 60,000 tribespeople prisoner, it was said that twice as many had died already.

If this was glory, Marius was not allowed to revel in it for very long. On returning to Rome, he was met with hostility from one of his former colleagues in the Senate, a man with aristocratic roots and a mulberry-coloured birthmark upon his face, Lucius Cornelius Sulla. The two men had first come into conflict a couple of years earlier while engaged in war against Numidia. The kingdom abutted the Roman province of Africa (formed following the defeat of Carthage) and was supposed to have been ruled conjointly by the late king Micipsa's adopted son Jugurtha, a grandson of Masinissa, and his two natural sons, Hiempsal and Adherbal. The untidy arrangement had unravelled when Jugurtha murdered Hiempsal and put Adherbal to flight. The Romans reacted to the appeals of the two surviving brothers by dividing the territory between them, but then Jugurtha had Adherbal assassinated, necessitating further intervention. Marius served as consul and won a triumph even though he had yet to bring the war to a conclusion. That achievement was claimed by Sulla, who arrived just as the conflict was nearing its end and handed Jugurtha over to Marius in chains.[25] The defeated king was dragged through Rome in the triumphal procession. Marius' men stripped him naked and ripped off his gold earring, taking his earlobe with it. They pushed him into a dungeon, probably the *tullianum*, a dark, foul-smelling chamber with a stone roof located almost four metres underground. There Jugurtha died in a state of hunger and mental degeneration. Sulla was so proud of his work that he had a picture of himself leading the Numidian king to Rome engraved on his seal ring. It made Marius sick to look at it.

Marius' relationship with Sulla began to deteriorate most seriously following his violent fallout with a tribune. After serving as consul every year between 104 and 100 BC, Marius was compelled to absent himself from Rome in the face of falling popularity. His return to the city saw him – and Sulla – sucked into one of the most serious wars Italy had witnessed in years.

Over the past few decades, the resettlement of war veterans on Italian soil had alienated many Italian people, especially those who lacked the rights of suffrage in Rome. It struck many returning soldiers as inherently wrong that they should have risked their lives for a city that had either denied them Roman citizenship in the first place, or transplanted them after their service to a place in which they had no hope of exercising it. The 'Social War' that erupted in 91 BC took its name from the Latin for 'allies', *socii*, and saw the peoples of wider Italy who lacked Roman citizenship revolt against the Romans and their enfranchised 'Latin' neighbours in Latium, Campania and beyond. While the women of Italy had no expectation of gaining the vote themselves, they were automatically embroiled in a political struggle that would ultimately leave many of them widowed.

The war – a civil war in everything but name – would last only a few years but lead to the deaths of more than 300,000 people according to one Roman author.[26] It began with the unlawful killing of a Roman praetor (elected magistrate) and his assistant in the south Italian town of Asculum and filtered steadily outwards into every district. Comparatively few non-Roman residents would have had the means of travelling to Rome in order to exercise their right to vote even if they had one, but they longed to have the choice, and were no longer prepared to be looked down upon by the inhabitants of Italy's dominant city. This was a war fought by people who believed more in the principle of holding Roman citizenship than in the practical benefits that citizenship bestowed. One group, the Samnites, made the depth of their passion particularly clear by minting silver *denarii* bearing the image of an Italian bull goring a Roman wolf to death.[27]

As far as the Roman people were concerned, Marius and Sulla excelled themselves in the field, the one quashing the Marrucini (of modern

Abruzzo) and the other confronting the Samnites and neighbouring tribes in the south. Marius, however, was advancing in years. Forced to retire from battle as a result of worsening rheumatism (he also suffered from varicose veins), he took himself off to Misenum to recuperate at the villa formerly owned by Cornelia.[28] The property, Plutarch snarled, was far too luxurious for a hardened man of war. Marius' replacement died in action, but Sulla succeeded in prevailing over the Samnites, and by 90 BC the Romans were in a position to pass a law rewarding the Italians who had refused to take up arms the right to acquire Roman citizenship. A second law, passed the following year, granted not suffrage but 'Latin rights' – including rights of trade – to the ordinary people north of the River Po. Only the male magistrates of these parts received full Roman citizenship. Such was the compromise. Much of the Italian mainland south of Gaul was now united with Rome in what even formerly sceptical Romans would have to admit was an advantageous arrangement. Rome could only be stronger as the *de facto* capital of a growing nation.

Sulla's success in the Social War earned him a consulship. As if this was not sufficient to antagonise Marius, the Senate then declared that Sulla, still sprightly at about fifty years old, would lead a command against Mithridates VI Eupator, king of Pontus, who posed a deadly threat to Roman interests in Asia Minor.

Mithridates was a Hellenised Iranian who claimed descent from Alexander the Great. His fertile kingdom lay just south of the Black Sea and Greek was its official language. Many years earlier, his mother, a Seleucid princess named Laodice, had ruled as regent. Her husband had died as a result of being poisoned, prompting young Mithridates to develop a lifelong fascination with toxins. Each day he ingested a small quantity of something deadly in the hope of developing immunity against potential attack.[29] While he might have turned his knowledge and paranoia against his mother and brother, Mithridates chose instead to have them imprisoned after seizing power himself. He married a sister, also called Laodice, who bore several of his children, but later had her executed under accusation of giving birth to another man's child. At least two of his other sisters, Roxana and Stateira, survived, but for reasons unknown remained single and childless into their forties.

Mithridates had already conquered the Crimea and north-east borders of the Black Sea when he approached Nicomedes, king of Bithynia, for assistance in annexing Paphlagonia. The territory lay directly between their two kingdoms and might feasibly have been shared between them. Before Nicomedes could launch his bid for land, however, Mithridates had grasped his kingdom too. The Romans tried to restore Nicomedes to his throne in 90 BC but were hampered by their unpopularity in the region. Since establishing the province of Asia in 133 BC, they had sent in streams of ruthless *publicani* or tax-farmers, who naturally earned the resentment of the native population. Mithridates had little difficulty in presenting himself as the Bithynians' liberator. He stirred up antipathy towards Rome not only here, but as far afield as Athens, his heart set on even greater domination.

Marius had probably met Mithridates in 98 BC when he travelled to Galatia, just south of Pontus, to pay honour to the Mother Goddess Cybele. Although now almost seventy years old and increasingly infirm, Marius was convinced that he was better placed than anyone, especially Sulla, to lead a command against Mithridates and his forces. He therefore came to an illicit agreement with an ambitious young tribune. In exchange for his support in putting through some difficult legislation, the tribune helped Marius to obtain Sulla's command by addressing the matter in the people's assembly. Sulla, naturally, was incensed, and when all other attempts to recover his power failed, ordered his legions to turn back towards Rome at forced march in what constituted an act of civil war. Nothing like this had ever been seen before. The bold tribune was killed and Marius, without time to build up an adequate defence force, retreated to North Africa, where he sought refuge with old friends. Rome had not seen the last of him.

By the time Sulla finally arrived in the east, Mithridates had caused unimaginable devastation. He had somehow managed to orchestrate a mass killing of Romans and Italians across not only the extent of Asia, but the Aegean islands as well. His orders were for all women, men, children and slaves of Roman and Italian blood to be slaughtered and left unburied.[30] Informers and slaves who betrayed their masters were rewarded with the gift of freedom. The most extraordinary thing of all was that Mithridates managed to have his message passed in secret across the lands in time for the murders to be carried out simultaneously. The people of Ephesus ripped Romans from the Temple of Artemis; the Pergamenese shot arrows at those who clung to statues of Aesculapius the god of healing; residents of Adramyttium, in Aeolis, drowned children in the sea. No mercy was shown to anyone seeking religious sanctuary. It was recorded that 80,000 people were killed in a single day.

The women who Mithridates chanced upon in the period of his murderous spree were powerless to reject his advances as he endeavoured to expand his already substantial harem and court. The king, who is believed to have had six wives, fathered at least a dozen children by the women he gathered around him, many of whom left no trace of themselves in the historical record. The majority of Mithridates' women were described as being either of royal birth or married to important officials, but intriguingly, those we know the most about were neither.

Stratonice was an impecunious harpist.[31] Mithridates was so mesmerised by her playing that he stole her away one night while her father was sleeping. The old man woke the next morning to find his daughter missing but his house laden with gold and silver, a retinue of slaves at the ready, and a royally caparisoned horse standing outside. Mithridates considered this a fair exchange for the woman. Stratonice would give birth to his son.

Another woman, Monime, came to Mithridates' attention while he was campaigning in Greece. She was probably born in Miletus, birthplace of Aspasia, but acquired a reputation across the wider Greek world for the resistance she initially put up to the king's advances. Monime was seemingly unmoved by Mithridates' gift of 15,000 pieces of gold. She would only accept him, she said, if he agreed to make her his wife and queen.[32] Monime would come to regret this request, for while Mithridates agreed to grant it, their ensuing marriage was nothing less than disastrous. A Greek source, which may well be biased against Mithridates, described the misery of their union and Monime's despair that her beauty had brought her a master rather than a husband and a life amid barbarians rather than civilised beings. She felt less like a wife than a slave.

Mithridates profited deeply from the Greeks. In addition to taking another wife, Berenice of Chios, most probably as a result of overrunning her island, he topped up his treasury following raids on Rhodes as well as Cos, where Asiatic Jews had concealed some 800 talents.[33] The women of Greece rued the day he led the Romans to their shores. It was on the Greek mainland that Sulla confronted the eastern king with five legions. Calling in supplies from Thessaly, Aetolia and further afield, Sulla made his way to Attica, his sights set on the Athenian port of Piraeus. While dispatching Lucullus, one of the ablest Romans in his charge, to procure fleets from Alexandria, Syria and Rhodes, Sulla maintained a long and merciless siege of the harbour. Although the people of Athens put up their stoutest defence, they were gradually reduced to famine, cannibalism and defeat. Sulla had every surviving woman and child put to death.

In 85 BC Sulla reached an agreement with Mithridates and the war was brought to an end. Mithridates came away with the title king of Pontus and ally of Rome, and Sulla with the authority to send even more *publicani* into the defeated cities to raise funds for his city. The result might have earned Sulla a hero's welcome upon his return home, but Marius had other ideas. The embittered older man had returned from Africa while Sulla was away and raised an army in Etruria. A great number of pro-Sullan senators had consequently lost their heads. In the climate of fear bred by these executions, Marius won a final, seventh consulship, but died just days after reprising the post. Civil war resumed, with some of the bitterest fighting taking place just outside Rome's Colline Gate, at the north-east end of the city. During the total breakdown of order Sulla appointed himself *dictator rei publicae constituendae* ('dictator for reconstituting the Republic').

Classical writers looked back on the years that followed as some of the darkest in Rome's history. Although women were not subject to having their names recorded on the 'proscription' lists in the forum, which condemned men to death or exile as inimical to the state, the confiscation of property belonging to their fathers, husbands and brothers left many of them bereft. Livia, the future wife of Augustus, first emperor of Rome, was just one of the women forced to flee Rome in the midst of the upheaval.

The apparent arbitrariness of the selection of victims instilled fear in the innocent. No one could be sure that his name would not appear on the proscription boards. As Sulla himself was supposed to have said, he would proscribe whomever he remembered that day, and more as their names came back to him.[34] In the first round, according to one source, he proscribed forty-odd senators and 1,600 equestrians. Another source put his initial proscriptions at eighty men without prior discussion with the Senate, 220 two days later, and so forth. Some were killed on the spot; others in temples; others were thrown through the air and tossed at Sulla's feet.[35] Some of the wealthiest women in Rome took their lives into their own hands as they conspired against the consuls and spared 'no effort or expense' to secure the return of proscribed Roman citizens.[36] It is a failing of the sources that we know more about the men who were banished than the women who came to their rescue.

Cornelia, daughter of Cinna, Marius' colleague and successor, certainly suffered as a consequence of Sulla's rise. She married Julius Caesar in about 84 BC and thereby strengthened the ties with the Marian camp that he already held as a nephew of Marius' widow Julia. As chaos enveloped Rome, Caesar made himself scarce by travelling to Bithynia to complete his military service and, if the gossips were to be trusted, to submit to the sexual whims of King Nicomedes IV. Cornelia for her part had more worrying issues than these alleged sexual peccadillos to contemplate, as Sulla stripped her of her dowry and Caesar of his inheritance. The couple had refused to divorce.

Sulla viewed what was happening as the necessary means to an end. He was of the old way of thinking that prized a unified, concordant Senate above an individual's right to freedom of expression. Dissenters were a disruption, an inconvenience, an impediment to the smooth running of society. They spoiled Rome for everyone else. Once he had cleared a path through the most obstinate corners of the city, he intended to set about implementing policies for reform, beginning with the Senate itself. He increased the body of the house from 300 to 600, though the new recruits were predominantly equestrians of proven loyalty to himself. To appease the old stalwarts, Sulla restored the senators' right to act as jurors in legal cases surrounding everything from bribery to murder, and took away the majority of the tribunes' powers, including their right to propose and veto laws in the popular assemblies, and to progress to higher office. Once he had done what he felt was necessary, Sulla relinquished his dictatorship and retired to Campania.

As a younger man, Sulla had depended upon a noble-born wife, another Julia, to lift him from obscurity.[37] Now in his dotage and several wives down, he came to the notice of a sprightly divorcee. Valeria was a niece of Hortensius, one of the great orators of the age, and shared her uncle's passion for literary acrobatics. Sulla was watching a gladiatorial show when Valeria strolled past, noticed a loose thread dangling from his toga and boldly plucked it away.[38] As he turned around to look at her, Valeria smiled and said something like *It's lucky!* Sulla had taken to calling himself Felix ('Lucky') in acknowledgement of his political achievements. Valeria's act of flattery enchanted him. The episode serves to illustrate that, just occasionally, noblewomen could and did break the rules of propriety and approach men in public.

The pair enjoyed a brief marriage before Sulla fell ill with a foul and unidentifiable disease which appeared to emanate from his bowels to his flesh in the form of parasites. He died in 79 BC at the age of sixty. In spite of widespread opposition, he was granted a state funeral, for which the women of the city supplied herbs and spices to use in the rites. Valeria, pregnant at the time of Sulla's death, gave birth to a daughter, named Postuma as daughters of deceased parents generally were. Neither she nor Valeria survived for very long.

One of the people who had been instrumental in securing Sulla a public funeral was Gnaeus Pompeius. His ruthlessness in putting down enemies in Africa and Sicily in the early part of his career had earned him the unenviable sobriquet *adulescentulus carnifex* ('The Teenage Butcher'), but Sulla had preferred to call him *Magnus*. Pompey the Great, as he would forever be known, now steadily emerged at the forefront of Roman politics. The young butcher's startling aptitude might have cost him a place in Sulla's will, but he had won a triumph and the attention of Rome, which was more than any ordinary benefaction could bestow.

The tough, rugged-mannered son of a wealthy senator assumed his place in the public consciousness after helping to stem a servile uprising in the south of Italy in 71 BC. In the course of the campaign, the gladiator Spartacus and his men used grapevines to lower themselves onto the plain beneath Mount Vesuvius and launch a surprise attack on the Romans.[39] Marcus Licinius Crassus, another of Sulla's former commanders who had benefited handsomely from the proscriptions, took the lead in putting down the revolt and had 6,000 of the participants crucified along the Appian Way. Pompey's claim to victory lay in supplying essential reinforcements in the final stages of the conflict. For this he won a triumph, whereas Crassus won an inferior ovation. There was no disguising the tension between the two men when they proceeded to a joint consulship the following year.

Pompey similarly felt no qualms about taking credit for Rome's final victory over Mithridates. War with Pontus resumed after the king of Bithynia died about 74 BC and bequeathed his territory to Rome. Pompey headed east, clearing the seas as he went of pirates, who had wrought havoc with Rome's grain supply. But it was louche Lucius Licinius Lucullus, a general under Sulla, who succeeded in quelling Mithridates' invasion of Bithynia and then driving him out of his own kingdom. Mithridates had just managed to find his way back again after taking refuge in Armenia when Pompey arrived and sent him scurrying to safety in Crimea.

Mithridates has often been pictured alone in his final days, abandoned by his people, usurped by one of his sons. But as he made his escape, he was joined by three companions, one of whom was Hypsicrateia, his concubine or perhaps wife.[40] Hypsicrateia dressed in men's clothes, wore her hair short, rode horses with ease, and performed the sort of exercises usually practised by the military.[41] Mithridates, evidently impressed by her efforts, addressed her using the masculine version of her name.

Hypsicrateia – or 'Hypsicrates' – was said to have adapted herself purposely to a male way of life in order to share as closely as possible in her lover's plight. This may have been true in part, but it is just as likely that she had been raised in the tradition of the earlier Scythian tribes, who had wandered the same geographical region for centuries with their pot-smoking tents and horsehair wigs. Like Penthesilea, Hippolyte, and the other Amazons of myth, Hypsicrateia was a woman of stamina and courage. She showed no signs of exhaustion as she accompanied Mithridates on horseback across the harsh landscape as far as Sinora in Lesser Armenia. Mithridates had a trove here containing treasure and poison. The former would be of relatively little use to him now but the poison – surely this was the time for it. The king distributed doses to each of his companions for safekeeping and carried on towards Colchis, the land of Medea, in modern Georgia.

Pompey would claim to have encountered Amazons himself in this region as he prepared to invade Armenia at the invitation of the son of its king. His mission was to pursue Mithridates beyond the mountain range of the Caucasus. His journey verged on the epic: he was forced to turn around as he neared the Caspian Sea by a congregation of venomous reptiles. More surprising, at least to those who knew him well, was his decision to turn his back upon the offer to have sex with Mithridates' concubines. Pompey was in no way prudish but it occurred to him that there could be a greater advantage in returning the women to their families than in taking them himself. True to expectation, Stratonice, the harpist's daughter, repaid Pompey's kindness by granting him use of one of Mithridates' strategic strongholds. Something even more appealing than sex awaited him inside. Mithridates' diaries, the love letters he had exchanged with Monime in the happier days of their relationship, and recipes and constitutions of various poisons were among the documents Pompey procured.

Mithridates' obsession with toxins eventually proved his undoing. Swallowing the contents of one of the vials he had removed from his trove might have been the quickest and easiest way out for him at this point, but his lifelong ingestion of minute quantities might also have rendered him immune to their worst effects. With no certainty the poison would work, Mithridates abstained from taking it and offered his body to the sword of one of his guardsmen instead. He was then in his early seventies.

The death of Mithridates in 63 BC meant the death of his sisters and his harem. Mithridates made sure of this. Before he committed himself to the sword, he dispatched a court eunuch named Bacchides to inform each woman that it was her time to die by whichever means she preferred.

Monime attempted to hang herself using the diadem Mithridates had given her as a wedding present. The irony of the headpiece breaking in the process was not lost on her. She spat on the fractured bauble, threw it across the room, and bravely offered Bacchides her bare neck.

Berenice chose poison. She gave her mother a deeper sip of the cup and endured the horrific sight of her dying while her own dose proved too weak. Bacchides made the decision to strangle Berenice, not to put her out of her misery, but because he was in a hurry to see the job completed.

Mithridates' sisters also chose poison, the family obsession, and drank it in one case silently, in the other cursing his name.

The nature of Amazonian Hypsicrateia's death is unknown.

The loss of these women meant little to the Romans, who rejoiced at the opportunity to establish a sprawling new province by combining Pontus with the kingdom of Bithynia, to be known as Bithynia-Pontus. The wars delivered them further territories – Armenia, Cappadocia, Media, Colchis, Iberia, Albania, Syria, Cilicia, Mesopotamia, Tyre, Phoenicia and Palestine, Judaea, Arabia, 'and everything the pirates had on land and sea that had now been overthrown'. In September 61 BC, coinciding with his forty-fifth birthday, Pompey the Great celebrated a triumph, his third, for his accomplishments. A cloak he claimed had been worn by Alexander the Great rested loosely on his shoulders.

Chapter XIV

Conspiring at Crossroads

Stop, stranger, and peruse what is written here.
A mother was not allowed to enjoy the company of her only daughter
Whom some god, I believe, I know not which, felt envious towards.
But since it was not allowed her to be adorned for marriage by her mother,
Her mother did this for her after she had died, at the end of time,
And for the daughter she loved she engraved this memorial.

Posilla Senenia, freeborn daughter of Quartus and Quarta Senenia, a former slave. Memorial inscription for a daughter, Monteleone, a Sabine city, first century BC, *CIL* 1, 1837

Mucia Tertia must have been surprised to receive divorce papers from Pompey following his return from the east. They had been married for almost twenty years and had raised two sons and a daughter. Mucia's half-brothers, Metellus Celer and Metellus Nepos, had assisted Pompey in the Mithridatic Wars and worked alongside him in the Senate. Anyone might have said they were the perfect Roman family. But then rumours began to spread that Mucia had been unfaithful to Pompey during his prolonged absences from Rome.

'Fertile is the seed of adultery,' smirked the poet Catullus, tickled by lewd talk of Mucia's misbehaviour.[1] The poet made no effort to disguise his own lack of moral probity on this front. He described himself in lusty verse cavorting with both women and boys in his quest for 'nine consecutive fucks' at midday.[2] Illicit sex was a favourite topic. Broken bedsteads, crumpled pillows, vanishing love-handles and secret safe houses – these were what made the romantic heart sing. Catullus claimed in one of his poems that Mucia had been carrying on with two different men as early as Pompey's first consulship in 70 BC. As time went on and Pompey grew more powerful, 'Maecilia', as Catullus called her, added exponentially to that number: 'The two remain, but a thousand men compete / Against each.' Among them, or so people said, was Julius Caesar.

About the time he delivered his funeral oration for his aunt Julia, Caesar had found himself delivering another one for his wife Cornelia, who died while still in her twenties. Many women her age lost their lives to post-partum infection, but, given that several years had passed since she gave birth to their daughter, another Julia, it seems more likely that Cornelia succumbed to a circulating illness. As the daughter of Cinna, the political successor of Gaius Marius, Cornelia had always been a recognisable figure in Rome, but in death she was treated with the reverence of a hero. No other woman her age had been commemorated with a eulogy from the Rostra (speaker platforms).

The eulogy no longer survives, but as a crowd gathered to hear it, few could have doubted the depth of Caesar's affection for his late wife. If the young politician did have an affair with Mucia – marriage would never impede his pursuit of other women – it most probably began after Cornelia's death and after he had wed for the second time. Pompey in either case chose to keep quiet about the rumours, which had first reached him in the east. Although he changed his mind upon returning to Italy and decided to divorce Mucia, he made no declaration of the grounds upon which he was doing so.[3]

The allegations concerning Mucia and Caesar were almost too convenient for Pompey. Success had very quickly gone to his head. In every way convinced of the Alexandrian quality of his new name, 'the Great' man was soon thinking of the other women he might profit from as he climbed the ranks of the Senate. Mucia's father, Quintus Mucius Scaevola, had been senior in the house and served as Pontifex Maximus, but he had been murdered many years ago in the Temple of Vesta. Marcius Porcius Cato ('Cato the Younger'), on the other hand, was not only alive, but thriving, and he had unmarried nieces. The situation could hardly have been worse for Mucia, who was related to the girls Pompey now set his heart on. While Mucia appears to have reacted to her ex-husband's fickleness with strength, Pompey did not repay her good grace. Mucia remarried and had another son but suffered further misfortune when her new husband was convicted of bribery during an unsuccessful bid to reach the consulship. Pompey did nothing to stop him from being sent into exile.

The breakdown of Mucia's family life provided the people of Rome with only so much distraction from more worrying events on their horizon. Very far from dissipating, the troubles which had plagued the city in the time of the Gracchi had resurfaced following the Social War of the Italian allies. Men who had fought for Sulla were settled on land confiscated from other men during the proscriptions, but 'settled' was the very last word anyone would have used to describe them, so inured were they to the taste of battle.

Legal cases arising from the proscriptions and the war for citizenship had propelled Marcus Tullius Cicero to the forefront of Rome's lawcourts for the first time. A man of humble beginnings, Cicero originally came from Arpinum, like Gaius Marius, and maintained a villa there. In 80 BC, at the age of twenty-six, he had successfully defended Sextus Roscius, a man falsely accused of murdering his own father, a victim of Sulla's dictatorship.[4] Cicero had notably also come to the assistance of a woman from Arretium (Arezzo) in a dispute over her citizenship.[5] He had completed military service under Pompey's father and supported Pompey's promotion to commander against the forces of Mithridates. Cicero had served under Sulla, too, but a soldier's life was never going to be for him. Following his defence of Sextus Roscius, he had travelled east to further his study of philosophy and rhetoric in Athens, Asia Minor and Rhodes, and stayed two years.

Accompanying him for at least part of his journey was his wife Terentia. Wealthy by birth, she brought to the marriage a dowry of 100,000 denarii, which would have qualified her as an equestrian had she been male. She owned rural land and at least two *insulae* (blocks of flats) in Rome, which she managed without the assistance of her husband. About a decade his junior, she appears in his letters as his 'light', his 'life', his 'most excellent wife'. Theirs was very much a meeting of minds. Terentia had little interest in domestic affairs and was inclined to change the subject if ever they arose.[6] Their conversation usually centred on politics. It was probably while they were in Greece that they conceived the first of their two children. Tullia was to hold a unique place in her father's heart. Cicero saw much of himself in her: she was, he wrote, 'the image of me in face and speech and mind'. The young family returned to Rome where Cicero embarked upon a political career. It was after his election to the consulship for 63 BC that tensions reached their crisis.

Rumours of a plot had been circulating for months. Dissatisfaction bred by an economic downturn in the wake of the wars had driven many Romans into a life of gambling and crime. As a proud *novus homo* ('new man'), the first in his family to scale the heights of the Senate, Cicero was ambitious to make his mark, even if the terrain was febrile. When a well-to-do woman approached him with information about a possible conspiracy, he therefore listened.

The woman's name was Fulvia and she had found herself in an abusive relationship. Her lover, Quintus Curius, had been discharged from the Senate on grounds of immoral behaviour.[7] Convinced that she was no longer interested in him, Curius tried to win her back by promising her mountains, but then became violently coercive. Fulvia's suspicions about him were raised when he returned home on the night of 6 November 63 BC looking unusually perplexed. Curius had never been good at keeping secrets, and Fulvia was able to extract from him that he had attended a meeting at the house of a man named Marcus Porcius Laeca in the quarter of Rome where the scythe-dealers lived.[8] A plan was afoot, Curius finally divulged, and it involved the assassination of Cicero.

Fulvia felt no great loyalty to her lover, but she did to her country, which was why she had been passing information to Cicero and others for some time. One name kept cropping up in Fulvia's intelligence, including the latest, and that was Lucius Sergius Catilina (Catiline).

Catiline was not an obscure figure. He was a member of one of the most eminent patrician families in Rome and had until recently been extremely wealthy. The historian Sallust described him as 'of great strength of mind and body, but of evil and depraved character', with a disordered brain that 'constantly hungered for what was excessive, incredible, a bridge too far'.[9] Catiline's egregious appetites extended to deflowering Vestal Virgins; Terentia's half-sister Fabia had suffered the ignominy of being accused of breaking her vow of chastity to satisfy his lust. When the crime was discovered, Catiline had a brief exchange with some of his allies in the Senate and saw the charges against him dropped. Fabia, by contrast, was tainted by the scandal forever after in spite of being acquitted. According to Cicero, who understandably nursed a vendetta, Catiline had murdered one wife in order to marry another. Catiline murdered his stepson, too, according to Sallust, because his fiancée was afraid of him.[10] Further scandal attended Catiline's handling of his personal finances; he had returned to Rome from a senatorial posting in Africa to face accusations of extortion.

Catiline's repeated failure to achieve the consulship had both exacerbated his debt and decided him on an extreme course of action. From what Fulvia said, he appeared to be intent on overthrowing the government, slaughtering its representatives and seizing power himself. Alarmed by what her lover had told her of Catiline's plans, Fulvia returned to Cicero, this time in haste, and relayed everything she knew. With some risk to himself and to her, Cicero approached the coercive Quintus Curius to verify what she said, and learned that it was true. Many of the conspirators who had gathered amid the scythe-dealers had blanched at the idea of toppling him, but at least two – an equestrian and a senator – had agreed to take the job in hand. They planned to call on Cicero's house on the Palatine Hill early the next morning.

The assassins were surprised to find the premises under close guard. They received no answer when they knocked. Cicero had heeded Fulvia's warning and kept himself safely tucked away. In retrospect it was clear: Fulvia had saved his life.

Within hours, the orator was standing before the Senate in the Temple of Jupiter the Sustainer near the forum, detailing in extremely dramatic fashion how close he had come to being assassinated. He did not name Fulvia publicly – it would have been detrimental to her safety if he had – but he knew in his heart that he owed everything to her intelligence. Fulvia's name ought to be synonymous with the failure of the Catilinarian Conspiracy.

When the moment came for Cicero to identify the perpetrator, Catiline had taken his seat. Looking him directly in the eye, Cicero pronounced the opening words of a speech that would become immortal. 'For how long, Catiline, will you persist in trying our patience?'[11] Cicero had actually considered Catiline as a running-mate for his election to the consulship for 63 BC. How his position had changed. By reaching the senior magistracy, Cicero had succeeded where Catiline had failed, and he now had the opportunity to prove that he, the equestrian man, was greater than him, the old-monied patrician man. Cicero continued: *o tempora, o mores*

('Oh what is the world coming to?'). Catiline was visibly confounded. He did not know what to say when Cicero asked him whether he had been at Laeca's house at the meeting. Insecurity turned to aggression, and after a few jibes at Cicero's social class, Catiline pleaded innocence before succumbing to senatorial pressure to leave Rome at once.

Catiline may have appeared to be compliant, but privately, as he made his way to Etruria, he was plotting his next move. He had amassed a significant following among certain groups of society during his previous campaigns for the consulship. If there was a certain tentativeness at Laeca's, among Sulla's veterans and the men they displaced there was much appetite for full-scale revolution. Pallid Catiline, his eyes bloodshot with ambition, appealed to them with his promises of eradicating debt, proscribing the rich, and leading Rome to a fairer future.[12] The least charitable writers categorised Catiline's followers as low lifes and petty criminals, gladiators and gamblers, murderers, debauchees and disaffected youths with hearts easily won.[13] But there were also senators, equestrians and women – in particular prostitutes who had fallen on hard times after exceeding the age of employability.[14]

One of the most interesting of Catiline's female followers conformed to none of the stereotypes. Sempronia, not to be confused with the sister of the Gracchi, hosted at least one of the conspirators' meetings. She was a wife, a mother and a polymath, with as many skills as there were evenings in the week to perform them.[15] She knew Greek and Latin literature, she wrote humorous poetry, she played the lyre, she danced; she was almost suspiciously accomplished. Sallust called her wanton and claimed that she had been privy to murder. Her 'masculine courage' certainly served her well against the threat of being identified as another wastrel adherent of Catiline. Her husband Decimus Brutus was away when she invited Catiline's Romans and members of the Gallic tribe of the Allobroges to the house to discuss the possibility of an alliance. The evening was not successful for the Catilinarians, whose offer to the Allobroges went unheeded. The tribesmen vocally pledged their allegiance to the existing government and secretly leaked the details of Sempronia's meeting to Cicero via an intermediary. They thereby provided the defenders of the Republic with valuable insight into whom Catiline was working with in Rome.

Cicero, already on his guard, was roused by evidence of further activity by the enemy in their midst. He had already persuaded the Senate that action was needed in the interest of national security. He had produced a bundle of letters, allegedly left at Crassus' door, opened them and read them aloud. These letters and news of Catiline's movements in Etruria provided the impetus the Senate needed to mount a robust defence.[16] Alarmed by reports of the armed troops Catiline had gathered after reaching the camp of a former centurion named Manlius, the senators voted Cicero and his partner in the consulship, Gaius Antonius Hybrida, the authority to raise an army if necessary for the defence of the Republic. Forces were dispatched to Faesulae in Etruria, Apulia, Capua and Pisa, while Cicero stood poised to defend Rome itself. Mucia's half-brother Quintus Metellus Celer, then praetor, dragged men from Gaul to Rome to stand trial before throwing them in prison.

The people of Italy were terrified at being plunged back into civil war. Women feared for their children as much as they did for their husbands and brothers. Terentia, Cicero's wife, was *exanimata* – so overcome with fatigue that she could faint.[17] Her daughter Tullia was newly married to a budding senator but united with her mother and younger brother in fear for Cicero's life. It seemed almost incredible that there were citizens among them who were prepared to destroy their own country at the call of one man. Thousands of Romans had been reduced to poverty under Sulla. Would thousands now overturn the state?

Some blamed Pompey and Crassus for the ructions that developed in the Senate. Had they not reinstated the powers of the tribunes of the plebs during their joint consulship, then Catiline might have been stopped. But even without the tribunes and their appeals to the popular vote, the Senate was highly divided. As a case in point, Cicero rejected the bribes of two senators to bring false accusations against a third, Julius Caesar, who found himself mired in scandal nonetheless.

The internal divisions of the house were plain for all to see when five conspirators were rounded up in Rome and the conversation turned to what to do with them. Caesar was staunchly in favour of imprisoning the accused and having them properly tried. The young praetor addressed the senators in the Temple of the goddess Concordia ('Harmony'), at the west of the forum, but he might sooner have pledged himself to *discordia*, such were the arguments that ensued. As Caesar stressed the need to put friendships and animosities aside, he spoke with fresh authority.[18] The previous year, his mother Aurelia had heard him say that he would either return from the latest elections as Pontifex Maximus, or not return at all. Aurelia was relieved when the ballots came out in his favour. Caesar now stood at the head of the most important priesthood in Rome. Imbued with the morality of his post, he urged his colleagues to carry out only what was strictly endorsed by law, no more. The five men ought to be incarcerated and deprived of their possessions rather than put to death in haste. This was not leniency, stressed Caesar, but rationality.

Caesar's speech was long and eloquent but failed to find favour with the more conservative elements of the house. Cato the Younger spoke for the opposite case and emphasised the unprecedented nature of the risk they faced. If the men were merely imprisoned, who was to say they wouldn't be rescued by accomplices remaining at large, especially if a mob became involved? Rome would be safer if they were dead.

The senators' choice lay between two different policies and two different men. Cato and Caesar were antitheses of one another: the first upright, abstemious, prosaic; the second liberal and loose to the point of being un-Roman. Caesar could hardly bear the restrictions of a belted toga which he was prone to hoisting up. Cato was observably austere – a natural hair-shirt candidate – in his bare feet, frugality and sexual continence. Caesar was the nephew of the wife of Gaius Marius. Cato had counted Sulla, enemy of Marius, as an old family friend. Caesar claimed descent from Venus via Aeneas. Cato's family was Sabine and his most famous ancestor was a mere mortal in the shape of his great-grandfather, the plebeian writer and conservative statesman Cato the Elder.

Cato's speech with its prevailing message of 'taking back power' worked on the restless minds of the senators. As consul, Cicero had particular sway, and he was adamantly in favour of the death sentence. The Senate now acted swiftly. The first of the conspirators was led down into the dark *tullianum* and strangled to death. The remaining four, no doubt hearing the cries of their ally, stepped forward to endure the same. Cicero delivered the news to the people of Rome with a restrained but powerful '*vixere*': they have lived; they are no longer living. It is arguable that none of this would have been possible without the intervention of Fulvia.

Catiline had meanwhile combined his forces with those of his ally Manlius to make up two legions. They proceeded towards Gaul as the loyalist Romans made their approach. Catiline resisted giving fight because he believed that he would soon be joined by the conspirators and their adherents in Rome. But then news reached his men of the death sentences. Panicked, many deserted their arms, convinced that they were doomed to fail and to die. Those who remained followed Catiline towards the Alps in the hope of finding sanctuary in Transalpine Gaul. To their horror, Mucia's half-brother Quintus Metellus Celer led three legions to the foot of the mountains to block their advance. The arrival of further forces from Rome ensured that the Catilinarians were firmly hemmed in. Catiline continued to rouse his men with the hope of victory. Manlius took the right wing, a man of Faesulae took the left, and Catiline and his freedmen took their places beside the eagle standard. Flooded with adrenaline, they pushed forward, Catiline replacing the wounded with fresh fighters and appearing wholly in control, even when his men were routed. At that moment he threw himself fearlessly into the enemy. They impaled him. He was still breathing, just a little, when his body was sought in the field.

Cicero gloried in the heroism of this moment. He was a saviour of the Republic, *pater patriae*, a consul to be remembered. But doubt lingered in many quarters over the legitimacy of the course he had taken. He had made the call to put Roman citizens to death before they had even been granted a trial. This would never be forgotten.

The women's festival of the Bona Dea – the Good Goddess – took place in early December each year at the home of one of the senior magistrates. The Vestal Virgins and prominent women of Rome would gather as darkness fell to conduct a series of rites to celebrate and nurture their fertility. No men were allowed to intrude upon these events or they risked upsetting their sanctity. Even paintings and statues of men were blanketed over around the house. The sense of secrecy that shrouded the occasion naturally intrigued many. In the second century, the satirist Juvenal would be carried away describing inebriated women shaking their hips to the cheering music of pan-pipes. He was not wrong to suppose that the festival of the Bona Dea was an uncorked, uncorseted affair.

Terentia had hosted the event the previous year and it had passed without too much comment. The Bona Dea of 62 BC was to be held at the home of the new Pontifex Maximus and his wife. As the granddaughter of Sulla, Pompeia had been an unlikely choice of bride for the widowed Julius Caesar, but their marriage served to draw a line under the traumas of recent decades. Little is known of her, and nothing at all of her feelings about the match, but if the rumours thrown up during the festival were true, Caesar was not the first man on her mind.

Pompeia had welcomed her mother-in-law and sister-in-law and the other celebrants of the Bona Dea when a troubling cry was heard from somewhere in the house. A suspiciously tall figure enveloped in a saffron gown with purple sashes and not-so-dainty upturned slippers stood among them. She was, it transpired, a gruff-voiced Publius Clodius Pulcher.

Clodius belonged to one of the oldest patrician families in Rome. He was descended from Claudia Quinta, who had tugged Cybele onto the Italian shoreline during the Punic Wars, and his innovative ancestor Appius Claudius 'The Blind' was still spoken of with reverence. It said a lot about their relationship with their heritage that Clodius and three of his sisters opted for the more fashionable plebeian spelling of their family name over the aristocratic *Claudius*. Rebellious Clodius had served under his successful brother-in-law, Metellus Celer, in the war against Mithridates. He was discharged after inciting a mutiny against another brother-in-law, Lucullus, who had since divorced his youngest sister. At thirty years old, Clodius was no less obstreperous, but he had managed to win a seat in the Senate for the following year as a quaestor (the entry-level position for men of patrician birth).

Clodius was supposed to be leaving for Sicily in the new year to carry out his duties. The women of the Bona Dea ensured that he stayed behind in Rome, for the moment, pending trial instead. Clodius had been ejected from the property the moment he was found, but he should never have entered in the first place, least of all in women's clothes. The charge brought against him was defined as *incestum*, which meant that he was recognised as having posed a threat to the chastity of the Vestal Virgins. Gossip soon spread that theirs was not the only chastity Clodius had mocked. If Pompeia and Clodius had wanted to conduct an affair, they could not have chosen a more theatrical setting than this. Clodius was not Catiline; he had no interest in deflowering holy virgins. Caesar's wife, on the other hand? Perhaps Pompeia had agreed to meet him that night; perhaps she had agreed to have sex with him while the other women were distracted; perhaps she had planned to let him out by the back door before he was recognised.

Perhaps, but it is unlikely that Pompeia would have arranged a liaison with Clodius when there was so much scope for scandal. Affairs among patrician Romans were commonplace, even expected, including among women, but there was an unspoken rule against causing undue disruption to another family. There was no excuse for Pompeia and Clodius re-enacting a scene from comedy.

Cicero, giving evidence for the prosecution, easily destroyed Clodius' alibi, and Caesar's mother and sister attended court to swear that Clodius was the man they had seen in the house. Lucullus, providing further testimony, went so far as to accuse his former brother-in-law of incest with his ex-wife. Incest was the rudest and most predictable slur one Roman could make against another and rumours of it very seldom carried any truth. Clodius was confident that he could triumph against the odds. The evidence of the women, in particular, was bound to be questioned when so much wine had been drunk that evening. With a shrug, Clodius 'Pretty Boy' Pulcher put his hand in his pocket, lent upon some powerful friends, and got himself acquitted. It was an embarrassing loss for the elite women of Rome and for Cicero, too, who would never live down his attempt to shame Clodius in court.

It was around this time that Clodius decided he ought to grow up. Roman men tended to wait to marry until they were thirty or thereabouts, which was also when they could enter the Senate. As they reached their age of maturity, their brides were usually only just beyond menarche and so roughly half their age. The teenage girl who came to Clodius' attention was unusually self-assured. Fulvia, not to be confused with Cicero's informant, came from Tusculum in the region of ancient Latium and was in possession of an attractive dowry. Her mother, Sempronia, may have been a close relation of the Sempronia who joined Catiline's conspiracy.[19] Her father, Marcus Fulvius Bambalio, was wealthy but 'a man of no consequence', according to Cicero.[20] He had a speech impediment – 'Bambalio' meant 'Stammerer' – which probably influenced Cicero's crude dismissal of him. Young Fulvia might have inherited this trait, for one of her cheeks was noticeably larger than the other, but in a woman the feature was considered endearing. A Sicilian teacher of rhetoric once wrote that Fulvia 'tempted the point of his pen'.[21] The same euphemism could have been used by passionate Clodius. The young couple quickly became inseparable.[22] Soon after they were married they produced a son, Publius Clodius, and a daughter, Claudia.

Marriages were being brokered and broken at an alarming rate among the wealthy families of Rome. In the wake of the Bona Dea scandal, Julius Caesar lodged for divorce from Pompeia despite there being no evidence that she had engaged in a dalliance with Clodius. There was little she could say when Caesar grandly declared that any wife of his needed to be 'above suspicion'. For the sake of a mere rumour he thereby resigned her to public censure. Cato, his mirror double, divorced his wife Atilia, mother of his two children, claiming that she too had been unfaithful. Add to these cases Lucullus' divorce of the youngest Clodia and Pompey's divorce of Mucia, and female infidelity was either rife, or the simplest excuse a man could make for forging more profitable connections.

Anyone in doubt as to how to interpret the sudden proliferation in high-profile divorces had only to consider the case of Cato. After leaving Atilia, he married a noblewoman named Marcia, only to give her up to the orator Hortensius who wanted her for himself. There is no indication that Cato's second marriage was failing. Marcia may even have been pregnant with her third child when Cato told her that she was to go to live with Hortensius. For Cato this was not an unattractive proposition. In addition to his house on the Palatine Hill, Hortensius kept a sprawling villa at Bauli near Baiae in the Bay of Naples, replete with fishponds filled with eels. Hortensius was very fond of eels. When he died a short time later, Marcia returned to Cato bringing with her everything she had inherited from her newer partner. Julius Caesar, always vying with the conservative fop Cato, could not help but point fun at the ludicrous farce. But, as Cato realised, Caesar was no better himself.

No sooner had his divorce from Pompeia been finalised than Caesar pursued an affair with Cato's half-sister Servilia. To anyone who knew of their rivalry it must have looked as though Caesar had deliberately begun courting her in order to antagonise Cato. It just so happened that Cato found out about the affair in the full glare of his senatorial colleagues. A private letter arrived for Caesar while he was in the Senate House and Cato intercepted it to his immediate regret.[23] The ordinarily buttoned-up senator threw his sister's passionate proclamation back to Caesar with the sort of language that prompted a man to smooth out his toga.

Cato not uncharacteristically overemphasised his importance in the affair. He did not see that Servilia had a natural affinity with Caesar. Not only was she his precise contemporary, but she had been twice married herself, first to a man who was killed by Pompey the Great – their son, Marcus Junius Brutus, a distant descendant of the Brutus who killed King Tarquin, understandably grew up loathing the man – and currently to Decimus Junius Silanus, a senator, by whom she had three daughters. She had no need to pursue Caesar for the sake of having more children. Their affair, thought to have begun shortly before her second husband died in 60 BC, would endure on its own strength for many years to come. Although Servilia was not the only woman Caesar was sleeping with (he had a particular liking for other senators' wives), she was his favourite, and he aimed to prove this to her by buying her a pearl for 6 million sesterces in 59 BC. The property qualification for entry to the senatorial class was 1 million sesterces. So overnight, Servilia became one of the richest women in Rome.

The money for the pearl probably came from Ptolemy XII Auletes of Egypt. Ptolemy had handed over a vast sum to members of the Roman Senate that year in a bid to be recognised formally as a friend and ally of the Roman people. His position in Egypt had become precarious owing to his egregious mismanagement of private and public finances. In the midst of a popular revolt, he absconded to Rome to seek political aid, leaving his daughters, Berenice IV and Cleopatra VI Tryphaena, as *de facto* rulers. Strikingly, given that the freedom of movement enjoyed by women in the earlier period had begun to be eroded, it was the people of Egypt who demanded that the two young women take control. Cleopatra VI died a short time after the transferral of authority, but Berenice was determined to fulfil her duty, even if that meant exercising violence. When a Seleucid prince was imposed upon her as a husband, she had him strangled and married a Greek man named Archelaus instead. The prospect of handing power back to her father one day increasingly filled Berenice with dread.

Caesar was able to grant Ptolemy the support he desired after reaching the consulship in 59 BC. The senator's promotion may have been beneficial for Ptolemy, but for Servilia it was guaranteed to make daily life more complicated. The rift between Cato, her half-brother, and Caesar, her lover, seemed to deepen with every passing week. Consuls were supposed to share power between them as part of a carefully calibrated system designed to prevent the development of an autocracy. Caesar's partner in the consulship, Marcus Calpurnius Bibulus, just happened to be married to Servilia's niece Porcia, a daughter of Cato. Servilia could not have known whether to be delighted or humiliated when the Roman people began speaking of 'the consulship of Julius and Caesar'.[24] Her loyalties were very publicly divided. Caesar became only stauncher in wresting power from his colleague in office. One day Bibulus, dripping from a bucket of excrement poured over his head, withdrew reluctantly to the safety of his house.[25]

Servilia might have married Caesar after being widowed, but at the age of forty-one, at a time when the onset of menopause was typically earlier than in later centuries, she perhaps accepted that she was less likely than a younger woman to provide her lover with a son. While Servilia contented herself with remaining his mistress, a younger woman named Calpurnia caught Caesar's eye. Calpurnia was the loyal teenage daughter of a senator named Lucius Calpurnius Piso Caesoninus. In the coming years she would show an interest in the meetings of the Senate. Knowing that her father was due to succeed him in the consulship the following year and that it could be useful to have him onside, Caesar brought about the match, again to Cato's fury.

Was it right, Cato asked, that a man's power could be determined by marriage? Was it right that *women* could secure men armies, even territories, simply by becoming brides?[26] Cato did not pause in his tirade to consider the burden such arrangements could place upon the women themselves. He had nonetheless recognised, albeit obliquely, that women had the power to influence political affairs. Caesar would marry Calpurnia in 59 BC and there was nothing he could do about it. She, like his long-serving mistress Servilia, would strengthen Caesar's political hand.

Cato had meanwhile poured water on Pompey's efforts to marry into his own family. No woman of Cato's house would stoop so low. In blocking Pompey's efforts to arrange a political marriage to one of his nieces, however, Cato proved himself to be remarkably short-sighted. Through his actions he inadvertently pushed Pompey into an alliance with Caesar and changed the course of Roman history. Another woman now emerged to unite two of the most ambitious men in Rome. She made Caesar and Pompey 'father- and son-in-law'.[27]

The bride, Julia, was Caesar's daughter by Cornelia. Julia was considerably younger than Pompey – about sixteen years old to his forty-six – and powerless to reject the betrothal, especially since her mother was deceased. She was, however, old enough to understand that by marrying Pompey she was helping her father. The political alliance brokered between the two men on the eve of the wedding was extended to a third, Marcus Licinius Crassus, who had profited during Sulla's proscriptions before allegedly lending his support to Catiline's conspiracy. All three stood to gain. Crassus was under pressure to satisfy the demands of equestrians who had lost money in their investments in the east. In exchange for political assistance he could supply Pompey with the riches he needed to reach an eastern settlement and find land for his veterans. Caesar could draw upon both of them for support as he endeavoured to extend his powers for the year following his consulship. The Senate had so far proposed to grant him the measly 'woods and tracks' of Italy to govern for his post-office *proconsulship*. Julia may have been a mere pawn in these arrangements, but even as a pawn she had cemented the alliance known to history as the First Triumvirate.

While deprived of the opportunity to select their magistrates each year, the women of Rome could not remain ignorant of the extraordinary powers the (unofficial) triumvirs – Caesar, Pompey, Crassus – invested in themselves. When Cato expressed his opposition to Caesar's plan to override the rights of the tribunes of the people and pass an agrarian law for Pompey's veterans, the women of his family urged him to back down and support the law instead.[28] Cato's female relatives were more vociferous than he led his senatorial colleagues to believe. Irritated, perhaps, by their intervention in the male world of politics, Cato stubbornly shrugged off the women's fears for his safety until Cicero approached him with similar advice. More experienced in the art of flattery, Cicero told him that Rome would never cope without him – that his safety was paramount – and thereby talked him round to the women's perspective.

As it happened, Cato and his nephew Brutus were shortly to leave Rome for Cyprus, which the Romans were hoping to annex. He could no longer be a thorn in the triumvirs' side. Caesar was leaving Rome too. Bypassing the limits imposed on him by the Senate, he had a law passed by the people granting him an army and command of Cisalpine Gaul and Illyricum, Teuta's former territory, for five years. The 'woods and tracks' of Italy held no interest for a man of his ambition.

The Sacred Grove and Dance Fresco: Sir Arthur Evans counted about 350 men and 120 women around the olive trees in this Minoan fresco from the Palace at Knossos on Crete. The men, as he observed, are largely transfixed by whatever they are watching, while the women talk among themselves. In the lower register of the painting (a replica of the original), bare-breasted women dance in flounced skirts. The walls surrounding their dance floor have been identified as the paths that cross the West Court of the excavated palace.

Mycenaean Woman: The nineteenth-century excavator of this striking plaster face believed it belonged to a sphinx. Uncovered near a shrine at Mycenae in Greece, and dated to the thirteenth century BC, it is now thought to represent a woman or a goddess. The red, sun-like markings on her forehead, cheeks and chin must have had religious significance.

Houmuwu Ding: From Shang dynasty China, a bronze cauldron, or 'ding', used for making ritual offerings to the dead. This one was made in honour of the militarily active royal consort Fu Jing. The quantity of metal used in its production – the object stands at 1.33 metres tall and weighs an extraordinary 833 kilograms – reflects the authority Fu Jing enjoyed in life.

Hatshepsut: Thought to have been only the third female pharaoh to rule Egypt in a space of 1,500 years, Hatshepsut came to power in the eighteenth dynasty. She chose to be depicted most often with a masculine physique, false beard, and the male *nemes* headdress and kilt. This empowered her to carry out religious roles usually performed by men and to put on a united front with her stepson and co-regent. Hatshepsut, whose name means 'Foremost of Noble Women', tended to retain her feminine grammatical forms in inscriptions, even where she resembled a king.

Granary Box: The grave of the ninth-century BC 'Rich Athenian Lady' was excavated near the Acropolis in 1967. This forearm-length chest, with a lid topped with five model granaries, was interred with her cremated remains. It has been proposed that the deceased was the wife or daughter of the local ruler and that the granaries symbolised her membership of the highest propertied class. The presence of stamp seals in her grave may suggest that she was also an agricultural businesswoman in her own right.

Bell Idol: Figurines of women known as 'Bell Idols' were made in Boeotia, central Greece, around the time Hesiod was composing his poems there, circa 700 BC. They take their name from their shape – the hollow terracotta torsos were made on potters' wheels – and have movable legs attached by wire. The tapestry design and swastikas painted on this model's dress are typical of the Geometric style. It is not known whether these idols were used in funeral rites or as decorative doll-like objects.

Etruscan Banqueter: One of five terracotta figures discovered seated in a rock-carved tomb at Cerveteri in Lazio in Italy. Three men and two women, each about 50 centimetres tall, have been identified from the fragments, which date to about 625 BC. In front of them were two tables and the woman here apparently reaches for some food or drink. The back of her head and her hairstyle are missing, but in her large hoop earrings and checked tunic, she looks extremely elegant.

The Bakers: Four women roll dough to the accompaniment of the flute in a sculpture from sixth-century BC Greek Thebes. It was traditional for women to bake bread for their families and communities at home in many parts of the world, including Egypt, where both flatbreads and conical loaves were popular. The first professional bakers arrived in Rome in 171 BC. Even after that time, says Pliny, baking continued to be done at home by women in most other cultures.

Spartan Runner: Ibycus, a Greek lyric poet from the toe of Italy, described Spartan women disapprovingly as 'thigh-flashers'. This Spartan woman, cast in bronze in the late sixth century BC as a decorative appliqué, is also a breast-flasher. Her minimal clothing would enable her to run, as here, wrestle, or jump in a popular Spartan heel-to-bottom exercise known as the *bibasis*.

Athenian Kore: One of a set of *korai* or 'maidens' erected in honour of Athena on the Acropolis at Athens. The sculptures were buried beneath the ground there after the Persians sacked the city during the Graeco-Persian Wars. Their long internment (they were excavated only in the late nineteenth century) helped to preserve significant patches of the original bright paint. This smiling woman, who is a little less than life-size, wears an elegant *peplos*.

Women Making Clothes: The Athens-based artist known as the Amasis Painter documented the weaving process on the body of this small *lekythos* (oil jar) from the mid-sixth century BC. A pair of women pass a shuttle through the threads of an emerging tapestry. The other side of the vase shows women preparing and spinning the wool with a distaff and holding the finished item.

Queen Atossa: Herodotus claimed that Atossa held 'the totality of power' in Persia. This bust of a woman from Persepolis has often been identified as her. The attribution is impossible to prove, but her hairstyle and headdress certainly give the impression of a woman of some standing. She was deemed important enough to have her likeness cast in expensive bronze.

A Domestic Scene: A collection of mid-fifth-century BC terracotta *pinakes* (tablets or plaques) was discovered in a sanctuary dedicated to Persephone in Locri, southern Italy. Most of the scenes capture traditional episodes in a young woman's coming of age. The woman depicted here puts a folded garment, perhaps her wedding dress, into a beautifully carved chest. She is surrounded by objects used for beautification and ritual, including a hand-held mirror, a *lekythos* for oil and a two-handled *kantharos*.

Aspasia: This is arguably the most accurate portrait of Aspasia in existence. Thought to have been copied from her grave monument, hence her solemn expression, it contrasts greatly with the literary portraits written in her lifetime. One male comic poet called Aspasia a 'dog-eyed concubine' and another, a 'whore'. A third was alleged to have tried to prosecute her for impiety but this was probably a fiction derived from one of his plays.

Olympias: Minted half a millennium after she lived, this gold medallion depicting Olympias was found with a number of others at Aboukir near Alexandria in Egypt. The reverse features Thetis, mother of Alexander's hero Achilles, riding a mythological seahorse.

Seianti Hanunia Tlesnasa: Analysis has revealed that the skeleton inside this Etruscan sarcophagus belonged to a woman who lived between about 250 and 150 BC and died at the age of about fifty. In spite of leg and pelvis injuries sustained in her youth, and worsening arthritis, she gave birth at least once. In later life, she was plagued by dental problems, which must have limited her ability to eat.

Cornelia: Immortalised as the devoted mother of the Gracchi, Cornelia sits at the centre of this 1795 neoclassical style painting by Joseph Benoît Suvée. The scene shows Cornelia with her children, or 'jewels' – Tiberius, Gaius and Sempronia – in a Roman hall with Doric columns.

Fulvia: Having a public face earned Fulvia notoriety. It was even slanderously alleged that she proscribed men out of lust for their beautiful houses.

The reverse of the coin shows the defiant goddess Athena and bears the name of the local magistrate in Eumeneia, Phrygia, who controlled the mint. This town briefly changed its name to Fulvia in her honour.

Livia's Garden Room: It was said that an eagle dropped a white hen with a laurel branch onto Livia after her marriage to Octavian. Her countryside villa at Prima Porta, north of Rome, was therefore known as 'White Hens' (*ad Gallinas Albas*). Laurel features heavily in the extraordinary frescoes, which adorned the walls of the villa's garden room and brought the outside, in.

Cleopatra: It is believed that this marble portrait was sculpted when Cleopatra was in Rome. She wears a diadem in her hair, which is curled and arranged in the so-called 'melon' style, as in another contemporary portrait housed at the Vatican. Her nose is noticeably less hooked than it is in some of her portraits on coins.

Antonia the Younger: Antonia was very young when her father, Mark Antony, abandoned her mother, Octavia the Younger, and began his affair with Cleopatra. In this portrait, Antonia looks wise, as befits a woman who managed her own business affairs. According to Suetonius, her grandson Caligula caused her death by refusing her a private audience and generally disrespecting her, but rumours also spread that he had her poisoned.

Former Slaves United in Death: A marble funerary monument from I BC featuring two women. Their names were Eleusis and Helena and they were kept as slaves – and then freed – by a woman named Gaia Fonteia. Their close bond is conveyed by their clasping of hands in a gesture usually reserved for married couples known as the *dextrarum iunctio*. The relief was perhaps repurposed; the portrait on the left appears to have begun as that of a man.

A Woman in Labour: Midwifery and gynaecology were broadly female professions in the ancient world. In this relief sculpture from Ostia in Italy, three stages of labour appear to be represented at once, with the woman on the right making the expectant mother comfortable, the woman in the middle delivering her baby, and the woman on the left holding it. Alternatively, the woman in the middle is delivering the placenta, or stemming bleeding.

Messalina and Britannicus: This sculpture fortunately survived the hammer and chisel following the Senate's instructions to remove all images of the empress from public view. The imagery contrasts sharply with the portraits composed by historians and satirists. This modestly attired Messalina is no *meretrix Augusta* ('whore Augusta'). She is presented as a reserved and loving mother.

Gemma Claudia: Unusually, the imagery on this Roman onyx cameo revolves around the family of one of the Julio-Claudian women, namely Agrippina the Younger. While she is depicted on the left with her husband, Emperor Claudius, her parents Germanicus and Agrippina the Elder emerge from the cornucopia on the right. The elder Agrippina wears a crested helmet, like that of Minerva, and the younger a crown associated with Cybele. Observe the famous Claudian overbite in everyone except Agrippina the Elder.

Eumachia: One of the wealthiest citizens of Pompeii, Eumachia represents what women could achieve by the mid first century AD, although her status was rare. She funded the construction of a large public building with a portico, as well as her own enormous tomb. The town's laundry-cleaners honoured her with this statue, in which she wears the traditional stola and mantle over her still-red hair. She also held authority as a priestess.

Sex in a Brothel: Prostitutes could sometimes be distinguished from other women on the streets of Rome by their clothes. In particular, they often wore togas, which aligned them more with men than with their 'respectable' female counterparts. On one level, stripping off made everyone equal, but on another, expectations of women varied. The woman in this brothel fresco, who wears nothing but a *strophium* (breast band), assumes what traditionalists would have considered a male sexual position. Not many Roman men would have publicly promoted the idea of their wives being on top.

Few people were closer to these events than the eldest of Publius Clodius Pulcher's sisters. Clodia – she too liked the plebeian spelling of her name – was fast becoming one of the most notorious women in Rome's political circles. It is widely believed that she inspired the figure of Lesbia in Catullus' love poems. 'Lesbia' was a metrically equivalent pseudonym for 'Clodia' and evoked the memory of Sappho. A pun on Clodia's brother's name and his alleged penchant for incest with his sisters – 'Lesbius is handsome Pulcher . . . Lesbia prefers him to you and all your people' – provided Catullus' contemporaries with a strong clue to her true identity.[29] Catullus evoked Lesbia often in his verse as his hot-and-cold mistress. He refused to love her in private. 'Give me a thousand kisses, then a hundred, / Then another thousand, then a second hundred. / Then – don't stop – another thousand, then a hundred,' he breathlessly demanded.[30] 'We should value at a penny all / The rumours of our elders – they are dourer than most.' Later Roman poets, most famously Propertius, Ovid and Tibullus, would develop the trope of the man hopelessly in thrall (indeed 'enslaved') to an unobtainable mistress. It was in poetry, more than in life, that women achieved sexual and romantic dominance.

The lines that Catullus wrote to Lesbia were imbued with subtle references to the works of Greek and Latin poets. They were intended for a highly literary woman. Befitting the name he gave her, the first poem Catullus sent Clodia/Lesbia was a free translation of one of Sappho's poems of jealous longing: 'Both my eyes are blinded by night'.[31] The agony of watching someone they loved being loved by someone else was an experience the two poets shared.

Clodia was still married to Metellus Celer when her affair with the poet began. Catullus filled the role of 'the other man':

Lesbia says a lot of cruel things to me in front of her husband.
The dolt finds considerable happiness in this.[32]

Clodia fulfilled an important role besides that of mistress and muse. While having an affair with Catullus, she remained heavily involved in her husband's work, which had taken him to Gaul to put down the Catilinarians and thence to the consulship for 60 BC. Her brother, Clodius, was also relying heavily upon her to persuade Metellus to help him to proceed in his own career. Held back by his senatorial enemies, the young aristocrat had conceived the unusual idea of having himself demoted to the plebeian class, which would enable him to run for the position of tribune of the plebs and bring legislation directly to the Roman people, thereby circumventing the barriers of the Senate. It was a highly unorthodox plan, but Clodia did her best to move her husband to help Clodius fulfil it. Metellus mounted a 'most distinguished opposition' to his brother-in-law's pursuit of power.

Clodia was caught in the middle of a fraught political dispute. She had made little headway in resolving the conflict when, in 59 BC, her husband suddenly died. With no obvious cause of death forthcoming, rumours quickly spread that Clodia had had him poisoned. In the coming years, Cicero would capitalise upon such empty talk and present Clodia to the people of Rome as an oversexed adulteress who would spare nothing in her desire for pleasure. In reality, Clodia could hardly have been willing to leave her husband for a self-avowedly penniless poet or become, in her mid-thirties, a widowed mother of one. The steady realisation of this began to niggle away at Catullus in the aftermath of Metellus' death.

Some said that Clodia had hoped to marry Cicero. Terentia was allegedly so jealous that she had encouraged her husband to speak as he had against Clodius during the Bona Dea trial.[33] This too was nonsense, but Terentia might well have been wary of Clodia – any woman might. Clodia was aristocratic, rich and possessed, by Cicero's own account, a pair of striking brown 'oxen eyes'. Cicero did not mean this flatteringly. The same description was used of Hera's eyes in the *Iliad* to convey her tempestuousness. As Catullus knew only too well, Clodia was a passionate woman, who could swing just as easily as he could from love to hate. She barked, she bit, she kissed then bit his lips again. Cicero was far too straitlaced to entice her. Clodia befriended his confidant Atticus in order to keep him abreast of Clodius' progress for the tribuneship, not because she wanted to become intimate with Cicero herself.

The death of Clodia's husband removed the 'most distinguished opposition' to Clodius' plans. In a ludicrous turn of events, the heedless demagogue had himself formally adopted by a twenty-year-old plebeian in a bid to extinguish his patrician roots. While Julius Caesar also benefited from the former senator's death by inheriting his territory, 'Further Gaul', as part of his commission for the following year, he almost immediately regretted waving through Clodius' request. For having won the tribuneship with promises of free grain for the masses, Clodius cast a shadow upon the legality of legislation that Caesar had passed the previous year to legitimise *collegia* (workers' guilds that had previously been banned), prompting in the process fresh waves of gang warfare across Rome.

Caesar was not the only man to feel perturbed by Clodius' radical programme. Clodius' most important new bill, which authorised Romans to outlaw any citizen who put another citizen to death without trial, had an obvious target. At first, Cicero prayed that it would simply evaporate, and that he would escape any charges for his execution of the Catilinarian conspirators. By the following spring, when the matter was put to the vote, he knew his luck had run out. Caesar took pity and offered him a position on his staff in Gaul. Cicero could not bear it. Pompey, ordinarily loyal, slunk away in cowardice. As the orator embarked upon his exile in Thessalonica, word reached him that he was not to come within 400 miles of Italy again or he would be in breach of Clodius' legislation. Anyone who tried to help him return was liable to be put to death.

Terentia now faced the prospect of a life alone with her children. She soon became a target for Clodian oppressors. On one occasion she was dragged violently out of the Temple of Vesta.[34] She ought to have been guaranteed safety within a religious precinct, especially one managed by other women, but old traditions were quickly being eroded. No one had seen Terentia cry before now. Clodius seized the handsome villa she had shared with Cicero on the Palatine Hill and began to speak of constructing a new house in its footprint. In an empty display of piety (which looked more like propaganda) he endeavoured to have part of the plot consecrated to the goddess Liberty.

Terentia received letter after tear-drenched letter from Cicero in the east.[35] News of her plight and her contraction of a fever reached him via friends and sent him into an even deeper depression.[36] Amid all her troubles Terentia tried to put on a brave face. When Cicero wrote to tell her that he was moving on to Dyrrachium (in modern Albania), she asked whether she could go with him. No, he said, she would be more helpful to him where she was.

All the while Terentia kept him abreast of political developments in Rome. Clodius could take away her house, but he could not take away her determination to help her husband, nor her appetite for hard news. There was no one Cicero trusted more to gauge the temperature of the tribunate when the candidates were proposed for the following year. In December 58 BC Clodius would be obliged to hand over his post to someone else. Here lay Cicero's best opportunity for recall. So desperate had he become for news that he arranged for a messenger to go to Terentia and carry to him as swiftly as possible any information she had garnered about the candidates. Terentia was ready to pounce the moment the new tribunes set out their plans for the year.

The omens were on Terentia's side. As she gathered what intelligence she could, she had the full support of Pompey, who had fallen out with Clodius and felt not a little guilt over his failure to save Cicero from exile in the first place. Working to bring about Cicero's return became a way of working against Clodius. A vote was held on his recall in the new year. Support for the proposal was unanimous. Terentia – and Pompey – had triumphed. After a difficult eighteen months, Cicero returned to Rome and reclaimed his plot on the Palatine Hill. The priest had failed to dedicate it to Libertas with due ceremony.[37] Freedom was Cicero's to exploit.

Short of taking revenge on Clodius directly, Cicero targeted Clodia, his long-suffering sister. In the wake of her husband's death, the oxen-eyed widow had embarked upon a relationship with Caelius Rufus, a (former) friend of Catullus. Caelius 'crept up on me,' the poet complained, 'ripped like a flame through my guts, and stole all I had'.[38] Tall and handsome with a fashionably trimmed beard, Caelius Rufus had studied under Cicero and enjoyed the guardianship of Crassus, but he was also a skilled poet. Thanks to his father's business interests in Roman Africa, he could afford to rent one of the luxurious apartments that Clodius owned on the Palatine Hill; this was perhaps where Clodia first met Caelius Rufus. Caelius was now facing trial for a series of offences. His defence, an opportunity to incriminate Clodia, was one of the first cases Cicero took on following his return to Rome.

Caelius Rufus stood accused of paying slaves to carry out the assassination of a member of a deputation of Alexandrians. Facing revolution from his daughter Berenice and her husband, Ptolemy XII Auletes had prevailed upon Pompey the Great and the Roman proconsul of Syria to help him reclaim his kingship, handing over yet more sums of money in the process.[39] A rival embassy had come to Rome to try to dissuade the Romans from granting him his request. The murder of the embassy leader, Dio, was carried out by a slave, whom Caelius Rufus was alleged to have paid using gold lent to him by Clodia.

The trial of Caelius Rufus took place in April 56 BC during the festival of the Mother Goddess Cybele. Clodia attended court to witness the prosecution. While Cicero promised to say as little about her as possible, he had soon 'made a slip' and referenced her alleged penchant for sex and incest at the seaside resort of Baiae. As he stood before her and the gathered crowd, he adopted the role of her illustrious ancestor Appius Claudius Caecus ('the Blind') to question her rhetorically over why she had been familiar enough with his client to lend him gold, yet so hostile that he had procured poison to silence her after she had done so.[40]

During the breakdown of their relationship, Catullus savaged Clodia in his poetry as a harlot in thrall to Caelius and many other lovers besides:

Caelius, our Lesbia, the Lesbia,
That *Lesbia, whom Catullus loved alone*
More than himself and all his family,
Now on crossroads and in alleys
Wanks the descendants of great-hearted Remus.[41]

Cicero now implied that Clodia had been spurned by Caelius Rufus following their brief affair. Her accusations against him, Cicero insisted, were those of a wounded tart – or a *quadrantia Clytemnestra* ('penny Clytemnestra'), to be more precise. Cicero was delighted with his phrase, which painted Clodia as not merely the murderer of her husband, as Clytemnestra was of Agamemnon, but also as a cheap common prostitute. It was the orator's equivalent to Catullus' description of Lesbia servicing men at crossroads. The image was particularly shocking at a time when the philosopher Lucretius advocated sexual restraint in women.[42] There was no advantage, Lucretius wrote, in a married woman behaving like a prostitute and moving lasciviously – or even at all – during sex, not least because doing so would dislodge the male seed and so hinder her chance of pregnancy. Women of high status such as Clodia were expected rather to stay still on all fours like a dog.

Cicero was not afraid to highlight the double standard that existed between women and men. Caelius Rufus was young, he said, he was entitled to a bit of sport. It was healthy for a young man to sprinkle some wild oats. The same had never been true of Clodia or any other respectably born woman. Placing the focus of his oration upon Clodia and her questionable morals, Cicero nimbly sidestepped the main issue of the accusation, which was that Caelius Rufus had been involved in a crime that might well have been engineered by supporters of Ptolemy.

The shocking acquittal of the defendant was to the ruler of Egypt's fleeting gain but Clodia's lasting detriment. A Roman-led army marched from Syria to Alexandria and restored Ptolemy to power. Berenice, ruler of Egypt for the past three years, was put to death at his command while her siblings stood by. Among them was her fourteen-year-old sister Cleopatra. By the end of the decade, Cleopatra would be sharing the throne with the increasingly infirm Ptolemy as a prelude to succeeding him together with her younger brother. The rise of the most famous Cleopatra in history came at the expense of Clodia's fall.

The trial of Caelius Rufus proved to be a last hurrah for the gossip-hungry *populus* before events took a more serious turn in Rome. The triumvirs did their best to put on a united front. They held a summit and renewed their alliance, agreeing that Pompey and Crassus should strive to return as joint consuls for 55 BC before proceeding to Spain and Syria respectively for their proconsular commands. Eight of the ten tribunes had already pledged loyalty to them. Caesar meanwhile committed to Gaul for another five years. The following spring would take him to Britain for the first time. Catullus was not alone in throwing doubts upon his progress. The Gallic Wars had threaded through his home town of Verona and wrought widespread devastation. Caesar exhibited no remorse over the deaths he caused while he continued to line his pockets.

What appeared on the surface to be a potent pact for power was, however, secretly crumbling. Pompey and Caesar had for some time had little to unite them beside their love for Julia. Her death in 54 BC while in labour with her first child broke their forced bond. The following year, Crassus followed Julia to the grave after invading Parthia, part of modern Iran, and employing a disastrous combination of tactics. His loss – and that of the Roman standards at Carrhae – was a grave blow to the fragile alliance.

The break-up of the First Triumvirate is usually attributed to Julia's death and the unravelling of male diplomacy. But there was in fact another woman who pushed the crisis beyond the point of repair. Fulvia had gained in confidence since her marriage to Clodius. It was an exaggeration to say, as Plutarch did, that she was ambitious to govern and rule, but her aptitude for leadership became only too apparent following an unexpected tragedy.[43]

Unusually, given how inseparable they were, Fulvia was not with Clodius when he was travelling in late 53 BC and encountered Milo, a candidate for the consulship, on the Appian Way near Bovillae in central Italy. As tribune of the plebs, Milo had been a vociferous supporter of the recall of Cicero and had consequently earned Clodius' distrust. While Clodius was proceeding on horseback with a guard of armed slaves, Milo was accompanied by his wife Fausta, a daughter of Sulla, her large retinue of serving women, and a team of gladiators.[44] The two parties clashed at the approach to a shrine to the good goddess Bona Dea. What started as a row developed into a scuffle and then a full-blown fight.

A short time later, a Roman senator was passing along the same stretch of road when he spotted a body, still fresh and bloodied. Clodius had been carried to an inn after being struck in the crossfire. The prospect of his making a recovery had decided Milo on an extreme course. His corpse now lay in the dust. Within hours, the passing senator had arranged for it to be carried back to Rome, where cries went up that Clodius had met his comeuppance for his desecration of the rites of the Bona Dea in his women's garb all those years before. Just as many laments were heard among the crowd of his plebeian supporters. People from both sides flocked to see his body being conveyed to the atrium of his house.

Fulvia would have been expected to close her doors at this point so that her husband's body could be cleaned in private. Instead, she flung them open, so that all of Rome could feast their eyes upon Milo's brutality. On the following day, she permitted the crowd to carry Clodius' corpse to the forum and place it on the speaker's platform, the gashes still visible in his flesh.[45] It has been speculated that Fulvia played a role in the organisation of Clodius' *collegia* or political gangs.[46] If she did, this was the most opportune moment to draw upon their support and incite hatred towards Milo. Supporters of Clodius responded to her cues and carried his body to the Senate House where they had it cremated. The rites were performed with such passion that the fire spread dramatically through the building and burned the surrounding edifices.

The Senate, panicked by the sight of their meeting place consumed by flames, passed an emergency decree authorising Pompey and the tribunes to do everything in their power to protect the city from further harm. Rather than heed popular calls to appoint Pompey dictator to settle the turbulence, the Senate voted him *sole* consul, so preserving a semblance of normality. Pompey had the experience to quell the rioters and suppress further outbreaks of violence. Even so, the city was deeply factionalised and divided over who the real criminal had been, Clodius or Milo.

The trial of Milo took place the following spring. Cicero, in a final act of enmity towards the late Clodius, took on Milo's defence. Virgin priestesses local to the area of Bovillae, where the brawl had erupted, made their way to Rome to deliver evidence. The priestesses testified that a woman they had never seen before had approached them in the wake of Clodius' death to pay a vow on Milo's orders. This was perhaps Milo's wife. His guilt seemed beyond question. Fulvia and her mother stepped forward in their mourning clothes to give further evidence and, 'with their weeping, greatly moved those who stood gathered'.[47] The trial held all of Rome in thrall. Expecting trouble the moment a verdict was reached, Pompey had the *tabernae* (inns) closed and guards posted around the forum. The pressure from the Clodian faction was so fierce that Cicero almost lost his thread while delivering his speech for Milo.

It was a difficult case to argue, but Cicero did his best to present Milo as under the thumb of his wife. The fact that Fausta was there when Clodius died, he asserted, offered good evidence that the attack had not been premeditated.[48] The jury was unconvinced by Cicero's line of argument. Convicted by a considerable margin, Milo left Rome for exile in Marseille suffering what was, all things considered, a lenient punishment. The outcome was not so much a failure on the part of Cicero, whose animosity towards the Clodii was well known, but a victory for Fulvia, who had roused the sympathies of Rome with the display of a bloodied corpse.

Chapter XV

From the Bed-Sack to the Bed

Be of good heart and have hope of recovering your good health
Terentia, quoted by Cicero, *ad Familiares* 14.4.5, first century BC

Fulvia's celebrity was yet to peak. Many more opportunities awaited her in what would prove to be one of the most politically anxious periods in Rome's history. Just three years after she presented Clodius' corpse to the people and to the forum, Julius Caesar did the unthinkable and crossed the Rubicon with the thirteenth legion and an imperious proclamation of *alea iacta est* ('the die is cast').[1] The river marked the boundary line between Cisalpine Gaul and Italy. By crossing it, Caesar was not only breaching senatorial authority, which dictated that his Gallic command had elapsed, he was declaring civil war. Panic swept the mainland. While men and women hastened to Rome in what was likened unimaginatively to a tidal wave, senators hostile to Caesar uprooted their families to save them from what Pompey insisted would amount to tyranny.[2]

Servilia, Caesar's long-suffering mistress, once again found herself in an impossible position as her brother Cato and son Brutus, lately returned from annexing Cyprus, went over to Pompey's side. Other senators preferred to throw in their lot with Caesar in abject hope than to abandon their city to uncertainty. These men felt vindicated in their decision to appoint Caesar dictator when they witnessed him adjust the interest rate to boost public confidence and hold elections for the following year. After just eleven days, Caesar relinquished the dictatorship and accepted his election to the consulship, sustaining the Republican fiction. His priority now was to remove the remaining threat to his political authority posed by Pompey the Great.

The two men confronted each other in Brundisium before resolving to carry on their war away from Italian soil. On 9 August 48 BC they met near Pharsalus, central Greece, Pompey leading an infantry of 45,000 and a cavalry of 7,000 relative to 22,000 and 1,000 on Caesar's side respectively. What Caesar lacked in numbers he made up for in tacticians. The son of one of his cousins, Mark Antony, had held a command in Gaul before reaching the tribuneship in his mid-thirties. He was handsome, and he knew it, with a nice beard and the sort of physique that might have been familiar to Heracles' wife.[3] Antony was the most skilled of Caesar's commanders, so while Caesar held the right wing, he held the left. Their subordinates were instructed to refrain from hurling their javelins in favour of stabbing Pompey's men in their eyes and faces.[4] The rationale was that these soldiers were peculiarly vain and would sooner run away than suffer scarring to their beautiful cheeks. Propelled more by pain, the wounded cavalrymen slunk back and fled the field. Pompey was so disheartened by the sight that he withdrew to his tent like Achilles at his most petulant.

Pompey's new wife Cornelia, a descendant of Scipio Africanus and former daughter-in-law of Marcus Licinius Crassus, was awaiting news of the battle at Mytilene, Sappho's quondam home. Like her earlier namesake, the mother of the Gracchi brothers, Cornelia was well educated, especially in philosophy, literature and, more unusually, mathematics. The law of probability dictated that Pompey should return to her in triumph, given his record, so, as the messenger approached, she was hopeful. It took only a few moments for her expression to change. Not only had Pompey's forces been thoroughly routed, but many of his men had either been taken alive and integrated into Caesar's legions, or killed. While Servilia received assurance in Rome that Brutus had been saved – Caesar's gift to her – Cornelia threw herself to the ground weeping that Pompey had not a single ship to his name.

In one deeply impressionistic portrait of the scene, Pompey was stooped over a river in the Vale of Tempe, his armour laid aside, brooding on the fact that in a single hour he had lost everything he had ever had.[5] He spent that night in a fisherman's hut before catching a boat to Lesbos. Cornelia had just about landed in his arms when she collapsed, more from emotion than from exhaustion at having run the distance from the city to the coast to find him. The people of Mytilene showed them compassion.

They must obey Caesar now, Pompey said, unable to deceive himself any longer.

Cornelia accompanied Pompey and his remaining friends to Asia Minor and thence to the one place they felt confident they would receive a warm reception: Egypt. Pompey had known Ptolemy XII Auletes for many years and helped to engineer his return to power. When Auletes died, of natural causes, in 51 BC, leaving the Romans to safeguard the continuation of his dynasty, Pompey took the copy of his will he had deposited in Rome and asked the Roman people to recognise Auletes' eighteen-year-old daughter, Cleopatra, and ten-year-old son, Ptolemy XIII, as his joint heirs. The siblings married in accordance with Egyptian custom and enjoyed the support of their people. But Pompey underestimated how uneasy the transition had been. In the first year of their rule, Cleopatra enjoyed sufficient authority to be depicted on a stele in male clothes, like the female 'king' Hatshepsut before her.[6] The monument had probably been intended for her father before he died, but the fact that it was rededicated to her, and not to her brother, suggests that she was very much seen as the primary ruler of Egypt at this point.[7] By the following year, Ptolemy XIII had begun to assert himself, and tensions developed with his sister. As a minor, Ptolemy was dependent upon a close circle of advisers for decision-making. Potheinus, his eunuch, Theodotus, a teacher of oratory, and his general, Achillas, were more concerned with bolstering Ptolemy's position relative to Cleopatra than investing in a once-powerful Roman. Supporting Pompey could only earn them the enmity of the more powerful Caesar. They knew whose side they needed to take.

As Pompey's boat drew near the coast of Pelusium, north-east Egypt, in 48 BC, Achillas made a pretence of welcoming him by inviting him aboard his own vessel. Cornelia was watching when, without warning, Pompey was run through with a sword, then a dagger, then another. She had only just embraced him. Pompey's body was thrown into the sea for his freedman to retrieve but his head was saved, together with his seal ring, to be presented to Caesar.[8] When he arrived in Alexandria a short time later, Caesar could only look askance at the greying visage of his former friend and weep. The day before Pompey died had been his fifty-ninth birthday. It need not have come to this. Cornelia carried what remained of his sea-swept corpse home to Italy as ashes in an urn. She would spend the rest of her life there as a widow.

By the time Caesar had recovered from the sight and issued instructions for the burial of Pompey's head, the co-rulers of Egypt had become embroiled in an aggressive power struggle, in which Cleopatra was driven from Alexandria by her brother and his rapacious advisers. She responded by drawing up an army in Syria to fight her way back to the throne. Caesar's first thought was to reconcile the siblings and honour their father's will, but the possibility of doing so felt remote when Ptolemy's advisers were so unyielding. The debt owed to Rome by the Alexandrian royal family stood at 17.5 million drachmas. The refusal of Potheinus to repay even half this sum to appease the veterans of Rome's recent war left Caesar with little choice but to approach Cleopatra directly.

The queen had so far communicated with Caesar purely through third parties. He may have thought that it was his idea to approach her, but Cleopatra had already decided that a meeting with Caesar would be beneficial. She had heard the rumours of his character and his susceptibility to women.[9] Seduction was not necessarily on Cleopatra's mind – she was not yet the confident woman she would become – but she had probably foreseen the value in becoming properly acquainted with Rome's prime representative. A man who was weak to a woman's beauty was likely to be susceptible to her persuasions.

Relatively little is known of Cleopatra's beginnings. She was born in late 70 or early 69 BC to Ptolemy Auletes and a mother whose name has not been recorded. Macedonian on her father's side, then, but on her mother's? No one can now say. If there was one characteristic most ancient writers agreed upon as they sought to describe her, it was the allure of her manner of speaking. The way she put words together was peculiarly attractive. Unlike the male Ptolemies who preceded her, Cleopatra was able to converse with Syrians, Ethiopians, Medes, Parthians and Jews as well as Egyptians, Macedonians and Greeks.[10] She spoke up to nine different languages and had the ability to incorporate traits and idioms into her own vernacular. We might imagine her sentences to have been thick and twisting. It would be unfair to describe her as chameleon-like, but she could mirror people like a child or the proverbial ape and make herself amenable to just about anyone. She was most adept at seeing what her interlocutors were like and meeting them in the style of conversation she perceived to be most natural to them. She sent Caesar a message in just the right tone for him to agree to risk meeting her in the palace at Alexandria without her brother's knowledge.

It was here that Cleopatra made her unforgettable entrance. One of her most trusted friends, a man from Sicily named Apollodorus, rolled her into a *stromatodesmon* – best translated from the Greek as a sack used for bed linen – and secured her in place with leather straps like sausage in a pastry.[11] As costumes went, it was decidedly out of vogue, but Cleopatra's priority was to gain entry to the palace without being detected by her brother. No one could have guessed that the carpet-like object they saw being lifted from a boat at dusk contained a living being. Over thirty years separated the Roman from the youthful queen of Egypt, but in that moment the distance between them dissolved. Caesar could not fail to be amused by so large and bewildering a present and so practical a piece of theatre.

What did he see when the linen was unwrapped? Was Cleopatra lovely to behold, was she striking, or was she plain? Her beauty has always been a matter of impossible dispute. The truth of it could no sooner be verified after she died than while she lived. Historians writing hundreds of years into the future relied on lingering hearsay to reach a verdict on her looks. Cassius Dio, a high-born second/third-century Roman historian of Greek extraction, found her to be very beautiful, but Plutarch, much closer to her in time, believed she had not been out of the ordinary. While several contemporary coins depict her with a large, rather hooked nose and heavy brow, a marble bust sculpted in her lifetime reveals a more attractive wide-eyed woman with a fleshy face, narrow chin, unremarkable nose, small mouth, shallow forehead and distinctive earlobes.[12] She wears her hair in plaits tied into a bun, with a small knot at the crown of her head, upon which there sits a diadem. The portrait is idealised, but there is a real woman's face behind the marble, and it is alert, determined – one would be tempted to add 'clever' – but as with any intuitive reading of a face, it is difficult to explain why. We sometimes find intelligence in each other's eyes, but these are now blank, though they would once have been painted. This Cleopatra holds us rather with the seriousness of her expression.

The queen would have been visibly made-up for her audience with Caesar. The make-up worn in Egypt was generally heavier than that worn in Rome and included kohl, which some believed protected their eyes from infection, antimony for brows, ochre for lips, and henna for hands and feet. Contrary to what male historians implied, there was nothing unusual in Cleopatra's decision to apply cosmetics for this meeting. There was no special face to put on to beguile Caesar; no magic potion to spread her allure. Wearing make-up was not, as Ovid once claimed, an act of treachery engineered to conceal reality from men, but an act of personal ceremony.

Cleopatra was determined to show Caesar two conflicting faces at once. She was beleaguered by her friends and family – a victim of the worst kind of betrayal – and yet solid in her capacity to govern her country. Caesar listened as Cleopatra described her claim to the throne. He was moved by her account of suffering at the hands of her brother and his men. He was moved, too, by his own shame at their crass removal of Pompey's head just a few days earlier.[13]

It was not daylight before Caesar had taken up the case of Alexandria's fractured monarchy. As planned, he sent a message to Ptolemy, intending to reconcile his sister to him and so reinstate her as monarch.[14] Shaken by Cleopatra's sudden re-emergence in the palace and the quick work she had apparently made of getting Rome on her side, Ptolemy fled, screaming that *he* had been betrayed. Caesar's troops seized the boy as he ran, but his people began to attack the palace. To calm the crowd, Caesar summoned an assembly and read aloud the will of Ptolemy XII Auletes, affirming the joint rule of Ptolemy and Cleopatra. The pair's younger siblings Arsinoë and Ptolemy XIV were appeased with the gift of Cyprus, but the eunuch Potheinus was much less easily satisfied. Envisaging trouble from Rome further down the line and bristling at Cleopatra's growing authority, he arranged for the general Achillas to draw up an army of 20,000 and besiege Caesar in the palace. Caesar, anticipating the siege, had Potheinus killed, but Achillas escaped in time to rouse his troops to proceed in what became known as the Alexandrian War.

The conflict witnessed the Alexandrian rebels attempt to dam up the canals and cut off the Roman fleet, to which Rhodes, Syria and Cilicia supplied ships.[15] Disaster struck when the Romans employed fire as a weapon to defend their hold on the harbour. Although wood was seldom used in the construction of buildings in Alexandria, the flames still spread unrelentingly inland. There was little anyone could do when the fire reached the great Library of Alexandria and began to engulf 700,000 of its precious books.

The siege was finally lifted following the arrival of Syrians and 3,000 Jews from Memphis. As the battle progressed to the Nile itself, the Alexandrian army was routed, and young Ptolemy, overwhelmed by events beyond his control, drowned. As for Achillas, his surviving adviser, he was put to death by the eunuch tutor of Arsinoë.[16] The princess momentarily declared herself ruler of Egypt, believing the throne to be vacant, but Caesar put her down and dispatched her to Rome as his captive.[17]

However she felt about the death and displacement of her siblings – her reaction is not recorded – Cleopatra was once again queen of Egypt, with her younger brother, Ptolemy XIV, as co-ruler. She was finally at liberty to enjoy Caesar's company or, as he put it, continue 'loyally in her friendship' with him.[18] They had perhaps a month before Caesar was compelled to leave. Their time together is not well documented, though for writers of a romantic disposition this was no great loss. The new lovers were to be pictured like the couple on a famous Alexandrian mosaic: floating up the river on Cleopatra's barge, gazing into each other's eyes, quaffing wine beneath a beautifully planted awning, musicians playing all around them while fishermen loaded boats with their catch.[19] Caesar might in reality have drifted away with Cleopatra as far as Ethiopia had his soldiers not grown impatient to return.[20] A flotilla of 400 ships sailed behind them.[21] Back on *terra firma*, the couple banqueted through the night until the sun broke the next morning.

Cleopatra was soon pregnant. It was probably too early for her to know this for certain, but Caesar's sudden departure has sometimes been read as a panicked reaction to the news of a baby. Dallying with the pregnant queen would have been disastrous for his reputation at home. What would people say? They would suppose that love alone had prevented him from transforming Egypt into a province, when, in truth, he feared doing so would inspire the Egyptians to revolt. Cleopatra's pregnancy probably had little to do with his decision to leave. More pressing was the fact that Pharnaces II, a son of Mithridates VI Eupator, had recaptured territory in Asia Minor. If Caesar did not act now, he risked losing Pompey's gains in the Mithridatic Wars. And so he ventured east, where he succeeded in driving Pharnaces out in the course of five days. Caesar's swift work in a battle at Zela (Zile, central Turkey) gave him ample justification to have the immortal words *veni vidi vici* inscribed on a placard at his ensuing triumph. News from Cleopatra would have to wait.

Meanwhile, Servilia's son-in-law, a consul named Servilius Isauricus, had had Caesar proclaimed dictator again. Mark Antony officially held equal authority as 'Master of Horse' when Caesar was away, but his failure to maintain order had resulted in a horrific outbreak of violence in the city. One of Antony's former friends, a tribune named Dolabella, had been trying to force through a law to cancel debt. In the process his supporters had occupied the forum.

Dolabella had lately become Cicero's son-in-law. After her first husband died, Tullia had married a man named Furius Crassipes, but the couple divorced for reasons now unknown. Cicero had formerly complained that Crassipes had used up his money on his travelling. The first century BC witnessed an increase in the number of women marrying *sine manu*, which meant remaining under the guardianship of their fathers, as opposed to entering that of their husbands *cum manu*. Dolabella at least appeared to be financially solvent. Cicero had his doubts, but he was away in Cilicia when Terentia selected Dolabella to be Tullia's new husband, and the couple were betrothed without his involvement. Unfortunately for Tullia, her father's anxieties proved to be well founded, and Dolabella emerged as a most profligate partner. While his fearsome supporters took over the forum in a bid to force his legislation through, Dolabella embarked upon an affair with Mark Antony's wife/cousin, Antonia Hybrida Minor.[22] Antony subsequently drove Antonia from their home and prepared to take up arms against Dolabella to block his law.[23]

On a personal level, Antony's reaction was hypocritical, for as everyone knew, he had been having affairs with several other women himself. His relationship with a former slave's daughter named Fadia had resulted in the birth of at least two illegitimate children.[24] Still more notoriously, Volumnia Cytheris, a mime actress and former slave, had captured his heart. She was also a favourite of Dolabella and Servilia's son Brutus.[25]

Cytheris' servile beginnings were obvious to anyone who knew her – she was obliged to take the name 'Volumnia' from her former master Volumnius – but she had transcended her class in a most spectacular way. People in Rome had seen her travelling in Antony's litter trailing a large entourage of her own slaves.[26] Influential men may have pursued her lustily, but she was known to have pursued men, too. According to Virgil, she enjoyed an affair with his fellow poet Gallus, who immortalised her in his verse as 'Lycoris'. The relationship came to an end when Cytheris left Gallus in order to wade through the snow of the Alps to reach another (unidentified) man.[27] Roman women, unlike their Greek counterparts, were permitted to dine openly with men, and Cytheris was often to be seen in the dining rooms of the rich. Cicero encountered her in one such setting and was perturbed by the lack of respect she showed his wife. Terentia said only that she found her rather hostile.[28]

Cytheris' relationship with Antony was serious enough for her to have moved some of her possessions into one of his houses, to which she had her own key.[29] Cicero once said that Antony kept Cytheris as a wife, intending this as a slur, but Cicero was not wide of the mark. Being installed in a house as a pseudo-wife to Antony was certainly preferable to being passed from man to man. For perhaps the first time, Cytheris had reason to hope for some stability in her life, until, all of a sudden, she found herself cast out as Antony set off in pursuit of yet another woman.

He may have met her earlier, but Antony probably only came to know Fulvia after she remarried following Clodius' murder. Fulvia's second husband, Gaius Scribonius Curio, had been a former consul who had commissioned an extraordinary double-theatre that could be pivoted together to form an amphitheatre and separated out again to form two interconnected D-shaped theatres. The invention would one day inspire Leonardo da Vinci. Unfortunately, Curio lost his life during a battle in Numidia not long after the wedding, leaving Fulvia widowed for a second time. Antony's passion for her was soon all-consuming.

Fulvia was hesitant when Antony made his approach. She knew about Cytheris and was unwilling to take second place to a woman engaged in a profession deemed as disreputable as acting. Other women might have dissembled this, but Fulvia made her feelings to Antony quite plain and stood firmly by her principles. One night, Antony came to her house in disguise, a hood pulled up over his face. He was, as often, quite drunk, but not so drunk as to give away his identity. He posed as a messenger with an urgent letter to deliver.[30] Fulvia, ordinarily known to be rather brusque, took the missive from him and read it with tears in her eyes. Antony had promised her that he had no intention of seeing Cytheris ever again. He pledged himself to Fulvia absolutely. Suddenly, he threw off his hood to reveal himself and wrapped his arms tenderly around her neck. They were married about 47 BC.

Cytheris was given no choice but to obey Antony's commands to gather her belongings, hand back her key, and leave his property. Such is the precariousness of a mistress's life. It is just possible that she reunited with him a few years later. In 44 BC Antony would find himself crossing the Alps with ambitions to govern Gaul. Was he the man she pursued poetically through the snow? It was a long way for a cuckolded woman to travel for love.

On 23 June 47 BC, Cleopatra gave birth to a boy, Ptolemy XV, though he was more commonly known as Caesarion ('Little Caesar'). Julius Caesar had not been in Alexandria for very long but the timing of the birth seemed to fit. Mark Antony told the Senate that Caesar had acknowledged the child to be his: the paternity of the baby, Antony said, was an open secret among friends. Some of Caesar's allies went to lengths to deny this in writing, but Caesar was content for the child to bear his name.[31] Caesarion's birth date was engraved upon a sculptural stele in Memphis, which helped to broadcast his Romanness. We can only imagine the effect this had upon Caesar's wife Calpurnia, who was yet to conceive a child of her own, as well as Servilia, his long-term mistress.

Cleopatra planned to come to Rome, but she was anticipated by her younger sister Arsinoë, who became the central attraction of Caesar's triumphal celebrations. The dictator's victories over Cleopatra's siblings and Mithridates' son were sweetened further by his progress in Gaul and defeat of King Juba of Numidia and consequently Cato. The rather highly strung, belt-and-braces senator had gone over to Africa to try to protect Utica (Utique, Tunisia) from Caesar's clutches. Civil war erupted between the two rival armies and, while Cato enjoyed the initial advantage, Caesar's legions prevailed. Cato escaped the ignominy of being added to Caesar's parade of captured prisoners but considered his life no longer worth living. He stabbed himself in the stomach, but not accurately enough to bring death: he resorted to gruesome disembowelment.

By the time Cleopatra herself reached Rome, the streets had been cleaned from the triumphal parades, and plans had been laid for a new forum and several new monuments to make the city worthy of its international reputation. The queen arrived to witness the dedication of a splendid new temple to Venus Genetrix, Caesar's illustrious ancestor in her guise as a nurturing mother. The new mother Cleopatra was to stay with her surviving brother/husband, Ptolemy XIV, at the *Horti Caesaris*, a large garden villa Caesar owned on the far side of the Tiber. A safe enough distance from the heart of the city to avoid idle spies; close enough that senators did not need to seek an excuse to visit her – they could just say they were passing. Mark Antony was almost certainly among the men who went to pay her court. He would have remembered himself to her if they had met when he campaigned to restore her father to the throne. For both parties this meeting would prove significant.

We do not know whether Cleopatra reprised her affair with Caesar in Rome. If she did, Caesar was under pressure to keep it as quiet as he could. His generous accommodation of the foreign queen grated on conservative Romans already.[32] 'Whore queen of lusty Canopus' was how one Roman poet described her.[33] Cicero, for his part, expressed strong feelings against her to his friend Atticus, writing, simply, 'I hate the queen'.[34] Cleopatra had apparently promised him something in her characteristically eloquent, 'word-loving' manner, and Cicero came away feeling flattered. Cleopatra had comported herself well, he told Atticus, speaking of their exchange in a public meeting. But it would appear that her promises did not hold, and Cicero was left feeling humiliated by her. He could not recall her stay in Rome without feeling a twinge of annoyance. She was, he reflected, *superba* – haughty and proud. Cleopatra had somehow outwitted him. Cicero could never have stood for that.

Egypt came too quickly and forcefully upon Rome for some people's liking. Cleopatra had her portrait made and a likeness produced in shining gilt. One might swear to have seen her face (or was it a reflection?) while walking through the city at night. Caesar chose this moment to draw upon the expertise of Sosigenes, a mathematician from the Alexandrian court, to reform the Roman calendar. The existing version had fallen out of step with the seasons because it was determined by the cycle of the moon. The Julian calendar was solar and divided the year into twelve months for the first time. Plans were also made for a major new library at Rome inspired by the prototype the Romans burned down.

Cleopatra's continuing presence and the influx of Alexandrian ideas did little to endear Caesar to the traditionalist quarters of the city. In the spring when the queen arrived, Caesar was granted a dictatorship for ten years, which was more than anyone who still believed in the good of the Republic could bear. Caesar gauged the mood and relinquished the conferral of power in favour of a string of consulships. But what difference did this truly make? When Pompey's sons Gnaeus and Sextus led forces against him, intent on avenging their father's death, Caesar acted as though he was making war on a foreign enemy. Gnaeus died in battle and Caesar assumed, wrongly, as it proved, that Sextus would simply slink away. Caesar's subsequent victory celebrations, which included the display of severed heads, left an ill feeling among the people of Rome who had endured decades of civil strife. Plutarch claimed that the population had more than halved since the civil wars began. His figures – a drop from 320,000 to 150,000 in the mid-50s BC – are not borne out by the official census statistics, but there can be little doubt that, with so many killed in battle, the female population of Rome now outnumbered the male.[35]

About this time, circa 46 BC, Terentia and Cicero divorced after more than thirty years of marriage. Cicero might have said that the signs were there when he sailed into Brundisium from exile and saw his daughter Tullia, but no Terentia, waiting to greet him off the boat.[36] Their relationship had not been the same since his return to Rome. They struggled to settle back into their old routine in an empty house: Terentia had had to sell furniture to pay off the debts that accumulated while he was away. The precariousness of their finances was almost certainly the prime reason for the breakdown of their marriage, but between them, they knew that there were other problems as well. Cicero felt that Terentia was distant. Terentia could not help but feel that Cicero had abandoned her, his head turned by somebody else.

Terentia's intuition proved to be fairly accurate. Soon after the divorce papers were signed, Cicero, now aged sixty, proposed marriage to Publilia, a girl of fourteen or fifteen. According to Terentia, he was charmed by her beauty, but most would have said that he was charmed by her money. His freedman secretary Tiro was certainly in no doubt that his employer needed to marry in order to pay his creditors.[37] Cicero already had control of Publilia's funds in the manner of a guardian and must therefore have known precisely what they totalled. He went through with the marriage in 46 BC with the encouragement of various friends and relatives but suffered no small amount of teasing in the process. Mark Antony, for one, could not help but taunt him for his callousness. Like all Roman virgins, Publilia would have dedicated her childhood clothes and dolls (mostly woman- rather than baby-shaped) to Fortuna or Diana prior to her wedding in a rite to mark her transition from *puella* to *matrona*. 'Tomorrow she will be a woman,' was Cicero's tasteless response to his detractors.[38]

We know little about Publilia's marriage to Cicero other than that it was short-lived. The girl had barely had time to digest what being Cicero's wife entailed before tragedy struck. In February 45 BC, just months after the wedding, Publilia's new stepdaughter, Tullia, died at the age of thirty-three.

Tullia's life as the daughter of the most recognisable public servant in the city had never been entirely her own. It followed the vicissitudes of her father's fortune, from the steady but unassured ascent of the *novus homo* to the heroic saviour of the city, then criminal, outlaw, pauper (the term was relative) and divorcé. Utterly unblemished in her father's eyes, she endured heartbreak, opprobrium and public scrutiny at every turn. Dolabella was not the husband she might have hoped for after two childless marriages. While angered by the fact that Cicero had failed to pay the full dowry he had promised, Dolabella had continued to be lavish in his spending and in his womanising besides. Tullia's marriage must have been truly terrible for her to have divorced him while pregnant. Their baby, a son, died shortly before she succumbed to complications of labour at a family home in Tusculum to the south-east of Rome.

Cicero had never been the most demonstrative man towards the people he loved, but in his grief for Tullia he was wholly unguarded. He was more public with his tears than most Roman men dared to be for the simple fact that he was incapable of holding them in. He sought distraction in his work as much as he could, embarking upon a new work of philosophy, the *De Finibus*, which found a supportive reader in one of his female friends. Caerellia, a wealthy woman with her own estates in Asia, had a passion for philosophy, but it was perhaps in part as a means of consoling Cicero that she tried to have a copy of the work made for herself.[39] The orator was increasingly cutting himself off from the world. He could not face seeing Publilia, let alone her family, and within months his new marriage had ended. Vicious rumours spread that Cicero divorced Publilia because she was secretly pleased at Tullia's death. Relations between a daughter and a stepmother half her age might have become difficult had there only been time, but there was not.

Cicero developed an obsession with constructing a funerary monument to loyal, wise, clever 'Tulliola'. When parents lost children in this period, they sometimes had emotional epitaphs inscribed on stone steles. A surviving example describes a girl named Cornelia Anniana who was just one year, three months and ten days old when she died; her parents wanted everyone who passed her grave to know that she was *dulcissima*, very sweet, and fond of babytalk.[40] Cicero had in mind a far grander and rarer monument to his daughter's memory. He wanted to build her a shrine.

He searched far and wide for a suitable plot to lay some foundations, but was repeatedly disappointed in his efforts to find one in the heavily built-up city. Such was his desperation that he began to eye some gardens owned by Clodia, widow of Metellus Celer. Unsurprisingly, given his unrelenting treatment of her at the trial of Caelius Rufus, she was unwilling to sell them to him.

Whether Cicero ever found a suitable location for the shrine is a mystery, but hundreds of years later, in 1485, the embalmed body of a young woman was exhumed from a marble tomb on the Appian Way and identified optimistically as that of Tullia. The corpse was put on display at the Conservatore in Rome where it was visited by some 20,000 people. Several onlookers wrote of their wonderment at seeing the woman's features so well preserved beneath the thick, herb-infused paste that covered her flesh. The boldest among them played with her like a doll which showed signs of coming to life. She had long hair and good teeth. Her eyes could be opened and closed and still had their lashes.[41] Her nose could be bent from side to side. Her cheeks lost their colour whenever they were pressed. Her tongue was still pink. A veil with gold thread covered her head. Naturally, the flesh began to deteriorate and blacken after a few days of being exposed to the air, especially in places where the paste was scraped away. Embalming was comparatively rare in Rome, and while it is not incredible that Cicero would have sought to preserve his beloved daughter in this way, there is no way of knowing whose body this really was.

Just over half a century after the body was exhumed it was announced that 'Tullia's funeral lamp' had been discovered still alight underground. It was not the first lit lamp to have been found in Rome, but its reappearance in the wake of the body's decay offered hope: flesh may be mortal but love can burn eternally. John Donne incorporated the burning lamp into a poem for the wedding of the Earl of Somerset and Frances Howard in 1613:

Now, as in Tullias tombe, one lamp burnt cleare,
Unchang'd for fifteene hundred yeare,
May these love-lamps we here enshrine,
In warmth, light, lasting, equall the divine . . .[42]

There is every indication in Cicero's letters that Tullia was loved as endlessly as this. She continued to occupy her father's heart while young Publilia vacated her ill-starred marital home.

Publilia was not the last woman to be divorced unexpectedly in Rome at this time. Brutus left his wife of more than a decade with similar abruptness. She belonged to the illustrious family of the Claudii and had done nothing to offend him, but the suicide of his uncle Cato had left a hole in the family, which she seemed unable to fill. Grief and mutual enmity can provide a strong impetus for friendship. Brutus and his cousin, Cato's widowed daughter Porcia, grew increasingly close.[43]

Their ensuing marriage put Servilia in an extremely awkward position. How could she maintain her relationship with Caesar when her own son (once rumoured to be Caesar's) was consumed by such hatred of him, the enemy of his new wife's late father? It was all Caesar could do to keep the peace between his bickering mistress and her new daughter-in-law. Caesar's feelings for Servilia had indeed shown no signs of cooling. He allowed her to help herself to estates auctioned off in Italy, including in Naples, at heavily reduced prices.[44] He even granted Brutus a prize praetorship for 44 BC and promised him the consulship later. Brutus could not have been deluded into thinking these anything other than gifts to his mother for her unwavering loyalty. The events that followed are best understood against the background of Servilia's relationship with Caesar, who in 44 BC became dictator 'for life'. They were in part the product of a familial strife that began with Pompey's killing of Brutus senior and escalated with Caesar's pursuit of Cato. Servilia played no direct role in their development but was to suffer the gravest of their consequences. We should never forget that the most cataclysmic episodes in Rome's history often affected women the most severely.

*

It was Porcia who first noticed that Brutus was looking troubled. All attempts to make him talk came to nothing and she began to worry that he was brooding over something serious. Her anxiety quickly peaked. In her bedroom she kept a small knife of the kind that hairdressers used to trim people's nails. She took hold of it and made a deep gash in her thigh. What she said to Brutus could only be imagined:

> I know that a woman's nature seems too weak to carry a secret, Brutus, but there's a strength that comes from being brought up well and keeping good company, and it is my good fortune to be both the daughter of Cato and the wife of Brutus. Previously I was less persuaded by this case but now I know that I am above pain.[45]

As blood gushed from her wound, Porcia hoped Brutus would accept that she was strong enough to bear not only whatever secret he was keeping, but any punishment that might be inflicted upon her should their life take a less fortunate turn.[46] Her heavy loss of blood and ensuing fever failed to shake Brutus from his silence.[47]

During the winter of 44/43 BC, Caesar was planning a campaign against Parthia, where Crassus had fallen a decade earlier. He hoped to follow this with an expedition to Scythia, country of the Amazons. A few nights before he was due to depart, Calpurnia woke him with the groans of someone suffering a nightmare.[48] She was not usually a suspicious woman, but a soothsayer, Spurinna, had warned Caesar to beware danger before or during the Ides of March.[49] It is probable that Spurinna's words were playing on her mind. The next morning, 15 March 44 BC – the Ides – Caesar was to attend a meeting of the Senate in the portico of Pompey's Theatre. Calpurnia asked Caesar whether they might delay, but, as one of his colleagues asked him mockingly, could the Senate really wait to conduct their business until his wife had more pleasant dreams?

Porcia, too, felt that something was not right. Of course, it was easy for historians to state this when they had the advantage of retrospect, but Porcia could well have had a premonition of impending trouble. Once Brutus had left the house, she fainted, though she was sitting down. Her female slaves screamed so loudly as she fell that neighbours rushed in from outside. Porcia had messengers on hand that morning to relay any news from the Senate. Amid the confusion, Brutus received a message declaring that Porcia was dead.[50] The report was corrected before he had time to choose between his wife and his mission, though in staying regardless of her collapse he effectively chose the mission.

The atmosphere around Pompey's Theatre was already tense. A senator was seen speaking quietly to Caesar (or was he passing him a note?). A dozen hands slipped beneath their togas. The slightest whisper in Caesar's direction – the slightest blink – would be taken as a sign that the plot was being leaked.

The senators filed into a room off the portico. As Caesar entered, they rose, and as he sat, they drew nearer. A man named Tullius Cimber stepped forward to issue a plea on behalf of his exiled brother. Caesar had begun to issue a rejection when Cimber laid hold of his shoulders with both hands and tugged open his robe. One of the senators standing behind Caesar drew a dagger and thrust weakly at his exposed shoulder. Caesar seized the handle of the weapon and asked him what on earth he was doing. But then Cimber took hold of his toga, allowing one of the Casca brothers to strike a blow. The chief conspirators, Marcus Junius Brutus, the son of Servilia, and Gaius Cassius Longinus, Servilia's son-in-law, had yet to move. Gladiators had been posted nearby in readiness. They were hardly needed. Thrust – there was Bucolianus. Thrust – there was Cassius. Thrust – Brutus stabbed Caesar in his thigh. *Kai su teknon* ('And you, my child?').

Caesar's final words (which could well have been mere historical invention) were full of disappointment and disbelief and akin to those of a stepfather to his stepson. Respect for Servilia had prompted Caesar to save Brutus after Pharsalus and appoint him to the consulship. He might still have made Brutus his heir. It would probably have made no difference if he had. Caesar had been betrayed by the son of the woman he arguably loved most in the world.

Brutus, Cassius and their fellow conspirators marched to the Capitol declaring that they had freed Rome from tyranny. For the time being they would be safe. The Senate passed an amnesty to protect them. Caesar would be given a state funeral, and a line would be drawn under the ugly circumstances of his death. But public feeling would begin to change as the reality of the assassination sank in. The sight of Caesar's heavily wounded corpse being carried to the forum, the reading of his will with its promises of lavish largesse for the people of Rome, would extinguish the fevered excitement of this moment. Driven by raw emotion, the crowd would build a hasty pyre in the forum and watch as Caesar's body burned itself into the sky, destined to fall again as a celestial body a short time later. Cleopatra, Servilia and Calpurnia remained in the city all the while. The sources are disappointingly thin on their reaction to the tragedy that united them.

Caesar had named his great-nephew Octavian, maternal grandson of his late sister Julia, as heir to three-quarters of his estate. The remainder went to two of his nephews and not to Cleopatra's son Caesarion. Octavian (full name Gaius Iulius Caesar Octavianus after his father Gaius Octavius) was also to be adopted posthumously as Caesar's son by a typical quirk of Roman law. The eighteen-year-old did not look much like Caesar, being rather short with fair wavy hair, bright eyes and a monobrow, but this would not stop him from cultivating an image of himself as his benefactor's biological son. He had been studying in Illyria when the news of Caesar's death reached him. His mother Atia was reluctant for him to travel to Rome when the political situation remained so febrile, but Octavian was determined and shrugged off her attempts to hold him back.

Rome was as chaotic and factionalised as Atia feared. While the so-called Liberators celebrated their success, Caesar's former allies, Octavian and kin set their hearts on avenging his murder. Mark Antony and Octavian were on the same side but quickly became rivals. Octavian shared the stronger blood relationship with Caesar, but where had he been all this time? Mutual loyalty to Caesar's memory led them to row over the distributions demanded by his will. In the most dramatic turn of events, Antony would be branded an enemy of the state for laying claim to a command over Cisalpine Gaul. Fulvia, Antony's wife, responded to the threat of his being outlawed with characteristic defiance and joined other members of his family in staying up all night to knock on the doors of other influential men in a bid to have the decision reversed.[51] The following morning, they blocked the entrance to the Senate House and, weeping in their mourning clothes, supplicated the senators. While Cicero stood firm, a fellow senator named Piso spoke in Antony's defence and might have saved him from his fate, but Antony refused to relinquish Gaul. A final showdown would take place at Mutina, where Antony laid a siege, in April 43 BC. The overthrow of Antony's forces by Octavian and his army forced his retreat and subjugation, but the effects were only temporary. It was to Antony that Calpurnia had entrusted her late husband's most precious belongings, valued at 4,000 talents, as well as his papers relating to decrees and the appointment of future magistrates.[52]

Caesar's appointment of Brutus and Cassius to the consulship had technically still held, but in the first instance the Senate had granted the two men a role in overseeing the distribution of Rome's corn supplies. Servilia had strong feelings about this, but, before she aired them, she had an important choice to make. Was she to join the Liberators, who included her son and son-in-law, even though they had been responsible for her lover's death? Or was she to align herself with their enemies and push for justice for Caesar, who in 42 BC was recognised formally as a god? If only a letter or diary survived to reveal the extent of Servilia's inner turmoil. Instinct says that she must have been emotionally rent over where to place her allegiance. But there is also the old adage that blood is thicker than water, and in Servilia's case this certainly held true. Whatever Caesar had meant to her in the past, the future of Brutus was what mattered to her now.

Servilia accompanied her daughter Junia Tertia, wife of Cassius, and Porcia to a meeting with Brutus, Cassius and Cicero in Antium, south of Rome. The Senate's appointment of the two principal assassins to the lowly position of overseeing the transport of corn had struck Servilia as deeply insulting. 'I shall remove the matter of the grain supply from the decree of the Senate,' she broke in, unprompted.[53] Her confidence that she could have a senatorial decree altered in spite of being barred from the Senate on grounds of her sex is extraordinary. It would appear that women of Servilia's rank could influence senatorial decisions by unofficial means if they were able to snatch a few words with senators acquainted with their relatives. Servilia was certainly vindicated in her decision to challenge the senators when they agreed to extend their allocation of her son and son-in-law's powers to control of Rome's eastern provinces.

Porcia bade farewell to Brutus as he left Rome for Athens. As she turned for home, a painting of Andromache and Hector caught her eye and she realised that she and Brutus were reliving the scene of the hero's departure in the *Iliad*.[54] One of Brutus' friends, noticing the same, quoted Andromache's address to Hector, in which she invokes him as her husband, father, mother and brother combined. Brutus listened and shook his head: he could never speak to Porcia as Hector spoke to Andromache: 'Go home and see to your tasks / At the loom and distaff, and order your servant women / To carry out their work . . .'[55] Porcia would never take kindly to receiving domestic instructions like that! The episode, so described by Plutarch, was first recorded in the memoirs of Porcia's son Bibulus. The memoirs are lost, but we can well believe that Brutus described Porcia in such affectionately bullish terms. She was equal to any man in her valiant defence of her country when Brutus stood on the brink of war with Caesar's defenders.[56]

Porcia's bravery was much-needed, for in 43 BC the Senate passed a law to track down and punish Julius Caesar's assassins as they scattered across the Adriatic, Asia Minor, and wherever they could reach. Mark Antony and Octavian, recently made a senator, came to an agreement with Marcus Aemilius Lepidus, formerly a close ally of Caesar, to forge what would be known to history as the Second Triumvirate. The alliance was this time legal and formalised by the Senate. Initially fixed at five years, it would enable them to rule the empire between them and present a strong front against the Liberators. Just as the First Triumvirate had been sealed by the marriage of Julia Caesar to Pompey, so the Second was sealed by a betrothal. Mark Antony's young-teenage stepdaughter Claudia, Fulvia's daughter by her late husband Publius Clodius Pulcher, became engaged to Octavian. Given that Octavian and Antony had met in conflict at Mutina just months earlier, this bond of marriage was arguably essential, and Fulvia was once again at the heart of events as both the wife of Antony and mother of Octavian's bride.

Cicero meanwhile doubled down on his efforts to besmirch Fulvia. His fourteen vitriolic *Philippics* presented her as a new Clodia Metelli, only more ruthless, bloodthirsty and tough. In the speeches she was described as standing by and allowing herself to be splattered by the blood of centurions slain by Antony during a revolt.[57] She was a natural-born killer, Cicero insinuated, with an unhealthy appetite for money. She was scandalously immoral. Worst of all, Antony had entrusted her with so much power that she had taken to auctioning off kingdoms and provinces at whim.[58] Cicero played a dangerous game in his wilful contortion of the truth. One of the men he had put to death without trial during the conspiracy of Catiline had been Antony's stepfather. His lifelong commitment to the Roman Republic and its freedoms besides made him a natural obstacle to the plans of the triumvirs. And so, when the three men agreed to reprise the process of proscription in Rome, Octavian failed to prevent Mark Antony from adding Cicero and his adherents to the list.

On 7 December 43 BC, Cicero was captured by Antony's soldiers near Formiae, on the coast of Latium (Lazio), where he kept a villa. He courageously submitted to their blows, which removed his head, then the hand with which he had written his offending speeches. The horror Publilia felt when Antony proceeded to have the body parts displayed on the speaker's platforms in Rome can only be imagined. Terentia, too, must have been devastated, for all that Cicero had put her through. It is not known for certain whether she remarried, but she would live to the age of 103. Fulvia, insensitive to their distress, allegedly picked up Cicero's head, spat on it, pulled out the tongue and pierced it with her hairpins.[59]

Although Fulvia became the subject of many cruel lies, some credible pieces of criticism were also levelled against her, particularly by other women. In the new year, with Cicero dead, the triumvirs published an edict instructing the 1,400 wealthiest women in Rome to donate a percentage of the value of their property to the state. As in times past, the financial burden of war fell upon those who had no right to fight in it, vote, or exercise a veto. The women called upon to open their purses were considerably more reluctant than their predecessors. Why should they be compelled to shore up the city? They immediately expressed their grievances to the women closest to the triumvirs in the hope that they would apply pressure to have the edict repealed. Octavian's sister, Octavia, and Antony's mother, Julia, agreed to try to help, but Fulvia curtly turned the women away. After all the threats that had been made against her family, Fulvia might simply have been cautious of causing further upset, but her reaction had the effect of alienating her from the other women of her class, to whom she appeared peculiarly cold and unfeeling.

Frustrated by their lack of progress with Fulvia, the women resolved to approach the triumvirs directly, selecting as their representative Hortensia, the highly persuasive daughter of the renowned orator. What purports to be her speech still survives, but it is in all likelihood an ancient reimagining of what she said. Composing speeches for real or legendary figures was a common literary exercise for students of rhetoric. Although the compositions were inauthentic, they were written to echo what was or ought to have been said, so are far from valueless today. The 'Hortensia' who composed this speech certainly did not hold back in her criticism of Fulvia and the financial demands imposed upon women. 'Proscribe us, if we have wronged you, just as you have our husbands,' she urged the triumvirs, 'but do not punish us if we are innocent.'[60]

The willingness 'Hortensia' showed to suffer the same physical punishment as the men of Rome was striking. The fact that there was little prospect of the triumvirs agreeing to proscribe women did not stop her from highlighting the lack of logic in their plans. Why was it, she asked, that women were being asked to pay taxes, when they were ineligible to receive the kind of honours conferred upon men? This orator, whoever he or she might have been, was astonishingly ahead of his or her time. The triumvirs were reminded that their own female ancestors had contributed to the wars against Carthage by willingly handing over their jewellery. But the situation this time was different. As free women in modern Rome they could not afford to part with their land, their dowries, their houses, all for the sake of a *civil* war.

Antony, Octavian and Lepidus were incensed that Rome's women should have organised a public meeting between themselves, and issued orders for it to be dispersed. They had not counted upon there being a second party of female protesters waiting in the wings. As the meeting was broken up, the crowd beyond began to roar, and the politicians found themselves frozen to the spot. Cowed by the unusual experience of a female mob, the triumvirs reluctantly agreed to postpone their decision over the edict until the following day. When they did reappear, they stipulated that only the 400 richest women need provide them with a valuation of their property and make a contribution, not 1,400 as formerly demanded.[61] To make up the shortfall, all *men* in possession of more than 100,000 denarii, be they natural citizens, immigrants or former slaves, would need to lend one-fiftieth of their property's value and pay a year's income to the war effort.

The women had triumphed. Although theirs was not a total victory, it came at the expense of their male counterparts, many of whom faced proscription already. Nor did it mark an end to the women's work in the civil war. Many of them now took up the challenge of trying to protect the innocent men who found their names added to the dreaded lists. Increasingly creative ways were sought to help the proscribed escape detection in the city. Some victims climbed into sewers, wells or chimneys.[62] One woman wrapped her husband in a laundry bag and had him shipped to Sicily as cargo as if he were Cleopatra. Another disguised her man as a coal-merchant. Roman women were not only weavers and dressers. Like Pandora and Penelope they were mistresses of guile.

Chapter XVI

This One's for Fulvia

Bunch of grapes, lying beneath the golden porch of
Aphrodite, brimming with drops of Dionysus:
No longer shall your mother put her lovely branch
Around you or flower fragrantly over your head.

Moero, a female poet of third-century BC Byzantium, *Greek Anthology* 6.119

While Brutus was away fighting with the Liberators, Porcia became unwell. Her illness may have been physical, stress-induced, possibly both, but it was serious enough to prompt Brutus to write to friends in Rome to berate them for failing to look after her.[1] In truth there was little they could do. Porcia had reached the stage where death begins to seem like a welcome reprieve when, in 42 BC, the worst news reached her. The forces of Octavian and Mark Antony had defeated her husband and his allies off the coast of Philippi, a city famous for its gold mines in eastern Macedonia. Cassius had taken his own life, but Brutus had asked a companion to stab him to death, believing he was no longer valuable to his country.

It was said that Porcia swallowed hot coals when she heard the reports, her slaves looking on in horror as she pushed blazing morsels down her throat.[2] It is far more likely that she succumbed to her illness than to suicide by internal combustion. Brutus had blamed his friends for aggravating her condition through neglect. Octavian gave orders for Brutus' head to be severed from his body, shipped back to Rome, and kicked at the foot of a marble statue of Caesar. Servilia was saved from enduring such an ignominy when her son's head was thrown overboard during a sea storm.[3]

While the triumvirs were able to transform Philippi into a Roman colony, their victory was not as total as it first appeared. Pompey the Great's surviving son Sextus, far from sinking into obscurity as Julius Caesar had expected, was on the rise, and for this he probably had Fulvia to thank. The Senate had authorised his promotion to Prefect of the Fleet and Coast, and during the proscriptions he had welcomed numerous ousted Romans to the shores of Sicily.[4] On hearing that he had been blacklisted, falsely, as an assassin of Caesar, Sextus had begun to build up his own navy. Fulvia and her mother-in-law were old friends of his and must have played a part in encouraging him to come to a mutually beneficial arrangement with Mark Antony. In exchange for providing Rome with grain and protecting the seas off Italy from piracy, Antony agreed that Sextus could retain Sicily and Sardinia.[5] Fulvia, as Antony's wife, was about to become even more prominent.

The triumvirs were now free to gather up all the cities they desired between Macedonia and the Euphrates, and each took a zone for himself. While Antony proceeded from Philippi to Athens and on to Asia Minor to manage the eastern provinces, Lepidus went to Africa, and Octavian, the youngest of the three, drew the short straw and returned home to resettle the soldiers. After fighting for their politicians, rather than their country, the veterans believed they were entitled to the very best land in Italy.[6] As Octavian set about evicting people from their estates to make room for the returning troops, the displaced flocked to Rome with their wives and children to lament the injustice of the situation. 'Look where civil war has landed the poor people!' cried a herdsman in one of Virgil's *Eclogues*, a set of ten bucolic poems reflecting the mood of the times.[7] Virgil's fellow poet Horace was among the many Italians forced to give up his ancestral land in the Italian countryside after fighting against Octavian at Philippi.[8] The upheavals led to street violence, murders, agricultural decline and famine.

Fulvia and her brother-in-law, Mark Antony's consul brother Lucius, sought to turn the situation to their advantage. They had originally planned to wait for Antony to return from the east and win glory by resettling his own soldiers. Fulvia was so eager to keep Antony in people's thoughts that she came before the military with their children to sing his praises.[9] Seeing how unpopular the resettlement process had made Octavian, however, Fulvia and Lucius changed their plan and cunningly resolved to champion the people he had dispossessed.[10] In this they were aided by Sextus Pompey, who drove the poorest into their arms by purposely cutting the grain supply to the mainland. Fulvia, at first reluctant to aggravate the situation, became the dominant force in the partnership.[11] Her primary objective was to strengthen Antony's position within the triumvirate by weakening Octavian's. Some writers, however, claimed that she was also purposely stirring up war against Octavian in a bid to bring Antony home.[12] News of certain extramarital affairs of her husband had begun to circulate in Rome.

Upon returning to Alexandria shortly after Caesar's death, Cleopatra had fortified her position in Egypt by poisoning her younger brother Ptolemy XIV, so that her son Caesarion became prominent. Although she had lost her primary connection to Rome with Caesar, she remained a powerful ally to the senators he left behind. Antony initially summoned her reproachfully for her apparent duplicity in supplying Caesar's murderer Cassius with funds ahead of Philippi. This was not what had happened, Cleopatra said, but she would be only too happy to explain the situation in person. Antony invited her to dinner. Cleopatra turned him down and told him that he should come to her instead.

The pair convened at Tarsus, Cilicia, in the summer after Philippi.[13] As ever, Cleopatra knew how to make an entrance, and adorned herself like Venus and her female attendants like nymphs. The sight of her reclining as the goddess on a motionless barge with purple sails, silver oars and a golden stern provided Antony with the merest foretaste of the luxuries that awaited him. The queen felt a deep affinity with Isis, protectress of women, healer of wounds, deliverer of magic. The meeting she laid on for Antony had the atmosphere of a celestial banquet. The room was hung with tapestries embroidered with gold and purple thread and glowed with the most extraordinary array of lights Antony had ever seen. Even the drinking vessels were gold and bejewelled.[14] Antony had recently enjoyed an affair with a Cappadocian woman named Glaphyra. She was soon a distant memory.

Classical historians wrote romantically of the latent passion that Cleopatra stirred in her Roman guest. As Antony looked at her, he 'was struck by her appearance and intelligence, and at once conquered by her, as if he were a youth, though in fact he was forty years old'.[15] Cleopatra, twenty-eight and supremely confident, listened when he spoke, charmingly picked up his military slang, and used it back to him. She had little difficulty in convincing him that she was not a traitor. Cassius had merely intercepted her gifts after she agreed to supply Dolabella, Tullia's widower, with legions in his capacity as proconsul of Syria. Dolabella had lost his life while fighting Cassius' troops a short time later.

Antony was only too pleased to put the matter aside. The day after their meeting, Cleopatra invited him and his friends to dinner, which was even more lavish than that of the night before. Guests were allowed to keep everything they touched, down to the very seats they reclined upon. As Horace observed, Cleopatra was a woman of no lowly tastes, *non humilis mulier.*

How was Antony to repay her kindness? He could not impress her with fine interiors as Alexandria was not his home. She had no need of gold drinking vessels. Only a present that would appeal to her intellect would do. Antony arranged for a collection of 200,000 scrolls from the library at Pergamum to be dispatched to Alexandria as if to compensate for those the Romans had burned.[16]

Antony and Cleopatra, soon becoming lovers, formed a new Society of Inimitables or 'Inimitable Livers' as the phrase is often translated from the Greek. Each day, at a previously undisclosed time, they would come together with other diners to feast at the spur of the moment, possibly in homage to the fun-loving Greek god Dionysus, a favourite of Antony. Cooks could be called upon any time to prepare the spread. Eight wild boars were deemed just about sufficient to feed twelve guests.

Antony was determined, seemingly to Cleopatra's amusement, to contribute further fare. It did not escape Cleopatra's notice that, while Antony very much enjoyed hunting and fishing, he was not terribly good at it. Antony, fearful that his new lover might discover his lack of prowess and tease him, went to some lengths to try to impress her. On one memorable trip, he had a fisherman dive into the water and surreptitiously attach someone else's impressive catch to his hook, which he then proceeded to lift from the water with noisy delight.[17] Cleopatra saw through the ruse but for the moment played along. The next time they went out, she invited some friends to witness the tremendous skill of her Roman friend. Hoping he might have better luck this time, Antony threw his line into the water and looked down to find a measly herring staring back at him. It did not occur to him that Cleopatra had turned the tables. This time, one of *her* friends had gone down and hooked the embarrassment on his line, and Antony hadn't even noticed. 'Hand over your rod to the fishers of Pharos and Canopus,' she urged him, 'your catch lies in cities and continents.'

There was a tender childishness in the way the couple cavorted. During one of their banquets, Cleopatra bet that she could consume 10 million sesterces before the meal was over, and Antony bet that she could not. As he watched, the queen dissolved an enormous pearl in a cup of vinegar and drank it down, winning the wager. The remaining pearl would later be split in two to make earrings for a statue of Venus in the Pantheon at Rome.

Money came so easily to Cleopatra that not having it was a game. She and Antony took to dressing up as slaves and peering into the windows of the city's poor to see how the other half lived.[18] They laughed as they went, fooling no one with their disguise of paupers' rags.

Plutarch believed that Cleopatra was indebted to Fulvia for teaching Antony to be obedient to domineering women.[19] As unfair as this was on all three, it was becoming fashionable among the Romans to speak of the steady emasculation of their toughest general. While he was in the east, Antony certainly appeared to be doing Cleopatra's bidding. Arsinoë, the queen's younger sister, had resided at the Temple of Artemis at Ephesus since Caesar's triumph and ought to have enjoyed religious sacrosanctity, but Antony agreed to send men to kill her as a potential threat to Cleopatra's authority.[20] Like her elder sister Berenice, Arsinoë had developed a taste for power, and fell victim to her own ambition. She was put down by Mark Antony upon Cleopatra's orders after calling herself queen. Cleopatra *was* queen and knew that her relationship with Antony had the potential to be mutually beneficial. As much as she required support from Rome, he required funds for his soldiers.

Fulvia's desire to extricate her husband from Cleopatra's grip, regardless of what people said, was surely secondary to her ambition to strengthen his position within the triumvirate and enhance his reputation more widely. Antony was behaving as though he had forgotten that Rome had a war to wage in Parthia and disputes to settle on the fields of Italy. Even after he secured Cleopatra's assistance against the Parthians, he seemed preoccupied, a million miles from home. If only he could regain his focus, Fulvia must have realised, he might take Octavian's place as the people's hero.

Try as he might, it was difficult for Antony to forget Fulvia while he was travelling. The likeness of a woman some historians have identified as her had begun to circulate on coins minted at Lugdunum (Lyon) in Gaul and Eumeneia in Phrygia, Asia Minor.[21] The woman's portrait was modelled on that of the goddess of Victory, but with her large eyes, slim nose and hair done up in a fashionable bun, she was clearly intended to resemble a notable mortal. Fulvia had certainly been increasingly prominent since the death of Clodius. Whether the portrait on these coins was always intended to represent her or, as others suggest, Octavian's sister Octavia, Fulvia was one of the first women to be represented on a coin. The imprint set an important precedent in showing that a woman did not even need to leave Rome to make an impression across the empire.

Back in the city, Octavian had taken to taunting Antony in his absence over his 'foreign affairs' and the impact they were having upon Fulvia. 'Because Antony fucks Glaphyra,' he spluttered in a poem, 'Fulvia set this punishment for me: that I should fuck her also.'[22] It is rare that we hear Octavian's voice in an unofficial and jocular capacity. Fulvia was his mother-in-law. He was hardly about to have sex with her. His poem jibed rather at Fulvia's dominance over him and the triumvirate more widely. Antony brushed aside the slur on his wife and his own manners. He was so nonchalant about his extramarital pleasures that Sextus Pompey felt at liberty to mock his affair with Cleopatra right under his nose. A joke about Glaphyra could not deter him from continuing his relationship with Cleopatra. If anything ought to have troubled him, it was the tension Octavian hinted at between himself and Fulvia.

In Octavian's poem, Fulvia goes so far as to threaten him, 'Either fuck me,' she says, 'or fight me'. These were strong words to put in her mouth but Octavian had every reason to believe that she might become combative. According to one historian, he even accused her and Lucius of aiming at supreme power.[23] At the end of the decade he told Fulvia that he was divorcing her daughter Claudia and sending her back home *virgo intacta* so that he could marry a twice-married woman named Scribonia instead. He swore on oath that the marriage had not been consummated, but this was of little consequence to Fulvia. For some time now she had been aggravated by Octavian's growing dominance. Her brother-in-law Lucius, still harbouring feelings for the Republic, was similarly moved to anger by the unevenness of the partnership.[24] Octavian's rejection of Fulvia's daughter proved to be the final trigger to war.

The Perusine War, as it came to be known, was truly Fulvia's war. Fought in 41–40 BC in the interest of altering the balance of power in the triumvirate and punishing Octavian for his acts of aggression, it would culminate in one of the bloodiest sieges in recent history and the deaths of innumerable innocent people. Although power ostensibly lay with Lucius, who was elected consul for 41 BC, the real power, according to the historian Cassius Dio, lay rather with Fulvia.[25] This might have read as a vast exaggeration and deliberate attempt to besmirch Fulvia, but Dio was not wrong to emphasise her authority at this juncture. Prior to the engagement Fulvia aided Lucius in raising the necessary legions in Italy.[26] She then personally travelled to Praeneste (Palestrina, northern Italy), where 'a sword was girded to her side and she gave signals to the soldiers and often even addressed them'.[27] Dio's description here was intended to highlight Fulvia's unnatural manliness. Fulvia did not pick up a sword in order to fight. If she held one at all, it was in a ceremonial manner to address the military, who were unaccustomed to taking instructions from a woman. Her role in the war which ensued in the city of Perusia (Perugia) was nevertheless crucial. She was the one to urge soldiers to travel from Gaul to Lucius' side when it was apparent that he needed reinforcements. She was the one to raise an army for Lucius when the forces he had proved unequal to the task.[28]

The war, indeed, did not go to plan. Fulvia and Lucius found themselves seeking refuge inside the city walls as Octavian's forces laid a siege and began to hurl missiles over the ramparts. Several of the lead bullets the men discharged from their slingshots were inscribed with crude messages for the enemy. 'I'm aiming for Fulvia's clit [*landica*],' reads one, which has miraculously been recovered from the site.[29] The clitoris was commonly thought of as an ugly malformed penis. To pleasure it was popularly considered disdainful and foul. The fact that the word was etymologically related to the Greek for 'hillock' and 'rub' as well as 'enclose', and that numerous paintings survive showing couples enjoying cunnilingus, reveal the hypocrisy of these viewpoints. 'I'm aiming for Octavian's bumhole,' read a counter missile, which was of such a size as to make the threat feasible, though extremely unlikely to be fulfilled.[30] A further missile shot over in Fulvia's direction. 'Bald Lucius Antonius and Fulvia,' it read, 'open your assholes.'[31]

Fulvia had become as notorious as her brother-in-law and former son-in-law. In deciding to *fight*, she had imperilled not only her position, but Antony's, their soldiers, and the people of Perusia. In early 40 BC Octavian mercilessly starved the citizens within the walls into submission. Fulvia and Lucius were spared, but many of the men who had fought for them were put to death, among them up to 300 senators and equestrians, who were allegedly sacrificed on the altar of Caesar himself.[32] The love poet Propertius would never forget the ensuing sack of Perusia.[33] Deprived during Octavian's land confiscations, and forced to bury his father before his time, he saw Perusia transformed into a tomb for his relatives and countrymen in his youth.[34] The whole city was razed but for a single statue of Juno that was carried off to Rome.

Antony was still with Cleopatra in Alexandria when news of Fulvia and the war reached him.[35] He made no hurry to return home. Cleopatra had become pregnant with his child, or rather, his children. Later that year, she would give birth to twins, Cleopatra Selene, named after the Moon, and Alexander Helios, named after the Sun. A third child, Ptolemy Philadelphus, would follow a few years later. Contrary to how it must have seemed to Fulvia, it was not Cleopatra's pregnancy that detained Antony, although he readily acknowledged his responsibility on that front, but his duties in the east. While his head was turned, the Parthians had begun to make great strides in conquering Asia Minor, their hearts set on seizing territory from Syria to Lydia and Ionia. If Antony did not confront the Parthian threat immediately, there was a good chance that the progress the Romans had made during the past two and a half decades would be entirely undone.

Antony had travelled as far as Phoenicia when a tearful letter arrived from Fulvia urging him to turn back. In the dismal aftermath of the war she had fought on his behalf, she was intent on coming to see him with their young children. Marcus Antonius Antyllus and little Iullus Antonius were about seven and three years old respectively. They barely knew their father. Fulvia wisely suggested to Antony that he meet them in Greece rather than Egypt. She and the boys would sail over with his mother Julia and await him. Antony agreed to this plan and they convened in Athens, but there was little time for a family reunion. Antony blamed Fulvia for the chaos of the Perusine War and showed little sign of hesitation in leaving her behind at Sicyon, near Corinth, when she was taken unwell. A message had arrived summoning him to Brundisium in the heel of Italy for a conference with Octavian. Antony crossed the waters that Fulvia had only lately crossed herself.

A series of tense negotiations had just begun between the two men in Italy when news arrived that Fulvia had died. If only she had stayed in Italy, she might have seen Antony there and saved herself a treacherous journey and a death far from home. Mark Antony could not help but feel partly responsible. It was perhaps only now that he understood how much Fulvia had done to promote him within the triumvirate and fortify his position while he dallied with Cleopatra in Egypt.

Classical historians were less forgiving of his ambitious wife. 'The death of this public affairs-obsessed woman who fanned the flames of war out of jealousy for Cleopatra,' wrote one, 'seemed extremely profitable for both parties, who were freed of her.'[36] The consensus remained that Fulvia had whipped up civil war in response to her husband's affair with Cleopatra alone. Her death was heralded for removing the main source of tension between the triumvirs, who proceeded to fortify their pact. Few could forget the chaotic scenes that attended the funeral of Fulvia's first husband Clodius a dozen years earlier. Time and again she had shown herself to be a nuisance to public order. As later events would show, predictions that the three men would get along swimmingly as soon as Fulvia was removed from the frame were ill-founded. It was all too convenient to lay blame for the fragility of the alliance upon the woman who had dared to stand between two of its members. Fulvia died a scapegoat, her loyalty and fortitude disregarded, as women's so often were.

The renewed agreement altered the responsibilities of the triumvirs. In accordance with its terms, Antony would focus on reducing the Parthians and avenging the death of Crassus; Octavian would preside over the western provinces, especially Sicily, where Sextus Pompey was still at large; and Lepidus would continue managing North Africa. As on previous occasions, the agreement was sealed with a betrothal, this time between Octavian's elder sister Octavia and Mark Antony.

Octavia was, by popular repute, 'a most wonderful thing'.[37] Beautiful, level-headed, a mother of three, she would have a good, calming influence upon wayward Antony, if anyone could. Or so people said. Octavia was still mourning the death of her first husband, Gaius Claudius Marcellus, but the Senate granted her permission to cut short her grieving period so as to marry the recently widowed Antony before the traditional ten months had elapsed. Antony was as enthusiastic as the rest of the population for the match.[38] 'Everyone proposed this marriage, hoping that Octavia, since she had dignity and intelligence on top of her considerable beauty, standing at Antony's side and feeling his affection, as was natural for such a woman, would be the salvation and solution for all their concerns.'[39] Antony made no effort to conceal from his bride his ongoing affair with Cleopatra.

Octavian also hoped to remarry. His relationship with Scribonia, for whom he had divorced Fulvia's daughter Claudia, had not proven as happy as he might have expected. Roughly a decade older than him, Scribonia had a daughter, Cornelia, by one of her previous marriages, but was yet to give Octavian a son. She was also rather dour – Seneca called her *gravis femina* ('a serious woman')[40] – but it counted for something that she was related to the wife of Sextus Pompey, who had until recently been a useful man for Octavian to have onside.[41] It could not have escaped Scribonia's notice that public opinion had turned against Sextus, whose blockade of the seas had triggered a shortage of food on the Italian mainland. As *de facto* rulers of Italy, the triumvirs were confronted with the ensuing popular backlash and more than a few stone pellets. The people of Rome grew so frustrated by their politicians' failure to alleviate the crisis that they turned on Sextus' mother Mucia and threatened to burn her to ashes if she did not persuade her son to release the grain.

The extraordinary episode showed just how easily the mother of a politician could become embroiled in her son's scandals. There was a genuine risk that Mucia might pay the ultimate price for Sextus' mistakes. To the triumvirs, Mucia's sudden involvement in the drama was less surprising, for Antony's mother Julia, too, was frequently drawn into political disputes. In recent years, Sextus had tended to communicate with Antony via Julia, and Julia had served as a go-between for Antony and Octavian. All three men knew only too well what mothers could do. Mucia certainly proved her power. It was at least partly as a result of her intervention that Sextus agreed to talk to Octavian and Antony, forge an agreement to cease war on land and sea, and allow the transport of goods to recommence unhindered so as to end the food-supply crisis. Later, when the treaty between them was broken, Octavian proclaimed victory over Sextus, who lifted the blockade he had again imposed but retained power over Sicily, Sardinia and Corsica. Gradually, some of the citizens who had sought refuge with Sextus during the proscriptions found themselves able to return to Rome. Legally they were entitled to recover just a quarter of their former property.[42]

It was in this context that Octavian found the new wife he had been craving. Livia Drusilla had sought refuge with Sextus in Sicily soon after the Perusine War. The daughter of Alfidia, a woman from Fundi in Latium, and Marcus Livius Drusus Claudianus, a distant relative of Clodia Metelli, she had been married at fifteen to one of her father's cousins, Tiberius Claudius Nero, a man three times her age. Their son, Tiberius, was born in 42 BC. In spite of his earlier allegiance – he had formerly commanded a fleet for Julius Caesar in Alexandria – Livia's husband stood firmly on the side of the Liberators.[43] Neither he nor his father-in-law could have been surprised to find themselves proscribed. The elder man took his own life after fighting on the losing side at Philippi, but Tiberius Claudius, determined to keep up the fight for the Liberators' cause, attempted to whip up a servile rebellion in Campania against Octavian following the siege of Perusia.[44] Livia and young Tiberius had gone on to seek the protection of Mark Antony in Greece. During their flight they were caught up in a forest fire in which Livia's hair and clothes were singed.[45]

That Octavian should have considered Livia as a potential wife was astonishing. Here was a woman who had been forced to flee her home with a baby in her arms at Octavian's command. A woman whose father gave his life defending what Octavian threatened to take away. A woman whose husband had made nomads of her family in their continuing fight for the Republic. A woman who lost three-quarters of her family wealth because Octavian did not like their name. What was more, Livia was expecting her husband's second child when she returned to Rome in 39 BC and Scribonia, Octavian's wife, had told him that she was expecting their first. The very idea that Octavian should pursue Livia at this juncture, or indeed at all, struck all around him as madness.

According to the Roman historian Tacitus, writing in the early second century AD, Octavian was driven 'by lust for [Livia's] body'.[46] This may have been so, but in portraits Livia is a paragon of modesty, her hair simply put back, her décolletage respectably free of extravagant jewellery. Octavian's lust was perhaps secondary to his admiration for her sophisticated, slightly austere manner, and the influence this would have upon his court. Scribonia might not have looked austere, but Octavian felt that she was frosty – a *gravis femina* such as Seneca described – and longed to be rid of her. And so, in the autumn of 39 BC, on the very day Scribonia gave birth to a daughter, Octavian walked away. When parents divorced in Rome the father was ordinarily given custody of the children. This was one reason women seldom initiated divorce. Scribonia's child, Julia, would be forced to grow up with her father.[47]

A few months later, on 17 January 38 BC, Octavian and Livia were married. Three months after that, Livia gave birth to Drusus, a brother for Tiberius. Octavian had become a father and a stepfather almost simultaneously. The rapid and peculiar sequence of events scandalised Rome. Octavian's desire to marry a pregnant woman seemed so inexplicable that some believed that his affair with Livia had begun earlier and that her ex-husband's child was actually his. Livia, like Scribonia, was legally obliged to give up her children to their natural father.

Their behaviour might have struck many as incomprehensible, but in cold, hard, practical terms, both Livia and Octavian had something to gain from their new partnership. He would enjoy a useful political connection to her illustrious family. She would be able to re-establish her wealth and status after her flight from Italy. Marriage to Octavian offered Livia the means of regaining something of the life she had known prior to the civil war. In an indication that an agreement satisfactory to all parties had been achieved, Tiberius Claudius Nero not only attended the wedding of his ex-wife to Octavian, but also in place of her father gave her away.[48] While he took care of the two boys, Livia was at liberty to give Octavian a child of his own. Little could either of them have foreseen that Julia, Scribonia's daughter, would be Octavian's sole surviving offspring.

Octavian's elder sister Octavia had enjoyed a good few years with Antony, largely in Athens, far from Cleopatra's gaze. By 37 BC, she had two young daughters, Antonia the Elder and Antonia the Younger, half-sisters to her children by her first husband, Marcellus, Claudia Marcella the Elder and Claudia Marcella the Younger. Yet Antony was liable to disappear without a moment's notice, as he had directly after the birth of their first daughter.[49] There were times when the Parthian War provided an excuse but there were also times when it did not. The more strained the relationship between Antony and Octavian became, the harder it was for Octavia to remain in their shadow. 'If the worst should prevail and war occur,' she told her brother, presciently, 'It is the fate of one of you to conquer and the other to be conquered – it is unclear which way this will go – but in either case, my life will be misery.'[50]

What an extraordinarily acute statement this was. Would it be worse to be the wife of the man who had killed her brother, or the sister of the man who had killed her husband? Only time would tell. In a bid to put off what already seemed inevitable, Octavia encouraged the two men to make a fresh pact when they met at the coastal city of Tarentum in southern Italy. To Octavia's relief a mutually beneficial agreement was reached. Her brother would provide Antony with two legions to send to Parthia in exchange for 100 bronze-beaked galleys for use against Sextus Pompey. Octavia herself secured twenty ships from Antony for her brother Octavian, and 1,000 soldiers for Octavian from Antony. The importance of the pact – and Octavia's instrumental role in its creation – became clear after 36 BC when Octavian's general Agrippa defeated Sextus off the Sicilian coast and Octavian saw Lepidus sent into permanent exile for attempting to launch his own bid for autocracy in Rome.[51] Octavia's husband and brother were the last of the triumvirs left standing but behaved as if the alliance-of-three was still in force.

Both Octavia and Livia received extraordinary honours in recognition of their proximity to power. They were the sort of privileges that ordinarily accompanied a man's promotion to the tribuneship: security and inviolability, the freedom to oversee their property and estates without the protection of a male guardian, and the right to be honoured with public statues.[52] But while raising them up, Octavian was determined to bat other women down, not least of all Cleopatra. This was less a game of gender politics than an exercise in gaining supremacy over Antony. For his part, Antony could not at first understand why Octavian was so troubled by his affair. He wrote him a letter to ask what objection he could possibly have to his sexual relationship with the queen: 'So do you sleep only with Livia Drusilla?' he asked. 'I salute you if, as you read this letter, you are not in bed with Tertulla or Terentilla or Rufilla or Salvia Titisenia, or all of them. Does it matter where, and in whom, you get it up?'[53] Octavian was by no means faithful to Livia, but of all the women he knew in his life, he was said to have loved her most of all.

Antony, while expressing a typically male view, had wilfully missed Octavian's point, which was that Cleopatra was not Roman. In carrying on with her publicly, in holding her in such high esteem, Antony was putting her above his Roman-born wife and political partner's sister. While receiving honours from her brother Octavian, Octavia had received very little from her husband, who meanwhile presented Cleopatra and her children with territories including Phoenicia and Cyprus. The people of Rome were repeatedly astonished by the inequality of this love triangle.[54] In 34 BC, at the gymnasium in Alexandria, Antony sat on a throne beside Cleopatra and their three children and named her Queen of Kings. Caesar's child, thirteen-year-old Caesarion, was proclaimed King of Kings and co-ruler. A *denarius* minted in Rome that year bore a portrait of a hook-nosed Cleopatra, 'Queen of Kings, who are sons of kings' on one side, and Antony on the other. Antony's children by Fulvia and Octavia received no such honours.

Octavia eventually took the initiative of sailing to Antony in an echo of Fulvia's actions following the Perusine War. Octavian was happy for his sister to go: if Antony was anything less than respectful towards her, he would have grounds for declaring war against him. Octavia arrived in Athens to a pile of letters from her errant husband. Antony asked that she proceed no further while he was on expedition. Frustrated but not deceived into believing that the Parthian War alone was keeping him, Octavia sent Antony a simple message in return. Where was she to send the luggage and the presents she had brought for the soldiers? Her kindness was characteristic and delighted Antony, but Cleopatra viewed it as a ruse to entice him away from her. Fearful that Antony would reunite with Octavia and abandon her, Cleopatra stopped eating and came before him looking gaunt, tearful and faint whenever he said that he had to leave.[55] The queen's attendants played their part in extracting empathy. At one point Antony was so afraid Cleopatra might commit suicide that he put off a military campaign in order to return to her in Alexandria.

After some time, Octavia felt that she had little choice but to turn around and sail back to Rome, her position as Antony's wife far from certain. Her worst fears were confirmed soon after she arrived home. She was instructed to leave the villa she shared with Antony and their children as soon as possible. Octavia, like the mime actress Cytheris, had been cast out of Antony's villa without so much as a warning. Maintaining her dignity in the public eye, Octavia agreed to leave the house, but added that she would continue to care for not only the children she had by Antony, but Antony's children by Fulvia, too. Octavia's growing popularity in Rome only exacerbated Antony's foul mood. In May 32 BC she received a final insult in the form of divorce papers.

While Antony had treated her appallingly, Octavia was adamant that her brother Octavian should *not* use her as an excuse to declare war on him, 'since it was no fine thing to hear that, of the most powerful rulers, one plunged the Romans into civil war out of love for a woman, the other out of resentment on a woman's behalf'.[56] The last thing Octavia wanted was to become a new Helen of Troy.

Octavian loved his sister dearly but he could not help himself. The opportunity to triumph over his political partner had finally come. The Vestal Virgins kept guard over Antony's will. Octavian made his way to the Temple of Vesta, scandalously retrieved the private document, and had it read aloud. Not only had Antony requested to be buried with Cleopatra when he died, it purportedly said, but he had appointed their children – not his Roman children – as his heirs. The Senate, fearing Egypt's dominance over Rome, responded in consternation and outlawed Antony immediately. There was neither the time nor the inclination to verify that the document Octavian was holding was legitimate. As a vote was passed to declare war on Cleopatra – and Cleopatra alone – Octavia's worst fears were fulfilled.

Cleopatra had recently supplied Antony with 200 ships and 20,000 talents for the next stage of the Parthian War. She had overcome the earlier challenges of her rule, including famine-inspired disaffection, to bring relative stability to her country. She was now in a position to help Rome. Disregarding his request that she retreat to Alexandria when the fighting resumed, she had remained with Antony at Ephesus in western Asia Minor, her intelligence in battle at least equal to that of many of the generals. As Octavian proceeded to engage Antony as an enemy, Cleopatra remained similarly close at hand. It was largely at her recommendation that the two men met at sea rather than on land.[57]

The queen sent galleys to Actium, off the north-west coast of Greece, and proudly looked over her fleet. It was smaller than Octavian's but contained larger vessels and, as far as she was concerned, superior manpower. On the morning of 2 September 31 BC the two sides met near the Ambracian Gulf, Cleopatra commanding her own reserve armada of sixty behind Antony as he prepared to confront Octavian's most trusted and talented commander, Marcus Vipsanius Agrippa. The battle might have been a predominantly masculine affair, but Cleopatra carried out a breakthrough when some of Antony's ships broke ranks and looked certain to endanger his life. Thwarted by Agrippa's naval expertise, Antony sailed after Cleopatra and away to safety.[58] This was not the engagement he had envisaged.

Cleopatra might have saved Antony's life but she could not save his dignity and position in Rome. Losses stood at over 5,000 on Antony and Cleopatra's side. Prows from the defeated ships were sent to Rome to adorn the Rostra outside the Temple of Divine Julius Caesar that had been constructed at the east end of the forum.

Some historians claimed that Cleopatra purposely led Antony to defeat in order to gain effective ownership of him as a partner. This is highly implausible, but she did ensure that she had a plan in place by which they might together elude servitude at the hands of Octavian. When Antony first heard of the extent of the losses at Actium and of a new alliance between Octavian and Herod of Judaea, he retreated to Pharos, home to the famous lighthouse in Alexandria. Cleopatra meanwhile arranged for her fleet to be raised from the isthmus that separated the Red Sea from the Mediterranean, hopeful that she and Antony might escape and settle outside Egypt. Antony stopped brooding and started drinking.

The pair killed off their Society of Inimitables and founded in its place the Partners in Death. It was said that Cleopatra began to research the efficacy of poisons by testing them on prisoners facing the death sentence. The fact that many of the substances brought on an agonising end allegedly prompted her to abandon her trials in favour of experiments with venomous animals. Instinct told her to prepare for the worst. Cleopatra's request that her children retain Egypt if Antony agreed to live as a private citizen in Athens was met with a lukewarm response from Octavian. At a meeting with her embassy in Asia the victor declared that she would be treated well if she ejected Antony at once or had him put to death. Octavian hoped and expected to drag Cleopatra back to Rome as a live trophy.

When Cleopatra heard that Octavian had taken Alexandria and that Antony had been deserted by his cavalry – and blamed her – she fled to the two-storeyed mausoleum her craftsmen had constructed for her and bolted the doors. Antony, not half as wily, believed her messengers when they told her she was dead. In his grief, he urged his trusted slave to kill him, but the improbably named Eros – Cupid, Love, Sexual Desire – killed himself instead. Misreading the situation once again, Antony interpreted Eros' suicide as a demonstration, and set his mind on dying by his own hand. He tried; he stabbed himself, but the blood was slow to leave his wound. Veins constrict when pulsed with fear. Cleopatra sent for him. Stunned that she was still alive, Antony bade his slaves carry him to her. In Plutarch's account, the most influential of all the sources written on this episode, Antony, bleeding more heavily, is led to the doors of his lover's tomb. Cleopatra does not come to the doors but appears at an upper window.[59] She and her two serving women, Iras and Charmion, use all their strength to hoist Antony up to them and lay him down.

Cleopatra knew that Antony was dying. Tearing her clothes and beating her breasts, she dipped her hands in his blood and smeared it on her face, then spoke to him as if he were her husband. Antony asked for some wine, drank it, and told Cleopatra which of Octavian's men she could most depend upon. He urged her to save herself. He was dying happy, he said, for he had held power and not fallen at another Roman's hands. A short time later he slipped away.

When Octavian heard that Antony was dead, he mourned him not as a colleague – he had become an enemy – but as a brother-in-law, albeit an unworthy one. His tears were not so free-flowing as to impede him from pursuing the next stage of his plan, to capture Cleopatra alive.

She was still in her tomb, bargaining with Octavian's men from behind barred doors, trying her utmost to negotiate the safety of her children. One man had entered her mausoleum when she tried to stab herself. He stopped her. A short time later a fever began to creep through Cleopatra's body. Whether she had sampled something deadly, or was simply in the grip of fear or blood-poisoning from her wound, is unclear. The Romans were under strict instruction to keep her alive. When Octavian came to speak to her in person a few days later, she allowed him in. He urged her to lie down while he sat. She asked him whether he would be merciful if she sent presents to Octavia and Livia. She had great treasures to bestow upon Rome and understood only too well the high esteem in which these women were held. She was told that she would be treated well.

Octavian went away believing that Cleopatra intended to live. She had deceived him. Once he had left, she had her two servants pour her a bath, laid out a sumptuous dinner, and carried in the dish of figs that had been delivered to her door. She had already written Octavian a letter when he came. She now dispatched it.

In her experiments, the queen had been most impressed by the efficacy of the asp, whose subtle bite induced sleepiness rather than spasms, peace rather than pain. An asp sat curled in the bottom of the fig basket. Cleopatra offered up her arm for it to bite her surreptitiously. An alternative death by lethal injection cannot be ruled out. Her arm was said to have been marred by a pair of puncture-marks.

Octavian opened the tablet. It contained the equivalent of a last request. Cleopatra wished to be buried with Mark Antony. Octavian immediately understood the subtext of the message: Cleopatra was intending to take her own life. Without a moment's pause, he sent messengers, only to hear that they were too late. By the time the men arrived, Cleopatra was lying lifeless on a golden couch. Her two women, who had accompanied her in her suicide, had laid her out with due ceremony and tenderly arranged a diadem on her head. Cleopatra had outlived Antony by nine days. She died in August 30 BC, aged thirty-nine.

Octavian was so angry that he had not taken her alive so as to parade her in his triumph at Rome that he allegedly summoned snake-charmers to suck the poison from her wound in a desperate attempt to revive her.[60] Nothing could be done. It took some time, but with reflection Octavian came to appreciate the extraordinary strength of Cleopatra's spirit, and agreed that she should be laid to rest with Antony as they had both requested.[61]

It is believed that a crypt holding the lovers' remains may lie just west of modern Alexandria. Over the past twenty years a criminal lawyer-turned-archaeologist from the Dominican Republic, Kathleen Martinez, has focused her search for their tomb on the sprawling Temple of Osiris in Taposiris Magna, 50 kilometres from Alexandria. The temple, dedicated to Cleopatra's patron goddess Isis and Isis' husband Osiris, a god revered by Mark Antony, has so far yielded six burial chambers, forty coins bearing portraits of Antony and Cleopatra, and a number of other objects. Part of the temple collapsed into the sea during a series of historic earthquakes, so it is possible that, if Antony and Cleopatra were interred here, their remains were long since swept away. The discovery by Martinez and her team of a 1,305-metre rock-cut subterranean tunnel in the same area as the temple in late 2022 has nevertheless renewed hopes that a tomb could be found.

In the aftermath of their deaths, statues of Antony were torn down, but statues of Cleopatra were kept up. It may be true that one of Cleopatra's friends bribed Octavian to preserve some of the monuments in Egypt, but it is possible that awe and a newfound respect for the late queen flourished even among the Romans. In her final days Cleopatra had exhibited a courage and magnanimity seldom associated with people living east of Rome. She had valiantly tried to save her children from sharing in her fate, to mixed results. Caesarion, her son by Julius Caesar, was deemed at the age of sixteen too grave a threat to Roman power and so was put to death. The eldest of Antony's seven children, Antyllus, a son of Fulvia, was similarly killed. Cleopatra's other children, however, were put under guard and led to safety. The ever-generous Octavia agreed to raise them with her own children, and those of Fulvia and Mark Antony. Cleopatra's two sons do not appear to have survived childhood, but Cleopatra Selene, the Moon twin, was proclaimed queen of Crete and Cyrenaica at the age of six. She was married nine years later to Juba, son of the late king of Numidia, future king of Mauretania, at Octavian's arrangement and upon Octavia's advice.

Cleopatra herself proved to be the last pharaoh of Egypt. While her defeat was ultimately a cause for celebration among the Romans, especially Octavian, who embraced her former country as his own, her life became an example to the women of the imperial household. Cleopatra had shown that it was possible to influence the actions of even the staunchest of Rome's leaders. First Julius Caesar, then Mark Antony had bowed to her commands, and in her final moments she had eluded Octavian, a man who thought he understood women, but was incontrovertibly proven wrong.

Chapter XVII

The Exiles

My wretched birthday is upon me, and sadly I have to spend it
In the horrible countryside without Cerinthus.
What is sweeter than the city? Could a villa or
A frosty river in rural Arretium really be suitable for a girl?

Sulpicia, 3.14, first century BC

Livia conceived a child with Octavian, but the baby was stillborn. As the years went by, the prospect of their becoming parents together steadily began to diminish. Octavian was guardian to Livia's sons by her first marriage to Tiberius Claudius Nero, namely Tiberius and Drusus, and began to take some interest in them when they came to live at his villa on the Palatine Hill following the death of their father. He might have preferred his own blood, but the two boys provided a contingency for the future, as they could be encouraged to procreate with members of his own circle. Octavian accordingly had Livia's ten-year-old Tiberius betrothed to Vipsania, the infant daughter of his right-hand man Agrippa and his wife Pomponia, and made Agrippa divorce Pomponia in order to marry his niece, Octavia's elder daughter, Claudia Marcella. Livia's younger son Drusus would marry Antonia the Younger, Octavia's daughter by the late Mark Antony, so making him part of Octavian's family. The marriage arrangements of the upper class were seldom less than dizzying.

Octavian was thinking seriously about the future of his family as he strove to fortify his political position in Rome. After Actium, he closed the gates to the Temple of Janus, prompting cheers from the war-wearied people. This was the first time the gates had been closed since the end of the First Punic War and Octavian would repeat the measure twice more in the course of his lifetime as he sought to cultivate a new era of peace, the Pax Augusta. He could neither restore the obsolete Republic, nor give the slightest impression of becoming a dictator like his adoptive father. Instead, he needed to consolidate his power as a *de facto* sole ruler by laying the foundations of a new kind of constitution, one that would be acceptable to both the Senate and the broader population of Rome.[1]

Octavian proceeded by a series of seemingly small steps. He would retain the office of consul after his term expired, so that by January 29 BC he had filled the post five times. He would proclaim himself 'First in the Senate', *princeps senatus*, so as to be seen to be working within established parameters, when really he was working outside and above them. Octavian would refer to himself increasingly as 'first citizen' of Rome, a manipulation of official parlance that left no doubt who was in charge.[2] In January 27 BC an official constitutional settlement was finally laid down. Octavian's resignation of military powers and restoration of authority over some of the provinces to the Senate were no more than republican gestures. In 23 BC he would receive *imperium maius quam proconsulare* (continuous authority to intervene in the provinces be it on a military or civic level) and the legislative and symbolic powers normally bestowed upon the tribunes of the plebs, only for life, 'a nomenclature of supreme authority rediscovered by [Octavian] so that he could avoid assuming the name of king or dictator, which nevertheless signified that his power was preeminent beyond all others'.[3] By this stage there was no pretending that a return to how things were was even possible. Octavian handed control over the provinces back to the Senate only to have his powers over half of them reinstated. He also received from the Senate a new name, Augustus (the 'serene' one, the 'revered' one, the one who deserved his honours piled high on a plate). Octavian-Augustus was Emperor of Rome.

The women of Augustus' family had an immediate part to play in his establishment of an imperial dynasty. While the idea of a principate that could be passed down from one man to another (as in the former Hellenistic world) was still hazy at Rome, the birth of sons within the family would provide some hope among his circle that, once Augustus had died, the constitution he was creating would survive. The onus fell first and foremost upon Julia as Augustus' only living child. In 25 BC she turned fourteen and was married to her first cousin, Octavia's son, Marcellus. The omens were not, however, promising. As eager as Augustus must have been for the match, he was unwell on the day of the wedding and, as on Julia's original birthday, made his excuses and stayed away.[4] Less than two years later, Marcellus became seriously unwell and died, possibly from plague. He was the first person to be interred in what would become the Julian family mausoleum, constructed as early as 28 BC in anticipation of the dynasty to come.

It was said that when Virgil came to read three books of his *Aeneid* to the family, Octavia fainted when she heard her son's name included among the glorious descendants of Aeneas destined to glorify Rome.[5] Octavia 'made no end to her weeping and mourning throughout the whole course of her life,' wrote Seneca. 'She remained always as she was at the funeral.'[6] The philosopher described her sitting alone in darkened rooms, rejecting new verses composed in Marcellus' honour and, later, brooding on the fact that Livia's elder son would assume the position Marcellus had held as the emperor's son-in-law. Rumours even spread that Livia had engineered Marcellus' death to divert Augustus' affections from his blood-nephew. There was nothing in them, of course, but the fact that this possibility was being discussed showed that Augustus was not alone in thinking of the future of Rome's first family. A dynasty was beginning to evolve. Octavia ensured that her son retained a symbolic place within it by opening a magnificent library in his name. She was evidently less reclusive in her grief than Seneca claimed.

There was no question in Augustus' mind that Julia should remarry as soon as possible. It was said to have been Octavia who first thought of Agrippa as a desirable new husband for the seventeen-year-old, in spite of there being one obvious obstacle. Agrippa was still married to the last woman Augustus had made him leave a wife for. He would have to agree to divorce Claudia Marcella, Octavia's own daughter, and make provision for the children they had been raising before he could even think about taking Julia's hand. Was this too much to ask? An emperor could never ask too much.

In 21 BC the widowed Julia found herself married, aged eighteen, to one of the most enquiring and enterprising men of the age. Building upon his earlier work to improve Rome's water supply – an impressive 500 fountains and 130 reservoirs had been constructed on his orders – Agrippa commissioned a new aqueduct, the Aqua Virgo, and new baths, though both were overshadowed by his basilica dedicated to Neptune, god of the sea.[7] Always broad-minded – Agrippa would one day compose a *Geography* and commission a map of the world – he also laid the foundations of a monumental building to house statues of the Olympian gods. Agrippa's Pantheon would be substantially remodelled after his death but rightly always bore his name. Augustus would claim to have found Rome built of brick and to have left it made of marble, but Julia's new husband was the king of cement.[8] The newlyweds moved into a lavish villa on the banks of the Tiber on the site later occupied by the Renaissance Villa Farnesina.

Julia, henceforth Julia the Elder, had developed an equally inquisitive spirit. She was known for her kindness and love of reading, her quick wit and lively turn of phrase.[9] Augustus had always kept a very close eye upon her. He sought to control every aspect of her life, from the friends she kept down to the clothes she wore. He told her more than a few times that she ought to tone down her appearance and be less conspicuous in the way she dressed and comported herself. He had been known to sneak in while she was having her hair styled to check that she was maintaining his desired levels of modesty. In surviving portraits Julia wears her hair scraped back with a neat quiff-like *nodus* (knot) or roll at the front. The style, also sported by Livia, was subsequently adopted by admiring women all across Rome. Even such simple styling carried its problems. On finding the hairdressers plucking some early grey hairs from her head one day, Augustus asked Julia whether she would prefer to be grey when she was old, or bald.

The emperor was forever drawing unfavourable comparisons between Julia and her stepmother. *Look at the honourable crowd that attends Livia whenever she leaves the palace*, he would say to her, *and look at the dandyish acolytes that follow you.* Julia had an answer ready: 'These men will be old one day too – when I am.'[10] Wit was the one tool Julia could use to disarm her dour and demanding father. 'How much more becoming is this look for a daughter of Augustus?' he once remarked, complimenting her on what she was wearing compared to the day before. 'Yes, because today I did myself up for the eyes of my father, yesterday for the eyes of my husband,' she retorted.[11]

Julia's brazen spirit and predilection for fashionable clothes prompted Augustus to question himself over her fidelity. The moment doubts crossed his mind, he would chastise himself, but his suspicions about Julia never went away. Her safe delivery of four children in quick succession –

Gaius (20 BC), Julia the Younger (19 BC), Lucius (17 BC) and Agrippina (15 BC) – offered him but fleeting comfort, for each bore some resemblance to their father.

Julia often accompanied Agrippa overseas. Travel across the empire naturally carried dangers. In 14 BC, the year after Agrippina was born, Julia ventured as far as Troy with an entourage of slaves.[12] Agrippa was already there as he was on his way home from Sinope in Bithynia-Pontus and realised, to his alarm, that Julia was arriving in the middle of a storm. The waters of the Scamander were rising as her ship approached the coastline. As far as Agrippa could see, there was a very real risk to life. Fortunately, Julia made it to land safely, but Agrippa was so shaken by the experience and by what he perceived as the local people's failure to assist her approach that he introduced fines to the region. This was probably the first time that legislation had been drawn up in the provinces in reaction to the perceived neglect of a woman. The bill was so punitive that the Bithynians had to prevail upon Herod the Great, king of Judaea, to persuade Agrippa to withdraw it.

Herod and his household were on friendly terms with the imperial family of Rome. His sister Salome turned to Livia for advice in some highly sensitive matters. Herod had ordered the execution of Salome's first husband, her uncle Joseph, after she accused him of having an affair with Herod's wife Mariamne, a Hasmonean princess. Salome's second husband, Kostobarus, was similarly executed after she informed upon him to her brother. More recently, Salome had fallen in love with Syllaios, acting ruler of Nabataea. She was desperate to marry him, but Herod had forbidden the union and was urging her to marry one of his dignitaries named Alexas instead.[13] Salome wrote to Livia for her opinion. Livia, less romantic than level-headed, advised her to agree to the match her brother proposed on the basis that it was important to stay onside with him. Herod, as Livia knew, exerted enormous control, and not only over his ten wives.

This might not have been the advice Salome wanted to receive, but she took it, married Alexas, and kept up her correspondence with Livia. Their friendship notably survived a serious diplomatic incident. Salome had given Livia a female slave, Acme, as a present. When it was discovered that Acme was leaking information to Herod from the Roman court, Augustus had her put to death. The possibility that the woman had been sent to Rome in order to spy on imperial affairs might easily have led to the friendship between Herod and Augustus being breached. Some careful diplomacy enabled Herod to re-establish contact following the incident. When Herod died around 4 BC, he left Augustus 10 million denarii and many of his treasures, and Livia some beautiful and expensive clothes.[14] When Salome died years later, in AD 10, she exceeded her husband in her generosity by leaving Livia a number of cities, including Iamneia in Judaea and Phaselis in Lycia. The two women thereby entered the world of diplomatic exchange cultivated most powerfully by the kings and satraps of the Persian Empire in centuries past.

Livia would have been delighted with these territories for she was as partial as Julia to seeing the world beyond Rome. In the 20s BC Augustus travelled across the empire to Gaul, Spain, Greece, Sicily and Asia Minor, and Livia accompanied him at least some of the way. She was certainly with him at Delphi, for next to the Temple of Apollo she made a curious dedication of the Greek letter epsilon, a short 'e', all in gold.[15] The meaning of this letter was unclear even in antiquity; an entire dialogue was composed puzzling over its significance. The Seven Sages were supposed to have dedicated a wooden letter at the site, which a group of Athenians replaced with a bronze edition. Livia had now made herself part of an ancient tradition. It is possible that the letter also had some private importance for her.

Livia probably also visited Sparta and Samos with her husband. She had spent time in the former during her flight from Rome in the civil war and was patron of the latter; her statue stood in the Samian Temple of Hera. It was to Livia that the people of Samos appealed for relief from paying tribute to Rome. While Livia's influence over her husband was considerable, Augustus could not grant the Samians their request, explaining that only the people of Aphrodisias in Asia Minor had attained this privilege, and they had supported him in wartime.[16] The emperor nevertheless expressed his approval of the favour they showed Livia for acting on their behalf.

One of the queens whom Augustus encountered in Samos proved more persuasive. Amanirenas was the ruler of Kush, which lay south of Egypt, in northern Sudan. Since the second century BC the kingdom had been ruled predominantly by queens, known as *kandakes*, who normally passed their power down matrilineally. The Romans, being unused to such traditions, viewed Amanirenas as suspiciously manly – 'a certain masculine woman, maimed in one eye'.[17] Her capacity for aggression was confirmed when she led her troops along the border of Egypt to capture Roman-held cities and forts.[18] The Roman governor of Egypt moved to confront her troops and the two sides engaged. Although the Romans claimed victory over the Kush city of Napata, intense heat forced them to withdraw before they could prevent Amanirenas' people from removing artworks from Egypt, including a bronze portrait of Augustus. The large bust was subsequently buried beneath the steps of a temple in Amanirenas' royal capital of Meroë. Either the queen intended to conceal it as treasure, or she had decided that the Roman emperor deserved nothing better than to be trampled underfoot. She finally met the emperor in the flesh at Samos to make a pact which released her people from the responsibility of paying the Romans tribute. Amanirenas was to rule until her death just over a decade later, when her kingdom fell to another *kandake*, Amanishakheto, possibly her daughter.

The episode provided a rare moment for pause in Augustus' otherwise breathless spate of empire-building. Over the years of his principate, the Romans achieved an almost unparalleled military record by conquering Cantabria, Aquitania, Pannonia, Dalmatia and Illyricum, Raetia and Alpine tribes, and finally recovering the Parthian standards lost with Crassus at Carrhae.[19] Indians and Scythians, 'nations of whom we knew then by hearsay alone', sent envoys to Rome to sue for friendship.[20]

Livia's interest in this work amounted to little more than interference in the eyes of ancient historians and later writers. 'Everyone knew that Livia kept Augustus in strict order and that, if not actually frightened of her, he was at any rate very careful not to offend her,' says Emperor Claudius in Robert Graves's fictionalised account of the family. Contrary to this and contemporary reports, Livia was no meddler in international affairs. She was the closest Augustus had to a partner in the principate aside from Agrippa. An anonymous poet would hail her as a *Romana princeps* – essentially first lady of Rome – and Ovid would describe her similarly.[21] If she liked someone, she would prevail upon Augustus to grant him Roman citizenship, regardless of where he came from. If she liked someone who was facing the death penalty, she would do all she could to save him.[22] It was with good reason that historians asserted that she was the power behind the throne, even if they did so only to malign her.

Livia was able to exert power while maintaining the veneer of matronly propriety admired by her husband. She made his clothes, always careful to ensure that they suited his ascetic tastes, but benefited personally from the services of many helpers. She employed numerous hairdressers, including a female slave from Capri named Dorcas;[23] a masseuse; a pearl-setter; a shoemaker; goldsmiths; a mirror-maker; a clothes-dyer.[24] Her retinue of slaves was quite enormous.

Livia's authority was apparent to even the ordinary people of Rome. She used to sit beside her husband in the imperial box to watch public entertainments, games and gladiatorial fights in the forum.[25] Other women were resigned to the back row when gladiators were performing, barred from attending the theatre before 10 o'clock in the morning, and prohibited from watching athletic contests altogether. There was one rule for Livia and another for everyone else of the female sex bar the Vestal Virgins, who were allocated special seating.

Augustus' efforts to limit women's movements in the city formed part of a broader strategy to 'correct' female morality. The emperor spent a considerable amount of time fretting over falling standards. It struck him that comparatively few wanted to marry any more or to remain married or even faithful to their spouses. Chastity? It was a forgotten virtue. Children? There ought to be more. Augustus' vision for the future of Rome was not as inconsistent as it appears to modern eyes. *Castitas* in the Roman mindset meant faithfulness to one's husband rather than sexual abstinence. It was the former, not the latter, that he wished to encourage.

Augustus introduced a range of laws to tackle the curse of adultery, promote marriage, and reward the birth of legitimate children among the upper classes. The impact of these laws upon the female population of Rome was particularly devastating. Under the *lex Iulia de adulteriis coercendis*, cases of alleged adultery were carried to court so that they could be scrutinised by a third party. Women convicted of adultery, now classified as a crime, were deprived of a third of their property and half their dowry, sent into exile, and prohibited from marrying again if their husbands divorced them, as they were strongly encouraged to do. A man was permitted to kill his daughter and her lover if he encountered them *in flagrante*. Meanwhile, a man who had sex with a non-servile virgin or widow without marrying her could be deprived of half his property if he was of high rank, or banished if he was of a lower status.[26]

There were penalties, too, for those who failed to marry in the green of youth. Augustus' *lex Iulia de maritandis ordinibus*, passed in 18 BC, rewarded women who became mothers to three or more children by releasing them from their male guardians so that they had greater freedom in their movements and management of their property.

Augustus' legislation provoked immediate dissent. Men took to betrothing themselves to the youngest girls they could find in order to put off marrying before they were ready. The emperor reacted by reducing the period that could elapse between engagement and marriage and increasing the rewards available to larger families. Widows and widowers were granted three years' grace before having to marry again. These policies principally affected upper-class women, but the *lex Papia Poppaea* of AD 9 also permitted freedwomen (former slaves) to make their own wills if they produced four children (the only catch was that they still needed to leave a share of their property to their former owners).[27]

Surviving tombstones and funeral orations from the period reveal that some women were able to skirt the limitations imposed by these laws. When a wealthy woman known as Turia died during Augustus' rule, she was commemorated by her husband of forty years with a long eulogy on her tomb praising her loyalty, piety and skill with wool – the usual female virtues – but also her legal victories and self-sacrifice.[28] Turia's parents had been murdered during the war between Julius Caesar and Pompey the Great. Her fiancé was away in Macedonia at the time, and her brother-in-law was in Africa, but Turia and her sister relentlessly pursued the killers and had them brought to justice. Turia then fought a successful battle to protect their patrimony from grasping relatives. She even withstood a physical attack by Lepidus' men while defending her husband's return to Italy during the fraught Second Triumvirate. She endured further sadness when she and her husband proved unable to have children. Feeling sorrier for him than for herself, she suggested that they divorce, so that he could find another woman to live in their house and provide him with a family. She would even help him to find such a woman, she said, and look upon the children as her own. They could divide their property but he could retain control of all of it. Turia's husband loved her too much to countenance any of her suggestions. The fact that Turia made them is a sign that women were making important decisions in their lives in spite of Augustus' laws.

Augustus hoped that his own family would set an example to other women. Julia was by no means the only member of the imperial household to be kept on a tight leash. The emperor 'forbade his daughter and granddaughters . . . from saying or doing anything except what could be listed openly in the daily chronicles'.[29] While Julia's daughters, Julia the Younger and Agrippina (the Elder), were for the most part kept occupied in weaving with other girls in the family, her sons Gaius and Lucius were adopted as Augustus' own and invited to read with him and to perfect their handwriting. The year of their adoption, 2 BC, was also the year of the dedication of Augustus' new temple to Mars the Avenger and the year in which the Senate conferred the title *pater patriae* ('father of his country') upon him, signalling to some degree their acceptance of a Julian royal family. The adoption of two boys, which would be followed by Augustus' successor, nevertheless reflected the election of two consuls and represented, perhaps, an effort to disguise the developing autocracy. Augustus' highly Periclean desire for women to be neither spoken nor written about touched Octavia and Livia the least. Both women were deemed virtuous enough to become part of the fabric of Rome itself with colonnades erected in their honour.

Augustus had grand ideas for improving the look of Rome and the function of its buildings. He commissioned a new forum for his temple to Mars the Avenger, providing a place for senators to meet to discuss war plans or claims for triumphs; governors destined for the provinces could formally gather there before leaving Rome. He cleared the Tiber, which was choked with rubbish; divided the city into wards; repaved the Flaminian Way at his own expense; restored temples which had fallen to ruin. He set fire to all verse alleged to be prophetic except for the Sibylline Books, which were deposited in the pedestal of a sculpture of Apollo on the Palatine Hill.

While Augustus proudly took credit for such a breadth of public works, Livia, too, was involved in the rejuvenation of the city. She oversaw the restoration of temples to Bona Dea, the Good Goddess, and Fortuna Muliebris, the deity who offered Fortune for Women, and dedicated shrines to Pudicitia (Chastity) and Concordia (Harmony). The latter formed part of a new public courtyard, the *Porticus Liviae*, which Livia is thought to have developed in conjunction with her son Tiberius. When the portico was dedicated in 7 BC, Tiberius hosted a dinner for the senators, and Livia a separate dinner for the women of the city.

The women of the wider imperial household found themselves on public display for the first time in 9 BC when Augustus unveiled a magnificent marble altar, almost 12 metres long, known to posterity as the Ara Pacis ('Altar of Peace'). Livia's birthday, 30 January, was chosen as an auspicious time to consecrate the monument, which was commissioned by the Senate and erected on the Campus Martius so that it could be seen by people entering the city from the north. On one level, the altar honoured the emperor's success in bringing peace and order to the wider empire, especially Spain and Gaul, and offered a place for priests and Vestal Virgins to offer annual sacrifice in thanksgiving.[30] On another, it stood as a vivid representation of Augustus' hopes for the future of his family.

The largest relief sculptures on the altar featured a family procession with senators and priests. Here was Augustus and there was Agrippa. Clearly visible were Livia, Tiberius, Drusus, Antonia the Younger, their young son Germanicus, Octavia, Octavia's daughter Antonia the Elder, Julia the Elder and her daughter Julia the Younger. Even one of Fulvia's sons by Mark Antony, Iullus Antonius, now married to Agrippa's ex-wife Marcella, was present. This was the first time that a state relief in Rome had featured men with their wives and children.[31]

It was to Augustus' enduring regret that the reality deviated from the paradigm. Work on the altar began in 13 BC. By the time it was finished, several of the people illustrated upon it had either died or stood on the verge of being cast out of the family altogether. In 12 BC, Agrippa lost his life in Campania following a military campaign in Pannonia, leaving Julia a widow once more. Their son was born later that year and named Agrippa Postumus in his honour. Agrippa's sister Polla celebrated her brother's memory by having his world map put on display. Augustus immediately set about arranging a replacement husband for Julia. Livia's son Tiberius was happily married to Agrippa's daughter Vipsania, who had given birth to a healthy son and was then pregnant with their second child. Tiberius made his reluctance to leave Vipsania perfectly clear, but Augustus forced him to divorce her and marry Julia instead. Livia could not have changed her husband's mind even if she tried. The year Julia was married to Tiberius, 11 BC, the emperor's sister Octavia died, in her fifties, from natural causes. Tiberius' brother Drusus followed her to the grave a couple of years later following a riding accident. He had travelled to

Germany to aid the campaign to push the Roman frontier north beyond the Rhine towards the River Elbe.

The death of Drusus, in particular, intensified the pressure upon the women of Augustus' family to strengthen the dynasty. Julia the Elder now had a duty to extend both Livia's and her father's family line by having a baby with Tiberius. In this she faced a considerable challenge, for her stepbrother-cum-husband was eager not only to leave Rome and prove himself on the battlefield, but to absent himself from her altogether. Tiberius made no secret of his misery at divorcing Vipsania. He could not stand Julia and the feeling was mutual. Julia, wrote Tacitus, 'despised him as unequal to her'.[32] As characters they could hardly have been less alike. She was literary; he was not; she was outgoing; he was not. They somehow managed to set aside their hatred of one another for long enough to conceive a child, but its death in infancy pushed the couple irreparably apart. Tiberius assumed his late brother's command on the Rhine and earned both a triumph and a consulship for 7 BC. The senior magistracy became an increasingly ceremonial role as the empire developed. The following year Tiberius left Rome – and Julia – and retired to the island of Rhodes.

Augustus had always tried to tell himself that his only daughter was deeply virtuous and maternal behind her colourful, playful persona.[33] But as the years went by and her marriage to Tiberius grew colder, rumours of her flirtations with other men had started to spread. It was said that Julia attended parties in the forum after dark.[34] There was no such thing as an innocent cup of wine with friends in Augustus' new age of puritanism. A married woman certainly had no business meeting men outside her husband's home. The very possibility that Julia had flouted the laws that carried her family's name appealed to anyone with an eye for irony. For the stern-browed writers of classical Rome the story wrote itself. 'Entirely unmindful of her great father and husband,' exclaimed one contemporary, 'she left no deed that a woman could perform or shamefully endure unblemished by extravagance or lust . . .'[35] The philosopher Seneca the Younger, always hard upon women he deemed to be disloyal to their husbands, wrote of Julia selecting the speaker's platform from which her father made his addresses as her preferred spot for sex. A statue of the satyr Marsyas, he elaborated, was her preferred pick-up point for prostitution.[36] The natural historian Pliny the Elder (AD 23/24–79) later interpreted a garland discovered behind the statue as long-lost evidence of Julia's sexual profanity.[37]

There was no originality in these men's claims of a well-known woman prostituting herself in the city. Clodia Metelli had been accused of just the same by Catullus half a century earlier. Julia's reputation as 'a paradigm of lust' nevertheless proved as immovable as rock.[38] A witticism no doubt falsely attributed to her offered an explanation as to why, in spite of so many sexual liaisons, she failed to become pregnant with various men's children: 'I never take on a passenger except when the ship is full.'[39] That was, she only ever had sex when she was already pregnant, which was less often than she might have hoped. She had no more children following the loss of her child by Tiberius. It would be highly optimistic to suppose that an emperor's daughter who had suffered a bereavement could jest so freely about her methods of birth control.

In keeping with the spirit of Augustus' laws against adultery, the names of Julia's alleged lovers were revealed publicly and included Quinctius Crispinus, Appius Claudius, Sempronius Gracchus, Cornelius Scipio and Iullus Antonius.[40] As the son of Fulvia and Mark Antony, late enemies of Augustus, Iullus Antonius was by far the most intriguing character on the list. A senator and former consul, he was still married to Agrippa's former wife Marcella and had three children by her. Unlike Tiberius he was fond of literature. Horace believed he showed particular promise as a poet and predicted that he would one day turn his hand to celebrating Augustus' achievements in verse.[41] Iullus Antonius' literary potential was of less interest to suspicious senators than his parentage. What did the young man mean by having an affair with the daughter of his parents' enemy? Who was to say that he had not seduced Julia as a first step towards seizing power?[42] While most of Julia's other alleged paramours were sent into exile, Iullus Antonius was sentenced to death.

Augustus was so aggrieved by the fiasco and the apparent confirmation of his worst fears about his daughter that he refused to receive visitors for some time. He wrote a letter on the matter to the Senate and took the extraordinary initiative of filing on Julia's behalf for her divorce from Tiberius.[43] By his own legislation against adultery, the emperor had turned what would once have been a domestic matter, to be settled in private, into a raucous public scandal. Under his own rules he had no option but to subject Julia to the harshest available punishment – second only to death.

In 2 BC, Julia was put on board a ship for Pandateria (Ventotene), a small volcanic island 70 kilometres off the west coast of Italy, just across the water from Naples. While at first approach one might have said it looked quaint, with vineyards enwrapping the land upon which Augustus' villa stood, any charms it had paled upon closer inspection. The island was so mouse-ridden that the fields had to be laid with traps.[44] Julia was to be kept under house arrest and deprived of all nice things. No wine, no sophisticated food, none of the beautifying clothes she liked to wear. As a prisoner she could receive no human company except by her father's express permission. Even then the emperor required a complete inventory of each visitor's particulars: age, height, distinguishing body marks, moles. Julia's mainstay was her mother.[45] Scribonia, the woman Augustus had abandoned in labour, voluntarily accompanied her daughter into exile.

Scribonia's decision to leave Rome was made easier by the fact that Julia was her sole surviving daughter. Julia's little-known elder half-sister, Cornelia, had died, but not before winning the admiration of Propertius. The poet composed a beautiful set of verses in her voice from beyond the grave. 'I was united with you in your bed,' she called up to her husband Paullus, a senator, from the depths of Hades. She spoke of her faithfulness, her nobility, her blamelessness, and of the children she bore. While presented as the work of a woman, the poem was tinged by values more commonly expressed by men. Propertius' Cornelia urges her daughter to marry and remain married for the rest of her life on the basis that this was 'the highest reward in a woman's glory, when wandering rumour can praise the marriage bed at the end of time'.[46] She begs her husband to play the role of a mother – to kiss the children when they cry, to grieve for her only when they are not looking. She regrets the pain she caused her own mother by dying. Most tellingly of all, revealed Propertius, this devout, honourable, quiet Cornelia earned Augustus' praise as 'a woman worthy of being sister to his own daughter'.[47]

Augustus indeed often prayed that his daughter had been someone other than Julia. He prayed that he might even have been father to her former slave Phoebe when Phoebe committed suicide. But Augustus' feelings about his daughter were not shared by the majority in Rome. Julia had barely been exiled from the city when petitions began to come in urging her recall. Augustus, rattled by the public outpouring of emotion, grunted that Rome would sooner see fire mixed with water than Julia returned. Julia's loyal followers responded by flinging lit torches into the Tiber.[48]

Infuriated by their persistence, Augustus threatened to curse the men among them with wives and daughters as troublesome as his own if they dared mention Julia ever again. He was predictably slow to soften and relent. It was five years before he agreed to transfer Julia to the mainland. From Pandateria she was to make her way to Rhegium on the toe of Italy. Livia, reacting perhaps to popular opinion, sent Julia some of her own slaves to make her exile more comfortable.[49] It is clear where her sympathies lay.

The political consequences of Julia's exile were more serious than either her father or her former husband could have anticipated. Tiberius' estrangement from Julia, and Julia's from Rome, opened up a gulf between Tiberius and Augustus and cast doubt upon the very future of the dynasty. Livia had every reason to grow concerned for her son's place in the imperial family. Julia's boys Gaius and Lucius, potential rivals to the throne, were looking increasingly promising. Not long after Julia was banished, Gaius travelled east to Syria and Parthia, where he dined with the king and conducted himself in a manner that befitted a Roman dignitary.[50] His younger brother Lucius was wise beyond his years and potentially more amiable than the comparatively charmless Tiberius.

The boys' sudden deaths only partially helped to heal the rift caused by Julia's absence. Lucius died in Marseille following a short illness in AD 2. Gaius lost his life a mere eighteen months later after sustaining a wound in battle. Their deaths were so convenient for Tiberius, who now became Augustus' most viable heir, that classical historians implicated his ambitious mother in the double tragedy.[51] 'Livia: a blight upon the nation as a mother,' wrote Tacitus with characteristic sharpness, 'a blight upon the house of Caesar as a stepmother.'[52] There was very probably no truth to the rumours of her involvement in the demise of Gaius and Lucius, nor in that of Marcellus previously, but it is plain to see why they gained currency. Three great rivals to the ever more remote Tiberius had been removed from the emperor's horizon. All had shared Augustan blood.

The emperor, no doubt prompted by Livia, adopted Tiberius as his own son 'for the sake of the *res publica*' in AD 4. At the same time, he adopted the surviving brother of Gaius and Lucius, his grandson Agrippa Postumus, Julia's son by Agrippa. Tiberius had the advantage of being old enough to hold tribunician power. Agrippa Postumus, still only fifteen, had the advantage of being a blood relative of Augustus. Fortunately for Tiberius, his stepson was not only immature, but reckless and uncultured, badly tempered, brutish, and observably hostile towards Livia. Still three years later the conduct of Agrippa Postumus left much to be desired. For reasons now unknown, Augustus had him transferred from Rome to Surrentum (Sorrento) and then to the island of Planasia in the Tyrrhenian Sea. Whatever the young man had done, it was deemed serious, for he was placed under armed guard and deprived of the opportunity to pursue his hobbies. It was particularly torturous for the keen fisherman to find himself surrounded by water but prohibited from throwing down a line. According to Tacitus, it was Livia, not Augustus, who gave the directions for Agrippa Postumus' miserable exile, but it seems unlikely that she would have made such an obvious attempt to thwart her son's chief rival.

Once the imperial family had exiled one of its members, it found it easy to repeat the process. While her mother, Julia the Elder, was confined to Rhegium, and her brother Agrippa Postumus languished on Planasia, Julia the Younger was making her own life in Rome. She had grown into a beautiful young woman with wide eyes, a small mouth, and long hair which she either curled and pulled back, or twisted into a chignon, if her surviving portraits are to any extent true to life. She had been married to a cousin, Lucius Aemilius Paullus, a senator and son of the late Cornelia, whom Propertius had eulogised. They shared a grandmother in Scribonia and a daughter named Aemilia Lepida. If the younger Julia had a weakness, it was for expensive property, lovely interiors and novelties; she kept a dwarf named Conopas, who at just two feet tall was the smallest man in Rome.[53] In this she was most unlike her father; ostentation for Augustus meant pinning a couple of enormous skeletons of extinct sea creatures to a wall and calling them 'giants' bones'.[54] When Augustus looked at his granddaughter's collections he despaired. He could not abide the all-over gaudiness of the villa she had built in the Italian countryside.

The emperor might have forgiven Julia the Younger her taste in candelabras and pillows had she not given signs of sharing her mother's taste in men. History began to repeat itself as rumours emerged of the younger Julia committing adultery behind her husband's back. There was no long list of lovers this time, only one with an alarming name, Decimus Junius Silanus.

Julia the Younger's affair with the ambitious senator allegedly began after she found herself alone in Rome. Her husband had been found guilty of treason and, like her closest relatives, sent into exile. It was not long before Silanus was facing banishment as well. The possibility that he had become embroiled in a plot against the emperor's life would be rendered only more credible by his relationship with Julia. A senator who sought to kill an emperor would be foolish *not* to pursue the emperor's granddaughter.

Rumours of affairs between imperial women and senators often proved to be empty. In this case, however, Augustus was probably right to be suspicious of Silanus and his familiarity with his granddaughter. There was more to this story than most people in Rome could possibly have realised. Julia the Younger, it seems, had been plotting to rescue her mother and brother from exile.[55] Two men, Audasius and Epicadus, were said to have agreed to abduct the elder Julia and Agrippa Postumus and take them to the legions overseas.[56] It is just possible that Silanus was not only Julia's lover, but her accomplice in this unlikely plan. Another Silanus, Marcus Junius Silanus Torquatus, went on to marry Julia the Younger's daughter Aemilia Lepida, which suggests a close relationship between Julia and the Silanus family. The possibility that a senator had lent his hand to a plot to undo Augustus' actions was far more threatening than a romantic affair. For all anyone knew, this was the beginning of a plan to reunite Julia the Younger with her mother and put her brother on the throne.

Silanus soon left for exile and Augustus saw to it that Julia the Younger was also removed from the public eye as swiftly as possible. Rather than send her to Rhegium, where she could be with her mother, Augustus dispatched her to the faraway Adriatic archipelago of Isole Tremiti.[57] Like her mother and brother before her, Julia the Younger had become an exile. Her extravagant Italian villa was razed to the ground.

The intrigue surrounding Julia's sudden fall from grace deepened as it transpired that the poet Ovid had also been sent into exile upon Augustus' orders. Ovid was, at fifty, the most famous writer in Rome. He had surprised readers with the subversiveness and explicit nature of his verse since his youth. In the *Amores*, which he is thought to have begun while still in his teens, he advised a young married woman to flirt with him surreptitiously across the dinner table. His advice to her, which included touching his foot, reading the secret messages he wrote for her in wine upon the tabletop, and stroking her cheek whenever sex crossed her mind, could easily be taken up by the young men and women he implored to be his readers. The publication of his more recent work, the *Ars Amatoria* ('Art of Love'), had proven even more scandalous with its recommendations of the sexual positions best suited to each female body type. The work effectively made a mockery of Augustus' moral crusade and risked overshadowing the poet's true genius. Ovid's magnum opus, the *Metamorphoses*, was nearing completion.

Ovid documented his miserable journey to the ends of the earth to take up residence in Tomis (Constanța, Romania) on the Black Sea coast, where nobody spoke Latin, only Greek; where nobody knew his name. The cause of his exile, he claimed, was *carmen et error*, 'a poem and a mistake'.[58] The poem was the *Ars Amatoria*, but the *error* remains a mystery and was arguably more serious, given that the *Ars Amatoria* had been available in Rome for almost a decade by now.

Ovid described having seen something by accident, a crime, which made his eyes 'guilty'.[59] What had Ovid seen? Was it Julia the Younger meeting Silanus or the men who planned to rescue her mother and brother from exile? It was largely bad luck that had landed him in exile, Ovid said, but there was also some fault he could not entirely defend himself over.[60] Had he been flirting with Julia? Or was he a coward, afraid to report what he saw, anxious to save himself from being implicated in a plot?[61] Whatever Ovid might have seen, it probably involved Julia, and was considered sufficiently serious for Augustus to send him as far away as possible, yet not so serious as to warrant his death. The poet's celebrity might well have helped save him. The incident inspired fear in Ovid's friends, most of whom scarpered, just when he needed them most.

While in exile, Julia the Younger delivered a baby, which Augustus refused to recognise.[62] A message was sent across the seas giving orders for the infant to be abandoned. Was the child her husband's, or her lover's, or was Julia raped upon arriving in exile? It is impossible to say. Livia sent her money, which may suggest she knew that Julia was suffering a worse punishment than she deserved.[63] The wateriness of the accusation brought against the young woman and its similarity to that brought against her mother give the impression that there was more to her exile than met the eye. It was almost too easy to represent the two Julias as riding roughshod over Augustus' legislation. The truth may never be discovered, but the possibility remains that Ovid had discovered what Julia the Younger was really up to, and that her liaison with Silanus was secondary to a plot to have her mother and brother brought home from exile. Augustus bore the situation as badly as he had every other drama in his family. If ever the name of Julia or Agrippa Postumus came up in conversation, he would quote Homer, 'If only I had remained unmarried and died a barren man.' Julia the Younger was never to see her mother or brother again. To Augustus they would forever remain, simply, his 'three pestilent growths'.[64]

Chapter XVIII

Empresses in the Shadows

You know the journey's a solemn weight lifted from your girl's mind?
I'm now allowed to be in Rome for my birthday.
May that day, the day of my birth, be a celebration for everyone,
For you did not expect to be so lucky when it came around.

Sulpicia, 3.15, first century BC

Julia the Elder never returned to Rome. In AD 14 she died in Rhegium in her fifty-third year, probably from starvation. In her final months she was deprived of even her limited allowances and put under strict house arrest. Two decades later, her youngest daughter Agrippina would die on her prison island and her elder daughter, Julia the Younger, would also die in exile.[1] The fates of all three women were determined by the rise of Augustus' successor.

Augustus predeceased Julia by a matter of months, dying in Nola, Campania, the same place as his father, on 19 August AD 14. The chroniclers believed that Livia hastened his end, fearful that he was experiencing a change of heart and intended to recall Agrippa Postumus, now aged twenty-five, and make him his heir in place of fifty-four-year-old Tiberius.[2] The death of Agrippa Postumus a short time later appeared to confirm their theory that Livia – and Tiberius – was on the warpath. There is no reason to suspect that Augustus died from anything other than natural causes. He was just shy of his seventy-sixth birthday and had recently caught a chill and suffered a bout of diarrhoea.[3] His lower jaw had also dropped, suggesting he might have had a stroke.[4] There were stronger grounds for suspecting that Livia had a hand in Agrippa Postumus' demise. As soon as her husband died, if the ancient historians are to be believed, she had the house and surrounding roads sealed by guards while Tiberius hastened home from Illyricum. Since there was no established protocol for transferring power under the new regime, Livia was able to have two announcements made simultaneously: Augustus was dead and Tiberius was emperor. The transition might have been more complicated had Agrippa Postumus survived to dispute it.

The Vestal Virgins opened the three sealed scrolls Augustus had placed in their care. At their reading in the Senate House, Livia and Tiberius were named as chief heirs to his estate, which was valued in excess of 150 million sesterces. Women in Rome were ordinarily prohibited from inheriting so much, but the Senate permitted the law to be waived so that Livia could receive one-third of the total. Livia was posthumously adopted into her husband's family and granted the seminal title Augusta. With Julia the Elder gone – Tiberius was responsible for removing her allowances and reinforcing her confinement – Livia became in both name and person the strongest living embodiment of Augustus and his ideals.

Livia's position as mother of the new emperor was nevertheless far from secure. News of Augustus' death and Tiberius' accession inspired mutiny among the legions on the Rhine, where many soldiers had been fighting for decades and grown weary of waiting for their retirement and pensions. A few brave souls attempted to flatter their commander Germanicus, son of the late Drusus and Antonia the Younger, by suggesting that he ought to succeed Augustus instead.[5] Germanicus (his father had held the same honorary name in acknowledgement of his victories in the country) did his best to ease tensions, but proved considerably less competent and persuasive than his wife.

Agrippina (the Elder), daughter of Julia the Elder and Agrippa, had followed her husband Germanicus to Germany with their toddling son. The soldiers, tickled by the sight of his miniature army footwear with its criss-cross laces, cooed over Gaius 'Little Boot' Caligula.[6] Their superiors did not want to see Agrippina endanger her life in the mutiny. They pleaded with her to withdraw to safety, first of all because she was the granddaughter of Augustus, second of all because she was heavily pregnant.[7] Agrippina did as she was told, but the sight of her making her way under heavy duress with the other generals' wives to seek sanctuary in the camp of a Germanic tribe shamed the Roman soldiers far more than did any of Germanicus' vituperative rhetoric. The soldiers quickly downed their weapons and Agrippina was permitted to turn back. She was nearing the period of confinement which Roman women traditionally entered before giving birth and (as Germanicus insisted) would be tucked away soon enough. In late AD 14 or 15 she would deliver a daughter, Agrippina the Younger, at Oppidum Ubiorum, a Roman settlement founded by Agrippa in 38 BC on the Rhine in modern-day Cologne. Another daughter, Julia Drusilla, would follow a year or so later at Ambitarvium (Koblenz).[8]

It was to her husband's military advantage that Agrippina the Elder remained in the camp. As Germanicus continued to push Rome's frontier deeper into Germany, reports arrived that his men had been surrounded and that a column of Germans was marching on Gaul. The Romans were so perturbed by the news that they contemplated destroying the bridge that lay over the Rhine at Vetera (Xanten) in order to protect themselves from attack. 'A woman of enormous spirit adopted during those days the duties of a general,' wrote Tacitus, describing the moment Agrippina stepped forward to stop the men from cutting themselves off on the riverbank.[9] The historian might not have approved wholeheartedly of her assumption of military authority, but he had to admit that she was immensely proactive, bestowing 'clothes and bandages on the helpless and wounded soldiers' in addition to intervening on the front line. Pliny the Elder, who conducted three tours of Germany as a young man, documented Agrippina's role in the army in his twenty-volume history of Rome's German Wars. Tacitus drew on Pliny's (since lost) account as he wrote of Agrippina standing at the very head of the bridge and lavishing praise and thanks upon the returning legions.

Agrippina's actions made a deep but unfavourable impression upon Tiberius. 'There was nothing left for the generals,' he complained, 'when a woman went among the troops, tended to the standards and tried her hand at bribery, as if it wasn't enough that she carried her son around in a common soldier's uniform and wished for him to be called Caesar Caligula.'[10] Tiberius had adopted Germanicus as his son in AD 4 upon Augustus' orders. His profound jealousy of Germanicus extended to jealousy of his wife Agrippina. Tiberius was so riled by reports of her capability that he convinced himself she 'had more power within the army than the legates and the generals'. Anger and insecurity made Tiberius exaggerate her hand, but Agrippina had, it was true, succeeded where

Germanicus had failed. She had helped to suppress a mutiny and saved his anxious men from making a rash and irreparable mistake.

The irritation Tiberius felt at Agrippina's assumption of authority was characteristic of his feelings towards women. On becoming emperor, he entered into what would become a lifelong dispute with Livia over their relative positions, not merely as mother and son and emperor and subject, but as man and woman. Livia's smallest actions grated. What did she mean by having her name inscribed before his on a statue to Augustus?[11] Why was she co-signing *his* correspondence?[12] What entitled her to host senators independently of him? Augusta had taken her title literally and assumed many of the late emperor's responsibilities. Tiberius did not need to be reminded that he owed his principate to her and her marriage to Augustus. When the Senate proposed adding the words 'Son of Livia' as well as 'Son of Augustus' to his honorific titles, he practically exploded.[13]

Tiberius quickly reached the conclusion that Livia wanted to co-rule. Ancient historians perpetuated the idea that they were engaged in a bitter power struggle, with domineering Livia striving to overshadow her son and usurp his role, and Tiberius fighting to wrest authority back from her. In truth, their struggle was more one of experience versus inexperience. Livia understood the workings of the empire better than Tiberius. He was determined to do things his own way. Livia tried to offer him guidance. Tiberius reminded her that she was a mere woman with no right to wade into the politics of men.

As unnerving as it was, the rise of Agrippina in Germany offered the emperor some distraction from the rise of Livia in Rome. An opportunity for Tiberius to redistribute the heroic couple and so re-establish his authority in the public eye came when Germanicus returned to Rome to celebrate a triumph for his progress. The Germanic campaign was far from complete, but Tiberius realised that it was beyond the scope of one man and believed that Germanicus (and Agrippina) would be better placed elsewhere. A dispute had arisen in Judaea, Syria and Armenia over the burdens of Roman taxation.[14] Germanicus and Agrippina would go east. Agrippina broke the journey at Lesbos to deliver her third daughter and final child, Julia Livilla.

The people of Mytilene, Sappho's former city, would later hail Agrippina as their benefactor and honour her with a statue.[15] What she could not have known at this stage was that the new Roman governor whom

Tiberius had sent to Syria, Gnaeus Calpurnius Piso, had made it his brief to challenge her husband at every turn. Piso had formerly served alongside Tiberius as consul and earned his trust. He was, nonetheless, 'a violent character, a stranger to compliance, with an engrained ferocity inherited from his father', and a pride inherited through both blood and marriage.[16] Piso's wife Plancina, whom he had to thank for much of his wealth, mirrored Agrippina in her readiness to become involved in military work. In the words of Tacitus, she 'did not adhere to the limits which befit women, but attended cavalry exercises and manoeuvres of the cohorts and hurled insults at Agrippina and Germanicus'.

The relationship between the two couples deteriorated at a distance. While Germanicus did his best to restore calm across the region, appointing a client king, Artaxias III, over Armenia, and converting Cappadocia into a Roman province in exchange for lowering taxes, Piso proved to be consistently stubborn to his commands. It took no more than a few meetings between them for an intense personal enmity to develop. When Germanicus fell ill in October AD 19 at Antioch, near what is now the Turkish-Syrian border, he immediately thought of poison, and of Piso. There was no other explanation for the sudden appearance of bruising all over his body.[17] Few ordinary maladies could cause a robust thirty-four-year-old to start frothing uncontrollably at the mouth.

A frantic search was made of everything around him. The discoveries were grim. Human remains had been hidden beneath Germanicus' floorboards and behind his walls. His name was found etched on curse tablets bearing evil spells.[18] Someone clearly wanted to do him harm. Naturally Germanicus' symptoms worsened as panic set in. While he could still speak, he told as many people as he could that he was dying at the hands of not only Piso, but his wife Plancina, too.

When Agrippina hastened to his bedside, Germanicus implored her to 'lay aside her ferocious spirit, to endure her savage fate, and not, when she returned to Rome, to enrage those stronger than herself through political rivalry'.[19] He said all this within earshot of his friends, hoping that they might hold her to it, before leaning in and whispering something in her ear. He then slipped away. During the cremation of his body, it was observed that the heart remained intact, as if saturated with poison.

Agrippina sailed home with her young brood. A great crowd of sympathisers, many still in shock, awaited them feverishly at Brundisium.

The sight of the young widow grasping a funeral urn in one arm and her children in the other bred feelings of hopeless despair. Even Tiberius was moved to send two praetorian cohorts with magistrates from southern Italy to pay their last respects to his deceased adopted son, though neither he nor Livia felt it appropriate to make a public appearance. As Germanicus' ashes were carried to the Mausoleum of Augustus, the silence of the crowd gave way to fervent mourning and cries of support and praise for Agrippina. Temples were stoned; altars of the gods were overturned; household gods were thrown into the streets; even newborn babies were exposed, as if deemed ill-omened.[20] Tiberius had little choice but to issue a proclamation to the Roman people to put an end to their excessive grieving.

The case against Piso and Plancina was referred to the Senate at Tiberius' instruction. A female poisoner from Syria named Martina, allegedly a friend of Plancina, was dragged to Rome under accusation of supplying the fatal dose. She died before she could testify. Tiberius knew that people suspected him of putting Piso up to the task of murdering Germanicus.[21] He assured his senators that he was giving them the opportunity to make up their own minds as to whether he was guilty or not. The prosecution addressed everything from the curses and spells to earlier charges of extortion which had little relevance to the current case.[22] Plancina initially pledged to share in her husband's fate and die with him if the jury found him guilty. But she then changed her mind and appealed to Livia for support. She did so publicly and to considerable scandal. Was it right that the mother of the emperor should grant an audience to the alleged killer of her grandson?[23]

Livia did grant an audience to the alleged killer of her grandson – and saw her acquitted. It is known for certain that Livia was responsible for securing Plancina's release because her intervention was recorded in a senatorial decree. Remarkably, the document, dated 10 December AD 20, was rediscovered in the 1980s. The Latin inscription, one of the longest ever found, included extraordinary details:

> Concerning the case of Plancina, against whom very many serious charges were made, since she confessed that she placed every hope in the compassion of our Princeps and Senate. Several times our Princeps took to ask that this board be satisfied with the punishment of

> Gnaeus Piso while sparing his wife and son Marcus. At the strong request of his own mother, he interceded on behalf of Plancina, and received his mother's reasons for her request that he do so. The Senate testified that Julia Augusta [Livia], most worthy of the Republic not only because she gave birth to our Princeps, but also on account of her many great deeds and acts of kindness to men of all orders, while she was in a position to ask with utmost authority what she liked of the Senate, used this right very sparingly; the great devotion of our Princeps towards his mother ought to be favoured and indulged; it is the Senate's pleasure that the punishment of Plancina be remitted.[24]

The senators' willingness to indulge Livia's 'strong request' on the basis that she seldom asked for anything was striking. The comment weighs against claims in the literary sources that Livia was constantly hosting senators and, by implication, meddling in affairs of state, prompting Tiberius to remove her from public business altogether.[25] Livia evidently believed that Plancina was innocent. Her failure to act similarly for Piso suggests that her impression of him was neutral at best and suspicious at worst.

Piso was duly condemned to death and subsequently slit his own throat. Evidence proving that Tiberius had issued the orders for Germanicus' murder was allegedly kept private.[26] Plancina was safe for as long as Livia was alive. Many years later, Tiberius would reopen the case against her as part of his mission to undo his mother's noble work, and Plancina would also take her own life.

Despite seeing justice for her husband's killer, Agrippina refused to 'lay aside her ferocious spirit, to endure her savage fate' and keep quiet. She was, in the words of Tacitus, *semper atrox*, always fierce, always fired-up.[27] She had every right to be angry over Germanicus' death. Tiberius, well aware of this, would ultimately punish her for her outspokenness by having her flogged. He initially supported her elder sons, Nero and Drusus, by commending them to the Senate. He then took the advice of Lucius Aelius Sejanus, Prefect of the Praetorian Guard (commander of a select band of troops drawn up for the emperor's protection), and began to move against them.

Sejanus, the son of a Roman equestrian of Tuscan descent, was a shady character, self-possessed, yet adept at feigning servility when it suited him. He enhanced the position of the Guard by having the battalions congregate in a single camp in the city on the pretence that they would be best placed that way to scramble in the event of an emergency.[28] Having any armed soldiers stationed within the *pomerium* violated laws that had been in place under the Republic. Power-hungry, he professed to act in Tiberius' interest: by demoting the kin of Germanicus, he might secure the succession of Drusus, Tiberius' natural son by his beloved first wife Vipsania. The sudden death of Drusus in AD 23, however, left only Tiberius' grandson Tiberius Gemellus (adopted by Tiberius and named his co-heir with Gaius) and Agrippina's sons as viable heirs. Some years later, Sejanus' wife Apicata would claim that her husband had poisoned the heir to the throne Drusus with the help of Drusus' wife. The woman in question was Sejanus' mistress Livilla.

Tiberius, unaware at this time of any suspicions surrounding the death of his son, was less supportive than Sejanus had hoped of his plans to marry Livilla. The emperor questioned the worthiness of the match between his guardsman and his former daughter-in-law and also niece. Suspecting, perhaps, an ulterior motive, he warned Sejanus that Livilla would never be satisfied with a mere equestrian like him and stressed that he could not support the marriage in the foreknowledge that it would aggravate Agrippina.

Sejanus played on Tiberius' apparent fascination with Agrippina and her influence by making her the object of his ensuing attack. With help from Livilla, the rumour was put about that the stout-hearted widow of Germanicus was intent on seizing power herself. To give life to this unlikely tale, Sejanus fabricated a 'party of Agrippina' among the common people and warned the Senate that its members and rival clans were so fervid that they could spark a civil war if the current situation went unchecked.[29] This would have been the first time that a political party formed around an imperial woman. While the novelty of the scenario failed to rouse Tiberius' suspicions, the historian Tacitus proved susceptible to the lie, describing Agrippina decades later as 'intolerant of equality, ambitious to rule, and in her mannish preoccupations, free of the defects of ordinary women'.

Sejanus did not doubt Agrippina's strength. He even targeted her friends and family in an effort to weaken her.[30] An innocent woman, Sosia Galla, was exiled and deprived of much of her property after her husband was accused of treason and driven to suicide. Agrippina's second cousin, Claudia Pulchra, was put on trial for treason, adultery and dabbling in dark arts, and convicted alongside her alleged lover.

Outraged by the proceedings, Agrippina went directly to Tiberius and began to rail at him just as he was performing a sacrifice to the now deified Augustus. What duplicity, she remarked, in honouring Augustus as a god while persecuting her, his granddaughter! 'It is not to voiceless statues that his divine spirit has been transposed,' she said, pointing to herself, 'the real thing, sprung from heavenly blood, here, perceives she's in danger . . .'[31] Agrippina recognised the attack on Claudia as an indirect attack upon herself. Tiberius laid hold of her and issued a firm warning in Greek tragic verse: 'Do you consider yourself injured, little girl, since you are not ruler?'

This episode and what followed were recorded in the memoirs of Agrippina's daughter. If only the younger Agrippina's writings had survived, they would surely have constituted the most fascinating record by a woman of the first century. We know that they included her account of her mother falling ill around this time and approaching Tiberius to ask his permission to remarry. We also know that Tiberius prevaricated and put off giving her a decision on the matter. It is probable that the man Agrippina desired was Asinius Gallus, the second husband and widower of Vipsania, Tiberius' first wife.[32] The emperor would later name Gallus as Agrippina's lover. The prospect of a marriage between Agrippina and a man whom the emperor naturally resented must have worried him. Agrippina's distress at Tiberius' inaction may well be imagined.

Sejanus convinced Agrippina that she should sooner expect a dose of poison from Tiberius than an answer to the question of her marriage. She subsequently grew so paranoid that she feared eating anything that was passed to her across the emperor's table. It is a sign of Agrippina's conviction over her importance within the imperial family that she believed herself to be a prime target for murder.[33] Her anxieties, overblown yet understandable, brought a wry smile to Tiberius' face. He momentarily laid aside his animosity towards his mother to indulge in a joke at Agrippina's expense. His relationship with his daughter-in-law would never recover.

Tiberius liked to talk of handing his powers down to the consuls one day and restoring the Republic, but most people now recognised this as a rhetorical trope rather than a promise.[34] Augustus had often tantalised his supporters with the prospect of abdicating. He never had. If there was a broad acceptance of the fact that the emperor as a figure was here to stay, Tiberius muddied public expectations by deciding to retire from public life – and from Rome – altogether.

The sixty-seven-year-old emperor – bald, stooped and ravaged by facial sores as well as, allegedly, his mother's quest for dominance – withdrew in AD 26 to Campania and then Capri to live a more relaxed, debauched and, so it was said, perverted life while ruling predominantly through letters and messengers from his twelve villas. Sejanus took on much of the day-to-day management of the empire in his place. As relieved as Agrippina might have been at Tiberius' departure, the rise of Sejanus spelled disaster for her and her sons, who now found themselves routinely followed and spied upon. Their every word was chronicled as though spoken in court.[35]

Tiberius grew tired of them all. A letter made its way from his desk to the Senate at Rome denouncing Agrippina for her 'arrogant mouth and haughty spirit' and accusing her of plotting to seek refuge with the armies in Germany.[36] This was a credible supposition given Agrippina's fear for her own life and continuing popularity with the military following her period on the Rhine. Her eldest son Nero Julius was accused in the same letter of performing depraved sexual acts with other men.

The Senate was divided over what to do, but the Roman people experienced no such crisis of conscience. While the senators sat in conference, protesters carried effigies of the accused around the circumference of the Senate House, insisting that the emperor's letter had been falsified and did not represent his true desires. They supported Agrippina and her boys and could not believe that Tiberius would turn so viciously against them. The public misjudged the relationship between the emperor and the family of the late Germanicus. Tiberius reaffirmed his orders and added that Agrippina and Nero Julius were to be exiled separately.

Agrippina need not have asked where she was going. Her mother Julia the Elder had spent five years on Pandateria before being moved to Rhegium. The prison island had space for a new recruit. Agrippina remembered what had happened to the elder Julia and was realistic about her own fate. And yet, she refused to leave quietly, and just as she had railed following her husband's death, she began to berate Tiberius for his cruelty. The emperor responded more staunchly this time by having a centurion physically assault her. The attack on Agrippina was so vicious that she lost an eye.[37] There was nothing she could do to help her elder sons. Nero Julius would be left to languish on the island of Pontia until his untimely and suspicious death in AD 31. Drusus would be imprisoned a short while later in a dungeon beneath the Palatine Hill. Deprived of food, he would eat the contents of his mattress and last eight days before finally succumbing to starvation.[38]

Unlike Drusus, Agrippina attempted to end her captivity as quickly as possible by going on hunger strike, only to be force-fed. She finally achieved her purpose a few years later, in the autumn of AD 33, when she died of malnourishment. Tiberius took credit for not having her strangled like Sejanus. The Praetorian, finally falling foul of Tiberius in the year of his first consulship, was executed together with his children. Since there was no precedent for strangling virgins, Sejanus' daughter was raped and then subjected to the noose with her brother. The bodies of all three were rolled down the steps from the Roman Capitol and into the River Tiber.

Agrippina's birthday was decreed a day of ill omen. Of her three sons, only the youngest, Caligula, survived. Following her exile, he and his sisters had gone to live with their great-grandmother Livia, who had notably saved Plancina during the trial of Germanicus' alleged killers, but not their mother. In his later years, Caligula would describe Livia, flatteringly yet pointedly, as 'Odysseus in a woman's stole'.[39] She was in her eighties then and had largely withdrawn from public life, but the revered Augusta remained formidable, a resourceful woman of many wiles.

Livia must have embraced the opportunity to forge a connection with her great-grandson after her relationship with her only living son had become irreparable. During their final row, she had lost her temper with Tiberius and produced a strong-box containing some of Augustus' letters. The late emperor had made no effort to conceal his disdain for his stepson. As rattled as he was by the unflattering portrait Augustus had drawn of him, Tiberius directed his anger rather at Livia for having hoarded such defamatory missives for so long.[40] He was stubborn to the last. Just one short meeting between Livia and Tiberius was recorded in the last years of her life. Tiberius did not return to Rome to visit her when she suffered a fall, nor did he attend her funeral after she died, in AD 29, at the age of eighty-six.[41] It was Caligula who mounted the speaker's platform in the Roman forum to deliver the funeral oration.

Unlike Tiberius, the people of Rome were deeply moved by Livia's death, so much so that they formally grieved for her over an entire year. In recognition of the lives she had saved, the children she had raised, the dowries she had helped to create for impecunious daughters, the senators voted to dedicate an arch in her name.[42] Livia was the first woman in Rome's history to be granted such an honour; however, Tiberius saw to it that the arch was never built.

Livia had been helping to raise Caligula when she died. The young man then passed into the care of his paternal grandmother, Antonia the Younger, daughter of Mark Antony and Augustus' sister Octavia. Widowed young following the riding accident of Tiberius' brother Drusus, Antonia had chosen to live at the imperial palace with her in-laws, Livia and Augustus, apparently because she was still so in love with her late husband.[43]

Financially, Antonia had no reason either to stay, or to go in search of a new husband. Her properties were already quite substantial enough. She had acquired the enormous villa with fishponds formerly owned by Hortensius at Bauli in fashionable Baiae and made her own very colourful additions. The fish had been famous since Republican times, but Antonia had a pair of earrings put on her favourite eel, to the horror of censorious writers.[44] The fact that eels lack distinctive ears offered no impediment: gills would serve perfectly well.

The playful gesture evoked the spirit of Cleopatra VII, whose former territory Antonia also now had a share in. Her landholdings in Egypt incorporated wheatfields, palm groves and farms for livestock, and were sprawling. It is very likely that she received much of this property via Augustus from the estate of her father Mark Antony. A piece of papyrus reveals that Antonia shared one of her Egyptian plots with Livia and was able to pass it down through her family after she died.[45] While she relied upon a number of estate managers to look after her land in her absence, including Alexander the Alabarch, a famously wealthy Jewish Alexandrian, prominent men relied in turn upon her considerable assets. Agrippa I, king of Judaea, prevailed upon Antonia's friendship and kindness to borrow 300,000 drachmas when he ran himself into debt.[46]

Antonia was close to Tiberius and had long enjoyed sway at court. She was able to persuade the emperor to grant one of Agrippa's freedmen a hearing, for example, when no one else would. Such was her confidence in Tiberius' character and good influence that she sent her new charge Caligula to live with him on Capri when he was eighteen. Tiberius admired Antonia, not only for her loyalty to his late brother Drusus' memory, but also for her loyalty to him. There is good reason to believe that he held her chiefly responsible for rescuing him from a coup led by Sejanus. In AD 31 rumours had reached Antonia of a plot against the emperor involving several senators and freedmen. Convinced that the rumours were true, Antonia wrote to Tiberius at Capri, informing him of Sejanus' involvement.[47] This was said to have been the final trigger to Tiberius' decision to put the Praetorian and his associates to death.

If there was one reason for Tiberius to pause over Antonia and her loyalty it lay in the conduct of her daughter. Sejanus' wife had committed suicide following the brutal killing of her husband and two children, but she had not died silently. Prior to her death, she incriminated Livilla as Sejanus' mistress and accomplice in the death of Drusus, Tiberius' natural son. Livilla was none other than Antonia's daughter.

There had been no question in Antonia's mind that the young woman needed to be punished. The new age of puritanism had not died with Augustus. Like his stepfather, Tiberius was eager to eliminate adultery while indulging in it quite spectacularly himself, and witnessed many an adulteress weeded out of society. The late Agrippina's daughter-in-law Aemilia Lepida committed suicide after a slave informed upon her for an affair.[48] Antonia took Livilla into her own hands and, according to one source, locked her in her bedroom until she starved to death.[49] Livilla subsequently became the first woman in the imperial family to suffer a fate analogous to that endured by disgraced dead emperors. On the orders of the Senate, her name and image were erased from public and private monuments in what constituted, in later terms, *damnatio memoriae* ('a condemnation of memory'). She was not only an adulteress but, on highly questionable evidence, an alleged accomplice in the murder of Tiberius' true heir. It would perhaps be more accurate to say that Livilla took the fall for Sejanus in the long term, her image tarnished, quite literally, in perpetuity. Antonia paid the price of her relationship with Tiberius – with her daughter's life. Given the allegations lodged against Livilla, however, it is doubtful Antonia could have saved her. Tiberius would surely have had the young woman put to death.

The hopes of Antonia's family now rested upon her younger son

Claudius, a man of impeccable credentials but, in his own time, questionable competence. As the grandson of both Livia and Octavia he was as blue-blooded as a Roman could be, and yet he had always struck his mother as rather slow, especially by comparison with his elder brother. Where Germanicus had been handsome and strong and good at everything he turned his hand to, be it poetry or war, Claudius was sickly and weak. He had a stammer and very probably suffered from epilepsy, if not also from cerebral palsy. Antonia considered him a monster; an abnormal being that nature had not quite finished forming.[50] He was just a baby when his father Drusus died in Germany. His remaining relatives, especially his grandmother Livia, mocked him for his disabilities.[51]

There was nevertheless something about Claudius that had made his family and friends think twice. Not only could he write, but he developed a passion for literature, which the historian Livy, for one, believed he ought to nurture. It was with Livy's encouragement that the young Claudius began to write his own Roman history. Even Antonia and Livia were impressed by the work. Far from dismissing it as a schoolboy exercise, they perceived that it could one day be published, and so issued Claudius some advice. It would be wise to omit the years of civil war that followed Caesar's death, they told him, for it was too soon to make an account of these public. The imperial women understood only too well how dangerous it could be to highlight the illegality of Caesar's acts and the murky development of their own dynasty.

A letter preserved in the imperial archives contained the essence of a conversation Augustus had with Livia over the best place to seat Claudius at some games.[52] If he was in command of his senses, Augustus felt, the boy could sit in full view of the crowd and more generally follow the usual path to adulthood, but, if he was not, he – and his family – needed to be protected from public mockery. Barred from public life in the ensuing years to save Augustus from embarrassment, Claudius kept up his literary pursuits into adulthood, producing in addition to his history of the Etruscans a formula for expanding the Latin alphabet. The three new letters he created sadly did not catch on.[53] Claudius' family were increasingly surprised by how comprehensive he could be both on and off the page. 'How one who speaks so ineloquently can possibly declaim so eloquently in public, and say all the things that needed to be said,' Augustus had once written to Livia, 'beats me.'[54]

Antonia had always shared Augustus' concern for the reputation of the family, but scandal had a habit of creeping up on her, much as it had upon Augustus. The death of her wayward daughter, the awkwardness of her surviving son, the depravity of her grandson Caligula, were all gifts to the gossipmongers of Rome.

Caligula's sexual misdemeanours were said to have developed while he was living with her as a young man. Antonia supposedly discovered him in bed with his youngest sister Drusilla who was still just a child. If his biographer is to be believed, Caligula committed incest with all three of his sisters, but Drusilla remained his favourite.[55] He even attempted to steal her away from her husband, his own former lover, when she married.

Antonia would have hoped that Caligula had outgrown the foibles of youth, as she might have described them, by the time he succeeded Tiberius in AD 37 at age of twenty-four. Some of his very first acts as emperor conveyed his gratitude towards her and the other female members of his family. Antonia was granted every honour that Livia had held including, for when she died, the title Augusta.[56] Caligula personally sailed to Pandateria to retrieve the ashes of his mother, Agrippina, which he placed in an urn with his own hands. The urn was conveyed ceremoniously by ship as far as Ostia, and thence up the Tiber towards Rome, where it was carried to the imperial mausoleum. The simple plaque made to commemorate her life still survives: 'The bones of Agrippina, daughter of Marcus Agrippa, granddaughter of Deified Augustus, wife of Germanicus Caesar, mother of Gaius Caesar Augustus Germanicus Princeps.' Sacrifices and games were performed in Rome to mark her final homecoming. From this moment forth, Caligula proclaimed, the names of Agrippina's daughters, Drusilla, Livilla and Agrippina the Younger, were to be included in all public and private oaths. Never before had such a privilege been bestowed upon Rome's women. The sisters were entitled to watch games with their brother from the imperial seats and were featured prominently on his coinage as allegories of Fortuna, Securitas and Concordia.[57]

The season of hope for Rome's women did not last very long. Just months into Caligula's principate, Antonia died, poisoned, or so some people said, upon his orders.[58] Drusilla followed Antonia to her grave the following year. Caligula was so devastated by his sister's death that he granted her a state funeral and moved to have her deified. A senator who swore that he had seen Drusilla's spirit ascend to the heavens earned 1 million sesterces for his devotion. Statues of her were subsequently erected in the Senate House and the Temple of Venus in the forum. A band of twenty priests and priestesses was formed to tend her cult. Drusilla's birthday became a festival. Cities across the empire were invited to venerate her in the form of a goddess named 'Panthea' ('the goddess of all' or All-Goddess).[59] It was only in AD 42, some thirteen years after her death, that Livia, the original Augusta, was transformed into a goddess herself.

The rare extravagance with which Drusilla was immortalised across the empire contrasted sharply with Caligula's treatment of his surviving sisters. Nine months after he became emperor, his sister Agrippina the Younger gave birth to a son in a difficult breech delivery. The boy was named Lucius Domitius Ahenobarbus but would later and more famously be known as Nero. His father, a grandson of Octavia, great-nephew of Augustus and something of a reprobate, died when Nero was just three. Caligula showed little compassion for his bereaved sister and nephew. Far from helping Agrippina, he denounced her, and produced forged letters as evidence that she was plotting with their other sister Julia Livilla to murder him and install Drusilla's widower in his place. Caligula's suspicions lacked foundation, but the paranoia of power directed the trial and execution of the widower, Marcus Aemilius Lepidus, and the exile of the sisters. Agrippina and Julia Livilla were deprived of their property and sent away from Rome to bear the same fate as their mother (Agrippina the Elder), grandmother (Julia the Elder) and aunt (Julia the Younger).

The principate of Caligula gradually proved to be as perilous for women outside the family as it was for those within. The Roman historians gave the impression that no woman who entered the court could be sure of leaving without first being snatched from her husband over dinner and ravished in a back room. One of Caligula's favourites was a mother of three named Milonia Caesonia. He used to parade her before the army in military uniform or naked before his friends, and took it as confirmation that he had fathered a child with her when she gave birth to a baby girl who scratched her siblings' faces. 'It is not easy to discern whether he forged, dissolved, or maintained his marriages more shamefully,' wrote Suetonius of lustful Caligula, who would eventually make Milonia Caesonia his fourth wife.[60]

The later Julio-Claudians showed little sign of following Augustus' example and marrying just once or twice. Claudius was less overtly lecherous than his nephew Caligula, but he could be just as insatiable and unpredictable in his behaviour towards women. Augustus had arranged for him to marry but the process was fraught with difficulties. An early engagement to Aemilia Lepida, eldest daughter of the outcast Julia the Younger, was broken off in favour of a union with the less well-connected Livia Medullina Camilla, which was in turn undone when Camilla suffered the misfortune of dying on her wedding day. Claudius was married in AD 9 to Plautia Urgulanilla, the granddaughter of one of Livia's closest friends, but divorced her on the unlikely grounds that she had been involved in both murder and adultery. He then married Aelia Paetina, the daughter of a former consul, only to divorce her on similarly 'watery' charges.[61] By now the father of two daughters and a son, Claudius married thirdly Valeria Messalina, the great-granddaughter of his grandmother Octavia, to further drama.[62]

Messalina's mother, Domitia Lepida, raised Nero after Agrippina was sent into exile. She was both business-minded and, like Antonia before her, extremely wealthy, with numerous estates. Ancient documents reveal that she owned granaries in the Neapolitan port town of Puteoli and charged grain merchants 100 sesterces a month to rent the storerooms within a 'Barbatian Warehouse' there to secure herself a steady income.[63] The facility must have originally belonged to her first husband, Messalina's father, Marcus Valerius Messalla Barbatus, who died soon after his daughter's birth.

It was very probably the widowed Domitia Lepida who arranged Messalina's marriage to Claudius. Messalina was young and, to judge from the few, admittedly impressionistic surviving portraits, incredibly beautiful, with a round, delicate, symmetrical face, big eyes, a neat nose, and small yet shapely lips. She wore her hair centrally parted and tightly curled, ringlets tickling her forehead all the way down to her ears. Middle-aged Claudius might not have been the love-match she had hoped for through her girlhood, but by the time of their marriage he had at least begun to shed his image as the stock of family jokes to become a viable member of the political class.

In AD 37, a year or so before he married Messalina, Claudius joined Caligula in the consulship. Having been forced to grow up in the shadows, the stammering Claudius was propelled to the very centre of the

Senate, where his aptitude for foreign policy and speech-writing could finally be appreciated. Even Caligula must have been surprised to find his uncle so eminently equipped for public life. Detractors would continue to pelt him with olives, fruit stones, curses and crusts of bread, but Claudius developed a thick skin and, with it, the admiration of many of the ordinary people including, most crucially, the Praetorian Guard. It was just four years after Caligula rose to power that their conspiracy against him was hatched. Caligula was assassinated together with his wife and daughter in AD 41 and condemned soon after to *damnatio memoriae*. The guardsmen allegedly found their preferred candidate trembling behind some curtains and fearing for his life. That same year, at the age of fifty, Claudius became shock emperor of Rome.

As first lady, Messalina knew what she wanted, both for herself, and for her husband. She would sooner share in his victories than suffer the slights against his name. When Claudius celebrated a triumph for his successful invasion of Britain in AD 44, she rode proudly behind him in her own special carriage.[64] It would be forty years before the Romans could truly claim to have conquered England and Wales, but Claudius had pushed further than Julius Caesar, and was therefore deemed worthy of a hero's welcome. While the first honours went to Claudius and his son by Messalina, Tiberius Claudius Caesar, known henceforth as 'Britannicus', the women of the family were allowed to share his limelight. On becoming emperor, Claudius recalled his nieces, Agrippina the Younger and Julia Livilla, from exile. While Messalina proceeded in her carriage and the British prisoners marched in procession, Agrippina assumed a position before the Roman standards. No Roman woman had ever enjoyed such a prominent position before.

One day, it came to Messalina's attention that Seneca the Younger, one of the most popular philosophers in the city, had been criticising her husband. A cruel satire of Claudius' life and rule, the *Apocolocyntosis* ('Pumpkinification') of Deified Claudius, would later be attributed to him. While it was arguably more politick to ignore the rumours than to rise to them, Messalina was disinclined to hold her tongue. In a bid to stymie Seneca's influence on popular opinion, she accused him of committing adultery with Julia Livilla, whom she allegedly envied, and thereby defeated two birds with one stone. Julia was sent back into exile – Claudius would condemn her to death for unspecified reasons a short time later – and the furrow-browed thinker was dispatched to Corsica.[65] Anyone who doubted Messalina's role in Seneca's downfall had only to turn to his book of *Natural Questions* in which he boldly acknowledged the friction between them.[66]

Seneca was by no means alone in falling foul of Messalina. It was entirely characteristic of the empress in the early part of Claudius' rule to take the initiative against potential foes. The difficulty is that the sources describing her defence of Claudius tend to take the form of attacks upon her character. The historians and satirists, especially Tacitus and Juvenal, were so hostile towards her that it can be dangerous to trust their testimony. Messalina's alleged incrimination of a prominent former consul and his mistress is a case in point. He, Decimus Valerius Asiaticus, was romantically linked to Poppaea Sabina, a woman of renowned beauty, and owned some beautiful gardens on Rome's Pincian Hill.[67] First laid out by Lucius Licinius Lucullus, the great tastemaker of the Late Republic, the *horti Asiatici* featured a number of self-contained dining rooms and were besides extremely opulent.[68] According to Tacitus, Messalina was so taken with the gardens, so covetous and eager to obtain them for herself, that she sought to incriminate Asiaticus for owning the assassination of Caligula in a public assembly and posing a threat to Claudius as well. Lending these claims some credibility was the fact that Asiaticus came from Vienna (Vienne) in Gaul and maintained forces there which he could feasibly lead against Rome.

It was said that Claudius reacted, as often, in blind panic, and sent troops of his own after Asiaticus. The luxuriant senator, far from rousing the military, was found idling in the louche resort of Baiae. Astonished by the sudden turn of events – and undoubtedly Messalina's part in them – Asiaticus was sent back to Rome in chains and came before Claudius in his bedchamber. Three accusations were levelled against Asiaticus while Messalina looked on. First, Asiaticus was told, he had corrupted the army; second, he had committed adultery with Poppaea; and third, he was 'soft of body', in other words he was a passive partner in homosexual affairs. Asiaticus offered a defence, and the imperial couple were moved, but not so moved as to save him. At one point, Messalina left the room in tears, stressing as she did so that Asiaticus was to face justice. The defendant, in recognition of his service to Claudius in Britain, was permitted to choose his own death. Unbeknownst to Claudius, Messalina then hired men to drive Asiaticus' supposed paramour, Poppaea Sabina, to suicide by threatening her with imprisonment.

The episode ought to be consigned to the large trove of stories spun about Messalina in the course of her life and long after her death. A similarly incredible tale would be told of Agrippina the Younger and her lustful quest for some gardens. Many more writers besides Tacitus would enter into the sport of describing the grossness of both women's appetites over the years. Pliny the Elder, a contemporary, set the tone by relating in his encyclopaedia of *Natural History* that Messalina once entered a competition with a prostitute to see who could have sex with more men in twenty-four hours. Pliny, always censorious, noted drily that Messalina came away the winner with a score of twenty-five.[69] Later, in the early second century, the satirist Juvenal bestowed the electrifying sobriquet of *meretrix Augusta* ('Augusta the Whore') upon Messalina in acknowledgement of her alleged fondness for prostituting herself.[70] The satirist unwittingly granted Messalina a promotion with his insult. Claudius had sanctimoniously spurned the conferment of 'Augusta' upon his wife as a title still most strongly associated with deified Livia.

The *meretrix* of Juvenal's text is, all the same, augustly bold. She travels through Rome by night wearing a blonde wig and hood over her dark locks and gold paint over her nipples beneath. Messalina the she-wolf in disguise then takes up position within the *lupanar*, a more natural home to her than the imperial palace, and outstays all the other prostitutes. No matter how much sex she has, Juvenal says, she is never satisfied. Even by the end of the night she is 'still burning with desire in her rigid clitoris'. Messalina finally returns to her husband's bed reeking of smoke from the oil lamps and everything else.

Not content with behaving like a whore herself, wrote Cassius Dio, Messalina compelled other women to follow her example and degrade themselves, even at the palace. She *forced* them to commit adultery while their husbands watched. She *tricked* any man who wavered over sleeping with her into doing so and *poisoned* the most defiant refuseniks.[71] She besides put many men to death upon false charges owing to personal vendettas. She was jealous, controlling, dangerous in bed and out of it. Reckless and promiscuous to the tentative and slightly odd Claudius, Messalina was, it must be said, a wildly exciting character to invent.

There was, however, one particular story that Tacitus absolutely insisted was true. This story, unlikely though it seemed, grew legs because it captured Messalina as she was believed to be naturally – in private and unfettered – while Claudius was away expanding his powerbase, overseeing public works or addressing problems overseas. At the beginning of his principate, the empire stretched from Hispania to Pontus, and by the end, it would also incorporate Thrace, Lycia, Noricum (Austria with some of Slovenia) and Mauretania in North Africa. The emperor's prolonged absences afforded Messalina considerable time alone, and it was while his back was turned that she was said to have fallen in love with the handsomest man in Rome.[72]

Gaius Silius was the surviving son of two of Sejanus' former victims, Sosia Galla, who was driven into exile, and her senator husband Gaius Silius, who was forced to commit suicide. Both had been friends of Agrippina the Elder. Following defiantly in his father's footsteps, Silius had climbed the ladder of the Senate and now stood as a consul-elect. He was married, and for obvious reasons wanted at first to keep his affair with Messalina private, but Messalina desired the very opposite. The ease with which she committed adultery and the tedium this caused her were cited as the reasons for her increasingly outrageous behaviour. Rather than have sex with Silius in secret, as most married aristocrats would, Messalina trailed her entire entourage to his house and filled the rooms with furniture from Claudius' home.

Silius could not refuse when she ordered him to divorce his wife. The tables were briefly turned against Messalina when Silius declared that he would like to marry her himself and adopt her son Britannicus as his own. At that, Messalina panicked, for while she was not averse to marrying Silius, the last thing she wanted was for him to do so and regret it. Could a wife retain the allure of a mistress? Steadily, it was said, Messalina came round to the idea. Whether she seriously believed that they might begin a new life together, or merely hoped that her affair would alter her relationship with Claudius for the better, she was running an enormous risk. By contrast with some of her other alleged paramours, who included a svelte actor-dancer named Mnester ('Wooer'), Silius posed a serious threat to Claudius' position by virtue of his noble blood and status as a senator. His desire to marry the emperor's wife and her apparent willingness to commit bigamy could only be construed by Claudius' advisers as the beginnings of a coup.

Messalina and Silius seized the opportunity to cement their bond while Claudius was away in Ostia overseeing the grain supply. The port had long served as the principal gateway for Rome's food imports but had lately begun to buckle under the demands of a growing population. A census undertaken during Claudius' principate revealed that the citizen population of Rome was nearing six million for the very first time.[73] Some of the women in the city, among them freedwomen, had accumulated sufficient private wealth to build boats. Faced with a desperate shortage of grain one year, Claudius appealed to them to aid the construction of new vessels for the import effort.[74] The women who agreed to assist were rewarded with the privileges ordinarily reserved for mothers of four or more children, namely freedom from male guardianship and the right to inherit property. The foundations of a large new harbour had been laid at Ostia to facilitate further trade.[75] Claudius had been travelling to and fro between Ostia and Rome often enough for Messalina to know that she had time to fulfil her audacious plan.

For the second time in her life, Messalina put on the saffron-coloured veil reserved for brides and joined hands with her new spouse. Sacrifices were performed and a banqueting table was laid. It was just as if a real wedding was taking place. The affair between Messalina and Silius might have been an open secret at court, even though Claudius remained strangely oblivious to it, but no one could have expected it to go this far. News of the 'wedding' propelled the emperor's chief advisers into action against a possible (if unlikely) power grab between the consul-elect and the empress.

Messalina might not have viewed her nuptials so crudely. She was almost certainly less enamoured of Claudius than Claudius was of her, at least physically, whereas Silius was the sort of man who might have inspired a woman to fulfil her most romantic dreams. Messalina was nevertheless familiar enough with the paranoid workings of the inner court to anticipate how her flamboyant relationship with Silius would be viewed.

Narcissus, a former slave employed as Claudius' private secretary, was equally astute, and knew that he would be less persuasive in this instance than those who knew Claudius intimately. He therefore approached two of the women Claudius kept as mistresses and bribed them to tell him all about the 'wedding' ceremony of his wife.[76] Calpurnia and Cleopatra duly informed upon Messalina. It seems clear that Narcissus was intent on bringing Messalina down. Claudius traced the story back to source and summoned his advisers. Narcissus would confirm the details and elaborate on the transferral of furniture and still tastier perks that Silius had enjoyed through Messalina's incomparable generosity.

Before Messalina's misdemeanours were brought to his attention, the emperor had been busy overseeing the construction of a new aqueduct, establishing a law to enable members of the Gallic tribe of the Aedui to become Roman senators for the first time, and performing his duties as censor, which included scrutinising the membership of the Senate to root out misfits. The office had elapsed in 22 BC, but Claudius had reinstated it with considerable enthusiasm. His treatment of a young equestrian who had become notorious for his infidelity and corruption provided some insight into his position on adultery. He permitted the equestrian to retain his post with a word of warning to go more carefully. 'Why,' he asked him, 'should I know who your mistress is?'[77] In his professional conduct, indeed, Claudius was more relaxed and realistic than his predecessors about the occurrence of adultery behind closed doors. Applying the same principles to his own life was always going to be more challenging. News that Messalina had not only been unfaithful, but feigned a marriage to another man, left Claudius incredulous. Repeatedly, he asked his officials whether the rumour was true, and if it was, whether it meant that he was no longer in power.

The authority of Narcissus and other freedmen advisers was consistently overemphasised by the ancient historians, who mistook Claudius' speech impediment for dithering indecision and supposed that the only way he got anything done was by heeding the advice of others.[78] In this case, however, it is credible that the advisers took the lead and prevailed upon the emperor to act decisively to protect his position, see off the interloper, and punish his wife. In the heightened emotion of the moment, Claudius oscillated between anger and remorse. His friends had often told him that Messalina was treacherous, but he had always made excuses for her because he loved her. His *amor* was *flagrantissimus*, not just ardent, but *superlatively* ardent, almost impervious to her reproach.[79] One moment he would curse Messalina's name. The next he would be lost in thought of their life together. Narcissus needed to persuade him one way, to focus on her misdemeanours.

Messalina was at a wine festival with Silius when she heard that Claudius had found out about their 'wedding'. It was autumn and the grape-harvest was in full flow, vats brimming with juice, presses straining, women flocking around them like maenads with wild hair and bacchic wands – or perhaps that was merely authorial fantasy.[80] As centurions arrived to lead their companions away as prisoners, Silius left for the forum and Messalina made her way with three escapees towards Ostia inside, of all things, a garden waste cart. She had decided to pre-empt Claudius' arrival by going to meet him and sending their son and young daughter Octavia to cuddle up to him. With remarkable clarity of mind, she also resolved to approach the chief Vestal Virgin, Vibidia, and implore her to urge the emperor's forgiveness on her behalf.

Claudius' emotions were still vacillating when Messalina arrived, tears flowing down her cheeks, desperate that he should hear what she had to say. She tried to speak, but Narcissus silenced her. The children tried to approach, but Narcissus had them dismissed. The freedman passed Claudius a list, no doubt largely spurious, of Messalina's lovers' names. Claudius had barely had time to digest it and visualise the men he would have to put to death before Vibidia attempted to intervene. The Vestal Virgin bravely stayed her ground when Narcissus tried to eject her too.

The Vestal Virgin reminded Claudius that it was unlawful for a man to put his wife to death without first giving her a fair hearing. This was not a law Claudius had always kept. At least two imperial women had already been put to death without trial during his rule, namely Julia, daughter of Tiberius' son Drusus, and Julia Livilla, daughter of Germanicus. Narcissus claimed that Messalina would have her chance to put her case to Claudius shortly. Vibidia was curtly dismissed with instructions to return to her religious duties.

The next challenge Narcissus faced was to persuade the emperor of the seriousness of the affair. Leading Claudius to the house of Silius, he flung open the door and began to point out to him in dramatic fashion all the pieces of furniture that had formerly stood in his home. A visit to the camp of the Praetorian Guard followed. Claudius was placed under incomparable pressure to act against his own wife.

Messalina had meanwhile returned to her gardens, where she was scrawling desperate letters and praying for mercy. That evening, Claudius sent a messenger to arrange for the 'poor wretch' (*misera*), as he called her, to be brought to him the following day so that she could offer her defence. Silius did not try his luck by asking for the same privilege. His only request was for a quick death.

The delay to Messalina's hearing and the audible distress of her children worried Narcissus. What if the emperor changed his mind overnight? Taking matters into his own hands, Narcissus criminally feigned orders from Claudius for the centurions to kill Messalina immediately.

Messalina was lying down in her gardens when the centurions approached. Her mother, Domitia Lepida, was lying with her, pleading with her to take her own life rather than submit to the force of the men who would inevitably come for her.[81] In tears, trembling, Messalina took hold of a dagger just as the soldiers were upon her. Messalina hesitated. The tribune nearest her forced the blade home. Domitia was left holding the bleeding body of her daughter.

Claudius heard the news of Messalina's death while he was at dinner. He appeared entirely emotionless in his shock. His own wife had been killed on the orders of someone impersonating him. He spent the following days in denial.

The Senate issued orders for statues and inscriptions bearing Messalina's name or image to be removed from public and even private view in what amounted to a process of *damnatio memoriae*. All memory of Messalina was to be erased before Claudius had even had time to digest that she existed in memory alone. Most of the paintings and statues of Messalina were obliterated or recarved. Her name has been erased, for example, from the surviving funerary inscription of one of her freedmen.[82] In the provinces, too, Messalina's name vanished from public monuments and even coins at the twist of a chisel. Two busts nevertheless survived total destruction. Attempts at mutilation are visible on both the Vatican portrait, which was probably also submerged in water, and the Dresden portrait, in which Messalina was depicted with a turreted crown and doomed look of defiance. The latter split into four pieces as a result of repeated hammer blows.[83] A third sculpture, full-length and showing Messalina veiled and holding the infant Britannicus, was illegally concealed and so saved from similar desecration.[84]

The first promise Claudius made himself once he had recovered his wits was that he would remain celibate in the aftermath of Messalina's death.[85] He even jested with his guard that they could kill him if he broke his word. Of course, celibacy was not an option as far as his court was concerned. The emperor needed to remarry in order to sustain the principate. A wife was crucial to the very survival of the empire. There were many women on the sidelines, including Lollia Paulina, the daughter of a former consul, and even Aelia Paetina, Claudius' previous wife.[86] But it was his niece, Agrippina the Younger, who won favour with the court and, to the astonishment of the Roman people, the emperor himself.

Chapter XIX

Broken Body, Valiant Mind

Under every stone, my friend, watch out for a scorpion.

Praxilla, quoted by a scholiast on Aristophanes *Thesmophoriazusae* 528

Agrippina was a tall, robust woman with a pronounced nose, straight brows and, according to Pliny, who had seen her in person, a double row of canine teeth on her right side, which was considered lucky.[1] Like Antonia, she parted her hair centrally and often had it tied in a low bun, but her curls were altogether tighter than Antonia's, and more extravagant. The historians claimed that she used feminine wiles to flirt with Claudius, to smother him with kisses, and so initiate their relationship, but they are hardly to be trusted on this subject.

It was Claudius who had arranged for Agrippina to remarry after she was widowed following the birth of her son Nero. Although she was said to have turned against her second husband, a rich and high-ranking senator, this was certainly not because she believed she could do better by marrying her uncle. There was no precedent for such relationships in Rome.[2] The very idea of such a union reeked of eastern extravagance. In order to proceed, Claudius needed the Senate to authorise marriages between uncles and nieces so that they were no longer classified as incestuous.[3] The Senate agreed, and a new law was introduced, but only two other couples were recorded as taking advantage of it.

When Agrippina married Claudius her first thought was for her son and his position in the dynasty. Nero became not only stepbrother to Britannicus, Claudius' son by Messalina, but fiancé to Britannicus' sister Octavia and the adopted son of Claudius himself. It was from this time that Nero ceased to be known as Lucius Domitius. Beyond these arrangements, there were early signs that Agrippina was leaning upon Claudius to make Nero his successor in place of Britannicus, the younger of the boys by three years. Vying with Messalina's bloodline for influence at court, Agrippina dismissed Britannicus' key supporters within the Praetorian Guard and appointed him new tutors. In the first act she was aided by one of Claudius' secretaries, Pallas, and in the second, by Claudius himself, who agreed that Britannicus ought to be disciplined for cheekily calling Nero by his birth name.

While Britannicus' former tutors were exiled or put to death, Seneca was recalled from Corsica at Agrippina's request to serve as Nero's tutor in rhetoric. The philosopher also, thanks to Agrippina, became a praetor or high-ranking magistrate in the Senate. The people of Rome were thrilled to see Seneca return and began to hope that Agrippina's rumoured dislike of Messalina and desire to reverse her deeds signalled brighter days ahead.[4] Their expectations were initially satisfied when news came that Messalina's mother had been sentenced to death. The accusations levelled against Domitia Lepida were highly suspicious. It was alleged that she had used magic and incited gangs of slaves to commit acts of violence in Calabria, where she was a well-established landowner. Domitia Lepida was not only Britannicus' grandmother, but the aunt who had raised Nero as a boy and thus a rival to his birth mother's affections. It is credible that Agrippina was the driving force behind Domitia Lepida's demise.

The episode was later viewed as a turning point in the history of imperial Rome. 'From that moment,' wrote Tacitus some decades later, 'the city changed, and everything bowed to a woman.' The later historian Cassius Dio would describe Agrippina as a new Messalina, but as Tacitus more accurately observed, Agrippina's influence and reputation were entirely her own.[5] 'She did not mock the Roman way of life by her lasciviousness as Messalina had done,' he proposed, but 'a rather masculine subjection was adduced: harshness and arrogance in public, yet no shamelessness at home, unless it was conducive to domination . . .'[6] Agrippina was recognised as the power behind the throne and traduced for initiating a darker period in Roman history. Behind Tacitus' patent misogyny lay genuine concerns over the balance of power between her and her husband.

Agrippina very quickly made her political presence felt far beyond the Roman capital. In AD 50 a new military settlement was established in her name at her birthplace in ancient Cologne. More significantly, two years later, she came to the defence of the Jews following a major international dispute.

The Galileans had approached the Roman procurator of Judaea, a man named Ventidius Cumanus, after the Samaritans killed some of their people as they travelled through their territory to a festival.[7] When Cumanus accepted bribes from the Samaritans not to pursue the murderers, the Galileans persuaded the Judaeans to take up arms in their defence and to regain their freedom from Roman control. Seeing their villages being plundered and destroyed, Cumanus armed the Samaritans and marched against the Jews, killing and imprisoning many of them in the process. The Samaritans also approached the Roman procurator of Syria and told him that the Jews were destroying their homes and disregarding Roman law. The Jews conversely blamed the Samaritans for starting the dispute and Cumanus for being corrupted. Quadratus, procurator of Syria, agreed to arbitrate. He believed that the Samaritans were to blame, but he was so perturbed by reports of the Jews' plans to revolt from Rome that he ordered Cumanus' captives to be crucified. Cumanus and the Samaritans were then sent to Rome so that the case could be put before Claudius.

The emperor's freedmen and friends generally took the side of the Roman, Ventidius Cumanus, and the Samaritans. Agrippina, on the other hand, championed the Jews, and so worked directly against her husband. Claudius had been in the business of expelling from Rome 'the Jews who were continually causing disturbance at the instigation of Chrestus', by which Suetonius surely meant early Christians, worshippers of Christ ('the anointed one' in Greek).[8] Agrippina faced a considerable challenge in persuading him to listen to the Jewish case. Eventually, she succeeded, and Claudius came to the conclusion that the Samaritans were guilty for their initial role in the fallout. The members of the deputation were put to death, Cumanus was sent into exile, and the people of Judaea received a new procurator named Antonius Felix. Victory also belonged to Agrippina. In recognition of her influence and support for the Jews, Felix had her name printed on the new set of coins he issued, ensuring that the people of Judaea remembered her.

The bias of the sources ensured that Agrippina's role in the international dispute was obscured by fictions surrounding her part in Claudius' death less than two years later. While intrigued by her growing prominence in the further corners of the empire, ancient historians were wholly absorbed by the idea that her relationship with the emperor had unravelled to such an extent as to drive her to murder.[9] The woman in the 'cloak all of gold', as Pliny once described her, was alleged to have poisoned Claudius, triggering his sudden death in AD 54.[10]

Agrippina, the historians said, did not want her crime to be detected, and so she approached the most dependable toxicologist in Rome. A woman named Locusta, originally from Gaul, had become notorious for educating her 'boorish' neighbours in the dark arts of killing their husbands.[11] Her vast knowledge of poisons had made her the chief culprit in a recently detected murder.[12] If anyone knew of a substance that would disturb a man's thoughts and bring death upon him gently, it was her.

Claudius was a true gourmand. He frequently ate to such excess that he needed to empty his stomach mechanically before the end of the day. A feather usually brought on the desired reflex.[13] His last supper, as anyone who inspected the contents of his bowl might have confirmed, featured his favourite mushrooms, *boleti*, probably porcini. The entire genus was such a delicacy that Cassius Dio felt compelled to explain to his readers that mushrooms were a type of vegetable.[14] The mushrooms that found their way onto the emperor's plate might well have been poisonous in themselves, but the historians did not trouble themselves with this possibility; the theory that Agrippina had spiked them with Locusta's toxin made for a better story.[15] Their reports of what came next varied slightly. Some said that Claudius lost his power of speech after dinner, ailed all night, and was dead by morning. Others claimed that he was sick from overeating and so given a second dose of poison in his gruel or by enema. It was also proposed that a further dose of poison was introduced to his throat on the feather he used to induce vomiting.[16] All that is certain is that by 13 October AD 54 Claudius was dead.

Agrippina's supposed motive for killing her husband was to secure the position of Nero at a time when Claudius seemed to favour his natural son Britannicus. It is entirely possible that the couple had rowed over the order of succession, but that Agrippina had a hand in Claudius' death is highly unlikely. The impact of the episode was nevertheless profound. In achieving this end, as Pliny put it, Agrippina did little more than give Rome a new poison in the form of a sixteen-year-old emperor.

Agrippina was recognised unofficially as co-ruler to young Nero in the early years of his principate. A relief sculpture carved at Sebasteion, Aphrodisias, in Asia Minor, showed her placing the crown upon his head, and coins minted at Rome in AD 54 depicted mother and son face to face. Life imitated art, for when a delegation arrived from Armenia, Agrippina sat beside Nero in the Senate House. This surprised everyone, not least Nero, who took Seneca's advice and greeted his mother politely. The pair were borne in the same litter in public, and on the day of his accession, Nero selected *Optima Mater* ('The Best Mother' or 'Best of all Mothers') as one of the watchwords for his security.[17] Steadily, however, as Nero assumed the responsibilities of the role, Agrippina faded from public view. A year after Nero came to power, her portrait was pushed to the background of his coinage, and a year after that, it had disappeared.[18]

Nero was of average height with blue eyes, fair hair, and rather a fat face.[19] He did not look like Augustus, but he was eager to present himself from the beginning as someone made in the same mould. He courted popularity by lowering taxes, distributing grain, putting on extravagant entertainments and, every politician's favourite trick, memorising the names of people as he met them.[20] His main passions, however, were chariot-racing, music and the arts. There came a time when he would sing in the theatre and forbid anyone from leaving until he had finished his performance. Women would be known to give birth in their seats or feign death so that they could be carried out on stretchers.

Locusta the toxicologist found herself in demand at court. From the beginning of his rule, Nero was eager to do away with his irritatingly popular stepbrother, who was fast approaching his fourteenth birthday and winning over even Agrippina in his maturity.[21] It would not be long before Britannicus exchanged his childhood clothes for the *toga virilis* ('toga of manhood') and entered public life. Locusta was at that time in custody facing charges of poisoning, but Nero approached the praetorian who kept guard over her, and ordered her to help him prepare a toxin for use against Britannicus. Locusta was in no position to refuse.

Achieving the desired strength of poison was by no means easy. Locusta's initial recommendation proved too weak and passed straight through Britannicus' bowels. In his ignorance, Nero threatened to beat her for supplying what appeared to be a digestive remedy.[22] Locusta, feistily leaping to her own defence, explained that she had purposely concocted a weaker toxin than she might have done in order to make Britannicus' reaction less suspicious. Nero arrogantly retorted that he had no reason to fear the law. Guardsmen were then led to a room adjoining his bedchamber to prepare a faster-acting poison under Locusta's instruction and demonstrate its efficacy.[23] The new tincture was tested on a goat kid but still found to be wanting; the kid took five hours to die. It was remixed and tested on a pig which perished instantly. The poison was ready.

Britannicus was enjoying his final days seated at the children's table at dinner. Like all key members of the court, he had a slave sample his food prior to eating it, just in case it was poisoned. As usual, his taster took a sip of his drink, to no ill effect, and passed it to Britannicus. Britannicus had a little but found it too hot so some cold water was added to the cup. His taster neglected to sample the water.[24] Britannicus probably suffered from epilepsy like his father, so when he ingested the poison and began to struggle, it was initially assumed that he was having another of his attacks. Death, however, came quickly. The young man's body was removed from the dining room and prepared for immediate cremation. All the while Agrippina and Octavia looked on and tried, as always, to conceal their emotions from the court. Their visible shock at this turn of events nevertheless suggested that neither was in on Nero's plan.

Locusta was duly rewarded for her services. Undeterred by the prospect of rousing further suspicion, Nero not only cancelled the charges against her, but made her a present of some estates and appointed her tutor to some pupils in toxicology.[25] She would live on until the reign of Nero's successor, Galba, who condemned her to death as an ugly legacy of an ugly ruler. Poison had been viewed as a woman's weapon of choice ever since Homer described Helen and Circe mixing dubious concoctions in his epics. Locusta had exceeded their fictionalised efforts by changing the course of Roman history. Had she not lent her services to Nero, Britannicus might yet have been promoted, Nero displaced, and the people of Rome saved from one of the most erratic rules they had ever endured.

Agrippina endeavoured to keep a close watch on Nero as he displayed the first signs of rebellion. The historians would describe the emperor as beginning well but steadily descending into every excess, especially from the late 50s AD. They applied a similar narrative arc to the lives of other emperors, including Tiberius, so echoing the Greek tragedians. In the fifth century BC, Aeschylus, Sophocles and Euripides had highlighted the precise turning points at which their heroes underwent a reversal of fortune in what was known as *peripeteia*. The envied became pitiable, the strong became weak, the good became bad. The Roman historians' accounts of Nero enduring a similar transition ought not to be read too literally. The emperor did not go from being the people's hero to arch-villain overnight. He remained highly popular with the lower classes throughout his life. His greatest misfortune was to alienate members of the old-monied elite, as well as many women, with what was construed as spontaneity and selfish excess. The historians who later wrote of him were typically equestrians and therefore economically upper class.

Rumours of all-day feasts, new clothes for each day and prostitutes titillated the memoirists. Nero's new palace, the Domus Aurea ('Golden House'), featured a mile-long colonnade, a revolving dining room, and a statue of the emperor the size of a giant. The wealthiest women of Rome were warned not to encroach upon such majesty. If they so much as attempted to emulate the emperor's ostentation, they could be stripped of their Tyrian purple finery, as well as their property.[26] Such was Nero's appetite for quashing female wealth that he launched a treasure hunt for a chest he believed that Dido, queen of Carthage, had concealed in some caves following her escape from Tyre. Its contents would have been welcome at a time when Rome's coffers were running dry. The expense of launching warships and rowers to retrieve the mysterious chest outstripped the rewards, for no treasure was ever found.

Tensions began to develop between Nero and his highly capable mother. These centred particularly upon Nero's choice of women. The emperor had quickly tired of Claudius' daughter Octavia, whom Agrippina had had him marry, wearying of her popularity and failure to produce an heir. His affair with a former slave named Acte drove a further wedge between him and his mother. Agrippina frowned upon Acte's lowliness and made her feelings on the pairing quite clear. After some time, however, she realised that Acte was harmless by comparison with some of the noblewomen her son might have courted. Agrippina therefore did her best to regain his trust by giving him use of a bedroom. Nero saw through his mother's duplicity and dismissed Pallas, the secretary she was rumoured to be sleeping with, to reassert his authority. His initiation of an affair with another woman only deepened the gulf between them.

Poppaea Sabina came from a wealthy family in Pompeii. Her father was a senator who had fallen into disgrace and her mother was the beautiful woman whom Messalina was said to have driven to suicide out of jealousy. She was intelligent, and would encourage Nero to show compassion towards the people of Judaea after the man she recommended to him as procurator proved to be so hostile to the Jews as to steal funds from their Temple, ultimately triggering the Jewish War. In later life she would marry Otho, who briefly served as emperor in AD 69 following Nero's death.

Surviving portraits dating from Poppaea's lifetime show a woman with a round, symmetrical face, large eyes, a neat nose but rather a hard mouth. The trend for portraying people with frowns and natural wrinkles had largely fallen away at the end of the last century. The real Poppaea Sabina could not have been quite as smooth-faced as her sculptors made her out to be. More than her face, it was her curled auburn hair that caught Nero's attention and inspired him as he composed a song in her praise.

Poppaea became not only Nero's muse, but his lover and, as time went on, a thorn in Agrippina's side. The relationship between the two women would grow increasingly strained in the mid-60s when Nero's popularity began to wane in the face of external pressures including the great fire. It was easy for Poppaea to work on Nero's insecurities so as to persuade him that he was paying the price of his mother's excess of power. Many of the honours bestowed upon Agrippina were wholly without precedent for women in Rome. She had been granted a priesthood in honour of Claudius, for example, and the use of two lictors or special attendants.[27] How she made use of either is a mystery. Without her memoirs we are solely reliant upon the accounts of the historians who sought, more often than not, to present her from the perspective of her son and Poppaea. She was meddlesome, interfering, a busybody who obstructed Poppaea's path and needed to be put out of the way.

Nero's opinion of his mother mattered to the historians because it dictated what became of her. Agrippina was stripped of her bodyguard and removed from the palace. Even then Nero complained that she would not leave him alone. From the Palatine Hill, Agrippina made her way to a riverside villa formerly occupied by Antonia, but that also proved too close for comfort. Despairing of her apparently endless involvement in his affairs, Nero had men board boats to shout through her windows and threaten her with lawsuits.[28] Agrippina simply closed her ears.

Agrippina's gravest mistake was to become embroiled in a politically charged love triangle. In a moment of imprudence, she warned her friend Silana's lover off her. Silana, she told the man, had a bad reputation and was too old to marry him. Agrippina believed she was acting in Silana's best interest. Without children, her wealth would fall to her new lover if she married him, and she might be left destitute. Silana however was so heartbroken that she decided to accuse Agrippina of inciting a distant cousin to revolt against the emperor. Rubellius Plautus was descended from Augustus by the same degree as Nero and therefore looked like a viable threat to the throne. To make the situation even more serious, a rumour was put about that Agrippina was besotted with Rubellius and desperate to marry him herself. The 'plot' was leaked to Nero by his favourite, a male ballet dancer named Paris, who had formerly served as a slave to his aunt Domitia. Such was Nero's trust in the man that he decided he needed to act against his mother once and for all.

It was said that the failure of the emperor's initial attempts to poison or crush Agrippina in bed while she was sleeping prompted him to seek a more ingenious method. One of the exercises he used to improve his rasping singing voice involved lying on his back with a sheet of lead pressed upon his chest. As Agrippina sailed across the Bay of Naples from a festival at Baiae, a similar lead weight would be placed upon the canopy of her boat, causing it to collapse. The plan was executed and might have achieved its aim, had not the sides of the couch on which Agrippina was resting resisted the weight and saved her from being smothered. With an injured shoulder, Agrippina swam to safety, but was then bludgeoned and stabbed to death. In a piece of theatre worthy of her son, she allegedly pointed to her womb, the source of the evil, and demanded to be struck right there.

Nero regretted her murder almost at once. While he tried to justify it to himself and to the Senate by emphasising Agrippina's desire to co-rule and further fabricating the story of her involvement in a plot against his life, he never truly recovered from his role in the incident. His decision to perform the part of Orestes the Matricide on stage sometime later would be a gift to proto-psychoanalysts.[29]

*

In AD 60, the year after Agrippina died, Nero was appointed co-heir to the estate of Prasutagus, leader of the Iceni tribe in Britain.[30] Unlike the Romans, the Britons were content to pass power down to women, and Prasutagus intended his two daughters to share his authority with Rome in an arrangement designed to safeguard his interests from external threat. As they were still young, the girls' mother Boudica would serve as regent. Prasutagus had hoped that this would satisfy the Romans' demands for repayment of funds lavished upon the Britons during Claudius' conquest, but it did not. While loans were called in and further financial restraints imposed upon the people of Britain, contempt for 'the remotest island in the west' filtered steadily upwards from the centurions to the Senate in Rome.[31]

Boudica's origins remain obscure, but she was said to have been tall with long, thick, red hair falling below her waist, determined eyes, and (the detail perhaps says more about the historian than her) a shrill voice.[32] She wore colourful clothes and a brooch and, as the same male author put it, she was cleverer than the average woman.[33] Boudica was not unique in standing at the head of a tribe in Britain. A woman named Cartimandua ruled over the Brigantes of northern England and would come to an arrangement with the Romans as a client queen. But as leader of the Iceni, a wealthy yet remote tribe centred at modern Norfolk and Suffolk – and as Prasutagus' widow and capable co-heir – Boudica struck the Romans as an impediment to their potential annexation of Britain.

The Romans launched their attack and mercilessly made after the Iceni. They scourged Boudica, raped her virginal daughters, enslaved other members of her family, and robbed the tribe of possessions. In so doing they enacted a punishment of Britain that had already been described in art. A temple dedicated to Aphrodite at Aphrodisias in Asia Minor bore sculptures of the Roman imperial family in triumph, one of which showed Claudius dressed in armour with his penis exposed. The emperor, who had celebrated a triumph for his work, was delivering the final blow to Britannia, who was depicted as a woman slinking desperately to the ground, clothes ripped, one breast released from her clothes. Her dishevelled appearance and the manner in which Claudius straddled and held her by the hair from behind transformed the scene into one of conquest and rape. The image was equivalent to that of the Italian bull goring Rome's she-wolf to death on silver coins issued after the Social

War of the first century BC. Boudica was now Britannia.

The queen remained defiant and responded to the sacrilege with as great a rebellion as she could muster. Forces were gathered from the Iceni and other tribes, especially the Trinovantes, who inhabited the area of modern Essex. Some 120,000 Britons came before her as she picked up her spear and made her address. Boudica faced little difficulty in persuading the Britons that they were living in abject slavery to Rome. Resentment towards the centre of the empire had been brewing for quite some time. It was one thing to revere a foreign emperor from afar, but quite another to live under the scrutiny of his legate, his procurator, his men on the ground.[34] Britons were forced to pay Roman taxes, to farm for the Romans, and to pay them death duties.[35] An *octostyle* temple measuring 32 metres long by 25 wide and dedicated to Claudius, deified after his death, stood menacingly over them at Camulodunum (Colchester) as a reminder of his invasion and Rome's dominance since AD 43.[36]

If only, exclaimed Boudica, the people of Britain had repelled the Romans then as they had in the time of Julius Caesar. But what good was there in dwelling on the past? In rousing rhetoric she urged her men not to fear the Romans. Britons, she said, were braver, stronger, hardier, more agile, and accustomed to harsher conditions and bad weather than Romans.[37] The queen suddenly released a hare from the folds of her clothes and, seeing it turn right, the side of good luck, raised her eyes to the heavens and invoked Andraste, a local goddess of war who featured on Icenian coins. Boudica's speech, as reimagined the following century, highlighted her virtues as a female ruler:

> I show you my favour, Andraste, and also invoke you, woman to woman, even though I do not bear the burdens of ruling the Egyptians, as Nitocris [a semi-legendary female 'king' of ancient Egypt] did, or the merchant Assyrians, as Semiramis did, for this we have now learned from the Romans. Nor indeed do I rule them in the way of Messalina then Agrippina and now Nero, who is a man in name, but a woman in deed, as evidenced by his cithara-playing and beautifying regime. But I do rule the men of Britain, who know not how to farm or to ply a trade, but to war with skill and share everything in common, even children and wives, on account of which the latter possess the same masculine virtues

> as the men. And so, as queen of men and women like this, I pray to you and implore you for victory and deliverance and freedom from men who are hubristic, unjust, insatiable, unholy . . .'[38]

The description of power resting with Messalina and Agrippina before Nero was as striking as the emphasis upon Nero's femininity which ran through the entire speech and reflected the pro-Roman prejudice of its writer. As much as Boudica might have wished to mock her enemy, her priority was to inspire her men, who remained alert to the slightest sign of a bad portent. The mysterious toppling of a statue of Victory at Camulodunum prompted the women around them to predict the very worst.[39]

Suetonius Paullinus, the Roman governor, was on Mona (Anglesey) when Boudica and her army began their advance. The sight of druids and women in dark robes brandishing torches among the enemy only reinforced how far the Romans were from home. No sooner had Suetonius' legions secured control of Mona than they were summoned to Camulodunum. The Britons had sacked the Roman show-town and begun to unleash their fury upon Verulamium (St Albans) and Londinium as well.

Londinium had developed into an important trading post about five years after Claudius' invasion. Located in the east of the modern capital, in the area of the City near Blackfriars, it spread out along the Thames and its subsidiary, the River Walbrook, a valuable conduit for goods. The earliest wooden buildings had gradually been replaced by stone constructions and a bridge had been thrown over the Thames. Wooden backs of wax tablets preserved in the ground where the Walbrook once flowed preserve references to the local brewing of beer. The earliest of the surviving tablet-backs, dating from AD 57, records the debt that one freedman owed another for the sale of supplies.

Suetonius had at his disposal the fourteenth legion, veterans of the twentieth, and auxiliaries – perhaps 10,000 men in total.[40] He was utterly merciless towards the Britons as he proceeded.[41] For all that he tried, he could not hold Londinium, far less save it from the fires that spread from building to building. As the Romans prepared to confront the enemy infantry and cavalry somewhere along Watling Street, the wives of the Britons rode along in wagons, Boudica and her daughters principally among them.

The queen wove among the tribes, reasserting the fact that it was usual for women to rule in this way, and that she was fighting for freedom, for vengeance for herself and for her daughters. Suetonius, far from being threatened, used the presence of so many women – weakling things – as impetus to spur his men on. The Romans advanced in silence, the Britons singing songs of battle.[42] The Romans charged, broke through the opposing ranks, and cavalry confronted cavalry. The Roman legionaries flung missiles then rushed out against the Britons in a column. Boudica's whereabouts in the heat of this engagement are unknown.

Tacitus recorded that 80,000 Britons fell, relative to just 400 Romans, but clearly this was a vast exaggeration on the Roman's part.[43] The historian's father-in-law, Gnaeus Julius Agricola, served under Suetonius Paulinus before becoming governor of Britain himself. Writing over half a century later, Tacitus reflected with pride on Rome's accomplishments, but others could not help but echo the feelings of shame the Romans had felt at having to confront a female-led uprising.[44] Cassius Dio, writing still later, emphasised the atrocities committed on Boudica's side against noble-born women. Hung up naked, he claimed, female captives were deprived of their breasts, which were sewn into their mouths, or impaled lengthways on skewers.[45] An army of 230,000 Britons had eventually been able to confront the Romans, but for many women, Boudica included, this came too late. The queen became unwell soon afterwards and died, probably as a result of taking poison.[46] The fate of her daughters is unknown.

Few who surveyed the landscapes of Britain in the coming years could have anticipated that recovery would be possible. Farming more or less ceased and Britain was soon in the grip of famine. As time went on, however, the survivors endeavoured to rebuild their scorched homes. Within a decade or so of the revolt, Londinium acquired a new forum (remains of a basilica/forum complex with foundations dating from about AD 70 have been discovered near modern Cornhill and Gracechurch Street, just east of where the Walbrook flowed), and the city's population reached about 60,000 at its height. There was an amphitheatre for staging gladiatorial contests and executions, and baths (beneath modern Cleary Garden), both deemed acceptable exports of an otherwise objectionable culture.

Nero had assumed that the death of his mother would facilitate his divorce of Octavia, but the process proved to be unexpectedly protracted and complex. The Roman people had always admired Octavia and were horrified to see her banished from the city on an obviously false charge of adultery. Her subsequent execution only served to inflame the passions of Nero's enemies. Poppaea was pretty and intelligent and a fine conversationalist, but the public could not accept her as Octavia's replacement when she married Nero in AD 62. As violence erupted in the streets in response to Octavia's fate, statues of Poppaea were toppled and stories invented to besmirch her for promiscuity. A tragic play entitled *Octavia* presented the new empress as corrupting Nero against Seneca's better judgement while Octavia prepared to leave for exile. In her sorrow, the condemned Octavia compares herself to Electra, daughter of Agamemnon, and her husband to a vicious lion. The only historical play in Latin to survive antiquity, *Octavia* was long believed to have been written by Seneca, but probably postdates Nero's life.

It was only many years later that Poppaea was recognised as a victim rather than a usurper. Her untimely death in AD 65 inspired classical historians to assert that she had been fatally kicked by her own husband after reproaching him for coming home late from the races. She was then pregnant with their second child (their first, a daughter named Claudia Augusta, had died in infancy). As with so many of the historians' claims about the emperor – his murder of a constipated aunt with a strong laxative was not the most outlandish – there was no evidence that this was true, and some indication that it was not. Nero loved Poppaea and hoped to have more children with her. He even had a boy castrated and dressed up as a woman to use as a sexual replacement until he remarried less than a year later. It is much more likely that Poppaea died from the complications of a miscarriage. Her body was carefully embalmed at Nero's instruction.

Romans who believed that Poppaea was responsible for Nero's fall from grace soon stood corrected. Her death had little impact upon the emperor's enduring reputation. He was still widely blamed for the fire that had broken out near the Circus the year before, AD 64, even though he had been away from the city when it started. His subsequent arrangements of a relief fund and opening up of the Field of Mars to the displaced had done little to improve morale.[47] In desperation, Nero blamed the city's Christians for the disaster, only to alienate himself further from his people. The crucifixion of members of what was still viewed as a strange, primitive cult, his violent use of Christian bodies as human torches, incited mainly pity among the pagans of Rome. Even his old tutor Seneca was implicated in a conspiracy against his life and cornered into committing suicide. The tragedy demonstrated just how isolated the emperor had become.

Ground down by attempts on his life, out of pocket, and despairing that he could do nothing right, the thirty-year-old was left with nowhere to turn. When the Senate declared him an enemy of the state, he emulated Seneca by choosing the Stoic way out, fleeing Rome for the house of a freedman. Locusta had supplied Nero with some poison which he concealed in a golden box. He might have taken it and shared in the fate of Britannicus had his men not already removed the vial and put it out of reach.[48] There were few options left open to him. With the help of his secretary, Nero took a dagger to his throat in AD June 68 and with it cut off the lifeblood of the Julio-Claudian dynasty. He had ruled for just under fourteen years. Two of the women who had nursed him in childhood, Egloge and Alexandria, joined his mistress Acte in depositing his ashes in a purple porphyry sarcophagus. A divisive figure, hated by the senatorial class, loved by the plebeians, his tomb would seldom be bare of flowers.[49]

The Julio-Claudian dynasty could have ended with Tiberius or Caligula or even with Augustus. That it lasted through five emperors and more than twice as many emperors' wives was astonishing considering the hatred of autocracy bred in Rome since the time of the last king. With each succession it became apparent that, to survive, a dynasty needed more than legitimate sons. Far more than the emperors realised, the success of a dynasty depended upon good direction from their wives, from the movements of wives in the shadows.

While the most powerful women were those at court, the period had witnessed the emergence of key insiders, including Locusta, whose expertise made them invaluable to male rulers. The unpredictable, unbridled, often brutish whims of the emperors had nevertheless made this a period of intense uncertainty for women of all classes. Turia might have successfully navigated the restrictions of Augustan law, but the majority of her female peers were beholden to rules designed to put them back to a generation that existed only within the emperor's imagination. To be a woman was, as ever before, to be a thread in a tapestry of unknowable, impossible extent.

Conclusion

The death of Nero resulted in a power vacuum into which four men passed in quick succession. AD 69 went down in history as the Year of the Four Emperors and culminated in the rule of Vespasian. The Flavian dynasty endured under Vespasian's sons, Titus and Domitian, before emperors Nerva, Trajan and Hadrian bridged the gap between the first and second centuries. These years would be characterised as a time of High Empire and, for imperial women, high hair but comparatively low expectations, as the letters of Pliny the Younger well attest.

In AD 67, the year before Nero died, the island of Crete, where the Minoans had flourished, was finally conquered by the Romans. Over the past 3,000 years, women had become intrinsic to the narrative of ancient history, though progress, to use the modern term, had been neither smooth nor linear. The Minoans had exhibited a reverence for women in their art that was difficult to discern under the Mycenaeans. Seventh-century BC Lesbos afforded Sappho more opportunities for finding fame than most women could enjoy in Athens 200 years later. Roman writers hailed Lucretia a heroine and Cleopatra a villain as if both belonged to the same not-quite-real world. The ability to understand women and view them in the round remained underdeveloped in even the most celebrated classical and contemporary historians. I hope to have gone some way towards bringing these women back to life.

Modern readers are well placed to appreciate the tangible ways in which women shaped the course of ancient history. It should matter to us today that the earliest named author was a female poet. The survival of Enheduanna's verse set a precedent for the triumph of art over violence that echoes through the intervening millennia. We ought to celebrate Cynisca of Sparta for becoming the first female victor at the Olympic Games while in her fifties. We may not know the names of the prostitutes who helped to finance the construction of Alyattes' tomb, nor what the baker

Croesus credited with smoothing his rise to power looked like, but the contribution these women made to the history of Lydia was paramount.

Cyrus the Great is remembered as the founding king of the First Persian Empire, but he would never have achieved his position without marrying Amytis, daughter of Astyages. The king's death at the hands of the Massagetae and defilement by Queen Tomyris cast a long shadow over his earthly achievements. Rare sources, including the Fortification Tablets, have revealed to us just how central women remained to the functioning of the Persian court. However negatively Herodotus intended his statement that Atossa held 'the totality of power' during the rule of her husband Darius, there is no ignoring the fact that she played a valuable role in international diplomacy.

Beyond the reports of courageous individuals such as Gorgo of Sparta, Telesilla of Argos and Artemisia of Halicarnassus, the sole female commander in the Graeco-Persian Wars, we have read of countless women becoming entrenched in battle. It says a lot about the position attained by Aspasia in Athenian society that she could be held responsible for the outbreak of the Samian War. The war that Olympias of Epirus waged against her stepson's wife ought to be remembered alongside her son Alexander's campaigns. The graffiti found on missiles in Perugia bring to life the siege engineered by Fulvia while Mark Antony pursued his affair with Cleopatra. It is high time these women became household names alongside Alexander the Great and Julius Caesar.

The sources have encouraged us to question whether Rome would have won the Punic Wars without the generosity and patience of its female population. Blamed repeatedly for the emergence of bad omens and for men's failure in the field, women parted with their money and possessions, only to carry on suffering the restrictions of sumptuary laws. The punishment of the sister of the man who lost Rome a fleet, for her simple wish that he might do so again in order to disperse the traffic, shows how suspiciously women were guarded. The honours enjoyed by Busa for her kindness to Rome's military were extremely rare.

Cornelia, mother of the Gracchi, unwittingly established a paradigm that mothers of the emperors would struggle to emulate. While Cornelia received praise for the political influence she exerted over her sons, Livia and Agrippina the Younger received only opprobrium and warnings to stay away. It was in the hands of each emperor to establish parameters for the women closest to him. The absence of hard-and-fast rules rendered the place of women a fraught issue far beyond the collapse of the Julio-Claudian dynasty. The crude and outlandish tales that came to be written of the two Julias and Messalina in particular said more about the novelty of female power and its reception by men than it did the realities of the court.

As historians we are always at the mercy of the material that has come down to us and the gaps and biases it contains. We may vent our frustration on behalf of all the women of antiquity whose lives were buried with them or twisted out of recognition, but like Xerxes lashing the sea, we risk overlooking the spirits swirling subtly beneath. Women are everywhere that antiquity raises its head. They are the authors of our history.

Notes

Introduction

Translations from the Greek and Latin throughout the book are the author's own.

1 Hesiod *Works and Days* 373–4.
2 *Ibid.* 63–4; *Theogony* 573–5.
3 Sappho Fr. 16 – P. Oxy. 1231 fr. 1 col. i 13–34, col. ii 1+2166(a) 2 + P.S.I. 123 1–2.
4 *Palatine Anthology* 9.506.
5 Strabo *Geography* 13.2.3.
6 The first-century poet Antipater of Thessalonica sang the praises of nine female poets: Praxilla, Moero, Anyte, Sappho, Erinna, Telesilla, Corinna, Nossis and Myrtis – *Greek Anthology* 9.26.

Chapter I

1 Photius *Bibliotheca* Codex 190, citing Ptolemy Chennus.
2 Eustathius, preface to commentary on the *Odyssey.*
3 S. Butler, *The Authoress of the Odyssey: Where and when she wrote, who she was, the use she made of the Iliad, and how the poem grew under her hands,* E.P. Dutton &. Co., New York, 1922 (first published in London in 1897), p. 143.
4 R. Graves, *Homer's Daughter,* Academy Chicago, Chicago, 1987 (first published in 1955), p. 25.
5 Strabo *Geography* 10.4.3.
6 *Ibid.* 10.4.5.
7 A. Evans and D.G. Hogarth, letter to the *Glasgow Herald,* 12 June 1899.
8 Evans's 'Minoan' was adapted from the German 'Das Minoische Kretas' of K. Hoeck, *Kreta,* vol. 2, Göttingen, 1825.
9 J.A. Lobell, 'The Minoans of Crete', *Archaeology,* vol. 68, no. 3, May/June 2015, pp. 28–35. Study by George Stamatoyannopoulos, University of Washington, on 37 mitochondrial samples on bones from a Late Neolithic and Minoan ossuary in the Hagios Charalambos Cave in Crete.
10 R. Castleden, *Minoans,* 1993, p. 11, citing P. Faure, *La Vie Quotidienne en Crète au Temps de Minos,* Hachette, Paris, 1973.
11 P.J.P. McGeorge, 'Health and Diet in Minoan Times', in R. Jones and H. Catling

(eds), *New Aspects of Archaeological Science in Greece*, BSA Occasional Paper 3, 1988, pp. 47–54, cited in L.V. Watrous, *Minoan Crete: An Introduction*, Cambridge University Press, Cambridge, 2021, p. 88.

12 P.J.P. McGeorge, 'Morbidity and Medical Practice in Minoan Crete', in G. Rethemiotakis, N. Dimopoulou-Rethemiotaki and M. Andreadaki-Vlazaki (eds), *From the Land of the Labyrinth: Minoan Crete, 3000–1100 BC*, Alexander S. Onassis Public Benefit Foundation, New York, 2008, pp. 119–21. Cited averages based on figures for Knossos MM.

13 McGeorge, 'Morbidity and Medical Practice in Minoan Crete', p. 123.

14 Castleden, *Minoans*, 1993, p. 14.

15 E. Adams, *Cultural Identity in Minoan Crete: Social Dynamics in the Neo-Palatial Period*, Cambridge University Press, Cambridge, pp. 163–4.

16 Thucydides *History of the Peloponnesian War* 1.4.1.

17 D. Blackman, 'Minoan Shipsheds', *Skyllis* 11, vol. 2, 2011, pp. 4–11.

18 E. Hadjidaki-Marder, *The Minoan Shipwreck at Pseira, Crete*, INSTAP Academic Press, Philadelphia, 2021; E. Bonn-Muller, 'First Minoan Shipwreck', *Archaeology*, vol. 63, no. 1, January/February 2010, pp. 44–7.

19 M.N. Pareja, *cit.* T. Whipple, 'Curious Tail of Monkeys Who Crossed the Ancient World', *The Times*, 10 December 2019.

20 B. Urbani and D. Youlatos, 'A New Look at the Minoan "Blue" Monkeys', *Antiquity*, vol. 94, no. 374, April 2020, published online by Cambridge University Press.

21 On her images see especially C.H. Roehrig (ed.), *Hatshepsut: From Queen to Pharaoh*, The Metropolitan Museum of Art, Yale University Press, New Haven; London, 2006.

22 Hatshepsut was succeeded by her nephew Thutmose III, who wrecked many of her works of art in an unsuccessful attempt to obliterate her memory.

23 W. Helck, *Die Beziehungen Ägyptens und Vorderasien zur Ägäis bis ins 7. Jahrhundert v. Chr.*, Darmstadt, 1979, p. 102.

24 Tomb of Rekhmire, Egyptian Thebes, Sheikh Abd el-Qurna, TT 100. The pictures of Minoan visitors are well captured in the facsimile reproductions of the fresco 'Cretans Bringing Gifts, Tomb of Rekhmire', by Nina de Garis Davies (1881–1965), tempera on paper, The Metropolitan Museum of Art, New York.

25 See D. Evely, 'The Potters' Wheel in Minoan Crete', *Annual of the British School at Athens*, vol. 83, 1988, pp. 83–126.

26 D.S. Reese, 'Palaikastro Shells and Bronze Age Purple-Dye Production in the Mediterranean Basin', *Annual of the British School at Athens*, vol. 82, 1987, pp. 203–6. Thousands of molluscs were required to colour part of a single garment.

27 'Town Mosaic' faience plaques discovered at Knossos.

28 Watrous, *Minoan Crete*, p. 84. J.L. Fitton, *Minoans*, British Museum Press, London, 2002, is an excellent introduction to the Minoans and their art and architecture.

29 Watrous, *Minoan Crete*, p. 48, provides a useful summary of the destroyed and abandoned sites which included Malia and Vasiliki.

30 J. Evans, *Time and Chance: The Story of Arthur Evans and His Forebears*, Longmans, Green and Co. Ltd., London; New York; Toronto, 1943, p. 144.

31 Information on the dispute between Kalokairinos and Evans retrieved during a visit to the Ashmolean Museum exhibition *Labyrinth* in Oxford in February 2023.

32 'that uncertain element' – A. Evans, *cit.* J.A. MacGillivray, *Minotaur: Sir Arthur Evans and the Archaeology of the Minoan Myth*, Hill and Wang, New York, 2000, p. 5. Iosif Hatzidakis helped Evans to purchase the plot.
33 P.W. Lehmann, 'Harriet Boyd Hawes: Introductory Remarks', *A Land Called Crete: A Symposium in Memory of Harriet Boyd Hawes 1871–1945*, Smith College, Massachusetts, October 1967, pp. 11–12. Several of the objects Boyd excavated were shipped to America and are now at the Metropolitan Museum of Art in New York, Penn Museum, and the Boston Museum of Fine Arts.
34 'In sport' – H.B. Hawes, 'Memoirs of a Pioneer Excavator in Crete', *Archaeology* 18, 1965, p. 97, *cit.* N. Marinatos, *Sir Arthur Evans and Minoan Crete: Creating the Vision of Knossos*, I.B. Tauris, London; New York, 2015, p. 180.
35 Homer *Odyssey* 11.568–71.
36 Euripides apparently suppressed Ariadne's role in Theseus' escape. Fragments of his lost play *Theseus* show Daedalus rescuing Theseus from the labyrinth instead.
37 See J.S. Major and C.A. Cook, *Ancient China: A History*, Routledge, London; New York, 2017, pp. 61–2. The slightly later Chinese city of Erligang, near Zhengzhou, would be home to the Shang dynasty (1600–1046 BC), who like the Minoans were literate, inscribing bone and shell with an early form of Chinese.
38 S. Marinatos to Ministry of Education, 16 May 1929, archives of twenty-third Ephoreia, no. 797/894, Heraklion, translated and cited by N. Marinatos, *Sir Arthur Evans and Minoan Crete*, I.B. Tauris, London; New York, 2015, p. 114.
39 E. Pottier, *cit.* MacGillivray, *Minotaur*, p. 205.
40 E. Waugh, *Labels: A Mediterranean Journal*, Duckworth, London, 1974 (first published in 1930), p. 136.
41 The image of a labyrinth appeared on a Linear B tablet discovered at Pylos around this date. The fresco dates to about 1700 BC.
42 On the double-axe at Knossos, Gournia and elsewhere, see M.L. Moss, *The Minoan Pantheon*, Hadrian Books, Oxford, 2005, p. 38.
43 See A. Shapland, 'Knossos Today', in A. Shapland (ed.), *Labyrinth: Knossos, Myth and Reality*, Ashmolean Museum, Oxford, 2023, p. 213.
44 Herodotus *Histories* 2.148.
45 The glorious bee pendant, now in the Heraklion Archaeological Museum on Crete, came from Chrysolakkos, the cemetery for the palace at Mallia, and dates from 1800–1700 BC.
46 Bull head rhyton, from Knossos, c. 1550–1500 BC, Heraklion Archaeological Museum, AE 1368.
47 Bull-leaper ivory figure from Knossos, Heraklion Archaeological Museum.
48 Late Minoan bronze bull sculpture, c. 1600–1450 BC, British Museum, 1966,0328.1.
49 J.A. MacGillivray, 'Labyrinths and Bull-Leapers', *Archaeology*, vol. 53, no. 6, November/December 2000, p. 54.
50 'Taureador Fresco', Knossos, perhaps 1450–1400 BC, Heraklion Archaeological Museum.
51 The date of the origins of the Phoenicians is much disputed, with many favouring 1200 BC, when their civilisation was probably already flourishing.
52 On the interaction between animal and human in this practice, see A. Shapland, 'Jumping to Conclusions: Bull-Leaping in Minoan Crete', *Society & Animals* 21, 2013, pp. 194–207.

53 Hesiod *Theogony* 477.
54 Moss, *The Minoan Pantheon*, p. 135. Mount Juktas is an equally important 'peak sanctuary'.
55 Homer *Odyssey* 19.188. Eileithyia was also worshipped at Inatos on Crete.
56 The Dumbarton Oaks Birthing Figure in the Robert Woods Bliss Collection of Pre-Columbian Art. Many believe the piece to be more modern than Aztec and perhaps even largely carved in the nineteenth century.
57 Figure of the Goddess with Upraised Arms, 1375–00 BC, from the Shrine of the Double Axes at Knossos, now in the Heraklion Museum. See G. Rethemiotakis, 'The Shrine of the Double Axes at Knossos and the Figure of the Goddess with Upraised Arms', in A. Shapland (ed.), *Labyrinth: Knossos, Myth and Reality*, Ashmolean Museum, Oxford, 2023, pp. 124–5.
58 See K. Lapatin, *Mysteries of the Snake Goddess: Art, Desire, and the Forging of History*, Houghton Mifflin, Boston; New York, 2002.
59 Goddess of Myrtos, c. 2500 BC, Archaeological Museum of Agios Nikolaos.
60 On both see B. Hinsch, *Women in Ancient China*, Bowman & Littlefield, Lanham; Boulder; New York; London, 2018, pp. 43–8.
61 See J. Younger, 'Minoan Woman', in S.L. Budin and J.M. Turfa (eds), *Women in Antiquity*, Routledge, Oxford; New York, 2016, pp. 573–94.
62 Terracotta circle of women from Palaikastro, c. 1350 BC, Heraklion Archaeological Museum.
63 Fresco, Room 3, Akrotiri, Thera, c. 1600 BC.
64 Gold ring found by Heinrich Schliemann at Mycenae – CMS 17.
65 Painted Sarcophagus in Heraklion Archaeological Museum.
66 Xeste 3.
67 H.J. Bruins, J.A. MacGillivray, *et al.*, 'Geoarchaeological Tsunami Deposits at Palaikastro (Crete) and the Late Minoan IA Eruption of Santorini', *Journal of Archaeological Science* 35 (1), 2008, pp. 191–212.
68 The connection between Santorini and Atlantis was made by Louis Figuier (*La Terre et les Mers*, Librairie de L. Hachette et Cie, Paris, 1864) and developed further in connection with Plato and Minoan societal collapse by Spyridon Marinatos ('The Volcanic Destruction of Minoan Crete', *Antiquity* 13, pp. 425–39) in 1939.
69 Plato *Timaeus* 24e–25d; *Critias* 108e; 113c–120e.
70 I. Lazaridis, A. Mittnik, *et al.*, 'Genetic Origins of the Minoans and Mycenaeans', *Nature*, vol. 548, 10 August 2017, pp. 214–30.

Chapter II

1 Pausanias *Description of Greece* 2.16.3. In an alternative legend, also related by Pausanias, Mycenae took its name from the cap (also *mykes*) of Perseus' scabbard falling here.
2 On the shipwreck and analysis see Y. Goren, 'International Exchange during the Late Second Millennium B.C.: Microarchaeological Study of Finds from the Uluburun Ship', in J. Aruz, S.B. Graff and Y. Rakic (eds), *Cultures in Contact: From Mesopotamia to the Mediterranean in the Second Millenium B.C.*, Yale University Press, New York, 2013.

3 The fact that Homer was later than the period he described was well known in antiquity.

4 A.E. Samuel, *The Mycenaeans in History*, Prentice-Hall, Inc., Englewood Cliffs, New Jersey, 1966, p. 49.

5 See G.E. Mylonas, *Mycenae and the Mycenaean Age*, Princeton University Press, Princeton, 1966, p. 17.

6 Pausanias *Description of Greece* 2.16.5.

7 Mylonas, *Mycenae and the Mycenaean Age*, p. 70.

8 S. Butler, *The Authoress of the Odyssey*, Longmans, Green & Co., London, 1897, p. 130.

9 Graves, *Homer's Daughter*, p. 8.

10 Fresco in the so-called 'Room with the Fresco Complex' at Mycenae.

11 Homer *Iliad* 2.612–14. Agamemnon also supplied 60 ships to the Trojan War on behalf of Arcadia. On the *wanax* and Homer see M.I. Finley, 'Homer and Mycenae: Property and Tenure', *Historia*, vol. 6, no. 2, April 1957, pp. 133–59.

12 Homer *Iliad* 2.489–90 and ensuing 'Catalogue of Ships'.

13 Homer *Odyssey* 4.708.

14 Geometric krater, probably Athenian, c. 740–30 BC, British Museum, 1899, 0219.1.

15 KBo 5.6 iv, from the Deeds of Suppiluliuma. Most identify the queen in question with Ankhesenamun but other contenders have been suggested.

16 Mummies 317a and 317b. J.A. Lobell, 'The Pharaoh's Daughters', *Archaeology*, September/October 2022 (online).

17 M. Wood, *In Search of the Trojan War*, BBC Books, London, 2008, was an early supporter of the theory that the king of Ahhiyawa was Mycenaean Greek. The connection between Achaea and Ahhiyawa was first made by E. Forrer, 'Vorhomerische Griechen in den Keilschrifttexten von Boghazkoi', *Mitteilungen der Deutschen Orient-Gesellschaft* 63, 1924, pp. 1–24.

18 AhT 20. The king was Mursili II.

19 CHT 214.12.A.

20 S.C. Murray, *The Collapse of the Mycenaean Economy: Imports, Trade, and Institutions 1300–700 BCE*, Cambridge University Press, New York, 2017, p. 37, citing tablets including AhT 19.

21 Alaksandu Treaty – clay cuneiform tablet recording the treaty between Muwattalli II and Alaksandu, British Museum 108569.

22 Homer *Iliad* 21.446–7.

23 *Ibid.* 6.242–4.

24 *Ibid.* 6.454–65.

25 'Dog-faced' – frequent, for example, Homer *Iliad* 3.180; *Odyssey* 1.145.

26 Homer *Iliad* 3.189.

27 The story of the Amazons fighting at Troy was told in the *Aethiopis*, part of the so-called Epic Cycle, now fragmentary.

28 Homer *Iliad* 2.138.

29 The grave of the so-called Griffin Warrior at Pylos housed the remains of a wealthy man in his thirties, about 5 feet 6 inches tall, who died about 1500 BC. It has been suggested that he was the *wanax* of the Pylian palace. He was buried with his sword and dagger on his chest and was surrounded by bronze and gold jewellery, drinking cups and seal stones.

30 Aeschylus *Agamemnon* 689–90.

31 On the Homeridae see especially Isocrates *Helen* 10.65; Hellanicus FGrH 4 Fr. 20; Strabo *Geography* 14.1.35.

32 KUB 21.38 (CTH 176) obv. 17–18, *cit.* T. Bryce, *Life and Society in the Hittite World*, Oxford University Press, Oxford, 2012, p. 94. For a summary biography of Puduhepa see C. Burney, *Historical Dictionary of the Hittites*, The Scarecrow Press, Inc., Maryland; Toronto; Oxford, 2004, pp. 230–1.

33 KUB 3.34 (CTH 165) rev. 15ff; *cit.* Bryce, *Life and Society*, p. 94.

34 Letter from Nefertari to Puduhepa, *cit.* K.A. Kitchen, *Pharaoh Triumphant: The Life and Times of Ramesses II*, Aris & Phillips Ltd, Wiltshire, 1982, p. 80.

35 Homer *Iliad* 6.168.

36 B.A. Olsen, *Women in Mycenaean Greece: The Linear B Tablets from Pylos and Knossos*, Routledge, Abingdon; New York, 2014, pp. 2, 6.

37 Homer *Odyssey* 20.106–9.

38 Ub 1318, *cit.* J.-C. Billigmeier and J.A. Turner, 'The Socio-Economic Roles of Women in Mycenaean Greece: A Brief Survey from Evidence of the Linear B Tablets', in H.P. Foley (ed.), *Reflections of Women in Antiquity*, Routledge, London and New York, 2004, p. 3.

39 See, for example, the Pylos tablet PY Aa 62, *cit.* Olsen, *Women in Mycenaean Greece*, p. 31.

40 D. Nakassis, *Individuals and Society in Mycenaean Pylos*, Brill, Leiden; Boston, 2013, pp. 8–9.

41 Streets – Samuel, *The Mycenaeans in History*, p. 76.

42 Homer *Iliad* 6.289–92.

43 J.-C. Billigmeier and J.A. Turner, 'The Socio-Economic Roles of Women in Mycenaean Greece', p. 5.

44 Billigmeier and Turner, 'The Socio-Economic Roles of Women in Mycenaean Greece', p. 6; L.R. Palmer, *Nestor*, 1 November (1977), 1082–3.

45 The names of several keybearers have been preserved: Ka-wa-ra (Qa 1289), Ke-i-ja (Qa 1303) and Erita, priestess of Pa-ki-ja-na (see Billigmeier and Turner, 'The Socio-Economic Roles of Women in Mycenaean Greece', p. 7).

46 The identification of Karpathia the keybearer with the Karpathia named in tablet Un 443 is made by D. Nakassis, in *Individuals and Society in Mycenaean Pylos*, Brill, Leiden; Boston, p. 130.

47 C.W. Blegen, 'Excavations at Pylos, 1953', *American Journal of Archaeology*, vol. 58, no. 1, January 1954, p. 28; Samuel, *The Mycenaeans in History*, p. 56.

48 Homer *Odyssey* 3.464–8.

49 C.W. Blegen and M. Rawson, with revisions by J.L. Davis and C.W. Shelmerdine, *A Guide to the Palace of Nestor*, American School of Classical Studies at Athens, Princeton, New Jersey, 2001, p. 22. The bathroom at Pylos measured 6.34 m by 2.56 m wide – see C.W. Blegen and M. Rawson, *The Palace of Nestor at Pylos in Western Messenia: Vol I: The Buildings and their Contents*, Princeton University Press, New Jersey, 1966, p. 186.

50 Samuel, *The Mycenaeans in History*, p. 56.

51 Olsen, *Women in Mycenaean Greece*, p. 89.

52 The description of the bathing of Odysseus in the *Odyssey* echoes that of the cleansing of Patroclus' body in the *Iliad*. Robert Graves takes this as further evidence of the 'feminine' nature of the *Odyssey* in his novel *Homer's Daughter*.

53 On Minoan child sacrifice there is a useful overview by E. Sapouna-Sakellaraki, 'A Human Sacrifice at the Minoan Temple of Anemospilia (Archanes)' in A. Shapland (ed.), *Labyrinth: Knossos, Myth and Reality*, Ashmolean Museum, Oxford, 2023, pp. 198–201. Evidence of Minoan-era ritual killing of humans has been found on the slopes of Mount Juktas at the Temple of Anemospilia, where it was seemingly carried out in an unsuccessful bid to avert an earthquake.

54 H. Gardner and F. Kleiner, *Gardner's Art Through the Ages: The Western Perspective*, vol. 1, Cengage Learning, Boston, 2017, p. 97, who notes that this dome remained the highest for a millennium and a half.

55 Grave Circle A at Mycenae.

56 A fresco at Mycenae, for example, features a figure-of-eight shield painted white with black cloud-like shapes, not dissimilar to cow-print.

57 Homer *Iliad* 10.260–5.

58 See M. Kramer-Hajos, *Mycenaean Greece and the Aegean World: Palace and Province in the Late Bronze Age*, Cambridge University Press, New York, 2016, p. 33.

Chapter III

1 Pylos An 1. An Aetolian city called Pleuron, possibly synonymous, appears in the *Iliad*.

2 Pylos An 610.

3 Pylos An 657.

4 Billigmeier and Turner, 'The Socio-Economic Roles of Women', p. 7.

5 Tawagalawas Letter, CTH 181.

6 The clay upon which the Tawagalawas Letter was written is thought to have come from the eastern Aegean and perhaps even Miletus itself – Y. Goren, 'International Exchange during the Late Second Millennium B C.: Microarchaeological Study of Finds from the Uluburun Ship', p. 60, in J. Aruz, S.B. Graff and Y. Rakic (eds), *Cultures in Contact: From Mesopotamia to the Mediterranean in the Second Millenium B.C.*, Yale University Press, New York, 2013.

7 Milawata Letter, CTH 182.

8 C.W. Blegen, J.L. Caskey and M. Rawson, *Troy III: The Sixth Settlement*, Princeton University Press, 1953, pp. 329–32. Blegen believed that Troy VIIa was destroyed around 1240 BC, but most scholars now date the event to 1180 BC.

9 A possibility M. Wood also weighs up, but in relation to the Trojan Horse, in *In Search of The Trojan War*, BBC Books, London, 2008, p. 281.

10 See, for example, C. Blegen, *Troy and the Trojans*, Barnes and Noble Books, New York, 1995, p. 182, and Wood, *In Search of the Trojan War*, p. 250, for a summary of the slingshots and other weapons found.

11 Pausanias *Geography* 1.23.8.

12 Homer *Iliad* 9.326–8.

13 *Ibid.* 5.638–43.

14 See P. Halstead and V. Isaakidou, 'Faunal Evidence for Feasting: Burnt Offerings from the Palace of Nestor at Pylos', in P. Halstead and J.C. Barrett (eds), *Food, Cuisine and Society in Prehistoric Greece*, Oxbow Books, Oxford; Philadelphia, 2004, pp. 143–50.

15 V.R. d'A. Desborough, *The Greek Dark Ages*, St Martin's Press, New York, 1972, pp. 19–20.
16 S.C. Murray, *The Collapse of the Mycenaean Economy: Imports, Trade, and Institutions 1300–700 BCE*, Cambridge University Press, New York, 2017, p. 237.
17 R. Osborne, *Greece in the Making: 1200–479 BC*, Routledge, London; New York, 1996, p. 31.
18 Homer *Odyssey* 19.177; Pindar *Isthmian* 9.1–4 claimed that the Dorians founded the Greek city of Aegina.
19 C. Thomas, 'Found: The Dorians', *Expedition Magazine*, vol. 20, no. 3, 1978: https://www.penn.museum/sites/expedition/found-the-dorians.
20 The Great Karnak Inscription (KIU 4246).
21 A.M. Snodgrass, *The Dark Age of Greece*, Edinburgh University Press, Edinburgh, 1971, p. 29.
22 R. Carpenter, *Discontinuity in Greek Civilization*, Cambridge University Press, Cambridge, 1966, pp. 60–1.
23 *Ibid.* p. 64.
24 Thucydides *History of the Peloponnesian War* 1.12.
25 *Ibid.* 1.2.
26 Herodotus *Histories* 1.146.
27 M.A. Liston and J.K. Papadopoulos, 'The "Rich Athenian Lady" Was Pregnant: The Anthropology of a Geometric Tomb Reconsidered', *Hesperia: The Journal of the American School of Classical Studies at Athens*, vol. 73, no. 1, 2004, pp. 7–38; E.L. Smithson, 'The Tomb of a Rich Athenian Lady, CA. 850 B. C.', *Hesperia*, vol. 37, no. 1, 1968, pp. 77–116.
28 Attic geometric grave-marker amphora by the Dipylon Painter, Athens, mid eighth century BC.
29 J. Boardman, *The History of Greek Vases*, Thames and Hudson, London, 2001, pp. 17, 28–9.
30 See S.C. Murray, *The Collapse of the Mycenaean Economy: Imports, Trade, and Institutions 1300–700 BCE*, Cambridge University Press, New York, 2017, pp. 205–9.
31 Boardman, *The History of Greek Vases*, p. 19.
32 Herodotus *Histories* 5.57–8.
33 The cup, now in the Museo Archaeologico di Pithecusae, is dated to 715 BC and linked to Teos by J.L. Fitton and A. Villing, 'Storytellers', pp. 29–30, in A. Villing, J.L. Fitton, V. Donnellan and A. Shapland, *Troy: Myth and Reality*, British Museum/Thames & Hudson, London, 2019.
34 Nestor's Cup, Villa Arbusto Museum, Ischia (my translation). The other Cup of Nestor, from Mycenae, is now in the National Archaeological Museum, Athens.
35 Homer *Iliad* 11.632–5.
36 See B. Hughes, *Venus and Aphrodite: History of a Goddess*, Weidenfeld & Nicolson, London, 2020, pp. 9–10. For my description of the development of Aphrodite I draw on a live discussion hosted between Hughes and myself by Blackwell's Bookshop online in October 2020.
37 See B. De Shong Meador, *Inanna: Lady of Largest Heart, Poems of the Sumerian High Priestess Enheduanna*, University of Texas Press, Austin, Texas, 2000.
38 Enheduanna, 'The Exaltation of Inanna'. The hymn is recorded across several Mesopotamian clay tablets. See for example, from c. 1750 BC, 1888: CBS 7847,

University of Pennsylvania Museum of Archaeology and Anthropology, Philadelphia.

39 *Ibid.* line 73, translation by Selena Wisnom, with thanks.

40 Akkadian disc, c. 2350–2300 BC, found in the Larsa Temple of Nin-Gal. The Penn Museum, B16665.

41 Mimnermus, Fr. 9.

42 Thucydides *History of the Peloponnesian War* 6.3.

43 *Ibid.* 6.2.6.

44 J. Swaddling, *The Ancient Olympic Games*, University of Texas Press, Austin, 1999, is a useful introduction to the Olympic Games.

45 Pausanias *Description of Greece* 5.6.7.

46 *Ibid.* 5.16.

47 *Ibid.* 3.8.

48 *Ibid.* 6.1.6.

49 *Iliupersis* – Proclus *Chrestomathy* 4 with Apollodorus 5.22 (M.L. West [ed.], *Greek Epic Fragments*, Harvard University Press, Cambridge, MA; London, 2003, p. 147). On the Locrian Maidens, see J. Fontenrose, *The Delphic Oracle*, University of California Press, Berkeley; Los Angeles; London, 1978, pp. 131–6; M. Dillon, *Girls and Women in Classical Greek Religion*, Routledge, Abingdon, 2003, pp. 63–6.

50 Aeneas Tacticus 31.24.

51 Plutarch *Moralia* - On the Delays of Divine Vengeance 12.

52 IG 9.12.3.706.

Chapter IV

1 Lesbos was 10 kilometres from Asia Minor and the third-largest island in the Aegean after Crete and Euboea. See D. G. Shipley, 'Lesbos', *Oxford Classical Dictionary* online, 2016. On the Mycenaean evidence see R. Stillwell, W.L. MacDonald and M.H. McAllister (eds), *The Princeton Encyclopedia of Classical Sites*, Princeton University Press, Princeton, New Jersey, 1976, p. 502.

2 Homer knew Lesbos as 'the abode of Makar', *Makaros hedos*, after its legendary first ruler, and described Odysseus journeying there to wrestle one Philomeleides in the *Odyssey* (P. Oxy. 2166(b) 10.3–17; Homer *Iliad* 24.544; Homer *Odyssey* 4.242–4). It was to Makar's son-in-law that Lesbos allegedly owed its name. On the complex mythological genealogy see Diodorus Siculus *Library of History* 5.81. Menelaus, too, was said to have made the crossing, and islanders spoke of Agamemnon enduring an uncertain voyage across the sea to make landfall on their beaches (Homer *Odyssey* 3.168–9; *P.S.I.* ii 123. 3–12 + P. Oxy. 1231 fr. 1 col. ii 2–21 + 2166(a) 3 [Ox Pap xxi p. 122] + 2289 fr. 9).

3 Homer *Iliad* 9.128–30. As it was, Achilles had already taken at least one Lesbian woman, 'Phorbas' daughter, Diomede of the beautiful cheeks' (*Iliad* 9.665), as his captive after sacking Lesbos on his way to Troy.

4 Alcaeus Fr. 130b – P. Oxy. 2165 fr 1 col. ii 9–32 + fr 2 col. ii 1.

5 The earliest painting of her, discovered on a Greek vase, dates to around a century after she lived. Depicted in flowing drapery and a cap and holding a lyre and plectrum, she is more stylised than realistic, as is to be expected from this period.

6 Sappho Fr. 1 – P. Oxy. 1800 fr. 1 (papyrus dating to the late second or early third century AD).
7 Demetrius *de Elocutio* 146. The outstanding man Sappho praises here is very probably Terpander, who took first prize at a new contest in Sparta in 676 BC and also triumphed at Delphi.
8 *Palatine Anthology* 9.50 (Plato *On the Muses*).
9 Spencer (2000), pp. 73–9, who discusses protection offered by Olympus too.
10 Aelius Aristides *Oration: In defence of the Four* 46.207.
11 Aristotle *Politics* 1311b. The overthrow of Penthilus by Megacles appears to have taken place when Alcaeus was still a child (P. Oxy. 1234 fr. 6).
12 Thucydides *History of the Peloponnesian War* 1.126.
13 Plutarch *Solon* 12.
14 Because the Athenians had killed suppliants under Cylon, the Spartans believed that they were cursed. Even just before the Peloponnesian War the Spartans referred back to this curse, hoping to eliminate Pericles and make the Athenians think that it was the *casus belli* – Thucydides *History of the Peloponnesian War* 1.127.1–2. See E. Foster, *Thucydides, Pericles, and Periclean Imperialism*, Cambridge University Press, Cambridge, 2010.
15 Scholiast on Aristophanes *Thesmophoriazusae* 401.
16 Hesiod *Works and Days* 63–4; *Theogony* 573–5.
17 Servius on Virgil *Eclogues* 6.42.
18 Maximus of Tyre *Orations* 18.9h.
19 Himerius *Orations* 9.4.
20 Sappho Fr. 98 – P. Haun 301 (third century BC papyrus).
21 Photius *Lexicon* 81.12s.
22 Hesiod *Works and Days* 73–5; Athenaeus *Deipnosophistae* 15.674e + P. Oxy.1787 fr. 33 (vv.1–5).
23 Sappho Fr. 94 – P. Berol. 9722 fol. 2, *Berliner Klassikertexte* 5.2 p. 12ss + Lobel Sigma. mu. p. 79.
24 Lucian *Dialogues of the Courtesans* 5.
25 Myson, fifth century BC, Museo Archaeologico Regionale, Syracuse. On the use of dildos with reference also to the Sappho fragment, see P. DuBois, *Slaves and other Objects*, The University of Chicago Press, Chicago; London, 2003, pp. 82–100.
26 The Hasselmann Painter, Attic pelike, 440–30 BC, British Museum 1865, 1118.49. This and similar vase scenes have been linked to the Athenian festival of the Haloa which honoured women's fertility.
27 Sappho Fr. 99 – P. Oxy.2291 (a). This papyrus fragment dates to the third century AD.
28 Suda Sigma 107.
29 Sappho, *cit.* Dionysius of Halicarnassus *On Literary Composition* 23 (+ P. Oxy. 2288).
30 See M. Williamson, *Sappho's Immortal Daughters*, Harvard University Press, Cambridge, MA; London, 1995, p. 51.
31 Maximus of Tyre *Orations* 18.9.
32 M.M. Patrick, *Sappho and the Island of Lesbos*, Methuen & Co., London, 1912, p. 103.
33 Sappho Fr. 214b – S 261A *S. L. G.* P. Colon. 5860 fr. 1 (Commentary on Sappho).

34 *Ibid.*
35 Maximus of Tyre *Orations* 18.9.
36 See M. Williamson, 'Sappho', *Oxford Classical Dictionary*, published online in 2016.
37 Alcman, *cit.* Athenaeus *Deipnosophistae* 13.600ff.
38 Aristotle *Rhetoric* 1367a. See also Hephaestion *Enchiridion* 14.4.
39 Vases include the Brygos Painter's Munich Krater (2416) from c. 500–450 BC.
40 There is an interesting article on this by G. Nagy, 'Did Sappho and Alcaeus Ever Meet? Symmetries of Myth and Ritual in Performing the Songs of Ancient Lesbos', Center for Hellenic Studies, Harvard University, published online: http://nrs.harvard.edu/urn-3:hlnc.essay:Nagy.Did_Sappho_and_Alcaeus_Ever_Meet.2007.
41 See P. duBois, *Sappho*, I.B. Tauris, London; New York, 2015, p. 18.
42 *Ibid.*, *Sappho*, p. 11. Aphrodite's temple on Lesbos stood in a peaceful grove of apple trees overgrown with roses beside a meadow of grazing horses (Ostracon Flor. [prim. ed. M. Norsa, Ann R. Scuola di Pisa vi, 1937, 8 ss] – potsherd of the third century BC).
43 Stillwell, MacDonald and McAllister (eds), *The Princeton Encyclopedia of Classical Sites*, p. 503. Sappho led women to dance in a precinct sacred to Hera at least once – *Palatine Anthology* 9.189.
44 Apollo Napaios – Stillwell, MacDonald and McAllister (eds), *The Princeton Encyclopedia of Classical Sites*, p. 503. The temple, the location of which is unknown, is mentioned by Strabo *Geography* 9.426. The people of Mytilene worshipped particularly Apollo Maloeis. Apollo protected colonists. This smaller temple is more likely than the Klopedi temple to have been in existence at Sappho's time.
45 N. Spencer, 'Exchange and Stasis in Archaic Mytilene', in R. Brock and S. Hodkinson (eds), 2000, p. 75, and see fig. 11 for a good diagram, in *Alternatives to Athens: Varieties of Political Organization and Community in Ancient Greece*, Oxford University Press, Oxford; New York, 2000, p. 75.
46 N. Spencer, 'Early Lesbos between East and West: A "Grey Area" of Aegean Archaeology', *Annual of the British School at Athens*, vol. 90, Centenary Volume, 1995, p. 298.
47 Homeric Hymn to Apollo 269, 300–4; Tyrtaeus (seventh century BC) Fr. 4.
48 Pausanias *Description of Greece* 10.6.6.
49 Athenian white-ground lekythos, c. 525–475 BC, Louvre, Paris, CA1915.
50 Archilochus Fr 19. On the changing meaning of *tyrannos* see V. Parker, 'Turannos: The Semantics of a Political Concept from Archilochus to Aristotle', *Hermes* 126, no. 2, 1998, pp. 145–72.
51 Herodotus *Histories* 1.13.
52 Alyattes waged war against Media in the second decade of the sixth century BC.
53 Herodotus *Histories* 1.25.
54 Sappho Fr. 98 – P. Haun 301; Homer *Iliad* 4.141–4, *cit.* G. Perrot and C. Chipiez, *History of Art in Phrygia, Lydia, Caria, and Lycia*, Chapman and Hall, Ltd., London; A.C. Armstrong and Son, New York, 1892, pp. 297–8.
55 Herodotus *Histories* 1.94; Xenophanes of Colophon, *cit.* Pollux 9.83.
56 Aristotle Fr. 611,37 (Rose).
57 See Y.A. Meriçboyu, 'Lydian Jewellery', in N.D. Cahill, *The Lydians and Their World*, Yapi Kredi Yayinlari, Istanbul, 2010.

58 Sappho, *cit.* Demetrius *de Elocutio* 140.
59 Athenaeus *Deipnosophistae* 1. 21bc.
60 Hephaestion *Enchiridion* 7.7.
61 Herodian *On the Declension of Nouns* (ap. Aldi *Thes. Cornucop.* 268V: v. Choerob. ii. lxv. 43s. Hilgard); see also Maximus of Tyre *Orations* 18.9d.
62 Strabo *Geography* 13.58 (on Assus and Lamponia).
63 Spencer, 'Exchange and Stasis in Archaic Mytilene', in Brock and Hodkinson (eds), p. 76.
64 Strabo *Geography* 17.1.33; Spencer, 'Early Lesbos between East and West', p. 293.
65 Herodotus *Histories* 2.178.
66 P. Oxy. 1800 fr. 1 (three brothers' names). Another brother of Sappho, Larichus, was an honourable cupbearer in the local *prytaneion* or government building in Mytilene (Athenaeus *Deipnosophistae* 10.425a), and the profession of Sappho's other brother Eurygius is unknown.
67 Herodotus *Histories* 2.134.
68 Sappho Fr. 5 – P. Oxy. 7 + 2289.6.
69 Alcaeus Fr. 117b – P. Oxy. 1788 frr. 4, 6, 11, 15 i + Ox. Pap. Xxi, pp. 140–2.
70 Sappho Fr. 213A – P. Oxy. 2506 fr. 43 col. ii (Commentary on lyric poets, first or second century AD).
71 See Ovid *Heroides* 15.63–70, 117–20.
72 What bothered Sappho was that, in being visited by Charaxus twice, Doricha would have reason to be boastful – Sappho Fr. 15 – P. Oxy. 1231 fr. 1 col. i. 1–12 + fr. 3; see also fragment P. Oxy. 2289 fr. 2.
73 *Palatine Anthology* 7.489.
74 Stobaeus *Anthology* (on folly) 3.4.12.
75 Herodotus *Histories* 2.135.
76 Athenaeus *Deipnosophistae* 13.596cd claimed that these spits were in fact the gifts of another woman also known as Rhodopis. The fact that Herodotus thought of them as belonging to Charaxus' Doricha, however, only goes to show that her ambition had been fulfilled.
77 Poseidippus, *cit.* Athenaeus *Deipnosophistae* 13.596cd.
78 Strabo *Geography* 13.38.
79 Plutarch *Solon* 17.
80 Diogenes Laertius *Lives of Eminent Philosophers* 1.74.
81 Strabo *Geography* 13.1.38.
82 *Ibid.*; Herodotus *Histories* 5.94–5.
83 Pittacus' father was from Thrace – Diogenes Laertius *Lives of Eminent Philosophers* 1.74. Alcaeus' brothers were Antimenidas and Kikis.
84 Plutarch *On the Malice of Herodotus* 858ab.
85 Diogenes Laertius *Lives of Eminent Philosophers* 1.74.
86 Conventionally dated c. 580 BC, this move could be later, given the reference to Croesus' involvement with Pittacus.
87 Alcaeus Fr. 70 – P. Oxy. 1234 fr. 2 i 1–13.
88 The word 'tyrant' in this context acquired shades of its later negative associations – see Parker, 'Turannos: The Semantics of a Political Concept from Archilochus to Aristotle', pp. 156–7.
89 Alcaeus Fr. 74 – P. Oxy. 1360 fr. 2 + 2166 c 31.
90 Aristotle *Politics* 1285a. Alcaeus' earlier exile was to Pyrrha.

91 Legend had it that Antimenidas excelled himself here by saving the people from an enemy just shy of five royal cubits tall – Strabo *Geography* 13.2.1.

92 This marriage accompanied a treaty between Cyaxares and Nebuchadnezzar after the sack of Nineveh in 612 BC – ABC Chronicle 3, 1.29, *cit.* M. Brosius, *Women in Ancient Persia, 559–331 BC*, Clarendon Press, Oxford, 1996, p. 39.

93 Berosus, *cit.* Josephus *Against Apion* 1.19; Josephus *Antiquities of the Jews* 10.11.1.

94 See F. Ferrari, *Sappho's Gift: The Poet and Her Community*, Michigan Classical Press, Ann Arbor, 2010, pp. 23–6.

95 Sappho's exile was recorded in the inscription on the Parian Marble, a stele originally measuring over two metres tall and attributed to a single anonymous author in 264/3 BC. The inscription reveals that she left for exile during the archonship of Critias, which places the date between 605 and 590 BC.

96 Sappho Fr. 20 – P. Oxy. 1231 fr. 9 + 2166(a)4A (Ox. Pap. xxi p. 122).

97 Alcaeus Fr. 6 – P. Oxy. 1789 l i 15–19, ii 1–17, 3 i, 12 + 2166e4. The poem is probably a metaphor for Alcaeus' struggles under Myrsilus, as Heraclitus suggests in *Homeric Allegories*.

98 Alcaeus, *cit.* Horace *Odes* 1.32-3-11.

99 Ovid *Metamorphoses* 5.525–6.

100 The Temple of Apollo, situated near the harbour, is thought to have been built c. 620–575 BC. There was also a Temple of Zeus at Polichne datable to c. 620–580 BC.

101 Alcaeus Fr. 129 – P Oxy 2165 fr. 1 col. I + 2166c 6.

102 Sappho Fr. 98b – P. Mediol, ed. Vogliano, *Philol.* 93 (1939) 277ss. The fact that 'exile' is also mentioned in this fragment suggests that Sappho's regret at failing to obtain the headband dates from this time.

103 Alcaeus Fr. 69 – P Oxy 1234 fr. 1 7–14 + 2166 c 1.

104 Diogenes Laertius, *Lives of Eminent Philosophers*, I 81.

105 Aristotle *Politics* 3.1285a.

106 Thales of Miletus, *cit.* Plutarch *Moralia* – Symposium of the Seven Wise Men 14.

107 Strabo *Geography* 13.2.3 (restoring autonomy); Diodorus Siculus *Library of History* 9.11 (lawgiver).

108 Aristotle *Politics* 1274 b.

109 Alcaeus – Fr. 38a P. Oxy. 1233 fr. 1 ii 8–20 + 2166 b 1; Horace *Odes* 1.37.1.

110 See R. Thomas, 'Pittacus, of Mytilene, c. 650–570 BCE *Oxford Classical Dictionary*, published online in 2016.

111 Diodorus Siculus *Library of History* 9.1.4.

112 Plutarch *Solon* 8.4. This is one version of events.

113 *Ibid.*, 21.

114 *Ibid.*, 15.

115 Plato *Protagoras* 343a–b; D. Sacks (ed.), *Encyclopedia of the Ancient Greek World*, 2005, p. 310. While the Sages were all male, Chilon's daughter, Chilonis, a follower of Pythagoras, was said to have been his equal in sagacity – see S. Pomeroy, *Spartan Women*, p. 11.

116 Pamphila *Historical Commentaries* 2, *cit.* Diogenes Laertius *Lives of Eminent Philosophers* 1.4.76.

117 Diodorus Siculus *Library of History* 9.12.3.

118 Aelian, *cit.* Stobaeus *Florilegium* 3.29.58.

119 *Palatine Anthology* 7.17 (Tullius Laurea *On the Same*). See also *Palatine Anthology* 7.15.

Chapter V

1 The tumulus of Alyattes has been named Koca Mutaf Tepe – see https://www.sardisexpedition.org for an introduction to the site.
2 R.U. Russin and G.M.A. Hanfmann, 'Lydian Graves and Cemeteries', in G.M.A. Hanfmann, assisted by W.E. Mierse, *Sardis from Prehistoric to Roman Times: Results of the Archaeological Exploration of Sardis 1958–1975*, Harvard University Press, Cambridge, MA; London, 1983, p. 56. The marble used in Alyattes' tomb does not appear to have come from either of the two nearest quarries, at Magara Deresi and Gölmarmara – see B.A. Barletta, book review of 'Lydian Architecture: Ashlar Masonry Structures at Sardis' by C. Ratté, *American Journal of Archaeology*, vol. 116, no. 3, July 2012, accessed online.
3 Herodotus *Histories* 1.93; Strabo *Geography* 13.627.
4 As far as I can tell. Russin and Hanfmann, 'Lydian Graves and Cemeteries', p. 56.
5 Herodotus *Histories* 1.93.
6 Athenaeus *Deipnosophistae* 12.515d–e quoting a lost fifth-century BC *Lydian History* by Xanthus; L. Matthews, 'Xanthus of Lydia and the Invention of Female Eunuchs', *Classical Quarterly*, New Series, vol. 65, no. 2 (December 2015), pp. 489–9. Gyges was said to have enjoyed the company of a female eunuch. The process might have involved genital cutting or possibly even the removal of the uterus and perhaps other gynaecological parts in an attempt to prevent girls from going through puberty.
7 Plutarch *On the Pythia's Oracles* 16.
8 See for example Aristotle *Generation of Animals* 763b–764a.
9 Hippocratic Corpus *De Mulierum affectionibus* 3.216.
10 See A. Taraskiewicz, 'Motherhood as *Teleia*: Rituals of Incorporation at the Kourotrophic Shrine', in L.H. Petersen and P. Salzman-Mitchell (eds), *Mothering and Motherhood in Ancient Greece and Rome*, University of Texas Press, Austin, 2012, pp. 54–8. Taraskiewicz notes that the festival of Eileithyia at Delos employed a baker and that terracotta sculptures pertaining to baking have often been found at sanctuaries associated with childbearing.
11 Sculpture in Louvre, Paris [see plates].
12 Herodotus *Histories* 1.51.
13 *Ibid.* 2.175; 1.29.
14 *Ibid.* 4.162.
15 *Ibid.* 2.181.
16 Diodorus Siculus *Library of History* 9.2.
17 Herodotus *Histories* 1.91.
18 On the fictionalisation of Cyrus' life in the ancient sources see A. Cizek, 'From the Historical Truth to the Literary Convention: The Life of Cyrus the Great Viewed by Herodotus, Ctesias and Xenophon', *L'Antiquité Classique*, Vol. 44, No. 2, 1975, pp. 531–52.
19 Xenophon *Cyropaedia* 1.3.
20 Cf. the third-century AD Justinus *Epitome of the Philippic History of Pompeius Trogus* 1.6, who suggests that Cyrus removed Astyages from power but then treated him well, appointing him governor of Hyrcania. Cyrus was then free to capture and loot the wealthy city of Ecbatana and carry its riches home to Anshan (Nabonidus Chronicle [ABC 7], col. ii.1–4).

21 1 Ezra 4: 29–31.

22 Ctesias. *FGrH* 688 F 9 (2), *cit.* Brosius, *Women in Ancient Persia*, p. 36. Cassandane was much mourned by Cyrus when she predeceased him: Herodotus *Histories* 2.1.

23 Ctesias. FGrH 688 F 9.

24 According to the Parian Marble, the first Pythian Games took place in 591/0 BC. According to Pausanias (*Description of Greece* 10.7.4–5) it was rather in 586 BC. Pausanias (*Description of Greece* 10.7.2) recorded further that the very first competition saw singers compete to hymn most beautifully to Apollo. Sport and athletic competitions were added later. The sporting competitions of the Pythian Games were mostly the same as those of the Olympics, but there were running races for boys in place of the four-horse chariot race. Women could participate in the music contests and would in later centuries go on to win stunning victories in the running races too.

25 Aeschines *Ctesiphon* 3.107–9; poisoning: Pausanias *Description of Greece* 10.37.7–8.

26 Herodotus *Histories* 1.51.

27 The discovery was made by the French archaeologist Pierre Amandry. See P. Amandry, 'Rapport préliminaire sur les statues chryséléphantines de Delphes', *Bulletin de Correspondence Hellénique*, vol. 63, 1939, pp. 86–119.

28 Herodotus *Histories* 1.53.

29 Plutarch *Moralia - Sayings of Spartan Women.*

30 Tyrtaeus fr. 5.7; P. Cartledge, *Sparta and Lakonia: A Regional History 1300–362 BC*, Routledge; London; New York, 2002, p. 103.

31 Cartledge, *Sparta and Lakonia*, p. 136.

32 Pausanias *Description of Greece* 4.16.9–10.

33 Herodotus *Histories* 1.66.

34 The bronze bowl the Spartans sent Croesus was of the same general type as a bowl discovered in the grave of a princess at Vix in France around AD 500 – Cartledge, *Sparta and Lakonia*, p. 137.

35 Sappho Fr. 16 – P. Oxy. 1231 fr. 1 col. i 13–34, col. ii 1+2166(a) 2+ *P.S.I.* 123 1–2.

36 Bacchylides *Ode* 3.

37 Attic red-figure 'Croesus on pyre' amphora by Myson, fifth century BC, Louvre, Paris.

38 See Russin and Hanfmann, 'Lydian Graves and Cemeteries', p. 57.

39 Bacchylides *Ode* 3.

40 Ctesias *Persica* – FGrH 688 F 9.

41 Bacchylides *Ode* 3.

42 Herodotus *Histories* 1.59–62.

43 For the separation of the three Coesyras I draw on T.L. Shear, Jr., 'Koisyra: Three Women of Athens', *Phoenix*, vol. 17, no. 2, Summer 1963, pp. 99–112.

44 Aristophanes *Clouds* 48.

45 Herodotus *Histories* 6.130–1.

46 Ostracon: H. Mattingly, *University of Leeds Review* 14, 1971, p. 283, *cit.* P.J. Rhodes, *A Commentary on the Aristotelian Athenaion Politeia*, Clarendon Press, Oxford, 1993, p. 204.

47 Shear, 'Koisyra: Three Women of Athens', p. 103.

48 Scholiast on Aristophanes *Clouds* 48, *cit.* Shear, 'Koisyra: Three Women of Athens', pp. 105–6.

49 Athenaeus *Deipnosophistae* 13.609 8c.
50 Aristotle *Athenian Constitution* 14.4; Herodotus *Histories* 1.60.
51 Farmers: Aristotle *Athenian Constitution* 16.2.
52 Plato *Hipparchus* 228b–c. Peisistratus' son Hipparchus was said to have been instrumental in the revival of Homer.
53 Aristotle *Athenian Constitution* 16.7.
54 Thucydides *History of the Peloponnesian War* 6.56.1.
55 Cf. Aristotle *Athenian Constitution* 18.
56 Pausanias *Description of Greece* 1.23.1–2; Plutarch *Moralia – On Talkativeness* 8.
57 Pliny *Natural History* 34.17; Pausanias *Description of Greece* 1.8.5. The statues were later stolen by Xerxes.
58 Epigram ascribed to Simonides by Aristotle and quoted by Thucydides.
59 Isocrates *de Bigis* 26.
60 Herodotus *Histories* 5.64.
61 Thucydides *History of the Peloponnesian War* 6.59.4.

Chapter VI

1 Herodotus *Histories* 1.205.
2 *Ibid.* 1.206.
3 *Ibid.* 1.214.
4 See for example Valerius Maximus *Memorable Deeds and Sayings* 9.10.
5 Herodotus *Histories* 4.66.
6 Ctesias *FGrH* 688.
7 Diodorus Siculus *Library of History* 2.13. Some scholars believe that the author was mistaken and was actually describing Darius' inscription and relief sculpture, but the descriptions of the image, and its placement on the cliff, are so different that I believe that both Semiramis and Darius adorned this cliff.
8 See Diodorus Siculus *Library of History* 17.71.
9 Herodotus *Histories* 7.2.2. Her name may have been Apame.
10 *Ibid.* 3.88.
11 Plutarch *Moralia* – Advice for Newly-weds 16.
12 Athenaeus *Deipnosophistae* 13.
13 Herodotus *Histories* 7.69.
14 See for example PF-NN 761 (20/X), *cit.* Brosius, *Women in Ancient Persia*, p. 125.
15 Sheep: Elamite tablet, Persepolis, Fort 6764 (19/1); Wine: PFT 1795 (19.1), both *cit.* Brosius, *Women in Ancient Persia*, p. 27.
16 Persepolis Fortification Seal 38. For commentary and bibliography see http://www.achemenet.com/en/item/?/achaemenid-museum/museums-and-institutions/the-oriental-institute/persepolis-fortification-seals-oip-117/2235342
17 Persepolis Fortification Seal 535, *cit.* L. Llewellyn-Jones, *Persians: The Age of Great Kings*, Wildfire, London, 2022, p. 185.
18 Mirandu: Elamite tablet, Persepolis, PFT 1835.
19 PFT 1236, *cit.* C.R. Yoder, *Wisdom as a Woman of Substance: A Socioeconomic Reading of Proverbs 1–9 and 31:10–31*, de Gruyter, Berlin; New York, 2001, p. 64.
20 Plutarch *Themistocles* 26.5.

21 Herodotus *Histories* 7.3.
22 Clement of Alexandria *Stromata* 1.16.76.10; Hellanicus of Lesbos *FGrH* 4 fr. 178, *cit.* P.A. Rosenmeyer, *Ancient Epistolary Fictions*, p. 25.
23 See Llewellyn-Jones, *Persians, ubique.*
24 Herodotus *Histories* 2.181.
25 *Ibid.* 3.134.
26 P. Demont, 'Herodotus on Health and Disease', in E. Bowie (ed.), *Herodotus – Narrator, Scientist, Historian*, De Gruyter, Berlin; Boston, 2018, pp. 178–9, citing also J. Jouanna, 'La maladie sauvage dans la *Collection Hippocratique et la tragédie grecque*', *Mètis*, 1988, pp. 356–9; J.S. Olsen, *Bathsheba's Breast: Women, Cancer and History*, Johns Hopkins University Press, Baltimore; London, 2002, pp. 3–4.
27 E.V. Stepanova, in St J. Simpson and S. Pankova (eds), *Scythians: Warriors of Ancient Siberia*, The British Museum, Thames & Hudson, London, 2017, p. 127, catalogue number 51.
28 *Ibid.*, p. 124, catalogue number 47.
29 On the Scythians' clothing see E.V. Stepanova and S. Pankova, 'Personal Appearance', in Simpson and Pankova (eds), *Scythians*, pp. 88–97.
30 Ps-Hippocrates *On Airs, Waters and Places* 18.
31 St J. Simpson and E.V. Stepanova, 'Eating, Drinking and Everyday Life', p. 155, who also quote the Ps-Hippocrates passage on the wagons. The wagon dated to the third century BC.
32 *Ibid.*
33 A.Y. Alexeyev, 'The Scythians in Eurasia', in Simpson and Pankova (eds), *Scythians.*
34 Herodotus *Histories* 4.64.
35 *Ibid.* 4.75.
36 As A. Mayor explains in her study of the Amazons, this idea was thought up by the author Hellanicus of Lesbos in the fifth century BC in an incorrect attempt to explain the etymology of the word 'Amazon' as 'lack breast'.
37 L.T. Yablonsky, 'New Excavations of the Early Nomadic Burial Ground at Filippovka (Southern Ural Region, Russia), *American Journal of Archaeology*, vol. 114, no. 1, January 2019, p. 133 – Kurgan 16, probably fourth century BC.
38 Kurgan 9, Chertomlyk, fourth century BC – A. Mayor, *The Amazons: Lives and Legends of Warrior Women Across the Ancient World*, Princeton University Press, Princeton, New Jersey; Oxford, 2014, p. 69.
39 Grave at Semo Swtchala, Georgia – see C. Baumer, *The History of Central Asia, vol. I: The Age of the Steppe Warriors*, I.B. Tauris, London; New York, 2018, p. 264.
40 Volute crater by Niobid Painter, c. 460 BC, from Ruvo, southern Italy, c. 460 BC. Naples 2421.
41 Neck-amphora signed by Exekias as potter and attributed to him as painter, 540–530 BC, Athens, BM Cat. Vases B 210.
42 Herodotus *Histories* 4.114.
43 On the discoveries here see E. Fialko, 'Scythian Female Warriors in the South of Eastern Europe', *Folia Praehistorica Posnaniensia* 22, p. 42.
44 Pomponius Mela *Description of the World* 3.30.
45 See K.V. Chugunov, T.V. Rjabkova and St J. Simpson, 'Mounted Warriors', in Simpson and Pankova (eds), *Scythians*, pp. 194–201.

Chapter VII

1 Herodotus *Histories* 5.51.
2 Plutarch *Moralia* – Sayings of Spartan Women, Gorgo 2.
3 Herodotus *Histories* 5.30–1.
4 *Ibid.* 5.49. On objections to Herodotus' 'too personal' account of the Ionian Revolt see G. Cawkwell, *The Greek Wars: The Failure of Persia*, Oxford University Press, Oxford, 2005, pp. 61–86.
5 Herodotus *Histories* 5.70. Initial calm: *The Cambridge Ancient History*, p. 303.
6 Herodotus *Histories* 5.51.
7 Plutarch *Moralia* – Sayings of Spartan Women, Gorgo 3.
8 Herodotus *Histories* 6.76.
9 Plutarch *Moralia* – Bravery of Women, 245d.
10 Fr. 717 *PMG.*
11 Antipater of Thessalonica *Palatine Anthology* 9.26.
12 Pausanias *Description of Greece* 2.20.8.
13 Tatian *Oratio ad Graecos* 33.
14 Lucian *Amores* 30.
15 Plutarch *Moralia* – Bravery of Women, 4.245e. In reality this festival probably pre-dated the event.
16 Herodotus *Histories* 5.37.
17 See the *Cambridge Ancient History* on the close association developed between freedom from Persia and freedom from tyranny.
18 Herodotus *Histories* 5.38.
19 *Ibid.* 5.99.
20 *Ibid.* 6.6.
21 *Ibid.* 6.20.
22 *Ibid.* 6.31.
23 *Ibid.* 6.106.
24 J.S. Mill, 'Early Grecian History and Legend (A Review of the first two volumes of "Grote's History of Greece")', *Edinburgh Review*, October 1846, reprinted in J.S. Mill, *Dissertations and Discussions, Political, Philosophical, and Historical*, reprinted chiefly from the Edinburgh and Westminster Reviews, vol. II, John W. Parker and Son, West Strand, London, 1859, p. 283.
25 Herodotus *Histories* 7.1.
26 Ctesias *Persica* – *FGrH* 688 F 13 (23).
27 Babylonian Tablet, Bit Sahiran: Evetts (1892), App. Nr. 2. – /–/acc., Xerxes, from 486 BC, *cit.* A. Kuhrt, *The Persian Empire*, vol. II, Routledge, London; New York, 2007, p. 601.
28 Tablet, *cit.* Llewellyn-Jones, *Persians*, p. 170.
29 Herodotus *Histories* 7.11.
30 *Ibid.* 7.187; Heracleides (FGrH 689 F I) suggests that there were 300 concubines at the Persian court. Deinon (*FGrH* 690 F 27) and Plutarch (*Artaxerxes* 27.2) suggest that there were 360 – almost one for every day of the year.
31 Esther 2:12–14.
32 Herodotus *Histories* 7.24.
33 On the archaeological evidence of the canal see B.S.J. Isserlin, R.E. Jones, S. Papamarinopoulos and J. Uren, 'The Canal of Xerxes on The Mount Athos

Peninsula: Preliminary Investigations in 1991–2', *Annual of the British School at Athens*, vol. 89 (1994), pp. 274–84.
34 Herodotus *Histories* 7.41.
35 *Ibid.* 7.46.
36 1.7m: Herodotus *Histories* 7.60.
37 *Ibid.* 2.239.
38 *Ibid.* 7.158.
39 Plutarch *Moralia* – Sayings of Spartans 225.
40 *Ibid.*
41 G.E. Markoe, *Phoenicians*, University of California Press, Berkeley; London, 2000, p. 80.
42 Herodotus *Histories* 7.175.
43 Athenaeus *Deipnosophistae* 13.89.
44 Plutarch *Pericles* 24.2. M. 2. 282.
45 Herodotus *Histories* 7.188.
46 Pausanias *Description of Greece* 10.19.1–2.
47 From the Tomb of the Diver, c. 470 BC.
48 Herodotus *Histories* 8.33.
49 *Ibid.* 7.140.
50 See R. Stoneman, *Xerxes: A Persian Life*, Yale University Press, New Haven; London, 2015, p. 142.
51 Herodotus *Histories* 7.99.
52 *Ibid.* 8.68.
53 Plutarch *Themistocles* 26.4.
54 PFa 5, *cit.* Brosius, *Women in Ancient Persia*, pp. 25, 92.
55 Herodotus *Histories* 8.73.
56 Polyaenus *Stratagems* 8.53. The friendly ship was Calydnian (from the border of Caria and Lycia).
57 Herodotus *Histories* 8.88.
58 Anon. *Tractatus de Mulieribus* 13. The work was possibly authored by the female historian Pamphila of Epidaurus, as suggested by D. Gera – see D. Gera, *Warrior Women: The Anonymous* Tractatus de Mulieribus, Brill, Leiden; New York; Cologne, 1997.
59 Polyaenus *Stratagems* 8.53.
60 Atossa's daughter Mandane lost three sons (Diodorus *Library of History* 11.57.2), as did Sandace.
61 Herodotus *Histories* 8.93.
62 *Ibid.* 8.103.
63 *Ibid.*
64 *Ibid.* 9.64.1.
65 *Ibid.* 9.76.
66 Pausanias *Description of Greece* 10.19.2.
67 *Ibid.* 3.11.3.
68 Ptolemy Chennus *New History*, *cit.* Photius *Bibliotheca* 190.
69 Plato *Alcibiades* 1 123b–c.
70 Herodotus *Histories* 9.109.
71 *Ibid.* 9.112.

Chapter VIII

1 Suda Pi 248.
2 Suda Eta 536.
3 Aristotle *Rhetoric* 3.9.
4 See R.V. Munson (ed.), *Herodotus: Vol. I: Herodotus and the Narratives of the Past*, Oxford University Press, Oxford, 2013, p. 7.
5 Greeks had settled at Croton, Sybaris and Cumae, among other places, between 725 and 700 BC.
6 Herodotus *Histories* 5.44–5.
7 M. Torelli, 'History: Land and People', in L. Bonfante (ed.), *Etruscan Life and Afterlife: A Handbook of Etruscan Studies*, Wayne State University Press, Detroit, 1986, p. 52.
8 Dionysius of Halicarnassus *Roman Antiquities* 1.27–8.
9 Herodotus *Histories* 1.94.
10 Alberto Piazza, paper at European Society of Human Genetics, 2007.
11 See M. Pellecchia, *et al.*, 'The Mystery of Etruscan Origins: Novel Clues from *Bos taurus* Mitochondrial DNA', *Proceedings of the Royal Society B: Biological Sciences* 274, 2007, pp. 1175–9, *cit.* M. Day, 'On the Origin of the Etruscan Civilisation', *New Scientist*, online, 14 February 2007.
12 C. Smith, *The Etruscans: A Very Short Introduction*, Oxford University Press, Oxford, 2014, p. 12.
13 Theopompus, *cit.* Athenaeus *Deipnosophistae* 12.517D.
14 Sarcophagus of Seianti Hanunia Tlesnasa, Poggio Cantarello, 250–150 BC, British Museum.
15 Tomb of the Painted Vases, Tarquinia, c. 530 BC. There is a good image (with discussion) in J. Toms, 'Dining and the Etruscans', in P. Roberts (ed.), *Last Supper in Pompeii*, Ashmolean, Oxford, 2019, pp. 27–8.
16 See for example the sarcophagus of Thankhvil Tarnai and Larth Tetnie, Vulci, 350–300 BC, Museum of Fine Arts, Boston.
17 Tomb 2, Olmo Bello Necropolis, Bisenzio, second half of the eighth century BC, cast bronze, Rome, Museo Etrusco di Villa Giulia, 57022/2.
18 S. Haynes, *Etruscan Civilization: A Cultural History*, The J. Paul Getty Museum, Los Angeles, 2000, pp. 21–4.
19 On Etruscan 'canopic' urns dressed in clothes see L. Bonfante, 'Mothers and Children', in J.M. Turfa, *The Etruscan World*, Routledge, London, 2013, p. 429.
20 Bronze Mirror, third–second century BC, Palestrina, Lazio, now in the British Museum, London, object no. 1898, 0716.4. Cited in L. Bonfante, 'Daily Life and Afterlife', in Bonfante (ed.), *Etruscan Life and Afterlife*, p. 241.
21 Tomb of the Gold, no. 5, Villanovan Necropolis (Museo Civico Archaeologico, 25676).
22 M.J. Becker and J.M. Turfa, *The Etruscans and the History of Dentistry: The Golden Smile through the Ages*, Routledge, London; New York, 2017, p. xv.
23 *Ibid.*
24 'Barrett I' – *ibid.*, p. 158.
25 For hoop earrings see the carved terracotta figures of the Tomb of the Five Chairs at Cerveteri. One of these figures, dated 625–600 BC, is in the British Museum, London: 1873,0820.637.

26 See L. Bonfante Warren, 'The Women of Etruria', in J. Peradotto and J.P. Sullivan (eds), *Women in the Ancient World: The Arethusa Papers*, State University of New York Press, Albany, 1984, p. 233.
27 P. Amann, 'Women and Votive Inscriptions in Etruscan Epigraphy', *Etruscan Studies*, vol. 22, nos 1–2, 2019, pp. 39–64.
28 See L. Bonfante, 'Daily Life and Afterlife', in Bonfante (ed.), *Etruscan Life and Afterlife*, pp. 240–1.
29 See S. Haynes, *Etruscan Civilization: A Cultural History*, The J. Paul Getty Museum, Los Angeles, 2000, pp. 174–80.
30 CIE 6314, 6316, Pyrgi, c. 500 BC, National Etruscan Museum, Villa Giulia – see K. McDonald, *Italy Before Rome: A Sourcebook*, Routledge, London; New York, 2021, pp. 44–6.
31 Amann, 'Women and Votive Inscriptions in Etruscan Epigraphy', pp. 39–64.
32 *Ibid.*
33 Nossis *Greek Anthology* 5.170.
34 *Ibid.* 6.265.
35 *Ibid.* 9.605.
36 *Ibid.* 9.332.
37 CIL 1 2 3556a, Pietrabbondante, c. 100 BC, Museo di Campobasso. See McDonald, *Italy Before Rome*, pp. 135–6.
38 Livy *ab urbe condita* 1.1. The story is the focus of Virgil's *Aeneid.*
39 *Ibid.* 1.3.
40 Osteria dell'Osa, Latium, burial 482. See A.M. Bietti Sestieri, *La Necropoli Laziale di Osteria dell'Osa*, Quasar, Rome, 1992, p. 687; D. Ridgway (ed.), *et al.*, *Ancient Italy in its Mediterranean Setting*, University of London, 2000, pp. 27–9; K. Lomas, *The Rise of Rome: 1000–264 BC*, Profile Books, London, 2017, p. 22, and R.D. Woodard and A.D. Scott, *The Textualization of the Greek Alphabet*, Cambridge University Press, New York, 2014, p. 60.
41 Pausanias *Description of Greece* 8.21.3.
42 See J.W. Stamper, *The Architecture of Roman Temples: The Republic to Middle Empire*, Cambridge University Press, Cambridge, p. 35.
43 Plutarch *Tiberius Gracchus* 15.
44 Livy *ab urbe condita* 1.4.
45 There may be a parallel between Roman images of the female wolf suckling Romulus and Remus, and Egyptian images of the goddess Hathor in the form of a cow suckling the female 'king' Hatshepsut.
46 Tacitus *Annals* 12.24; K. Lomas, *The Rise of Rome: 1000–264 BC*, Profile Books, London, 2017, p. 43.
47 Cicero *de re Republica* 2.10.
48 Livy *ab urbe condita* 1.8.
49 *Ibid.* 1.9.
50 Plutarch *Romulus* 9.
51 Ovid *Ars Amatoria* 1.4.
52 Livy *ab urbe condita* 1.13.
53 Dionysius of Halicarnassus *Roman Antiquities* 2.45.
54 The Caenians – Romulus slaughtered their king.
55 After the First Punic War and after the Battle of Actium. Augustus (*Res Gestae* 13) boasted of having closed the doors three times.

56 G. Forsythe, *A Critical History of Early Rome: From Prehistory to the First Punic War*, University of California Press, Berkeley; London, 2006, p. 88.
57 Tabula Lugdenensis (Lyons), AD 48.
58 Pliny *Natural History* 35.152. See also Dionysius of Halicarnassus *Roman Antiquities* 3.46ff.
59 Livy *ab urbe condita* 1.34.
60 Donatus ad. Terence *Hec.* 135 (in Ennius *Annales* Loeb, 147).
61 Some 77 per cent of female burials at Tarquinii contained textile tools – S. Lipkin, 'Textile Making in Central Tyrrhenian Italy – Questions Related to Age, Rank and Status', in M. Gleba and J. Pásztókai-Szeöke (eds), *Making Textiles in Pre-Roman and Roman Times: People, Places, Identities*, Oxbow Books, Oxford; Oakeville, 2013, p. 20.
62 Plutarch *Roman Questions* 31.
63 When Marcus Varro saw it. See also Pliny *Natural History* 8.194; bronze statue: Plutarch *Roman Questions* 30. Some dispute this was Tanaquil. The temple was that of the Sabine god Sancus on the Quirinal Hill.
64 Pliny *Natural History* 8.194. Emperor Claudius identified Servius Tullius with Mastarna, who had been driven out of Etruria after a military campaign (CIL 13 1668, Claudius, Tabula Lugdenensis, AD 48. See S.J.V. Malloch, *The Tabula Lugdvnensis: A Critical Edition with Translation and Commentary*, Cambridge University Press, Cambridge, 2020, pp. 106–7. See also Tacitus *Annals* 11.23–4). A rare painting of Mastarna appears on a fourth-century BC Etruscan tomb painting, the so-called François Tomb, near Vulci, which housed the remains of a number of wealthy Etruscan warriors. Many ornate frescoes drawn from history and myth adorned the tomb walls. Mastarna was shown freeing his friend, Caelius Vibenna, from a prisoner's bonds. This scene of heroism was presumably well known in the local area.
65 Cicero *de re Republica* 2.38.
66 According to Dionysius of Halicarnassus *Roman Antiquities* 4.13.2, whose account I favour here over Livy who adds the Quirinal Hill to the list of additions.
67 Livy says that they were sons, but Dionysius of Halicarnassus says they were rather grandsons.
68 See R. Thomsen, *King Servius Tullius: A Historical Synthesis*, Gyldendal, Copenhagen, 1980, pp. 281–3.
69 Livy *ab urbe condita* 1.47.
70 Law passed to confirm authority: Cicero *de re Republica* 2.38.
71 See J.W. Stamper, *The Architecture of Roman Temples: The Republic to Middle Empire*, Cambridge University Press, Cambridge, p. 36.
72 Livy *ab urbe condita* 1.58.
73 Valerius Maximus ('On Chastity') 6.1.1.
74 *Ibid.*
75 Seneca *de consolatione ad Marciam* 16.2.
76 See for example Silius Italicus *Punica* 13.824–7; Valerius Maximus ('On Chastity') 6.1.2.
77 Dionysius of Halicarnassus *Roman Antiquities* 8.56.2.
78 20,000–30,000 – C. Ampolo, 'La Formazione della Città nel Lazio', Rome, 1980, p. 27.

Chapter IX

1 J.B. Connelly, *The Parthenon Enigma: A Journey into Legend*, Head of Zeus, London, 2014. The play Connelly identifies as of significance to the narrative of the frieze is Euripides' *Erechtheus*. In the play, Athena issues her commands for the constructions in lines 87–100.
2 Pausanias *Description of Greece* 5.11.
3 Plutarch *Pericles* 13.9.
4 Pausanias *Description of Greece* 1.24.5–7.
5 Plutarch *Pericles* 31.2–5. Plutarch claims that Phidias was imprisoned and died in Athens, but work attributed to him at Olympia postdates his prosecution, so it is highly probably that he fled there.
6 Thucydides *History of the Peloponnesian War* 2.45.2.
7 'elders of the tribesmen' – Plutarch *Lycurgus* 16.1.
8 About one in three – see M. Golden, *Children and Childhood in Classical Athens*, Johns Hopkins University Press, Baltimore, 1990, p. 71. On childbirth and mortality see N. Demand, *Birth, Death, and Motherhood in Classical Greece*, Johns Hopkins University Press, Baltimore, 1994.
9 Hippocrates *Peri Parthenon* 1.
10 Hippocrates *On Generation* 4.
11 See A. Taraskiewicz, 'Motherhood as Teleia: Rituals of Incorporation at the Kourotrophic Shrine', in L. H. Petersen and P. Salzman-Mitchell (eds), *Mothering and Motherhood in Ancient Greece and Rome*, University of Texas Press, Austin, 2012, p. 44.
12 Sophocles *Tereus* Fr. 583 (Loeb), *cit.* A. Taraskiewicz, 'Motherhood as Teleia: Rituals of Incorporation at the Kourotrophic Shrine', in Petersen and Salzman-Mitchell (eds), *Mothering and Motherhood in Ancient Greece and Rome*, pp. 44–5.
13 Hippocrates *On Generation* 8.
14 On maternity clothes see M.M. Lee, 'Maternity and Miasma: Dress and the Transition from *Parthenos* to *Gune*', in Petersen and Salzman-Mitchell (eds), *Mothering and Motherhood in Ancient Greece and Rome*, pp. 23–42.
15 Attic grave stele, c. 330 BC, Harvard Art Museums, 1905.8. The stele is discussed by Petersen and Salzman-Mitchell (eds), *Mothering and Motherhood in Ancient Greece and Rome*, p. 9.
16 Pausanias *Description of Greece* 1.27.3.
17 Xenophon *Symposium* 2.10.
18 Xenophon *Oeconomicus* 7.32–39.
19 *Ibid.* 4.42.
20 *Ibid.* 3.12.
21 *Ibid.* 7.3.
22 Andocides *On the Mysteries* 124–7, *cit.* F.D. Harvey, 'The Wicked Wife of Ischomachos', *Echos du monde Classique: Classical Views*, vol. 28, no. 1, 1984, pp. 68–70.
23 Plutarch *Pericles* 24.
24 Aspasia as a teacher: Plutarch *Pericles* 24.4; Suda, alpha 4202; Socrates visited her: Plutarch *Pericles* 24.3.
25 Plato *Menexenus* 235.
26 *Ibid.* 236b.

27 A. D'Angour, *Socrates in Love: The Making of a Philosopher*, Bloomsbury, London, 2019.
28 Plutarch *Pericles* 24.5.
29 Cratinus, *cit.* Plutarch *Pericles* 24.6.
30 Plutarch *Artaxerxes* 26.
31 On Thargelia in a philosophical context see Lucian *Eunuchus* 7. Thargelia's political acumen was generally treated with suspicion. Aspasia's was likewise.
32 Ps-Demosthenes *Against Neaera* 59.122.
33 Plutarch *Pericles* 25.1.
34 Plutarch *Cimon* 14.4.
35 Plutarch *Pericles* 28.
36 The verse Pericles quoted was Archilochus Fr 205 (West).
37 Plutarch *Cimon* 4.5.
38 Plutarch *Pericles* 24.1.
39 Cratinus *Dionysalexandrus* – P. Oxy. 663, 45–7.
40 Aristophanes *Acharnians* 526–7.
41 Pericles, *Funeral Oration* – Thucydides *History of the Peloponnesian War* 2.44.
42 Thucydides *History of the Peloponnesian War* 5.18.
43 *Ibid.* 5.84.
44 *Ibid.* 6.8.
45 *Ibid.* 6.27–8.
46 Plutarch *Alcibiades* 8.
47 Thucydides *History of the Peloponnesian War* 7.87.
48 Plutarch *Nicias* 29.
49 Euripides *Trojan Women* 474–90.

Chapter X

1 Demosthenes *Philippics* 3.9.31.
2 Diodorus Siculus *Library of History* 16.91.6.
3 Satyrus, *cit.* Athenaeus *Deipnosophistae* 13.557.
4 Plutarch *Alexander* 2.1.
5 *Ibid.* 3.8.
6 *Ibid.* 77.7–8.
7 *Ibid.* 7.3. Philip had since restored Stageira to its people.
8 Diogenes Laertius *Lives of Eminent Philosophers* 5.10.
9 Plutarch *Alexander* 9.1.
10 On Thebes see P. Cartledge, *Thebes: The Forgotten City of Ancient Greece*, Picador, London, 2021 (revised edition; first published in 2020).
11 On the Sacred Band and the mass grave see J. Romm, *The Sacred Band: Three Hundred Theban Lovers Fighting to Save Greek Freedom*, Scribner, New York, 2021.
12 Athenaeus *Deipnosophistae* 13.557.
13 *Ibid.*
14 Made wine last: Plutarch *Alexander* 23.1.
15 Pausanias *Description of Greece* 5.20.10.
16 Diodorus Siculus *Library of History* 16.92.1.
17 *Ibid.* 16.92.5.

18 *Ibid.* 16.93.6. The battle was against the Illyrians.
19 Plutarch *Alexander* 10.6.
20 It was formerly believed that Philip was buried in Tomb II at Vergina. Recent research places him rather in Tomb I.
21 A. Bartsiokas, J. Arsuaga, *et al.*, 'The Lameness of King Philip II and Royal Tomb I at Vergina, Macedonia', *Proceedings of the National Academy of Sciences* 112 (32), 11 August 2015, pp. 9844–8. The authors identify a knee ankylosis and hole.
22 Deaths of Eurydice and son: Pausanias *Description of Greece* 8.7.7.
23 Plutarch *Alexander* 11.5.
24 *Ibid.* 12.
25 Arrian *Anabasis* 1.23.
26 Strabo *Geography* 14.2.17.
27 Diodorus Siculus *Library of History* 17.24.2.
28 Plutarch *Alexander* 22.4.
29 Arrian *Anabasis* 2.3.
30 Diodorus Siculus *Library of History* 17.37.3.
31 Plutarch *Alexander* 21.1; Curtius *History of Alexander* 3.12.
32 It was perhaps out of consciousness of his stature that Alexander only ever permitted a small number of trusted artists to paint and sculpt him. Lysippos was his principal sculptor and Apelles was his painter. Alexander was allegedly so friendly with Apelles that he bestowed one of his favourite Greek mistresses upon him. Her name was Campaspe.
33 Diodorus Siculus *Library of History* 17.37.6; Plutarch *Alexander* 21.2.
34 Diodorus Siculus *Library of History* 17.67.1.
35 Dicaearchus, *cit.* Athenaeus *Deipnosophistae* 13.557.
36 Plutarch *Alexander* 30.1.
37 Diodorus Siculus *Library of History* 16.52.3; Curtius *History of Alexander* 6.5.2.
38 Diodorus Siculus *Library of History* 17.23.5.
39 Plutarch *Alexander* 21.4.
40 Curtius *History of Alexander* 4.4.16–17. Curtius notes that 15,000 other Tyrians found refuge with the Sidonians among the Macedonian forces.
41 A million – Plutarch *Alexander* 31.1.
42 *Ibid.* 43.7.
43 Cleitarchus, *cit.* Athenaeus *Deipnosophistae* 13.576e; Plutarch *Alexander* 38; Diodorus Siculus *Library of History* 17.72.
44 In Plutarch *Alexander* 38.2, Thaïs is Ptolemy's hetaera but in Athenaeus *Deipnosophistae* 13.576e she is identified as his wife.
45 SIG3 314. Their daughter Eirene would marry a Cypriot king and one of their sons would storm to victory in a chariot race in Lycaea in Greece.
46 Arrian *Anabasis* 7.12.
47 Plutarch *Alexander* 39.7; Arrian *Anabasis* 7.12.
48 Diodorus Siculus *Library of History* 18.49.4.
49 SEG IX 2; Lycurgus *Against Leocrates* 26.
50 SEG XXIII 198.
51 For a useful overview see M. Wood, *The Story of China: A Portrait of a Civilisation and its People*, Simon & Schuster, London, 2020, pp. 87–9.
52 Plutarch *Alexander* 68.4.
53 *Ibid.* 47.4; Arrian *Anabasis* 4.19.

54 Plutarch *Moralia* – Precepts of Statecraft 818b–c.
55 Arrian *Anabasis* 7.4.
56 Chares *History of Alexander* 10, *cit.* Athenaeus *Deipnosophistae* 12.54.
57 Plutarch *Alexander* 75.
58 Fragmentary cuneiform tablet, British Museum, 1881,0706.403.
59 Plutarch *Alexander* 74.
60 Ps-Callisthenes, *The Alexander Romance*.
61 Diodorus Siculus *Library of History* 118.3.
62 Antonias Bartsiokos, *cit.* N. Romeo, 'Was This Really the Tomb of Alexander the Great's Father?', *National Geographic*, 21 July 2015, online.
63 Polyaenus *Stratagems* 8.60.
64 Arrian *Events after Alexander* 22 (Photius).
65 Diodorus Siculus *Library of History* 18.49.3. In 317 BC.
66 *Ibid.* 19.11.
67 Athenaeus *Deipnosophistae* 13.10.
68 See E.D. Carney, *Olympias: Mother of Alexander the Great*, Routledge, New York; London, 2006, p. 16.
69 Diodorus Siculus *Library of History* 19.51.
70 *Ibid.* 37.5.
71 *Ibid.* 20.21.

Chapter XI

1 Toothless: Plutarch *Pyrrhus* 4.
2 *Ibid.* 5.
3 *Ibid.* 22.
4 Virgil *Aeneid* 1.340–52; 4.20–1.
5 Justinus *Epitome of the Philippic History of Pompeius Trogus* 18.5.
6 Virgil *Aeneid* 1.357–68.
7 Timaeus, *cit.* Dionysius of Halicarnassus *Roman Antiquities* 1.74.
8 Menander of Ephesus, *cit.* Josephus *Against Apion* 1.18.
9 C.R. Krahmalkov, 'The Foundation of Carthage, 814 B.C. The Douïmès Pendant Inscription', *Journal of Semitic Studies*, vol. 26, no. 2, October 1981, pp. 177–91.
10 Virgil *Aeneid* 1.336–7.
11 Silver tetradrachm, c. 320–10 BC.
12 CIS 1, 5948, *cit.* G. Markoe, *Phoenicians*, University of California Press, California, 2000, p. 92; M. Woolmer, *A Short History of the Phoenicians*, Bloomsbury, London, 2002, p. 76.
13 Pliny *Natural History* 6.200. The skins survived until Rome's sack of Carthage in the second century BC.
14 Ps.Scyllax *Periplus* 112.
15 Virgil *Aeneid* 4.365–8.
16 Justinus *Epitome of the Philippic History of Pompeius Trogus* 18.6.
17 D. Gera argues persuasively that the anonymous *Tractatus de Mulieribus*, a selection of short biographies of historical women, was written by Pamphila. Dido is among the women to feature. See D. Gera, *Warrior Women: The Anonymous* Tractatus de Mulieribus, Brill, Leiden; New York; Cologne, 1997.

18 Virgil *Aeneid* 4.624.
19 Polybius *Histories* 3.22.
20 Plutarch *Pyrrhus* 23.
21 Polyaenus *Stratagems* 8.68.
22 Plutarch *Pyrrhus* 23.
23 Polybius *Histories* 1.9.
24 Pindar *Olympian* 1.
25 Polybius *Histories* 1.10.
26 Diodorus Siculus *Library of History* 20.14.6.
27 Quintus Curtius *History of Alexander* 4.3.23.
28 Polybius *Histories* 1.20.
29 Valerius Maximus *Memorable Deeds and Sayings* 8.1d.4.
30 Suetonius *Tiberius* 2.3 (first woman put on trial for treason by the people and her wish); Aulus Gellius *Attic Nights* 10.6.3 (25,000 asses). The aediles were Tiberius Sempronius Gracchus and Gaius Fundanius.
31 Livy *ab urbe condita* 24.16.19.
32 Polybius *Histories* 1.56.
33 *Ibid.* 1.74.
34 Aelian *Historical Miscellany* 2.41. Agron had been bribed by the Macedonians into aiding the Greek town of Medion against the Aetolian Greeks who had laid siege to it. Hearing his forces were victorious, the king became drunk, developed pleurisy and died.
35 Polybius *Histories* 2.4–5.
36 *Ibid.* 2.8.8.

Chapter XII

1 Polybius *Histories* 2.1.
2 Polybius *Histories* 2.13
3 Silius Italicus *Punica* 1.79–80.
4 *Ibid.* 3.61–96.
5 Livy *ab urbe condita* 24.41.7. The city was founded by Castalius of Delphi and named after his own mother.
6 Polybius *Histories* 3.35.
7 *Ibid.* 3.78 (wigs, some of which were designed to make him look like an old man, and others like a young man).
8 The first dictator was Quintus Fabius Maximus Verrucosus, who was granted four legions for emergency use. He quarrelled with the second dictator, Marcus Minucius Felix, and the two men were replaced in the next elections by consuls Lucius Aemilius Paulus and Gaius Terentius Varro.
9 Livy *ab urbe condita* 22.1.8–13.
10 Valerius Maximus *Memorable Deeds and Sayings* 4.8.2.
11 Livy *ab urbe condita* 22.54.4.
12 *Ibid.* 22.54.3.
13 On the impact of Busa's generosity in allowing the Romans to re-equip their forces see R.A. Bauman, *Women and Politics in Ancient Rome*, Routledge, London; New York, 1994, p. 23.

14 Livy *ab urbe condita* 34.6.
15 *Ibid.* 22.57.
16 *Ibid.* 29.10.
17 Ovid *Fasti* 4.
18 Suetonius *Tiberius* 2.3.
19 Livy *ab urbe condita* 29.14.
20 Ovid *Fasti* 4.
21 Cassius Dio *Roman History* 17.57.51.
22 Appian *Punic Wars* 6.27.
23 Livy *ab urbe condita* 30.7; Appian *Punic Wars* 6.27.
24 Livy *ab urbe condita* 30.12.
25 *Ibid.* 30.14.
26 Another source: Appian *Civil Wars* 6.28.
27 D. Hoyos, *Mastering the West: Rome and Carthage at War*, Oxford University Press, Oxford; New York, 2015, p. 206.
28 Valerius Maximus *Memorable Sayings and Deeds* 6.7.1.
29 Polybius *Roman History* 31.26.
30 On Cato and luxury see A.E. Astin, *Cato the Censor*, Clarendon Press, Oxford, 1978, especially pp. 94–103.
31 Livy *ab urbe condita* 34.2.
32 Plutarch *Cato the Elder* 23 – he advocated a strict diet of green vegetables, duck, pigeon and hare, and believed in the strictest bodily and mental discipline.
33 Appian *Civil Wars* 4.33.
34 Law prohibited women from being made heirs: Augustine *City of God* 3.21. Vestal Virgins alone could now appoint female beneficiaries.
35 See for example Cicero *In Verrem* 2.1.106; *Republic* 3.17.
36 Polybius *Roman History* 31.26.2.
37 Pliny *Natural History* 21.2.
38 There was 'a time lag of at least a century' before Latin became the lingua franca – A. Wilson, 'Neo-Punic and Latin Inscriptions in Roman North Africa: Function and Display', in A. Mullen and P. James (eds), *Multilingualism in the Graeco-Roman Worlds*, Cambridge University Press, Cambridge, 2012, p. 268.
39 Pliny *Natural History* 18.22.
40 *Ibid.* 33.57.

Chapter XIII

1 Livy *ab urbe condita* 38.57.5. Plutarch (*Tiberius Gracchus* 3) claims that this story related rather to the betrothal of Claudia, daughter of Appius Claudius the censor and Antistia, to Tiberius Gracchus the Younger.
2 Pliny *Natural History* 7.57.
3 Cicero *Brutus* 104.
4 Plutarch *Tiberius Gracchus* 1. Ptolemy supposedly offered to share his throne with Cornelia.
5 Valerius Maximus *Memorable Deeds and Sayings* 4.4.
6 Quintilian *Institutio Oratoria* 1.1.6; Cicero *Brutus* 211.
7 Aulus Gellius *Attic Nights* 10.3.

8 Plutarch *Tiberius Gracchus* 8.
9 Cornelia, *cit.* Cornelius Nepos Fr. 1 (Loeb).
10 Plutarch *Gaius Gracchus* 4.
11 *Ibid.* 12.
12 Appian *Civil Wars* 1.115.
13 Pliny *Natural History* 33.48.
14 Cost: Plutarch *Gaius Marius* 34.
15 *Ibid.* 19.
16 Appian *Civil Wars* 1.20.
17 Plutarch *Gaius Gracchus* 4.
18 CIL VI 10043, Capitoline Museums, Rome. This inscription dates to the Augustan period.
19 Valerius Maximus *Memorable Deeds and Sayings* 3.8.6.
20 Plutarch *Gaius Marius* 6.
21 Cicero *de oratore* 2.44, *cit.* M. Dillon and L. Garland, *Ancient Rome: A Sourcebook*, Routledge, London; New York, 2005, p. 362.
22 Plutarch *Gaius Marius* 11.
23 In 102 BC.
24 Plutarch *Gaius Marius* 27.
25 Sallust *War with Jugurtha* 113.5.
26 Velleius Paterculus *Roman History* 2.15.3.
27 Silver denarius of C. Papius Mutilus, 90–89 BC, British Museum, R. 12820.
28 Varicose veins: Plutarch *Gaius Marius* 9.
29 On the so-called 'Poison King' see A. Mayor, *The Poison King: The Life and Legend of Mithridates, Rome's Deadliest Enemy*, Princeton University Press, Princeton, New Jersey, 2010.
30 Appian *Mithridatic Wars* 5.22.
31 Plutarch *Pompey* 36.2–3.
32 Plutarch *Lucullus* 18.3.
33 Josephus *Antiquities of the Jews* 14.7.2.
34 Plutarch *Sulla* 31.4.
35 Appian *Civil Wars* 1.95.
36 *Ibid.* 1.63.
37 Obscurity: Sallust *War with Jugurtha* 95.3.
38 Plutarch *Sulla* 35.
39 Plutarch *Crassus* 9; Appian *Civil Wars* 1.116.
40 Plutarch *Pompey* 32.8.
41 Valerius Maximus *Memorable Deeds and Sayings* 6e.2.

Chapter XIV

1 Catullus *Carmina* 113; Suetonius *Caesar* 50.
2 Catullus *Carmina* 32.
3 Plutarch *Pompey* 42.7.
4 Cicero *Pro Roscio Amerino*. Cicero took the unlikely line that two relatives of Roscius had helped him and were the real murderers.
5 Cicero *Pro Caecina* 97.

6 Plutarch *Cicero* 20.
7 Sallust *War with Catiline* 23.
8 Cicero *In Catilinam* 1.4.
9 Sallust *War with Catiline* 5.
10 *Ibid.* 15. The wife in question was Aurelia Orestilla.
11 Cicero *In Catilinam* 1.1.
12 Catiline's appearance: Sallust *War with Catiline* 15.
13 *Ibid.* 14; gladiators, gamblers, adulterers, see also Cicero *In Catilinam* 2.5; 2.10.
14 Women: Sallust *War with Catiline* 24.
15 Sallust *War with Catiline* 25.
16 Cicero *In Catilinam* 3.5.
17 *Ibid.* 4.3.
18 Sallust *War with Catiline* 51.
19 It is possible that Fulvia was a niece of Sempronia the conspirator, as suggested by R. Syme, *Sallust*, University of California Press, Berkeley; Los Angeles; London, 1964, p. 135.
20 Cicero *Philippics* 3.16.
21 Suetonius *On Rhetoricians* 29.
22 Cicero *Pro Milone* 28.
23 Plutarch *Cato the Younger* 24.2. Plutarch appears to date the beginning of the affair between Servilia and Caesar a few years too early.
24 Suetonius *Caesar* 20.2.
25 Plutarch *Cato the Younger* 32.2.
26 Plutarch *Caesar* 14.8.
27 Catullus *Carmina* 29; Plutarch *Antony* 2.1.
28 Plutarch *Cato the Younger* 32.4.
29 Catullus *Carmina* 79.
30 *Ibid.* 5.
31 *Ibid.* 51.
32 *Ibid.* 83.
33 Plutarch *Cicero* 29.2–3.
34 Cicero had not even left the shores of Italy when he began to spill tears over his pages for Terentia – *ad Familiares* 14.2.
35 See for example Cicero *ad Familiares* 14.4, letter to Terentia written from Brundisium (Brindisi).
36 *Ibid.* 14.8.
37 C.E. Schultz, *Fulvia: Playing for Power at the End of the Roman Republic*, Oxford University Press, New York, 2021, p. 39.
38 Catullus *Carmina* 77.
39 Cassius Dio *Roman History* 39.55.
40 Cicero *Pro Caelio.*
41 Catullus *Carmina* 58.
42 Lucretius *De Rerum Natura* 4.1263–78.
43 Plutarch *Antony* 10.3.
44 Cicero *Pro Milone* 28.
45 Asconius *Commentary on Cicero's Pro Milone* 3; Schultz, *Fulvia*, 2021, pp. 43–4.
46 C.L. Babcock, 'The Early Career of Fulvia', *American Journal of Philology*, vol. 86, no. 1, January 1986, p. 21.

47 Asconius *Commentary on Cicero's Pro Milone* 10.
48 Cicero *Pro Milone* 54.

Chapter XV

1 Plutarch *Caesar* 32.8. The quotation was taken from the Greek poet Menander.
2 *Ibid.* 33–4.
3 Plutarch *Antony* 4.1–2.
4 Plutarch *Caesar* 45.
5 Plutarch *Pompey* 73.
6 Stele, on which Cleopatra worships Isis, 2 July 51 BC, now in the Louvre, Paris.
7 See discussion in J. Tyldesley, *Cleopatra: Last Queen of Egypt*, Profile, London, 2009, pp. 45–6.
8 Plutarch *Caesar* 48.2.
9 Cassius Dio *Roman History* 42.34.
10 Plutarch *Antony* 27.3–4.
11 Plutarch *Caesar* 49.
12 'Vatican Cleopatra', marble, c. 40–30 BC, Vatican Museums, Rome.
13 Florus *Epitome of Roman History* 2.13.56.
14 Cassius Dio *Roman History* 42.34.
15 Attr. Hirtius *Alexandrian War* 1.
16 *Ibid.* 6.
17 Julius Caesar *Civil War* 3.112.
18 Julius Caesar *Alexandrian War* 33.
19 Mosaic, first century BC, found in Praeneste, Italy, now in the Staatliche Antikensammlungen, Munich.
20 Suetonius *Julius Caesar* 52.
21 Appian *Civil War* 2.90.
22 On the rumours see C.E. Schultz, *Fulvia: Playing for Power at the End of the Roman Republic*, Oxford University Press, New York, 2021, p. 39.
23 Plutarch *Antony* 9.1.
24 Cicero *ad Atticum* 16.11.
25 Aurelius Victor *de viris illustribus* 82.
26 Plutarch *Antony* 9.4.
27 Virgil *Eclogues* 10. And see Servius' commentary on the possible identification of the rival suitor with Antony.
28 Cicero *ad Familiares* 14.16.
29 Cicero *Philippics* 2.69.
30 *Ibid.* 2.77.
31 Suetonius *Caesar* 52.
32 Cassius Dio *Roman History* 43.27.
33 Propertius *Elegies* 3.11.39. Canopus was a coastal Egyptian town.
34 Cicero *ad Atticum* 15.15, 13 June 44 BC.
35 Plutarch *Caesar* 55.5.
36 Plutarch *Cicero* 41.
37 *Ibid.*
38 Quintilian *Institutio Oratoria* 6.3.75.

39 Cicero *ad Atticum* 13.21A.2.
40 CIL 14, 2482, Castrimoenium, Italy, Imperial period, *cit.* E.A. Hemelrijk, *Woman and Society in the Roman World: A Sourcebook of Inscriptions from the Roman West*, Cambridge University Press, Cambridge, 2021, p. 52.
41 Antonio de Vaseli, 1485, who states that this body was found at Santa Maria Nova in Campagna, and Daniele da San Sebastiano, both *cit.* R. Lanciani, *Pagan and Christian Rome*, Houghton, Mifflin and Company, Boston; New York, 1982, chapter 6, fol. 48.
42 John Donne, *Eclogue*, 1613, December 26.
43 On Porcia's affection for Brutus see Plutarch *Brutus* 13.4.
44 Suetonius Caesar 50; Cicero *ad Atticum* 14.21.3.
45 Plutarch *Brutus* 13.9.
46 See further K. Tempest, *Brutus: The Noble Conspirator*, Yale University Press, New Haven; London, 2017, p. 89, on Porcia's demonstration of her ability to handle potential torture.
47 Plutarch *Brutus* 13. Cassius Dio *Roman History* 44.13 suggests that Brutus divulged the plot to Porcia.
48 Plutarch *Caesar* 63.
49 Suetonius *Caesar* 81.2–3; Plutarch *Caesar* 63.5.
50 Plutarch *Brutus* 15.5.
51 Appian *Civil Wars* 3.51.
52 Plutarch *Antony* 15.1–2.
53 Cicero *ad Atticum* 15.12.
54 Plutarch *Brutus* 23.
55 Homer *Iliad* 6.490–2.
56 See later Plutarch *Moralia* – Bravery of Women, 243c.
57 Cicero *Philippics* 3.4; Cassius Dio *Roman History* 45.12.
58 Cicero *Philippics* 5.11.
59 Cassius Dio *Roman History* 47.8.
60 Appian *Civil Wars* 4.32.
61 See S. Treggiari, *Terentia, Tullia and Publilia: The Women of Cicero's Family*, Routledge, London; New York, 2007, p. 149.
62 Appian *Civil Wars* 4.13.

Chapter XVI

1 A letter written by Brutus before Porcia died reveals that she had become unwell during his absence – Plutarch *Brutus* 53.6. The letter no longer survives.
2 Appian *Civil Wars* 4.136; Plutarch *Brutus* 53.4.
3 Suetonius *Augustus* 13 (head sent); Cassius Dio *Roman History* 47.49 (head sank).
4 Cassius Dio *Roman History* 48.17.
5 Plutarch *Antony* 32.
6 Appian *Civil Wars* 5.2.17.
7 Virgil *Eclogues* 1.71–2.
8 Horace *Epistles* 2.2.49–51.
9 Appian *Civil Wars* 5.14.
10 Cassius Dio *Roman History* 48.6.

11 Livy *Periochae* 125.2.
12 Appian *Civil Wars* 5.3.19.
13 *Ibid.* 5.1.8.
14 Socrates of Rhodes, *cit.* Athenaeus *Deipnosophistae* 147F–148.
15 Plutarch *Antony* 26.4.
16 *Ibid.* 58.5.
17 *Ibid.* 29.3–4.
18 *Ibid.* 29.
19 *Ibid.* 10.3.
20 Appian *Civil Wars* 5.1.9; Josephus *Jewish War* 15.4.1. Appian claims that Arsinoë was actually at Miletus.
21 Lugdunum coin: RPC 1, 513; Eumeneia coin: RPC 1, 3139. See discussion in C.E. Schultz, *Fulvia: Playing for Power at the End of the Roman Republic*, Oxford University Press, New York, 2021, pp. 14–16, who suggests that an identification with Octavia may be likelier.
22 Octavian, *cit.* Martial *Epigrams* 11.20.
23 Cassius Dio *Roman History* 48.5.
24 Appian *Civil Wars* 5.5.43.
25 Cassius Dio *Roman History* 48.4.
26 Appian *Civil Wars* 5.3.24 said that Lucius had 6 legions and 11 of Antony's against Octavian's 4.
27 Cassius Dio *Roman History* 48.10.
28 Appian *Civil Wars* 5.4.33.
29 ILLRP 1106. The 'Glandes Perusinae', Archaeological Museum of Perugia.
30 *Ibid.* 1108.
31 *Ibid.* 1112.
32 Cassius Dio *Roman History* 48.14.
33 Propertius *Elegies* 1.22.4–5.
34 *Ibid.* 4.1.127–30; 1.22.4–5.
35 Plutarch *Antony* 30.
36 Appian *Civil Wars* 5.6.59.
37 Plutarch *Antony* 31.1.
38 Appian *Civil Wars* 5.9.76.
39 Plutarch *Antony* 31.
40 Seneca *Epistulae Morales* 70.10.
41 Appian *Civil Wars* 5.6.53.
42 In accordance with the Treaty of Misenum.
43 Tiberius Claudius was formerly betrothed to Tullia, but a difficulty in timings led her to marry Dolabella instead.
44 Cassius Dio *Roman History* 48.15.
45 Suetonius *Tiberius* 6.
46 Tacitus *Annals* 5.1.
47 Octavian recorded sending the baby to Tiberius Claudius Nero – Cassius Dio *Roman History* 48.44.
48 *Ibid.* 48.44.
49 Appian *Civil Wars* 5.10.95.
50 Plutarch *Antony* 35.
51 Appian *Civil Wars* 5.13.126; Suetonius *Augustus* 16.

52 Cassius Dio *Roman History* 49.38.
53 Suetonius *Augustus* 69.
54 Cassius Dio *Roman History* 49.32.
55 Plutarch *Antony* 53.
56 *Ibid.* 54.
57 *Ibid.* 63.
58 See J. Bleicken, translated by A. Bell, *Augustus: The Biography*, Allen Lane, London, 2015, p. 248.
59 Plutarch *Antony* 77.
60 Suetonius *Augustus* 17.4.
61 Plutarch *Antony* 86.

Chapter XVII

1 Suetonius *Augustus* 28.
2 See J. Bleicken, *Augustus: The Biography*, Allen Lane, London, 2015, pp. 282–3.
3 Tacitus *Annals* 3.56.
4 Cassius Dio *Roman History* 53.27.5. Agrippa attended Julia's wedding in Augustus' place.
5 Donatus *Life of Virgil* 31; Virgil *Aeneid* 6.883 (*tu Marcellus eris*).
6 Seneca *De Consolatione ad Marciam* 6.2.4.
7 Pliny *Natural History* 36.121.
8 Suetonius *Augustus* 29.
9 Macrobius *Saturnalia* 2.31.2. Although Macrobius was writing centuries after Julia lived, he drew upon sources from the Augustan period, including the writings of Domitius Marsus, so his profile of Julia has credibility.
10 *Ibid.* 2.31.6.
11 *Ibid.* 2.31.5.
12 Nicolaus of Damascus F134.
13 Josephus *Antiquities* 17.1.1.
14 *Ibid.* 17.8.1.
15 Plutarch *On the E at Delphi* 3.
16 Marble inscription in theatre in Aphrodisias – J. Reynolds, *Aphrodisias and Rome*, SPHS, London, 1982, no. 13.
17 Strabo *Geography* 17.54.
18 Cassius Dio *Roman History* 54.5.
19 Suetonius *Augustus* 20.
20 *Ibid.* 21.
21 *Consolatio ad Liviam* (unknown authorship and date), line 356. See also Ovid *Tristia* 1.6.25 (*femina . . . princeps*).
22 Suetonius *Augustus* 40 – Livia helped to secure Roman citizenship for a Gaul; Cassius Dio *Roman History* 55.22, 58.2.
23 *CIL* 6.8958.
24 The *Monumentum Liviae* is a mass tomb containing the cremated remains of almost 100 people on Livia's staff.
25 Suetonius *Augustus* 45.
26 Julian *Institutes* 4.18.4.

27 Ulpianus *Epitome* 29.3.
28 CIL 6.1527; 6.31670; 6.37053; CIL 6.41062 (the so-called Laudatio Turiae) from c. 9 BC. The name of the woman is unknown, but she is referred to as Turia owing to her mild resemblance to a woman of that name mentioned by Appian in his *Civil Wars* (4.44) and by Valerius Maximus (6.7.2). See E.A. Hemelrijk, *Woman and Society in the Roman World: A Sourcebook of Inscriptions from the Roman West*, Cambridge University Press, Cambridge, 2021, pp. 17–18. The eulogy makes for an interesting comparison with that for Murdia (CIL 6.10230), which praises the deceased's virtue predominantly. For a reconstruction of Turia's life, drawing on the work of Mommsen, see J. Osgood, *Turia: A Roman Woman's Civil War*, Oxford University Press, Oxford; New York, 2014.
29 Suetonius *Augustus* 64.
30 Augustus *Res Gestae* 12.
31 D.E.E. Kleiner, *Roman Sculpture*, Yale University Press, New Haven; London, 1992, p. 92.
32 Tacitus *Annals* 1.53.
33 Macrobius *Saturnalia* 2.31.9.
34 Cassius Dio *Roman History* 55.10.12.
35 Velleius Paterculus *Roman History* 2.100.
36 Seneca *De Beneficiis* 6.32.1.
37 Pliny *Natural History* 21.9.
38 *Ibid.*
39 Macrobius *Saturnalia* 2.31.4.
40 Velleius Paterculus *Roman History* 2.100.
41 Horace *Odes* 4.2.
42 Cassius Dio *Roman History* 55.10.15.
43 Suetonius *Augustus* 11.
44 Varro *On Agriculture* 1.8.5.
45 Velleius Paterculus *Roman History* 2.100; Cassius Dio *Roman History* 55.10.14.
46 Propertius *Elegies* 4.11.71–2.
47 *Ibid.* 4.11.59–60.
48 Cassius Dio *Roman History* 55.13.
49 Rhegium inscription (AE 1975.289). On this inscription and its interpretation of the slaves see J. Linderski, 'Julia in Rhegium', *ZPE*, 72, 1988, pp. 181–200, and J.F. Gardner, 'Julia's Freedmen: Questions of Law and Status', *Bulletin of the Institute of Classical Studies*, no. 35, 1988, pp. 94–100. The slaves involved were apparently a man, his wife and their son, although it is not certain which members of this family were directly under Julia's control.
50 Velleius Paterculus *Roman History* 2.101.
51 Tacitus *Annals* 1.3.2; Cassius Dio *Roman History* 55.10.4 says that suspicion fell on Livia.
52 Tacitus *Annals* 1.10.
53 Pliny *Natural History* 7.75.
54 Suetonius *Augustus* 72.
55 See B. Levick, 'The Fall of Julia the Younger', *Latomus*, vol. 35 no. 2, April–June 1976, pp. 335–7.
56 Suetonius *Augustus* 19.
57 Tacitus *Annals* 4.71 – Trimerus.

58 Ovid *Tristia* 2.1.207.
59 *Ibid.* 2.102–3.
60 *Ibid.* 3.5.51–2.
61 Ovid *Ex Ponto* 2.2.17.
62 Suetonius *Augustus* 65.
63 Tacitus *Annals* 4.71.
64 Suetonius *Augustus* 65.

Chapter XVIII

1 Suetonius *Tiberius* 53. Julia the Elder's remains were excluded from the royal mausoleum in Rome.
2 Tacitus *Annals* 1.5; Pliny *Natural History* 7.150.
3 Suetonius *Augustus* 100 (birthday); 97 (ailments).
4 *Ibid.* 99.
5 Suetonius *Caligula* 1.
6 *Ibid.* 9.
7 Tacitus *Annals* 1.40.
8 Pliny, *cit.* Suetonius *Caligula* 8. Altars were erected to honour Agrippina's childbearing.
9 Tacitus *Annals* 1.69.
10 *Ibid.*
11 *Ibid.* 3.64.
12 This and the following: Cassius Dio *Roman History* 57.12.
13 Suetonius *Tiberius* 50.
14 Tacitus *Annals* 2.43. Germanicus' appointment was authorised by the Senate.
15 IG 12.2.204.
16 Tacitus *Annals* 2.43.
17 Suetonius *Caligula* 1.
18 Tacitus *Annals* 2.69.
19 *Ibid.* 2.72.
20 Suetonius *Caligula* 5. This all allegedly happened on the day of Germanicus' death, but it's likely that it followed his death, given that it would have taken time for the news to reach Rome from Antioch.
21 *Ibid.* 2.
22 Tacitus *Annals* 3.13.
23 See *ibid.* 3.17.
24 Senatus Consultum de Gnaeus Pisone patre 109–20.
25 Cassius Dio *Roman History* 57.12.
26 Suetonius *Tiberius* 52.
27 Tacitus *Annals* 4.52.
28 *Ibid.* 4.2.
29 *Ibid.* 4.17.
30 *Ibid.* 6.25.
31 *Ibid.* 4.52.
32 See B. Levick, *Tiberius*, Routledge, New York; London, 1999.
33 Levick, *Tiberius*, p. 167.

34 Tacitus *Annals* 4.9.
35 *Ibid.* 4.67.
36 *Ibid.* 5.3.
37 Suetonius *Tiberius* 53.
38 Tacitus *Annals* 6.23.
39 Suetonius *Caligula* 23.
40 Suetonius *Tiberius* 51.
41 Cassius Dio *Roman History* 58.2.
42 *Ibid.*
43 Valerius Maximus *Memorable Deeds and Sayings* 4.3.3.
44 Pliny *Natural History* 9.172.
45 C9, *cit.* N. Kokkinos, *Antonia Augusta: Portrait of a Great Roman Lady*, Routledge, London; New York, 1992, p. 72.
46 Josephus *Antiquities of the Jews* 18.4.
47 *Ibid.* 18.6.
48 Tacitus *Annals* 6.40.
49 Cassius Dio *Roman History* 58.11.
50 Suetonius *Claudius* 3.
51 Suetonius *Augustus* 83. Augustus was suspicious of anyone who looked different, especially dwarfs, whom he considered to be unlucky.
52 Suetonius *Claudius* 4.
53 *Ibid.* 41; Tacitus *Annals* 11.14.
54 Augustus, *cit.* Suetonius *Claudius* 4.
55 Suetonius *Caligula* 24.
56 *Ibid.* 15; Cassius Dio *Roman History* 59.3.4. Coins minted at Rome after her death labelled Antonia as Augusta.
57 Sestertius, copper, AD 37–8, Rome, British Museum, London, R.6432.
58 Suetonius *Caligula* 23.
59 Cassius Dio *Roman History* 59.11.
60 Suetonius *Caligula* 25.
61 Suetonius *Claudius* 26.
62 According to Suetonius, Claudius later denied being the father of Claudia, daughter of Plautia Urgulanilla.
63 TPSulp 46, see H.L.E. Verhagen, *Security and Credit in Roman Law*, Oxford University Press, Oxford, 2022, pp. 183–4.
64 Suetonius *Claudius* 17. The *carpentum*.
65 According to Cassius Dio (*Roman History* 60.8.5), Messalina was angry with Julia for failing to show her sufficient respect, and also because she was pretty.
66 Seneca *Natural Questions* 4.13.
67 Tacitus *Annals* 11.1.
68 Plutarch *Lucullus* 41.
69 Pliny *Natural History* 10.172.
70 Juvenal *Satires* 6.118.
71 Cassius Dio *Roman History* 60.27.
72 Tacitus *Annals* 11.12.
73 *Ibid.* 11.25.
74 Suetonius *Claudius* 19.
75 Tacitus *Annals* 11.26–7; Cassius Dio *Roman History* 60.11.

76 Tacitus *Annals* 11.29.
77 Suetonius *Claudius* 16.
78 *Ibid.* 25, 29.
79 *Ibid.* 36.
80 Tacitus *Annals* 11.31.
81 *Ibid.* 11.37.
82 CIL 6.4474.
83 See E.R. Varner, *Mutilation and Transformation: Damnatio Memoriae and Roman Imperial Portraiture*, Brill, Leiden, 2004, p. 96.
84 The sculpture is in the Louvre, Paris (MR 280/N 1539).
85 Suetonius *Claudius* 26.
86 Tacitus *Annals* 12.5.

Chapter XIX

1 Pliny *Natural History* 7.71.
2 Tacitus *Annals* 12.5.
3 Suetonius *Claudius* 26.
4 Tacitus *Annals* 12.8 on Agrippina's recall of Seneca.
5 Cassius Dio *Roman History* 60.33.
6 Tacitus *Annals* 12.7.
7 Josephus *Antiquities of the Jews* 20.6.
8 Suetonius *Claudius* 25.
9 *Ibid.* 43.
10 Pliny *Natural History* 33.63; Tacitus *Annals* 12.56.
11 Juvenal *Satires* 1.71–2.
12 Tacitus *Annals* 12.66.
13 Suetonius *Claudius* 33.
14 Cassius Dio *Roman History* 60.34.
15 *Ibid.* 61.34.
16 Tacitus *Annals* 12.67.
17 Suetonius *Nero* 9.
18 Coinage information retrieved during the Nero exhibition at British Museum, London, 2021.
19 Suetonius *Nero* 51. The fatness of Nero's face is evident in numerous portraits.
20 *Ibid.* 10.
21 Tacitus *Annals* 13.15; Suetonius *Nero* 33.
22 *Ibid.*
23 Suetonius *Nero* 33; Tacitus *Annals* 13.15.
24 Tacitus *Annals* 13.16.
25 Suetonius *Nero* 33.
26 *Ibid.* 32.
27 Tacitus *Annals* 13.2.
28 Suetonius *Nero* 34.
29 *Ibid.* 21.
30 Tacitus *Annals* 14.31.
31 Catullus *Carmina* 29.

32 Cassius Dio *Roman History* 62.2
33 *Ibid.*
34 Tacitus *Agricola* 15.
35 Cassius Dio *Roman History* 62.3.
36 Tacitus *Annals* 14.31.
37 Cassius Dio *Roman History* 62.5.
38 *Ibid.* 62.6.
39 Tacitus *Annals* 14.32.
40 *Ibid.* 14.34.
41 Tacitus *Agricola* 16.
42 Cassius Dio *Roman History* 62.12.
43 Tacitus *Annals* 14.37.
44 Cassius Dio *Roman History* 62.1.
45 *Ibid.* 62.7.
46 Tacitus *Annals* 14.37.
47 Suetonius *Nero* 38. Nero also had affordable food shipped in from Ostia.
48 *Ibid.* 47. Locusta would be executed under Nero's successor Emperor Galba – Cassius Dio *Roman History* 63.3.
49 Suetonius *Nero* 57.

Bibliography

Adams, E., *Cultural Identity in Minoan Crete: Social Dynamics in the Neo-Palatial Period*, Cambridge University Press, Cambridge, 2017

Akyeampong, E.K., and H.L. Gates Jr., (eds), *Dictionary of African Biography*, Oxford University Press, Oxford, 2012 (published online: Oxford Reference)

Amandry, P., 'Rapport préliminaire sur les statues chryséléphantines de Delphes', *Bulletin de Correspondence Hellénique*, vol. 63, 1939, pp. 86–119

Amann, P., 'Women and Votive Inscriptions in Etruscan Epigraphy', *Etruscan Studies*, vol. 22, nos 1–2, 2019, pp. 39–64

Ampolo, C., 'La Formazione della Città nel Lazio', *Dialoghi di Archeologia*, vol 2, pp. 165–92, Rome, 1980

Aruz, J., S.B. Graff and Y. Rakic (eds), *Cultures in Contact: From Mesopotamia to the Mediterranean in the Second Millenium B.C.*, Yale University Press, New York, 2013, especially: Y. Goren, 'International Exchange during the Late Second Millennium B.C.: Microarchaeological Study of Finds from the Uluburun Ship', pp. 54–61

Astin, A.E., *Cato the Censor*, Clarendon Press, Oxford, 1978

Atila, C., 'The Ahhiyawa Question: Reconsidered', *Belleten Türk Tarih Kurumu*, vol. 85, no. 303, August 2021, pp. 333–59

Aubet, M.E., *The Phoenicians and the West: Politics, Colonies and Trade*, translated from the Spanish by M. Turton, Cambridge University Press, Cambridge, 2001 (second edition)

Babcock, C.L., 'The Early Career of Fulvia', *Athenian Journal of Philology*, vol. 86, no. 1, January 1965, pp. 1–32

Barletta, B.A., review of 'Lydian Architecture: Ashlar Masonry Structures at Sardis' by C. Ratté, *American Journal of Archaeology*, vol. 116, no. 3, July 2012, accessed online: www.ajaonline.org/book-review/1145

Barrett, A.A., *Agrippina: Sex, Power, and Politics in the Early Empire*, Yale University Press, New Haven; London, 1999

Bartsiokas, A., J.-L. Arsuaga, *et al.*, 'The Lameness of King Philip II and Royal

Tomb I at Vergina, Macedonia', *Proceedings of the National Academy of Sciences* 112 (32), July 2015, 9844–48

Bauman, R.A., *Women and Politics in Ancient Rome*, Routledge, London; New York, 1994

Baumer, C., *The History of Central Asia*, vol. I: *The Age of the Steppe Warriors*, I.B. Tauris, London; New York, 2018

Beard, M., *SPQR: A History of Ancient Rome*, Profile Books, London, 2015

Becker, M.J., and J.M. Turfa, *The Etruscans and the History of Dentistry: The Golden Smile through the Ages*, Routledge, London; New York, 2017

Berger, S., *Revolution and Society in Greek Sicily and Southern Italy*, Franz Steiner, Stuttgart, 1992

Biers, W.R., *The Archaeology of Greece: An Introduction*, Cornell University Press, Ithaca, New York, 1980

Billigmeier, J.-C., and J.A. Turner, 'The Socio-Economic Roles of Women in Mycenaean Greece: A Brief Survey from Evidence of the Linear B Tablets', in H.P. Foley (ed.), *Reflections of Women in Antiquity*, Routledge, London; New York, 2004 (first published 1981), pp. 1–18

Blackman, D., 'Minoan Shipsheds', *Skyllis*, vol. 11, no. 2, 2011, pp. 4–11

Blegen, C.W., *Troy and the Trojans*, Barnes and Noble Books, New York, 1995

— 'Excavations at Pylos, 1953', *American Journal of Archaeology*, vol. 58, no. 1, January 1954, pp. 27–32

Blegen, C.W., J.L. Caskey and M. Rawson, *Troy III: The Sixth Settlement*, Princeton University Press, Princeton, 1953

Blegen, C.W., and M. Rawson, with revisions by J.L. Davis and C.W. Shelmerdine, *A Guide to the Palace of Nestor*, American School of Classical Studies at Athens, Princeton, New Jersey, 2001

— *The Palace of Nestor at Pylos in Western Messenia: Vol. I: The Buildings and their Contents*, Princeton University Press, New Jersey, 1966

Bleicken, J., translated by A. Bell, *Augustus: The Biography*, Allen Lane, London, 2015

Boardman, J., *The History of Greek Vases*, Thames and Hudson, London, 2001

Boatwright, M.T., *Imperial Women of Rome: Power, Gender, Context*, Oxford University Press, Oxford, 2021

Bonfante, L. (ed.), *Etruscan Life and Afterlife: A Handbook of Etruscan Studies*, Wayne State University Press, Detroit, 1986, especially: M. Torelli, 'History: Land and People', pp. 47–65, and L. Bonfante, 'Daily Life and Afterlife', pp. 232–78

Bonn-Muller, E., 'First Minoan Shipwreck', *Archaeology*, vol. 63, no. 1, January/February 2010, pp. 44–7

Booms, D. and P. Higgs, *Sicily: Culture and Conquest*, British Museum Press, London, 2016

Bowie, E., (ed.), *Herodotus – Narrator, Scientist, Historian*, De Gruyter, Berlin; Boston, 2018, especially: P. Demont, 'Herodotus on Health and Disease', pp. 178–9

Bowra, C.M., *Greek Lyric Poetry: From Alcman to Simonides*, Oxford University Press, Oxford; New York, 1936

Brereton, G. (ed.), *I am Ashurbanipal, king of the world, king of Assyria* (British Museum exhibition catalogue), Thames & Hudson; British Museum, London, 2018

Brock, R., and S. Hodkinson (eds), *Alternatives to Athens: Varieties of Political Organization and Community in Ancient Greece*, Oxford University Press, Oxford; New York, 2000, especially: N. Spencer, 'Exchange and Stasis in Archaic Mytilene', pp. 68–81

Brosius, M., *Women in Ancient Persia, 559–331 BC*, Clarendon Press, Oxford, 1996

Bruins, H.J., J.A. MacGillivray, *et al.*, 'Geoarchaeological Tsunami Deposits at Palaikastro (Crete) and the Late Minoan IA Eruption of Santorini', *Journal of Archaeological Science* 35, no. 1, 2008, pp. 191–212

Bryce, T., *Life and Society in the Hittite World*, Oxford University Press, Oxford, 2012

— *The Kingdom of the Hittites*, Oxford University Press, Oxford; New York, 2005

Budin, S. L. and J.M. Turfa (eds), *Women in Antiquity*, Routledge, Oxford; New York, 2016, especially: J. Younger, 'Minoan Woman', pp. 573–94

Burn, A.R., *The Lyric Age of Greece*, St. Martin's Press, New York, 1960

Burney, C., *Historical Dictionary of the Hittites*, The Scarecrow Press, Inc., Maryland; Toronto; Oxford, 2004

Butler, S., *The Authoress of the Odyssey: Where and when she wrote, who she was, the use she made of the Iliad, and how the poem grew under her hands*, E.P. Dutton & Co., New York, 1922 (originally published by Longmans, Green and Co., in London in 1897)

Cahill, N.D. (ed.), *The Lydians and their World*, Yapi Kredi Yayinlari, Istanbul, 2010, especially: Y.A. Meriçboyu, 'Lydian Jewellery', pp. 157–76

Carney, E.D., *Olympias: Mother of Alexander the Great*, Routledge, New York; London, 2006

— *Women and Monarchy in Macedonia*, University of Oklahoma Press, Norman, 2000

Carpenter, R., *Discontinuity in Greek Civilization*, Cambridge University Press, Cambridge, 1966

Cartledge, P., *Thermopylae: The Battle that Changed the World*, The Overlook Press, New York; Woodstock, 2006

— *Sparta and Lakonia: A Regional History 1300–362 BC*, Routledge, London; New York, 2002

Castleden, R., *Minoans: Life in Bronze Age Crete*, Routledge, London; New York, 1993

Cawkwell, G., *The Greek Wars: The Failure of Persia*, Oxford University Press, Oxford, 2005

Cerchiai, L., L. Jannelli and F. Longo, *The Greek Cities of Magna Graecia and Sicily*, J. Paul Getty Museum; Arsenale Editrice, Los Angeles, 2002

Cizek, A., 'From the Historical Truth to the Literary Convention: The Life of Cyrus the Great Viewed by Herodotus, Ctesias and Xenophon', *L'Antiquité Classique*, vol. 44, no. 2, 1975, pp. 531–52

Coldstream, J.N., 'The Rich Lady of the Areiopagos and Her Contemporaries: A Tribute in Memory of Evelyn Lord Smithson', *Hesperia: The Journal of the American School of Classical Studies at Athens*, vol. 64, no. 4 (October–December 1995), pp. 391–403

Connelly, J.B., *The Parthenon Enigma: A Journey into Legend*, Head of Zeus, London, 2014

D'Angour, A., *Socrates in Love: The Making of a Philosopher*, Bloomsbury, London, 2019

Day, M., 'On the Origin of the Etruscan Civilisation', *New Scientist*, online, 14 February 2007

De Angelis, F., *Archaic and Classical Greek Sicily: A Social and Economic History*, Oxford University Press, Oxford; New York, 2016

Demand, N., *Birth, Death, and Motherhood in Classical Greece*, Johns Hopkins University Press, Baltimore, 1994

Desborough, V.R. d'A., *The Greek Dark Ages*, St Martin's Press, New York, 1972

Dillon, M., *Girls and Women in Classical Greek Religion*, Routledge, Abingdon, 2003

Dillon, M., and L. Garland, *Ancient Rome: A Sourcebook*, Routledge, London; New York, 2005

— *Ancient Rome: Social and Historical Documents from the Early Republic to the Death of Augustus*, Routledge, London; New York, 2015 (second edition)

Doob, P.R., *The Idea of the Labyrinth: From Classical Antiquity through the Middle Ages*, Cornell University Press, Ithaca; London, 1990

DuBois, P., *Sappho*, I.B. Tauris, London; New York, 2015

— *Slaves and Other Objects*, University of Chicago Press, Chicago; London, 2003

Dunn, D., *Not Far From Brideshead: Oxford Between the Wars*, Weidenfeld & Nicolson, London, 2022

— *In the Shadow of Vesuvius: A Life of Pliny*, William Collins, London, 2019

— *Catullus' Bedspread: The Life of Rome's Most Erotic Poet*, William Collins, London, 2016

Evans, J., *Time and Chance: The Story of Arthur Evans and his Forebears*, Longmans, Green and Co. Ltd., London, 1943

Evans, R., *Ancient Syracuse: From Foundation to Fourth-Century Collapse*, Routledge, London, 2016

Evely, D., 'The Potters' Wheel in Minoan Crete', *Annual of the British School at Athens*, vol. 83, 1988, pp. 83–126

Faure, P., *La Vie Quotidienne en Crète au temps de Minos*, Hachette, Paris, 1973

Ferrari, F., *Sappho's Gift: The Poet and Her Community*, Michigan Classical Press, Ann Arbor, 2010

Fialko, E., 'Scythian Female Warriors in the South of Eastern Europe', *Folia Praehistorica Posnaniensia*, vol. 22, 2018, pp. 29–47

Figuier, L., *La Terre et les Mers*, Librairie de L. Hachette et Cie, Paris, 1864

Finley, M.I., *Early Greece: The Bronze and Archaic Ages*, W.W. Norton & Co., New York, 1970

— 'Homer and Mycenae: Property and Tenure', *Historia: Zeitschrift für Alte Geschichte*, vol. 6, no. 2, April 1957, pp. 133–59

Fitton, J.L., *Minoans*, British Museum Press, London, 2002

Foley, H.P. (ed.), *Reflections of Women in Antiquity*, Routledge, London; New York, 2004 (first published 1981), pp. 1–18

Fong, W. (ed.), *The Great Bronze Age of China: An Exhibition from the People's Republic of China*, The Metropolitan Museum of Art, Alfred A. Knopf, Inc., New York, 1980

Fontenrose, J., *The Delphic Oracle*, University of California Press, Berkeley; London, 1978

Forrer, E., 'Vorhomerische Griechen in den Keilschrifttexten von Boghazkoi', *Mitteilungen der Deutschen Orient-Gesellschaft* 63, 1924, pp. 1–24

Forsythe, G., *A Critical History of Early Rome: From Prehistory to the First Punic War*, University of California Press, Berkeley; London, 2006

Foster, E., *Thucydides, Pericles, and Periclean Imperialism*, Cambridge University Press, Cambridge, 2010

Fraser, A., *Warrior Queens: Boadicea's Chariot*, Orion, London, 2002

Freeman, P., *Julius Caesar*, Simon & Schuster, New York, 2008

Gabba, E., 'The Perusine War and Triumviral Italy', *Harvard Studies in Classical Philology*, vol. 75, 1971, pp. 139–60

Gardner, H., and F. Kleiner, *Gardner's Art Through the Ages: The Western Perspective*, vol. 1, Cengage Learning, Boston, 2017

Gardner, J.F., 'Julia's Freedmen: Questions of Law and Status', *Bulletin of the Institute of Classical Studies*, no. 35, 1988, pp. 94–100

Gera, D., *Warrior Women: The Anonymous* Tractatus de Mulieribus, Brill, Leiden; New York; Cologne, 1997

Gleba, M., and J. Pásztókai-Szeöke (eds), *Making Textiles in Pre-Roman and Roman Times: People, Places, Identities*, Oxbow Books, Oxford; Oakeville, 2013, especially: S. Lipkin, 'Textile Making in Central Tyrrhenian Italy – Questions Related to Age, Rank and Status', pp. 19–29

Golden, M., *Children and Childhood in Classical Athens*, Johns Hopkins University Press, Baltimore, 1990

Graves, R., *Homer's Daughter*, Academy Chicago, Chicago, 1987 (first published 1955)

— *I, Claudius*, Random House, New York, 1961 (first published 1934)

Griffin, M.T., *Nero: The End of a Dynasty*, Routledge, London; New York, 2001

Hadjidaki-Marder, E., *The Minoan Shipwreck at Pseira, Crete*, INSTAP Academic Press, Philadelphia, 2021

Halstead, P., and V. Isaakidou, 'Faunal Evidence for Feasting: Burnt Offerings from the Palace of Nestor at Pylos', in P. Halstead and J.C. Barrett (eds), *Food, Cuisine and Society in Prehistoric Greece*, Oxbow Books, Oxford; Philadelphia, 2004, pp. 136–54

Hanfmann, G.M.A., assisted by W.E. Mierse, *Sardis from Prehistoric to Roman Times: Results of the Archaeological Exploration of Sardis 1958–1975*, Harvard University Press, Cambridge, MA; London, 1983

Harvey, F.D., 'The Wicked Wife of Ischomachos', *Echos du Monde Classique: Classical Views*, vol. 28, no. 1, 1984, pp. 68–70

Hawes, H.B., 'Memoirs of a Pioneer Excavator in Crete', *Archaeology*, 18, 1965, pp. 94–101

Haynes, S., *Etruscan Civilization: A Cultural History*, The J. Paul Getty Museum, Los Angeles, 2000

Helck, W., *Die Beziehungen Ägyptens und Vorderasien zur Ägäis bis ins 7. Jahrhundert v. Chr.*, Darmstadt, 1979

Hemelrijk, E.A., *Woman and Society in the Roman World: A Sourcebook of Inscriptions from the Roman West*, Cambridge University Press, Cambridge, 2021

Hinsch, B., *Women in Ancient China*, Rowman & Littlefield, Lanham; Boulder; New York; London, 2018

Hoeck, K., *Kreta*, vol. 2, Göttingen, 1825

Holloway, R., *The Archaeology of Ancient Sicily*, Routledge, London, 2000

Hoyos, D., *Mastering the West: Rome and Carthage at War*, Oxford University Press, Oxford; New York, 2015

Hughes, B., *Venus and Aphrodite: History of a Goddess*, Weidenfeld & Nicolson, London, 2019

James, S.L., and S. Dillon (eds), *A Companion to Women in the Ancient World*, Wiley-Blackwell, West Sussex, 2012

Keith, A., 'Lycoris Galli/Volumnia Cytheris: A Greek Courtesan in Rome', *Eugesta Revue*, no. 1, 2011, pp. 23–53

Kent, P.A., *A History of the Pyrrhic War*, Routledge, Oxford; New York, 2020

Killen, J.T., 'The Wool Industry of Crete in the Late Bronze Age', *Annual of the British School at Athens*, vol. 59, 1964, pp. 1–15

Kitchen, K.A., *Pharaoh Triumphant: The Life and Times of Ramesses II*, Aris & Phillips Ltd., Wiltshire, 1982

Kleiner, D.E.E., *Roman Sculpture*, Yale University Press, New Haven; London, 1992

Kokkinos, N., *Antonia Augusta: Portrait of a Great Roman Lady*, Routledge, London; New York, 1992

Krahmalkov, C.R., 'The Foundation of Carthage, 814 B.C. The Douïmès Pendant Inscription', *Journal of Semitic Studies*, vol. 26, no. 2, Autumn 1981, pp. 177–91

Kramer-Hajos, M., *Mycenaean Greece and the Aegean World: Palace and Province in the Late Bronze Age*, Cambridge University Press, New York, 2016

Kuhrt, A., *The Persian Empire: A Corpus of Sources from the Achaemenid Period*, vols I–II, Routledge, London; New York, 2007

Isserlin, B.S.J., R.E. Jones, S. Papamarinopoulos and J. Uren, 'The Canal of Xerxes on The Mount Athos Peninsula: Preliminary Investigations in 1991–2', *Annual of the British School at Athens*, vol. 89 (1994), pp. 274–84

Lanciani, R., *Pagan and Christian Rome*, Houghton, Mifflin and Company, Boston; New York, 1982

Lane Fox, R., *Alexander the Great*, Penguin Books, London, 2004

— *The Classical World: An Epic History of Greece and Rome*, Penguin Books, London, 2006

Lapatin, K., *Mysteries of the Snake Goddess: Art, Desire, and the Forging of History*, Houghton Mifflin, Boston; New York, 2002

Lazaridis, I., A. Mittnik, *et al.*, 'Genetic Origins of the Minoans and Mycenaeans', *Nature*, vol. 548, 10 August 2017, pp. 214–30

Lehmann, P.W., 'Harriet Boyd Hawes: Introductory Remarks', in *A Land Called Crete: A Symposium in Memory of Harriet Boyd Hawes 1871–1945*, Smith College, Massachusetts, October 1967

Leighton, R., *Sicily Before History: An Archaeological Survey from the Paleolithic to the Iron Age*, Cornell University Press, Ithaca, New York, 1999

Levick, B., *Tiberius: The Politician*, Routledge, London; New York, 1999

— 'The Fall of Julia the Younger', *Latomus*, vol. 35, no. 2, April–June 1976, pp. 301–39

Linderski, J., 'Julia in Rhegium', *ZPE*, 72, 1988, pp. 181–200

Liston, M.A., and J.K. Papadopoulos, 'The "Rich Athenian Lady" Was Pregnant: The Anthropology of a Geometric Tomb Reconsidered', *Hesperia: Journal of the American School of Classical Studies at Athens*, vol. 73, no. 1, 2004, pp. 7–38

Llewellyn-Jones, L., *Persians: The Age of Great Kings*, Wildfire, London, 2022

Lobell, J.A., 'The Pharaoh's Daughters', *Archaeology*, September/October 2022 (online)

— 'The Minoans of Crete', *Archaeology*, vol. 68, no. 3, May/June 2015, pp. 28–35

Lomas, K., *The Rise of Rome: 1000–264 BC*, Profile Books, London, 2017

MacGillivray, J.A., 'Labyrinths and Bull-Leapers', *Archaeology*, vol. 53, no. 6, November/December 2000, pp. 53–5

— *Minotaur: Sir Arthur Evans and the Archaeology of the Minoan Myth*, Hill and Wang, New York, 2000

MacLachlan, B., *Women in Ancient Rome: A Sourcebook*, Bloomsbury, London; New York, 2013

Major, J.S., and C.A. Cook, *Ancient China: A History*, Routledge, London; New York, 2017

Malloch, S.J.V., *The Tabula Lugdvnensis: A Critical Edition with Translation and Commentary*, Cambridge University Press, Cambridge, 2020

Marinatos, N., *Sir Arthur Evans and Minoan Crete: Creating the Vision of Knossos*, I.B. Tauris, London; New York, 2015

Marinatos, S., 'The Volcanic Destruction of Minoan Crete', *Antiquity*, 13, 1939, pp. 425–39

Markoe, G.E., *Phoenicians*, University of California Press, Berkeley; London, 2000

Matthews, L., 'Xanthus of Lydia and the Invention of Female Eunuchs', *Classical Quarterly*, New Series, vol. 65, no. 2, December 2015, pp. 489–99

Mayor, A., *The Amazons: Lives and Legends of Warrior Women Across the Ancient World*, Princeton University Press, Princeton, New Jersey; Oxford, 2014

— *The Poison King: The Life and Legend of Mithridates, Rome's Deadliest Enemy*, Princeton University Press, Princeton, New Jersey, 2010

McDonald, K., *Italy Before Rome: A Sourcebook*, Routledge, London; New York, 2021

McGeorge, P.J.P., 'Health and Diet in Minoan Times', in R. Jones and H. Catling (eds), *New Aspects of Archaeological Science in Greece*, BSA Occasional Paper 3, 1988, pp. 47–54

Meador, B. De Shong, *Inanna: Lady of Largest Heart, Poems of the Sumerian High Priestess Enheduanna*, University of Texas Press, Austin, 2000

Mill, J.S., *Dissertations and Discussions, Political, Philosophical, and Historical*, reprinted chiefly from the Edinburgh and Westminster Reviews, vol. II, John W. Parker and Son, West Strand, London, 1859

Moss, M.L., *The Minoan Pantheon: Towards an Understanding of its Nature and Extent*, British Archaeological Reports 1343, Hadrian Books, Oxford, 2005

Mullen, A., and P. James (eds), *Multilingualism in the Graeco-Roman Worlds*, Cambridge University Press, Cambridge, 2012, especially: A. Wilson, 'Neo-Punic and Latin Inscriptions in Roman North Africa: Function and Display', pp. 265–316

Munson, R.V. (ed.), *Herodotus: Volume I: Herodotus and the Narratives of the Past*, Oxford University Press, Oxford, 2013

Murray, S.C., *The Collapse of the Mycenaean Economy: Imports, Trade, and Institutions 1300–700* BCE, Cambridge University Press, New York, 2017

Mylonas, G.E., *Mycenae and the Mycenaean Age*, Princeton University Press, Princeton, New Jersey, 1966

Nagy, G., 'Did Sappho and Alcaeus Ever Meet? Symmetries of Myth and Ritual in Performing the Songs of Ancient Lesbos', Center for Hellenic Studies, Harvard University, published online: http://nrs.harvard.edu/urn-3:hlnc.essay:Nagy.Did_Sappho_and_Alcaeus_Ever_Meet.2007

Nakassis, D., *Individuals and Society in Mycenaean Pylos*, Brill, Leiden and Boston, 2013

Olsen, B.A., *Women in Mycenaean Greece: The Linear B Tablets from Pylos and Knossos*, Routledge, Abingdon; New York, 2014

Osborne, R., *Greece in the Making: 1200–479 BC*, Routledge, London; New York, 1996

Osgood, J., *Turia: A Roman Woman's Civil War*, Oxford University Press, Oxford; New York, 2014

Parker, V., 'Τύραννος: The Semantics of a Political Concept from Archilochus to Aristotle', *Hermes* 126, Bd., H. 2, 1998, pp. 145–72

Patrick, M.M., *Sappho and the Island of Lesbos*, Methuen & Co. Ltd., London, 1912

Pellecchia, M., *et al.*, 'The Mystery of Etruscan Origins: Novel Clues from *Bos taurus* Mitochondrial DNA', *Proceedings of the Royal Society of Biological Sciences*, vol. 274, 2007, pp. 1175–9

Peradotto, J., and J.P. Sullivan (eds), *Women in the Ancient World: The Arethusa Papers*, State University of New York Press, Albany, 1984, especially: L. Bonfante Warren, 'The Women of Etruria', pp. 229–40

Perrot, G., and C. Chipiez, *History of Art in Phrygia, Lydia, Caria, and Lycia*, Chapman and Hall Ltd., London; A.C. Armstrong and Son, New York, 1892

Perry, L., *Ariadne's Thread: Awakening the Wonders of the Ancient Minoans in our Modern Lives*, Moon Books, Hampshire, 2013

Petersen, L.H. and P. Salzman-Mitchell (eds), *Mothering and Motherhood in Ancient Greece and Rome*, University of Texas Press, Austin, 2012, especially: M.M. Lee, 'Maternity and Miasma: Dress and the Transition from *Parthenos* to *Gune*', pp. 23–42, and A. Taraskiewicz, 'Motherhood as Teleia: Rituals of Incorporation at the Kourotrophic Shrine', pp. 43–70

Pomeroy, S., *Goddesses, Whores, Wives, and Slaves: Women in Classical Antiquity*, Robert Hale & Co., London, 1976

Pomeroy, S. (ed.), *Women's History & Ancient History*, University of North

Carolina Press, Chapel Hill; London, 1991, especially: D. Delia, 'Fulvia Reconsidered', pp. 197–217

Poo, M., *Daily Life in Ancient China*, Cambridge University Press, Cambridge, 2018

Potter, D., *The Origin of Empire: Rome from the Republic to Hadrian 264 BC–AD 138*, Profile, London, 2019

Reese, D.S., 'Palaikastro Shells and Bronze Age Purple-Dye Production in the Mediterranean Basin', *Annual of the British School at Athens*, vol. 82, 1987, pp. 201–6

Relaki, M., and Y. Papadatos (eds), *From the Foundations to the Legacy of Minoan Archaeology*, Oxbow Books, Oxford, 2018

Rethemiotakis, G., N. Dimopoulou-Rethemiotaki and M. Andreadaki-Vlazaki (eds), *From the Land of the Labyrinth: Minoan Crete, 3000–1100 BC*, Alexander S. Onassis Public Benefit Foundation, New York, 2008, especially: P.J.P. McGeorge, 'Morbidity and Medical Practice in Minoan Crete', pp. 118–27

Reynolds, J., *Aphrodisias and Rome*, Journal of Roman Studies Monograph, London, 1982

Rhodes, P.J., *A Commentary on the Aristotelian Athenaion Politeia*, Clarendon Press, Oxford, 1993

Ridgway, D. (ed.), *et al.*, *Ancient Italy in its Mediterranean Setting*, University of London, London, 2000

Ring, T. (ed.), *International Dictionary of Historic Places*, vol. 3: Southern Europe, Fitzroy Dearborn Publishers, Chicago; London, 1995

Roberts, P. (ed.), *Last Supper in Pompeii*, Ashmolean, Oxford, 2019, especially: J. Toms, 'Dining and the Etruscans', pp. 27–32

Roehrig, C.H. (ed.), *Hatshepsut: From Queen to Pharaoh*, The Metropolitan Museum of Art, Yale University Press, New Haven; London, 2006

Roller, D.W., *Cleopatra: A Biography*, Oxford University Press, Oxford; New York, 2010

Romeo, N., 'Was This Really the Tomb of Alexander the Great's Father?', *National Geographic*, 21 July 2015, accessed online

Romm, J., *The Sacred Band: Three Hundred Theban Lovers Fighting to Save Greek Freedom*, Scribner, New York, 2021

Rosenmeyer, P.A., *Ancient Epistolary Fictions: The Letter in Greek Literature*, Cambridge University Press, Cambridge, 2004

Russin, R.U., and G.M.A. Hanfmann, 'Lydian Graves and Cemeteries', in

G.M.A. Hanfmann, assisted by W.E. Mierse, *Sardis from Prehistoric to Roman Times: Results of the Archaeological Exploration of Sardis 1958–1975*, Harvard University Press, Cambridge, MA; London, 1983, pp. 53–66

Sacks, D. (ed.), revised by L.R. Brody, *Encyclopedia of the Ancient Greek World*, Facts on File, Inc., New York, 2005

Samuel, A.E., *The Mycenaeans in History*, Prentice-Hall, Inc., Englewood Cliffs, New Jersey, 1966

Schiff, S., *Cleopatra: A Life*, Virgin Books, London, 2011

Schofield, L., *The Mycenaeans*, British Museum Press, London, 2007

Schultz, C.E., *Fulvia: Playing for Power at the End of the Roman Republic*, Oxford University Press, New York, 2021

Scott, M., *Delphi: A History of the Center of the Ancient World*, Princeton University Press, Princeton; Oxford, 2014

Scullard, H.H., *From the Gracchi to Nero: A History of Rome from 133 BC to AD 68*, Routledge, London; New York, 2006 (first published 1959)

Sestieri, A.M.B., *La Necropoli Laziale di Osteria dell'Osa*, Quasar, Rome, 1992

Shapland, A., 'Jumping to Conclusions: Bull-Leaping in Minoan Crete', *Society & Animals* 21, 2013, pp. 194–207

— *Human-Animal Relations in Bronze Age Crete: A History Through Objects*, Cambridge University Press, Cambridge; New York, 2022

— (ed.), *Labyrinth: Knossos, Myth and Reality*, Ashmolean Museum, Oxford, 2023

Shear, Jr., T.L., 'Koisyra: Three Women of Athens', *Phoenix*, vol. 17, no. 2, Summer 1963, pp. 99–112

Shelmerdine, C.W. (ed.), *The Cambridge Companion to the Aegean Bronze Age*, Cambridge University Press, Cambridge, New York, 2008

Shipley, D.G.J., 'Lesbos', *Oxford Classical Dictionary* online, 2016

Simpson, St J., and S. Pankova (eds), *Scythians: Warriors of Ancient Siberia*, The British Museum, Thames & Hudson, London, 2017, especially: A.Y. Alexeyev, 'The Scythians in Eurasia', pp. 16–31; E.V. Stepanova and S. Pankova, 'Personal Appearance', pp. 88–151; St J. Simpson and E.V. Stepanova, 'Eating, Drinking and Everyday Life', pp. 152–91; K.V. Chugunov and T.V. Rjabkova and St J. Simpson, 'Mounted Warriors', pp. 192–255

Smith, C., *The Etruscans: A Very Short Introduction*, Oxford University Press, Oxford, 2014

Smithson, E.L., 'The Tomb of a Rich Athenian Lady, CA. 850 B.C.', *Hesperia*, vol 37, no. 1, 1968, pp. 77–116

Snodgrass, A.M., *The Dark Age of Greece*, Edinburgh University Press, Edinburgh, 1971

Spencer, N., 'Early Lesbos between East and West: A "Grey Area" of Aegean Archaeology', *Annual of the British School at Athens*, vol. 90, Centenary Volume (1995), pp. 269–306

Stamper, J.W., *The Architecture of Roman Temples: The Republic to Middle Empire*, Cambridge University Press, Cambridge, 2005

Steadman, S.R., and G. McMahon, *The Oxford Handbook of Ancient Anatolia*, Oxford University Press, Oxford, 2011

Stillwell, R., W.L. MacDonald, and M.H. McAllister (eds), *The Princeton Encyclopedia of Classical Sites*, Princeton University Press, Princeton, New Jersey, 1976

Stoneman, R., *Xerxes: A Persian Life*, Yale University Press, New Haven; London, 2015

Strauss, B., *The Trojan War: A New History*, Simon & Schuster, New York, 2006

Swaddling, J., *The Ancient Olympic Games*, University of Texas Press, Austin, 1999

Swaddling, J., and J. Prag, *Seianti Hanunia Tlesnasa: The Story of an Etruscan Noblewoman*, British Museum occasional paper No. 100, British Museum, London, 2002

Syme, R., *Sallust*, University of California Press, Berkeley; Los Angeles; London, 1964

Tempest, K., *Brutus: The Noble Conspirator*, Yale University Press, New Haven; London, 2017

Thomas, C., 'Found: The Dorians', *Expedition Magazine*, vol. 20, no. 3, 1978: https://www.penn.museum/sites/expedition/found-the-dorians

Thomas, R., 'Pittacus, of Mytilene, c. 650–570 BCE', *Oxford Classical Dictionary*, published online in 2016

Thomsen, R., *King Servius Tullius: A Historical Synthesis*, Gyldendal, Copenhagen, 1980

Treggiari, S., *Servilia and her Family*, Oxford University Press, Oxford, 2019

— *Terentia, Tullia and Publilia: The Women of Cicero's Family*, Routledge, London; New York, 2007

Tsetskhladze, G.R. (ed.), *Greek Colonisation: An Account of Greek Colonies and Other Settlements Overseas*, vol. 1, Brill, Leiden; Boston, 2006, especially: J. Vanschoonwinkel, 'Mycenaean Expansion', pp. 41–113, and J. Vanschoonwinkel, 'Greek Migrations to Aegean Anatolia in the Early Dark Age', pp. 115–41

Tyldesley, J., *Cleopatra: Last Queen of Egypt*, Profile Books, London, 2009

— *Daughters of Isis: Women of Ancient Egypt*, Viking, London, 1994

Urbani, B., and D. Youlatos, 'A New Look at the Minoan "Blue" Monkeys', *Antiquity*, vol. 94, no. 374, April 2020, published online by Cambridge University Press

Varner, E.R., *Mutilation and Transformation: Damnatio Memoriae and Roman Imperial Portraiture*, Brill, Leiden, 2004

Verhagen, H.L.E., *Security and Credit in Roman Law*, Oxford University Press, Oxford, 2022

Villing, A., J.L. Fitton, V. Donnellan, and A. Shapland, *Troy: Myth and Reality*, British Museum/Thames & Hudson, London, 2019

Watrous, L.V., *Minoan Crete: An Introduction*, Cambridge University Press, Cambridge, 2021

Waugh, E., *Labels: A Mediterranean Journal*, Duckworth, London, 1974 (first published in 1930)

Wharton, H.T., *Sappho: Memoir, Text, Selected Renderings*, David Stott, London, 1887

Williams, E.H., 'Notes on Roman Mytilene', *Bulletin Supplement (University of London. Institute of Classical Studies)*, no. 55, The Greek Renaissance in the Roman Empire: Papers from the Tenth British Museum Classical Colloquium, 1989, pp. 163–8

Williamson, M., 'Sappho', *Oxford Classical Dictionary* online, 2016

— *Sappho's Immortal Daughters*, Harvard University Press, Cambridge, MA; London, 1995

Wood, M., *In Search of The Trojan War*, BBC Books, London, 2008

— *The Story of China: A Portrait of a Civilisation and its People*, Simon & Schuster, London, 2020

Woodard, R.D., and A.D. Scott, *The Textualization of the Greek Alphabet*, Cambridge University Press, New York, 2014

Woolmer, M., *A Short History of the Phoenicians*, Bloomsbury, London, 2002

Yablonsky, L.T., 'New Excavations of the Early Nomadic Burial Ground at Filippovka (Southern Ural Region, Russia)', *American Journal of Archaeology*, January 2010, vol. 114, no. 1, pp. 129–43

Yoder, C.R., *Wisdom as a Woman of Substance: A Socioeconomic Reading of Proverbs 1–9 and 31:10–31*, de Gruyter, Berlin; New York, 2001

Picture Credits

Plate:

1: © Alamy (*all*)

2: © Shutterstock (*top*); © Alamy (*bottom*)

3: © Giovanni Dall'Orto (*top*); © Alamy (*bottom*)

4: © The Trustees of the British Museum (*top*); © Marie-Lan Nguyen (*bottom*)

5: © The Trustees of the British Museum (*top*); © Alamy (*bottom*)

6: © The Met/Fletcher Fund (*top*); © Bridgeman Images (*bottom*)

7: © Alamy

8: © Alamy (*top*); © The Walters Art Museum (*middle*); © The Trustees of the British Museum (*bottom*)

9: © Alamy

10: © Alamy (*all*)

11: © Alamy (*all*)

12: © The Trustees of the British Museum (*top*); © Science Museum Group (*bottom*)

13: © Alamy

14: © Bridgeman Images

15: © Alamy

16: © Shutterstock

Acknowledgements

I conceived the idea for this book a long time ago. Over the years it has taken to research, the world has witnessed a resurgence of interest in classical women, particularly the women of Greek myth. I was eager to turn my attention to those overlooked historic women whose voices are for the most part lost to us, but whose legacies live on in the world they helped to create. These women have always been the true history-makers for me.

I feel proud to have read Classics at the last of the women's colleges at Oxford. My previous book, *Not Far From Brideshead: Oxford Between the Wars*, which I wrote alongside this one, brought home just how long female scholars had to wait to achieve anything close to equality with their male counterparts. It was sometimes disheartening to discover how many of the challenges encountered by women in antiquity remained unchanged in the twentieth century. Readers of *The Missing Thread* may well detect enduring parallels between the past and the present. I owe considerable thanks to my tutors at St Hilda's for first nurturing my interest in women's history as an undergraduate – Rebecca Armstrong, Katherine Clarke and Emily Kearns – as well as Teresa Morgan and Mary Whitby.

While the women of this book have been close companions for the duration of this project, I have many women – and men – to thank in the modern world as well. To Alan Samson, Ed Lake and Maddy Price, my editors at Orion, and Terezia Cicel, my editor at Viking in the US, I am immensely grateful. My thanks also to Richard Mason, my sharp-eyed copyeditor, Anne O'Brien for proofreading, my publicist Elizabeth Allen, Georgia Goodall and Lily McIlwain. This book would not have been possible without the support of my agent Georgina Capel, and everyone at the agency; thank you Rachel Conway, Irene Baldoni, Polly Halladay and Simon Shaps.

Thank you to Carcanet Press for permission to reproduce work by Robert Graves and to Graham Stewart and Christopher Montgomery of *The Critic* for permission to draw on reviews I have written for them.

Enormous thanks to Connor Beattie, Lesley Fitton, Lady Antonia Fraser, Jasper Gaunt, Fra Lidz, Nicholas Purcell, the late Julian Sands, Selena Wisnom and to Paul Cartledge, always. To the staff of The London Library, The Combined Library of the Institute of Classical Studies and the Hellenic and Roman Studies, Engelsberg Ideas and The Axel and Margaret Ax:son Johnson Foundation for Public Benefit – thank you. I could not have finished this book without the love and faith of my family.

Index

Achaeans 33, 212
Achaemenes 88
Achillas 277, 280, 281
Achilles 36, 37, 41, 47, 61, 186
Acme 321
Acropolis 155–6
Acte 368, 376
Ada 186–7
Adea-Eurydice 194–6
Adherbal 242
Aedui 358
Aemilia Tertia 225–6, 229, 231
Aeneas 138, 139, 140, 202, 204–5, 215
Aeneas Silvius 139
Aeolians 48
Aeschylus 42, 119, 129, 155, 368
Aesculapius 245
Aesop 71, 81
Aetolians 211, 212
Agamemnon 32–3, 37, 41–4, 61, 63, 156, 166, 208
Agariste 93, 154
Agathyrsi 109
Agricola, Gnaeus Julius 374
Agrippa I of Judaea 347
Agrippa, Marcus Vipsanius 310, 313, 317, 319–20, 321, 327, 332
Agrippa Postumus 327, 332, 333, 336–7
Agrippina the Elder 321, 326, 336, 337–46, 350, 351
Agrippina the Younger 338, 344, 350, 351, 353, 355, 361, 362–73
Agron 211
Ahenobarbus, Lucius Domitius *see* Nero
Ahhiyawans 34, 46
Ahmose-Nefertari 22
Ahuramazda 101
Ajax 59
Akarai, Asi 3
Akhenaten 24, 34
Akkadians 55
Alcaeus 62, 63, 66, 72, 74–8, 79, 81
Alcestis 156
Alcibiades 171, 172–3, 176–7
Alcmaeonids 93, 96, 97, 154
Alcman 66
Alexander Helios 305, 316
Alexander I of Epirus 179
Alexander IV 194, 195
Alexander the Alabarch 347
Alexander the Great 167, 180–2, 184–98
Alexandria 376
Alexas (dignitary of Herod I) 321
Allobroges 216, 257
Alyattes 68–9, 78, 82, 91
Amanirenas 322–3
Amanishakheto 323
Amasis II 71, 85, 86
Amazons 36, 40, 100, 107–9, 153, 202
Ambrones 241–2

Amenemhat III, of Egypt 20
Amestris 118, 130–1
Amica 137
Amytis (Cyrus' wife) 87–8, 100
Anaximander 112, 162
Anchises 138
Andocides 161
Andraste 372
Andromache 35–6, 40, 47, 215, 293–4
Andromeda 66, 70, 76
Ankhesenamun 34
Ankhnesneferibra 86
Anna (Dido's sister) 204
Anteia of Lycia 39–40
Antigone 156
Antigonus II 206
Antigonus the One-Eyed 197
Antimenidas 76
Antipater 186, 191, 193, 194, 195
Antonia Hybrida Minor 282
Antonia the Elder 309
Antonia the Younger 309, 317, 337, 347–50
Antonius Antyllus, Marcus 305, 316
Antonius, Iullus 305, 329
Antonius, Lucius 299, 303–5
Antony, Mark 6, 276, 282–6, 292–6, 298–303, 305–16
Anyte 3, 9, 199
Apame 87
Aphrodite 54–5, 65–7
  Alcaeus prays to 77
  Diomedes wounds 44
  feared 56
  Pandora and 1
  Phaon and 81
  Sappho and 64, 71
  statues of 86, 137
  temples to 115, 371
Apicata (Sejanus' wife) 343
Apollo 59, 68, 89, 92, 114
  temples to 67, 78, 88, 322
Apollodorus 164, 279
Arabians 121
Arcesilaus 85
Archedice 96
Archias 57
Arethusa 77, 114
Argileonis 90
Argives 33, 115
Ariadne 17, 18, 205
Aristagoras, tyrant of Miletus 112, 113–14, 115–16
Aristarete 4
Aristogeiton 95–6, 125
Aristonice (priestess at Delphi) 125
Aristophanes 93, 167, 168, 174–6
Aristotle 133, 180–1
Arrhidaeus, Philip III 179, 180, 194, 195, 196
Arsames 121
Arsinoë (sister of Cleopatra VII) 280, 281, 284, 302
Artaxerxes 118
Artaxias III, of Armenia 340
Artaynte 130
Artazostre 104
Artemis 77, 89, 114
  dedications to 42, 72, 88, 90
  temples to 245, 302
Artemisia, of Halicarnassus 126–9, 130, 132
Artystone, of Persia 102–3
Aryenis, of Lydia 69
Ascanius 138–9, 204
Asiaticus, Decimus Valerius 354–5
Aspasia 162–6, 167–8, 170, 177
Assyrians 39, 53, 55, 121
Astarte 202
Astyages 87, 88

Astyanax 215
Athena 1, 33, 64, 88, 93, 186
temples to 78, 153–4, 155, 192
Atia 292
Atilia 263
Atlantis 27
Atossa 102, 103–6, 111–31
Attalus 182, 184
Attalus III, of Pergamum 235
Atthis 66, 70
Atticus, Titus Pomponius 268, 285
Attis 221
Audasius 333
Audata 179
Augustus, Emperor 144, 318–35, 336–9, 344–7, 349–52
as Octavian 292, 294, 296, 298–300, 302–16, 317–18
Aurelia, Cotta 259
Axiothea, of Cyprus 197
Ay 34

Baal Hammon 57, 208
Babylonians 39, 55, 76, 118
Bacchides 251
Bacchus 77
Bactrians 121
Bambalio, Marcus Fulvius 262
Bardiya (Smerdis) 101
Barsine 189, 192
Battus III, of Cyrene 85
Baucis 3–4
Bellerophon 39–40
Berenice I, of Egypt 199
Berenice IV, of Egypt 264, 270, 272, 302
Berenice of Chios 246, 251
Bias 81
Bibulus, Marcus Calpurnius 265, 294
Bithynians 85, 321
Biton 86
Black-Cloaks 109
Blossius, Gaius 232
Boii 217
Boji 80
Bona Dea festival 260–1, 273, 326
Boreas 124
Boudica 371–4
Boyd, Harriet (*later* Hawes) 17–18, 21
Brasidas 90
Brigantes 371
Briseis 37, 41, 47, 61
Britannia 371–2
Britannicus 353, 356, 359, 362–3, 365, 366–7, 371, 376
Brutus, Decimus 257
Brutus, Lucius Junius 150
Brutus, Marcus Junius 264, 266, 275, 289, 290–1, 293–4, 298
Brutus, Publius Iunius 226, 228
Busa 218–19
Butler, Samuel 10, 11, 31
Byzantine period 2

Caecus, Appius Claudius 206
Caelius Rufus, Marcus 270–2
Caerellia 287
Caesar, Julius 240, 248, 258–66, 268–9, 275–82, 289–94
Cleopatra and 278–80, 284–6
family 240, 248, 253, 272
Caesar, Nero Julius 342, 346
Caesarion 284, 292, 300, 311, 316
Caesonia, Milonia 351
Caligula, Emperor 337, 338, 346–7, 348, 350–3, 354
Callicrates 154
Callisthenes 193
Calpurnia 265, 284, 290, 292, 293
Calpurnius Piso Caesoninus, Lucius 265

Calypso 4
Cambyses 87, 100, 104
Camilla, Livia Medullina 352
Candaules 67–8
Carians 186
Carthaginians 201–11, 219, 229–30
Cartimandua 371
Cassandane 87
Cassander 193, 195, 196–7, 200
Cassandra 42, 59
Cassius Longinus, Gaius 291, 293, 298, 300, 301
Castor 32
Catiline (Lucius Sergius Catilina) 255–8, 259–60, 262, 266
Cato the Elder 226–9, 259
Cato the Younger 253, 259, 263–5, 266, 275, 284, 289
Catullus 252–3, 267, 268, 271, 329
Centaurs 153
Chaeronea, Battle of (338 BC) 181
Charaxus 71–2, 73, 77
Charmion 314, 315
Charmus 94
Chians 116
Chilon 81
Chimera 40
Cicero, Marcus Tullius 232–3, 254–8, 259–60
  Cato and 266
  on Cleopatra 285
  Clodia and 270–2
  Clodius and 262
  on Cornelia (Gracchi) 235
  on Cytheris 283
  Fulvia and 292, 294–5
  Milo's trial 274
  on Rome 141
  Servilia and 293
  on Servius Tullius 146
  Terentia and 268–70, 275, 286
  Tullia and 254, 282, 286–8
  on women 228
  De Finibus 287
Cilicians 116
Cimber, Lucius Tullius 291
Cimbri 241, 242
Cimon 154, 165, 169
Cinna, Lucius Cornelius 248, 253
Claudia Pulchra 209
Claudia Quinta 222
Claudia (Octavian's wife) 294, 303
Claudianus, Marcus Livius Drusus 308
Claudius, Emperor 145, 323, 349, 351–65, 369, 371–2
Claudius, Appius 'The Blind' 206, 207, 234, 261, 271
Claudius Nero, Tiberius 308, 309, 317
Claudius Pulcher, Publius 209
Cleisthenes 93, 113, 115
Cleito 27
Cleobis 86
Cleobulus 81
Cleombrotus 127
Cleomenes I, of Sparta 97, 111–14, 121
Cleon 170
Cleopatra (VII) 277–81
  Antony and 6, 300–3, 305–7, 309, 310–16
  children 284–5, 292
  Clodia and 272
Cleopatra II 232
Cleopatra III 232
Cleopatra VI Tryphaena 264
Cleopatra of Macedonia 178, 179, 180, 183, 184, 191–2, 195, 197
Cleopatra Selene 305, 316
Clodia (Metelli) 267–8, 269, 270–2, 329

Clodius Pulcher, Publius 261–3, 267–70, 273, 274
Clytemnestra 32, 42, 43, 156, 166, 271
Coesyra 93–5, 96
Collatinus 149, 151
Concordia 258, 326, 350
Confucius 80
Conopas 332
Corinna 214
Corinthians 57, 117, 127, 170
Coriolanus, Gaius Marcius 152
Cornelia (Gracchi) 231–9
Cornelia Anniana 288
Cornelia (Augustus' stepdaughter) 307, 330
Cornelia (Julius Caesar's wife) 248, 253, 265
Cornelia (Pompey's wife) 276–7, 278
Crassipes, Furius 282
Crassus, Marcus Licinius 249, 258, 266, 272, 276, 306
Cratinus 163
Creusa 138
Critias of Athens 76
Croesus 78, 81, 83–9, 91–2, 96, 97
Cumanus, Ventidius 364
Cupid 204
Curio, Gaius Scribonius 283
Curius, Quintus 255, 256
Cyaxares, of Media 76
Cybele 67, 116, 221, 245, 261
Cyclopes 30–1
Cylon 63
Cynane 179, 194
Cynisca 58
Cypriots 116, 201
Cyrus the Great 87–9, 98–102, 105
Cyrus the Younger 163
Cytheris, Volumnia 282–4

Daedalus 18
Damatria of Sparta 153
Danaans 33
Danaë 29
Darius the Great 101–6
  children 118, 119, 121, 123, 126, 130
  war 109, 110, 111, 112, 117
  wives 97, 118
Darius (Xerxes' son) 118
Deinomache 171
Delphians 123–4
Demaratus, of Sparta 121
Demeter 77, 79, 174
Demetrius I, of Macedon 200
Democedes of Croton 105
Demodocus 37
Demosthenes 178
Detfri 137
Di Xin, King 51
Diana 147, 238, 287
Dido 201–5, 215, 237–8, 368
Dio Cassius 279, 304, 355, 363, 365, 374
Diomedes 44
Dionysus 62, 67, 155–6, 180, 301
Diophanes 232
Diotima 162
Dolabella 282, 287, 301
Domitian 377
Donne, John 288–9
Dorians 48–9
Doricha 71–2, 73, 88
Draco 73, 79, 80
Drusilla, Julia 338, 350–1
Drusus, Julius Caesar 343
Drusus, Nero Claudius 309, 317, 327–8, 337
Drusus Caesar 342, 346
Drypetis 187, 192, 194

Egloge 376

Egyptians 15, 34, 39, 116, 118, 157
Eileithyia 23, 137, 139
Electra 375
Elpinice 165–6
Enheduanna 55–6
Ephorus 165
Epic Cycle (poems) 59, 62
Epic of Gilgamesh 38, 55
Epicadus 333
Eratosthenes 33–4
Erechtheus 154
Eretrians 116, 117
Erinna 3–4, 29, 98
Eris (Strife) 33
Eros 64, 77
Eros (servant) 314
Esther 119
Esther, Book of 119
Ethiopians 121
Etruscans 133–9, 141, 144–5, 146–8, 152
Euboeans 57
Euboule 61
Euphiletos 161, 161–2
Euripides 154, 155, 173, 174–5, 203, 368
Europa 22, 182, 184
Eurydice (mother of Philip II of Macedon) 178
Eurydice (wife of Philip II of Macedon) 182, 184
Eustathius 9
Evans, Sir Arthur 12, 16, 17–20, 24, 25
Eve 2
Ezra, Book of 87

Fabia (Terentia's sister) 255
Fadia 282
Fausta (Milo's wife) 273, 274
Felix, Antonius 364
Floronia 220
Fortuna 147, 152, 287, 326, 350
Fu Hao 25
Fu Jing 25
Fulvia
  children 294, 311, 312, 316
  Clodius' wife 262, 273, 274, 275
  Curio's wife 283
  Mark Antony's wife 6, 283, 292, 294, 295, 299–300
  Perusine War 302–7
Fulvia (Cicero's informant) 255, 256, 259

Gaia 55
Gaius Caesar 321, 326, 331
Galba, Emperor 367
Galla, Sosia 343, 356
Gallus 282
Gamoroi 78
Gemellus, Tiberius 343
Germanicus 337–43, 346, 349, 350
Giambologna 143
Gilliéron, Émile 20
Gisco, Hannibal 208, 209–10
Glaphyra 300
Glaucus 39
Gobryas 126
Gorgo 70, 111–12, 113–14, 121–3
Gracchus, Gaius 231, 233, 234, 235–8, 239–40
Gracchus, Tiberius 231, 233–5, 236, 240
Graces 1, 64
Graeco-Persian Wars 111–31, 132, 163, 169, 177, 378
Graves, Robert 10, 11, 31, 323
Gyges, of Lydia 67–8, 92

Hades 18, 77, 81, 184
Hadjidaki-Marder, Elpida 14

Hadrian, Emperor 377
Hamilcar Barca 210–11, 214
Han Chinese 229
Hannibal 214–18, 220, 225
Hanno (general) 208, 216, 217
Hanno (*Periplus*) 203
Harmodius 95–6, 125
Hasdrubal Barca 225
Hasdrubal Gisco 223
Hasdrubal the Fair 214
Hatshepsut 14–15, 25
Hattusili III 39
Hawes, Charles 21
Hector 35–6, 47, 215, 293–4
Hecuba 173–4
Helen 32–3, 36–7, 40, 42
Hephaestion 188, 192
Hephaestus 1
Hera 32, 33, 58, 67, 137, 322
Hercules 108
Hermes 1, 172
Hermodike 69
Herod the Great 321–2
Herodotus
  Artemisia and 126–7
  on Atossa 103, 105
  background 132–4, 137–8
  on Darius the Great 101
  Doricha and 71, 73
  on the Greeks 129
  Hippias and 117
  on Lydians 82–3
  Persians and 120, 130
  on the Scythians 107
  wars and 33, 39, 100
  Histories 86, 113, 169
Hersilia 143–4
Hesiod 1, 2, 51, 54–5, 57, 64
Hiempsal I 242
Hiero I, of Syracuse 138, 207
Hiero II, of Syracuse 207–8
Hipparchus 94, 95
Hipparete 172
Hippias 94, 95, 96, 97, 115, 117
Hippocrates of Cos 104
Hippocratic Corpus 158–9
Hippolyte 108, 250
Hippolytus 156, 166
Histiaeus, of Miletus 110
Hittites 34–5, 39, 45–6, 49, 56
Homer 35–8
  on the Amazons 108
  Augustus quotes 335
  characters 367
  on Eileithyia 23
  on Lesbos 65
  performances of epics 95
  Phantasia and 9, 11
  on Troy 35
  works 9–10, 30, 32, 37–40, 39
  Iliad 47, 59, 61, 293–4
    characters 41, 54, 69, 215
    Trojan War 30, 33
    warriors 43, 44, 72
  Odyssey 2, 40, 42, 44, 72
Horace 79, 301, 329
Horai 64
Hortensia 227, 295–6
Hortensius 248, 263
Hybrida, Gaius Antonius 258
Hydna 124, 130
Hypsicrateia 250, 251
Hystaspes 118

Iaia 4
Icarus 18
Iceni 371–2
Ictinus 154
Illyrians 180, 211–13
Imilce 215–16

Inanna 55–6
Indians 121, 323
Iolas 193
Ionians 48, 110, 116
Iphigenia 42, 208
Iras 314, 315
Irdabama 104
Irene 4
Isagoras 113
Isauricus, Publius Servilius 282
Ischomachus 160–1
Isis 85, 300, 315
Ithaca 37

Janus 317
Jason 166
Jews 76, 98, 246, 281, 364, 369
Jocasta 156
Juba, of Numidia 284, 316
Jugurtha 242–3
Julia Livilla 351, 353
Julia (Marius' wife) 240–1, 248
Julia (Mark Antony's mother) 295, 307
Julia (Pompey's wife) 265–6, 272, 294
Julia the Elder 309, 318–21, 326, 327–35, 336, 337, 345, 351
Julia the Younger 321, 326, 332–3, 334–5, 336
Juno 202, 203, 204, 217, 221, 230
Jupiter 217, 230
Justinus 205
Juvenal 355, 360

Kallo 137
Kalokairinos, Minos 17
Kanuta 136
Kerkulas 65
Kleis 65, 66, 75
Kora of Corinth 4
Kronos 22, 55, 87

Ladice, of Cyrene 85, 86, 104
Laertes 31
Laius, of Thebes 157
Lamachus 172
Lanassa, of Syracuse 200
Laodice 244, 251
Laodice VI (Seleucid) 244
Larentia 140
Larthia Ateinei 137
Latinus Silvius 138, 139
Lavinia 138–9
Leaena 96
Leaena ('Lioness') 96
Leda 32
Leonidas 121, 122
Lepida, Aemilia 332, 352
Lepida, Domitia 352, 370
Lepidus, Marcus Aemilius 294, 296, 299, 306, 310
Leptines 207
Lesbia 267
Lesbos 61–81
Lesches 62
Leto 88, 89
Leukothea 137
Lex Voconia 228–9
Licinia (Gaius Gracchus' wife) 238
Livia 320–4, 326–8
  children 317, 319, 331–2, 336–7, 339
  Cleopatra and 310, 314
  deification 351, 355
  flees Rome 247
  grandchildren 341–2, 346–7, 349
  Julia the Younger and 334
  Marcellus and 319
  wife of Octavian/Augustus 308–9
Livilla (Tiberius' niece) 343, 348
Livilla, Julia (Germanicus' daughter) 339, 350, 353, 359

Livy 138–9, 142–3, 148, 215, 218–19, 223–4
Locusta 365, 366–7, 376
Lord, Albert 38
Lucius Caesar 321, 326, 331
Lucretia 148–52, 377
Lucretius 271
Lucullus, Lucius Licinius 238–9, 246–7, 250, 261, 262, 263, 354
Lucumo 145
Lugal-anne 56
Lutatius Catulus Quintus 240
Lycurgus 90, 92
Lydians 68–9, 78, 82–92
Lygdamis 132
Lysander 177
Lysias 161
Lysicles 170
Lysimache 175
Lysimachus 197, 200
Lysistrata 175–6

Macedonians 117, 178–97
Mago 230
Mandane 87
Manlius, 258, 259, 260
Marathon, Battle of (490 BC) 117–18
Marcella the Elder, Claudia 309, 317, 319
Marcella the Younger, Claudia 309
Marcellus, Gaius Claudius 306, 309
Marcellus, Marcus Claudius 318–19
Marcia 263
Mardonius 117, 126, 128–9, 130
Marinatos, Spyridon 20
Marius, Gaius 240–5, 259
Marius, Marcus 233
Marrucini 243–4
Mars 140
Marsyas 328
Martina 341
Martinez, Kathleen 315
Masinissa 223–5
Massagetae 98–100
Meda 179
Medea 156, 166, 174
Medes 76, 121
Medusa 29, 155
Megabates 112
Megacles 92–3, 94–5
Megalostrata 66
Megarians 79, 167, 168
Mela, Pomponius 109
Melanchrus 63
Melinno, 'Ode to Rome' 231
Menander of Ephesus 202
Menelaus 32, 33, 36, 42, 69
Meritneith 14
Merneptah of Egypt 49
Mesopotamians 56
Messalina, Valeria 352–60, 369, 372
Messalla Barbatus, Marcus Valerius 352
Messenians 90
Metellus Celer, Quintus 252, 258, 260, 261, 267–8
Midas, King 69
Milesians, 51, 71, 114, 115–16, 123, 165
Mill, John Stuart 118
Milo 273, 274
Milto 163
Mimnermus 57
Minerva 230
Minoans 11–28, 136, 377
Minos, King 11, 12, 18, 19, 22
Minotaur 11, 144
Mithridates VI Eupator 244–7, 249–51
Mnester 356
Moero 298

Monime 246, 251
Mucia Tertia 252–4, 263, 307
Murray, Gilbert 156
Muses 1, 77
Mycenaeans 27–8, 29–44, 45–52, 59, 377
Mynes 37
Myrsilus 75
Myrtis of Boeotia 45
Myson 81
Mytilenaeans 74–5, 78–9, 95

Nanna 55
Naram-Sin 56
Narcissus (courtier) 357–60
Naucrates 9
Nausicaa 10
Neaera 164
Nebuchadnezzar II, of Babylon 76, 193
Nefertari 39
Nefertiti 24, 34
Nekhbet 24
Neoptolemus I, of Epirus 179
Nepos, Cornelius 235
Nepos, Metellus 252
Nereids 71, 124
Nero, Emperor 130, 351, 362–3, 365–71, 372–3, 374–6
Nerva 377
Nestor 41, 42, 43–4, 54, 57
Neuri 109
Niceratus 115
Nicesipolis 179
Nicias 170, 171, 172, 173
Nicomedes IV, of Bithynia 244–5, 248
Nikandre 72
Nike 125, 155, 207, 303
Nitocris 372
Nossis 132, 137
Numa Pompilius 144
Numidians 217, 223, 224
Numitor 139, 140
Nyssia 67–8

Ocrisia 146
Octavia, Claudia 359, 362, 367, 368, 374–5
Octavia the Younger 306–7, 309–12
  children 316, 317, 318–19
  death and legacy 326, 327
  Fulvia and 295, 303
Octavian *see* Augustus
Octavius, Marcus 236
Odysseus 44, 50
Oedipus 87, 156, 157
Olympias 4, 178–98
Olympias II of Epirus 200
Olympic Games 57, 58–9, 63, 180, 377
Opimia 220
Opimius 238
Oppian Law 219, 226, 228
Oreithyia 124
Orestes 63
Orpheus 62
Osiris 315
Otanes 121
Otho 369
Ouranos 55
Ovid 2–3, 72, 143, 267, 323, 333–5
Oxyartes 192

Paetina, Aelia 352, 361
Pallas 363, 368
Pamphila 81, 205
Pamphylians 85
Pandora 1, 2, 36, 64, 155
Pantaleon 83
Pantarces of Elis 154

Panyassis 133
Paris 33, 35, 36, 41
Paris (ballet dancer) 370
Parmys 102
Parry, Milman 38
Parthians 121
Parysatis 190, 192
Pasiphaë 11, 18, 21
Paulina, Lollia 361
Paullus, Lucius Aemilius 330, 332
Pausanias 43, 46–7, 183–4
Peisistratids 96, 97, 98
Peisistratus 92–5
Peleus 33, 124
Peloponnesian War (431–404 BC) 167–77
Penelope 31, 32, 37, 40, 50
Penthesilea 36, 202, 250
Pericles 4, 93, 154–5, 156–7, 162–3, 164–71, 174
Pericles the Younger 177
Persephone 72, 77–8, 174, 184, 206
Perseus 29
Persians 99–110, 115–30
Perusine War (41–40 BC) 304–5
Phaeacians 37
Phaedra 156, 166, 174
Phaedyme 100–1, 102
Phantasia 9–11, 31, 38
Phaon 81
Pharnaces II, of Pontus 281
Pheidippides 117
Pheretime, of Cyrene 85–6, 131
Phidias 154, 155
Phila of Elimeia 179
Phile of Priene 4
Philinna 179, 180
Philip II, of Macedon 178–85, 189, 191, 194, 195
Philistis 207
Phoebe 330
Phoenicians 22, 41, 53–4, 57, 116, 119, 123, 137, 165, 201–3
Photius 9
Phratagune 102, 123
Phrygians 85
Phryne 185
Phrynon 74
Phye 93–4
Pindar 185
Piso, Gnaeus Calpurnius 340, 341–2
Pittacus 74–6, 78–9, 81, 83
Plancina 340, 341–2, 346
Plato 27, 81, 162
Pliny the Elder 4, 203, 328–9, 338, 355, 362, 365
Plutarch
  on Aspasia 163
  on Cleopatra 302
  Gorgo and 114
  on Marius 244
  Myrtis of Boeotia 45
  Olympias and 182
  on Persian men 126
  Porcia and 294
  quotes Eurydice I of Macedon 178
  on Rome's population 286
  on the Sabines 143
  Parallel Lives 90
  Sayings of Spartan Women 153
Polla, Vipsania 327
Polyarkhis 137
Polybius 210, 226
Polycaste 42
Polydeuces 32
Polygnotus 165–6
Polyneices 156
Polyperchon 195
Pompeia (Julius Caesar's wife) 261–2, 263

Pompeius Magnus, Gnaeus 286
Pompeius, Sextus 286, 299, 300, 306, 307–8, 310
Pompey the Great
  Caesar and 272, 275–8
  marriages 252–4, 263, 265–6
  Pompey's Theatre 290–1
  Senate and 258, 274
  Terentia and 269, 270
  Mithridatic Wars 249–51
Pomponia, Attica 317
Poppaea Sabina (the elder) 354–5
Poppaea Sabina (the younger) 369, 375
Porcia 289, 290–1, 293, 298
Porcius Laeca, Marcus 255
Poseidon 27, 32, 35, 46, 153
Posidippus 73
Potheinus 277, 278, 280
Potnia 32
Prasutagus 371
Praxilla 82, 362
Priam 36, 42, 186
Prometheus 1–2
Propertius 267, 305, 330, 332
Ptolemy Chennus ('the Quail') 10–11
Ptolemy Philadelphus 305, 316
Ptolemy (Pyrrhus' son) 200
Ptolemy VIII Euergetes II Physcon 232
Ptolemy I Soter 197, 199–200
Ptolemy XII Auletes 264, 270, 272, 277, 278, 280, 281
Ptolemy XIII 277, 278, 279, 280
Ptolemy XIV 280, 281, 284, 300
Ptolemy XV *see* Caesarion
Puabi 56
Publilia 286–7, 289, 295
Pudicitia 326
Puduhepa 39
Punic Wars 207, 210, 214–30
Pygmalion, of Tyre 201
Pyrrhus, of Epirus 199–201, 204, 205–7, 218
Pythia (at Delphi) 96–7, 123–4
  advice to Telesilla 114
  bribery of the 121
  Croesus and 89, 91
  Cybele and 222
  Gyges' family 68, 92
  Spartans and 122

Qin dynasty 191
Quadratus, Gaius Ummidius 364
Quintilian 232–3

Rameses the Great 39
Rameses III 49
Ratahsah 118
Remus 140–1
Rhea 22–3
Rhea Silvia 139–40
Rhodogune 118
'Rich Athenian Lady' 52–3
Romulus 140–4
Roscius, Sextus 254
Roxana 192, 194, 196
Roxana (Mithridates' sister) 244, 251
Rubellius Plautus 370

Sabines 142–4
Sallust 255, 256
Salome 321, 322
Samian War (440–439 BC) 165–6, 378
Samians 322
Samnites 243–4
Sappho 3, 61–81
Sargon 55

Sauromatae 109
Scaevola, Quintus Mucius 253
Schliemann, Heinrich 43
Scipio Aemilianus 229, 239
Scipio Africanus, Publius Cornelius 216, 218–19, 222–3, 224–6, 229, 231
Scipio, Gnaeus Cornelius 208–9
Scipio Nasica, Publius 235
Scribonia 303, 307, 308–9, 330
Scyllias 124, 130
Scythians 98, 100, 106–10, 117, 121, 250, 323
'Sea Peoples' 49
Seasons 1, 64
Securitas 350
Seianti Hanunia Tlesnasa 134
Sejanus, Lucius Aelius 342–3, 344, 345, 346, 348
Seleucids 198, 230
Seleucus 197, 200
Semiramis 101, 372
Semonides 2
Sempronia (Catiline's conspiracy) 257
Sempronia (Fulvia's mother) 262
Sempronia (Gracchi sister) 231, 239
Seneca the Younger 151, 307, 319, 328, 353, 363, 375–6
Senenia, Posilla 252
Servilia 263–5, 275, 276, 282, 284, 289, 291–3, 298
Seven Sages of Greece 81, 322
Shalamana 103
Shiboulet 203
Sibyl of Cumae 220
Sibylline Books 220–1, 326
Sicilians 173, 201, 203
Silana 370
Silanus, Decimus Junius (Julia's 'lover') 333, 334, 335
Silanus, Decimus Junius (Servilia's husband) 264
Silanus Torquatus, Marcus Junius 333
Silius, Gaius 356–60
Silius Italicus 215–16
Silvius 139
Simaitha 168
Simonides 96, 123
Sisygambis 187, 188, 190, 194
Smerdis 100–1
Social War (91–87 BC) 243–4
Socrates 160, 162, 171
Solon 79–81, 85, 86–7, 88, 92, 113
Sophocles 155, 157, 368
Sophonisba 223–5
Sosigenes 285
Spargapises 98, 99–100
Spartans 89–91, 96–7, 121–3, 127, 129, 167–71, 177
Spurinna 290
Stateira 187, 188
Stateira II 187, 192, 194
Stateira (Mithridates' sister) 244, 251
Stephanus 164
Stratonice 246, 250–1
Strepsiades 93
Suetonius 351, 364
Suetonius Paullinus 373–4
Sulla, Lucius Cornelius 242–50, 254, 258, 259, 266, 273
Sulpicia 317, 336
Sumerians 55
Suppiluliuma, King 34
Sychaeus (Acerbas) 201
Syphax 223, 224
Syracusans 78
Syrians 281

Tacitus
on Agrippina the Elder 338, 342, 343
on Agrippina the Younger 355, 363
on Julia the Elder 328
on Livia 331, 332
Messalina and 354, 355, 356, 363
on Octavian 308
on Plancina 343
on Rome 374
Tanaquil 144–7
Tanit 208
Tarentines 199, 200, 204
Tarpeia 143
Tarquinius, Arruns 147
Tarquinius Priscus, Lucius 146, 147, 148
Tarquinius, Sextus 148–50
Tarquinius Superbus, Lucius 147, 148, 220
Tashlultum 55
Tauri 109
Tawagalawas 46
Telemachus 42
Telesilla 111, 114–15
Telesippa 66
Tentkheta 86
Terentia 254, 258, 260, 268–70, 275, 282, 286, 295
Terpander 62
Teuta 211–13
Teutones 241
Thaïs 190
Thales 81, 112, 162
Thargelia 123, 163
Theano 61
Thebans 170, 185
Themistocles 127
Theodotus 277
Theseus 18, 205
Thessalians 123
Thessalonice 179
Thetis 33, 124
Thracians 62, 85, 117, 185
Thucydides 50, 169, 170
Thutmose II, of Egypt 14
Tiberius, Emperor 308, 309, 317, 326–9, 331–2, 337–48
Tiberius Sempronius Longus 217
Tibullus 267
Timarete 4
Timas 72
Timocleia 185–6
Tiro 286
Titans 1
Titus, Emperor 377
Tomyris, Queen 98–100
Trajan, Emperor 377
Trinovantes 372
Trojan War 9, 11, 30, 32–7, 39, 45–7, 50, 202, 204
Trojans 30, 33, 35, 39, 56, 59
Tullia (Cicero's daughter) 254, 258, 282, 286, 287–9
Tullia the Elder 147
Tullia the Younger 147–8
Tullius, Servius 146–8
Turia 325, 376
Turnus 138
Tutankhamun 34
Tyrians 189, 202
Tyrrhenus 134

Uni 137
Urgulanilla, Plautia 352

Valeria (Coriolanus' wife) 152
Valeria (Sulla's wife) 248–9
Venus 138, 201, 204, 284, 351
Verginia 151–2

Vespasian, Emperor 377
Vesta 140, 219, 269
Vestal Virgins 139–40, 219–20
  Antony and 312
  Augustus and 327, 337
  Catiline and 255
  Claudia Quinta and 222
  Claudius and 359
  Clodius and 261
  Livia and 324
  rites 260
Vibidia 359
Vipsania 317, 327, 328, 343
Virgil 202, 282, 299
  Aeneid 138–9, 204–5, 215, 319
Volscians 152, 227

Wadjet 24, 85
Walmu, King 46
Waugh, Evelyn 20

Xanthippe 160
Xanthippus 154
Xenophon 160–1
Xerxes 104, 118–23, 125, 126–31

Zannanza 34
Zerubbabel 87
Zeus
  children 153
  Crete and 22–3
  Danaë and 29
  Delphi and 88
  Leda and 32
  Mount Olympus 77, 155
  Olympic Games 57
  overthrows father 87
  Pandora and 1, 2
Zhou dynasty 51, 80